CONSUMER BEHAVIOUR

CONSUMER BEHAVIOUR

SECOND EDITION

ISABELLE SZMIGIN & MARIA PIACENTINI

OXFORD
UNIVERSITY PRESS

Great Clarendon Street, Oxford, OX2 6DP,
United Kingdom

Oxford University Press is a department of the University of Oxford.
It furthers the University's objective of excellence in research, scholarship,
and education by publishing worldwide. Oxford is a registered trade mark of
Oxford University Press in the UK and in certain other countries

First Edition 2015
Impression: 1

Published in the United States of America by Oxford University Press
198 Madison Avenue, New York, NY 10016, United States of America

British Library Cataloguing in Publication Data
Data available

Library of Congress Control Number: 2017956302

ISBN 978-0-19-878623-8

Printed in Great Britain by
Bell & Bain Ltd., Glasgow

To Janusz, Alex, Nick, Claire, and Anna
To Bob, Sandro, and Rosa

CONTENTS IN BRIEF

CONTENTS IN FULL

PREFACE

Why consumer behaviour is important

All over the world people are consuming—every minute of every day, 365 days of the year. Countries as diverse as China, Russia, Brazil, and Sweden rely on consumption for their economic development and progress. In some countries people have little to consume and barely enough to survive from day to day, while in other countries people are able to consume much more than they need, so much so that their health can be affected, particularly by the excessive consumption of food and alcohol or the choice of unhealthy or even illegal substances. So, while understanding consumer behaviour is at the heart of economic development and business, and particularly marketing, it also produces some concerns. In this book we hope to give you a broad understanding of consumer behaviour—both its benefits and some of its problems. However, above all we hope to show how consumer behaviour is at the heart of marketing.

For students of business, and especially marketing, consumer behaviour is a critical area that practitioners need to know about. Central to the marketing concept is the need for organizations to understand the factors that shape and influence people's behaviour in different environments. Marketers have to recognize and appreciate how consumers respond to the various aspects of their offerings. This implies that business needs a solid grasp of consumer behaviour in many different settings and contexts, which means thinking about all types of individual consumers, including different age groups and different social and cultural settings. We require knowledge of how the individual makes decisions and how the market 'makes' decisions. We take a global perspective in this book by ensuring the inclusion of examples and cases from a range of countries, including China, India, Mexico, Japan, Korea, Australia, Germany, Austria, the Netherlands, and the UK. We also play close attention to trends and developments in technology and social media and how organizations use these as they interact with consumers. Current research is also incorporated, including sustained treatment and inclusion of studies from consumer culture theory.

The framework for our book is logical and developmental. Our model (Figure P.1) begins from the inner circle with Part 1, which comprises two chapters that look at the *historical and contemporary context* of consumer behaviour. In Chapter 1 we ask the question: how did we arrive here? We do this in terms of the role that consumer behaviour now plays in business. In particular, we consider the disciplines and changes in marketing that led to the development of consumer behaviour as a discipline that is so important to business and marketing. In Chapter 2 we move on to explore some contemporary trends in consumer behaviour. Part 2 consists of five chapters, which we have termed the *micro-view*, and in this part we consider elements of the individual that impact consumption from the nature of their decision-making through to how their attitudes are developed and changed. Part 3 is entitled the *macro-view*. Here we look at consumers in a broader context, from how they operate in groups and as part of a culture to how they function as a whole within the marketplace, i.e. the impact of the decisions of thousands of consumers on the market. Part 4 consists of one chapter, which considers *future trends* in consumer behaviour. This chapter is entitled 'Where are we going?'. Although this part contains only one chapter, it is a very important conclusion to the book, since it looks at some of the current opportunities in terms of how we view consumers and the technologies that will impact on consumer behaviour today and in the near future.

In order to consider further why we study so many elements of consumption, let us consider just one product—coffee. The 1990s TV show *Friends* popularized the idea of the coffee shop as a place to hang out with friends, and many people share this view of coffee shops as a social space, as a place to get together with friends or even to meet new people through organized events. But did you know that coffee houses in the Ottoman Empire in the 1550s served a similar, perhaps more transgressive, function? At that time coffee houses provided an important meeting place for people to engage in a range of transgressive behaviours (such as gambling, taking drugs, discussions against the state) and were often banned by the state. Despite this, coffee houses survived and flourished, and their discourses often challenged the authority of the state and religion and led to changes in society. The first coffee houses in England appeared in the 1650s, and in 1675 Charles II tried to suppress them (unsuccessfully) because they had become such important centres for political discussion. Thus, both the Ottoman and the British coffee house culture could be said to represent an early example of consumer activism, which highlights how powerful

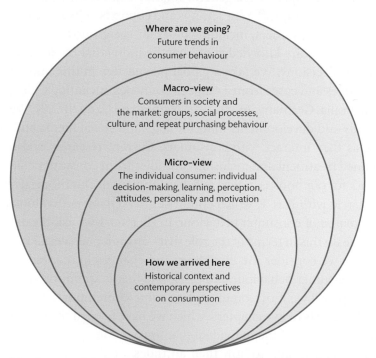

Figure P.1 Organizing framework for how this book approaches consumer behaviour

one product can be! So here we have insights on coffee consumption, and consumption more generally, that come from historical reflection and understanding of consumers, and this is the kind of issue we explore in Part 1.

If we think of ourselves as individual coffee consumers, we might consider how we buy and prepare coffee ourselves. Companies are interested in the process of individual decision-making, from choosing which coffee shop to go to, to which size and combination of coffee and milk you choose on that day and in that shop. The influences that affect this decision-making (Chapters 3–7) can include many aspects related to the appearance of things, down to what tastes we prefer. So here we might think about the experience of going into coffee shops. The smells and sounds within the coffee shop assault our senses, and help us form an impression of the place and the coffee on sale. The noise of the coffee machines, the aroma of coffee beans roasting, the look and appearance of other consumers, the music being played, the crockery used, the coffee flavour itself—all these are perceived by us and combine to help us develop a preference for particular coffee brands. We learn what sizes and types of coffee are served at different places, and we may form attitudes to different coffee brands. Coffee companies also try to connect with their customers through various initiatives that help to form more personalized relations with them. In 2012, Starbucks brought the policy of writing customers' names on their cups to the UK. By writing your name on a cup, and creating a more customized experience (of what is actually a highly standardized offering), Starbucks aimed to build consumer loyalty by forming relationships with their customers. All these points show the importance of understanding the range of individual influences on consumption.

We have already mentioned some of the social elements of coffee consumption, and the social and cultural aspects of consumption that we deal with in Chapters 8 and 9 often influence our individual consumption choices. Thinking about culture and its impact on consumption, if we asked consumers from different cultures what coffee means to them, we would not only learn how coffee is viewed, but would also gain some insights into what it is like to live in that culture. While French consumers may talk about espresso machines and smoky brasseries, and American consumers may think more about bookstores and large milky drinks, in Asian countries coffee is more likely to be routinely sold by street vendors and is an entirely different concoction, made with both condensed and evaporated milk, often chilled in ice bags and drunk through a straw. And do you know where and when the 'flat white' was created? It was in Australia and New Zealand in the 1980s. Recently the major coffee chains have introduced cortados (from Spain) and macchiatos (from Italy) into their product ranges, effectively appropriating different products from around the globe. The different approaches to coffee reflect the geographical and sociocultural aspects of different countries, and the role that consumption occupies within different cultures. But there is another aspect to the macro-view of coffee consumption. All businesses need to know how their consumers are choosing their product rather than the many others available to them. What does the whole market look like? How does the market share of Caffe Nero compare with that of Costa or Starbucks? What is influencing our loyalty and how often do we switch between brands and why? This aspect of understanding consumers is covered in Chapter 10. You might like to consider for a moment how your own loyalty in buying coffee is influenced. Many of us own loyalty cards that we use in coffee shops, which are used by companies to encourage our repeat business. We might have these loyalty cards because we really do feel a positive emotional connection to the brand, which is great for that company. But at other times we use coffee shops for reasons not really down to our choice, but more through convenience and location—buying a coffee from whichever coffee outlet is available at the station we use to get to work. It makes sense to have a loyalty card for this, since we are repeat buyers, but it is not necessarily our favourite choice of coffee. And what about the future of coffee? Now you can make coffee in many different ways from powdered to filter to instant espresso machines. There are many different apps dedicated to coffee lovers. For example, Coffee Buzz lets you check into your favourite coffee shops and share what you are drinking, and Beanhunter finds the nearest coffee shops to your location.

As we can see from this analysis of coffee consumption, there are very many aspects impacting on what people are doing, and all have something useful and valuable to offer to organizations interested in knowing their consumers better.

In this book, we aim to show and explain the range of ways of thinking about and examining consumers. The latest issues in behavioural, psychological, and sociological approaches are presented alongside important techniques such as neuromarketing, and their application to marketing is discussed. There are many new trends, research, and discoveries occurring in such fields as economics and psychology, and new ways of understanding how and why people behave socially and culturally in a changing world, that are helping us to understand the factors that shape and influence people's behaviour in different environments. Many of these new approaches have been embraced by marketing practitioners, and in this book we provide various examples and illustrations of these theories being used in practice through our practitioner insights where we ask people actually involved with consumer behaviour what they think and do.

This book will take you through the key issues associated with developing a deep understanding of consumers, drawing insights from contemporary theory and marketing practice to ensure that you have a comprehensive appreciation of contemporary consumer behaviour.

How the book is organized

In Part 1, Chapters 1 and 2 provide an overview of the historical context for understanding consumption and also outline the different perspectives on consumption. Chapter 1 is important in providing a *historical perspective* on this subject, showing how our understanding of consumers has evolved and examining some of the debates around how we view consumers. In the second complementary chapter we consider *contemporary perspectives on consumption* that have had an impact on our understanding of how consumers are behaving in the twenty-first century and their importance for the theory and practice of consumer behaviour.

Part 2, comprising five chapters, provides a micro-view of consumption. Chapter 3, which focuses on *consumer decision-making*, is the first of five chapters that look at the individual. We continue the focus on the individual in the following four chapters and take a closer look at some of the psychological aspects of consumption. Chapter 4 considers the processes of *learning*, the different approaches to learning theory, and how these impact on consumption decisions. Chapter 5 focuses on *perception* and the processes underpinning the ways that consumers perceive and absorb marketing messages. In Chapter 6 we consider *attitude formation and change*, discussing some of the ways that both marketers and policy-makers use attitudes in practice. In Chapter 7 we turn to *personality, self and identity, and motivation* and consider how these impact on consumption, and discuss the sociocultural aspects of identity.

Part 3, which comprises three chapters, provides a macro-view of consumption. In Chapters 8 and 9 we move on to consider important cultural and social influences on aspects of consumption. In Chapter 8, we look at specific *social groups*, and the processes within and across groups that may impact upon how people consume, while in Chapter 9 we consider *culture* and how this shapes consumption. Chapter 10 complements Chapter 3 in terms of considering decision-making, but rather than looking at the individual it considers the macro-aspects of decision-making and what all the thousands of decisions made every day mean for companies. We consider actual purchasing behaviour mostly derived from large (often in the thousands) consumer panels and give close consideration to *patterns of repeat buying behaviour* and how this tells us what consumption actually looks like in the marketplace.

Part 4 focuses on where the field is going, and in the final chapter, Chapter 11, we consider the *future for consumer behaviour*, thinking about developments on the horizon and their implications for marketing practice.

How the book works

As discussed above, the book is in four parts and can be used in different ways depending on the structure of your consumer behaviour course (Figure P.2).

While we are suggesting above that one way to use this book is to move from Part 1 directly through to Part 4 starting with the historical context and current perspectives through micro and then macro influences to future trends, reading the book in different ways will not hinder your understanding of consumer behaviour. An alternative approach is to follow the first two chapters, then Part 3 (the macro-view) and Part 2 (the micro-view). This approach will take you from the broadest aspects of understanding consumption to the specifics of individual behaviour and how this is observed in the market.

Each chapter is organized in line with this framework, and at the start of each chapter we show how this topic fits with our overall understanding of consumer behaviour. We have provided learning objectives at the beginning of each chapter to help you follow the material covered, and navigate you through the chapter.

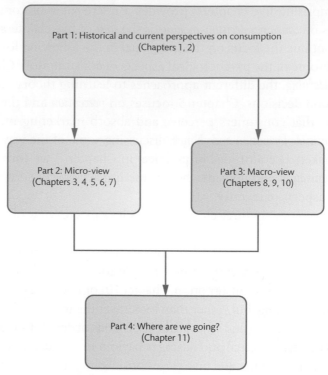

Part 1: Historical and current perspectives on consumption
(Chapters 1, 2)

Part 2: Micro-view
(Chapters 3, 4, 5, 6, 7)

Part 3: Macro-view
(Chapters 8, 9, 10)

Part 4: Where are we going?
(Chapter 11)

Figure P.2   Pathways for organizing your course using this book

One of the key aims of this book is to bring together leading thinking on consumers, alongside insights and examples from contemporary marketing practice. To do this, we have developed a set of 'insights' from research, marketing practice and consumer situations, which run throughout the book.

We bring cutting-edge thinking to your understanding of consumer behaviour in every chapter by featuring *Research Insights*, which provide a flavour of the current big ideas in the field and some of the important historical research findings and hint at where things are going. These Research Insights draw on academic work from around the world, and provide a combination of classic studies and others recently published in major international journals, including those from consumer culture theory. We hope that you will be sufficiently interested and encouraged to go to the original sources to discover the full import of the Research Insight.

One of the best ways of explaining consumer behaviour theory is through examples, and in this book we provide many different types of example to help you develop your understanding of consumers. Throughout each chapter many examples are integrated into the main text. Each chapter contains a number of *Consumer Insights*, which are mini-case examples, and include topics such as social networking in China, Sri-Lanka's mod-tradi consumers, Danish Hygge, the worldwide growth of discount stores, the use of celebrities to support sports brands such as Nike, and attitudes towards breaking the speed limit among drivers in

Australia. Additionally, every chapter includes an extended *Case Study* covering topics such as Snapchat, Havaianas, Oreo, lifestyle in India, and repertoire shopping in China, which bring together the themes discussed in the chapter, and help you to connect with the material.

To bring these theoretical approaches and ideas to life, every chapter contains *Practitioner Insights*, which are commentaries from marketing and advertising professionals who discuss consumer behaviour issues for their organization. Companies and organizations such as Dettol, Kantar Millward Brown, Ipsos, Thinkbox, and BrandSense all provide real-world views on the topics being discussed.

This book uses a variety of tools to help you understand consumer behaviour from a range of perspectives. We build on the traditional psychological approach to acknowledge more holistic perspectives of consumer behaviour and incorporate new areas of research, all of which are impacting on our understanding of this fascinating subject.

About this book (for lecturers and tutors)

The format and main features of this book have already been described. The book is designed to be worked through systematically, over a period of 10 or 11 weeks. Each chapter is accompanied by PowerPoint presentations covering key aspects and including additional illustrations and animations that bring the concepts to life. As we have already discussed, while we have suggested a structure and approach moving from historical influences on consumer behaviour through the micro- and then macro-view, we do not feel that the book imposes this structure on any course and it will easily accommodate a range of course structures.

Each chapter contains *Review Questions*, which students can use to check their base knowledge from the chapter. In addition, we provide a set of challenging *Discussion Questions* at the end of each chapter, which can be incorporated into workshops. The Case Studies in each chapter are also intended for use in workshop/seminar settings, and solutions are provided as part of the tutor pack.

New to the second edition

For this new edition of the book, we have updated the text in response to reader and lecturer feedback, as well as reflecting trends and shifts in the wider economic and social environment. We have added new coverage of sustainability and ethical issues in consumer behaviour, as well as substantially increasing the coverage of digital consumption and online consumer behaviour. These themes run through the whole book, developed through the examples and cases we use, and are reinforced through some of our research, consumer insights, and practitioner insights. Alongside this, we have extensively revised all the key features of our book, with new practitioner insights, new consumer insights and new case studies. Finally, we have thoroughly updated the book to reflect the latest research throughout, and over half of the research insights are new or updated.

GUIDED TOUR OF THE BOOK

Learning and applying understanding

> **LEARNING OBJECTIVES**
>
> Having read this chapter, you will be able to:
>
> 1. Evaluate the **early history of consumption** and the role of econ development of consumer behaviour.
>
> 2. Understand **how consumption became a part of everyday l** conspicuous consumption.
>
> 3. Recognize the **key trends in the development of shops and s** of **motivational research**.

Learning objectives

Clear and concise learning objectives help you to place the content of the chapter in context and allow you to identify the key topics and skills you will gain from working through the chapter. These are then revisited in the chapter conclusions. The learning objectives can also help you plan your revision to ensure you identify and cover all of the key concepts.

> **Review questions**
>
> 1. Define attitudes, and comment on the various componen
>
> 2. What do you understand by the term 'hierarchy of effect of your own from four different contexts, mapping these chy of effects outlined in the chapter.
>
> 3. Describe balance theory, and comment on how it is usefu two different illustrations of balance theory.

Review questions

There is a set of review questions at the end of every chapter, designed to test your knowledge of the key concepts in each chapter and consolidate your learning. Use them in your revision to ensure you understand the primary issues, theories, and developments.

> ## GLOSSARY
>
> **Absolute threshold** is the minimum amount of stimulation that can be picked up by any of our senses.
>
> **Acceptance/rejection** is when the consumer considers existing choice criteria and elaborates the message received to reach a point of acceptance or rejection of the information.
>
> **Attitude** is a learne a consistently favour relation to some obje
>
> **Attitude object/a** the attitude is held, a ideas, people, and be

Glossary of key terms

The key terms you need to know are highlighted in **bold** when they first appear in the chapter and defined in a glossary at the end of the book. The glossary provides an easy and practical way for you to revise and check your understanding of definitions, and provides quick reference for reviewing unfamiliar terms.

Consumer behaviour in practice

> **CONSUMER INSIGHT 9.3**
>
> ### *Hygge*: myth or reality?
>
> Sometimes an aspect of a country's culture can become so influen commodity. This has been the case with the concept of Danish *hygg* and how much reality? *Hygge* has been described as a feeling of c and the desire for *hygge* has become a fashion and lifestyle pheno least it is definitely reality.
>
> In 2016 Denmark was ranked first in the *World Happiness Rep*

Consumer insights

Every chapter contains a number of consumer insights, which explore issues such as celebrity endorsement, attitudes towards digital marketing, and social media. Well-known companies and organizations such as Nike, Samsung, and Ikea are used to illustrate these mini-case examples, while some consumer insights focus on specific regional markets, such as Uniqlo in Singapore and Abercrombie & Fitch in the US. The consumer insights are accompanied by questions which encourage you to think critically about how consumer behaviour theory is applied in a variety of contexts.

PRACTITIONER INSIGHT 9

Jeremy Rix, Managing Director, OKO

Do you care about how the meat you eat is produced? To what extent do you think about animal welfare when you're in the meat aisle at your local supermarket? Choosing to buy and eat meat is associated with many different beliefs and customs which manufacturers need to understand in order to identify the appropriate messages that resonate with their consumers' values.

Practitioner insights

Learn from the real-life experiences of people in business, advertising, and government to understand how they embrace new developments in marketing. Each practitioner insight focuses on a different aspect of consumer behaviour, from neuroimaging and consumers' use of technology and social media, to the ways that marketers use buyer behaviour data and principles to inform everyday business decisions. The practitioner insights help you understand exactly how the theories and developments play an important role in key organizations.

CASE STUDY 2

Snapchat—authentic and transient?

Launched in 2011, Snapchat (Figure 2.16) is a mobile app that allow [...] tures that self-destruct within a few seconds of their being viewed. It [...] users could engage with thoughts and pictures without concern that [...] them, as they were not permanent—friends had 10 seconds to vie[...] disappeared from their phone.

By May 2014, 700 million snaps a day were being sent (www.pock[...]

Case studies

An extended case study is provided at the end of every chapter, covering companies such as Snapchat and Havaianas, and topics such as lifestyle issues relevant to Indian consumers and gym culture in the UK. The case studies conclude with thought-provoking questions encouraging you to think about how developments in consumer behaviour theory impact organizations in practice.

Take your learning further

RESEARCH INSIGHT 1.1

Patsiaouras, G., Fitchett, J.A., and Davies, A. (2016), 'Beyond the c[...] character readings into narcissism and denial', *Marketing Theory*, 16, [...]

In this paper, the authors develop a psychoanalysis of the consumptic[...] the central characters, Jay Gatsby and Willy Loman, from the classic [...] *Death of a Salesman*. Using a Freudian psychoanalytic methodologi[...] how psychoanalysis can be used to bring fresh insights to contempo[...]

 Access the online resources and follow the web links to learn more.

Research insights

A number of research insights are included in every chapter to encourage you to read around the topic discussed and learn more about the current big ideas in consumer behaviour and some of the most important historical research findings. These research insights draw on academic work from around the world, and provide a combination of classic studies and others recently published in major international journals, including those from consumer culture theory. Around half of the research insights are brand new for this edition.

Discussion questions

1. Identify some examples of what you would consider t[...] sumption today. In your opinion what are such goods off[...] consume them?

2. Do you consider that consumption has a moral dimensi[...] major moral issues concerning consumption in the twent[...]

3. Look at the advertising for three brands of soap. Analyse[...] and consider whether they relate to Dichter's utilitarian o[...]

Discussion questions

Discussion questions can be found at the end of every chapter and have been designed to help you develop your analytical and reasoning skills, and encourage debate.

GUIDED TOUR OF THE ONLINE RESOURCES

The online resources that accompany this book provide students and registered adopters of the textbook with ready-to-use teaching and learning materials. These resources are designed to maximize the learning experience. Visit www.oup.com/uk/szmigin_piacentini2e/ to find out more.

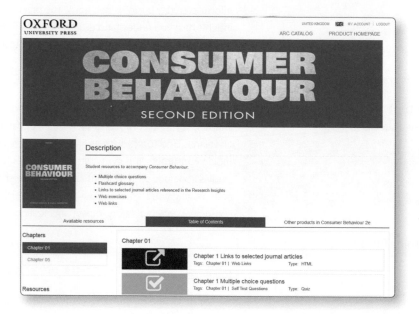

Student resources

Web exercises

Arranged by chapter, the web exercises help you to undertake online research and enhance your understanding of key consumer behaviour concepts with a variety of exercises.

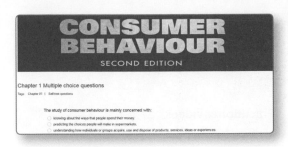

Multiple choice questions

Interactive multiple choice questions for every chapter give you instant feedback, as well as page references, to help you focus on the areas that need further study.

Flashcard glossary

Learning all the jargon related to consumer behaviour can be a challenge, so these online flashcards have been designed to help you understand and memorize the key terms used in the book.

Research insights

Follow the links to read the abstract and access the full paper of articles and books covered in the research insights.

Web links

Follow the web links to learn more about the companies and organizations covered in the book.

Lecturer resources

These resources are password protected, but access is available to adopters of the book.

Practitioner videos

Brand new for this edition, the practitioner videos are thought-provoking clips featuring some of the professionals from the practitioner insights in the book. The practitioners discuss contemporary issues in consumer behaviour and marketing and how they relate to the work they do. Full transcripts from the videos are also provided.

Instructor's manual

The instructor's manual is a substantial and superior ready-to-use online package of supplementary teaching resources that provides you with:

- notes on the case studies in the book and guidance on how to use them in class;
- additional questions for seminars or for assessment with indicative answers, and;
- additional questions and discussion points on the practitioner insights in the book.

Learning activities

This feature includes a range of more detailed workshop-based activities, shorter lecture-based in-class exercises, and suggestions for assessment approaches.

PowerPoint slides

Accompanying each chapter is a suite of customizable and illustrated PowerPoint slides for you to use in your lectures.

ACKNOWLEDGEMENTS

Authors' acknowledgements

The authors would like to thank the practitioners who took time to talk about their work to illustrate how important the understanding and application of consumer behaviour is to marketing products and services: Lord Mitchell (House of Lords), Simon Harrop (BRANDsense), Simon Tunstill (Thinkbox), Rachel Hartley (Nutracheck), Frederique Hull (Dettol), Edward Langley (Ipsos), Graham Staplehurst (Kantar Millward Brown), Andrew Tenzer (Trinity Mirror), Jeremy Rix (OKO), Tom Lloyd (Metametrics), and Lucy Milosavlovich (Grant Thornton UK LLP). They also thank Professor Byron Sharp (Director of the Ehrenberg-Bass Institute for Marketing Science, University of South Australia) for reading and commenting on Chapter 10, Lee Swinnerton (Lancaster University) for assisting with Case Study 8, and Dr Ahmad Daryanto (Lancaster University) for providing input on perceptual maps (Chapter 5).

The authors would like to thank the team at Oxford University Press for their support and guidance throughout this process. In particular, they thank Nicola Hartley and Caroline Mitchell for their editorial assistance.

Isabelle Szmigin would like to thank students at the University of Birmingham and the Singapore Institute of Management for 'trying out' the text. She would also like to thank Andrea Solomons, Kate Goldrick, and Jane Robertson for their support and advice.

Maria Piacentini would like to thank her students at Lancaster University, who have provided valuable feedback on the exercises and material contained in this book. She also thanks Emma Banister, Katy Mason, and Imogen Tyler for professional support and advice through this process. She also thanks her husband Bob and children Sandro and Rosa for providing a welcome distraction from the book and offering so many thoughts and insights as twenty-first century consumers.

Publisher's acknowledgements

The publisher would like to thank the practitioners and professionals who gave their time to provide us with an insight into how consumer behaviour theories play an important role in the real world

The publisher would also like to thank the very long list of people who kindly granted permission and supplied the images to illustrate this textbook: Kirklees Image Archive, George Aye at Hubwear, Le Bon Marché, Tesco Stores Ltd., Margy N. Javier, Canoe Inc., Waitrose, Bob Cromwell, Marie-Hélène Cingal, LazyTown Entertainment, John Cairns and the Department of Engineering Science at the University of Oxford, AB InBev, Cadbury's Ltd, FreshMinds, Karina Minteer, Appleby Westward Group, Selfridges & Co., Dollar King, United Biscuits, Boden, Eat Big Fish, McCann and Metro Trains Melbourne, Barry Doyon, Havaianas, the NSPCC, Zandera, Robert Opie and the Museum of Brands, Audi, Ogilvy & Mather, Brandon Ford, Nutcase Helmets, Paul Carrington, Triodos Bank, Honcho PR, Chillblast, Reckitt Benckiser, Oase Outdoors, Marks & Spencer, Springer, Wallop Design, Jung von Matt, Kantar Millward Brown, Cartier, Casio, Zizzi, Nicoletta Reggio, The American Marketing Association, Nike Inc., Strategic Business Insights, Pop Chips, Volvo Cars, Ecover, Beattie McGuinness Bungay, Gozogomo, Uniqlo, Unilever, Cognation, Atelier Opa, Mayer/McCann Erickson, Slovakia, and Miele, Sanrino, The Victoria Tea Room, Phillips Taiwan, INTAGE Ltd., Frankie Roberto, Nestlé, MyNetDiary Inc., Martin Thuresson, Pocket-Lint, Jo Hodge, Martin Thuresson, Nest Labs Inc., Hiut Denim, Harvard Business Review, Statista, Kantar Media CIC, CrowdOptic, Ipsos Mori, Under Armour, Emerald Group, Gatorade, TBWA/Chiat/Day Inc, SCSC, iD Agency, Roger Blackwell, National Environment Agency Singapore, John Lewis, Taylor & Francis, Open International Publishing Ltd., the Fairtrade Organisation, Christopher Terry, Coca-Cola Retailing Research Council Eurasia & Africa, American Psychological Association, Goldman Sachs Global Investment Research, the NHS, McCain, adam&eveDBB, Tuesday's Child Agency, Dennis Publishing Ltd, Revistadonna, Lloyds Banking Group, and Datapine.

Every effort has been made to contact copyright holders, but in some instances this was not possible. We will be pleased to clear permission with any copyright holders we were unable to contact in the first instance.

Editorial advisors

The authors and Oxford University Press are immensely grateful to the following reviewers, who provided invaluable feedback at multiple stages throughout the writing of this text to inform its development and help us ensure that it fulfilled its aims.

James Blackmore-Wright, University of Northampton
Catherine Canning, Glasgow Caledonian University
Dr Laura Chamberlain, University of Warwick
Dr Polymeros Chrysochou, Aarhus University
Dr Farooq Chudry, University of the West of England
Dr Carl Clare, Leeds Beckett University
Andrew Corcoran, Aston University
Dr Dianne Dean, University of Hull
Dr John Desmond, University of St Andrews
Dr Athina Dilmperi, Middlesex University
Dr Amanda Earley, University of Leicester

Professor Anita Eves, University of Surrey
Dr Stephanie Feiereisen, City, University of London
Dr Clare Foster, Keele University
Tim Froggett, Anglia Ruskin University
Dr Ayantunji Gbadamosi, University of East London
Dr Alvina Gillani, University of Surrey
Dr Diana Gregory-Smith, University of Birmingham
Dr Alexander Gunz, University of Manchester
Dr Anne Harbisher, Staffordshire University
Dr Jason Healy, Dublin City University
Dr Paul Hewer, Strathclyde University
Professor Chanaka Jayawardhena, University of Hull
Dr Sarah Maddock, University of the West of England
Donald McFetridge, Retail Analyst, Author and Broadcaster
Dr Miriam McGowan, Bangor University
Dr Sally McKechnie, University of Nottingham
Dr Christina O'Connor, Maynooth University
Dr Andrew Perkins, Canterbury Christ Church University
Dr Brendan Richardson, University College Cork
Professor Peter Scott, University of Reading
Professor Jaywant Singh, Kingston University London
Professor Peeter W.J. Verlegh, Vrije Universiteit Amsterdam
Dr Markus Wohlfeil, University of Stirling
Dr Dorothy A. Yen, Brunel University London
Dr Anita Lifen Zhao, Swansea University

PART 1

HISTORICAL AND CURRENT PERSPECTIVES ON CONSUMPTION

Where are we going?

Future trends in
consumer behaviour

Macro-view

Consumers in society and
the market: groups, social processes,
culture, and repeat purchasing behaviour

Micro-view

The individual consumer: individual
decision-making, learning, perception,
attitudes, personality and motivation

How we arrived here

Historical context and
contemporary perspectives
on consumption

1

A HISTORICAL CONTEXT FOR UNDERSTANDING CONSUMPTION

Introduction

Consumption is a core part of our everyday lives. From the minute we wake up we are confronted with situations that have some element of consumption to them. Just getting ready to go to a college or university class in the morning, you face many consumer decisions: What to eat for breakfast? Which clothes to wear? What fragrance to put on? Which form of transport to use? What music to listen to (and in what form)? Which books to take, and in which bag? These are just *some* of the consumption-related decisions consumers have to think about, and most of these take place within 30 minutes of getting up!

Marketing practitioners and policy-makers need to understand consumer behaviour. Central to the marketing concept is the need for organizations to recognize the factors that shape and influence people's behaviour in different environments. The cultures of those of us living in affluent societies are influenced by consumption. We shop, consume, and compare ourselves with others through the products and brands we use. What food we eat and how much exercise we take may have a long-term impact on our health and well-being, which is also of importance to government and policy-makers. Businesses want to understand how and why consumers shop and consume in the ways they do both to develop products and to effectively communicate with customers. Arnould et al. (2004: 5) describe consumption as 'individuals or groups acquiring, using and disposing of products, services, ideas or experiences'. But to gain a solid appreciation of consumer behaviour, it is important to look to the past to understand how people thought about and practised consumption, and to think about how this has moulded the ways we consume today.

LEARNING OBJECTIVES

Having read this chapter, you will be able to:

1. Evaluate the **early history of consumption** and the role of economics and philosophy in the development of consumer behaviour.

2. Understand **how consumption became a part of everyday life**, including the rise of conspicuous consumption.

3. Recognize the **key trends in the development of shops and shopping**, as well as the rise of **motivational research**.

4. Evaluate the role of **consumerism** in the development of consumption.

5. Learn how **consumers can be classified** and identify types of consumers.

6. Explain what a **postmodern consumer** is.

7. Analyse the **different approaches to studying consumers**.

An early history of consumers and consumption

Hundreds of years ago most people would have produced their own food and clothing, primarily concerned with sourcing what they needed to survive. They had no opportunity to make choices between alternative products or brands, partly because there was so little to choose from and because few would be living above subsistence level. If surplus was produced, then it may have been exchanged for other goods. This contrasts sharply with contemporary living; as we shall see in Chapter 3, today we have more choice than ever before. Trentmann (2016) begins his history of consumers by remarking that a typical German today will own 10,000 objects, while a British adult will have roughly 100 items of clothing, a quarter of which never leave the cupboard. It is important, however, to remember that in many parts of the world subsistence level consumption still exists. In Tanzania, for example, many people farm small plots of land which provide most of their food and engage in alternative forms of economic exchange to meet their various day-to-day needs (Figure 1.1).

In medieval times there were traditional patterns of exchange through sharing and bartering, often within a fixed geographical location such as a village. Today the exchange and swapping of unwanted consumer items goes beyond geographical boundaries, with much of it done online. Often, as in the case of the Malaysian online swapping site Swap.me, reuse and recycling are actively encouraged and such exchange may be seen as a way to promote sustainability (Brohier, 2014). Once goods are being made specifically to be bought and consumed by others, we begin to see one of the most important aspects of marketing: the relationship between production and consumption. Companies produce goods and services for people to buy; in order to buy, con-

Figure 1.1   Subsistence farming in Tanzania
Source: © iStock.com/nwbob.

sumers have to see value in these goods and services, so that they are prepared to exchange money for them. We shall discuss some of the issues that have arisen from the development of the process of exchange later in this chapter when we consider Karl Marx's views on the relationship between production and consumption.

Historians and economists debate over when consumption, and hence consumer behaviour, became a feature of society (Benson, 1994; Stearns, 2001). Table 1.1 gives a brief overview of some key points in the development of consumption. The term originated from the Latin *consumere*, which became used in Europe from the twelfth century onwards to refer to the using up of something such as food, candles, and firewood (Trentmann, 2016). Early

	Historical consumer milestones
12th century	The word *consumere* is used in Latin
15th century	Europeans import spices from East
16th century	The Royal Exchange Shopping Gallery opened in London
17th century	Social codes of dress become part of court life More products available to consume
18th century	The Industrial Revolution The term *middle class* first appears. Adam Smith publishes *The Wealth of Nations*
19th century	John Stuart Mill criticizes 'unproductive consumption' Karl Marx publishes ideas on product and labour value
20th century	Rationing of consumption during the First and Second World Wars Influence of Freud and Dichter in motivational resarch Keynes advises government to find ways to increase consumption The term *consumer sovereignty* first used
21st century	UN's 17 Sustainable Development Goals published

Table 1.1   Timeline of some key consumer behaviour milestones

accounts prioritized production over consumption, but consumption has clearly been a feature of human society and culture since the earliest times. The growth of trade, and more latterly globalization, has been a key element in the development of consumption beyond subsistence. Spices were one of the earliest traded goods and were highly valuable; for example, nutmeg was worth more by weight than gold (Szczepanski, 2013). This trade dates back to pre-Roman times, but became highly significant across Europe and Asia in the medieval period. In the late Middle Ages the wealthy developed a taste for sugar, which led to an increase in production, with sugar plantations established in European colonies.

Products such as sugar were the privilege of the elite, and their widespread consumption did not begin to pick up until the rise of the urban middle classes in western Europe. The idea of a middle class of society purchasing consumer goods only emerged in the late nineteenth century (Loftus, 2011), although the term 'middle class' was first used in the eighteenth century. Those able to afford such goods before this time were primarily members of the aristocracy. In aristocratic circles, consumption was a required and visible part of daily life. For example, in the court of the French King Louis XIV (1638–1715) there was a social code that required discretionary spending on frivolous items such as silverware, jewellery, and handkerchiefs (Kroen, 2004). The Elizabethans also recognized some 'must-have' fashion items. As Neil MacGregor (2012), the former Director of the British Museum, notes, the man of fashion needed his rapier and dagger just as today he would want his watch or trainers. Courtiers had to conform to social norms which required spending large amounts of money on fashions dictated by the monarch (see Figure 1.2).

Recent historical accounts have challenged the view that most consumption of luxury goods was restricted to the elites. New evidence suggests that the consumption of goods such as tea and coffee (and the utensils required for their consumption) grew rapidly throughout the eighteenth century and was on a scale that suggests widespread consumption (McCants, 2007). Not only was consumption extensive, but it also proved a key stimulant of the Industrial Revolution, and therefore, arguably, the rise of contemporary mass consumerism as local attempts at producing exotic goods multiplied. Associated with this revision has been an emphasis on the global aspects of consumption, with an increased understanding of the role of trade with Asia, a source of many of the groceries and manufactured goods consumed at this time. Global influence is also nothing new; Trentmann (2016) describes how in the mid-nineteenth century Indian officials under colonial British rule began to wear suits (although usually with turbans rather than hats). Today people are increasingly aware of the impact of climate change from buying globally sourced items and often choose to purchase locally produced

Figure 1.2   Portrait of King Louis XIV

Source: © iStock.com/hrstklnkr. Original painted by Hyacinthe Rigaud (1701).

goods. In response, retailers are sourcing food products from local suppliers, which can simplify their supply chains and transportation costs and build popularity with their community and committed local shoppers who have been referred to as 'locavores'. The local food market in the USA is forecast to be as much as $20.2 billion by 2019 (Goller, 2016).

As the rate of consumption increased, so did its critics. Historically, the rise in consumerism has been accompanied by the development of various critiques of consumption attitudes and behaviour, from early Christian and Judaic asceticism through Puritanism to present-day ideas around anti-consumption and voluntary simplicity. Some of these ideas have been enshrined in law. An interesting aspect of early consumption was the development of **sumptuary laws**, which are laws that attempt to *'regulate expenditure, especially with a view to restraining excess in food, dress, equipage, etc.'* (*Oxford English Dictionary*, 2013).

Throughout history, sumptuary laws have played a role in many countries as a way of regulating people's expenditure and curbing conspicuous consumption. For example, sumptuary laws in China can be traced back to the Qin dynasty (221bc), embodying the Confucian virtue of restraint. In medieval England, sumptuary laws were important for distinguishing ranks within society, with an emphasis on the clothing that different social groups could or could not wear, thus reinforcing social hierarchies. For example, knights were not allowed to wear gold or ermine (Berry, 1994). In renaissance Italy, sumptuary laws focused on women's clothing, restricting the wearing of low necklines and jewelled sable furs as accessories (Killerby, 2002). These laws are a manifestation of an important theme found in many studies of consumer behaviour that centre around the idea of the 'right' or 'best' way to consume. Today, while some people are accused of excessive, wasteful, or conspicuous consumption, others are concerned about ethical consumption and the impact that their behaviour has on the environment and on people living in socio-politically oppressive regimes. Throughout the history of consumption we see this juxtaposition of conspicuous or inappropriate consumption against more considered or thoughtful ways to consume. We begin to see some of these concerns expressed in the work of the Scottish economist Adam Smith, which we discuss in the next section. Consumer Insight 1.1 explores some of these issues in the context of sugar and chocolate production.

CONSUMER INSIGHT 1.1

Slavery, sugar, and chocolate

Along with the enjoyment of sugar came the responsibility of growing it. In the eighteenth century, this work was undertaken by slaves. Some anti-slave campaigners compared sugar consumption to cannibalization, suggesting that it was like consuming the flesh of the slaves who had grown it. Although boycotting of slave-grown sugar became a transatlantic movement, it did not last long. The abolition of slavery in 1833 led to a moral retreat to the extent that when the media turned the spotlight on slave-produced cocoa in the early twentieth century, there was little response from consumers (Grant, 2005).

Unfortunately, slave labour in the production of cocoa, usually child slave labour, continues to this day in West Africa. It has been argued that the huge chocolate industry has not taken significant steps to end the use of child labour through incentives such as paying cocoa farmers a living wage (Fair Trade USA, 2017).

Consumers today cannot be sure that the chocolate they buy has not been produced using child labour or slavery. There are many different labels on chocolate bars such as fair trade certifications and the Rainforest Alliance Certification, but they cannot guarantee that exploitation has not been involved. In 2009, the founders of the fair trade certification process had to suspend several of their Western African suppliers due to evidence that they were using child labour.

Multiple government and non-governmental organization (NGO) programmes have been developed in an attempt to address the root causes of child labour and slavery in West Africa. However, the success of these efforts will depend greatly on the genuine support or lack thereof from the chocolate industry over the coming years.

Questions

1. What do you consider to be the responsibility of chocolate manufacturers in the issue of the production of chocolate?

2. What do you consider to be the responsibility of consumers in the purchase of chocolate?

3. Examine the pros and cons of boycotting a chocolate brand that might have been produced by child labour.

Sources: Sussman (2000); Grant (2005); BBC (2010); Fairtrade Labelling Organizations International (2012); Trentmann (2016); Fair Trade USA (2017).

 Access the online resources and follow the web links to learn more.

Economists, philosophers, and consumption

Adam Smith's *Wealth of Nations*, first published in 1776, is credited with first articulating the relationship between consumption, production, and democracy that has been central to the concept of the consumer in the twentieth and twenty-first centuries (Kroen, 2004). Smith lived at a time when the priorities of economists lay largely in issues around production. However, he began to look for the connections between consumption and production, writing that 'Consumption is the sole end and purpose of all production; and the interest of the producer ought to be attended to, only in so far as it may be necessary for promoting that of the consumer' (Smith, 1776/1981: 660). Smith was very concerned that justice and some degree of fair distribution of wealth were assured. He was particularly anxious that labourers with little education and many physical needs would always be at a disadvantage in the marketplace as they did not have the resources to better themselves. We shall see concern for the disadvantaged consumer again when we look at 'types' of consumer later in this chapter. In this quotation we also see one of the first discussions of the relationship between production and consumption. In this case Smith made it clear that producers had a responsibility to their consumers.

In the *Wealth of Nations*, Smith recognized that consumption could help to stimulate an economy. While he suggested that consumption be restricted to promoting economic growth, he also believed that luxury consumption could prevent stagnation. Luxury consumption was a concern of another philosopher and economist, John Stuart Mill, who criticized the purchase of luxuries such as gold, lace, pineapples, and champagne as 'unproductive' consumption (Mill, 1848/2004). Such unproductive consumers were placed in opposition to the productive ones whose consumption helped the working man, who in turn would buy necessities which would further assist working people. Today, consumption is more complex. We may recognize that some goods such as branded trainers are not essential for children, but we are also aware that without the appropriate clothing they may be victimized or feel inferior in some way to their peers at school (Elliott and Leonard, 2004).

In the nineteenth century, Karl Marx was concerned that people did not recognize the value of the commodities they consumed (Marx, 1867/2000). For Marx, a commodity was primarily a product of labour. Wood cannot become a table unless it has been turned into a useful object through the process of someone working on the wood. As workers moved into factories, rather than producing goods at home or locally, they had no control of how much they were able to sell their labour for and so were open to exploitation from the rich factory owners who controlled their employment. Consider today the people who make cheap clothes for high street shops; they too have no control over how much their labour is worth to the factory owners or to us, the end consumers.

Value is a hard idea to pin down, so consequently there are a number of different conceptions of it. A common concept of value for a good or service is **exchange value**, which in most circumstances is the same as the market price. Exchange value can be said to *represent what the value of a good is to the consumer and therefore what it could be exchanged for, usually its price*. We expect uniform exchanges in shops—we expect the same T-shirt to be priced consistently. In a competitive market, the price balances the maximum consumers will pay against the minimum suppliers will take, so exchange value is critical in how markets function. **Use value** is another notion of value that adds a further dimension. It means the satisfaction we get from a good or service, which is usually thought of as being determined by a set of attributes that define its quality (e.g. for a car this might include fuel economy, performance, and boot space). Use value can be described as *the value of a good to the consumer in terms of the usefulness it provides*. Use value is necessary for exchange value, but can be above it or below it for an individual buyer or seller. Most home-owners do not have their house on the market; its use value to them is higher than its exchange value. You might decide not to buy a jacket because it is too expensive, meaning that the exchange value is higher than its use value to you. These traditional economic concepts treat the consumer as self-contained, unconcerned about how others view them. Today, however, we also talk about the **sign or symbolic value** which is *the symbolic meaning consumers attach to goods to construct and participate in the social world*; in doing so they consume the idea of the good to signal identity in social relationships. This can turn the traditional categories on their heads, so that a higher price signals that a good is exclusive and may make purchase attractive even if in traditional functional terms its use value may be similar to an alternative that is cheaper or has a lower exchange value. Purchase can be important because it sends a social message about how you want to be seen in society.

Imagine the actual cost of making a handbag compared with the price for which it can be sold in a designer store, such as Prada or Gucci. The *exchange value* of that handbag does not represent its *use value*, because the function could just as easily be provided by a much cheaper alternative. However, the *sign value* of such handbags is probably higher for those who purchase them than either the exchange value or the use value. Of course, for most of us today these are difficult concepts to grapple with, as many of the objects we consume are defined by their sign or symbolic value more than their use value. Although Marx lived at a time before the proliferation of designer handbags, he recognized that once goods had lost the link with their nature of production and their use value, they took on a mysterious quality that he termed the **fetishism of commodities** (Marx, 1876/1976) which can be described as '*the disguising or masking of commodities whereby the appearance of goods hides the story of those who made them and how they made them*' (Lury, 1999: 42).

During the First World War, rationing of consumption became a reality; consumption was restricted not only by the scarcity of goods but also by government actions such as wage restraints, tariffs, and 'buy national' campaigns (de Grazia, 2005). After the war, the British liberal economist Maynard Keynes began to consider how wages could be increased to aid people's purchasing power. Keynes recommended that the British government should find ways to increase consumption as a means to economic recovery, and developed the concept of the **consumption function** which *maps the relationship between disposable income and level of wages*. In particular, it showed that the rich saved proportionately more of their income and therefore consumed relatively less than the remainder of the population. Therefore it was necessary to find ways to encourage the rich to spend or invest their savings in the production of goods to be consumed.

Such encouragement to spend emerged again after the global financial crisis of the early twenty-first century, and consumers were encouraged to spend to ensure continuing production to aid fiscal recovery.

Consumption becomes part of everyday life

The first half of the nineteenth century saw a major economic transformation. The Industrial Revolution of the eighteenth century led to the increased production of goods and to forms of manufacture that produced more goods quickly, which meant that prices dropped and more people could purchase them. At the same time, the marketing environment began to develop with improved forms of distribution, retailing, and advertising.

Before the Industrial Revolution much production and consumption had been through cottage industries, small-scale farming, bartering, and buying from neighbours, at fairs, and from hawkers or others who travelled the country selling door to door. Markets were the most formal site for buying and selling. Shops were barely recognizable in the medieval period. They had no glass windows, but were open during the day, often with a simple stall outside, and protected with shutters at night. More recognizable shops began to appear in the seventeenth century, and spread in the eighteenth century with the development of new methods of producing glass. The first shopping mall or gallery, the Royal Exchange Shopping Gallery, appeared in the UK in 1568; the still thriving London store Fortnum and Mason was founded in 1707. Accompanying these developments were new approaches to marketing. Goods could now be displayed in shop windows to entice customers into shops to purchase (see Figure 1.3). Advertising began to develop, and the first shopping arcades appeared in the late eighteenth century in Paris.

The types of product sold also changed. Industrialization and early global trading provided a hugely expanded range of goods. Manufacturers and shop owners realized they could persuade people to buy more than they needed. For example, new fashions in clothing could be introduced to ensure that people bought items regularly. Department stores became the place to shop in urban areas, and mail-order companies emerged as a way to transport a wider range of goods to rural consumers. In Bejing, China, in the early twentieth century, Tianquia ('Bridge of Heaven') was like a modern day mall with over 300 shops and a leisure complex with acrobats, singers, roller skating, and bowling on offer (Trentmann, 2016).

Figure 1.3　A Victorian grocer's shop　　*Source:* Image courtesy of Kirklees Image Archive (www.kirkleesimages.org.uk).

The increase in the range and nature of products was influenced by industrial innovations in all aspects of human life. Some of these were in materials such as plastic, which was introduced around the middle of the nineteenth century, and artificial fibres such as rayon, nylon, and viscose. These gave expanded possibilities for the design and manufacture of consumer goods. Transport was the site of successive waves of innovation, from steam to air travel, with the car in particular proving a consumer success on a massive scale. Household appliances multiplied, and food and cooking were revolutionized by inventions such as canning and freezing (see Consumer Insight 1.2). Technological innovations in electronic products have meant that computers have become much smaller but with more capacity. But perhaps more importantly, computers, mobile phones, and the internet have built a new need among consumers to be continually connected with one another—friends, family, and places of work—and in turn this has led to different modes of working, shopping, and keeping in touch with people on a 24-hour, 7 days a week basis.

CONSUMER INSIGHT 1.2

How innovation changed the way we eat and live

Most of us include at least some convenience food in our diets. Innovations such as canned food were introduced to Britain after the First World War, and frozen foods, introduced in the USA in the 1920s by Clarence Birdseye, meant that storing food became much easier. By 1961 over 60 Birds Eye products, including fish fingers, were available to UK consumers (Hardyment, 1995). Such innovations meant that many people had a better and greater variety of food. It also meant that women did not have to spend so much time at home cooking, and working outside the home increased. In 1900 only 21 per cent of American women worked outside the home; by 1999 this had increased to 60 per cent, and so innovations such as the microwave were invaluable. However, they also changed the way people ate. Convenience meals could be heated quickly, and different members of the family could easily cook their meals at any time of the day. In 1989 fewer than 20 per cent of the French population had microwaves at home, but by 1995 over half did (Fernandez-Aremesto, 2001). In the 1980s India saw the introduction of convenience brands such as Maggi instant noodles which offered mothers convenience and children fun and novelty. However, there are critics of the increase in convenience food. Nestle (2003: 20) comments: 'Many food products relegate cooking to a low-priority chore and encourage trends toward one-dish meals, fewer side dishes, fewer ingredients, larger portions to create leftovers, almost nothing cooked "from scratch", and home-delivered meals ordered by phone, fax, or internet'.

Questions

1. Outline the main advantages of convenience foods.

2. What do you think have been the main societal impacts of convenience food?

3. Take another product class, such as books or cars, and consider how changes over the years have impacted on how we use them.

Sources: Hardyment (1995); Fernandez-Armesto (2001); Nestle (2003).

 Access the online resources and follow the web links to learn more.

While product innovation has meant that consumers have more and better products to choose from, it has also led to what is often termed planned or built-in obsolescence, where a product has a limited lifespan and is regularly replaced with new versions. Early car-makers were concerned with producing standardized and durable cars, but by the 1920s and 1930s they were introducing regular (often annual) model changes. Often just superficial changes to the appearance of the car, they were designed to encourage people to feel that their car was out of date and needed replacing. This practice is now common in consumer behaviour; we regularly update our wardrobes, mobile phones, computers, and furnishings long before they no longer work or are worn out. Therefore today many of us are not only able to buy more types of goods, but we buy the same item many more times than previous generations. Increasingly, however, firms, consumers, and even governments are becoming more aware and responsive to the need to reduce unnecessary waste (see also Chapters 3 and 11). The Swedish government is introducing reductions on VAT rates for the repair of household items such as washing machines and bicycles as well as clothes and shoes (Orange, 2016).

Conspicuous consumption

American economist Thorstein Veblen introduced the idea of 'conspicuous consumption', where goods represented a way to compete and gain social recognition, in his book *Theory of the Leisure Class* (Veblen, 1899/2007). Veblen was concerned with the very wealthy and how they consumed and compared themselves with one another through their mansions, furnishings, carriages, and clothes. The possession of goods signified esteem; without them an individual was nobody. An important aspect of Veblen's analysis of this leisure class was their ability to be extravagant and wasteful; they could pay huge amounts of money for clothes that they would rarely wear or food that they would not consume. Today we are encouraged not to be wasteful, and the waste that consumer society produces has itself caused huge problems in landfill sites and impact on the environment. It might be that some people in countries where there is serious poverty and people are malnourished would see Western society as a modern day equivalent of Veblen's leisure class. Also, consumers in former Eastern Bloc countries, other former communist countries, and developing countries are playing catch-up in order to experience the pleasure and novelty of being able to consume in the way that the West has done for so long. It may be difficult for such people to hear others exhort them not to consume excessively when so many of us have been able to do so for so long. Consumer Insight 1.3 considers how consumption is currently used to signify status.

CONSUMER INSIGHT 1.3

Needs versus wants

Alain de Botton, in his book *Status Anxiety* (de Botton, 2005), uses Veblen (1899/2007) as a starting point for considering what material goods are necessary for happiness. Today, many people are concerned not only about the goods they possess, but also about whether they are the 'right' products and brands. Trendwatching.com (2010) describes five features of the 'statusphere', the term used to describe the diverse ways that consumers are finding to express their status in the twenty-first century. These include consuming bigger, better, and harder than other consumers, showing one's green consumption credentials, or having knowledge and skills as ways of displaying status. Just as traditional luxury symbols still signify status (as illustrated by the continued popularity of luxury cars in China, with 32 per cent growth in Mercedes car sales in 2016 (Chua Kong Ho, 2016)), so too is it important to show that you have relevant consumer knowledge and skills, facilitated greatly by technology and the use of apps by consumers, which place them 'in the know'. The Bandsintown Gig Finder app helps users to find local music and includes recommendations based on what's in your library, searches for shows by location, and provides venue directions and ticketing links. Similarly, in 2009/10, the Adidas Urban Art guide was launched as a guide to the best graffiti in Berlin and Hamburg where users could retrieve images and information about graffiti artists. Some goods can provide understated status. For example, Hubwear produces customized T-shirts that show the airport codes of the wearer's memorable trips. While to those 'not in the know' this may just look like a T-shirt with a series of letters, to the wearer it is truly meaningful. Can you work out the two destinations in Figure 1.4?

Figure 1.4 A Hubwear T-shirt
Source: Image courtesy of George Aye at Hubwear (http://hw.santheo.com/shop/?ams).

Questions

1. Think of ways in which people might use products or services to signify their status. How do you think that this differs by culture and age?

2. Can you think of any items that have been used for status but are no longer perceived in this way?

3. Trendwatching.com talks about 'unconsumption' as being a potential status tool. How do you think people would use this to provide status?

Sources: Veblen (1899/2007); de Botton (2005); www.hubwear.com www.trendwatching.com

 Access the online resources and follow the web links to learn more.

Figure 1.5   Le Bon Marché in the nineteenth and twenty-first centuries
Source: Images courtesy of Le Bon Marché. Image to the right is copyright Gabriel de la Chapelle.

Key trends in the development of shopping

To satisfy people's desires for more and different goods, a greater variety of shopping sites began to appear in the nineteenth century. Le Bon Marché in Paris opened its doors in 1838 (see Figure 1.5). To begin with, it was just a mix of clothing stores grouped together a bit like a modern shopping mall, but by the 1850s it was recognizable as a modern department store. Gradually, items other than clothes were added—furniture, kitchen goods, and toys. The department store offered the consumer huge choice, with the opportunity to browse and look at items other than those they had intended to buy.

New ways to shop

Department stores developed ways of enticing consumers with sales and special promotions and exciting new window displays built around seasons and festivities such as Easter, Thanksgiving, and Christmas. Other famous department stores, such as Macy's in New York, and Harrods and Selfridges in London, opened soon after, with the department store concept spreading rapidly to other countries, such as El Corte Ingles in Spain, GUM in Russia, Edgars in South Africa, and METRO in Singapore. An important feature of department stores was that the customer became anonymous. Previously, in local shops and markets, the customers were known to the store or stall owner; in department stores they were not, and indeed the shop assistants were not encouraged to develop such relationships. Alongside the development of department stores other new ways of shopping were introduced. With a large rural population unable to get to department stores, catalogue shopping became particularly popular in the USA at the end of the nineteenth century. Through catalogues, department stores could be brought directly into their customers' homes. Today people still shop in department stores or from catalogues, alongside new opportunities such as shopping on the web using their computer or mobile phone. What has changed is the variety of opportunities to shop, the variety of items available through such different channels, and that every part of the day is now available for shopping.

From service to self-service

While department stores increased the personal distance between the customer and the retailer, this found its most extreme form with the introduction of self-service in the development of the supermarket in the USA in the 1930s. Customers were required to find what they wanted in the shop and place their shopping in a trolley, which was able to carry more than the traditional basket, thus encouraging more purchasing. In her book *Carried Away by Shopping*, Rachel Bowlby describes the effect of supermarkets as signalling the difference between 'doing' and 'going' shopping: 'doing the shopping involves definite articles, a necessary task; going shopping is out of the way, open-ended, a diversion' (Bowlby, 2000: 32). This is an important point in the history of consumer behaviour, as it signals that even grocery shopping no longer needed to be purely functional but could be something more akin to leisure. Impulse purchasing was encouraged by the supermarket, where a customer would see an item that they had not previously been aware of or thought that they needed and put it into their basket. The location of goods and their apparent easy availability, such that the shopper could pick them up without having to ask an assistant, was an important feature and a major opportunity for retailers and producers in developing packaging and point-of-sale material. The suburban shopping mall, as we recognize it today, appeared after the Second World War and was designed to overcome customers' problems with parking and the weather. As more women were in the workforce people became time poor, and daily grocery shopping was replaced by weekly shopping facilitated by the car.

Today most Western consumers have access to diverse shopping environments. High street shops, farmers' markets, charity shops, shopping malls, express supermarkets, vending machines, and out-of-town supermarkets are all part of the shopping environment. Examples of all these modes of shopping can be found across the world. Dubai, known for its mega-malls and shopping complexes, is beginning to develop a market for more individual and artisan food shops (such as Baker & Spice and Secrets Fine Foods http://secretsfine-food.com), and in 2013 held its first farmers' market, selling organic produce sourced from the United Arab Emirates (UAE) region (Hirsch, 2013). Developments in vending machine technology have resulted in a vast range of foodstuffs being sold this way, including a live crab vending machine in China, a vending machine selling bouquets of flowers in Japan (see Figure 1.6), and an

Figure 1.6   A vending machine in Japan selling bouquets of flowers
Source: Image kindly supplied by Margy N. Javier.

egg, milk, and cheese vending machine in Germany (Knutson, 2013). Increasingly technological advances are helping to innovate how we shop.

While buying online has never been easier, it often lacks the visual experience of being in a store. This is where virtual reality (VR) comes into its element. A number of companies have introduced virtual stores; for example, Australian department store Myers linked up with eBay to introduce what they are calling the world's first virtual department store, with over 12,000 products with prices and stock information updated in real time. Customers wear the VR headset and can browse products in a three-dimensional setting before purchasing.

One of the most recent phenomena in retailing has been pop-up shops, and 'pop-upping' (see www.Trendwatch.com) has also spread to pop-up food outlets and pop-up brands. The first pop-up shops appeared in the late 1990s, but recent global recessionary pressures have stimulated the pop-upping phenomenon with the increased availability of cheap retail space and the lack of capital to invest in longer-term projects. Pop-up stores offer consumers surprise and novelty, and because their lifespan is limited they introduce an element of urgency among consumers and, in the case of food outlets, almost a cult following. Mostly these are small-scale shops or food trucks that offer producers the opportunity to engage with customers without the capital cost of a restaurant or shop, but others are more sophisticated. When Kanye West launched his *Life of Pablo* album in 2016, he also opened 21 simultaneous pop-up stores around the world for the Yeezy/Life of Pablo clothing range. Fashion pop-up stores are very popular, with examples including the Tribe Pop-Up Shop in Kenya, based at the boutique Tribe Hotel and showcasing the work of local designers (Lati, 2012), and the Love Story Pop-Up shop in Sydney, which sells designer clothes, typical of many fashion pop-ups.

In 2011, the first pop-up mall, Boxpark, appeared in London's East End (Figure 1.7). On a site which had been derelict for the previous 40 years, 60 recycled shipping containers form the shops which make up the mall. Boxpark offers small brands 'low-risk retailing' where they can sign up to stay for between one and five years, when the lease on the site will run out. Box Park has already become popular with locals and a tourist destination.

A similar logic underlies the way that big brands have taken to marketing products as limited editions, where they introduce a new product for a limited time to encourage a sense of urgency among their customers. KitKat introduced a number of limited edition Chunky bars including Double Choc, peanut, orange, and white chocolate flavours. Consumers were encouraged to vote on Facebook for their favourite as only one of the flavours would survive.

Motivational research—from the rational to the emotional

After the First World War a divide in terms of consumption appeared between the USA and Europe. While in Europe the horse-drawn carriage was still a means of travel, in the USA the car was taking over the roads. The USA had embraced mass production, which led to a virtuous circle of investment, production, and wealth creation, while providing more goods to more people at lower prices. As a country at the forefront of production and consumption, it was US companies that first embraced the latest thinking from Europe of Sigmund Freud, the Austrian founder of psychoanalysis, and his followers. They applied

Figure 1.7 Pop-up shops in Boxpark, Shoreditch   *Source*: Image kindly supplied by Canoe Inc.

Freud's psychoanalytical research to help them understand why consumers did or did not buy their products (see Research Insight 1.1). When goods were scarce and few people had the money to buy more than what was necessary for their survival, there was no need to understand consumer psychology. Once mass production increased what was available, and consumers began to have disposable income, they were able to choose how to spend their money and so businesses had to compete for buyers. Research Insight 1.1 demonstrates the use of Freudian psychoanalytic theory in contemporary consumer research.

RESEARCH INSIGHT 1.1

Patsiaouras, G., Fitchett, J.A., and Davies, A. (2016), 'Beyond the couch: psychoanalytic consumer character readings into narcissism and denial', *Marketing Theory*, 16, 1, 57–73.

In this paper, the authors develop a psychoanalysis of the consumption desires and consumer lives of the central characters, Jay Gatsby and Willy Loman, from the classic book *The Great Gatsby* and play *Death of a Salesman*. Using a Freudian psychoanalytic methodological approach the authors show how psychoanalysis can be used to bring fresh insights to contemporary consumer theory.

 Access the online resources and follow the web links to learn more.

An important aspect of Freud's psychoanalytic research was that he suggested that people's behaviour was often determined by irrational and unconscious motives and by socialized inhibitions (Berlin, 2011). Freud believed that unconscious thoughts were as important as conscious ones. A number of researchers put Freud's ideas and influence into action, aiming to understand how and why consumers liked or did not like certain products and brands. If choice was determined by motives other than the purely conscious and rational, asking straightforward questions as to why you liked or did not like a product were unlikely to reveal the real reasons for behaviour.

In his book *The Hidden Persuaders* (Packard, 1957), Vance Packard describes how a brewery was trying to find out what kinds of people drank their two types of beer, a regular brew and a light version. The brewery asked people (whom it knew favoured the brand in general) whether they drank light or regular beer. They found that those saying they preferred the light beer outnumbered those saying they liked the regular beer by more than three to one. This was despite the fact that the brewery produced nine times more regular than light beer every year to satisfy demand. According to Packard, what appeared to be happening was that the company was effectively asking: 'Do you drink the kind preferred by people of refinement and discriminating taste, or do you just drink the regular stuff?' (Packard, 1957: 38). What marketers needed to do was to find a way of uncovering consumers' more subconscious desires that they were less able or willing to articulate.

The rise of motivational research

A key figure among the researchers who took Freud's ideas into the marketplace was the Austrian-American psychologist Ernst Dichter, who in the 1930s developed so-called motivational research to help companies understand some of the more irrational motives for choice (see Research Insight 1.2). Motivational research will be discussed further in Chapter 7. Perhaps the most important characteristic of this period was the recognition of both the role of emotions in our choice decisions and that these decisions could not always be analysed or explained from a rational viewpoint. There are many examples of how Dichter applied his theories to consumer behaviour. He often used 'in-depth interviews' to identify people's real motives for using certain products or choosing a particular brand. He found from such in-depth research that bathing could be seen as a ritual that allowed a woman a few moments of indulgence (see Figure 1.8). He also recognized that the choice of brand of soap did not necessarily depend on its price or even its smell, but rather on how the consumer perceived the personality of the soap. This in turn was dependent to some extent on the consumer's personality, such that the brand acted as a mirror or extension of them. As a result he was able to classify the personalities of soaps then on the market. One named Ivory was perceived as representing purity, while another named Camay was perceived as a seductress (Samuel, 2010) (Figure 1.8).

Figure 1.8 An advertisement for Camay showing bathing as an indulgence
Source: Image supplied by Heritage Images.

RESEARCH INSIGHT 1.2

Dichter, E. (1947), 'Psychology in market research', *Harvard Business Review*, 432–43.

In this paper Dichter is appealing primarily to the business community and explaining how motivational research could help them better understand their consumers. He outlines his approach to motivational research, the techniques he uses, content analysis, in-depth interviewing, laboratory experiments, field observations, and statistical tests, and some of the projects they have been used on.

 Access the online resources and follow the web links to learn more.

One of Dichter's most famous uses of motivation research was for the marketing of Chrysler's Plymouth car, which had not been selling well. Dichter spoke with potential customers and also studied the existing advertising, which proclaimed that its cars were 'different from any other one you have ever tried'. He concluded that by using this advertising message, potential customers were put off the car as they were fearful of the unknown in a market where familiarity was equated with safety. He also found that although convertibles were bought by very few customers—in 1939 only 2 per cent of the market was accounted for by convertibles—it was frequently the dream of middle-aged men to own one. Convertibles could be put in dealership windows to lure potential male buyers. Indeed, when they were used in this way more men visited the dealership. Inevitably when they returned with their wives they were more likely to actually buy a sensible saloon car, reflecting the importance of wives in the decision-making process. Dichter interpreted wanting a convertible as symbolizing youthfulness and freedom, even the desire for a mistress, but also not something that they often take seriously and actually buy. In this way Dichter helped Chrysler with their Plymouth in two ways. By putting the convertible version in the windows, it drew the attention of the males and brought them into the dealership to enable further selling. In addition, they started to advertise in women's magazines with a line that presented a reassuring and familiar message for the brand. Their campaign informed the consumer that after 'only a few minutes' they would feel at home with their Plymouth (*Economist*, 2011).

Critiques of motivational research

In the 1950s there was increasing fear that, as the marketing industry grew, consumers were being 'sold' things they neither needed nor really wanted but bought only to fulfil their consumerist lifestyle. Vance Packard's *The Hidden Persuaders* (1957) remains a powerful critique of marketing and advertising at a time when an increasing range of psychological techniques were being tried out. Some thought that such techniques invaded the minds of consumers and persuaded them to buy using inappropriate secret methods such as subconscious advertising. Packard identified four major complaints against the kind of motivational research that Dichter had used for his commercial clients.

1. Motivational research could not be a cure-all for all marketing problems.

2. Taking diagnostic tools from clinical psychiatry and applying them to consumer behaviour was not wholly valid.

3. Motivational research relied too heavily on the person making the interpretation with few standardized or validating testing procedures.

4. The findings of motivational researchers had not been subjected to objective confirmation by conventional methods before they were applied to business situations.

While these are all reasonable criticisms of motivational research, and indeed reflect questions raised by others regarding the validity of such research today, the most significant criticism was presented by Packard in his final chapter, entitled 'The Question of Morality', which dealt with the issue of whether these techniques were not only commercially but also morally appropriate.

> On the other hand, a good many of the people manipulating activities of persuaders raise profoundly disturbing questions about the kind of society they are seeking to build for us. Their ability to contact millions of us simultaneously through newspapers, TV, etc., gives them the power, as one persuader put it, to do good or evil 'on a scale never before possible in a very short time'.
>
> (Packard, 1957: 209)

Although motivational research suffered from the attacks of Packard and others, particularly in light of the difficulty of making valid inferences from the data, it has in one way or another continued to be used by many companies up to the present day, and researchers recognize the contribution motivational research has made to understanding consumer behaviour (Tadajewski, 2006).

From consumers to consumerism: the politics of consumption

The late nineteenth and early twentieth centuries saw an increasing number of people able to purchase goods, and to purchase more of them. This period also saw the development of a more active consumer, with increasing concern that governments should protect the rights and safety of other consumers, particularly with regard to the safety of the products they bought. Ideological activists had been involved in consumption issues from the late eighteenth century (e.g. the abolition of the slave trade), while in the nineteenth century much activity revolved around issues relating to the welfare of those producing the goods to be sold, such as working conditions in factories.

The term 'consumer sovereignty' was first coined in the 1930s (de Grazia, 2005) and came to represent the exercise of freedom that people could have through consumption. Consumer rights organizations also began to increase, and in 1957 Michael Young founded the Consumers' Association (now known as Which?) in the UK. There are now a number of similar organizations operating in many countries, such as the Consumer Federation of Australia, the Consumers' Association of Canada, the Consumer Guidance Society of India, the Uganda Consumer Action Network, and the National Consumer Agency in the Republic of Ireland. All share the goal of ensuring that consumers are protected in their marketplace dealings.

This focus on consumer protection subsequently became an issue of concern to both companies and governments, and many countries introduced legislation to protect consumers. In the UK, the Consumer Credit Act 1974 was introduced to allow consumers paying by credit to have a period of time in which to change their mind regarding the purchase they had made. Other countries have consumer legislation in place to protect the interests and safety of consumers, including the Republic of China's Consumer Protection Law 1994, the Indian Consumer Protection Act 1986, and, in Europe, the European Charter of Fundamental Rights 2000. Today, protection of consumers with regard to credit (and in particular the interest that they have to pay) continues to be a major social and political issue, as highlighted in Practitioner Insight 1.

One of the most famous consumer activists is American-born Ralph Nader who famously took on the car industry in an article he wrote in 1959 for *The Nation* entitled 'The safe car you can't buy'. Nader continued his campaigns against the US car industry in the 1960s with attacks on General Motors, whose cars had been involved in numerous accidents. Over the years Nader's work produced results at a national level, and to some extent it has been activists like him who have changed the perspective of producers away from the concept of *caveat emptor*, i.e. 'buyer beware', to recognizing that producers and retailers have a responsibility to the consumer not only in producing goods but in ensuring that they are safe, fair, and of the value promised. Nader helped to bring about national laws improving vehicle safety, in particular heralding the introduction of additional safety features.

Today, many people are actively involved in campaigning for better, safer products and fairer working environments. In 2000, Naomi Klein's book *No Logo* was published with an overtly anti-corporate and 'alter-globalization' message (Klein, 2000). Klein discusses the appalling acts of multinational companies, including the use of sweatshops and the rise of short-term contracts and 'McJobs'. Many people also think that the consumer should assume some responsibility, as we consume too much or inappropriately. This has led to boycotting and anti-consumption movements. In 2004, independent film-maker Morgan Spurlock's film *Supersize Me* chronicled the impact of his weight gain and psychological well-being from spending 30 days eating only food from McDonald's, as well as documenting the fast-food industry's wider influence on the nutrition of the American public.

Alongside this increased activism, consumers now have access to large amounts of information that allow them to make better and informed choices. A quick search on the internet will reveal not only price comparison websites but also whether the company has been involved in dubious or unethical practices. One of the most significant issues that consumers and producers face is the sustainability of a world where production and consumption are damaging the planet. The effect of landfill sites, pollution, climate change, and diminishing resources are all key issues that face current and future generations. Equally, it can be argued that people in developing countries living in poverty should have the same opportunities to consume as their counterparts in the developed world. In January 2016, the 17 Sustainable Development Goals adopted by world leaders at a historic UN Summit in 2015 officially came into force. Over the next 15 years these will fight inequalities and tackle climate change.

Classifying consumers

Early attempts to classify consumers centred on classic variables such as age, gender, occupation, and income, with efforts aimed at facilitating the segmentation and targeting of products and brands to different consumer needs. Increasingly, as consumers have understood that businesses were marketing goods to them in ways that were not always straightforward, they have become more sophisticated in the manner in which they respond to marketing, product innovations, pricing, advertising, promotions, and offers. This, in turn, has led to a range of new attempts to classify types of consumer. Such classifications have generally involved the development of wider-ranging variations, not necessarily mutually exclusive but still often with some categories in opposition to one another. These typologies are examined in more detail in this section. One of the most cited classification of consumers is that of Gabriel and Lang (1995, 2006) who have defined nine types which are detailed in Table 1.2.

If we examine the brief descriptions in Table 1.2, we can see that Gabriel and Lang's typology of consumers is really describing trends and ways of consuming (or not) rather than types of people. We can be hedonistic in our consumption on one day, but that does not preclude us from being an activist on another. Aldridge (2003) criticized the typology-for being underdeveloped and having overlapping categories—one might see similarities between the consumer as activist and as rebel. However, as an indicator of the roles and positions that consumers may take, this can be a useful typology. Typologies such as this, while not necessarily developed from direct empirical data, can be useful for marketers. In

Consumer type	Description
Chooser	The rational problem-solving consumer, requiring genuine options, finance options, and information.
Communicator	Uses goods to communicate. Material objects are used for the messages they convey, often relating to status or taste.
Explorer	Consumers increasingly have places to explore, and often we explore with little idea of what, or even if, we wish to buy.
Identity-seeker	Creating and maintaining personal and social identity through consumption.
Hedonist/artist	Consumption as pleasure: consumption can fulfil needs for emotional aesthetic pleasure and fantasy.
Victim	The exploited consumer: the consumer may lack knowledge or be unaware of choices, or they may have limited choice because of their socio-economic situation
Rebel	Using products in new ways as a conscious rebellion: this can include consuming differently, or less, or boycotting, and can also refer to active rebellion (e.g. joyriding, looting, taking over consumption spaces).
Activist	Presented historically from the cooperative movement, the value-for-money movement, especially fighting against corporate greed and political activism, seeking more ethical consumption.
Citizen	Consumers are also citizens with rights and responsibilities: awareness that consumerism encroaches on areas such as housing, healthcare, and education as well as consumer goods.

Table 1.2   A typology of consumers   *Source*: Adapted from Gabriel and Lang (1995, 2006).

particular, typologies help marketers to identify the types or segments that they may wish to target or even avoid. Today marketers are also interested in identifying whether such typologies are different for digital consumers. For example, in 2013 GroupM Next identified six different segments of digital consumers. The most important of these is the Digitally Driven segment which uses every digital tool available, from the start of the consumer decision process to the end (see Chapter 3); they are most concerned about convenience and tend to avoid physically going to shops (Richards, 2014).

Consumer victims

Gabriel and Lang's 'consumer as victim' is an interesting category, and resonates with Bauman's (2007) idea of the 'flawed' consumer—someone who is effectively excluded from consumer society because of their economic or social position. We can all feel as though we are consumer victims at times, but certain groups in society are particularly vulnerable, perhaps because they live on a low income or have a disability. Some people are effectively excluded from the opportunity for choice or for exploring or from engaging in hedonistic consumption; they may be excluded through their economic position or their inability to engage with the expectations of modern consumer society. Consider how those who do not have access to or cannot use the internet are excluded, not only from shopping opportunities but also from financial deals which might be economically advantageous. Consumers living on low incomes, who have to borrow money at high interest rates, can find themselves in very difficult financial situations, which can be particularly damaging, as Lord Mitchell explains in Practitioner Insight 1.

PRACTITIONER INSIGHT 1

Lord Mitchell, House of Lords, UK

Lord Mitchell told us about the work he had been doing with short-term loan companies, often referred to as payday loan companies.

One of my greatest successes since being in the House of Lords was to get an amendment to the Financial Services Act 2012. This meant that the Financial Conduct Authority (FCA) was given powers to cap the total amount charged by short-term loan companies. In addition, this amendment meant that borrowers would also be prevented from repeatedly rolling over loans, and lenders who failed to comply with the FCA's rules would not be able to enforce repayment. Non-compliance would have drastic consequences for payday lenders. In addition, in March 2013 the Office for Fair Trading (OFT) came out with hard-hitting recommendations. They cited most of the industry as acting illegally and gave them 60 days to sort themselves out or risk losing their licences.

Why is this so significant for consumers? Since 2008 the payday loans industry has grown significantly as households have struggled to balance rising bills with falling wages and retail banks have resisted offering unsecured loans. There are some consumers who are more vulnerable than ever before and we need to recognize that this may lead them to make decisions that ultimately do not serve them well. In Rochdale in 2010 the BBC *Panorama* reporter Richard Bilton found it easy to collect nearly £1,000 from moneylenders with no security. Also, consider the example I gave in the House of Lords of a friend whose son with mild attention deficit disorder had taken out two payday loans totalling £800, only to find that in just a few months the amount had escalated to £5,000. Yet the OFT guidance for creditors on irresponsible lending pointed out that: 'All assessments of affordability should involve a consideration of the potential for the credit commitment to adversely impact on the borrower's financial situation, taking account of information that the creditor is aware of at the time the credit is granted'.

We must remember that payday lenders fill what in today's climate is an important gap, but when we hear stories of lenders charging an annual percentage rate (APR) in excess of 4,000 per cent we have to find ways to protect vulnerable consumers from becoming victims, while providing them with financial services that will allow them to continue a reasonable quality of life.

Since the introduction of a price cap on payday loans in January 2015, Citizens Advice reports a 45 per cent reduction in clients accessing advice about payday loan issues (https://www.citizensadvice.org.uk/Global/CitizensAdvice/Debt%20and%20Money%20Publications/For%20publication%20-%20Part1-Overviewofthetrendsinthepaydaymarketreport.pdf).

There have been other attempts to classify consumers. Edwards (2000: 13) differentiates between five 'perceptions' of the consumer, which are all 'to some extent at least, stereotypes, yet contain a grain of truth'. They are the consumer as king, victim, criminal, anti-consumer, and voyeur. Dagevos (2005) argued that modern consumers defy traditional segmentation by age, gender, or income, and that classical criteria to distinguish homogeneous groups (with corresponding behavioural intentions and patterns) have lost much of their explanatory power. Instead, Dagevos proposed four consumer 'images' which are based on two key dimensions, materialistic/non-materialistic and individualistic/collectivist, as shown in Figure 1.9.

These consumer types capture the relations between consumers and products, and Dagevos characterized them as follows.

- *Calculating* is rational, mainstream, efficient, and effective, 'Keep up with the Joneses', concerned with convenience.

- *Traditional* is conformist, cost-conscious, self-disciplined, fearful of new things, community-oriented.

- *Unique* is described as fun and impulsive, seeks variety, seeks status, distinction, and new things.

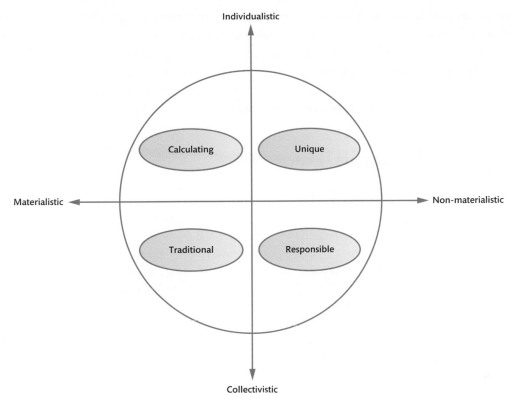

Figure 1.9   Four images of the consumer

Source: Dagevos (2005), 'Consumers as four-faced creatures. Looking at food consumption from the perspective of contemporary consumers', *Appetite*, 45, 1, 32–9. Copyright © 2005, Elsevier.

- *Responsible* is captured by involvement, altruistic, 'Keep down with the Joneses', informed, environmentally aware.

Overall, consumer typologies are popular in commercial and academic research. While these typologies are interesting and useful in terms of recognizing differences among consumers, few have been based on empirical research and therefore we must be circumspect in their application.

The postmodern consumer

The progressive nature of the consumerist movement could be said to represent modernity and progress, but alongside this arose the concept of the postmodern consumer (Firat and Venkatesh, 1995; Goulding, 2003; Simmons, 2008). An important feature of postmodern consumers is their fragmented nature. Rather than being one 'type', as described in the section on 'Classifying consumers', the postmodern consumer truly crosses many types and it is difficult to tell when he/she will be one or the other. No longer does consumption provide support to a unified idea of a person framed by their work, gender, moral choices, and achievements. Rather, postmodern consumers do not seek a unified theme, but want to explore different and separate identities to match the fragmenting markets and the proliferation of products. This suits not only the different segments but also the different moods of the consumer and can take many forms around the world, as demonstrated in the example of the mod-tradi consumer discussed in Consumer Insight 1.4.

CONSUMER INSIGHT 1.4

Sri Lanka's mod-tradi consumer

Bernard Cova (1999) suggested that we no longer have expectations of what people do and what they buy based on their class or occupation. He illustrates this by saying that a government minister could as easily be driving a Citroen 2CV as an unemployed person could be driving a BMW. Other commentators identify postmodern consumption as deconstructing patterns of old shopping behaviour, erasing the boundaries across price, image brand, and location (Fassnacht, 2007), such that you might eat your lunch at McDonald's and your dinner at a five star restaurant, or buy cheap socks at a discount shop and an expensive iPod at the Apple store.

Different cultures respond in a variety of ways to new sociocultural forces that shape behaviour and consumption. In Sri Lanka the seemingly opposing forces of traditionalization and modernization have in fact been converging to produce a response that Liyanage (2011) refers to as the mod-tradi consumer. Identifying the lines of fusion between the traditional and modern is a challenge to marketing in Sri Lanka in terms of identifying not only disparate sociocultural groups but also urban–rural groups and how they are impacted. Sometimes different social groups show a preference for the traditional or the modern. For example, higher social groups may choose cement floors and traditional furniture, while lower socio-economic groups prefer the convenience of glossy floor tiles. In some cases old and new become fused. Young people may wear faded branded jeans and a T-shirt while also wearing the *pirith nool*, a string around the right wrist, which is believed to ward off evil and is an important traditional religious symbol. Food is also subject to mod-tradi consumption, with traditional food being eaten alongside sausages at home and trips to McDonald's.

Questions

1. Can you find examples of mod-tradi consumption in your own lives?

2. How have marketing companies used such preferences for the new and the traditional?

Sources: Cova (1999); Fassnacht (2007); Liyanage (2011).

 Access the online resources and follow the web links to learn more.

Firat and Shultz (1997) represent the fragmentation of postmodern consumers as a result of a loss of a central core of being where multiple selves can address the same product category. Baudrillard (1981) suggested that consumers use goods to create and manage identities. We can use brands to make us appear as one thing in the morning and something else later in the day—we have learnt to use the market and what it offers to change who we appear to be. There is no longer any logic to production being important in the Marxist sense; instead, the only thing that matters is the signs that are represented through consumption. A pair of jeans could be considered only in terms of their strength and durability (related to their use value), which was the focus of the original advertisements for Levi jeans. Today, however, use value is of less significance, and instead it is the sign and hedonic value communicated through wearing Levi's (or some other high-fashion brand) that is important for consumers.

Central to understanding of contemporary postmodern consumers is the assumption that we live in a complex social and cultural world, and that meaning is individually created based on our shared experiences (Brown, 1993). Bourdieu's (1984) thesis, as summarized by Gronow and Warde (2001: 221), presents the consumer as using goods to act 'as signs of inclusion and exclusion: people like me or us, prefer objects like ours whereas the 'others' choose, dress or design and use theirs otherwise'. While the postmodern consumer has appeared as a powerful theme in much academic literature, the question raised by some has been how relevant this concept actually is to real people's consumption experiences (Miles, 1999; Goulding, 2003). If anything, it is a concept of use to marketing and advertising in terms of the amount and variety of products and images available to us that encourage consumption in increasingly competitive markets.

Some have critiqued the idea of postmodernism as having been appropriated by late modern forms of capitalism for their own managerial purposes (Boje, 2006). Boje uses McDonald's as an example of a company that has used a clever juxtaposition of engaging with children and parents with both cartoons and celebrities to construct the idea of fast food being nutritious, but also using scientific-seeming charts of fat and nutrition content with endorsements from fitness experts. McDonald's uses a range of discourse types (both visual and fun, cognitive and scientific) to 'story themselves to customers and employees' (Boje, 2006: 31). On the other hand, Boje classifies other companies, such as Blackspot Sneakers and No Sweat clothing, as postmodern organizations because they are critical of some of the features of modern capitalism such as global sweatshops. Blackspot began as a consumer cooperative where consumers pooled orders for trainers and found a unionized factory with a long-standing history in the shoe industry employing men and women, young and old. Their marketing and advertisements clearly position Blackspot as anti-Nike; the high-top Hemp boot is called the 'Unswoosher'—a direct reference to the Nike Swoosh—and tagged 'the most Earth-friendly shoe in the world'.

Postmodernism in marketing was seen as breaking down the divide between production and consumption, leading to the idea of co-creation of value, whereby the consumer plays a constructive and value-creating role, not only in consumption but also in production, by creating their own products or taking part in production through connections with the firm. The most extreme version of this is the creation of one's own products with no engagement with a firm. Boje (2006) describes building his own motorcycle using what he describes as 'after-market products'. See also Research Insight 1.3 for an interesting example of consumption and production coming together in the context of the football manager simulation game *Football Manager*.

RESEARCH INSIGHT 1.3

Skandalis, A., Byrom, J., and Banister, E. (2015), 'Brand scouting: co-creation of value in the Football Manager community', *Advances in Consumer Research*, 43, 409–14.

This qualitative, in-depth study provides a good example of the blurring of production and consumption in a consumer context. Focusing on the *Football Manager* game community, the authors explore collective value co-creation processes, and show how consumers are enlisted to undertake unpaid research work for the brand in order to enhance their consumption experience.

 Access the online resources and follow the web links to learn more.

Post postmodernism

Some academics now suggest the end of postmodernism as a theme in consumer research (e.g. Cova and Maclaran, 2012). This is partly because it has become subsumed by consumer culture theory (Arnould and Thompson, 2005) and possibly because both researchers and consumers have moved beyond it. Cova and Maclaran see the new fields of interest as being cultural (consumer culture theory), neuromarketing, and the material turn. Consumer culture theory will be discussed further in Chapter 2, and will be referred to throughout this book where relevant. Neuromarketing will also be covered in Chapter 2. The material turn refers to the role of non-human objects (things) in shaping behaviour. For example, we might consider how we use shopping trolleys and the implications of their invention for the size of supermarkets and how much we buy (Cochoy, 2009). What is clear from these and other studies is that theories that describe and aim to understand consumer behaviour will continue to be developed, just as consumers themselves will develop new ways of behaving in the market that will need to be explained.

Approaches to studying consumers and consumption

Interdisciplinary perspectives on consumption

Just as there are different ways of thinking about consumption and how it is classified, it is also useful to think about how different social science perspectives lead to different approaches to studying consumer behaviour. While many academic disciplines are relevant to the study of consumers, the main perspectives we see in consumer research relate to anthropology, sociology, psychology, and economics, with history and geography also making a contribution.

Anthropology is concerned with people as they live in their society and culture. When applied to consumer contexts, this perspective tends to focus on consumers' behaviours and practices, looking at how rituals, myths, and symbols all contribute to understanding the meaning and significance of consumption to consumers. The sociological perspective on consumption contributes insights into the social forces that influence individual and group consumption, including the social structural concepts of social class, ethnicity, gender, and lifestyles. Perhaps the most influential social science in understanding consumers is psychology—the scientific study of mental processes and behaviours. We have already seen how aspects of psychology were incorporated in the work of the early motivational researchers. The ideas of personality, the self, and the individual, how we learn and perceive the world around us—ideas essential for the study of the consumer—are derived from psychology. It has also been influential in terms of the research methods used in consumer research. Economics also has a role to play in understanding consumption. Classic microeconomic theory is the source of the utility-maximizing framework used to explain some aspects of how we process information and make decisions. Macroeconomics provides indicators of consumption behaviours that are very useful in understanding global differences in consumption. History and geography help in our understanding of the origins and development of consumer culture, including marketing communications and advertising, and the impact of marketing institutions and practices on urban and suburban landscapes, especially retail spaces.

To see this holistic approach to studying consumption in action, it is useful to look at the issue of excessive alcohol consumption that represents a very real and significant public health problem for many societies. Different perspectives on studying this issue may focus on different things. Anthropologists might focus on the ritualistic practices around socializing. Sociologists might focus on how local community policing influences the behaviour of young people in the night-time economy. Psychologists might examine the links between personality type and alcohol consumption, whereas economists might be interested in how alcohol consumption might change following the introduction of minimum unit pricing. A historical perspective might consider how patterns of alcohol consumption have changed over time, and geographers might undertake an audit of off-licence shops (which sell alcohol) in local communities and relate this to consumption levels.

Relating perspectives to methods of studying consumers

While many disciplines may be interested in consumer behaviour, approaches to investigating consumers tend to be divided into two broad research orientations: the positivist approach and the interpretivist approach.

The **positivist approach** to consumer behaviour emphasizes *the objectivity of science and the consumer as a rational decision-maker* (Calder and Tybout, 1989). This approach sees the world as having an external objective reality, and the goal of research using this perspective is to understand consumers in terms of theories that have been rigorously tested and can explain this external reality. Methods from this perspective often focus on examining relationships between key factors (or variables) that explain some aspect of consumer behaviour, and research tools allow relationships to be observed and quantified in some way. For this reason, most methods involved in this approach to consumer research tend to be quantitative, with qualitative methods being used in a limited supporting role. Many commercial companies use this approach, and typical techniques include structured questionnaires, experiments (laboratory-based and field experiments), consumer panels, and hall tests.

The **interpretivist perspective** *stresses the subjective meaning of the consumer's individual experience and the idea that any behaviour is subject to multiple interpretations rather than one single explanation.* This approach is driven by a need to develop a deep understanding of people's lives and behaviours, recognizing that the researcher interprets this data in terms of a particular system of ideas and assumptions about the nature of reality. This approach recognizes that reality is socially constructed, and that the researcher is an active participant in the research process (rather than viewed as some objective bystander). The unstructured depth interview is a classic method used in interpretivist research, allowing the researcher to adopt a flexible approach to the interview and to probe more deeply areas of particular interest to the consumer being interviewed. Other methods include ethnography, personal introspections, participant observations, and narrative analyses. These approaches are more associated with qualitative methodologies, although it is important to note that not all qualitative research is interpretivist.

Conclusions

This chapter has introduced you to some of the key aspects relating to the ***early history of consumption***, examining the historical links between consumption and social class. Our discussion of the sumptuary laws during the period of the Qin dynasty in China, medieval England, and renaissance Italy showed that historically there have been concerns about the moral implications of consumption, something that continues to the modern day.

Examining the ***role of economics and philosophy*** in the development of consumer behaviour, we considered how production and consumption are connected, and the way that value has evolved. Analysing designer handbag consumption, we showed how the different types of value are interrelated, concluding that many objects we consume today are defined by their sign or symbolic value more than their use value.

It is important to ***understand how consumption became a part of everyday life***. As shops appeared, shopping became a pleasurable experience, and this led to increased investment in production as manufacturers recognized that people were prepared to spend more on goods above their needs. Consumer Insight 1.2 mapped how innovations in domestic technology influenced the ways that consumers eat and live. We also introduced the concept of **conspicuous consumption**, looking at the example of Hubwear's customized T-shirts (Consumer Insight 1.3) as a way for consumers to signal status.

We examined some **key trends in the development of shops and shopping**, such as global innovations in online shopping and the trend towards pop-up shopping due to its 'low-risk' nature, particularly in the fashion sector. The twentieth century saw major changes in our understanding of consumers, and in particular this occurred as a result of an interest in the work of Sigmund Freud. **Motivational research** has been important for studying consumer behaviour as it recognizes that not all consumer decisions can be explained by rational or economic arguments.

Nowadays, **consumerism** is part of everyday life. For a range of reasons, some groups of people have rejected the marketing message and become active in attacking businesses that they believe are producing inappropriate, dangerous, or simply too many products. Examining consumer protection legislation across the world, we discussed a range of issues associated with consumer activism.

Classifying and identifying 'types' of consumer is important for marketing practice, and this is looked at in more depth in Case Study 1, which examines how different groups of supermarket shoppers use branded and own-label goods during a recession.

As consumers became more familiar with marketing, they became more sophisticated, and some refer to the **postmodern consumer** as encapsulating the uncertainty and playfulness of behaviour, image, and identity in consumption in the twenty-first century. The mod-tradi Sri Lankan consumer was discussed as an example of the postmodern consumer.

Changes in understanding consumption and consumers over time have led to many **different approaches to studying consumers**. Much consumer behaviour is now manifested online. Consumers discuss brands and products, and recommend or complain about the choices they have made on social networking sites and internet communities. As a result much more research uses online ethnography or netnography (Kozinets, 2010) to study such behaviour.

Review questions

1. Define and explain the following terms: exchange value, use value, and sign value. Are exchange and use value still helpful in understanding consumption today?

2. Identify the main economic and philosophical arguments regarding production and consumption that are relevant to understanding consumer behaviour today.

3. Explain the significance of 'wastefulness' in Veblen's *Theory of the Leisure Class*.

4. Outline Packard's four criticisms of motivational research. What do you think of these criticisms in relation to what you understand of marketing today?

5. Using Gabriel and Lang's typology, suggest which you think are the most common consumer types today and explain why you think this is so.

Discussion questions

1. Identify some examples of what you would consider to be conspicuous consumption today. In your opinion what are such goods offering to the people who consume them?

2. Do you consider that consumption has a moral dimension today? Examine the major moral issues concerning consumption in the twenty-first century.

3. Look at the advertising for three brands of soap. Analyse the messages they use and consider whether they relate to Dichter's utilitarian or indulgent types. What other kinds of message are used today?

4. Consider how car advertisements are presented in a range of women's and men's magazines today. Compare and contrast the messages used to convince women and men of the value of the car brand.

5. Jeans, cars, and handbags could all be said to encapsulate sign value. Take one of these product categories and choose three brands. Explain which sign value, in your opinion, each brand represents.

Access the online resources to test your knowledge further and complete the Multiple Choice Questions for Chapter 1.

CASE STUDY 1

Supermarket responses to the recessionary consumer

This case looks at how consumers adjust their approach to supermarket shopping as the result of recession. The case considers how, following the global financial crisis of 2008, retailers responded to market research on shopping behaviour and highlights how people's use of branded and own-label goods changed. The questions ask you to consider the likely preferences and behaviour of different types of shopper. In doing this you should also reflect on what you have learned about consumers and their behaviour in the chapter.

What changes might one expect in consumers' attitudes and behaviours following a recession? A number of organizations have looked at consumer behaviour in times of economic hardship, and this work goes back to around 2009, following the major global recession of 2008. In 2009, shop-percentric.co.uk undertook a study of over 1,000 individuals in the UK to see how the recession had affected them. They identified four types of reactions to the recession.

- **Unaffecteds**—13 per cent claimed to be unaffected but were making small changes.

- **Planners**—15 per cent were not affected yet but were making changes in case they were. They had noticed that their household costs had risen. Their focus was on price, avoiding temptation, and economizing by making meals from scratch.

- **Soft reactors**—48 per cent made changes to household spending but the changes were small. They may have switched to a reliance on own-label brands and large shops, and avoiding top-up shopping. They are price aware, avoiding waste and temptation.

- **Strong reactors**—24 per cent were making major changes, and were moving between stores for best prices.

When this study was revisited in April 2012, there were some marked changes: Unaffecteds remained steady at 12 per cent, Planners went down to 6 per cent, Soft Reactors was at 46 per cent, and Strong Reactors increased to 35 per cent. Perhaps surprisingly, Planners were somewhat lower, but Strong Reactors, i.e. those making major changes, were up by 11 per cent. This may indicate the long-term impact that the recession had on some consumers, whether they were choosing to be more prudent with their spending or because felt they had no choice but to make these changes.

Recent data from Nielsen (2016) on the grocery shopping behaviour of millennials has also shown how the recession of 2008 'fundamentally changed' consumer shopping habits, with 57 per cent of Millennials in this study feeling personally affected by the recession. There was a greater effect for older millennials (26-34 year olds) than younger ones (18-25 year olds). Interestingly, this effect was mainly in terms of reducing their spending on eating out and entertainment, and only 8 per cent felt it impacted on their grocery shopping. The report notes: 'According to our data, to counteract it and save, they're dining out less and opting to eat at home more. This is why there hasn't been a sizable decline in grocery shopping, post-recession. Lost restaurant trips should ultimately benefit grocery retailers.'

Among the population more widely, post-recession developments include openly looking for bargains, taking time to get the best purchase (i.e. maximizing), looking for free offers, reducing wasteful consumption, seeking transparency in dealings with big companies, and using their mobiles for everything—shopping, communicating, playing. The impact on living standards in the financial crisis, with increases in food and fuel prices, is also thought to have made supermarket shoppers more discerning, searching for lower prices, special deals, and bargains. However, the picture may be somewhat more complex than this.

UK research on grocery shopping from 2012 (Chahal, 2012) reported that low-income families often prefer premium branded goods and services over retailers' own brands. When asked about the importance of price, many people living on lower incomes said that price was a conscious factor influencing choice. However, when their actual purchases were inspected, it was seen that consumers with lower incomes preferred more premium brands; brands like Birds Eye, McCain, Kellogg's, and

Coca-Cola did well. According to this report, buying premium brands enables low-income consumers to assert their social position when other means—such as surroundings, income, and education—are inaccessible to them. Jo Ruddock, head of consumer and market insight at Kellogg's, also recognizes the status role that branded goods may play for lower-income families: 'This is a hugely complex area with a large number of factors at play but I think there is an element of "what a brand says about us" that determines brand choices'. This, she says, may apply more for public categories that are seen by others. Savvy shoppers choose branded products in categories that matter most to them (Chahal, 2012).

According to Nick Canning, Director for People and Customers at Iceland, the key to understanding this trend is an appreciation of the risks inherent in food shopping when living on a low income. According to Canning, 'They [lower income customers] would rather buy something they know the quality and taste of, as opposed to something they are not 100 per cent sure about'. Research in nutritional science supports this, showing that low-income consumers tend to be more risk averse in their food shopping since the costs associated with foods not being acceptable to their families are high.

So how do businesses respond to such changes in consumer behaviour?

John Lewis is a famous British high street department store with a grocery arm, Waitrose. The profile of Waitrose is of a store catering primarily to the middle classes; as *The Guardian* noted, it is often perceived as 'posh but pricey'. It stocks a full range of grocery items, including many upmarket brands. It prides itself on quality, but knows that some shoppers will only purchase certain items from Waitrose and go to cheaper stores for commodity shopping. In 2009 it recognized the impact of the recession on its consumers by introducing 'Essential Waitrose', a cheaper own-brand alternative. The aim was to encourage more existing customers to do their full shop with Waitrose and to give a cheaper offering without compromising on their quality reputation. At the same time, they did not want to alienate their loyal customers who might be suspicious of 'down-market' offerings. The Essential Waitrose product range included over 1,000 fresh and everyday staples, and also involved rebranding 1,200 existing own-label products. Waitrose made their Essential Waitrose products more visible and relevant to customers at a time when their competitors had been building their competitive advantage by developing what had been Waitrose's key areas of differentiation. These included improving product quality, sourcing standards, and ethics, but they too had recognized the recessionary trends and had been moving their emphasis back to price and value. So Waitrose's biggest challenge was to ensure that their new Essential Waitrose products offered both quality and value, and that this was evident to customers in the way the products were labelled and the packaging designed. In choosing the name, they avoided the language of 'value' or 'basics' so as to reassure customers of the maintenance of the quality of the products. The *Oxford English Dictionary* defines essential as 'Absolutely necessary, indispensably requisite', and hence Essential Waitrose was seen as appropriate to indicate the everyday staple nature of both food and non-food items.

In the past other supermarkets have launched product lines aimed to offer value to customers affected by recessionary times. Perhaps the best known of these was Tesco's Value range launched following the recession of the early 1990s. In 2012 Tesco announced that they were rebranding as Everyday Value. The supermarket's stark blue and white striped Value range was seen as too basic in comparison with other supermarket ranges such as Waitrose's Essential range, emphasizing affordable quality in the classier packaging and attracting what *Management Today* called 'the increasing volume of cash-strapped yet status-conscious shoppers' (see Figure 1.10). Some customers also questioned the quality of the Tesco brand, and its distinctive blue and white packaging was perhaps more obvious in their shopping basket than they might have liked (Haslett, 2010).

Research with low-income consumers tells us that they have greater trust in brands and believe that there is a difference between national brands and retailer's own-label brands. The 2012 Aldi campaign tackled this head on by showing consumers who liked both the national brand and Aldi's own-label version of the product. Aldi's advertising shows people comparing a main-line brand and Aldi's own-label version (see Figure 1.11). The price is always clearly visible in the advert, with Aldi's product usually about half the price of their branded competitor. The adverts are light-hearted and, interestingly, do not suggest that the own-label brand is better than the branded version. In one advert an older lady says that she buys the branded tea (at £3.00) for her husband, and then says that he also likes the Aldi own-label brand (at £1.99). She finishes by saying that she doesn't like tea, she likes gin.

Figure 1.10   Essential Waitrose and Tesco Everyday Value product lines

Sources: Waitrose and Tesco Stores Ltd.

Aldi simply puts across the results of price checks and taste tests. These results show that, despite Aldi's own-label products costing about half the price of their branded competitors, many people 'also like them'. So Aldi presents the parity of the products, but with Aldi's being considerably cheaper. Data from Nielsen (2014) shows that 71 per cent of UK respondents to their global survey of private labels believe that the quality of own-brand products has improved. The 2016 US data from Nielsen tells a similar story—70 per cent of US households think private store brands are a good alternative to branded product (Nielsen, 2016).

A number of UK supermarkets have introduced price match initiatives to ensure that customers will pay no more for cupboard staples like washing powder and baked beans than they would at other supermarkets. Campaigns such as Waitrose's Brand Price Match initiative, Asda's Price Guarantee, and Sainsbury's Brand Match generate (refund) coupons at the till if branded goods can be bought cheaper elsewhere.

HEINZ 570g
£1.95

ALDI 563g
69p

Prices checked 7 Feb on mysupermarket.com. Details at aldi.co.uk.
In taste tests, 163 liked Heinz, 64% of them also liked Aldi.

Figure 1.11   Aldi advertisement   *Source*: Image supplied by The Advertising Archives.

The big supermarkets have also used the internet to offer price comparisons, with both Asda and Tesco running internet-based price-checking facilities, and increasingly shoppers are using their mobiles and tablets to order their food online. Although many of Britain's supermarkets offer delivery to your house, at the time of writing, Waitrose is the only store to offer it free of charge.

Questions

1. Compare and contrast the four types of recessionary shopper described. What particular needs might each type have?

2. How might the way they do their supermarket shopping differ for each type? What would be different about their behaviour and how might supermarkets use this information?

3. Consider any of Gabriel and Lang's types of consumer in relation to supermarket shopping. How might they differ from those described in the Case Study and what kind of supermarket consumer behaviour would you think they would exhibit?

Sources: Haslett (2010); Collins (2012); Chahal (2012); Wood (2012); Leyland (2012); Steiner (2012); Nielsen (2016); www.shoppercentric.co.uk

References

Aldridge, A. (2003), *Consumption*, Oxford: Polity Press.

Arnould, E.J. and Thompson, C.J. (2005), 'Consumer culture theory (CCT): twenty years of research', *Journal of Consumer Research*, 31, 4, 868–82.

Arnould, E.J., Price, L., and Zinkhan, G. (2004), *Consumers*, New York: McGraw-Hill.

Baudrillard, J. (1981), *For a critique of the political economy of the sign*, St Louis, MO: Telos.

Bauman, Z. (2007), *Consuming life*, Cambridge: Polity Press.

BBC (2010), 'Tracing the bitter truth of chocolate and child labour', http://news.bbc.co.uk/panorama/hi/front_page/newsid_8583000/8583499.stm (accesssed 4 December 2016).

Benson, J. (1994), *The rise of consumer society in Britain, 1880–1980*, London: Longman.

Berlin, H.A. (2011), 'The neural basis of the dynamic unconscious', *Neurophsychoanalyis*, 13, 1, 5–71.

Berry, C. (1994), *The idea of luxury: a conceptual and historical investigation*, Cambridge: Cambridge University Press.

Boje, D.M. (2006), 'What happened on the way to postmodern?', *Qualitative Research in Organizations and Management*, 1, 1, 22–40.

Bourdieu, P. (1984), *Distinction: a social critique of the judgement of taste* (transl. R. Nice), Cambridge, MA: Harvard University Press.

Bowlby, R. (2000), *Carried away by shopping*, London: Faber & Faber.

Brohier, M. (2014) Bartering in the 21st Century http://www.frecmalaysiatoday.com/category/money/2014/07/01/bartering-in-the-21st-century/ (accessed 25 June 2016).

Brown, S. (1993) 'Postmodern marketing?', *European Journal of Marketing*, 27, 4, 19–34.

Calder, B.J. and Tybout, A.M. (1989), 'Interpretive, qualitative and traditional scientific empirical consumer behaviour research', in E.C. Hirschman (ed.), *Interpretive consumer research*, Provo, UT: Association for Consumer Research, pp.199–208.

Chahal, M. (2012), 'Lower income consumers snap up big brands', *Marketing Week*, 11 October, http://www.marketingweek.co.uk/trends/lower-income-consumers-snap-up-big-brands/4004162.article (accessed 6 December 2012).

Chua Kong Ho (2016), 'China auto sales growth accelerates on rising SUV demand', *Bloomberg News*, 8 July 2016 http://www.bloomberg.com/news/articles/2016-07-08/china-auto-sales-grow-at-faster-pace-on-suv-electric-car-demand (accessed 21 December 2016)

Cochoy, F. (2009), 'Driving a shopping cart from STS to business and the other way round: on the introduction of shopping carts in American grocer stores (1936–1959)', *Organization*, 16, 1, 31–55.

Collins, D. (2012), 'Honest upfront message is making the brand relevant to the British shopper', *Marketing Magazine*, 4 July, http://www.marketingmagazine.co.uk/article/1139369/adwatch-webwatch-july-4-top-10-recall-aldi (accessed 8 April 2014).

Cova, B. (1999), *'From marketing to societing: when the link is more important than the thing'*, in D. Brownlie, M. Saren, R. Wensley, and R. Whittington (eds), *Rethinking Marketing*, London: SAGE, pp.64–83.

Cova, B. and Maclaran, P. (2012), 'Rethinking consumer culture after postmodernism: in search of a new "turn"', presented at *McDonald's Consumer Culture Theory Conference*, University of Oxford, August 2012.

Dagevos, H. (2005), 'Consumers as four-faced creatures: looking at food consumption from the perspective of contemporary consumers', *Appetite*, 45, 1, 32–9.

de Botton, A. (2005), *Status anxiety*, Harmondsworth: Penguin.

de Grazia, V. (2005), *Irresistible empire: America's advance through 20th century Europe*, Cambridge, MA: Belknap Press.

Dichter, E. (1947), 'Psychology in market research', *Harvard Business Review*, 432–43.

Economist (2011), 'How Ernest Dichter, an acolyte of Sigmund Freud, revolutionised marketing, http://www.economist.com/node/21541706 (accessed 7 December 2011).

Edwards, T. (2000), *Contradictions of consumption: concepts, practices and politics in consumer society*, Maidenhead: Open University Press.

Elliott, R. and Leonard, C. (2004), 'Peer pressure and poverty: exploring fashion brands and consumption symbolism amongst children of the "British poor" '. *Journal of Consumer Behaviour*, 3, 1, 347–60.

Fairtrade Labelling Organizations International, 25 March 2012, http://www.fairtrade.net/new/flo-response.html (accessed 4 December 2016)

FairTrade USA (2017), 'Is there child labor in your chocolate?', http://www.huffingtonpost.com/fair-trade-usa/is-there-child-labor-in-y_b_9169898.html.

Fassnacht, M. (2007), 'Postmodern shopper', *Marketing Geek*, 28 January, http://marketinggeek.blogspot.co.uk/2007/01/postmodern-shopper.html (accessed 4 January 2013).

Fernandez-Armesto, F. (2001), *Food: a history*, London: MacMillan.

Firat, A. and Shultz, C. (1997), 'From segmentation to fragmentation: markets and marketing in the postmodern era', *European Journal of Marketing*, 31, 3/4, 183–207.

Firat, A. and Venkatesh, A. (1995), 'Liberatory postmodernism and the reenchantment of consumption', *Journal of Consumer Research*, 22, 3, 239–67.

Gabriel, Y. and Lang, T. (1995), *The unmanageable consumer*, London: SAGE.

Gabriel, Y. and Lang, T. (2006), *The unmanageable consumer* (2nd edn), London: SAGE.

Goller, L. (2016), 'Local foods drive massive growth in retail', https://www.rangeme.com/blog/local-foods-growth-in-retail/ (accessed 25 May 2016).

Goulding, C. (2003), 'Issues in representing the postmodern consumer', *Qualitative Research*, 6, 3, 152–9.

Grant, K. (2005), *A civilised savagery: Britain and the new slaveries in Africa, 1884–1926*, New York: Routledge.

Gronow, J. and Warde, A. (2001), *Ordinary consumption*, London: Routledge.

Hardyment, C. (1995), *A slice of life: the British way of eating since 1945*, Harmondsworth: Penguin.

Haslett, E. (2010), 'Now John Lewis' online customers won't be knowingly undersold (kind of)', *Management Today*, 27 September, http://www.managementtoday.co.uk/news/1030995/John-Lewis-online-customers-wont-knowingly-undersold-kind-of/ (accessed 8 April 2014).

Hirsch, J. (2013), 'Dubai's first farmers market', *Modern Farmer*, 17 July, http://modernfarmer.com/2013/07/dubai-farmers-market/ (accessed 8 September 2013).

Killerby, C.K. (2002), *Sumptuary law in Italy 1200–1500*, Oxford: Oxford University Press.

Klein, N. (2000), *No logo*, London: Flamingo.

Knutson, A. (2013), '24 vending machines you won't believe exist', *Buzzfeed Food*, 14 January, http://www.buzzfeed.com/arielknutson/vending-machines-you-wont-believe-exist (accessed 8 September 2013).

Kozinets, R.V. (2010), *Netnography: doing ethnographic research online*, London: SAGE.

Kroen, S. (2004), 'A political history of the consumer', *Historical Journal*, 47, 3, 709–36.

Lati, M. (2012), 'Fashion shop is seeking platform for local designers', *Business Daily Africa*, 28 November, http://www.businessdailyafrica.com/Fashion+shop+is+seeking+platform+for+local+designers/-/539444/1632194/-/9i5adk/-/index.html (accessed 7 April 2014).

Leyland, A. (2012). 'Hot topic: Waitrose has shifted from high-low pricing to something more knowing', *The Grocer*, 5 May, http://www.thegrocer.co.uk/opinion/the-grocer-says/waitrose-has-shifted-from-high-low-pricing-to-something-more-knowing/228916.article (accessed 8 April 2014).

Liyanage, U. (2011), 'Sri Lanka's new mod-tradi consumer', *Sunday Times*, 30 January, http://www.sundaytimes.lk/110130/BusinessTimes/bt09.html (accessed 23 May 2013).

Loftus, D(2011), 'The rise of the Victorian middle class', *BBC History*, 17 February, http://www.bbc.co.uk/history/british/victorians/middle_classes_01.shtml (accessed 2 July 2013).

Lury, C. (1999), *Consumer culture*, Cambridge: Polity Press.

McCants, A.E.C. (2007), 'Exotic goods, popular consumption, and the standard of living: thinking about globalization in the early modern world', *Journal of World History*, 18, 4, 433–62.

MacGregor, N. (2012), *Shakespeare's restless world*, London: Allen Lane.

Marx, K. (1867/2000), *The culture industry: enlightenment as mass deception*, in J.B. Schor and D.B. Holt (eds), *The consumer society reader*, New York: New York Press.

Marx, K. (1876/1976), *Capital: a critique of political economy*, Vol. 1, Chicago, IL: Charles H. Kerr.

Miles, S. (1999), 'A pluralistic seduction: postmodernism at the crossroads', *Consumption, Culture and Markets*, 3, 145–63.

Mill, J.S. (1848/2004), *The principles of political economy*, New York: Prometheus.

Nestle, M. (2003), *Food politics*, Berkley, CA: University of California Press.

Nielsen (2014), 'UK shoppers turn to supermarkets' premium own-brands', http://www.nielsen.com/uk/en/press-room/2014/uk-shoppers-turn-to-supermarkets-premium-own-brands.html (accessed 2 October 2017).

Nielsen (2016). 'Retail resonance: upping the private label game among multicultural Americans', http://www.nielsen.com/us/en/insights/news/2016/retail-resonance-upping-the-private-label-game-among-multicultural-americans.html (accessed 2 October 2017).

Orange, R. (2016), 'Waste not want not: Sweden to give tax breaks for repairs', https://www.theguardian.com/world/2016/sep/19/waste-not-want-not-sweden-tax-breaks-repairs (accessed 25 May 2017).

Packard, V. (1957), *The Hidden Persuaders*, London: Penguin.

Patsiaouras, G., Fitchett, J.A., and Davies, A. (2016), Beyond the couch: psychoanalytic consumer character readings into narcissism and denial. *Marketing Theory*, 16, 1, 57–73.

Richards, H. (2014), 'The six types of digital consumer', https://www.intelligenthq.com/marketing/the-six-types-of-digital-consumers/(accessed 2 October 2017).

Samuel, L.R. (2010), *Freud on Madison Avenue*, Philadelphia, PA: University of Pennsylvania Press.

Simmons, G. (2008), 'Marketing to postmodern consumers: introducing the internet chameleon', *European Journal of Marketing*, 42, 3/4, 299–310.

Skandalis, A., Byrom, J., and Banister, E. (2015), 'Brand scouting: co-creation of value in the *Football Manager* community', *Advances in Consumer Research*, 43, 409–14.

Smith, A. (1776/1981), *An inquiry into the nature and causes of the wealth of nations*, Indianapolis, IN: Liberty Press.

Stearns, P.N. (2001), *Consumerism in world history: the global transformation of desire*, London: Routledge.

Steiner, R. (2012), 'Tesco ditch basic range after admitting shoppers are "too embarrassed" to buy the blue and white striped products', *Daily Mail*, 24 September.

Sussman, C. (2000) *Consuming anxieties: consumer protest, gender and British slavery 1713–1833*, Stanford, CA: Stanford University Press.

Szczepanski, K. (2013), 'Nutmeg: the unsavory history of a tasty spice', http://asianhistory.about.com/od/colonialisminasia/p/Nutmeg-Unsavory-History.htm (accessed 25 November 2017).

Tadajewski, M. (2006), 'Remembering motivation research: toward an alternative genealogy of interpretive consumer research', *Marketing Theory*, 6, 4, 429–66.

Trendwatching.com (2010), 'Statusphere', http://www.trendwatching.com/trends/statusphere/ (accessed 16 September 2017).

Trentmann, F. (2016), *Empire of things: how we became a world of consumers, from the fifteenth century to the twenty-first*, London: Allen Lane.

Veblen, T. (1899/2007), *The theory of the leisure class*, Oxford: Oxford University Press.

Wood, Z. (2012), 'Waitrose matches Tesco prices with "never knowingly undersold" pledge', *The Guardian*, 2 May, http://www.theguardian.com/business/2012/may/02/waitrose-johnlewis (accessed 7 December 2017).

2

CONTEMPORARY PERSPECTIVES ON CONSUMER BEHAVIOUR

Introduction

In 2010, the UK government set up a Behavioural Insight Team (BIT), under the guidance of behavioural economics experts, to improve public services and to help people make better choices for themselves (www.behaviouralinsights.co.uk). Similar initiatives have followed in Canada, Australia, and the USA. The use of behavioural economics provides just one example of the new ideas, discoveries, and research studies that are emerging from fields such as economics and psychology which enable us to understand the factors that shape and influence people's consumption behaviour in different environments. Marketing professionals have embraced these new approaches, and there are many examples of how they are used in practice. At the same time the discipline of consumer behaviour is developing in other ways, and researchers are examining consumers from a range of different perspectives, such as how they experience consumption activities and relate these to their social contexts. In this chapter we shall consider some recent developments that have impacted on our understanding of consumer behaviour in the twenty-first century, and their importance for the theory and practice of consumer behaviour. We draw on a range of ideas from other disciplines—such as economics, psychology, and sociology—to show how the field of consumer behaviour is evolving. We then move on to exploring some of the contemporary challenges around thinking about the role of technology for consumers and how social media features in this area. We also examine how the new techniques developed from neuroscience are being applied to marketing.

LEARNING OBJECTIVES

Having read the chapter, you will be able to:

1. Identify key topics from **behavioural insight thinking** and how they may impact on consumer behaviour.

2. Understand the theories and practices of **experiential consumption and consumer culture theory**.

3. Evaluate **the role of technology** in influencing consumer behaviour.

4. Identify the ways in which **neuromarketing** can help marketers explain how consumers behave.

5. Analyse the difference in the **nature of innovations**, and understand how and why innovations are adopted and rejected.

6. Recognize ways in which **social media** can be used to understand and influence consumer behaviour.

Behavioural insights

Traditionally, economists have presented consumers as behaving rationally, making logical decisions about their consumption based on factors such as price and quality. However, behavioural economists and psychologists increasingly recognize that human behaviour is more complex in terms of how we assess the costs and benefits of our choices. This has led to the development of a field of study around behaviour insights, also known as behavioural economics, where the focus is on the **contexts of decisions**, placing emphasis on the *environment within which consumption choices take place*. For example, you may be on a diet, but when invited to a dinner party you eat more because of the social nature of the occasion and because you do not want to offend your host. The behavioural economics perspective recognizes different modes (or ways) of behaving, and how these influence our behaviour in different ways.

Automatic and reflective modes

Researchers in behavioural economics refer to two modes of thinking, automatic and reflective. When in the **automatic mode** *you are operating routinely with little effort and no feeling of voluntarily being in control*. You smile when you see a baby, flinch or jump when you hear a sudden loud sound. In the same mode you may pick up a bar of chocolate at the checkout almost without thinking about it, even though you may wish to lose weight. When in the **reflective mode**, however, *you give effortful attention to a mental activity, and this is often associated with considered choice and concentration.* If you were working out the relative price per gram of two different-sized packs of pasta you would be operating in reflective mode; it would take some effort and concentration. In terms of understanding behaviour we would conclude that the automatic mode is more involved with the context of a situation, whereas the reflective mode represents the cognitive information-processing aspect of decision-making, which will be further discussed in Chapters 3 and 4. Figure 2.1 highlights some of the differences between the two modes.

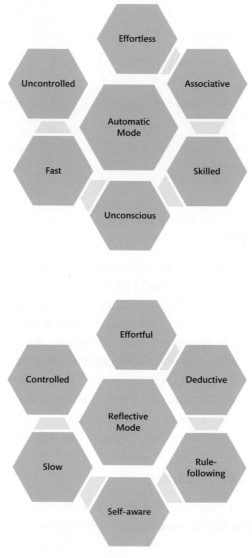

Figure 2.1　The word associations of the two cognitive systems: automatic mode and reflective mode

An example helps to illustrate the two modes. Imagine going to a new supermarket for the first time; you will most likely go around slowly in a controlled manner, identifying the appropriate aisles for the goods you want to buy. The whole experience may be quite an effort; you are operating in reflective mode. However, after a couple of visits you are familiar with the location of items on the shelves; the process takes less effort and you can almost go around unconsciously knowing where things are. You have switched to automatic mode.

Researchers consider the context of a decision to nudge people towards a particular behaviour; often this requires only minor changes to the environment or context in which the behaviour takes place. This frequently involves what is called **choice architecture**, which describes *how the way a choice is presented influences the choice made*.

Figure 2.2   The black house fly at the base of the Schiphol airport urinal

Source: Image courtesy of Bob Cromwell, http://toilet-guru.com.

One example of the use of choice architecture is the 'house fly target', introduced at Schiphol Airport to help reduce unnecessary spillage in the men's toilets (see Figure 2.2). The image of a black housefly was etched onto the bowls of the airport's urinals. This resulted in an 80 per cent decline in spillage. Houseflies and other targets (e.g. football goals) are now appearing in urinals all over the world. A minor change in the environment, in this case giving men something to aim at, made a significant reduction in mess.

Such measures have had a significant impact on governments and policy-makers who are wanting to find the most effective ways to change people's behaviour in areas such as saving for retirement, or moderating eating and drinking behaviours. Similarly, it has been traditional for supermarkets to place confectionery products at eye level where they know people will spend most time looking and are likely to pick up items in automatic mode. Other important aspects of behavioural economics that can affect consumer behaviour include mental accounting, loss aversion, norms, defaults, and priming, which are discussed in the following sections.

Mental accounting

Mental accounting *is when individuals allocate assets into separate, non-transferable groupings to which they may assign different levels of utility*. How people save provides a good example of mental accounting; for instance, parents may have a current account, a savings account, and an account earmarked for medical bills or their children's education. We use these accounts to help us control our lives; parents will think carefully before removing money from a child's account to pay for some immediate household need. Sometimes this results in irrational behaviour, such as putting money into a savings account while continuing to pay a higher rate of interest (than the savings account provides) on outstanding credit card debt. Gross and Souleles (2002) found that a typical US household had around $5,000 in savings accounts earning less than 5 per cent interest, while also holding $3,000 on credit card balances that often carried an interest rate of 18 per cent or more.

Consumers may follow similar processes in how they think about money more generally. For example, you may be willing to spend time waiting in line for a reduction of £10 off a £30 shirt, but be less keen to queue for a £10 reduction off a £500 television. The reason we engage in mental accounting is because it acts as a way to frame and keep things under control within our cognitive limitations. While it might not always be the most economically sensible way to behave, mental accounting can help us feel more secure. If you are on a limited budget, allocating a small amount every week for pleasurable activities, such as going to the cinema, may make your life more worthwhile even if you still have debts to pay.

Incentives and loss aversion

Another important aspect of human behaviour is known as **loss aversion** and refers to *how we generally dislike losses more than we like gains of an equivalent amount*. Often companies and governments will try to change behaviour through the use of incentive schemes offering rewards. However, this may not be the best way of achieving change if an incentive is not perceived to be as important as a loss. Ebhohimhen and Avenell (2008) looked at ways of treating obesity which involved financial incentives, but found no significant effect on participants' long-term weight loss or maintenance. An alternative might have been to frame the incentives as a charge imposed if people fail to do something. An example of this kind of 'reverse' incentive was used in a study examining another method for trying to help people lose weight (Volpp et al., 2008). Participants were asked to deposit money into an account, which was returned to them (with a supplement) if they met weight-loss targets. After a number of months this group showed significant weight loss, while the weight of participants in a control group without this incentive did not change. It appears that this was a classic case of the loss acting as a greater incentive than the gain. Not reaching a goal can also act as a loss. A student might be saving up for a pair of shoes in a sale, but they are sold before she has saved enough money to buy them; this can feel like a loss even though she never actually owned the shoes.

Norms

Norms refer to the kinds of behaviour that we see around us and consider to be appropriate. **Norms** *can be defined as informal rules that govern behaviour*. Norms are cultural and social, and may be rule-driven—for example, not smoking in a pub, train, or plane. Often they are generally known in a social or cultural group. For example, forms of greeting vary from country to country, based on the social norms of different cultures. In European cultures, such as Italy, Spain, and France, the usual form of greeting is to kiss on the cheeks, which contrasts with the more formal handshake that is customary in the USA and UK, and again with the forms of bowing witnessed in China (a nod or bow), Japan (a bow from the waist), and Korea (a slight bow). Social influence through information or peer pressure can impact norms. With regard to information, if we see or hear a number of people doing something, we may use this as information and follow their lead. If we visit a foreign country, we may observe how people operate in train stations or shopping queues and use this information to help us navigate new and strange environments. Peer pressure works when we care what others think about us; you might go along with the crowd to avoid punishment or to stay in their favour. We shall see some of the effects of peer pressure when we consider groups in more detail in Chapter 8. An example of how a social norm can be introduced is recycling towels in hotels. One US study (Goldstein et al., 2008) found that a sign asking clients to recycle towels to help the environment led to 35.1 per cent recycling. But when the sign said that most previous occupants of the room had reused towels during their stay, recycling increased to 44.1 per cent.

Norms can work both positively and negatively. In a study of energy use in 300 US households, Schultz et al. (2007) informed the householders how much energy they had used in recent weeks alongside information about the average consumption in their area. In the following weeks the above-average users decreased their use, but unfortunately the below-average users increased their consumption. This is known as a 'boomerang effect' and reveals the danger of showing people that their behaviour is better than the existing social norm (Thaler and Sunstein, 2009). Interestingly, when householders were shown visual representation (in this case, emoticons) as well as being given information there was an even greater impact on their reduction in energy use. Therefore when high users received an unhappy emoticon they decreased energy use even more. However, the boomerang effect was removed for below-average users when they received a happy emoticon. Research Insight 2.1 considers the application of nudge theory in the context of sustainable consumption, while in Consumer Insight 2.1, we look at the use of nudge theory for improving children's health.

RESEARCH INSIGHT 2.1

Lehner, M., Mont, O., and Heiskanen, E. (2016). Nudging–a promising tool for sustainable consumption behaviour? *Journal of Cleaner Production*, 134, 166–77.

This paper focuses on how consumers can be nudged into making better decisions for themselves and society at large. Drawing on studies from behavioural economics and behavioural sciences, the authors describe the range of nudge activities that have informed policy in consumption domains of energy use in the home, food, and personal transport behaviour. They outline a range of nudge tools, such as the use of social norms to provide information about others' transport behaviour and ideal-type behaviour, simplification and framing of information to provide informative energy bills and meter readings, and changes to the physical environment, such as road and lane planning to influence transport decisions.

 Access the online resources to read the abstract and access the full paper.

CONSUMER INSIGHT 2.1

Nudging for better health?

Obesity is a global problem, and many countries are developing various campaigns to help manage this public health issue. Concerns about the 'obesity epidemic' led New York State to pass legislation in 2009 to make restaurants note the calorific content of all regular menu items. However, initial studies found no noticeable change in calories purchased after the introduction of labelling (Elbel et al., 2009). About half of the respondents reported noticing calorie information, and only a quarter of these reported that the information influenced their food choices. One reason might be that the information did not mean much as many people are not aware of what levels of calories are good or bad for them. New York State subsequently introduced an educational campaign informing residents that 2,000 calories a day was the most that adults should eat. In 2015 the US Food and Drug Administration introduced a requirement for many food establishments to list calorie information for standard menu items. However, there are mixed results in changes to calorie intake. Dumanovsky et al. (2011) found that although total calories had not reduced following calorie labelling, one in six lunchtime customers were using the calorie information and making lower-calorie choices. Recent work (Behavioural Insight Team, 2016) explored people's record of calorie intake in Britain. Official statistics recorded that calorie intake had reduced and yet as a nation obesity is on the rise. Their research found that people were underestimating the calories they consumed and this was exacerbated when on a diet—a case of wanting to consume less calories rather than actually consuming less!

Other initiatives have been used to try to encourage people to eat more healthily. For example, in a pilot study conducted by the New Mexico State University College of Business yellow tape was put on supermarket trolleys and shoppers were asked to put their fruit and vegetables in front of the line of tape. This doubled purchases of fruit and vegetables (Cabinet Office, 2010). Putting fruit by the lunch checkout in a school increased fruit bought by 70 per cent (Just and Wansink, 2009). Another interesting initiative is the use of musical stairs to encourage people to walk up steps rather than take escalators. Examples of these can be found in Stockholm, San Francisco, and Paris (Figure 2.3).

In Iceland, children have been encouraged to exercise and eat healthier food by Sportacus, the hero of the children's TV show *LazyTown* (see Figure 2.4). In one of their campaigns children

Figure 2.3   Musical stairs in Montparnasse Station in Paris

Source: Image kindly supplied by Marie-Hélène Cingal.

and parents can sign an 'Energy Contract' where they are rewarded for healthy eating and being active. One supermarket labelled its fruit 'Sports Candy'—*LazyTown's* name for fruit and vegetables—and increased sales by 22 per cent (www.lazytown.biz). *LazyTown* has seen similar results in other places around the world, including the UK and Mexico. Iceland is one of the few places in the world to have seen levels of child obesity starting to fall (Cabinet Office, 2010; Ly and Soman, 2013).

Questions

1. Imagine that you have been asked to develop a plan to encourage schoolchildren to eat more fruit at school. How might you use social or cultural norms in this plan? From your reading of Lehner et al. (2016), what other mechanisms from behavioural economics could be used to nudge schoolchildren towards eating more fruit?

2. The BIT team found that people were underestimating their food consumption. How might a government help people to better estimate their calorie intake?

3. For each of the examples suggested in this consumer insight, identify what problems you might have in implementing the measures more widely.

Figure 2.4 The character Sportacus from *LazyTown*

Source: Image courtesy of LazyTown Entertainment. All rights reserved, © 2014.

Sources: Elbel et al. (2009); Just and Wansink (2009); Ly and Soman (2013); Cabinet Office (2010); Dumanovsky et al. (2011); Harper and Hallsworth (2016); http://www.rolighetsteorin.se http://www.lazytown.com

 Access the online resources and follow the web links to learn more about how nudge theory has been used in public health campaigns.

Defaults

Every day we accept default options because our environment is set in a particular way. A **default** is *a preselected option without active choice*. Default behaviour relies on our inertia, i.e. it is more bothersome to have to do something than to remain with the status quo. Yet as consumers we are often the losers because of our inertia, while companies gain from an understanding of defaults. For example, many people do not change their savings accounts even when there are better interest rates elsewhere. Similarly, many companies offer 'free' magazine subscriptions for a period of time, and unless you cancel the subscription after the free period you will continue with it, which of course have to pay for.

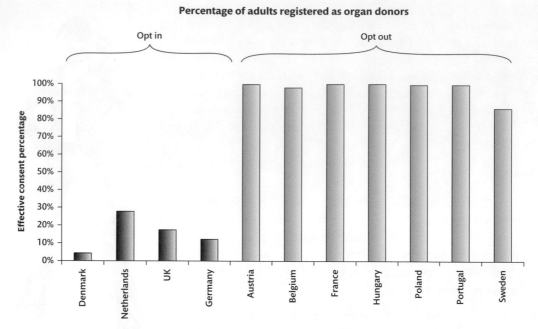

Figure 2.5 Comparison of organ donation registration in opt-in and opt-out systems
Source: Johnson and Goldstein (2003).

Another important example that helps us to understand default behaviour is 'opting in or opting out'. This is particularly important for government initiatives; if you are automatically considered to be in some kind of scheme and have to make an effort to opt out, you are probably likely to remain in it unless you feel very strongly against it. Similarly, if you have to do something to opt in you may just not find the time to complete whatever paperwork is required. In Figure 2.5 we can see one very powerful effect of opt in versus opt out for registered organ donors across countries. There are far fewer registered organ donors in those countries where you are required to opt in than in those where you have to opt out.

Priming

Think about how certain actions may be linked to how you feel (and vice versa). Feeling happy makes you smile, and just smiling can make you feel happier. This kind of association is a form of priming. It is a highly useful concept in the understanding of behaviour and has the potential to be used to manipulate our behaviour. **Priming** *is the alteration of people's behaviour outside their conscious awareness as a result of their first being exposed to certain sights, words, sensations, or activities.* In other words, priming people with certain cues without their being conscious of this happening can change behaviour or feelings. See Consumer Insight 2.2 for a discussion of some studies that have included priming.

One of the most striking things about priming is that people do not appear to be aware of the effect of the different cues on their behaviour (see Research Insight 2.2). This clearly has major implications for the use of subliminal or other manipulative techniques that may affect behaviour. As well as marketers, political leaders may use priming to try to control a population or induce a particular kind of behaviour. Figure 2.6 shows a poster of Lord Kitchener used in Britain during the First World War to recruit soldiers. The poster's powerful imagery, staring at passers-by, arguably affected young men to join up to fight (Surridge, 2001).

Figure 2.6   Recruitment poster for the First World War

CONSUMER INSIGHT 2.2

How easily are we influenced?

The UK Government's Cabinet Office has produced a report that discusses in detail how behavioural economics can be used to help design various features of choice contexts to prompt people to make choices that are in line with their underlying motivations (Cabinet Office, 2010). A number of stimuli can be used to influence behaviour.

1. **Words**—studies have revealed how powerful words can be in influencing the way people act. When people were exposed to words relating to the elderly (e.g. 'wrinkles'), it was shown that they subsequently walked more slowly when leaving the room and had a poorer memory of the room (Dijksterhuis and Bargh, 2001). This effect is explained by the fact that these people had been 'primed' with an elderly stereotype and behaved accordingly. In a similar vein, asking participants to make a sentence out of scrambled words such as fit, lean, active, and athletic made them significantly more likely to use stairs rather than lifts (Wryobeck and Chen, 2003).

2. **Sights**—what people see can influence their behaviour. For example, we know that the size of food containers primes our subsequent eating. Movie-goers ate 45 per cent more popcorn

when it was given to them in a 240g container than in a 120g container. Situational visual cues, such as walking shoes and runners' magazines, may prime a 'healthy lifestyle' in people (Wansink and Kim, 2006).

3. **Smells**—in a canteen setting, exposure to the scent of an all-purpose cleaner had an effect on the ways that people interacted with the space. A Dutch study showed that people were more prone to keeping their table clean as they ate in the canteen than when not exposed to this scent (Holland et al., 2005).

4. **In-store environments**—a recent study by Tal and Wansink (2015) showed how situational in-store interventions (such as free samples) could be used to nudge consumers to make healthy choices. They demonstrated this by providing consumers with free samples of apples in store (and comparing their subsequent purchases with those who had not received a sample or had received a chocolate chip cookie). The shoppers receiving the free apple sample went on to make greater purchases of fruits, vegetables, and other healthy foods (compared with the other shoppers).

Questions

1. Consider how you might use what you have learnt about priming to try to increase children's reading.

2. Think of some examples of how manufacturers use priming to encourage us to purchase their products. Are there instances where this has been used in ways that might be considered unethical, e.g. to encourage increased consumption of unhealthy food? What are your thoughts on this?

Sources: Dijksterhuis and Bargh (2001); Wryobeck and Chen (2003); Holland et al. (2005); Wansink and Kim (2006); Cabinet Office (2010); Tal and Wansink (2015).

 Access the online resources and follow the web links to learn more.

RESEARCH INSIGHT 2.2

Hastorf, A.H. and Cantril, H. (1954), 'They saw a game: a case study', *Journal of Abnormal Psychology*, 49, 129–34.

This classic study reported how the fans of two American college football teams perceived completely different actions by the team they supported compared with their rivals. The match had been rough, and what was seen as fair play by one side was viewed as foul by the other, and vice versa. Clearly, both sides had seen the match only from their perspective.

 Access the online resources to read the abstract and access the full paper.

Experiential marketing

Focusing on perspectives of consumption rooted in social contexts, Morris Holbrook and Elizabeth Hirschman first proposed experiential marketing in 1982. Their purpose was to shift emphasis from the consumer as rational decision-maker to a model where the consumer was viewed as an experience-seeker. Their work aimed at offering a way of analysing and explaining experiential consumption acts in consumer behaviour terms. Focusing on the consumption of the arts, entertainment, and other leisure activities as forms of consumer experience (rather than consumer behaviour), Holbrook and Hirschman (1982) emphasized the sensory and hedonic aspects of consumers rather than thinking of them as problem-solvers seeking to maximize decision-making effectiveness through rational processes. Their work highlighted the multisensorial aspect of consumption. This approach offered insights into consumption not revealed through other models. For example, if you attempt to analyse the purchase of tickets for your favourite band or football team, you will quickly see that a purely rational approach does not do justice to the strong emotional connections you feel. If you consider going to see a band you really love, what are you consuming when you see them? On one level it is the band itself, but the experience of the performance coupled with the sense of being part of the audience sharing an unrepeatable moment are also important aspects of the consumption experience. If you think about the things that you enjoy doing, whether it is going to the gym, the cinema, or a music festival or volunteering, you can start to see how central the idea of experience is to these activities.

Although these ideas first surfaced in the 1980s, the effect came to the attention of the wider business community through books such as *The Experience Economy* (Pine and Gilmore, 2011), and its impact has been enduring, mainly in shifting companies' emphasis away from consumers as buyers to a focus on consumer experiences with services and goods. Increasingly, brands are trying to introduce experiences into their marketing, such as when the TV station TNT launched in Belgium in 2012 and created mayhem in a quiet town square to tie in with its 'We know drama' tagline. In the centre of the square was a button labelled 'push to add drama'. When an unwitting cyclist did just that, a real life cops-and-robber scene unfolded in the square, much to the bemusement of the locals (see Figure 2.7). The YouTube video has received over 50 million views.

But experience is just as much about how you are treated when you ring up a call centre; waiting a long time or being dealt with poorly can severely affect your experience, and marketers need to think about how they can stop bad experiences just as much as creating new and novel ones. Charities have also benefitted from experiential approaches to engage consumers. fiftyfifty, a German organization focused on addressing the needs of the homeless during the cold winter months, turned down the room temperatures in cinemas across Germany in December and January to enable people to experience how difficult it is for homeless people in the winter. Donations could be made via QR-codes on distributed blankets, with links to a microsite set up to support the campaign.

Figure 2.7 Still from the TNT YouTube video 'We know drama'

Source: Turner Benelux (2012). A dramatic surprise on a quiet square (online). YouTube. Available at: youtube.com/watch?v=316AzLYfAzw (accessed 22 September 2017).

Neuromarketing

People often make choices at a subconscious level, and those choices do not always appear to be rational. In some cases people may not know why they choose a particular product or brand. Traditionally, market researchers have used either direct questions to ask people which brands they prefer, or motivational techniques such as those suggested by Ernst Dichter (see Chapters 1 and 7). The problem with direct questioning is that we find out what people *think* but not necessarily what they *do*. There is also the problem that respondents may give answers that reflect favourably on them or which they think are acceptable to the researcher, as in the case of the 'light' or 'regular' beer example described in Chapter 1. People are often asked to report on things that have happened in their past, and sometimes they find it difficult to reconstruct and interpret past actions, thoughts, and emotions in retrospect (Bagozzi, 1991).

Neuromarketing is a relatively new field of marketing research which uses brain-imaging techniques such as functional magnetic resonance imaging (fMRI) to identify brain activity through changes in blood flow. It directly examines how the brain works and the choices it makes without requiring the consumer to participate consciously (Morin, 2011). In other words, it identifies the choices the brain is making without the social, rationalizing, or other activities that can get in the way. **Neuromarketing** is '*the application of neuroscientific methods to analyze and understand human behaviour in relation to market and marketing exchanges*' (Lee et al., 2007: 200).

The relationship between the brain and our social and cultural environments and preferences is complex. Consider the following description of a restaurant meal devised by McClure et al. (2004: 379):

> A salad of perfectly grilled woodsy-flavored calamari paired with subtly bitter pale green leaves of curly endive and succulent petals of tomato flesh in a deep, rich balsamic dressing. Delicate slices of pan-roasted duck breast saturated with an assertive, tart-sweet tamarind-infused marinade.

For many, this lush description triggers appealing memories of food experiences, although if you were a vegetarian or disliked calamari your response might be different. Nevertheless such a description can fire our imagination so that we can almost taste the imaginary meal. McClure and his colleagues used this knowledge of the importance of social and cultural cues to recreate a neuromarketing version of the Pepsi Challenge. From 1975, Pepsi instigated a blind taste test in shopping malls as part of a promotional campaign directly attacking their chief competitor Coca-Cola. Shoppers were faced with two unmarked cups, one containing Pepsi and the other Coca-Cola, and were invited to taste both and select the one they preferred. Their brand preference was then revealed. The results showed a general preference for the taste of Pepsi even though Coca-Cola had the larger market share.

The problem with the Pepsi Challenge is that while it may be testing people's *taste* preference, it is not testing their *brand* preference. Flavour is a composite sensory perception, which is made up of taste and experience. In the experiment performed by McClure et al. (2004), people's brains were scanned to uncover their neural responses not only to the taste of carbonated drinks but also to the brand image. They found that when there was no brand information, i.e. the participants did not know whether they were drinking Pepsi or Coke, there was little difference in their neural responses. However, when those who described themselves as preferring Coke were cued that the drink they were tasting was actually Coke, there was significant activity in key areas of the brain. A possible explanation is that the brand effectively has a life of its own in people's minds, recognizing that preference is more than just taste (Ariely and Berns, 2010) or, perhaps more controversially, that the idea of the brand itself actually tastes like something (Montague, 2006).

Such research tells us that it is virtually impossible to find a purely objective response to brands. We cannot experience a brand purely in terms of its physical qualities because our brains also process the imagery that has been built up around it. Consider, for example, the impact that knowing the price of an object may have on our interpretation of its taste. In one study neural responses were measured when people sipped wine. Particular neural responses were heightened when the participants were told that the wine was expensive versus inexpensive. Indeed, the responses correlated with self-report preferences, i.e. the participants preferred the 'expensive' wine even though it was the same as the 'inexpensive' one (Plassmann et al., 2008).

Marketers are interested in such research as they hope to access people's hidden desires and preferences, just as Ernst Dichter did nearly 100 years ago. Thus one might consider showing subjects pictures of new product designs or concept advertising and measuring their brain activity to see which looked likely to be most favourable (Erk et al., 2002). Various foods have been tested using the MRI scanner, and different perceptions of taste, smell, texture, and even sound have been mapped onto areas of the brain to identify their contribution to the overall experience. For example, using chocolate as a reward and a motivation to continue eating, researchers identified different brain areas for reward and punishment (Small et al., 2001). Companies could use such techniques to design more appealing food products. Such developments have a downside; companies could create foods so carefully linked to neural responses that individuals would over-eat (Ariely and Berns, 2010).

Another technique used by neuromarketing companies is electroencephalography (EEG), which identifies brain activity from electrodes placed on a person's scalp. This method gives real-time information, but an EEG cannot locate exactly where the activity in the brain's reward or emotional centres is coming from. However, from a consumer behaviour and marketing context this may not be necessary, as the following example illustrates. An international cosmetics company pretested two versions of an advertisement for a skincare product. They differed only in that in one version the model looked passively at the camera and in the other she briefly touched her cheek with the back of her hand. Viewers preferred the version where the model touched her cheek. It appeared that this gesture enhanced the effectiveness of the advertisement even though focus group participants were unable to articulate why. The researchers used EEG to monitor skin conductance and registered significant changes in neurophysiological reactions in the scene with the gesture. What this meant was that the simple gesture brought about a brief but powerful emotional impact in this version of the commercial; consumers' brains can show different reactions to marketing stimuli even if they are not able to identify this at a conscious level (Ohme et al., 2009). Such research offers the possibility for companies to diagnose in the pre-campaign stage whether new advertisements can produce the kinds of response they are looking for (see Figure 2.8). Although it is still early days, results from experiments also indicate that recognizing what happens in the brain may be a better indicator of preference than asking people directly, as Research Insight 2.3 suggests.

Figure 2.8   Two people watching a Blu-Ray disc whilst researchers monitor their neurophysical responses
Source: Image courtesy of Pocket-lint.com.

RESEARCH INSIGHT 2.3

Vezich, I.S., Gunter, B.C., and Lieberman, M.D. (2017). The mere green effect: an fMRI study of pro-environmental advertisements. *Social Neuroscience*, 12, 400–8.

A classic problem in the study of sustainable consumer behaviour is the disconnect between consumers' stated positive attitudes and preferences for 'green' products over standard ones, but this is not translated in their purchase behaviour. This study used magnetic resonance imaging (MRI) to track consumers' brain activity in response to 'green' and 'standard' ads. When asked about their preferences for the ads, the consumers stated they preferred the green ads over the standard control ads. However, the functional MRI data suggested an opposite pattern—the participants showed greater activation in regions associated with personal value and reward in response to control ads relative to green ads. In addition, participants showed greater activity in these regions to the extent that they reported liking the control ads, but there was no such trend for green ads. So, although consumers might say they liked the green ads more, this may be down to social desirability effects, and in a purchase situation the personal values and rewards associated with standard products overwhelm their purchase decisions.

 Access the online resources to read the abstract and access the full paper.

This research suggests that neuromarketing has great potential in key areas of business and marketing such as product design, the development of advertising, brand image, pricing, and other applied areas such as the optimum store layout. However, some neuroscientists are unconvinced of the usefulness of neuroscience to marketing, and the area remains relatively under-researched. A recent study (Venkatraman et al., 2015) suggests that most of the purported techniques have little evidence to support them, with fMRI currently producing the most helpful results. The increasing applications of imaging techniques are discussed by Simon Harrop in Practitioner Insight 2.

PRACTITIONER INSIGHT 2

Simon Harrop, Brandsense

Simon Harrop talks about how Royal Mail used neuroimaging to assess consumers' responses to marketing material.

The UK's Royal Mail wanted to discover the different ways in which consumers responded to a piece of marketing information, presented with exactly the same layout, when it was delivered either on paper or digitally. To do this they used neuroimaging techniques to identify consumers' brain responses to the two forms of communication. What was found was that those areas in the brain that highlight emotional responses were more active when the stimulus was presented on paper than when it was presented in digital form. It appears that there is something about reading a message on paper that is associated with a physical locality that gives an object a place in space and time which resonates with people. Research such as this also reveals what is termed 'super-additivity'. Here, the emotional response is non-linear. So if you have a document and add texture to it and then smell, the increased emotional response may be greater than each element's contribution, i.e. rather than 1+1 equalling 2, it produces 3. What seems to happen is that additional emotional response is created by the synergy of the elements.

Rory Sutherland from Royal Mail describes physical post as producing high attention processing (HAP). Although direct mail will be thrown away by some, if people open it, they look at it, and may file it and look at it again; unlike digital forms of communication, you do not often look at it while doing something else or flicking through different web pages. Now BRANDsense is working with Royal Mail to develop Sensation-alMail where direct mail communications include other sensory elements such as fragrance and sound.

Consumer culture theory

Alongside this development in thinking about consumers as experience-seekers was a shift in how consumer behaviour was investigated, with a move towards greater use of qualitative methods and a more holistic examination of the factors affecting consumption. This shift is illustrated in important papers by authors such as Belk et al. (1988, 1989), Rook (1988), and O'Guinn and Faber (1989). This early work paved the way for the consumer culture theory approach to consumption (Arnould and Thompson, 2005), which is discussed in the next section.

Consumer culture theory (CCT), a term first proposed by Eric Arnould and Craig Thompson in 2005, aims to capture an approach to the study of consumers that emphasizes the social and cultural aspects of consumption. The CCT approach places consumers in a wider context than previous research. For example, a CCT investigation into consumer food shopping behaviour might focus on the various practices around food shopping to develop a rich and wide understanding of consumption. Therefore this might include looking at menu planning and list-making, how foods are stored in homes, the availability and use of different foods, family routines and practices around shopping, and cooking arrangements in order to develop a full and deep account of how these various aspects of food shopping come to influence the acts of purchasing food. Arnould and Thompson (2005) organized key studies from consumer culture research over the last 20 years into four main strands of research (see Table 2.1). Common to the studies that are classified as CCT is an emphasis on sociocultural processes and structures and how these are linked to consumption.

Another important aspect of the CCT approach is that it has developed new ways of thinking about how to approach research with consumers, some of which have been transferred into commercial marketing practice. Some of the research approaches now being used are detailed in Table 2.2.

CCT theme and explanation
1. **Consumer identity projects** This research has focused on consumers seeking to develop their identity through their consumption behaviour. Identity projects relate to the idea that throughout our life we are engaged in a process of construction of a story (or narrative) of ourselves, and use consumption to mark this story. Jewellery often serves this function for consumers. The Danish jewellery company PANDORA markets its charms and charm bracelets with the promise 'You're certain to find one for each of your special moments in the PANDORA range of charms'.
2. **Marketplace cultures** This strand focuses on how consumers interact with the marketplace, how their particular consumption needs are served by it, and how consumers become influencers and producers of culture. Nightclubs provide a good illustration of a marketplace culture—the fashions and trends in music, styles of dancing, clothes worn, and drinks and drugs consumed are influenced and shaped by both clubbers and club promoters.
3. **The socio-historic patterning of consumption** This strand looks at how the institutions and social structures in our lives influence consumption, and draws on more sociological understandings of consumer lives. This approach might typically consider how representations of consumption have evolved over time, and how these are supported in society. Efforts to understand sociocultural influences on men's eating habits, for example, may systematically analyse representations of men, food, eating, and health in various media over a historical period of time to gain a sense of the ways that this has evolved.
4. **Mass-mediated marketplace ideologies and consumers' interpretive strategies** This research strand is concerned with how consumers make sense of marketing messages and develop responses to them. From this perspective, consumers are active agents, engaged with meaning-creating activities. Examples of this type of activity may focus on the ways that consumers subvert and resist marketing messages that they find offensive in some way, as found in the Canadian anti-consumerist campaigning group Adbusters and its offshoot organizations around the world.

Table 2.1   Themes of consumer culture theory

Method	Explanation
Ethnography	Ethnography is a qualitative research method which aims to understand the cultural phenomena reflecting the knowledge and meaning systems associated with the everyday life of a cultural group. This method aims for deep immersion in the culture of interest. Examples of ethnography include studies of desire in the USA, Turkey, and Denmark (Belk et al., 2003) and studies of domestic use of kitchen cupboards and storage space (Coupland, 2005).
Introspection	Introspection is a form of structured self-reflection, and has been used to examine a range of consumption practices, including music consumption (Shankar, 2000), consumer value (Holbrook, 2006), and a long-term visit to Sweden (Montanari, 2012).
Narrative analysis/inquiry	Narrative analysis stems from literary criticism, and from this perspective the 'consumer story' is viewed as a repository for emotional, cognitive, and affective responses to brands, advertising, and interpersonal exchange. Examples include narrative analysis of sports shoe purchase experience (Stern et al., 1998), Australian consumers' use of brands to construct their self (Schembri et al., 2010), and Chinese tourists' evaluations of their travel dining experiences (Chang et al., 2011).

Table 2.2   Some research methods favoured in the CCT approach

Companies using experiential, ethnographic, and CCT approaches

Experiential approaches to, and ethnographic methods of, understanding consumer behaviour are not only used by academic researchers (see Research Insight 2.4). Businesses have realized the importance of different approaches in helping them to understand consumers. Collecting ethnographic data has become easier for companies as people use selfies, fitness trackers, and wearable video cameras to monitor their own lives and those of their

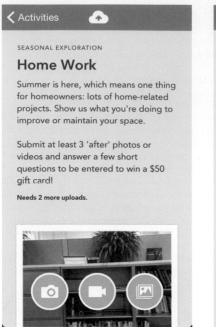 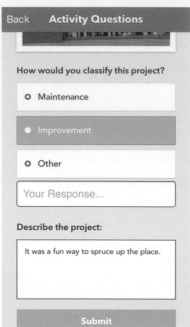

Figure 2.9 Ethnographic research

Source: Reprinted with permission from 'August 2017 *Harvard Business Review Digital* article, 'Use your customers as ethnographers' by Julie Wittes Schlack.

families and friends. People are used to uploading photos and videos, and so this makes the process easier for market research companies. For example, when Proctor & Gamble was developing its Secret range of deodorants they asked women to use a mobile ethnography app to upload photos and videos illustrating scents that brought them pleasure during a week alongside a few sentences to explain why. The results, which included Play-Doh and freshly mown grass, helped the product developers to develop a new sub-brand for the Secret line of deodorants (Schlack, 2015) (Figure 2.9).

RESEARCH INSIGHT 2.4

Cayla, J. and Arnould, E. (2013), 'Ethnographic stories for market learning', *Journal of Marketing*, 77, July, 1–16.

This paper offers insights into the ways that companies use ethnographic approaches to bring stories of consumers' lives into the boardroom. Drawing on data from a consumer goods company selling cleaning products and a financial services company, the authors argue that ethnographic stories provide an important and valuable way of understanding the complexity of consumer culture. They also explore ethnography as a means to learn about and understand market contexts.

 Access the online resources to read the abstract and access the full paper.

Technology and consumer behaviour

Another important aspect of understanding consumers in context is appreciating the role of technology as an influence and driver of consumption. Technological developments are a key force for social change, and as technology stabilizes, its design begins to influence user's practices and behaviours in relation to it.

Technology in a sociocultural context

Technology is changing the infrastructure of business and markets, but it has also dramatically altered the social fabric of consumer lives. The extent to which technology reflects and responds to consumer needs is a matter of debate, and it is often difficult to envisage the full social and economic impact of new technology. In 2016, Amazon opened its first food store in Seattle, USA, with no checkouts; purchases are automatically charged to the customer's Amazon account. The Amazon Go stores use a technology system which detects when a shopper takes an item from the shelf, and then syncs the data to a handheld device. The system logs the items as they are shopped, which eliminates the need for a traditional checkout and the system senses when they are leaving the store. The social consequences of this technology are huge, not least on employment, as some analysts predict that such technology could eliminate up to three-quarters of grocery store jobs.

One of the most significant technological advances of recent years has been the development of the smartphone, which has had a major impact on consumer behaviour. Its emergence around 2001 fuelled a major shift in practices and behaviour around mobile phones. With consumers now interacting with their phones as mobile computing devices, the result was a new set of consumption behaviours involving the consumption of web-based media and the purchase of dedicated software—apps. These behaviours imply a high level of downloading, and thus have implications for mobile operators in terms of pricing, speed, and access. When interacting with mobile technology and social media, consumers have come to experience a sense of immediacy which impacts on their expectations of consumption experiences; they expect speed and ease of access as the norm, as further discussed in Consumer Insight 2.3. Humans start to respond to the technical parameters and constraints that existing technology imposes on the consumer, with their attitudes, views, and buying behaviours feeding back to the manufacturers and their development teams.

CONSUMER INSIGHT 2.3

What does innovation do for the consumer?

In 2016 Samsung had to withdraw its new 2.5m Galaxy Note 7 smartphones from circulation. It is not the Galaxy's octa-core processor, 4GB of RAM or its clear 5.7 inch display that will be remembered but rather its exploding batteries. The iPhone 7 was also launched in 2016 with its dual camera and 'taptic' home button, but what most people remarked on was that the analogue headphone jack had been removed. What is noticeable is that smartphones have changed relatively little in the last few years but the real innovations are coming through the things you can do with them—pay for your coffee, find your way in a new city, learn a language, or organize meetings.

According to Gartner Research, technology is placing greater power in the hands of the customer. Armed with their smartphones, consumers are becoming more savvy in all aspects of the shopping experience, as they have unparalleled access to the information they need to make more informed consumption decisions. But is this true? Nagiah (2013) argues that the idea of consumer power is illusory, and companies are giving consumers the feeling of being in control (facilitated by technology), when actually companies have considerable knowledge about and power over consumers.

Questions

1. Consider what you can do with your smartphone. How has it changed in the last year or two? What other things might you want to be able to do with it?

2. What are the drawbacks for companies who decide to change something that customers have become used to, such as the analogue headphone jack? As a customer, how do you feel when something is updated in this way?

3. Read the article by Nagiah (2013). Do you think that consumers are really empowered?

Sources: Nagiah (2013); Bevan (2016); http://www.gospelware.co.uk/ http://www.gartner.com/newsroom/id/1984415

 Access the online resources and follow the web links to learn more about the concept of consumer power.

Types of technological innovations

Innovations are best classified in this context by a product-oriented classification, where the focus is on the degree of novelty in the product and the effect that this has on consumer behaviour. This perspective helps us consider some of the central issues for consumers responding to technological developments in the marketplace. **Continuous innovations** *are those that tend to create little change in consumption patterns, and generally involve the introduction of a modified product rather than a totally new one.* Examples are the introduction of a new version of software (such as the launch of Windows 10) or minor improvements or modifications to existing equipment, such as an updated version of a tablet. This approach of minor improvements and modification is typical of many markets, not just technology, and it is a way that companies can keep their products fresh and relevant for consumers, while responding to their changing needs. The BabyHub SleepSpace is a good example of such an innovation—it is a relatively lightweight travel cot that can safely be used by standing babies and can be reused as a play tepee (https://www.babyhubshop.com). **Dynamically continuous innovations** *create some change in behavioural patterns, but the magnitude of change is not very great.* This might involve the creation of a new technological innovation or the modification of an existing one, but is best thought of as evolutionary rather than revolutionary; the product tends to be used in the same way as its predecessors were used. The introduction of digital cameras is a good example of a dynamically continuous technological innovation; consumers can still take photos in the same way they did with a film camera, but the practices around printing (developing) and sharing photographs are very different, and require different support structures.

Figure 2.10   The Oxford University RobotCar

Source: John Cairns and the Department of Engineering Science at the University of Oxford.

The final type of innovation is **discontinuous innovation**, *which has a disruptive effect, and will require the establishment of new behavioural patterns.* Such innovations are very likely to be technology based, and would be characterized as revolutionary—so new that we have never known anything like it before. Examples of discontinuous innovations include the internet and email. Recently, there has been a great deal of interest in the development of the computer-controlled car, commonly known as the 'driverless car' (see Figure 2.10). The driverless car is an auto-driving system that can navigate entirely without human input, and Google's prototypes are already on the roads of California. Driverless cars are likely to be commercialized in the near future, radically altering how we approach driving. Benefits associated with this technological advancement include fewer road accidents, more productive commutes, and fewer traffic jams. But there are still questions about the extent to which these driverless cars would be received by consumers, and how the various infrastructural and regulatory aspects of motoring would assist or hinder the acceptance of this technological innovation (Araujo et al., 2012). Innovations such as this always come with risks, and a fatal accident involving a car in autonomous mode (like a self-driving car) is likely to affect consumer acceptance.

Adoption of new technology

When discussing the adoption of new forms of technology, the milestone of reaching 50 million users is often mentioned. The radio took 38 years, TV 13 years, the internet 4 years, and Facebook approximately 3.5 years to reach 50 million users. In 2012, it took the Angry Birds Space app 35 days to reach 50 million users (Annan, 2012), and Pokemon Go (Figure 2.11) reached it in just 19 days (sensortower.com). Not all new technologies will enjoy quite this type of pattern of adoption and uptake, and these social technologies are closely linked to the overall increased processing power of

Figure 2.11   Pokemon Go   *Source*: Matthew Corley/Shutterstock.com.

computers, but it is useful for firms to consider what it is that makes consumers adopt innovations and new ideas.

The most influential work on the diffusion of innovations is by Everett Rogers (1995) who argued that an innovation is communicated through certain channels over time among the members of a social system. Within the context of rural farmers, he proposed that an innovation must reach a critical mass in order to sustain itself. Rogers suggested that there are five main categories for adopters based on their readiness and desire to adopt innovations and new ideas: innovators, early adopters, early majority, late majority, and laggards. This model and approach has informed much marketing thinking and analysis of consumer adoption of new technology, and is still used today to understand the nature of adoption. Table 2.3 provides an overview of how the main categories of consumer adoption apply in contemporary technological innovation contexts, along with approximate indications of the size of each segment within the market.

A study in the USA by First Direct focused on how consumers use and adopt financial services technology. Along similar lines to Rogers' classification, the research identified six distinct categories of banking consumer based on key demographic, behavioural, and attitudinal measures, including their inclination to use banking technology products and services.

- Fast trackers—young family types who rely on smartphones and banking apps.

- Young aspirationals—singles with varied interests and little banking loyalty.

- Simplifiers—middle-aged lower-income wage earners loyal to their local banks.

- Middle of the roaders—middle-aged wage earners who wait until technology is proven.

Category	Characteristics
Innovators (2.5%)	Visionary imaginative individuals, who are technology enthusiasts. They want to be the first to get new technological products.
Early adopters (13.5%)	Genuinely enjoy the process of discovering new technologies and love talking to others about it. They are likely to embrace new social technologies before most people do.
Early majority (34%)	These consumers deliberate a little longer over adoption and take their cues from 'innovators' or 'early adopters' they know personally. They tend to look for innovations offering incremental predictable improvements on existing technology. They do not like risk, care about the reputation of the innovator, are fairly price sensitive, and like to see competitors entering the market so that they can compare features.
Late majority (34%)	Conservative, somewhat sceptical, cautious of new products and progress, preferring and relying on tradition. They fear high-tech products and usually adopt new technologies only when forced.
Laggards (16%)	Exhibit similar characteristics to the late majority (bound in tradition; sceptical) but even more so. Likely to be found among older consumers and consumers with lower socio-economic status.

Table 2.3   Characterizing the categories of adoption   *Source*: Based on Rogers (1995); Huh and Kim (2008); Hoyer and MacInnis (2008).

- Value seekers—older, well-educated, and financially comfortable customers; little interest in technology.

- Conventional stalwarts—fixed-income retirees who prefer paper statements and live tellers.

Factors influencing technological impact on consumption

What are the factors influencing technological impact on consumption? One major issue relates to how disruptive the technological innovation is; the example of the driverless car is a good illustration of the extent of change in the sociotechnical context that is needed to support new technology. Technological developments occur within a complex matrix of infrastructural elements and stakeholders or actors, and consumers are just one set of actors in this matrix. Environmental factors can also impact on technological advancements, since many are developed in response to environmental and ecological conditions (see Consumer Insight 2.4). Linked to this is an understanding of the cultural and social systems within which the technology is developed. The Tata Nano was originally launched as a cheap car, aimed at people in India and China who were looking to buy their first car in place of a motorbike or scooter (Chang, 2008). However, environmental critics were concerned that the increase in the car market in India would lead to even more traffic congestion, as well as adding to India's pollution problems. But these fears were premature; as of April 2012, only 175,000 Nanos had been sold in India (which has a population of 1.2 billion) and the most recent sales figures show a steep decline. The car has now been repositioned as a smart car, offering good value for money (BBC, 2013).

CONSUMER INSIGHT 2.4

Wind farms: good or bad?

Wind farms provide a good illustration of technological advances in response to environmental concerns, but also how acceptance is influenced by social and cultural factors. The Eurobarometer Standard Survey, conducted biannually, has shown a positive picture with regard to renewable energies and, in particular, there is support for wind energy in some European countries, notably Denmark, Greece, and Poland (http://www.wind-energy-the-facts.org/). Nevertheless, there is still resistance to wind farms in many countries. The visual impact on the landscape has been considered to be a major influence on attitudes to wind farms and a key motivation to opposition (Warren et al., 2005). One study identified harmony with the environment as the most critical perceptual dimension, with those who view turbines as having a high degree of unity with the landscape showing less opposition to them. Studies in the UK, The Netherlands, and Ireland found preferences for smaller-scale turbine installations (Devine-Wright, 2005).

Wind farms are a source of great debate in the UK. Those in favour argue that they provide a clean source of renewable energy, with no pollution and no waste products; they have a small footprint (the base occupies only a small area and farmers can still cultivate the land around them); they create jobs (manufacturing, installation, and maintenance); and they can be built offshore beyond the horizon line, meaning that they are not visible from the land.

Conservation groups and members of local communities living near proposed sites often argue against wind farms saying that they and their associated infrastructure (such as roads and tracks) are an eyesore, spoiling the natural beauty of the landscape and causing noise pollution; that they are expensive and at current levels not as efficient as fossil fuel or nuclear energy; and that turbines can cause disruption to TV and radio signals, and even the migration of birds, when not positioned correctly. Others have considered the impact on the bird population, including loss of habitat as well as death from collision with the wind turbine. Opponents also claim that turbines are only cost-effective as a result of extensive government subsidies. Clearly, the arguments are not expressed purely in terms of environmental impact, but rather reflect the complexity of issues involved, and the actors affected, when introducing such a disruptive new technology.

Questions

1. From your understanding of the issues, what advice would you give the Department for Business, Energy and Industrial Strategy to convince local people of the benefits of having a wind farm in their community?

2. What other innovations can you think of that have caused major debate and differences of opinion? Consider what the major reasons for people to resist innovations are in each case. Do you find similarities and/or differences?

Sources: Drewitt and Langston (2006); Carrington (2012); Kirkup (2012); www.energychest.net; www. wind-energy-the-facts.org

 Access the online resources and follow the web links to learn more about wind farms in the UK.

Finally, technological innovations often have unanticipated social and economic consequences. The effects of technological innovations are not always positive. As smartphone technology has evolved, often with high-specification digital cameras, many consumers have shunned dedicated cameras in favour of such multipurpose devices (Mintel, 2012). This move towards people using their smartphones for digital photography, and the shift towards people sharing photos online via social media (rather than having them printed), has contributed to the decline in the popularity of film-based photography and the closure of specialist shops and services that support it (e.g. the closure in the UK of Jessops camera stores). To survive and prosper businesses have to keep pace with technological change and see how consumers are responding to it. However, it is difficult for businesses to predict how consumers will react to innovations—they embrace some, and reject others—and recognizing what changes in behaviour mean to business is essential for survival.

Social networks and consumer behaviour

We are all familiar with the power of social networks around the world. The rise of social media use has been incredibly fast, and has changed the ways that we socialize and interact with each other; over 90 per cent of marketers use social media in some way. From a consumer behaviour perspective, these new forms of communication with millions of people around the world have changed not only the way we communicate with one another, but also how we comment on, complain about, and recommend brands. As social media is a global phenomenon, it is incumbent on companies to understand how it is used in different countries and cultures; as Consumer Insight 2.5 shows there can be particular cultural differences. Companies have little control over this behaviour. However, they can use social networks to listen to what consumers say to one another, and watch what people are doing. Companies can also create platforms for buyers to engage with, either to find out more about their consumers or to offer the opportunity to develop and market products and services to them. Celebrity blogging is a recent phenomenon, and a number of recent studies have looked at the new ways that consumers are connecting with celebrities through blogs and vlogs via more participatory approaches (Gannon and Prothero, 2016; Cocker and Cronin, 2017). Figure 2.12 demonstrates the continued popularity of Facebook, but other popular sites, including VK (Russia), WeChat (China), and Snapchat, are increasing in importance.

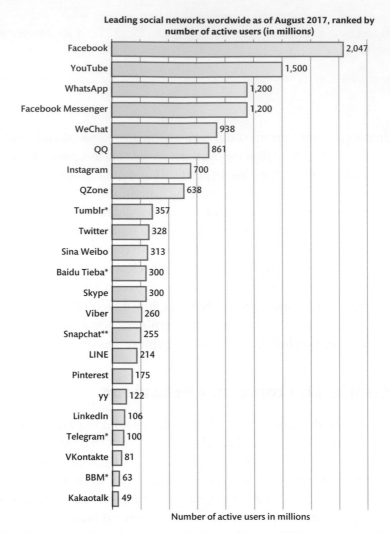

Figure 2.12   Most famous social network sites worldwide as of August 2017, ranked by number of active users (in millions)

Source: Image courtesy of Statista.

CONSUMER INSIGHT 2.5

Social networking in China

In China, there are around 634 million internet users, and 91 per cent of Chinese online users have a social media account. In comparison, around 67 per cent of the online population in the USA have a social media account. It is estimated that Chinese 'netizens' spend an average of 46 minutes on social media platforms every day. Chinese netizens interact with brands, following on average eight brands each, and make purchasing choices based on recommendations that they find on social media. Many new platforms have appeared, and big players such as Alibaba and Tencent have increased their presence. Nevertheless, new social networks emerge all the time, with China offering grants and incentives for new networking platforms which inevitably means a fragmentation of media. Some examples of the new platforms are Nice, which is a photo app similar to Instagram, and 'Meipai', which is a video app. Nice has 30 million users and has attracted many Western brands including Ray-Ban, Audi, and Kate Spade because of its photo-tagging function where users can tag what they are wearing and share their photos. Brands also use the app to run campaigns that include prizes and discounts. The app allows users to find photos using geographical locations and trending topics. Meitu Pic has over 400 million users and caters to the fondness of the Chinese for selfies. It has a huge portfolio of editing apps that allow users to edit and enhance photos and videos, from removing blemishes to elongating legs and introducing Snapchat-type face filters. Wolf (2012a) noted that young people in China may be uncomfortable meeting strangers in a face-to-face situation and find that social networking sites offer them the opportunity to have low-risk interactions where they are able to craft their profile and persona in advance. The sheer scope of Chinese social media is evident in Kantar's Chinese Social media landscape (Figure 2.13).

More mundane products are also successful on social media. Chinese kitchenware brand Supor promoted its rice cooker using cartoon-type stories on WeChat and Weibo. The cartoons typically told stories of tensions between a mother and daughter-in-law that were resolved through

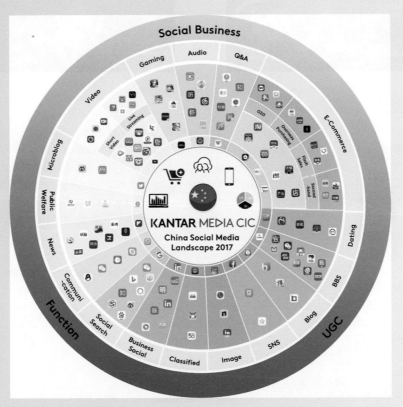

Figure 2.13   Chinese social media landscape, 2017   *Source*: Image courtesy of Kantar Media CIC.

Figure 2.14 Promotion for 'I do' campaign   *Source*: Image courtesy of AB InBev.

the daughter-in-law preparing perfect rice. Social campaigns have also proved successful. In 2015 WeChat, together with China's Child Safety Emergency Response Foundation launched a charity app to help prevent child abduction, a major social issue in China. With a database of more than 600 million users, WeChat moment feeds were dominated by the charity message, which was widely talked about and shared. Another social campaign, launched by InBev's Budweiser in 2010, used Sina Weibo and the Baidu search engine to engage consumers and gain participation by asking drivers to commit to not drinking and driving, which would win them an exclusive 'I do' badge for their personal page. This allowed people to identify as potential designated drivers. In 2012, the 'I Do' campaign (Figure 2.14) moved to a new level. Following the premiere launch of the mini-movie, AB InBev China kicked off an online charity campaign called 'Exchange one commitment for another' on weibo.com. AB InBev committed to building a Hope School in the Jiangsu Province when over half a million 'netizens' posted or forwarded the Budweiser 'I Do' commitment link. They donated 500,000RMB ($78,125).

Questions

1. Consider the kind of social media campaign that works most effectively in your country. What are the particular features of social media that make it useful for such a campaign?

2. Take a look at how brands engage with users on your favourite social media platforms. What methods do they use to engage you and what do you think is most successful and least successful and why?

3. Social media in China is fragmenting. What challenges do you think that presents to companies? Consider the social media platforms that are available to marketers in your country: How are they used? Are some better for certain types of brands and/or messages?

Sources: Wolf (2012a,b,c); Rapp (2016); Tsang (2016); www.ab-inbev.cn

 Access the online resources and follow the web links to learn more about social networking in China.

Companies have a major presence on social networking sites as this allows them to interact with their current and potential consumers in new ways that are different from traditional advertising. Games, competitions, quizzes, and other interactive approaches enable an engagement with consumers that would not be possible in other media. Apps also offer some added function or amusement and ensure that the name of the brand is kept in front of the consumer in a much more consistent way than can be achieved through other forms of advertising.

Twitter is another important development for consumer behaviour, largely because it is an almost instant medium of communication. Twitter search, a powerful feature with searches based on real-time tweets, is perhaps one of the most important features for consumers. At the time of writing, there were over two billion searches on Twitter every day (http://www.statisticbrain.com/twitter-statistics/). Social networking sites have been important in terms of developing two-way (both consumer to consumer and consumer to supplier) rather than one-way (supplier to consumer) conversations. It is easy for consumers to share information with each another, and importantly people want to participate and talk about the brands and products they love and/or hate.

It is important to recognize the differences between those consumers who have grown up surrounded by computers, mobile phones, and digital technology and those who have not. An interesting, although contentious, view is offered by Prensky (2001), who compares what he calls 'digital natives' and 'digital immigrants'. In his view, the importance of the distinction is this: as digital immigrants learn to adapt to their environment, they always retain, to some degree, their 'accent', i.e. their foot in the past. The 'digital immigrant accent' can be seen in such things as turning to the internet for information second rather than first, or in reading the manual for a program rather than assuming that the program itself will teach you to use it. Marketers have to remember that they are dealing with a range of people who have learned about technology in different ways. Research Insight 2.5 examines the role of social media and digital marketing in consumer behaviour.

RESEARCH INSIGHT 2.5

Stephen, A.T. (2016). The role of digital and social media marketing in consumer behavior. *Current Opinion in Psychology*, 10, 17–21.

This review article examines literature consumers in digital and social media environments, to identify five main themes in this research: (i) consumer digital culture, (ii) responses to digital advertising, (iii) effects of digital environments on consumer behaviour, (iv) mobile environments, and (v) online word of mouth (WOM). The paper provides new insights and thinking around the digital consumer experience, although notes that a disproportionate amount of work has focused on WOM, and that future research might usefully think about issues around the antecedents and consequences of online WOM, the effect of different digital environments (e.g. social media compared with mobile phone), impact on various consumer outcomes, and also privacy issues in the context of digital marketing and social media.

 Access the online resources to read the abstract and access the full paper.

Mobile technology

In 2012, the World Bank estimated that three-quarters of the world's population has access to mobile technology (World Bank, 2012). Some of the outcomes of the adoption of mobile technology are highlighted below (Martin and Willmott, 2014).

1. **Pressures on prices**—Digital technologies make pricing transparent, such that it is easy for consumers to switch between digital brands and retailers. Examples of such apps, which allow consumers to scan barcodes and identify best pricing information, include Etao.com (China) and the ShopSavvy app (UK/USA). In South Korea, the OK Cashbag app pools product promotions and loyalty points to allow customers easy access to more than 50,000 merchants.

2. **New businesses emerge from unexpected places**—Barriers to entry are low in digital and there is no need to build distribution networks, so companies can move into new areas easily. For example, in Japan the web retailer Rakuten is using its existing network to move into financial services

3. **The importance of alpha fans**—Companies increasingly nurture their 'alpha fans', who interact with others to build a buzz that can spread rapidly across the digital world. McKinsey uses the example of telecoms start-up Free, whose digital community is largely supported through fans and advocates because of their approach to nurturing key 'alpha fans' (see Chapter 8).

4. **Rapid integration of products and services**—Digital allows the rapid integration and assemblage of items. For example, new portals in the travel industry

can rapidly assemble trips including flights, hotels, car rentals, and even holiday excursions.

5. **Location-based services**—Zipcar (Zipcar.com) is a service for people who want to be able to drive a car but not own one. It has a free app (which engages GPS and Google Maps) to allow users to locate, reserve, and unlock Zipcars.

6. **Deep discounts**—gilt.com has online 'flash' designer sales with deep discounts, offered on an invitation only basis for a limited time.

7. **Immediate gratification**—books, music, and films are all now available instantly or within seconds, often through subscription models such as Spotify.

An example of how such mobile technology can be used effectively is a promotion by L'Oréal Canada, when it paired up with CrowdOptic to create a virtual art exhibition during the Luminato Festival in Toronto (Bernstein, 2013) (Figure 2.15). Augmented reality technology was used to devise this virtual art gallery, based around the Lancôme brand (a subdivision of L'Oréal), which could only be seen with an app created exclusively for the project. As people walked around the space, virtual works of art were displayed on their phones depending on their location.

Figure 2.15   L'Oréal/Lancôme's virtual reality art exhibition   *Source*: Image courtesy of CrowdOptic.

Conclusions

In this chapter we have examined a range of very different contemporary ways of looking at how consumers behave. We identified key topics from **behavioural economics** and how they may impact consumer behaviour. In Consumer Insight 2.1 we described a number of examples from the health domain to show how behavioural economics is becoming increasingly popular as a way of influencing behaviour, but also the difficulties that may be encountered. We also looked at research into recycling behaviour in hotels, and demonstrated how emphasizing social norms in marketing communications leads to greater behavioural change.

We explored the theories and practices of **experiential consumption** and **consumer culture theory**, and how these are changing how consumers relate to products and services and how researchers study consumers. An increasingly important area of marketing research is neuromarketing, and we looked at how it is currently being used to identify people's preferences and, in Practitioner Insight 2, how Royal Mail has used the insights from neuroimaging to understand consumer responses.

Appreciating the **role of technology**, and how it impacts on consumption, is very important to help understand how consumption practices develop and change over time. In Consumer Insight 2.3 we discussed the evolution of smartphone technology, how companies are using technology to interact with consumers, and how this has empowered consumers. This illustrates some of the ways that new technologies can shape behaviour.

The **nature of innovations** was explored in depth, and we considered a range of examples, including the driverless car. We showed that the extent to which the new technology disrupts established patterns of behaviour will have most impact on how consumers react to and interact with new technological innovations.

New technological platforms have allowed the development of novel **social media**, and businesses are learning how consumers are behaving with these media and what opportunities they may offer. We considered the example of the use of the Chinese social networking site Sina Weibo to promote Budweiser among young people, and we take an in-depth look at Snapchat in Case Study 2. Social media will be used differently by different demographic groups and so offers many opportunities, but we must also recognize that some consumers will be more resistant or less able to use them. Above all we recognize that we cannot rely on a simple unified approach to consumer behaviour, and marketers who want to succeed in the complex marketplace need to draw on a range of theories, resources, and techniques to better understand their consumers. New social media platforms have introduced a degree of uncertainty into the marketing landscape, which will require companies to identify how to engage with the different consumers and recognize how and why consumers use the platforms they do.

Review questions

1. Explain the difference between the automatic and reflective systems.

2. Discuss the concepts of mental accounting and priming, and explain what these concepts tell us about consumer behaviour.

3. Briefly explain what is meant by loss aversion and mental accounting.

4. Provide a definition of the term 'experiential consumption', and provide your own examples of how it applies in consumer behaviour.

5. Define and describe the four main research themes underpinning the consumer culture theory approach to consumer behaviour.

6. Identify three ways in which new technology has affected consumer behaviour.

7. Explain what neuroimaging can tell the marketing manager that other research methods cannot.

8. What is the difference between a 'digital native' and a 'digital immigrant'? How might their consumer behaviour differ?

Discussion questions

1. Using behavioural economics to inform your discussions, consider campaigns that might be successfully developed for:

   a) encouraging people to take some exercise during their working day

   b) putting litter into litter bins

   c) keeping to the speed limit.

   Remember that incentives, choice, and feedback can be useful for successful choice architecture.

2. Where do you think your government might consider an 'opt-out' rather than 'opt-in' method for changing consumer behaviour. What might be the problems with doing this? Are there ethical issues that we should consider?

3. MyFitnessPal.com is an app designed to allow people to work out how many calories they consume in a day. Go to their website http://www.myfitnesspal.com/ and consider what benefits consumers get from using this app and website. Based on your understanding of consumer behaviour, what recommendations would you make to the company to enhance the way they connect with consumers through their website?

4. Use the four stages of consumption experience (Arnould et al., 2002) to describe a recent purchase. Try to identify what was special or ordinary about each experience stage.

5. Watch the short ethnographic film showing a consumer's daily London commute (https://www.youtube.com/watch?v=i7VokQv79i8). Analyse in terms of your understanding of consumer culture theory. As part of this analysis, think about and comment on how this material is relevant for marketing practice.

6. Consider what products or services you have adopted recently and which you have not. What attracts you to the ones you have adopted? Why have you not adopted others? List the factors for and against two products or services and consider what changes would need to be made to the one you have not adopted to make it more attractive to you.

7. Plan a social media campaign for a charity or cause of your choice. Consider all the ways that you would engage the consumer—what would be your target audience and why, and which social media and message would you use? What problems might you encounter?

8. Why might neuromarketing techniques be superior to traditional market research techniques? Where are they limited? How might marketers make best use of neuromarketing methods, alongside other methods available?

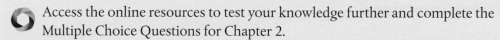 Access the online resources to test your knowledge further and complete the Multiple Choice Questions for Chapter 2.

CASE STUDY 2

Snapchat—authentic and transient?

Launched in 2011, Snapchat (Figure 2.16) is a mobile app that allows users to send videos and pictures that self-destruct within a few seconds of their being viewed. It was developed as a place where users could engage with thoughts and pictures without concern that they would come back to haunt them, as they were not permanent—friends had 10 seconds to view the video or picture before it disappeared from their phone.

By May 2014, 700 million snaps a day were being sent (www.pocket-lint.com), mostly by teens and young adults. Celebrities and marketers, including Gigi Hadid, Selena Gomez, Justin Bieber, and many more, have also been catching on to the possibilities of using Snapchat (Gillam, 2016). By 2016, the number of users was estimated to be around 200 million (Oremus, 2015), with the age demographic creeping upwards (Dredge, 2016). It has surpassed Instagram and Tumblr as the fastest growing social app (Global Web Index). There is a whole terminology linked to Snapchat including 'snapchatters' (Snapchat users), snapback (a reply to a snap), lenses, which add real-time special effects and sounds, and a snapstreak which is an exchange of snaps on a run of consecutive days.

Photos and videos can be enhanced with captions, stickers, and filters, or the 'snap' can be added to your 'story' which is a 24-hour collection of snaps. Despite its essentially ephemeral nature, you can take screenshots or save the snaps as pictures. Recently, Snapchat launched an archive feature called 'Memories'. Using this feature, you can save snaps to share again, and find photos from your camera roll to use on Snapchat.

Figure 2.16   The Snapchat app   *Source*: Wachiwit/Shutterstock.com.

The filters that Snapchat lets you apply include lighting effects, turning everything to black and white, and overlaying time and temperature. The stickers, fun lenses and geo-filters are all designed to keep Snapchat fun. Videos can be speeded up, slowed down, and reversed. Snapchat also includes a chat screen where you can find the snaps sent to you by friends; this is where Snapchat has similarities with WhatsApp and Skype because it allows chatting by text or video call with WiFi.

Snapchat is much less structured than other social media and images appear without framing to remind you where you are, so the experience is much more immersive (Kar, 2016). There is also no 'like' function, which makes it much less of a popularity contest. Therefore the transient nature of Snapchat means that you can post more intuitively and not worry too much about what you have said and what it looks like—you are not going to be reminded of what you have posted in years to come.

Some people have also suggested that it is more authentic than other platforms such as Instagram, where styling seems to be everything. However, Snapchat does include a 'beauty' filter which some have suggested introduces a look that moves toward Western mainstream norms of beauty. The filter makes the face slimmer, the eyes bigger, and the nose narrower (Strange, 2016).

So the character of Snapchat is all about creating content to send to others (it's about making rather than consuming), and the products that have been developed, such as Live Stories, are all developed around this active feature of Snapchat. In Live Stories, Snapchat curators pick snaps from a particular location, such as a sports event or videogame expo, and turn it into a story. The focus on creating rather than consuming has paid off; CEO Evan Spiegel recently reported that the service was getting 10 billion video views a day, up from 2 billion in May 2015.

It was thought that Snapchat wouldn't work well for advertisers because of its fundamentally transient nature, but the Discover feature is proving popular with some advertisers. Discover allows marketing through articles and videos, and by tapping on the publications button the latest commercial stories are revealed. Brands on Discover include *Vogue*, *Cosmopolitan*, and even the *Economist*. It also has sponsored geo-filters and lenses. Currently it is the Discover feature which generates 43 per cent of the company's advertising revenue. As yet, however, Snapchat has not gained huge advertising revenues, with eMarketer (2016) estimating that currently it has around a 2.3 per cent share of social

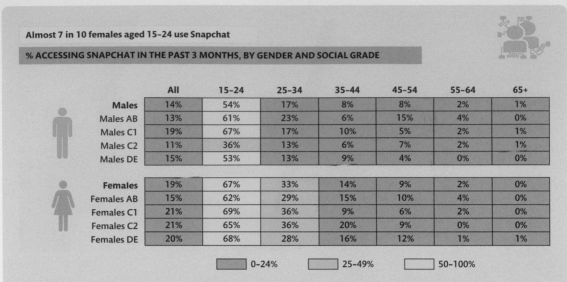

Figure 2.17   Snapchat usage by age, gender, and social grade

Source: Reproduced with permission from Ipsos Connect TechTracker Quarterly Release: Q2 2017.

network spend in the USA, but it should be remembered that it only established its advertising platform in mid-2015. It is sure to face further challenges as it competes with the more established players Facebook and Twitter. However, Kar (2016) suggests that Snapchat has benefits over Twitter and Facebook, which he says have become overloaded with content you don't want, whereas Snapchat has a lot of content but it is limited to those you want to follow. It has effectively side-tracked news and marketing content by having it in the separate Discover section, rather than intruding on your threads. It has technical benefits as well; before Snapchat, you often had to watch videos on your phone horizontally, but Snapchat has changed this and vertical orientation has now become the de facto format for other social networks. Facebook has already tried to copy the Snapchat formula with Slingshot, but this failed and the app was shut down (Newton, 2015).

How has Snapchat grown? Primarily it would seem, through word of mouth, although it has done some marketing. The networking effect has made it easier for Snapchat to continue to attract and also keep users. And it has had an impact on other social media; eMarketer (2016) estimates that Snapchat is about to see an explosive growth in its advertising revenues, potentially making nearly $100 million in 2017. Advertisers reportedly like its ability to attract the often hard to reach Millennial group. According to Ipsos Mori, it still has a strong young female orientation in the UK (see Figure 2.17).

Snapchat has recently opened an office in Shenzhen, China, which focuses on the development of Snapchat's recently released video camera sunglasses, known as Spectacles. China also manufactures the devices. Spectacles integrate a camera into the hinge and wirelessly transfer recordings to a smartphone's Snapchat app. This move has happened despite the fact that Snapchat and other social networks, such as Twitter and Facebook, are blocked in China. Nevertheless, the Chinese tech giant Alibaba invested $200 million in Snapchat last year, and Tencent has also reportedly invested in the company.

Perhaps one of the major reasons that young people like Snapchat is because of the privacy it affords. This is not about keeping your details secure, rather it is about how content is shared and with whom. It is an inherently private medium, leaving the user to decide who to share their information with. You can privately message or make it public to your followers. This is different to other platforms and of course Snaps disappear. When you send a Snap you are prompted to send to your friends, but you can also decide to make it a Story which will make it visible to followers for 24 hours. Miller et al. (2016) found that among British teenagers it constituted the most intimate social media platform, with most school-age users maintaining around 10–20 contacts that they regularly shared images with—many of these were 'ugly', joky self-portraits which necessarily relied on trust among friends. These images were often reminiscent of emojis, representing how the sender felt at the time but also contributing to a vast increase in visual images in communication.

It is the very visual aspect of the platform that led the World Wildlife Fund (WWF) to use Snapchat to raise awareness among Millennials. WWF's campaign reflected the character of Snapchat where images disappear in seconds, just like many of the endangered animals that WWF aims to protect. They subverted the selfie meme, creating #LastSelfie, and used the 'timed message' functionality to highlight that time is running out for endangered species. On its first day, the campaign was seen and shared by millions of users globally.

Questions

1. What can we learn about consumers from Snapchat?

2. Given the nature of the Snapchat platform, what are the possibilities for marketers to use it and what types of products do you think will be most successful on it?

3. Go to Snapchat and identify the brands that are present. How do marketers use it and what kind of messages are they using? What are the opportunities and problems for marketers using the platform?

Sources: Betters (2015); Oremus (2015); Dredge (2016); eMarketer (2016); Gillam (2016); Kar (2016); Miller et al. (2016); Strange (2016); https://www.globalwebindex.net

References

Annan, G.K. (2012), 'Radio took 38 yrs to get 50 million', https://visual.ly/community/infographic/technology/reaching-50-million-users (accessed 2 July 2017).

Araujo, L., Mason, K., and Spring, M. (2012), 'Self-driving cars: a case study in making new markets', *Big Innovation Centre*, 4 December, http://www.biginnovationcentre.com/Publications/25/Selfdriving-cars (accessed 2 July 2017).

Ariely, D. and Berns, G.S. (2010), 'Neuromarketing: the hope and hype of neuroimaging in business', *Nature Reviews Neuroscience*, 11, 4, 284–92.

Arnould, E., Price, L., and Zinkhan, G. (2002), *Consumers*, New York: McGraw-Hill.

Arnould, E.J. and Thompson, C.J. (2005), 'Consumer culture theory (CCT): twenty years of research', *Journal of Consumer Research*, 31, 4, 868–82.

Bagozzi, R.P. (1991), 'The role of psychophysiology in consumer research', in T.S. Robertson and H.H. Kassarjian (eds), *Handbook of consumer behavior*, Englewood Cliffs, NJ: Prentice Hall, pp.124–61.

BBC (2013), 'Tata Nano: world's cheapest car gets image makeover', 22 August, http://www.bbc.co.uk/news/world-asia-23792196 (accessed 13 December 2017).

Behavioural Insight Team (2016), 'Counting calories: how under-reporting can explain the apparent fall in calorie intake', http://www.behaviouralinsights.co.uk/publications/counting-calories-how-under-reporting-can-explain-the-apparent-fall-in-calorie-intake/ (accessed 2 October 2017).

Belk, R. (2010), 'Sharing', *Journal of Consumer Research*, 36, 5, 715–34.

Belk, R.W., Ger, G., and Askegaard, S. (2003), 'The fire of desire: a multisited inquiry into consumer passion', *Journal of Consumer Research*, 30, December, 326–51.

Belk, R.W., Sherry, J.F., and Wallendorf, M. (1988), 'A naturalistic inquiry into buyer and seller behavior at a swap meet', *Journal of Consumer Research*, 14, 4, 449–70.

Belk, R.W., Wallendorf, M., and Sherry, F.J., Jr (1989), 'The sacred and the profane in consumer behavior: theodicy on the Odyssey', *Journal of Consumer Research*, 16, June, 1–38.

Bernstein, P. (2013), 'CrowdOptic powers Lancome Virtual Gallery app, crowd-powered heat map', *Tech Zone*, 3 June 2013, http://www.techzone360.com/topics/techzone/articles/2013/06/03/340432-crowdoptic-powers-lancome-virtual-gallery-app-crowd-powered.htm# (accessed 13 September 2017).

Betters, E. (2015), 'What's the point of Snapchat and how does it work', http://www.pocket-lint.com/news/131313-what-s-the-point-of-snapchat-and-how-does-it-work (accessed 12 December 2016).

Bevan, K. (2016), 'Why innovation in consumer technology does not always work', *Financial Times*, 16 October, http://dare-think.com/2016/11/why-innovation-in-consumer-technology-does-not-always-work/ (accessed 20 December 2016).

Cabinet Office (2010), 'Applying behavioural insight to health', Discussion Paper, Cabinet Office Behavioural Insights Team, London, December, https://www.gov.uk/government/publications/applying-behavioural-insight-to-health-behavioural-insights-team-paper (accessed 2 July 2017).

Carrington, D. (2012), 'Why there's only one honest objection to wind farms', *Guardian*, 21 June, http://www.guardian.co.uk/environment/damian-carrington-blog/2012/jun/21/wind-power-subsidies (accessed 2 July 2017).

Cayla, J. and Arnould, E. (2013), 'Ethnographic stories for market learning', *Journal of Marketing*, 77, July, 1–16.

Chang, R.C., Kivela, J., and Mak, A.H. (2011), 'Attributes that influence the evaluation of travel dining experience: when East meets West', *Tourism Management*, 32, 2, 307–16.

Chang, R.S. (2008), 'Tata Nano: the world's cheapest car', http://wheels.blogs.nytimes.com/2008/01/10/tata-nano-the-worlds-cheapest-car/ (accessed 17 December 2017).

Cocker, H.L. and Cronin, J. (2017), 'Charismatic authority and the YouTuber: unpacking the new cults of personality', *Marketing Theory*, available online at http://journals.sagepub.com/doi/pdf/10.1177/1470593117692022.

Coupland, J.C. (2005), 'Invisible brands: an ethnography of households and the brands in their kitchen pantries', *Journal of Consumer Research*, 32, 1, 106–18.

Devine-Wright, P. (2005), 'Beyond NIMBYism: towards an integrated framework for understanding public perceptions of wind energy', *Wind Energy*, 8, 125–39.

Dijksterhuis, A. and Bargh, J.A. (2001), 'The perception–behavior expressway: automatic effects of social perception on social behavior', *Advances in Experimental Social Psychology*, 33, 1–40.

Dredge, S. (2016), 'New to snapchat? Here's how to join the conversation', https://www.theguardian.com/technology/2016/sep/25/how-to-use-Snapchat-tips-join-conversation (accessed 2 July 2017).

Drewitt, A. and Langston, R.H.W. (2006), 'Assessing the impacts of wind farms on birds', *IBIS*, 148, 1, 29–42.

Dumanovsky, T., Huang, C.Y., Nonas, C.A., et al. (2011), 'Changes in energy content of lunchtime purchases from fast food restaurants after introduction of calorie labelling: cross sectional customer surveys', *British Medical Journal*, 343, d4464.

Ebhohimhen, P.V. and Avenell, A. (2008), 'Systematic review of the use of financial incentives in treatments for obesity and overweight', *Obesity Review*, 9, 4, 355–67.

Elbel, B., Kersh, R., Brescoll, V.L., and Dixon, L.B. (2009), 'Calorie labeling and food choices: a first look at the effects on low-income people in New York City', *Obesity* 28, 6, w1110–21.

eMarketer (2016) https://www.emarketer.com/Article/Snapchat-Ad-Revenues-Reach-Nearly-1-Billion-Next-Year/1014437 (accessed 2 July 2017).

energychest.net (nd), http://www.energychest.net/energy_sources/activity_centre/windofchange.html (accessed 2 July 2017).

Erk, S., Spitzer, M., Wunderlich, A.P., Galley, L., and Walter, H. (2002), 'Cultural objects modulate reward circuitry', *NeuroReport*, 13, 18, 2499–503.

Gannon, V. and Prothero, A. (2016), 'Beauty blogger selfies as authenticating practices', *European Journal of Marketing*, 50, 9/10, 1858–78.

Gillam, R. (2016), '42 celebrities you need to follow on Snapchat', http://www.instyle.co.uk/celebrity/news/celebrity-Snapchats (accessed 13 December 2016).

Global Web Index (nd), https://www.globalwebindex.net/blog/topic/Snapchat (accessed 29 December 2016).

Goldstein, N.J., Cialdini, R.B., and Griskevicius, V. (2008), 'A room with a viewpoint: using social norms to motivate environmental conservation in hotels', *Journal of Consumer Research*, 35, 3, 472–82.

Gross, D.B and Souleles, N.S. (2002), 'Do liquidity constraints and interest rates matter for consumer behaviour? Evidence from credit card data', *Quarterly Journal of Economics*, 117, 149–85.

Harper, H. and Hallsworth, M. (2016), http://38r8om2xjhhl25mw24492dir.wpengine.netdna-cdn.com/wp-content/uploads/2016/08/16-07-12-Counting-Calories-Final.pdf (accessed 13 December 2016)

Hastorf, A.H. and Cantril, H. (1954), 'They saw a game: a case study', *Journal of Abnormal Psychology*, 49, 129–34.

Holbrook, M. (2006), 'Consumption experience, customer value, and subjective personal introspection: an illustrative photographic essay', *Journal of Business Research*, 59, 6, 714–25.

Holbrook, M.B. and Hirschman, E.C. (1982), 'The experiential aspects of consumption: consumer fantasies, feelings and fun', *Journal of Consumer Research*, 9, 2, 132–40.

Holland, R.W., Hendriks, M., and Aarts, H. (2005), 'Smells like clean spirit: non-conscious effects on of scent on cognition and behaviour', *Psychological Science*, 16, 9, 689–93.

Hoyer, W.D. and MacInnis, D. (2008), *Consumer behavior*, Boston, MA: Cengage Learning.

Huh, Y.E. and Kim, S.-H. (2008), 'Do early adopters upgrade early? Role of post-adoption behavior in the purchase of next-generation products', *Journal of Business Research*, 61, 1, 40–6.

Johnson, E.J. and Goldstein, D. (2003), 'Medicine: do defaults save lives?', *Science*, 302, 5649, 1338–9.

Just, D. and Wansink, B. (2009), 'Smarter lunchrooms: using behavioral economics to improve meal selection', *Choice*, 29, 3.

Kar, I. (2016), 'What exactly is so great about Snapchat?', http://qz.com/706692/why-is-Snapchat-so-appealling/ (accessed 20 December 2016).

Kirkup, J. (2012), 'Living next to a wind farm is good for you, says minister Ed Davey', *Daily Telegraph*, 12 March, http://www.telegraph.co.uk/earth/energy/windpower/9137224/Living-next-to-a-wind-farm-is-good-for-you-says-minister-Ed-Davey.html (accessed 2 July 2017).

Lee, N., Broderick, A.J., and Chamberlain, L. (2007), 'What is neuromarketing? A discussion and agenda for future research', *International Journal of Psychophysiology*, 63, 7, 199–204.

Lehner, M., Mont, O., and Heiskanen, E. (2016), 'Nudging—a promising tool for sustainable consumption behaviour?', *Journal of Cleaner Production*, 134, 166–77.

Ly, K. and Soman, D. (2013), 'Nudging around the world', m.es/documents/1922922/1973600/Nudging+Around+The+World.pdf/3af04386-ba8b-4742-b339-73626bf2be94 (accessed 2 July 2017)

McClure, S., Li, J., Tomlin, D., et al. (2004), 'Neural correlates of behavioral preference for culturally familiar drinks', *Neuron*, 44, 379–87.

marketingtochina.com (nd), 'How to promote your brand on social media in China', http://marketingtochina.com/promote-brand-social-media-china-2/ (accessed 19 December 2016).

Martin, H. and Willmott, P. (2014), 'Strategy for competing in the digital age', *McKinsey Quarterly*, https://www.mckinsey.com/business-functions/strategy-and-corporate-finance/our-insights/strategic-principles-for-competing-in-the-digital-age (accessed 5 October 2017).

Miller, D., Costa, E., Haynes, N., et al. (2016), *How the world changed social media*, London: UCL Press.

Mintel (2012), 'Digital cameras UK', http://store.mintel.com/digital-cameras-uk-may-2012 (accessed 2 July 2017).

Morin, C. (2011), 'Neuromarketing: the new science of consumer behavior', *Society*, 48, 2, 131–5.

Montague, R. (2006), *Why choose this book?*, New York: Dutton.

Montanari, A. (2012), 'Beyond subjective to confirmatory personal introspection: interpreting events and meaning of a long-term visit in Sweden', *Journal of Business Research*, 66, 11, 2363–8.

Nagiah, N. (2013), 'Consumer empowerment is an illusion', *Huffington Post*, 23 July, http://www.huffingtonpost.com/navin-nagiah/consumer-empowerment-is-a_b_3635067.html (accessed 2 July 2017).

Newton, C. (2015), 'Facebook shuts down its experimental Creative Labs division', *The Verge*, https://www.theverge.com/2015/12/7/9865624/facebook-creative-labs-shutdown (accessed 5 October 2017).

O'Guinn, T.C. and Faber, R.J. (1989), 'Compulsive buying: a phenomenological exploration', *Journal of Consumer Research*, 16, 2, 147–57.

Ohme, R., Reykowska, D., Wiener, D., and Choromanska, A., (2009), 'Analysis of neurophysiological reactions to advertising stimuli by means of EEG and galvanic skin response measures', *Journal of Neuroscience, Psychology, and Economics*, 2, 1, 21–31.

Oremus, W. (2015), 'Is Snapchat really confusing, or am I just old?', http://www.slate.com/articles/technology/technology/2015/01/Snapchat_why_teens_favorite_app_makes_the_facebook_generation_feel_old.html (accessed 13 December 2016).

Pine, B.J. and Gilmore, J.H. (2011), *Welcome to the experience economy*, Brighton Watertown, MA: Harvard Business Review Press.

Plassman, H., O'Doherty, J., Shiv, B., and Rangel, A. (2008), 'Marketing actions can modulate neural representations of experienced pleasantness', *Proceedings of the National Academy of Sciences of the USA*, 105, 1050–4.

Prensky, M. (2001), 'Digital natives, digital immigrants: Part 1', *On the Horizon*, 9, 5, 1–6.

Rapp, J. (2016), '10 Chinese photo-sharing apps luxury marketers need to know', https://jingdaily.com/10-chinese-photo-sharing-apps-luxury-marketers-need-know/ (accessed 20 December 2016).

Rogers, E.M. (1995), *Diffusion of innovations* (4th edn), New York: Free Press.

Rook, D.W. (1988), 'Researching consumer fantasy', *Research in Consumer Behavior*, 3, 247–70.

Schembri, S., Merrilees, B., and Kristiansen, S. (2010), 'Brand consumption and narrative of the self', *Psychology and Marketing*, 27, 6, 623–37.

Schlack, J.W. (2015), 'Use your customers as ethnographers', *Harvard Business Review*, August, 2–9.

Schultz, S.P., Nolan, J.M., Cialdini, R.B., et al. (2007), 'The constructive, destructive, and reconstructive power of social norms', *Psychological Science*, 18, 429–34.

sensortower.com (2016), 'Pokémon GO hit 50 million downloads in record time, now at more than 75 million worldwide', https://sensortower.com/blog/pokemon-go-50-million-downloads (accessed 3 December 2016).

Shankar, A. (2000), 'Lost in music: subjective personal introspection and popular music consumption', *Qualitative Market Research*, 3, 1, 27–37.

Small, D.M., Zatorre, R.J., Dagher, A., et al. (2001), 'Changes in brain activity related to eating chocolate: from pleasure to aversion', *Brain*, 124, 1720–33.

Stephen, A.T. (2016), 'The role of digital and social media marketing in consumer behavior', *Current Opinion in Psychology*, 10, 17–21.

Stern, B., Thompson, C., and Arnould, E. (1998), 'Narrative analysis of a marketing relationship: the consumers' perspective', *Psychology and Marketing*, 15, 3, 195–214.

Strange, A. (2016), 'Why Snapchat and smartphone beauty filters need a culturally inclusive update', http://mashable.com/2016/08/13/Snapchat-beauty-filter-culture/#hBVbK.nOn8qR (accessed 30 December 2016).

Surridge, K. (2001), 'More than a great poster: Lord Kitchener and the image of the military hero', *Historical Research*, 74, 185, 298–313.

Tal, A. and Wansink, B. (2015), 'An apple a day brings more apples your way: healthy samples prime healthier choices', *Psychology & Marketing*, 32, 5, 575–84.

Thaler, R.H. and Sunstein, C.R. (2009), *Nudge: improving decisions about health wealth and happiness*, London: Penguin Books.

Tsang, J. (2016) 'How to create great earned social media campaigns for China', https://www.clickz.com/how-to-create-great-earned-social-media-campaigns-for-china/92259/ (accessed 19 December 2016).

Venkatraman, V., Dimoka, A., Pavlou, P.A., et al. (2015), 'Predicting advertising success beyond traditional measures: new insights from neurophysiological methods and market response modeling', *Journal of Marketing Research*, 52, 4, 436–52.

Vezich, I.S., Gunter, B.C., and Lieberman, M.D. (2017), 'The mere green effect: an fMRI study of pro-environmental advertisements', *Social Neuroscience*, 12, 400–8.

Volpp, J., John, L.K., Troxel, A.B., et al. (2008), 'Financial incentive-based approaches for weight loss: a randomized trial', *JAMA*, 330, 22, 2631–7.

Wansink, B. and Kim, J. (2006), 'Bad popcorn in big buckets: portion size can influence intake as much as taste', *Journal of Nutrition, Education and Behavior*, 37, 5, 242–5.

Warren, C.R., Lumsden, C., O'Dowd, S., and Birnie, R.V. (2005), 'Green on green: public perceptions of wind power in Scotland and Ireland', *Journal of Environmental Planning and Management*, 48, 6, 853–75.

Wolf, D. (2012a), 'China's social networks: choosing the right site', http://www.warc.com

Wolf, D. (2012b), 'Marketers and China's microblogs: Sina Weibo vs Tencent Weibo', http://www.warc.com

Wolf, D. (2012c), 'Social media in China: a marketer's guide', http://www.warc.com

World Bank (2012), http://www.worldbank.org/en/news/press-release/2012/07/17/mobile-phone-access-reaches-three-quarters-planets-population (accessed 2 July 2017).

Wryobeck, J. and Chen, Y. (2003), 'Using priming techniques to facilitate health behaviours', *Clinical Psychologist*, 7, 2, 105–8.

PART 2

MICRO-VIEW OF CONSUMPTION

Where are we going?

**Future trends in
consumer behaviour**

Macro-view

**Consumers in society and
the market: groups, social processes,
culture, and repeat purchasing behaviour**

Micro-view

**The individual consumer: individual
decision-making, learning, perception,
attitudes, personality and motivation**

How we arrived here

**Historical context and
contemporary perspectives
on consumption**

£10 SUMMER DINNER FOR TWO

Starter/dessert + main + side + drink/chocolates

Shop offer

3

DECISION-MAKING AND INVOLVEMENT

Introduction

When you buy a product for the first time, how much do you think about what you are buying? Do you ever go shopping in the supermarket intending to buy one brand and come out with a completely different one? Do you find that you buy something different when you are with your partner or friend than when you are on your own?

When and how we shop, the decisions we make about whether or not to purchase, and what we buy and how we feel after we have bought something are the concerns of this chapter. How rational are consumers in their choices? Do we use shortcuts to make decisions? And how involved are we with what we purchase? These are all questions important to marketers in understanding consumer behaviour and for finding the best marketing strategy to ensure that their products and brands are purchased, and purchased again.

LEARNING OBJECTIVES

Having read this chapter, you will be able to:

1. Explain **decision-making** in low and high involvement situations.

2. Understand the nature of **involvement**, how this affects people's decision-making and how to increase it.

3. Analyse the *stages in the decision-making process*.

4. Identify different types of *shopping behaviour* and consumer shopping motives.

5. Explain the problems that people have with choice, and the strategies used to deal with choice situations such as *satisficing and maximizing behaviour, and the use of heuristics, anchoring, and framing*.

From choice to decision-making

We make decisions every day. While some of these are important and may have a long-term impact on our lives (such as choosing which university course to take), many are trivial (such as whether to have toast or cereal for breakfast) and sometimes we may not even notice that we have made a decision. The decision-making process assumes that we seek to solve a problem or achieve a desired goal. We may want to lose weight or move to a new city. We may feel thirsty or hungry. While the solutions to some of these may be relatively simple, others are more complex and involve a number of decisions regarding choices and actions to achieve our goal. There will be significant differences in how the decision comes about depending on the problem to be solved and the nature and context of the person deciding. The level of involvement consumers have with a purchase is a key factor influencing the decision-making process. **Involvement** *is the perceived relevance of a purchase to the consumer.*

Some decision-making, such as choosing our university course, is important as it will affect aspects of our life (such as the career we can follow). We refer to these as high involvement decisions. Other decisions are of less importance. When a consumer is thirsty they are likely to choose a pleasant tasting drink that quenches their thirst. If they do not like the drink chosen, they may buy another or not buy that brand again, but the outcome is not likely to be very important. Such decisions are referred to as low involvement. Figure 3.1 provides a simplified comparison of decision-making in low and high involvement contexts.

What are the differences between these two decision-making processes? The main difference of significance to marketers is that in the high involvement decision a choice is made following a process of search and evaluation, where some kind of evaluative criteria will be applied. In the low involvement decision the choice is made without these intervening steps. Obviously there are shades of grey, and some researchers distinguish between what is referred to as extended problem-solving (high involvement) and habitual decision-making (low involvement). Limited problem-solving occurs in situations where the consumer is less motivated to search for information or evaluate alternatives in as rigorous a way as they would for an extended problem-solving choice. In such cases consumers may use simple evaluation criteria or decision rules such as 'it must be under £5' or 'it must fit

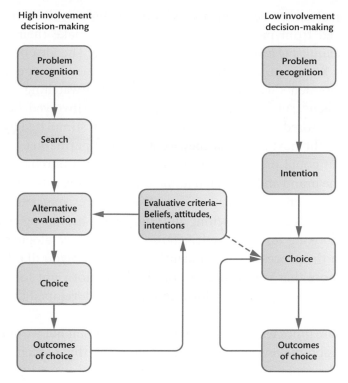

Figure 3.1   High and low involvement decision-making

into the space in the corner'. In the low involvement decision the outcomes of the purchase may also affect evaluative criteria, although the impact may be more limited (identified by the dashed line in Figure 3.1). A key difference between high and low involvement from a marketing perspective is that in high involvement consumers are in an active manner as outlined in Table 3.1.

In the consumer behaviour context **active learning** *involves the acquisition of knowledge before purchase, and therefore extensive information search* (Erdem et al., 2005). Here we want to learn more about the brands we are considering buying because the purchase decision is important to us, i.e. it is one of high involvement. Although problem recognition

Low involvement hierarchy	High involvement hierarchy
Brand beliefs are formed through passive learning	Brand beliefs are formed through active learning
A purchase decision is then made	Brands are then evaluated
The brand may or may not be evaluated	A purchase decision is made

Table 3.1   Learning in low and high involvement decision-making

occurs in a low involvement decision, just as it does in high involvement, the consumer uses beliefs formed from passive learning in order to make their choice. **Passive learning** *is the acquisition of knowledge without active learning.* The idea of passive learning was developed by Krugman and Hartley (1970) who studied how people watched TV and which advertisements were recalled. They found that watching TV required little effort from the audience; viewers did not need to be actively involved. Messages received by consumers were stored in a passive dormant state until stimulated by recognition of the brand, perhaps the next time that they went to the supermarket. Awareness of the brand at this point could produce behaviour resulting in a purchase. Once the consumer had tried the brand and evaluated it, their attitudes towards it would be formed. An important aspect of passive learning is an absence of resistance to what is learned. As active learning is by its nature exciting and engaging, it may bring about more resistance. If you are looking for a new refrigerator you search catalogues, internet sites, and shops, and in the process you will identify brands that you like (e.g. Smeg, Neff, Miele), but also those that you dislike or you think are not right for your needs (e.g. Beko, Indesit, LEC). This represents a form of resistance developed through the active search process.

However, there are times when the decision is still important but we do not go through the extensive decision-making process outlined earlier in this section. When someone buys a new car they may spend considerable time looking at different brands and types within their price bracket and evoked or consideration set. The **evoked set** refers *to all brands they are aware of which might meet their needs*, while the **consideration set** refers *to those they might actually consider buying*. Alternatively, they may already have a well-formed intention of what they want to buy. Perhaps their current car is a BMW Mini and the only reason they want to change is because it has reached a high mileage. In this case they may limit themselves to looking at new models of the Mini. They have a well-formed intention to make a particular choice, and this process is shown in Figure 3.2 where intention comes directly after problem recognition. Of course, if as a result of this purchase they are not happy with their choice, they will probably reconsider and revert to a more actively oriented decision process as shown in Figure 3.1. In Figure 3.2, however, for the purchase to become a more routine decision, a positive outcome has to feed back to a future intention to buy the same brand.

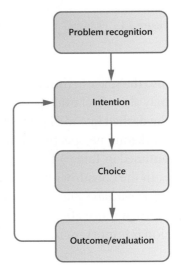

Figure 3.2   Routine decision process in a high involvement situation

Before examining the stages in the decision-making process in more detail, other types of involvement that might impact decision-making and the importance of involvement to marketing are considered in more detail (see Research Insight 3.1).

RESEARCH INSIGHT 3.1

Arsel, Z. and Bean, J. (2013), 'Taste regimes and market-mediated practice', *Journal of Consumer Research*, 39, 5, 899–917.

This paper considers an aspect of consumers' decisions that influences how and what they consume—the concept of taste. Taking a consumer culture theory approach, the authors explore how consumers develop a sense of good taste in interior design and how they incorporate it into their homes. By analysing a popular home design blog, Apartment Therapy, the authors undertake a qualitative and quantitative investigation of participants' involvement on this blog to develop a deeper understanding of how consumers develop their sense of taste.

 Access the online resources to read the abstract and access the full paper.

Involvement and decision-making

As discussed already, the level of involvement and relevance of purchases for consumers can bring about different decision-making processes, as shown in Table 3.2.

In a low involvement process, where there are few differences between brands, a consumer may not be too concerned about their choices. This could result in inertia which may manifest itself in apparent loyalty, i.e. buying the same brand of tinned tomatoes every week. While the consumer may appear loyal, a price promotion on a similar brand may find them switching brands. Similarly, a consumer may equally follow a random choice routine where they pick up the first brand they notice within their price range or that appeals to them because of packaging or promotion. However, if the choice is a high involvement decision which may include an element of risk, the consumer is likely to engage in dissonance reduction strategies (see Chapter 6) to ensure that they make the right choice. This may mean that they engage in an extended search and look for reassurance after purchase that they have made the right choice.

In a recent advertisement for Swinburne University of Technology in Melbourne, Australia, the copy in the advertisement states 'Am I making the right choice or the safe one?', thereby asking the prospective student if they are confident enough to look beyond the

	Low involvement (low price, low risk)	High involvement (high price, high risk)
Few differences between brands	Inertia or spurious loyalty Random choice	Complex decision-making and dissonance reduction
Significant differences between brands	Variety seeking Random choice Experimentation	Complex decision-making or brand loyalty

Table 3.2   High and low involvement purchases

hype and choose a university based on its merits. This approach reflects Swinburne's recognition that university choice is difficult and that older more established names may be seen as a safer bet. Swinburne tackled high involvement choice head on by trying to alleviate the dissonance a student might feel by emphasizing that Swinburne may be the right (if not the safe) choice. Of course there may be some students who wish to choose a safe option, but many young people will be influenced by an argument that attacks the 'safe' position.

When there are many differences between brands in a low involvement decision there is more incentive for the consumer to engage in variety seeking and try different brands, as noted in Table 3.2. This is often the case in products such as soft drinks, confectionery, and ready-to-eat cereals. Variety-seeking behaviour provides an important opportunity for businesses to develop new flavours, formulations, and packaging, as consumers may be prepared to experiment because the cost of disappointment is low. Equally, as it is a low involvement purchase, they may also follow the random choice process highlighted in Table 3.2. In the high involvement situation the consumer has more reason to engage in active decision-making to ensure that they examine all possibilities. However, they may also follow a routine process once they have found their preferred brand, as described in Figure 3.2, reducing the effort that they put into the new purchase.

Other forms of involvement

While we categorize decision-making by high or low involvement, a consumer's level of involvement will depend on how relevant the purchasing decision is to them. Different people will exhibit varying levels of involvement with regard to the same product because of differences in their personality, socio-economic and demographic factors, previous experience, and the product's relevance to them and their situation (Antil, 1984). In this section we shall consider the following types of involvement.

- **Product involvement** *is the perceived personal relevance of the product, based on needs, values, or interest* (Zaichkowsky 1985, 1986).

- **Message-response involvement** *reflects the consumer's interest in marketing communications* (Batra and Ray, 1983).

- **Enduring involvement** is *'the pre-existing relationship between an individual and the object of concern'* (Houston and Rothschild, 1978: 3).

- **Ego involvement** is *when consumers perceive products or brands as relevant to their personal interests* (Foxall, 1993).

While companies are often concerned with developing advertisements to convince consumers to purchase a product, advertising agencies know that it is often most important to get the consumer involved with the message as persuasion may follow (see Consumer Insight 3.1).

Foxall's (1993) research reminds us that involvement is a relationship between the product and the consumer, and that some consumers may be more involved with a typically low involvement product field. While personal factors and a long-term interest in a product may affect our level of involvement, such factors may also change depending upon the purchase situation. Situational involvement tends to depend on some particular event or time in our lives. Buying a bottle of wine as a gift is different from buying a bottle of wine to drink at home at the weekend. This reflects our different levels of involvement. If we are buying wine as a gift, we might visit a specialist wine retailer (such as Oddbins or Indigo, an online wine merchant), and we might seek expert advice from magazine reviews to ensure that we buy the 'right' gift. Wine bought to drink at home might be purchased at the supermarket, perhaps influenced by price deals and expert recommendations (a trend in supermarkets is to note 'As recommended by …' alongside wines on display).

CONSUMER INSIGHT 3.1

How to achieve enduring involvement through emotion

The advertising agency Fallon was tasked with building a feeling of love towards Cadbury's Dairy Milk, especially among younger consumers who had not grown up with Cadbury's Dairy Milk being the 'default' chocolate bar as their parents' generations had. The agency felt that the brand needed what they referred to as 'fame'. The creative brief was to 'Give people the feeling they have when eating our chocolate'; they needed to imbue the advertisements with emotion. The juxtaposition of a gorilla playing drums to a track by the former Genesis drummer and vocalist Phil Collins was designed to make people smile (see Figure 3.3). In testing the advertisements the key criterion of success was generating a smile; the agency recorded facial expressions. In further quantitative analysis the impact and involvement for the advertisement was high, with spontaneous brand recall at 80 per cent.

A very different approach was used by John Lewis in an advertisement showing a woman's life from a baby to an elderly woman, supported throughout with products from the department store and accompanied by the song *Always a Woman*. The advertisement illustrates how it is possible to resonate with the nature of both a customer's product and enduring involvement. The campaign is aimed at reinforcing in consumers' minds that the company makes a lifelong commitment to quality, fair pricing, and excellent service.

It was a phenomenally successful campaign, and Robert Bain, the Head of Strategy for John Lewis, put its success down to how the advertisement reflected the 'lifelong commitment and emotional bond that people build with the brand. It's the idea that John Lewis is there throughout all key stages of your life—a birth, a wedding, moving home. They're events that stir strong emotion, and I think the advertisement was able to reflect that. Part of the foundation of what we believe John Lewis offers is trust. The ability to come back over all those stages of your life and get the same level of service, the same quality of goods is important. The emotional affinity people felt with the advertisement made it the success it was' (Bain, 2010)

Figure 3.3   Screen shot from the Cadbury's 'Glass and a Half Full Production'
Source: Image printed with permission from Cadbury's Ltd.

Questions

1. Look at the two advertisements on YouTube. How do they engage with the consumer?

2. What different techniques are used in the advertisements?

3. Do you think they are successful? Why do you think this?

Sources: Barreyat-Baron and Barrie (2008); Bain (2010); www.utalkmarketing.com

 Access the online resources and follow the web link to learn more about achieving enduring involvement through emotion.

How to increase involvement

Marketers want to increase involvement with both their products and their messages so that customers have positive associations with them when making high or low purchase decisions. There are a number of ways that they can achieve this.

Figure 3.4   Increasing involvement through hedonism   *Source*: Image supplied by The Advertising Archives.

Link the brand to hedonic needs Häagen Dazs ran a series of advertisements that directly associated the eating of ice cream with sex, while Pot Noodles presented their brand as a dark and rather naughty pleasure (Figure 3.4). For some time Pot Noodles used the line 'the slag of all snacks', but this had to be removed after a number of complaints. Nevertheless, this positioning as a cheap and easy form of instant food gratification has continued.

Use distinctive or novel ways of communicating your product The packaging for the Korean laundry detergent Spark (Figure 3.5) is distinctive and novel, quickly facilitating communication about the product and its use. In addition, the packaging allows the consumer to see how much is left in the box, making re-purchase easier.

Figure 3.5   Using novel ways of communication to increase involvement

Source: Image printed with permission of Aekyung Industrial Co., Ltd.

Figure 3.6   Misty Copeland for Under Armour   *Source*: Image courtesy of Under Armour.

Use celebrities Celebrities can be very useful for creating greater involvement with a brand (see Consumer Insight 3.2). To engage their audience, celebrities have to create impact. Holt (2016) describes how Under Armour's campaign 'I will what I want' used celebrity to challenge convention and expected ideas of gender and social norms. The campaign focuses on the ballet dancer Misty Copeland, who grew up in poverty and was told that her body would be wrong for ballet. Such pushing of gender norms is as important as the use of the celebrity to engage with consumers who are bombarded with images of celebrities daily. Under Armour, having made the successful connection with Misty Copeland have developed the strong imagery of their original ads with their recent 'Unlike Any' campaign (Figure 3.6).

CONSUMER INSIGHT 3.2

Finding the right celebrity endorser around the world

In Asian countries American celebrities have extensively endorsed local brands. In Japan, Arnold Schwarzenegger has advertised Nissin instant noodles, while Keanu Reeves promotes Suntory Reserve. China is particularly celebrity prone, although the use of some celebrities such as Bill Clinton, Warren Buffet, and Bill Gates has clearly been achieved without their permission. Brands like L'Oréal have used a successful mix of local and global ambassadors, including actor Andy Lau and movie star Li Bingbing in China, and former Miss World and Bollywood actress Aishwarya Rai in India.

In Taiwan Magiclean used a celebrity mum to advertise their cleaning products. A successful TV star and mother of three children, Dee Hsu was seen as epitomising the modern Taiwanese working woman trying to strike a balance between family and career. According to this campaign, people like Dee Hsu don't have much time to clean their kitchens and bathrooms and are looking for a quick and easy solution, which Magiclean provides.

The internet and social media have led to celebrity endorsement being extended across channels, critical in these times when young people are using their mobile phone screens for media consumption. Fans of celebrities will purchase the brands they endorse, collecting and sharing information through social media. Fans will post reactions to new commercials on social media and blogs, and will visit the corporate sponsors to watch the advertising in which their idol is represented. One such idol in Japan is Ninomiya Kazunari, a member of the boy band Arashi. On the corporate webpage for Nisshin OilliO, the cooking oil he endorses, fans can view longer commercials and videos of the making of the commercials as well as downloadable PC wallpaper and recipes for their idol's favourite food.

Questions

1. What do you think are the advantages and disadvantages of using local celebrities to increase involvement?

2. Think of ways that you might use social media to increase involvement with celebrities for:
   - a new brand of chocolate bar
   - public transport.

Sources: Lee (2012); www.asiapacificmemo www.guardian.co.uk www.howstuffworks.com

 Access the online resources and follow the web links to learn more about campaigns that have used celebrities.

Tell a story This is particularly effective when there is a longer period of time to present a narrative, such as in cinema advertising or on the internet. Google's Reunion ad centres on the story of an Indian man explaining to his granddaughter how he and his friend had not seen one another since the partition between India and Pakistan. The grand-daughter tracks his friend down with the help of Google and the friends are reunited. The ad, which has received over 13 million views on Youtube, works as a poignant story but ensures that the viewer engages with how Google was central to the happy ending. Nescafé Philippines told stories of community spirit and passion for music in their Red Mug Sessions, which show inspiring stories and experiences of Filipino musicians that were shared on Nescafé Philippines social media platforms. Nescafé was linked to supporting local talent and giving musicians an outlet for their music, but importantly these videos were not used as a vehicle for highlighting Nescafé's attributes although the beverage was always in the background. The Red Mug Sessions achieved over 500,000 views on YouTube and over 1.8 million fans on Facebook (Quek, 2013).

Build a relationship Companies that invest in a particular communications message can build a relationship between the viewer and that message. Whether or not the consumer is involved with the brand, they will, over time, build knowledge of what the brand stands for. BT have used a modern romance that both tells the story of a couple (Adam and Jane meeting, falling in love, and marrying) and builds a relationship with the viewer (by getting the viewer to choose what happens in the next advertisements). In 2011, viewers were asked to vote, through a Facebook page, for Jane's wedding dress and car. Throughout the series of advertisements BT align products with the story; for example, as the couple are about to move house, BT links this with a new easy form of telephone connection for people moving home. The internet and social media platforms are increasingly important for building relationships, but as Research Insight 3.2 reveals it is increasingly difficult for brands to manage this against the range of alternative digital entertainment available.

RESEARCH INSIGHT 3.2

Holt, D. (2016), 'Branding in the age of social media', *Harvard Business Review*, March, 41–50.

This conceptual paper highlights how consumers are rejecting the branded content of big brands like McDonalds, Coca-Cola, and even Red Bull, who try to develop online relationships; instead young people's online relationships are with digital broadcasters and vloggers. Holt discusses the video gaming as entertainment sector, with its star vloggers (many of whom are not widely heard of) achieving massive online presence very quickly and thus having significant impact; the YouTube channels of these star gamers typically have subscriptions in the region of tens of millions. This compares with McDonald's, one of the largest social media spenders, which has just over 204,000 subscribers.

 Access the online resources to read the abstract and access the full paper.

In the age of digital, is TV still important? It certainly is, as Simon Tunstill explains in Practitioner Insight 3.

PRACTITIONER INSIGHT 3

Simon Tunstill, Head of Communications, Thinkbox

There are many ways we can watch TV these days—on buses, on beaches, in bed, and beyond. But the majority of the TV we watch continues to be watched on a TV set, generally in the company of others while sitting on the sofa in our living rooms.

This 'normal' way of watching TV is sometimes described as a 'passive' or 'lean back' experience. The theory goes that, unlike holding and

reading a book or scrolling, browsing, and clicking your way around the internet, with TV you nestle into your sofa and let it all wash over you. There's not much more to do beyond choosing your channel and adjusting the volume. But our brains are very much in motion; they are incredibly active. The term 'passive' doesn't quite do justice to the time we spend watching TV and deciphering plots, or chewing over quiz questions, or being gripped by a match, or laughing at jokes, or following a recipe, or any of the other countless things our brains process when we watch TV.

The blend of conscious and semiconscious activity that goes together to enable us to enjoy TV is described by Dr Robert Heath in *The Hidden Power of Advertising* as 'low involvement processing'. Much of it involves 'implicit' learning which takes place without us knowing that we are learning. This sort of information is filed in our long-term memory without any of the conscious filtering which would increase the risk of rejection. As such, it is an incredibly effective way of increasing a set of associations around a brand and is well suited to thematic or brand messages that need to be remembered over the long term.

The way our minds interact with TV and its advertising is at the heart of why TV advertising is so powerful and memorable, and central to this is the emotional connection TV creates between viewer and brand. The key role of emotion in advertising has risen to greater prominence in recent years, as what is clear from research is that emotion is fundamental to advertising effectiveness. Just ask John Lewis.

The context in which we normally watch TV is also very important. TV is generally a shared experience; we watch it with other people (either in the room with us or connected to us via the internet and social media—more of that later). Almost half (45 per cent) of our TV viewing is shared with loved ones in the room with us (sometimes with unloved ones too).

Because we share the experience, TV creates conversations—both immediately as we watch and subsequently in our daily discourse. TV has always been one of our favourite topics of conversation, and this devotion to discussing what we've watched is another reason why TV is so memorable. And these conversations are often about brands as well as programmes— that pasta sauce, visit that website, adopt that meerkat. They can also lead to instant personal recommendations ('I've tried that, it was great. You should try it'), which is a very powerful motivator. Thinkbox's POETIC research—'Paid, Owned, Earned: TV's Influence Calculated'—revealed that TV advertising creates 51 per cent of new conversations about brands (new as in over and above the ongoing base level of conversations people have about brands). Nothing else comes close.

In recent years the power of the shared TV experience has increased because now, thanks to the internet, we are sitting on a virtual sofa as well as on our actual sofa. Even if we are not watching TV with someone else in the room, we can connect with people across the globe to share our views and opinions—good or bad—about what we're watching via a companion screen such as a laptop, tablet, or smartphone.

Multi-screening, as this is known, enables us to chat, play, discover, and buy things as we watch TV. We can upload our own pastiches to YouTube, join TV-related Facebook groups, and follow and comment on TV-associated hashtags on Twitter. Multi-screening has expanded the world of TV.

This is a new form of an established human trait. People have always multi-tasked when watching TV—multi-screening is the latest accompaniment, albeit an incredibly complementary one. Multi-screening is now a mainstream activity. According to the IPA's Touchpoints study, 75 per cent of adults in the UK multi-screen each week on average for 39 minutes a day.

The most common multi-screening activity is using social media, which accounts for 46 per cent of multi-screening time. Because of the immediate public—potentially global—sharing of TV that can now happen, social media offers a great window into the effects that broadcast TV creates. Broadcasters and programme-makers can use these insights and interactions to shape output and market TV in an agile cost-effective way.

However, it is worth being cautious about acting on what you discover that people are saying online. People tend to be more negative online and Keller Fay, the US word-of-mouth specialist, has estimated that 90 per cent of brand conversations happen offline anyway.

For TV advertisers, multi-screening means that many viewers have a device to hand primed for response to their advertisements. One of the key findings from Thinkbox's 'Screen Life' research into multi-screening was that multi-screeners are even more open, welcoming, and positive about advertising than single-screeners. It also revealed that multi-screening keeps viewers present for advertisement breaks, encourages more TV viewing, does not affect advertisement recognition, brings people closer to TV and its advertisements, and even appears to encourage more shared and family TV viewing. It is good news for marketers.

So, with multiple screens come multiple opportunities. TV is now a point-of-sale medium; the living room can be the high street, and viewers are able to act and transact on what they see on TV immediately via a second screen. The ad break now enables viewers to go straight from engagement with a TV ad to interaction with it to purchase. So much for passive TV viewing.

Get the consumer to participate Brands seem to be more successful when they can get active involvement from consumers, and social media offers them many opportunities to do this. The Singaporean communications company SingTel engaged in a real-time marketing experiment on Twitter, asking followers to describe useful situations for a high speed 4G mobile connection. Within nine hours the company had turned the suggestions into improvised comedy sketches on YouTube and tweeted the contributors. The #Need4GSpeed hashtag was trending for more than 24 hours and increased traffic for the 4G website by 39 per cent (Quek, 2013). In 2015, Lee Jeans launched a campaign across 32 cities in China promoting heat-retaining denim. Consumers were encouraged to get outside (even in the cold) and explore their cities while tracking their movements with the Warmth Tracker WeChat app. Warmth Index points were accumulated when users scanned QR codes at scattered locations. By collecting points, users could earn denim products and access exclusive events.

Having looked at involvement and ways to increase it in detail we shall now look at the stages in the decision-making process, starting with problem recognition.

Stages in the decision-making process

Problem recognition

Problem recognition *is a realization that a problem needs to be solved through purchase.* It may be triggered by internal factors such as hunger or thirst, or external factors such as having to buy a birthday pres-ent. Problem recognition occurs in high and low involvement decision-making when we recognize (not necessarily consciously) the differ-ence between our actual state and an ideal state. Figure 3.7 shows two ways in which problem recognition may manifest itself. In each case there is a difference between the actual and the ideal state. The need recog-nition example shows a situation where one moves easily between an actual and an ideal state, and that is why the top circle is labelled as both ideal and actual. A person can readily

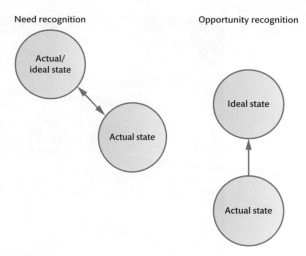

Figure 3.7   Need recognition versus opportunity recognition

bring themselves back to the ideal state through a simple consumption decision. So when hungry (actual state) at lunchtime, we buy a sandwich and some fruit and are no longer hungry (ideal state); although our actual state was, briefly, not our ideal one, we were able to rectify it easily. Opportunity recognition, however, is a situation where the consumer may recognize a lack in their actual state that they were not aware of before. Perhaps they see an advertisement for a new mobile phone, or a friend tells them about the holiday that they are about to go on. Although previously content with their actual state, seeing the advertisement or having the conversation affects them so that they wish to upgrade their phone or book a holiday to bring about the ideal state, which may take considerable effort and cost. Therefore opportunity recognition as illustrated in Figure 3.7 shows the distance between the actual and ideal states as greater and the arrow pointing in one direction.

Information search

Information search *is the process by which we identify appropriate information to help aid our choice in a decision-making situation.* In the case of need recognition our information search may be quite simple. We may already know from previous experience (ongoing search) the loca-tion of the nearest preferred sandwich bar. Our search is mostly at the point of sale in terms of choosing what we want, and here marketers help us choose by clearly presenting a vari-ety of different food deals to help us decide (see Figure 3.8).

In an opportunity recognition situation our search may be more complex as we may not have the information necessary to make the decision. While we may use pre-purchase search to facilitate decision-making for a specific goal, many of us are searching with no particular plan to buy (Bloch, 1986). Such ongoing search occurs independently of a spe-cific immediate purchase problem (Bloch et al., 1986). Information search is not purely

Figure 3.8 Food-to-go counter   *Source*: Image courtesy of Appleby Westward Group.

functional; it is often just fun to browse the shops, trying things on and comparing different possibilities. Vogt and Fesenmaier (1998) identified five classes of information need: functional, hedonic, sign, innovation, and aesthetic.

- *Functional needs* are the acquisition of knowledge from one's own experiences and those of others, and through stimuli such as advertising or articles to increase knowledge and reduce risk. These act as a way of educating the consumer about the product's utility, attributes, and applications.

- *Hedonic needs* relate to the elements of pleasurable experiences that may occur during decision-making.

- *Sign needs* are the social and identity aspects of information search—what the product might say about us. Information may be passed on or sought as part of signifying our social position (see Chapter 1 on sign value).

- *Innovation needs* relate to the search for something that is new or different to the consumer.

- *Aesthetic needs* are where information is viewed as a stimulus to visual thinking, to imagining the product and how it looks in your life.

We may already have resources from previous experiences to draw upon (internal search), while a novel or difficult purchase may require an external search. While much searching will be deliberate, i.e. actively looking for information, we often also receive incidental information through talking to people or noticing an advertisement or editorial when we

Figure 3.9　Dinner for two from Waitrose　*Source*: Image courtesy of Waitrose.

are not actively seeking information. Marketers have to consider carefully when, where, and how often they place advertisements in the hope that they will initiate needs in their customers.

Alternative evaluation

Following an information search we face choice alternatives. These may not just be different brands or products; they might include make or buy decisions, such as hosting a dinner party and considering whether to make or buy a dessert. Marketers can exploit these choice situations through campaigns such as Waitrose's '£10 Summer dinner for two' campaign (see Figure 3.9) which offers the option of a ready-made dinner rather than having to make the dinner from scratch.

There may be brands that you are familiar with and brands you have used before. Your information search may also have resulted in new unfamiliar brands. At this point we can place the results of the information search into different categories (Narayana and Markin, 1975).

- The **evoked set** includes *all brands the consumer is aware of which might meet their needs.*

- The **consideration set** includes *brands from the evoked set that the consumer might actually consider buying.*

- The **inept set** are *those brands that the consumer may have come across during their search or from previous experience but would not consider for this decision.*

- The **inert set** includes *those brands not under consideration at all.*

An example of such a categorization might be when a consumer is purchasing a fragrance for their mother. The inert set might include brands that they are aware of but which they would just never consider buying, say in this case Katie Price's Besotted. There may be certain brands that they like but do not think would be suitable for her (inept) such as Taylor Swift's Wonderstruck. Inevitably brands that are familiar are likely to be in a consumer's evoked set; here it might be Chanel No. 5 and Elizabeth Arden, and this in turn means that businesses need to ensure that consumers are familiar with their brands and that these are readily available to them. This is important for both how much a company spends on marketing communications and its distribution strategy.

Evaluation

In an active decision-making situation we may consciously use **evaluative criteria** which are *those factors that we use to compare offerings to help make a choice*. Figure 3.1 includes beliefs, attitudes, and intentions. As we shall see in Chapter 6, the formation of beliefs and positive attitudes can lead to an intention to purchase. These will be part of one's evaluative criteria, but it does not necessarily follow that a person will purchase a product that they have positive attitudes towards or even an intention to buy (see Research Insight 3.3). For example, after much consideration a consumer may have decided to buy their mother Chanel No. 5 perfume but may find that the store does not have it in stock. At this point they may go to another store or choose to purchase their second-choice brand Elizabeth Arden.

RESEARCH INSIGHT 3.3

Edelman, D. and Singer, M. (2015). 'The new consumer decision journey', http://www.mckinsey.com/business-functions/marketing-and-sales/our-insights/the-new-consumer-decision-journey

In this development from McKinsey's earlier 'The consumer decision journey' (Court et al., 2009), which questioned the traditional funnel approach, the updated article shows how firms can use automation, proactive personalization, contextual interaction, and journey innovation to build customer value during the decision-making process. The new consumer decision journey can be viewed in Figure 3.10. From this, we can consider examples, such as how automation might be using a phone image rather than a paper ticket. Proactive personalization means using information you have on a customer to give them a better experience, such as an automatic upgrade for a loyal customer, contextual interaction can be as simple as keeping a customer updated on where their order is, and journey innovation is looking for useful synergies and innovations such as an airline app that integrates with a taxi service to pick them up at the airport.

 Access the online resources to read the abstract and access the full paper.

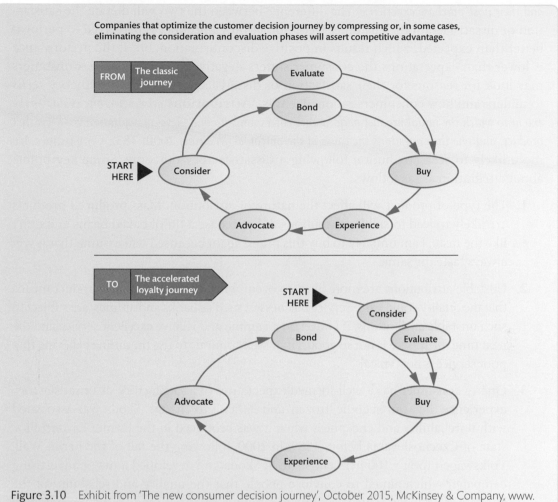

Figure 3.10 Exhibit from 'The new consumer decision journey', October 2015, McKinsey & Company, www.mckinsey.comgr.3.10

Outcomes of choice

Businesses are concerned that their customers are happy with their purchase. Generally that is the main concern of marketing, but an outcome of purchase may ultimately be disposal, whether it is throwing something away when it is no longer working or useful, or selling it on when you want a replacement such as with a car or house. There are a number of outcomes of decision-making that impact on marketers, including disposal, which we examine.

Both happy and unhappy customers may tell others about their purchase experience (word of mouth) as in the example in Consumer Insight 3.3. The **disconfirmation paradigm** is *the difference between a consumer's pre-purchase expectations of the product's performance* *and their post-purchase experience.* The difference between the two will dictate the satisfaction or dissatisfaction the customer feels. Sometimes a product is perceived to perform better than expected, which results in positive disconfirmation, but if the performance is lower than expectations the consumer suffers negative disconfirmation. Consumers may look for reasons for their satisfaction or dissatisfaction. Attribution theory seeks to understand how consumers rationalize this. '**Attributions** *arise when one evaluates the extent to which the initial product performance corresponds to one's level of aspiration vis-à-vis that product, and one then questions the cause of the outcome'* (Weiner, 2000: 383). Consumers are more likely to seek attribution following a dissatisfactory outcome. Some key points about attribution are as follows.

1. The type of product will affect the nature of attribution. Mass produced products are likely to lead to stable attributions. If I purchase a tin of baked beans and don't like the taste, I am unlikely to buy this brand again because I will assume that it will always taste the same.

2. Unstable attributions are more likely to occur when the nature of the product means that the quality could vary. Service businesses, such as banks and airlines, are subject to such unstable attributions. If I travel on an airline and receive excellent service and the next time the service is not so good, I may well continue to use the airline believing that poor service is not typical.

3. Once a consumer has a well-formed expectation of a satisfactory or unsatisfactory experience they can become 'frozen' and difficult to change. Škoda was associated with unreliability and cheapness when it was produced in the former Eastern Bloc state of Czechoslovakia before 1989. In 2000, following the fall of the Berlin Wall, Volkswagen took a 100 per cent share in Škoda and developed a major advertising campaign which aimed to convince people that the quality and reliability of the Škoda had changed. This was done in a tongue-in-cheek manner, where potential customers would test drive the car but could not come to terms with a car that good being a Škoda and so were shown running away from the car dealership—a clear case of an attempt to shift a 'frozen' image.

4. Causal locus is where the cause of the attribution is with or outside the control of the consumer. Therefore on occasion we may blame ourselves for our decision such as, 'I'll never get the hang of this mobile phone', or we may attribute the problem to the product such as, 'The instructions with this mobile phone are incomprehensible'. Marketers need to be aware of the likely type of attribution their products will be subject to and ensure that they respond appropriately. Commodity products such as margarine need to be regularly taste-tested so that they meet consumers' preferences. Service businesses often use 'mystery shoppers' to ensure that they are providing the appropriate level of service. In both cases the issue is that if standards are not maintained, eventually the customer will reassess their attribution.

It is important to remember that decisions are not always made in isolation, and we are often influenced by the people we care about, particularly family members (see Chapter 8). Gorlin and Dhar (2012) have classified four types of decision-making: (1) making decisions together to produce one outcome, such as choosing a restaurant where you will eat together; (2) making decisions together but consuming separately, such as doing the weekly shop which includes ingredients for one partner's packed lunches; (3) making decisions separately but consuming together, such as choosing an experience weekend for a partner's birthday that you are going to enjoy too; and (4) making decisions separately and consuming separately. What marketers would often like to know is to what extent the beliefs and attitudes of one partner can influence the other and to what effect in the decision process. It is important, therefore. to remember that we are often not alone when making a consumption decision and in some cases we may do what we think an important other would want us to do.

CONSUMER INSIGHT 3.3

Happy with your purchase?

Today it is relatively easy to get a refund for something you don't like or doesn't fit you. But what if you want to complain about your purchase? A number of research studies (summarized in Figure 3.11) have examined what we might do in such situations. 'Action/no-action' discrimination (Day and Landon, 1977) is the first step of complaining behaviour. The most basic distinction in complaining is exit or voice division (Hirschman, 1970): does the consumer decide to respond to their unsatisfactory experience through exiting, i.e. not purchasing again, or with voice, i.e. communicating their dissatisfaction? If the latter, they may do it publicly, to the company or to other third parties such as regulatory authorities or the media, or privately, to family and friends. Finally, the consumer may seek redress, which might include monetary compensation, again from either the company or third parties.

Today one of the most popular and seemingly successful ways of complaining is using social media. Leading companies now have dedicated Twitter accounts for customer feedback. Companies are concerned about the viral capacity of social media, but it can also act as an opportunity. The BBC (Wallis, 2014) reported that when one train customer complained about the cold train she was travelling on, the operators alerted the driver and the heating was switched on. Another business decided to respond to a customer complaint in the same street style as the complainant had used (we gettin' sum more PS4 tings in wivin da next week, y'get me), getting them a huge number of retweets within an hour.

Questions

1. Do you complain? When would you complain to the company and when to friends and family? What methods do you use to complain?

2. How is complaining on social media different to complaining in person?

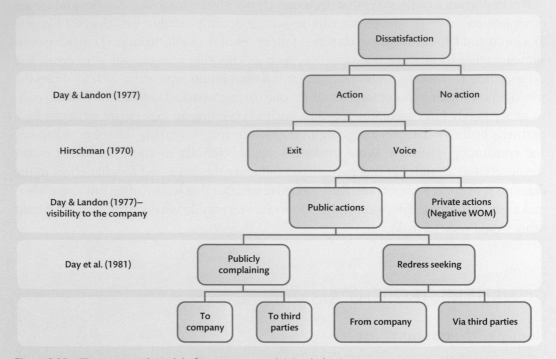

Figure 3.11 The integrated model of customer complaining behaviour

Source: Adapted from Istanbulluoglu, Leek and Szmigin (2017). Reproduced with permission from Emerald Group Publishing Ltd.

3. Check some company websites/twitter feeds, etc, to see how easy it is to complain. How do companies do this well and not so well?

Sources: Hirschman (1970); Day and Landon (1977); Wallis (2014); Istanbulluoglu et al. (2017).

 Access the online resources and follow the web links to learn more about how consumers register their complaints.

Disposal of goods

At a time when environmental concerns are of greater importance than ever before, marketers need to be aware of how their customers dispose of goods. When we purchase something we are probably not thinking about when or how we are going to dispose of it. We dispose of packaging every week when we shop, and increasingly we are encouraged to recycle such packaging. For some consumers the choice of product or brand may depend on the amount of packaging—for example, choosing loose fruit and vegetables rather than pre-packaged. We dispose of things in numerous ways and some are listed here:

1. to friends and family or given away freely through specialized sites such as Freecycle (http://uk.freecycle.org/)

2. to charity

3. direct disposal either in general rubbish or recycled

4. by exchanging for another item

5. through car boot sales, private advertisements, and auction sites.

One issue to consider is the impact our consumption has on the environment. One message that has been used across continents is 'Reduce, Reuse, Recycle' (Figure 3.12). The idea is that before we think about recycling we also need to consider whether our consumption could be reduced and whether we have products that could be reused by either ourselves or others. For example, this might mean mending clothes rather than throwing them away if they have a tear. Of course, there are forces that work against this approach, such as the increased availability of cheap clothes, and the fact that many products are made with built-in obsolescence, meaning that they either stop working after a period of time or that new more fashionable versions are introduced.

Figure 3.12   Reduce reuse, recycle
Source: © Yobidaba/Shutterstock.com.

One of the biggest problems of consumption is the environmental impact of waste. Plastic in the world's seas is killing, and changing, marine life. Some countries, such as Ireland, Israel, and Uganda, are using legislation to reduce waste. In 2002 Ireland became the first country to introduce a tax on plastic bags, the Plas Tax. The Plas Tax had a dramatic impact, with reduction of around 90 per cent in plastic bag consumption and less litter (Harrison, 2013). In October 2015, the UK also introduced a charge for plastic carrier bags and their use has since reduced by around 80 per cent (Whitmarsh, 2016). Although East African countries banned certain types of plastic bags in 2007, implementation has proved tricky where it is difficult to ensure compliance. In countries in South America and Africa waste is a much more complex problem. Many countries place their refuse in huge dumpsites where people scavenge for plastic waste which they sell on to contractors. Others benefit, meaning that waste provides jobs for some of the poorest in these societies, thus making waste a productive product for some.

Although the idea of the circular economy goes back to the 1970s, many people are still trying to find ways to keep resources in use for as long as possible and regenerate materials at the end of their life. Lacy and Rutqvist (2015) identify four forms of waste: resources (materials and energy that cannot be regenerated), life cycles (products with artificially short working lives), capability (products that are idle), and embedded values (materials that have not been recovered from products that have been disposed of, such as a plug on a lamp that no longer works). They recommend improving product life extension through repairing, upgrading and sharing platforms where people can share, rent, or swap idle goods, and recovery and recycling where the production and consumption systems are designed to exclude all waste (see Figure 3.13). In 2016 the city of Cape Town's municipal authority upgraded its Integrated Waste Exchange (IWEX) to make it easier for individuals and businesses to connect and recycle waste items such as furniture and computers through a portal that allows images and details to be easily uploaded and viewed.

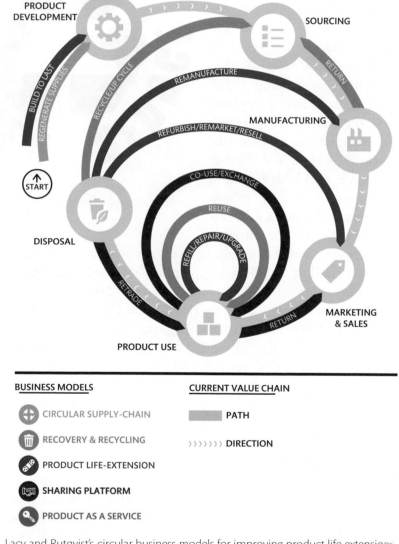

Figure 3.13 Lacy and Rutqvist's circular business models for improving product life extensions

Source: Peter Lacy and Jakob Rutqvist, *Waste to Wealth*, published 2015, Palgrave Macmillan, reproduced with permission of SCSC.

Is decision-making different online?

Is decision-making different between online and offline purchases? While we may go through the same or similar decision stages, there is no doubt that it is quick and easy to shop online if you have a credit card, debit card, or PayPal account. When you shop online you are not restricted to the shops in your location and in turn the establishments online have potentially limitless shelves and do not necessarily have to have the expense of a high street presence. Of course it does not mean that you will look through all their shelves (or pages). It is much easier to screen out products that you want in your consideration set online and similarly you can readily compare products at the same time rather than having to move from shop to shop.

But there are also difficulties for both consumer and marketer. If you are looking for an appliance such as a breadmaker that you had never bought before, an initial Google search might provide too much information and lead to confusion. Haubl and Trifts (2000) found that, once on a product website, if you do not find the product appealing within just a few seconds you will move to another site. So, from a marketing perspective, companies have to get you to their online store and then find ways to keep you there. Firms can create personalized customer interfaces for consumers designed to adapt to the specific interests and preferences of shoppers often derived from algorithms. Such personalized product recommendations can be based on the behaviour of other buyers (e.g. Amazon) or a knowledge of the consumer's preferences from their previous behaviour.

A benefit to marketers of the personalized shopping environment that can be created in online marketing is its potential for customer loyalty. It has been thought that the ease of moving between sites would make consumers more promiscuous (Bakos, 1997), but the reality is somewhat different. Research has shown that customers can become very loyal shoppers because they grow accustomed to and experienced in a particular website, and so the search effort required to shop is much less (Haubl and Trifts, 2000).

The marketer needs the customer to trust the site and the product that is being sold, and that is why including online reviews is important. Where you cannot physically engage with the item, another person's positive description of the colour, smell, or texture can be extremely useful to the consumer and the marketer. Of course, you also have to accept that not all reviews will be positive. Companies need to invest in technologies such as TrustPilot and Feefo to get reviews for the products on their website.

A disadvantage of purchasing online for the consumer is that they cannot see or touch the product and, as we shall see in Chapter 5, these sensory aspects of consumer decision-making are important. Increasingly, though, retailers are investing in high quality web content with true colour representations that help to manage expectations. But an advantage is that they can take their time to assess what they have bought in the comfort of their home and if they don't like it they can return the item. Hewitt (2017) suggests that, although it is costly, it is strategically advantageous to make it easy to return products as this has the potential to increase customer loyalty to the extent that 75 per cent of customers are more likely to use a retailer who offers free returns. Additionally, some companies are finding cost efficient ways of managing delivery and returns through click and collect methods.

Shopping behaviour

To make our purchases we have to shop, whether with a major retailer, on the internet, or in a local shop or market. Researchers have considered how and why people shop and the role that shopping plays in their lives. For most people there is a difference between 'going shopping' and 'doing the shopping'. The former is often a pleasurable activity, where you may spend time and money, perhaps with a friend or partner, just enjoying the experience of shopping, whereas 'doing the shopping' is often an obligation or a routine chore (Bowlby, 1997).

A study by Ganesh et al. (2007) found five different types of shopper:

- **apathetic shoppers**—indifferent to shopping

- **enthusiasts**—enjoy all aspects of shopping

- **destination shoppers**—focused on finding the right place to buy the brand or product they are after

- **basic shoppers**—those with a clear idea of what they want who shop quickly and easily, having no interest in the social or experience aspects of shopping

- **bargain-seekers**—motivated to find a good deal and to achieve choice optimization.

Those who are very involved with the shopping experience are known as 'market mavens' (Feick and Price, 1987). Market **mavens** are *active information-seeking consumers or smart shoppers (similar to the recreational shoppers and information seekers identified in other studies), and they like to communicate, providing information to others on a broad variety of goods, services, and marketplace characteristics* (Slama and Williams, 1990). As we shall see in Chapter 8 they are important for passing on information to other consumers.

Shopping motivation—online and offline

The pleasure we get from shopping and how our motivations and even personalities affect how we shop are important to marketing (see Research Insight 3.4). Knowing how and why consumers shop the way they do enables marketers to provide the appropriate shopping experience. In 1972, Tauber published an exploratory review of 30 people aged between 20 and 47, and from this hypothesized both personal and social motives for shopping. Here we discuss how relevant these may be for the twenty-first century consumer.

RESEARCH INSIGHT 3.4

Close, A.G. and Kukar-Kinney, M. (2010), 'Beyond buying: motivations behind consumer's online shopping cart use', *Journal of Business Research*, 63, 9–10, 986–92.

In this paper, the authors examine motivations for placing items in an online shopping cart with or without buying. The authors identified a number of utilitarian and hedonic motivations for online cart use including securing online price promotions, obtaining more information on certain products, organizing shopping items, and entertainment.

 Access the online resources to read the abstract and access the full paper.

Personal motives for shopping

Role playing According to Tauber (1972), shopping is related to certain roles in society, and for some women grocery shopping offered the opportunity to express their housewife role. Today the internet provides one way for time-constrained working consumers to enact the traditional role of household shopper since they can do so at a time that is convenient for them (Parsons, 2002).

Diversion Tauber suggested that shopping can be a recreational activity, a diversion from everyday life. The development of shopping malls, where many shopping, entertainment, and catering resources are commonly in one place protected from the weather, shows how marketing has responded to this. Similarly, online window-shopping may act as a diversion for people at any time of the day within their own homes. The internet also gives consumers a chance to shop at store types that would otherwise be unreachable because of their location or opening hours.

Self-gratification Shopping may offer a compensation for other problems in consumer's lives. Escapism and reward are part of this type of shopping motivation. When only offline shopping was available, we had to make a certain amount of effort to go out and shop, but now consumers can reward themselves whenever they want by just logging on to their favourite shopping sites.

Learning about new trends Going around the shops allows people to keep up to date with new trends. If you go into most city centres in Western economies at the weekend you will see young people checking out what the shops have to offer and also what their peers are wearing. Computer and electronics shops let people 'play' with their products to get an idea of what they can do. Whereas in the past we had to search out new trends, the internet means that they are brought to us on a daily basis. If you sign up for any shopping site you will get regular updates of 'What's New'.

Physical activity This refers to people shopping for physical exercise, and indeed there is a trend towards the shopping mall as a place for exercise, with reports from Doha, Qatar, of

Figure 3.14 Christmas at Selfridges   *Source*: Image courtesy of Selfridges & Co.

initiatives to encourage consumers to use the mall as a place for exercise (Nordland, 2013). Clearly, internet shopping detracts from this physical activity, although using the internet to shop could free up time for physical exercise (Parsons, 2002).

Sensory stimulation Walk into a big department store in any major city and you will be bombarded with sights, sounds, and smells. Christmas shopping in Selfridges in London is enlivened by Christmas carol singers and food tastings to add to the Christmas feeling (see Figure 3.14). Clearly it is more difficult to achieve this sensory experience online, but increasingly companies are enhancing their sites by using music, videos of their products, and even real-time fashion shows. Advertisers on Snapchat have realized that they have to appeal to a generation that expects high levels of sensory stimulation. The soft drinks company Gatorade, which has partnered the US Open Tennis Championships for many years, introduced an old school video game with 22 levels on Snapchat that could be played directly on the app (see Figure 3.15).

Figure 3.15   Gatorade's 'Serena Match Point' video game
Source: Image courtesy of Gatorade and TBWA/Chiat/Day, Inc.

Social motives for shopping

Social experiences Some shopping situations may become social events. When pressed for time, shopping for food for dinner may not seem very social. However, a Sunday morning trip to a farmers' market can be a very different food shopping experience, with both buyers and sellers often happy to discuss the produce and interact in a relaxed fashion. On a Sunday in Singapore you will often see families eating picnics outside shops, waiting for them to open. Social media has become one of the biggest opportunities for sharing social experiences as consumers contact one another about new products, or show themselves wearing, using, or even eating their purchases.

Communicating with others who have similar interests Special interest and sports shops often employ staff with a particular expertise so that they can talk knowledgeably to customers. If you go into an electronics or gaming shop, or a specialist running store, you will see much interaction alongside the act of purchasing, and often the store environment is set up to encourage this. Again, the internet has become an important vehicle for shared interest, particularly on community sites dedicated to sharing information about favourite brands. In their study of the Zara virtual brand community, Royo-Vela and Casamassima (2010) concluded that brand communities can be used by companies to increase customers' levels of satisfaction and commitment, and enhance positive word of mouth communication.

Peer group attraction In some cases people are attracted to certain shops because they associate them with an aspirational group. If you read a celebrity magazine and see a picture of a pop star shopping in Gucci or Prada you might wish to go there for some of the celebrity glamour to rub off, even if you don't end up buying anything! The same peer group attraction effect can be achieved on the internet with fashion sites such as ASOS Fashion Finder, which matches looks worn by celebrities with their own products.

Status and authority Some shops still have shop assistants attending to your needs, which may give you the feeling of being special. If you have a suit made in London's Savile Row you would expect such service. While you might imagine that the internet would not be able to offer such personal service, a number of sites now offer web chat to help customers make the best choice when shopping online.

Pleasure of bargaining There are still many opportunities for people either to haggle or to feel that they can get a bargain (see Figure 3.16). eBay and other auction sites allow you to bid for goods, while car boot sales allow direct bargaining.

Although all these motivations can be important, shopping is a cost-incurring activity. As Consumer Insight 3.4 shows, consumers around the world are still concerned about the price they pay for goods, with many cash-strapped shoppers motivated by the desire to find a bargain.

Is shopping different on the internet?

Do we shop differently on the internet and how does it compare with shopping in person? Researchers have developed consumer categorizations specific to internet shopping habits to help understand what motivates people to use the internet for shopping and whether

Figure 3.16 Haggling at a street market in Singapore   *Source*: Image courtesy of Isabelle Szmigin.

they shop differently there. In research with online grocery shoppers, Rohm and Swaminathan (2004) identified four groups of online shopper.

1. The **convenience shopper** (11 per cent of the sample) was motivated by the convenience of online shopping, was less concerned with immediate possession of goods, and didn't particularly seek variety across retail channels.

2. The **variety seeker** (41 per cent) was most interested by variety seeking across retail alternatives, products, and brands, while still motivated by online shopping convenience.

3. The **balanced buyer** (33 per cent) showed a lower likelihood to plan purchases and therefore might be a more impulsive online shopper.

4. The **store-oriented shopper** (15 per cent) showed the lowest level of online shopping convenience, preferring the physical orientations of the store and the immediate possession of goods.

Shopping online is a different experience from shopping in store where you can touch and smell goods and ask assistants for advice. Online stores aim to replicate some of the advantages of bricks and mortar stores by having online assistants to answer questions, and reduce the risk of making the wrong decision through ease of returning goods. 'Blended shopping' is increasing, where consumers mix and match between the internet and the online store, sometimes ordering online and collecting in store, or doing their information search in store and then making their final choice online. Brashear et al. (2009) looked at six countries and found that online shoppers share many similar commonalities, which include a desire for convenience, having more favourable attitudes to direct marketing and advertising, being wealthier, and being heavy users of both email and the internet. They also tend to be more impulsive.

CONSUMER INSIGHT 3.4

The growth of the discount store

There has been a huge growth in discount stores such as Poundland in the UK, Dollar King in Australia (Figure 3.17), and 100 yen shops in Japan. Recent analysis has suggested that this trend will outlive the recession (*Economist*, 2013). What is sold in these stores varies greatly over time depending on the purchasing strategies and abilities of their owners. The names of these stores are usually based on the price points at which they sell, and in some places, such as Hong Kong, this in itself has become a point of competition with 10 dollar, 8 dollar, and even 2 dollar shops opening.

   Countries all over the world have shops whose rationale is a price level offer. Such shops first opened in the USA in the 1950s. Poundland offers many branded goods, such as Heinz, Cadbury's, and Colgate, at prices less than those in supermarkets. While Poundland draws most of its customers

Figure 3.17   Dollar King store in Australia   *Source*: Image courtesy of Dollar King.

from lower socio-economic groups, people from higher income groups are increasingly shopping there. This trend is similar to that found in Case Study 1, as more people regularly shop at discount supermarkets such as Aldi and Lidl. A recent poll by *The Guardian* newspaper found that 72.4 per cent of people would accept discount stores in more upmarket shopping malls as they reflected our changing shopping habits, and only 27.6 per cent said that shopping centres are supposed to offer a more upmarket retail experience.

Source: Kollewe (2012); Roberts (2012); Wood (2012); *Economist* (2013).

Questions

1. Refer back to the shopping types illustrated at the end of Case Study 1. How do you think the different groups will use the discount stores described in this Consumer Insight?

2. What other factors might affect consumers' decisions to shop in such stores?

3. Recently Poundland has been selling items for over £1. What problems might this create for the brand and consumers?

 Access the online resources and follow the web links to learn more about the growth of discount stores around the world.

Shopping on impulse

Most of us will have had the experience of **impulse purchasing** described by Rook (1987) *as a sudden, powerful urge to buy a product with little regard to the consequences of what we are buying.* There is normally little outcome if we buy a low value item, such as a bar of chocolate or some make-up, but we can also impulse purchase much higher value goods such as clothes or even a car. The environment we shop in may increase our likelihood to impulse purchase—for example, buying clothes on the internet.

Other researchers have tried to identify types of impulse purchasing. Bayley and Nancarrow (1998) identified four styles of impulse shopping.

1. **Accelerator impulse**—consumers are motivated to stockpile, purchasing in advance of some future need. Sales promotions such as BOGOF (buy one get one free) appeal to this type of impulse, as consumers can rationalize the purchase as likely to be used in the future.

2. **Compensatory impulse**—consumers make impulse purchases as a reward for success or as compensation for failure. Advertisements for confectionery or snacks often suggest that we deserve compensation or reward through food. An example of this is the 'Have a break, have a KitKat' slogan where the marketer makes the association of a rest from work with a chocolate snack.

3. **Breakthrough impulse**—this type of impulse relates to the sudden need to make a purchase, often triggered by some kind of unconscious problem or issue. The researchers suggest that it can be life changing, as well as dealing with particular issues suffered by the person. For example, on impulse a man may see a ring in a jewellery shop, buy it, and propose to his girlfriend. Advertisements shown around Valentine's Day often try to encourage such impulsive behaviour.

4. **Blind impulse**—this refers to impulse buys that are not easily explained or rationalized by the consumer. Often this occurs when a consumer is overwhelmed by the product and feels that they just have to have it immediately, without any thought for the cost implications. In research undertaken in Singapore, Mattila and Wirtz (2008) found that stimulating customers in-store led to increased impulse purchases. Environmental factors such as the tempo of music (fast and high volume), warmth of colours (oranges and reds), and ambient scents (citrus) could increase stimulation levels. They also found that employee friendliness could interact positively with such environmental factors.

Is choosing a problem?

In the twenty-first century those of us living in the developed world face more choice in terms of products and brands we can buy than ever before. But is having such choice always a good thing? Choice means that we can have more variety in style, price, and content, but some think that it leads to confusion and even discomfort. In the opening chapter of *The Paradox of Choice* (Schwartz 2009: 1), the author describes buying a pair of jeans. This is his interaction with the sales clerk:

> 'Do you want them slim fit, easy fit, relaxed fit, baggy, or extra baggy?' she replied. 'Do you want them stonewashed, acid-washed, or distressed? Do you want them button-fly or zipper-fly? Do you want them faded or regular?'

He goes on to list the 61 varieties of suntan lotion and 80 different pain relievers in the pharmaceutical aisle of his supermarket to add to his argument that more choice can lead to confusion as we cannot check out all the alternatives. Marketers need to understand when choice is good for the consumer and when it may lead to problems such as confusion or information overload. The lessons for marketers will be discussed further in the following sections.

Satisficing and maximizing

Have you ever stood in front of a display of shampoos unsure which to buy? You may be wondering whether your hair is fine, coloured, heat damaged, or all three. You may consider whether you need a separate conditioner and shampoo, or even just what size to buy.

Some people will take the time to look at the ingredients on the bottles and others will use heuristics (discussed in the following sections) to help them make a decision, but for many of us a good enough decision will suffice. So rather than assume, as traditional economics might, that consumers have complete information about the costs and benefits of all possible choices, information itself may be considered a commodity with its own price, whether in money or time or effort (Schwartz et al., 2002).

When we make such 'good enough' decisions we are doing what Herbert Simon (1956) referred to as 'satisficing'. We are almost always limited by the complexity of the environment and our own cognitive limitations, i.e. how we manage to keep and recall information and do the mental calculations to arrive at the 'best' choice. A satisficer will choose a brand based on some kind of threshold, such as price. In future they may find another brand that surpasses their original choice and so reject their previously chosen item. We might buy a spray window-cleaning product on one occasion and then on the next we may buy cleaning wipes and find that we prefer them because they are easier to use. Marketers use the information from purchasing statistics to identify where to invest and what products to keep in production and what to phase out, or indeed whether it is better to offer consumers a range of choice.

Maximizers tend to be people who consider all alternatives and seek the best option. Research shows that in some situations consumers are more likely to make a purchase if fewer choices are made available to them. Iyengar and Lepper (1999, 2000) found that too many choices could be demotivating, and consumers were more likely to choose and buy goods (in their studies, jams and chocolate bars) when fewer options were available. There may be some problems for those consumers who maximize their options. First, it is often difficult to assess whether all alternatives have been considered, and if it is not practical to examine all options they may have doubts as to whether they have made the best choice. This may mean that they are less happy with their choice (Schwartz et al., 2002). Finding the 'best' may just be very difficult, especially in environments where there is a lot to choose from. Although maximizers may achieve better objective outcomes, they may not feel that they have made a better choice because of the high bar they set themselves, and where an exhaustive search is just not possible they may suffer regret at the 'better' options they may have chosen. There are some situations where being a maximizer is probably the best approach—for example, when one is looking for medical treatment. If it is a matter of life or death, most people will be looking for something better than 'good enough'. So companies need to identify when they should be providing the best and when 'good enough' will do.

Heuristics to aid choice

Heuristics are *methods to aid decision-making to arrive at satisfactory solutions by simplifying the complexity of assessing the probability and prediction of value in a choice situation.* They are often referred to as mental short cuts or rules of thumb to help aid decision-making. Heuristics are particularly useful for consumers in situations where there is a lot of choice but little difference between brands and the outcome of the choice will not matter greatly, perhaps because the item is relatively cheap. Consumers use heuristics for effort reduction (Shah and Oppenheimer, 2008). There are many different categories of heuristics, but we shall consider a few of particular interest to how consumers behave. Jansson-Boyd (2010) categorizes heuristics into four types: prediction, persuasion, choice, and compliance.

- **Prediction heuristics** are *where the consumer is trying to predict an outcome such as 'If I buy a new mobile phone now, when will I need to update it'*. Important examples of prediction heuristics are the availability and representativeness heuristics.

  - The **availability heuristic** *refers to a situation where people judge the likelihood or frequency of something happening in the future by how easy it is to remember similar events*. Consumers use the mental images they have available to act as a cue for the likelihood of an event. An important aspect of the availability heuristic is its salience or vividness, with more salient and vivid images coming more easily to mind in consumption contexts. Therefore if you have a strong memory of news reports of accidents at funfairs this may make you fearful of attending such fairs.

  - The **representativeness heuristic** is when we *judge something on the basis of how similar it is to something else*. We often make decisions about the probability of an event by assessing it against some stereotypical case. A problem with this is that it ignores other information to help make a better decision. Tversky and Kahneman (1974) found that people typecast features and make assumptions on the basis of stereotyping. We make assessments using the representativeness heuristic all the time in our purchase decisions, choosing products or brands because they look similar to others and therefore we have an expectation of their performance or taste.

- **Persuasion heuristics** refers to how *consumers take short cuts when processing advertisers' messages*. Rather than processing all the information available, people may refer to previous experiences or other cues to reduce demands on their thinking. Consumers may follow the consensus rule (Chaiken et al., 1989) where a majority opinion is used for guidance, such as when an advertisement suggests that in trials the majority of people will use a particular brand. Similarly, expertise (e.g. using a dentist in an advertisement to recommend a brand of toothpaste) or, as in Figure 3.18, showing an endorsement by farmers responsible for growing the wheat for the bread may act as a short cut to assuming that the brand must be better than if advertised by an actor (Ratneshwar and Chaiken, 1991).

- **Choice heuristics** *allows us to reduce the number of attributes to be considered for the possible alternative choices*. Choice heuristics are orientated towards reducing

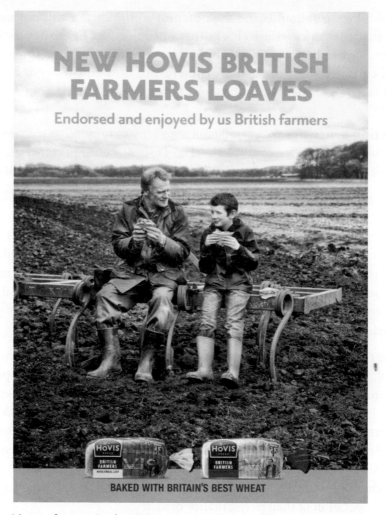

Figure 3.18 Hovis's use of persuasion heuristics   *Source*: Image supplied by The Advertising Archives.

cognitive effort, particularly in situations where the product class is not very important or where there are a lot of brands to choose from. People often use what is known as the lexicographic heuristic (Fishburn, 1974). Here consumers decide which attribute is the most important (e.g. price) and then select which brand offers the best value for this attribute. If a number of brands tie, then consumers will look to the second most important attribute and so on until a choice is made.

- **Compliance heuristics** *are those built around the likelihood of choosing something based on complying with a request.* The knowledge that people will do this is used extensively in marketing. One compliance heuristic, scarcity (Brannon and Brock, 2001), means that we place higher value on something judged to be rare or scarce; websites often have messages saying 'Hurry low stock!' to encourage us to purchase. Another compliance heuristic, reciprocity (Langer, 1989), involves the apparent return of a favour, so if a sales person does the make-up for a customer in store, the customer may reciprocate by purchasing products.

While these heuristics may appear quite different, with some based on functional aspects such as specific attributes and some on attitudinal or even emotional responses, the key to their commonality is that they all act to reduce the effort associated with decision-making. By understanding how people make such short cuts, marketers can design communications to take such behaviour into account. Of course, it could also be said that marketing exploits this knowledge, and as consumers we should also be aware that using such heuristics may not always give us the 'best' solution.

Other methods we use to help us choose—anchoring and framing

Some methods to help us choose, such as satisficing and heuristics, aid decision-making in complex situations, whilst others may determine, apparently arbitrarily, what we are prepared to pay for a product. This is known as anchoring. We often compare the prices of goods on the basis of other items in the same store. A person may see one pair of shoes in a shop for £200 when all the others are priced at over £300 and think that the £200 pair is a bargain. But if this same person were to look at other stores and see that similar shoes were priced under £100, they might not feel that the £200 pair was such a good deal. Such **anchoring** *is over-reliance on one piece of often irrelevant information to make a decision*. Anchoring is also referred to as arbitrary coherence. The initial price of the pair of shoes was arbitrary; the person could have started their shoe search in a cheaper or more expensive shop. However, once the price is established in our minds, this shapes what we are willing to pay for this and similar items, and hence becomes coherent (Arierly, 2008). So within one shop we expect to see similar prices, and such anchoring may lower our resistance to purchasing.

Framing refers to how we make a decision *through the context in which a choice is presented to us*. Perception, language, and the way items are ordered may all make us see things differently. Tversky and Kahneman (1981), in their study of framing decisions, compared this to travelling in a mountain range. As you move through the range you notice that the apparent relative height of the mountain peaks appears to vary depending on where you are; at one point a mountain peak may look higher than others, but as you move forward this will change as the relative positions of the mountains change. Framing produces the same effect, such that the relative attractiveness of options changes when presented or framed differently. If you imagine that you want to book a cheap flight on the internet, you might come across a message such as this on a website:

Pay by debit card for a £20 discount.

Another website might have the following announcement:

All credit card transactions are subject to a £20 surcharge.

Effectively both sites are presenting the same offer, but they are framed differently. In the first you are drawn to the idea of a discount if you use a debit card, but effectively it is the same as the second offer because if you pay with a credit card (the only other payment option) in the first example you will be paying £20 more than if you paid with your debit card. Framing effects may be used to manipulate decision-making. This is most obvious in how the content of food products is described. Advertisers have learned that labelling a food product 75 per cent fat free is likely to have a more favourable impact on sales than labelling it as having a 25 per cent fat content.

Conclusions

Understanding **decision-making**, and how the nature of **involvement** in the purchase may impact it, is important in terms of what, how, and when marketers communicate with consumers along the decision-making journey. We examined a range of examples to show the complexity of consumer involvement. Companies generally aim to increase involvement with their brand in an attempt to make it more likely to be purchased, and while Consumer Insight 3.1 explained how the Cadbury's Gorilla advertising campaign was used to increase enduring involvement with the brand, Research Insight 3.2 suggests that it will be increasingly difficult for brands to engage with consumers in a crowded online world where celebrity bloggers and entertainers are more compelling.

We examined the **stages in the decision-making process**, drawing on a range of examples to illustrate the stages. We have discussed similarities and differences between decision-making online and offline. It is important to recognize the similarities and differences and what this means for marketers in their online and offline presence. In Research Insight 3.3 we introduced the concept of the consumer decision journey to show how companies might benefit from thinking in terms of consumers engaged in a more circular journey. In Case Study 3, a real life decision-making process is presented to help you think through the practical implications of a decision that can depend on many factors.

We have looked at different types of shoppers and **shopping behaviour** alongside consuming behaviour and how digital shopping may differ from shopping in a store. Shopping motivations were examined in more detail, and we compared the different motives for online and offline shopping. The growth of the discount store was the focus of Consumer Insight 3.4, where we looked at this phenomenon across the globe.

Whether we have too much choice in the market place today is open to question: while some consumers think that it would be easier to have less choice, many others feel that they benefit from the range and variety available. In some situations, consumers are prepared to accept a good-enough solution, known as **satisficing**, while in others we need to be more sure that we are really getting the best solution to a problem. In such cases we are **maximizing** our choices. Understanding how consumers behave in different contexts and buying decisions is very important for what is communicated to them.

Decision-making may be thoughtful or impulsive, and may be affected by many factors including heuristics, **anchoring**, and **framing**. At times people's behaviour when they are using heuristics may appear irrational, but often there are reasons, some conscious and others unconscious, for the decisions made. It is important to remember that we all use heuristics in everyday decision-making.

Review questions

1. Compare and differentiate low and high involvement decision-making.

2. Explain the difference between need and opportunity recognition.

3. Explain the difference between enduring involvement and situational involvement

4. Consider the stages of the decision-making process. How would you influence consumers at different points in the process?

5. Identify three motivations for shopping.

6. Distinguish between different types of impulse purchasing.

7. What are the key differences between a maximizer and a satisficer? Identify a situation where it would be better to be a maximizer and one where it would be better to be a satisficer.

8. Explain the difference between heuristics, framing, and anchoring.

Discussion questions

1. Take a look at https://www.realsimple.com/work-life/money/saving/smart-shopping-101 What tactics do you use when shopping to keep the cost of your shopping down? Can you recognize situations where you are a different kind of shopper to others? Use any of the categories of shopper identified in this chapter and consider an incident when you have shopped in that way. Are there different ways that you shop which are not mentioned in any of the typologies?

2. Consider an impulse purchase that you have made. Does it fall into any of the categories discussed in this chapter? Was it a low or high value item? Try to recall how you felt when you bought it and how you felt afterwards. Did you keep it or return it? Were you pleased that you made the purchase?

3. Think of a situation where a consumer might use an availability heuristic, a compliance heuristic, and a lexicographic heuristic. Examine how using such

heuristics in the situations you have chosen can be explained by the effort reduction they offer.

4. Gorlin and Dhar (2012) highlight the differences between joint and individual decision-making. Consider how their different categories of decision-making might be influenced by marketing and by the joint decision makers themselves.

5. Think of two or three brands that you regularly buy. Consider the type of involvement you have with them. Do you remember the advertisements (message response)? Are they high or low involvement products for you? Do you have enduring involvement with these brands? Also think about situations where you might buy different brands of the same product category. What influences your different choice of brand?

6. Telling a story is a method that is being increasingly used in digital media such as YouTube. Take a look at a few (e.g. on http://ozcontent.com/blog/best-corporate-storytelling-examples/). What do you think makes a successful story and why?

Access the online resources to test your knowledge further and complete the Multiple Choice Questions for Chapter 3.

CASE STUDY 3

George and Lucy buy a new kitchen

While we have considered decision-making from a theoretical perspective of high and low involvement, it is important to recognize that people vary in how they make decisions based on many factors. In this case we see one example of a fairly ordinary decision, but one which appears to be dependent on many different factors. One issue to consider in this case is how closely George and Lucy's decision process matches those we have studied in this chapter. It also gives you an opportunity to consider the advantages and disadvantages of buying online.

George and Lucy had moved into their house two years ago. The kitchen they had inherited was a bit old and tired, but they had managed to work in it. Then one Sunday when they had invited Lucy's parents round for dinner the cooker stopped working and the tap that had been a bit wobbly fell off. They decided that they needed to invest in a new kitchen. Both George and Lucy worked full time, so finding the space in their busy lives to search for the kitchen units and equipment was difficult. They devoted one Saturday to going around showrooms for the units but the cooker and fridge were more difficult. They had never bought these items before and to begin with had no idea what they might need. George rather liked large American style fridges with ice-making machines but Lucy said it would be far too big. She preferred the idea of one that could be covered with a fascia from the kitchen units. They decided that a smaller one would be more practical and they didn't really need an ice maker.

Before they started looking in earnest they talked to their friends and families and checked out what people had in their kitchens. Lucy's mother suggested that they should get a fridge that defrosted automatically, while her friend suggested that moving to induction hobs for the cooker would be a good idea. They soon found out, however, that most modern refrigerators had an automatic defrost function, while induction hobs required you to use special saucepans which they thought would be an extravagance. They also measured the space for the cooker and found that it was not a standard size. They realized that this was going to be the most important factor in their choice of cooker.

Given their time constraints they decided to search online. They had different views of the best way to search for their kitchen. Lucy wanted to do it via her favourite department store, which had an online presence. She was convinced that because they were so well known they would only stock reputable brands and so some of the work would already be done for her. She also had a store card which provided gift tokens when one had spent a certain amount of money. George favoured more general search sites such as Google shopping as he said it was much easier to put in their requirements and quickly identify a shortlist of available brands as well as compare the prices at different outlets. They searched individually for a few days but both of them were overwhelmed by the brands. They were getting short of time as their kitchen units would soon be ready and their fitter was asking them whether they wanted the cooker and fridge put in at the same time; if they wanted a fridge with a fascia they would have to decide quickly so as not to incur additional delivery costs. So the following Saturday afternoon they sat down together and looked at the department store website. They decided to split the work, with George looking at the refrigerators and Lucy the cookers. George could see the benefit of actually having less to choose from and that most people who had bought products had left extensive reviews. Luckily for Lucy the constraint on size of cooker actually reduced the available choices considerably. She then spent a lot of time reading the 25 reviews that one brand had received including one reviewer who wrote:

> I think I have fallen in love. My new induction cooker is the best thing ever. Nothing burns and no more dirty ceramic hob; the hob doesn't get hot so spills are really easy to clean. The dials make it simple to adjust the temperature. I also love the way the oven opens sideways—somehow it seems so much more practical.

This brand had a five star rating and had also been recommended by a consumer magazine, but was more expensive than many of the other brands. She began to wonder if an induction hob would be more useful and perhaps investing in new pans would be worthwhile, but she was unsure what George would think about this as the saucepans had been a present from his aunt.

Meanwhile George had found a refrigerator and freezer which would be perfect in the kitchen but was a brand he had never heard of. Nevertheless it had good reviews and he assessed that if it was covered with a kitchen unit door nobody need know the make of the brand. What was more, it was on special offer for one week. He showed Lucy the fridge–freezer, and she was won over as she hadn't thought they would be able to get both a refrigerator and freezer into the space they had and she liked the idea of the fridge being incorporated into the units. Delivery was free and interest-free credit was also available. They decided to buy it and take the offer of interest-free credit for a year.

They still had not decided on the cooker and that evening they went to friends for dinner. Coincidentally the friends had an induction hob and showed George and Lucy how easy it was to use. They also had some very attractive saucepans and told George and Lucy where they had bought them.

On the way home, George suggested to Lucy that they get the induction oven she had found and buy some new saucepans. They could always sell the old ones at a car boot sale or give them to his younger sister who was about to start university.

The following day Lucy's mother called round and suggested that before they made a final decision they really ought to see the cooker. 'What if you don't like it when you actually see it?' she said. Lucy and George disagreed; the website was excellent and had a detailed explanation of the various knobs and switches. Lucy replied 'Mum it is only a cooker'. She showed her Mum the cooker on the website and noticed that since she had last looked the stock had gone down from 5 to 2. She decided that she should buy it there and then. She bought it with her store card knowing this would mean that it would go towards her next set of gift vouchers from the store.

The cooker and refrigerator were delivered free of charge. The store had recently switched its delivery to a company who delivered at weekends for a small extra charge, which was perfect for George and Lucy. They just had to wait in their sitting room for a few days until the rest of the kitchen was fitted. All in all they were very happy, although Lucy did notice that the colour of the glass on her cooker was darker than she had expected from the website. She made sure that she put a review up on the department store website after they had used the cooker for a month. This is what she wrote:

Fantastic, I love my cooker and I love this website. If I hadn't read these reviews I would never have known how wonderful induction cooking was. As a young working couple having convenient weekend delivery made a big difference. I shall always come back to check the offers in your store. Just a small point, the cooker glass is in reality slightly darker than it appears on the website.

Questions

1. Outline George and Lucy's decision-making process. How does their decision-making process compare with those outlined in the chapter?

2. How many decisions did they make?

3. Identify any heuristics used in their decision-making.

4. What were their key evaluative criteria?

5. Are there any lessons to be drawn for companies marketing their products on the internet and for those who do not?

References

Antil, J.H. (1984), 'Conceptualization and operationalization of involvement', *Advances in Consumer Research*, 11, 203–9.

Arierly, D. (2008), *Predictably irrational: the hidden forces that shape our decisions*, London: Harper Collins.

Arsel, Z. and Bean, J. (2013), 'Taste regimes and market-mediated practice', *Journal of Consumer Research*, 39, 5, 899–917.

Bain, R. (2010), 'In partnership', *Research*, http://www.research-live.com/magazine/in-partnership/4004253. article (accessed 15 May 2014).

Bakos, J.Y. (1997), 'Reducing buyer search costs: implications for electronic marketplaces', *Management Science*, 43, 12, 1676–92.

Barreyat-Baron, M. and Barrie, R. (2008), 'Cadbury—how a drumming gorilla beat a path back to profitable growth: a real-time effectiveness case study, IPA Effectiveness Awards', WARC https://www.warc.com/Content/ContentViewer.aspx?MasterContentRef=ded7d8eb-9cfd-460b-9d17-b2f91fb9238a&q=AID per cent3a88470&CID=A88470&PUB=IPA (accessed 15 February 2012).

Batra, R. and Ray, M.L. (1983), 'Operationalizing involvement as depth and quality of cognitive responses', *Advances in Consumer Research*, 10, 309–313.

Bayley, G. and Nancarrow, C. (1998), 'Impulse purchasing: a qualitative exploration of the phenomenon', *Qualitative Market Research*, 1, 2, 99–114.

Bloch, P.H. (1986), 'The product enthusiast: implications for marketing strategy', *Journal of Consumer Marketing*, 3, 3, 51–62.

Bloch, P.H., Sherrell, D.L., and Ridgway, N. (1986), 'Consumer search: an extended framework', *Journal of Consumer Research*, 13, 1, 119–26.

Bowlby, R. (1997), 'Supermarket futures', in P. Falk and C. Campbell (eds), *The shopping experience*, London: Sage.

Brannon, L.A. and Brock, T.C. (2001), 'Norms against voting for coerced reform', *Journal of Personality and Social Psychology*, 64, 347–55.

Brashear, T.G., Kashyap, V., Musante, M.D., and Donthu, M. (2009), A profile of the internet shopper: evidence from six countries, *Journal of Marketing Theory and Practice*, 17, 3, 267–82.

Chaiken, S., Liberman, A., and Eagly, A.H. (1989), 'Heuristic and systematic processing within and beyond the persuasion context', in J.S. Uleman and J.A. Barg (eds), *Unintended thought*, New York: Guilford Press, pp.215–52.

Close, A.G, and Kukar-Kinney, M. (2010), 'Beyond buying: motivations behind consumer's online shopping cart use', *Journal of Business Research*, 63, 9–10, 986–92.

Court, D., Elzinga, D., Mulder, S., and Vetvick, O. (2009), 'The consumer decision journey', www.mckinseyquarterly.com (accessed 9 January 2013).

Day, R. and Landon, L. (1977), 'Towards a theory of consumer complaining behavior', in A. Woodside, J.N. Sheth, and P. Bennett (eds), *Consumer and industrial buying behavior*, Amsterdam: North-Holland.

Day, R., Grabicke, K., Schaetzle, T., and Staubach, F. (1981), 'The hidden agenda of consumer complaining', *Journal of Retailing*, 57, 3, 86–106.

Economist (2013), 'Shopping habits: in for a pound', *Economist*, http://www.economist.com/news/britain/21578107-middle-classes-are-turning-keen-bargain-hunters-pound (accessed 9 July 2013).

Edelman, D. and Singer, M. (2015), 'The new consumer decision journey', http://www.mckinsey.com/business-functions/marketing-and-sales/our-insights/the-new-consumer-decision-journey (accessed 9 November 2016).

Erdem, T., Keane, M.P., Sabri Öncü, T., and Strebel, J. (2005), 'Learning about computers: an analysis of information search and technology choice', *Quantitative Marketing and Economics*, 3, 3, 207–47.

Feick, L. and Price, L. (1987), 'The market maven: a diffuser of marketplace information', *Journal of Marketing*, 51, 1, 83–97.

Fishburn, P.C. (1974), 'Lexicographic orders, utilities and decision rules: a survey', *Management Science*, 20, 142–7.

Foxall, G.R. (1993), 'The influence of cognitive style on consumers' variety seeking among food innovations', *British Food Journal*, 95, 9, 32–6.

Ganesh, J., Reynolds, K., and Luckett, M. (2007), 'Retail patronage behaviour and shopper typologies: a replication and extension using a multi-format, multi-method approach', *Journal of the Academy of Marketing Science*, 35, 3, 369–81.

Gorlin, M. and Dhar, R. (2012), 'Bridging the gap between joint and individual decisions: deconstructing preferences in relationships', *Journal of Consumer Psychology*, 22, 3, 320–3.

Harrison, S. (2013), 'Northern Ireland bag levy could reduce litter', BBC News, 8 April, http://www.bbc.co.uk/news/uk-northern-ireland-22037034 (accessed 25 November 2012).

Haubl, G. and Trifts, V. (2000) 'Consumer decision making in online shopping environments: the effects of interactive decision aids', *Management Decision*, 19, 1, 4–21.

Hewitt, M. (2017), 'Returns are where under-fire retailers can fight back', *Daily Telegraph* http://www.telegraph.co.uk/business/2017/06/01/returns-under-fire-retailers-can-fight-back/ (accessed 5 June 2017).

Hirschman, A. (1970), *Exit, voice, and loyalty: responses to decline in firms, organizations, and states*, Cambridge, MA: Harvard University Press.

Holt, D. (2016), 'Branding in the age of social media', *Harvard Business Review*, March, 41–50

Houston, M.J. and Rothschild, M.L. (1978), 'Conceptual and methodological perspectives on involvement', in S. Jain (ed.), *Research frontiers in marketing: dialogues and directions, 1978 Educators' Conference Proceedings*, Chicago, IL: American Marketing Association, pp.184–7.

Istanbulluoglu, D., Leek, S., and Szmigin, I. (2017), 'Beyond exit and voice: developing an integrated taxonomy of consumer complaining behaviour, *European Journal of Marketing*, 51, 1109–28.

Iyengar, S.S. and Lepper, M.R. (1999), 'Rethinking the value of choice: a cultural perspective on intrinsic motivation', *Journal of Personality and Social Psychology*, 76, 349–66.

Iyengar, S.S. and Lepper, M.R. (2000), 'When choice is demotivating', *Journal of Personality and Social Psychology*, 79, 995–1006.

Jansson-Boyd, C.V. (2010), *Consumer psychology*, Maidenhead: Open University Press.

Kollewe, J. (2012), 'Discounters take over UK malls', *Guardian*, 18 April, http://www.theguardian.com/business/2011/apr/18/discounters-take-over-uk-malls (accessed 9 April 2014).

Krugman, H.E. and Hartley, E.L. (1970), 'Passive learning from television', *Public Opinion Quarterly*, 342, 184–90.

Lacy P. and Rutqvist, J. (2015), *Waste to wealth: the circular economy advantage*, London: Palgrave Macmillan.

Langer, E.J. (1989), *Mindfulness*, Reading, MA: Addison-Wesley.

Lee, W. (2012), 'Magiclean: Celebrity mom kidnapping', http://www.warc.com/Content/ContentViewer.aspx?ID=e68b68f3-b312-4701-949a-8196417ddf17&MasterContentRef=e68b68f3-b312-4701-949a-8196417ddf17 (accessed 17 August 2013).

Mattila, A.S. and Wirtz, J. (2008), 'The role of store environmental stimulation and social factors on impulse purchasing', *Journal of Services Marketing*, 22, 7, 562–7.

Narayana, C.L. and Markin, R.J. (1975), 'Consumer behavior and product performance: an alternative conceptualization', *Journal of Marketing*, 39, 4, 1–6.

Nordland, R. (2013), 'Too hot to exercise (and who really wants to?)', *New York Times*, 7 July, http://www.nytimes.com/2013/07/08/world/middleeast/in-qatar-too-hot-to-exercise-and-who-really-wants-to.html?_r=0 (accessed 9 April 2014).

Parsons, A.G. (2002), 'Non-functional motives for online shoppers: why we click', *Journal of Consumer Marketing*, 19, 5, 380–92.

Quek, C. (2013), 'Make your brand story meaningful', *Harvard Business Review*, http://blogs.hbr.org/2013/06/make-your-brand-story-meaningf/ (accessed 30 July 2014).

Ratneshwar, S. and Chaiken, S. (1991), 'Recognition is used as one cue among others in judgement and decision making', *Journal of Experimental Psychology: Learning, Memory and Cognition*, 32, 150–62.

Roberts, H. (2012), 'Top of the shops: discount stores are booming in recession as thrifty customers seek out bargains', *Daily Mail*, 3 April, http://www.dailymail.co.uk/news/article-2124263/Discount-stores-thrive-recession-thrifty-seek-bargains.html (accessed 9 April 2014).

Rohm, A.J. and Swaminathan, V. (2004), 'A typology of online shoppers based on shopping motivations', *Journal of Business Research*, 57, 748–57.

Rook, D. (1987), 'The buying impulse', *Journal of Consumer Research*, 14, 2, 189–99.

Royo-Vela, M. and Casamassima, P. (2010), 'The influence of belonging to virtual brand communities on consumers' affective commitment, satisfaction and word-of-mouth advertising: the Zara case', *Online Information Review*, 35, 4, 517–42.

Schwartz, B. (2009), *The paradox of choice: why more is less*, New York: HarperCollins.

Schwartz, B., Ward, A., Monterosso, J., et al. (2002), 'Maximizing versus satisficing: happiness is a matter of choice', *Journal of Personality and Social Psychology*, 83, 5, 1178–97.

Shah, A.K. and Oppenheimer, D.M. (2008), 'Heuristics made easy: an effort-reduction framework', *Psychological Bulletin*, 134, 2, 207–22.

Simon, H.A. (1956), 'Rational choice and the structure of the environment', *Psychological Review*, 63, 129–38.

Slama, M. and Williams, T. (1990), 'Generalization of the market maven's information provision tendency across product categories', *Advances in Consumer Research*, 17, 48–52.

Tauber, E.M. (1972), 'Why do people shop?', *Journal of Marketing*, 36, 4, 46–9.

Tversky, A. and Kahneman, D. (1974), 'Judgement under uncertainty: heuristics and biases', *Science*, 185, 4157, 1124–31.

Tversky, A. and Kahneman, D. (1981), 'The framing of decisions and the psychology of choice', *Science*, 211, 4481, 453–8.

utalkmarketing.com (2008), Editor's pick: John Lewis 'Always a Woman' advert, http://www.utalkmarketing.com/pages/CreativeShowcase.aspx?ArticleID=17464&Filter=0&Keywords=&Order=LATEST&Page=1&Title=Editor%E2%80%99s%20Pick.%20John%20Lewis%20%E2%80%98Always%20a%20Woman%E2%80%99%20advert (accessed 30 July 2014).

Vogt, C.A. and Fesenmaier, D.R. (1998), 'Expanding the functional informational search model', *Annals of Tourism Research*, 25, 3, 551–78.

Wallis, L. (2014), 'Why it pays to complain on Twitter', http://www.bbc.co.uk/news/business-27381699 (accessed 1 June 2017).

Weiner, B. (2000), 'Attributional thoughts about consumer behaviour', *Journal of Consumer Research*, 27, 3, 382–7.

Whitmarsh, L. (2016), 'Saving the planet?', *Society Now*, Summer, p.3.

Wood, Z. (2012), 'Discount stores boom as upmarket shoppers boast of saving money', *Observer*, 26 August, p. 43, http://www.theguardian.com/business/2012/aug/26/discount-stores-boom-upmarket-shoppers (accessed 9 April 2014).

Zaichkowsky, J.L. (1985), 'Measuring the involvement construct', *Journal of Consumer Research*, 12, 341–52.

Zaichkowsky, J.L. (1986), 'Conceptualizing involvement', *Journal of Advertising*, 15, 2, 4–14.

4

LEARNING AND MEMORY

Introduction

When Apple introduced the iPhone in 2007, the company spent time and effort showing consumers how to use it, with every advertisement showcasing one individual iPhone feature. This process of teaching consumers how to use a relatively new product category was important for bringing smartphones to the mass market, and for helping consumers engage with other devices such as tablets. How consumers learn is the focus of this chapter. We are all familiar with the rigours of learning, whether it is cramming for an exam or trying to master a new language. Learning extends into many areas, and is linked with other human characteristics, including personalities, motivations, perception, and attitudes.

Consumption inevitably has a learning aspect, and there are various dimensions to this learning. Businesses rely on consumers remembering brand names, their attributes, how they can be used, what price they are compared with their competitors, and of course how they feel about the brand. For consumers to retain this information they need to store it in their memory, and to do this they must have gone through the process of learning about the brand. Marketers need to know how consumers learn to enable them to communicate appropriately with buyers. In particular, they need to identify the best ways to reinforce learning about their brands, while being aware of the limitations of consumers' cognitive capacity to take many new ideas on board.

LEARNING OBJECTIVES

Having read this chapter you will be able to:

1. Demonstrate understanding of the **main approaches to learning**.

2. Understand what is meant by **behavioural learning**, and the difference between classical and operant conditioning.

3. Describe the different **modes of cognitive learning**.

4. Explain the different functions of **sensory, short-term, and long-term memory**.

5. Understand and evaluate the role of memory in **retaining and retrieving information**.

6. Explain the issues around **social learning**, including observational and vicarious learning.

Main approaches to learning: behavioural and cognitive learning

Learning *is the activity or process of acquiring knowledge or skill by studying, practicing, or experiencing something.* Learning is important in the field of consumer behaviour as it often leads to changes in attitudes, beliefs, or behaviour. Figure 4.1 identifies the different branches of learning theory that will be discussed in this chapter. We focus on two major categories: behavioural and cognitive learning. **Behavioural learning** *is concerned with learning as a response to changes in our environment.* A behavioural view of learning expects a consumer to respond to an external stimulus, such as seeing a brand of soft drink for sale and, having had a previous positive experience with the brand, making a decision to buy it again. Here, environment is the key to shaping learning and behaviour. This model of learning has its limitations, but there is a long tradition of its use in marketing since the 1950s, and it has been widely used as a model for the interpretation and understanding of advertising.

Cognitive learning *theories focus on learning through internal mental processes and conscious thought.* Such theories regard learning primarily as a process of mental activity where we are thinking through our actions to some degree. This is particularly true for information processing, discussed later in this chapter. A consumer deciding whether to buy a major household appliance, such as a new washing machine, might carefully read advertisements and customer reviews, talk to people, consider all the key attributes, and evaluate what is best for them, engaging in the high involvement decision process discussed in Chapter 3. During this decision process the consumer is accessing and learning new information, some of which will be committed to memory. With cognitive learning, we

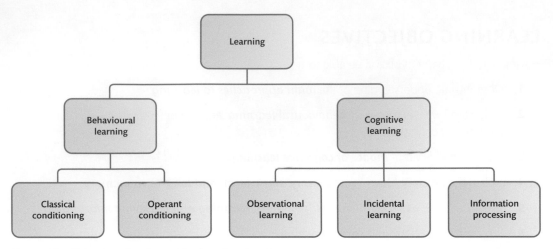

Figure 4.1 Behavioural and cognitive learning theories

might expect consumers to have gone through a process of search and evaluation from their memory of previous experiences (internal) and from new information available to them (external).

Behavioural learning

Classical conditioning

In this section we consider classical conditioning, a form of behavioural learning, and explain the concepts of first-order conditioning and higher-order conditioning. We examine stimulus generalization and discrimination as part of classical conditioning. These theories stem originally from Ivan Pavlov, a Russian physiologist who was researching digestive processes in dogs when he identified a process now known as classical conditioning. Pavlov noted that when an assistant entered the dogs' room they began to salivate because they associated the assistant with feeding time. Salivation is a reflexive process, not within the control of dogs or, more usefully, humans. Imagine coming home hungry after a long walk, entering your house, and smelling enticing cooking smells; your salivary glands are probably activated in a similar fashion to those of Pavlov's dogs. What was unusual was that the dogs began to salivate when the assistant entered the room, even when there was no food present, and this could not be explained physiologically. Pavlov then experimented with a bell which was rung each time food was presented, and again the dogs salivated as they were about to be fed. After a period of time of repeatedly ringing the bell in the presence of food, the bell was rung but no food was given to the dogs. The dogs still salivated, suggesting that the salivation process had been conditioned by the presence of the bell. This led Pavlov to explain the link between the unconditioned stimulus (US)—the food—and the conditioned stimulus (CS)—the bell. The dogs' physiological response to food is unconditioned and is

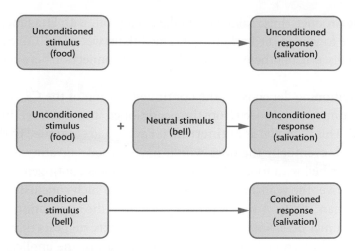

Figure 4.2   Producing a conditioned response

referred to as the unconditioned response (UR). When the dogs salivated and there was no food present, clearly they had been conditioned by the previous contiguity of the bell and the food, thus producing a conditioned response (CR).

Figure 4.2 provides an explanation of these links between the unconditioned, neutral, and conditioned stimuli and responses. The unconditioned stimulus produces an unconditioned response, and the unconditioned stimulus (food) linked with a neutral stimulus (bell) produces an unconditioned response. Over time, this repeated pairing results in the bell acting as a conditioned stimulus which produces a conditioned response (salivation).

First-order conditioning

The example of Pavlov's dogs is known as **first-order conditioning**, and occurs when *a conditioned stimulus acquires motivational importance by being paired with an unconditioned stimulus, which is intrinsically aversive or rewarding,* such as a painful shock or food (Gewirtz and Davis, 2000). In first-order conditioning the US needs to come almost immediately before exposure to the CS, which is typically a biological stimulus, such as food, sex, or pain, that elicits a natural physiological response. This may explain why sexual images are so often used in advertising for products such as expensive fast cars. In such advertisements, a woman (US) is directly associated with the sports car (CS), suggesting to the viewer that the two are connected. Sex is a basic biological instinct (see Chapter 7), and the association here is between driving an expensive car and the appeal that this will have to the opposite sex. Women are not excluded from such sexual connections; for a number of years, Diet Coke has used the image of an attractive and fit young man drinking Diet Coke while being watched, longingly, by women. The most recent of these types of advertisements was devised to mark the 30th anniversary of Diet Coke, emphasizing the associations between Diet Coke and sexual attractiveness. In this 2013 advertisement, a group of women send a can of Diet Coke rolling down a hill in the direction of a 'hunky' gardener, who opens the can, spraying himself with the product, thus making him take his top off, with Etta James singing 'I just wanna make love to you' in the background. The link between Diet Coke and sex may be more difficult to discern, but there is a direct biological connection between a diet product and a fit body!

Classical conditioning depends on the continued pairing of the CS and the US. If the unconditioned stimulus is removed from the conditioned stimulus, over time the response will be removed. This is known as **extinction**. If Pavlov had continued to ring the bell but not produce food, eventually the dogs would have ceased salivating as they would no longer connect the bell with food. Classical conditioning is contingent on many factors, and experiments over the years have not always provided such conclusive results as those of Pavlov (Bitterman, 2006). A recent investigation into the application of classical conditioning in consumer behaviour and advertising contexts suggests that its effectiveness may be exaggerated (Pornpitakpan, 2012). For examples of the application of classical conditioning to advertising see Consumer Insight 4.1.

CONSUMER INSIGHT 4.1

Celebrity endorsers and classical conditioning

Celebrity endorsement is widely used in advertising (see Figure 4.3). The 'match-up' hypothesis (Till and Busler, 2000) suggests that celebrities are most useful when there is commonality between them and the product they are endorsing. So, while Rihanna would be an unlikely endorser of Halford's bikes, the four-time Olympic gold medal winner Laura Trott matches up with the product and brings credibility to the endorsement. Nike makes extensive use of celebrity endorsement across the world, with Liu Xiang (the Chinese Olympic hurdler) as an endorser of Nike to promote the spirit of Nike— 'Nike: Find Your Greatness'. More recently, the tennis player Li Na has launched an exclusive line of Nike sportswear for Chinese women. More recently, we see celebrity endorsement associated with more political and environmentally oriented causes, such as Emma Watson endorsing the Green Carpet Challenge (http://eco-age.com/gcc-brand/gcc-brandmark-brands/), a campaign to raise the profile of sustainable and ethical fashion.

In experimental studies Till et al. (2008) found support for the use of celebrities as unconditioned stimuli. They also found that highly congruent celebrities would result in greater conditioning. Associating the basketball player Michael Jordan with a sports drink resulted in stronger conditioning than when the sports drink was paired with actor Pierce Brosnan. When thinking about how celebrity endorsement impacts on consumer brand learning, a key mechanism is **evaluative conditioning**, defined as *the changes in the liking of a stimulus (e.g. brand) linked to the pairing of that stimulus with other positive or negative stimuli (e.g. celebrity)*. Celebrities are chosen because they are well liked or have other desirable properties, and they are often paired with the brand in a manner that should promote evaluative conditioning.

There are drawbacks to using celebrities for classical conditioning; if a celebrity has built up a strong connection with one brand, it may be difficult to use the same celebrity for another product

Figure 4.3   David Beckham advertising Kent & Curwen clothing
Source: Image supplied by The Advertising Archives.

as the previous connection could suppress the formation of a new association (Pornpitakpan, 2012). However, there are some celebrities for whom the unconditioned response is carried across readily from one brand to another. Cara Delevingne endorsed the sports clothing brand Puma, but has also endorsed Rimmel, and both brands were enhanced by their links with the model. The unconditioned stimulus Cara Delevingne is readily linked with a variety of conditioned stimuli from fashion/sports clothing to make-up.

Questions

1. Pick three or four different brands that use celebrity endorsers and assess their 'match-up'. Try to pick different product types and also consider different celebrities who are used by different brands in the same product class.

2. Assess to what extent you think congruency matters in the use of celebrity endorsement. Are there any apparently mismatched celebrities whom you still think work as unconditioned stimuli?

Sources: Till and Busler (2000); Till et al. (2008); Pornpitakpan (2012).

 Access the online resources and follow the web links to learn more about the use of celebrity endorsements.

Higher-order conditioning

Whereas first-order conditioning relies on the connection between the unconditioned and conditioned stimulus, **higher-order conditioning** *is the pairing of two conditioned stimuli.* Higher-order conditioning can occur when a conditioned stimulus (CS1) acquires associative strength through being connected to a second conditioned stimulus (CS2) (rather than an unconditioned stimulus). The pairing of CS1 and CS2 may occur before or after the first conditioned stimulus (CS1) is paired with an unconditioned stimulus (US).

Music acts as a particularly powerful form of higher-order conditioning. The use of well-known songs in advertising has become increasingly popular and successful. In the media this trend is known as 'synchronization', which reflects the appropriate pairing of song and brand (*Economist*, 2003). In the 1960s, Bob Dylan released the song 'Blowin' in the Wind', which was an anti-establishment anthem for young people of that era, asking when change would come about. This song was already conditioned in (older) people's minds, associated with the need for change for the better. In 2009, Dylan granted permission for the UK-based group The Co-operative to use it in an advertisement. The advertisement carefully linked visually with the song from the opening shot of a dandelion blowing its seeds in the wind, which blew across many countries showing people working to produce goods sold by the Co-Op (see Figure 4.4). The closing lines of the advertisement were: 'From community projects to a share of the profits. From renewable energy to Fair Trade products. The Co-operative believes that when benefits are passed on it's good for everyone', thus successfully pairing the associations of The Co-operative with the already conditioned

Figure 4.4   Still from The Co-operative's 'Blowin' in the Wind' advertisement
Source: Image supplied by The Advertising Archives.

song as a movement for change. Hence, two conditioned responses (anti-establishment conditioning associated with the song and community orientation associated with The Co-operative) produce a powerful associative response.

Stimulus generalization

Stimulus generalization *occurs when a stimulus similar to a conditioned stimulus elicits a similar conditioned response.* Stimulus generalization stems from the fact that people often respond in the same way to stimuli that are similar. The importance of stimulus generalization to marketing is shown in the ways that consumers respond to brand extensions and private-label marketing. Consumers form impressions and judgements about new product lines and extensions based on their general feeling towards the brand, largely derived from previous experiences with that brand. Brand extensions are important for companies as they allow them to innovate, increase market share, and move into other markets, but they are also risky for companies in terms of consumer acceptance. Where there is transfer of positive feelings from the parent brand to the extension, the risk will be reduced. Stimulus generalization is a mechanism for such positive transfer (Till and Priluck, 2000), and will be dependent on the quality of the parent brand and the fit with the brand extension (Völckner and Sattler, 2007)

Heinz is a brand that has successfully managed product innovation while benefiting from stimulus generalization. From ketchup to beans to baby food, the Heinz brand is well known. If Heinz brings out new products such as hot sauces, the process of stimulus generalization acts as insurance to the consumer and may encourage them to try something new. In Figure 4.5 we see three products from Heinz. Most people will be familiar with the

Figure 4.5   Heinz product extensions   *Source*: © iStock.com/cnicbc.

shape of the bottle and label on Heinz ketchup, and this has been transferred to two other products—relish and mustard. Therefore the familiarity of the ketchup bottle and labelling is transferred to the other products in this stimulus generalization example. Heinz often uses tag lines such as 'It has to be Heinz' to enforce the reassurance of choosing a quality brand even if the product is unfamiliar.

Another area where stimulus generalization has an impact is private-label marketing. Many retailers offer private labels in their stores to compete with national brands. These private-label products often use similar colours, fonts, package shapes, etc. to those of the major brands with which they are competing. Consumers may be confused or pick up own-label brands quickly, or through stimulus generalization the private-label brands may simply benefit from a transfer of positive attitude from the main-line brands. Major companies, such as Proctor & Gamble and United Biscuits (see Consumer Insight 4.2), have successfully sued private-label brands that they see as feeding off the goodwill of their name (Narisetti, 1994).

CONSUMER INSIGHT 4.2

Passing off: Penguin versus Puffin

Passing off is *the marketing of a good in a way that enables it to be mistaken for another brand, and it relies on the phenomenon of stimulus generalization.* From a legal perspective, the essence of passing off is that the goodwill of one brand is taken advantage of by another to the detriment of the first. Passing off relies on consumers associating the benefits of a well-known brand with another brand that looks similar through stimulus generalization (Warlop and Alba, 2004). Typically, such 'copycat' brands use perceptual elements, such as colour, shape, and imagery, from the brand they are imitating (Miceli and Pieters, 2010). An important case of passing off was between United Biscuits, the makers of the Penguin chocolate biscuit, and UK supermarket Asda, who sold an own-label biscuit called Puffin in their stores 1997. This was the first time that a copycat case had gone to trial. It was also interesting because United Biscuits products were sold in Asda stores. Penguins were chocolate-coated biscuits sold in red packaging with a yellow band across and the brand name horizontally placed in black lettering, and the packs also displayed images of penguins (see Figure 4.6). United Biscuits used the slogan 'Pick up a Penguin' in its advertising. The Asda lookalike brand was also in red packaging with black lettering and had a cartoon Puffin on the front. In promotional material Asda used the phrase 'Pick up a Puffin'. Puffin was sold in Asda stores alongside Penguin, but at a lower price. In a BBC Money Programme, Justin King, then the product development manager of Asda, said, 'We feel it is very important that we are able to continue to offer the value that own-label products deliver to our customers'. Two witnesses said that they had thought they were buying Penguins when they were actually buying Puffins, and another two witnesses said that they thought the same company that made Penguin must make Puffin.

Figure 4.6   Penguin packaging
Source: Image courtesy of United Biscuits.

In this case the judge upheld the complaint by United Biscuits of misrepresentation, recognizing the similarity between the packaging and the use of a bird similar to a penguin (marketingweek.com). The judge said that had the Asda product been called Bison, with an appropriate cartoon, the case would never have been brought and concluded, 'The Puffin packaging and get up was, in the material sense, deceptively similar to those of the Penguin' (Burrell, 1997).

Questions

1. Despite the ruling in 1997 there are still many lookalike brands. Choose a couple of own-label brands from a supermarket that you think look particularly similar to leading brands. Identify what elements are similar (e.g. size and shape of packaging, the name, the colours used). What is the price difference?

2. For your chosen brands, assess whether you think your chosen brands are passing off or that customers would recognize the differences. Why?

Sources: Burrell (1997); marketingweek.com (1997); Warlop and Alba (2004); Miceli and Pieters (2010)

 Access the online resources and follow the web links to learn more about brand misrepresentation.

Stimulus discrimination

Just as we can generalize from one stimulus to another, we can also learn to discriminate between similar stimuli. For example, dogs can be trained to discriminate so that they only respond to the particular sound of their owner's whistle. If a conditioned stimulus is not followed by an unconditioned stimulus, the response will decline and hence we discriminate against that conditioned stimulus. If we buy an own-label product and find that it does not perform to the same standards as the branded product, we are likely to discriminate against this product by switching back to the manufacturer's brand. Manufacturers have a vested interest in consumers recognizing their brand in a sea of own-labels and competitor brands, and will often indicate their distinctiveness and quality with lines such as Tetley's 'Original and the best' slogan. Manufacturers can also use stimulus discrimination more positively to enable consumers to distinguish between products in their brand range. Typically, cosmetics manufacturers choose one or two colours with which to associate their brand, but introduce more variety in packaging, such as tubs, jars, and tubes, to enable consumers to recognize additions to their product range easily.

Operant conditioning

Operant conditioning, also known as instrumental learning, was identified by B.F. Skinner (1953). **Operant conditioning** *is the changing of behaviour through reinforcement following a desired response.* Skinner showed that learning occurs when behaviour is changed, or modified, as a result of the outcome of previous behaviour. Skinner kept a number of pigeons in

	Condition	Response	Outcome
Strengthens response	Positive reinforcement	Shopping at a retail outlet you find many shops and bargains on designer brands	This increases the likelihood that you will return to shop at the outlet
	Negative reinforcement	You suffer from hay fever but when you take antihistamine tablets your symptoms decrease	You ensure that you have antihistamine tablets with you during the hay fever season
Weakens response	Punishment	The boots you bought for winter let in water and don't keep you warm	You will not return to the shop from which you bought the boots
	Extinction	The internet site that offered free shipping and returns removes this service feature	Decreases the likelihood of your using this site

Table 4.1   How operant conditioning works

a box, always at three-quarters of their ideal weight to ensure that they were hungry. In the box was a lever that dropped food when pushed. The pigeons learnt to press this lever to receive food. The behaviour of pressing the lever was reinforced by the appearance of the food. Table 4.1 describes the different responses and outcomes that are found in operant conditioning.

Imagine that a new coffee shop opens on your way to work. You decide to try it one day instead of your usual shop. You find that the coffee is very good and cheaper than that you usually buy, so you decide to go there again. Here you have acquired learning through behaviour, which has produced a positive outcome, known as positive reinforcement. Your behaviour may also be affected by negative reinforcement. This is where something unpleasant is removed following a particular behaviour, or where you behave in a certain way to avoid something unpleasant. You might have a stain on your favourite shirt and find a product that removes it—this is an example of negative reinforcement. In addition, some behaviours may neither increase nor decrease the likelihood of repetition; perhaps the behaviour was not important enough or the response was neutral. You might buy some stock items such as biscuits or tea; if there was nothing particularly good or bad about them you might not notice the brand, and next time you might or might not buy them again. These are referred to as **neutral operants**. Some responses decrease the likelihood of repeating the behaviour; i.e. they lead to a weakening response. If you buy a new flavour of ice cream and neither you nor your family like it, you are effectively being *punished* for your choice and are unlikely to purchase it again. Finally, if a behaviour is repeated but no longer leads to a positive outcome, extinction will occur and the behaviour will be less likely to continue.

Marketers want to create positive reinforcement for their brands. Free samples are a useful way of encouraging consumers to try products and, if the brand meets consumers' expectations, act as a form of positive reinforcement for them. Free samples have to be used carefully to encourage trials in realistic situations. Alpro, who produce soya products,

Figure 4.7   Alpro breakfast bags   *Source*: Image courtesy of iD Agency.

presented morning commuters with breakfast bags which included their milk, cereal, and a spoon, while in the afternoon they provided a soya pudding, thus making the free sample into a whole experience (Figure 4.7).

At the most basic level companies want to be sure that their brand is good enough for the item to be purchased again, but they may also provide other positive attributes that may help in a customer's choice and repeat purchasing. Internet retailers typically offer free delivery and returns to customers, effectively giving them a reduction in price and an incentive to shop. This may act as a positive reinforcement, especially if it is offered all the time or regularly as in the case of the internet fashion company Boden (Figure 4.8).

Figure 4.8   Using free delivery to reinforce purchasing   *Source*: Image courtesy of Boden.

Reinforcement schedules

An important aspect of operant conditioning relates to how and when reinforcement is applied to behaviour. Reinforcement schedules can be continuous or variable.

- A **fixed ratio schedule** *applies reinforcement after a specific number of responses.* Many loyalty schemes will make it clear how much you have to spend before you get a financial reward. Caffe Nero stamps your card every time you buy a drink (see Figure 4.9), and once it is stamped for nine drinks you are rewarded with a free one. See Research Insight 4.1 for research into how this works.

- A **fixed interval schedule** *is when reinforcement is provided after a specific known period of time.* A store may advertise that it has a sale three times a year, and customers may decide only to shop there at those times.

RESEARCH INSIGHT 4.1

Nunes, J.C. and Drèze, X. (2006), 'The endowed progress effect: how artificial advancement increases effort', *Journal of Consumer Research*, 32, 4, 504–12.

In this paper, Nunez and Drèze examine and compare the level of effort and commitment involved in filling a loyalty card for a carwash. They conducted an experiment to look at the factors influencing whether or not consumers stick with reward cards to get them completely filled up (and receive the reward). They found that those who receive two free stamps on a loyalty card exert more effort and are more committed to using the same carwash than those receiving no free stamps. They documented this effect as the 'endowed progress effect' whereby people provided with artificial advancement towards a goal (e.g. the two free stamps) exhibit greater persistence towards reaching the goal.

 Access the online resources to read the abstract and access the full paper.

- **Variable schedules** *are where reinforcement is provided on an irregular basis.* Skinner suggested that gamblers are particularly susceptible to variable schedules. This is when reinforcement is present after a variable (unknown to the person behaving) number of responses. If you play a slot machine you may win a little at one time and a lot at another, but you have no control over the response. It is the unknown but potentially positive outcome that keeps gamblers playing.

- Finally, a **variable interval** *is when the reinforcement occurs at some unknown but consistent rate.* In the lead-up to festivals, such as Diwali in India, companies typically have a range of deals and special offers to coincide with the festival. The Indian e-commerce

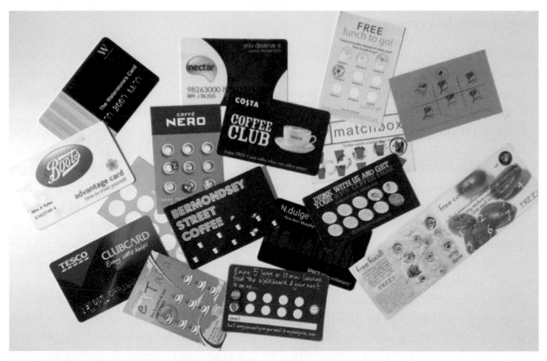

Figure 4.9   Fixed ratio cards from Caffe Nero and other food and drink outlets
Source: Image courtesy of Eatbigfish (www.eatbigfish.com).

portal Snapdeal runs Diwali sales on an annual basis. Customers expect such sales but they do not know exactly when, and so they may be encouraged to regularly shop and visit websites to ensure that they don't miss an offer. The Samsung campaign for Diwali 2013 was typical of this kind of promotion. With the slogan 'Samsung Home Happy Home', the company invited consumers to choose Samsung household goods (such as flat panel televisions, air conditioners, and refrigerators) to make their home a happy place for the festive season.

Learning history

An important element of behavioural learning is our learning history. This is developed from similar or related experiences that the consumer has had before, and when they encounter new settings they call upon these experiences to guide behaviour. The first time you visit a gym, you may feel uncertain about what to do, how the machines work, or the gym etiquette. But you may have some experience of using sports facilities in another context, say from school, that you can draw on to help you. After you have been a few times you become familiar with the environment and feel much more comfortable. It is our past experience of these situations and their consequences that help us understand new environments. We use this experience, which comprises our learning history, to adopt appropriate behaviour (Foxall et al., 1998). Therefore it is advantageous to marketers to try to ensure that it is easy to learn how a product or service environment works.

Cognitive learning

Cognitive learning is concerned with internal mental processes, which contrasts with behavioural learning and its focus on learning as a response to external cues in our environment. Cognitive learning has the potential to explain much more complex behaviour and decision-making processes than is possible with the behaviourist approach.

For our purposes, the key feature of cognitive learning is that it is based on the view that humans are broadly rational and use the information available in their environment to make decisions. Our responses to our environment can include a complex set of processes including gathering, processing, and interpreting information, assigning it meaning, and storing it in our memory. Cognitive learning manifests itself in many aspects of our lives. It can operate in high or low involvement situations (see Chapter 3) and can be conscious or unconscious. While in some situations we may be aware of collecting information in a conscious manner, on other occasions we learn through what Krugman (1965) termed passive learning, i.e. we are not conscious that we are learning.

There are various conceptions of cognitive learning theory, but some key elements can be identified, such as an insistence that although we cannot directly observe the workings of the mind we can make inferences from behaviour, and that we create knowledge based on our experience rather than passively receive it. At the heart of most cognitive learning theory is the information processing model.

Information processing

The information processing model explains how communications are received by the consumer and then interpreted, stored in the memory, and later retrieved in a logical and sequential fashion. Information processing in high involvement situations (see Chapter 3) became of increasing interest to researchers in the late twentieth century, particularly as computers became widespread. Researchers such as Bettman (1970) and Newell and Simon (1972) often referenced explanations of how computers worked to illustrate human information processing.

When information processing takes place the consumer uses information received from the environment, which passes through a cognitive process. In the case of deciding whether or not to purchase a particular brand, this involves not only new or repeat information from their environment, but also a mental assessment as to the brand's suitability, given the consumer's evaluative criteria and its integration with information stored in the memory. The process can be summarized as follows, using the example of a consumer, Jim, buying a gift, and is illustrated in Figure 4.10.

- **Exposure** *involves sensory detection and registration through receptor organs.* Jim wants to buy a birthday present for a friend. As he looks around he is exposed to many advertisements in magazines and on the internet. At this stage, incidental exposure to products and brands can occur, thus facilitating implicit learning, a form of learning that takes place in the absence of an intention to learn.

- **Attention** *requires the focusing of attention, leading to perception and categorization of stimuli.* Jim doesn't notice most of the information to which he is exposed, but he

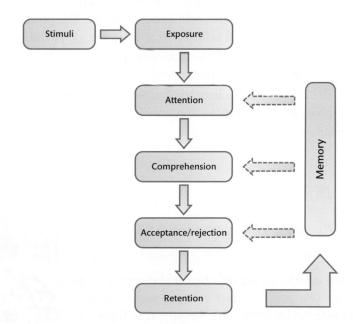

Figure 4.10   A five-stage process of information processing   *Source*: Adapted from Blackwell et al. (2006).

regularly receives an email alert from an internet bookshop and as he knows his friend is interested in history he pays more attention to this site.

- **Comprehension** *is where the consumer searches (and identifies) meaning.* Jim looks at the site in more detail and compares the information with what he has in his memory regarding his friend's taste in books and what he knows he has read. He also reads some of the reviews in more detail so that he starts to distinguish what might be the best choice.

- **Acceptance/rejection:** *the consumer considers existing choice criteria and elaborates the message received to reach a point of acceptance or rejection of the information.* Jim shortlists two books and is convinced that one of them is likely to be particularly appealing to his friend.

- **Retention:** *learning has to be retained in the memory for future use.* Jim has learnt a number of things—how to navigate the website, where to find reviews on books, and that the bookstore was offering free shipping on orders over €30. He will retain some or all of this in his long-term memory.

To reach the consumer's long-term memory, information has to go through the stages outlined in Figure 4.10. Typically, successful exposure to a stimulus depends on how closely it conforms to a consumer's past experiences and current beliefs, that it is not too complex, that it is believable, and that it relates to their current needs. However, it is worth noting that we may perceive and take note of information that is not immediately believable or that relates to our current needs, but is novel or just interesting. Advertising often captures our attention with novel stimuli (see Chapter 5). We may not be immediately interested in the service or product but are attracted by the advertisement and its content. The problem that marketers face is whether such information will be rejected at a later stage of the process, or will be understood and accepted so that it becomes a long-term memory. Novel stimuli can often gain the consumer's attention, but may not survive their information processing. In Practitioner Insight 4, Rachel Hartley tells us how the Nutracheck tool helps people to learn about their calorie intake through a process that aids comprehension and retention in their memory to enable them to manage their food intake.

PRACTITIONER INSIGHT 4

Rachel Hartley, Business Development & Marketing Director, Nutracheck

In 2005, Nutracheck developed the UK's first mobile phone program to track what you ate. Its latest barcode scanning app, together with the interactive food diary website, is designed to

track your food intake and empower you with the knowledge to make better choices to manage your diet—whether your goal is to lose weight, gain it, or eat better for good health.

Managing your diet is all about learning. Many people genuinely have no idea about the calorie content of foods and how many calories their body actually needs. Nutracheck has a food database (UK foods) of over 200,000 products. As well as packaged food, we also have data for foods that don't carry nutritional labelling, such as coffee shops, alcoholic drinks, take-aways, and eating out places.

Nutracheck is an app with a dedicated website designed to help people track what they eat by keeping a food diary—either via the barcode scanning app or online. It is an educational tool to make people more aware of how their food choices contribute to their daily calorie allowance—and in turn affect their weight. As well as calories, Nutracheck tracks six important nutrients—protein, carbohydrates, sugar, fat, saturated fat, and salt. A simple bar chart shows users how their diet stacks up against recommended guidelines for healthy eating. Keeping a food diary is a very important aspect of learning and building up knowledge through repetition. All you do is scan the product you ate or search for it in the Nutracheck food database (which also shows photos for easy recognition) and add it to the food diary which keeps track of how many calories you've consumed. Once a member has learned the basics of simply recording what they eat and staying within their calorie allowance, there are many quick short cuts they can use to speed up keeping the food diary (e.g. saving favourite foods and copying their diary ahead) and this helps to make learning easier. Users estimate that it only takes around 10 minutes a day to add food.

Another important aspect for people concerned about their weight and nutrition is how to reinforce their behaviour. We use award rosettes for every pound lost. When a user hits a milestone goal of 7 pounds or 1 stone, they are rewarded with a silver or gold rosette. These can be displayed on their forum profile so that other members can congratulate them, and a printable version is sent to them by email. A special weigh-in and progress board in the forum allows members to share their successes. Our nutritionist runs regular team challenges with prizes where members pledge how much they wish to lose during the four- to six-week challenge and are allocated into teams. Members earn points for their team through participation in weekly mini-tasks set by the nutritionist and their weight loss. We post the teams' weekly progress in the forums. The challenges combine an element of competition with a collaborative team effort in which members support one another. Such support is also provided by Diet Buddies who can communicate with one another through a private messaging service to help someone through a similar experience to them, such as losing baby-weight or getting ready for a special event.

Above all, learning about nutrition is the aim of Nutracheck, and once members have become familiar with the nutritional content of food and the calories they consume, this is knowledge they are unlikely to forget (especially the high calorie counts that have shocked them!), and the more they fill in their food diaries and check the nutrition content the better the information will stay in their memories.

Memory

Once a consumer has been through a learning process it is important that the information is retained in their memory to enable them to use it later. This is particularly important for marketing, where companies are spending vast sums of money to get people to remember their brand. This section explores the various stages involved when information is contained and retrieved from memory via a process of encoding, storage, and retrieval. A simplified summary of how memory works is presented in Figure 4.11.

Memory *is a system and a process whereby information is received, sorted, organized, stored, and retrieved over time.* Memory is central to understanding how consumers make decisions; marketers are eager to get their brands remembered and enable retrieval from consumers' memories during the purchase decision process. However, they have to recognize the many limitations on getting their message remembered. Alongside the issues associated with perceiving a stimulus (see Chapter 5), people are often exposed to advertisements weeks or months before they intend to buy. Therefore the chance of their remembering much of the original message is low. There are three critical steps to information being remembered: encoding, storage, and retrieval.

Encoding *refers to how information enters the memory.* Advertisers want their brands and communications to be distinctive and different, but their messages must be comprehended unambiguously for consumers to be able to make sense of, and store, this information. Such comprehension can be facilitated by the use of brand names that incorporate the main benefit of the product and can be easily encoded, such as Mr Sheen household polish or Head & Shoulders shampoo, where key characteristics of the brands are encapsulated in the brand name. Remember that in different countries very different sounding brand names may appear memorable. In France the brand Pschitt is onomatopoeic, recognized by consumers as sounding like the opening of a bottle—in English-speaking countries it has quite different connotations and associations. Brands can also present themselves in a simple form to avoid any ambiguity. If you look at the campaign for the Ronseal brand, each advertisement is very pared down and direct in its message, and the tag line 'Does exactly what it says on the tin' appears as the actor presents the tin with the product description to the camera.

Storage *is how the encoded information is retained in the memory.* Once in the memory the new information is connected with other information that may impact on how and when it is retrieved. Our memories include memorable nostalgic experiences, such as

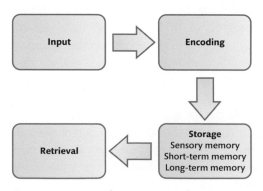

Figure 4.11   How the memory works

an important birthday or graduation (Wildschut et al., 2006). Zauberman et al. (2008) identified that people will use strategic memory protection in order to protect their ability to remember such important experiences. Memory pointers, such as photographs or mementos, may be used to help them recall these events. We may also practise memory protection through avoidance, so that our special memories are protected. For example, you might not want to go back to the restaurant where your partner proposed to you with business colleagues because the new situation may sully the memories of the more important experience. We shall see later in this chapter, in the section 'Retrieval of memory', how marketers aim to get consumers to retrieve these memories. In Consumer Insight 4.3 we explore how repetition and learning are used in advertising.

CONSUMER INSIGHT 4.3

Repetition and learning in advertising

Krugman (1965) identified that most people are unlikely to be involved with much of the commercial information they receive through television, but some of that information may move into their long-term memory just from repeated exposure. This does not mean that we have been persuaded about the product or that our attitudes have changed. Krugman advised marketers to repeat brand names and slogans as often as possible, given their finite promotional budgets, because beliefs and associations stored in the memory over time may form the basis for brand choice. It is at the moment when we are at the point of purchase and see the brand that our memories are jogged, even though we may not have considered the brand consciously until then. Krugman described this as the catalyst that brings to the fore the passive learning that has occurred just from repeated contact with mass media. In such low involvement situations marketers are looking for methods to help their messages penetrate the memories of their audience.

Jingles and distinctive visual imagery may help in this process. Learning through repetition is referred to as rote learning, and is one of the easiest ways that we learn. Often we find jingles or words from songs in our memories even though we have not consciously memorized them. Most people are able to memorize information that is heard or seen repeatedly. Such information can be visual (iconic rote memory) or aural (echoic rote memory). Businesses may use words or phrases that are simple but memorable.

An example of a business that successfully combines echoic and iconic rote memory is comparethemarket.com. It uses the powerful imagery of talking meerkats to increase iconic rote memory while continually raising the apparent confusion between the fictitious 'compare the meerkat.com' and its own name, thus pursuing an echoic rote memory route as well. The company has repeatedly used this combination in its advertising, such that for many it is difficult to think of meerkats without thinking of comparethemarket.com.

Questions

1. Do you think that there are there any disadvantages of repetition for consumers? If so, what are they?

2. Think of some other examples where iconic and/or echoic rote memory are utilized. Are there particular types of imagery that are powerful and why?

Sources: Krugman (1965); www.comparethemarket.com

 Access the online resources and follow the web links to learn more about repetition and learning in advertising.

Memory systems

Memories are not stored in discrete areas of the brain. Although we talk about sensory, short-term, and long-term memory, these are ways of describing how we remember rather than the physical storage of memories. While not universally accepted, this model of three levels of memory—sensory, short-term, and long-term—helps us to understand how and why some things are remembered and some are not. This system is referred to as the multiple store of memory.

Sensory memory

Here information is received in its sensory form—sight, smell, touch, taste, or hearing—and retained for a very brief period, no longer than the amount of time that the sensation is experienced. Imagine that you are walking through a fairground. You will pass many colourful sights, fascinating smells, and noisy sounds, you may taste a bit of your friend's candyfloss, and touch a teddy bear that someone has won, but all these moments are fragmentary. When you get home you may have a general sense of what you experienced and one or two things may have stayed with you (transferred to short-term memory), but much will have been forgotten as visual information only stays in the sensory memory for about half a second and auditory information for about two seconds (Jansson-Boyd, 2010). The reason for this is that sensory memory is essentially automatic and does not involve any particular attention or interpretation.

Short-term memory

This is where current information is processed. An important aspect of short-term memory is that it is limited to holding small amounts of information in mind for short periods of time. In a classic study from the 1950s, Miller (1956) conducted a number of experiments where he found that in a one-dimensional task (i.e. where a person is being asked to remember one type of thing at a time, such as numbers, loudness, etc.) most people can remember a series of up to seven items plus or minus one or two. Around seven items in some kind of sequence appears to be the maximum capacity of the short-term memory. One way that marketers can help their messages to be retained is through **chunking**, *which is the grouping together of similar or meaningful pieces of information* (MacGregor,

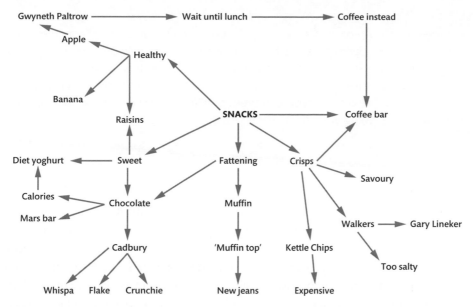

Figure 4.12 An associative network

1987). A chunk may be small or large, but as long as it is meaningful it can be remembered as a whole; people can remember around seven chunks of such information (see Research Insight 4.2). Imagine that someone writes down their phone number for you. It might look like 0204256543, but to remember it you might recall it in three chunks of three or four numbers 020 425 6543; the latter is much easier for the brain to process and remember. Take a look at the debit or credit card in your wallet; the long number will be presented as four chunks of grouped numbers, which are easier to read, say aloud, and remember.

Long-term memory

Our long-term memory has the potential to remember for ever. But first, memories have to get to the long-term memory and few do, otherwise we would be overloaded with mostly useless memories. Getting memories into the long-term memory is achieved by encoding them through **engrams** *which are neural networks connecting new memories with old* (Schacter, 1996). This involves the rehearsal of information in the short-term memory and linkage of this information with that stored in the long-term memory. Heath (2012) suggests that an engram for a brand would connect with its advertising and with that of other brands and their advertisements to produce an extensive network of interlinked memories or associative networks as shown in Figure 4.12.

RESEARCH INSIGHT 4.2

Vanhuele, M., Laurent, G., and Drèze, X. (2006), 'Consumers' immediate memory for prices', *Journal of Consumer Research*, 33, 2, 163–72.

Taking an experimental approach, Vanhuele et al. (2006) found two important properties that helped consumers to remember prices. One was the verbal length of the price stimulus and the other was the nature of its pattern. Consumers may aid retention of prices in their memory by using different recall strategies that decrease the number of syllables they have to remember. A price of $173 may be remembered as 'one hundred and seventy-three', 'one hundred seventy-three', 'one seventy-three, or 'one seven three'—anything from four to eight syllables.

 Access the online resources to read the abstract and access the full paper.

Memory can be affected by the processing effort required, with more effort (deep processing) more likely to result in long-term memory. It is probably best not to think of long-term memory as being completely discrete from short-term memory as there is much movement between the two. Information can be envisaged as being stored in the memory in a complex set of linked packets of information forming what is referred to as an associative network (Anderson, 1993). The networks are made up of nodes, which are concepts such as a place, time, person or brand, taste, smell, etc., and they are linked through different associations and pathways to form a network. Some associations may be stronger than others. and some elements may have more links to items than others. One of the typical packets of information, and a key element in how memory works, is the schema, which is an abstraction about an entity based on a range of experiences with that entity. So we may have a café and restaurant schema which contains such information as the various features of tables, chairs, menus, counter, coffee machine, till, and toilets, and also information about the typical spatial arrangement of these features, such as the counter being near the entrance and the toilets at the back. Associated with this may well be a script. This is a special type of schema where we have a well-developed concept of what to do in a certain situation. This may be built up from our learning history (see the section on 'Operant conditioning') where, from experience, we know what we will do in certain situations. Therefore in this example we may have a script for going to a café that involves elements such as reading the menu, attracting the waiter's attention, ordering, waiting, eating, and paying the bill. Figure 4.12 shows a possible associative network for someone thinking about a snack. The first words that occur in the memory might include crisps, healthy, and sweet—the person might like a bag of crisps but is also thinking of something healthier to have and that an alternative might be something sweet. Each of these words is linked to other items, perhaps specific products such as an apple (healthy) and chocolate (sweet), and in turn these can be linked to specific types (e.g. New Zealand Braeburn apples or Japanese Crispin apples) or brands (e.g. Cadbury's Dairy Milk or Hershey's Milk Chocolate), but may also be linked to consequences (e.g. satisfying; fattening). Some of the links may even lead to people, such as the healthy apple and Gwyneth Paltrow (her daughter's name is Apple), and for the crisps there may be similar associations such as footballer Gary Lineker, who has been a celebrity endorser for the Walkers brand of crisps in the UK, or Saif Ali Khan, the Indian actor who endorses Lay's crisps in India.

A company interested in identifying what an associative network might look like can use a number of research techniques. One is the response-time method where statements regarding a brand can be presented and respondents agree or disagree. Not only can the links with statements be mapped out visually but the response times can be measured, with longer times suggesting that the association is further away and vice versa. Another approach is the Kelly Repertory Grid (Kelly, 1955). This method is used to map associations with brands and allows respondents to identify the stimulus brands, and then assess the dimensions on which to compare and differentiate the brands. Respondents can then compare groups of three brands at a time. Here they are asked in what way two brands are alike and the third is different. So if the research was looking at snacks, one triad of brands might be Twiglets, Frito-Lay's potato chips, and Cadbury's Dairy Milk chocolate. An obvious similarity would be between the first two as savoury snacks, while the final one is sweet. Another might be Cadbury's Dairy Milk with Picnic and Mars Bar; here a respondent might group the last two together as chocolate bars for eating on your own and the Cadbury's Dairy Milk for sharing. Over multiple combinations, dimensions can be identified along which the brands can be evaluated and positioned on associative maps. Marketing managers can then use the associative maps to better understand the links that consumers make between different brands, different products, when they are used, and who or what they are associated with. This kind of map helps marketers understand how consumers actually see connections between different products, brands, and other associations, and can be used for new product development and marketing communications.

Types of long-term memory

The long-term memory can be subdivided into two types of memory: knowing how to do things (*procedural memory*) and memory of events that have taken place (*declarative memory*), as shown in Figure 4.13.

- **Procedural memory** *is involved with knowing how to do things, and allows us to remember how to perform tasks and actions—e.g. riding a bike, typing on a computer, making a cup of tea.* We learn how to tie our shoelaces as children, and it is often difficult to remember when we learned this as it has become an automatic action.

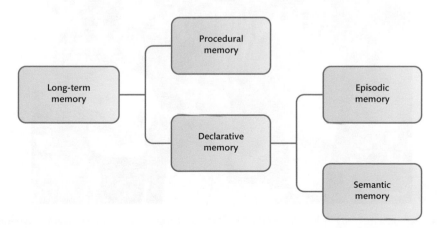

Figure 4.13   The organization of long-term memory

- **Declarative memory** *is specifically about knowing things.* It is made up of two different types of memory systems (episodic memory and semantic memory) which remember different types of event.

  ○ **Episodic memory** *refers to our memories of specific events and experiences, which have formed our autobiographical time line.* We remember significant events in our lives, perhaps getting examination results, an important boyfriend or girlfriend, and our graduation or wedding (see Figure 4.14). Places, times, the season when a significant event happened are all associated with other contextual elements to form these memories, which are often emotionally charged.

  ○ **Semantic memory** *involves structuring of specific records, facts, concepts, and knowledge about the world we live in.* It can include factual data, such as who was the first man on the Moon or the names of capital cities, and can also include generally held customs or how to play games or more abstract ideas, such as the meanings associated with certain people or well-known characters (e.g. Harry Potter or Bart Simpson). Heath (2012) suggests that the reason specific advertisements are difficult to remember is that they involve episodic memory, which requires more thorough encoding than semantic memory. He says that in order to recall an advertisement we have to have encoded it sufficiently to have a picture in our mind and possibly an idea of when we saw it. This may explain why advertisers have increasingly used nostalgia in their advertisements, attempting to link their brands with happy memories from our past. In the UK, Robinsons Barley Water tried to create the feeling of being young again with this copy: 'Think about it, a hot day in an endless summer and you're waiting expectantly for a large frothing glass, you drain it to the

Figure 4.14   Episodic memory includes important life events   *Source*: © iStock.com/monkeybusinessimages.

last drop and wipe the barley moustache from your lips. A butterfly circles and lands on your arm'. This represents a clear attempt to encode Robinsons through the memory of a hot summer day as a child, probably for most people a pleasant memory that they would be happy to recreate. Cartoons and catchy music were used to great effect in the Australian social marketing campaign for rail safety 'Dumb Ways to Die', explored in Consumer Insight 4.4.

CONSUMER INSIGHT 4.4

'Dumb Ways to Die'—learning through songs

Metro Trains, Melbourne, Australia, released a three-minute cartoon message designed to encourage young people to behave safely around trains. Generally this might be considered a rather boring message and not one to which young people are going to pay attention. But this cartoon showed a number of 'jelly bean' men meeting a range of sticky ends, including being hit by a train, all to the catchy tune 'Dumb Ways to Die'. Animated gifs were released on Tumblr, on radio, in posters, and throughout the Metro Trains network. Within days the YouTube video amassed millions of views and was on the front page of Reddit for hours, and had 'gone nuts on Tumblr' (John Mescall, McCann ECD, who wrote the advert).

Why did it work so well? It has a catchy song that leaves the safety message right until the end. It is likeable—you want to share it because of the lovely jelly bean characters who all find dumb ways to die (e.g. offering their private parts as piranha bait or poking a stick at a grizzly bear) and yet all continue to sing and dance even with no heads or bodies (see Figure 4.15). Above all it is not didactic; it

Figure 4.15   'Dumb Ways to Die'

Source: Image printed with permission of McCann and Metro Trains Melbourne and screenshot taken from http://www. dumbwaystodie.com

is not telling young people what to do, but having a laugh with them about dumb things they might just consider doing.

The use of strong visual imagery and a catchy song (iconic and echoic rote memory) help to make a difficult message memorable. Now 'Dumb Ways to Die' has been released as a ringtone and a smartphone app where you have to save as many of the characters as you can. You have to flick the piranhas away from the private parts and swat the wasps as quickly as you can, remove forks from toasters carefully, and above all keep idiots away from the platform edge.

Questions

1. Identify any theories used in this chapter so far which indicate why this should be such a successful campaign.

2. What other marketing techniques might be used to extend the value of this marketing communication?

3. This ad uses humour to aid learning, but many other campaigns use different approaches. Consider some other approaches that you are familiar with to communicate safety messages and comment on what you consider their pros and cons are compared with 'Dumb Ways to Die'.

Sources: theinspirationroom.com (2012); econsultancy.com (2012).

 Access the online resources and follow the web links to learn more about this campaign.

Retrieval of memory

Retrieval *is the process whereby we remember and access our stored memories.* There are different ways that we retrieve information from our memories including recollection, recognition, and relearning.

- **Recollection** *is when we reconstruct memory through a range of different narratives and bits of memory.* If we are in a store we may see a product, remember someone telling us about it, and then recall having seen an advertisement in a magazine; the partial memories come together to form a greater whole.

- **Recognition** *requires the memory to retrieve information by experiencing it again.* So you may be looking in the supermarket for snacks and recognize a new product that you had seen advertised on TV. You had to visually recognize the product to recall it.

- **Relearning** *is when you relearn something that you had previously learned, and the process of relearning helps with remembering and retrieval.* You may have used the automatic check-in at an airport but often you have to relearn how to use it if some time has elapsed between uses. The more you use the check-in, the easier it is to retrieve the information you need to help you manage it easily.

In some cases it may be beneficial for a company if their customers forget things. Consider all the different attributes that you had to learn when choosing a new mobile phone. A year or two after going through this learning process a new product type is launched on the market, and that means learning new product features in order to decide which brand to buy. When trying to remember the new and important attributes of a product, some of the older features may interfere with the most recent ones. This is a process known as *proactive interference*. On the other hand, *retroactive interference* is when new information you have had to learn excludes previously learnt old information, which may still be important to product choice. If you only remember the new attributes plus any of the old ones that are still pertinent, you are experiencing what has been termed the *benefit of forgetting*, i.e. the right balance of remembering the old and the new. Such intentional forgetting can be useful to marketers as it means that customers are making room in their memories for new information about brands (Shapiro et al., 2006).

Explicit and implicit memory

Researchers distinguish between explicit and implicit memory. **Explicit memory** *is the conscious recollection of an experience* while **implicit memory** *is remembering without conscious awareness*. Explicit memory requires a conscious recollection of something. Market research agencies will often measure explicit memory in day-after recall tests where they may ask you how much you can remember of an advertisement you watched on the television the previous night. You will use explicit memory through recognition or recall. Marketers use devices such as colours, packaging, and logos to aid your recognition. Sometimes it may be confusing when in a supermarket to immediately identify the brand you want to buy, and so you may rely on the marketers' devices to aid rapid recognition by looking for the familiar colour or logo. Children can often readily pick out logos that they are familiar with (Figure 4.16).

Implicit memory occurs when previous experiences help performance of a task despite the person involved having no memory of a prior event. People may be unaware of using information they have recently been exposed to when performing a subsequent task. Imagine you were walking through a department store (e.g. Debenhams in the UK or El Corte Ingles in Spain) and to get to the department you wished to visit, you passed through the sports section. You did not consciously look at anything, but later when a friend asks you for ideas of where you might buy tennis shorts you bring to mind the section in the department store you passed through. The impact of implicit memory often depends on whether or not the consumer has existing strong brand preferences, as a dominant brand is more likely to be chosen because it is both more preferred and more easily accessed in the memory (Lee, 2002). So while you might have passed a number of different brands, it may only be well-known brands like Adidas and Nike you remember. From a marketing perspective it is important to remember that exposure to stimuli is often momentary, and failure to remember does not mean that the consumer has not been affected by this

Figure 4.16   Recognition of a cereal   *Source:* © iStock.com/monkeybusinessimages.

exposure (Holden and Vanhuele, 1999). This explains why companies continue to spend money on billboards that may only be glanced at.

Aiding memory

Marketers ultimately want their products and brands remembered, and they want consumers to recall them at the time of purchase or at other important points during the decision-making process. Research suggests that a number of techniques can help the retrieval of memory and therefore are useful for marketers to understand in order to capitalize on them in their marketing.

Repetition and spacing

If a consumer is repeatedly exposed to marketing stimuli for a particular brand, their likelihood of recalling it increases. Unnava and Burnkrant (1991) found that this does not have to be exactly the same message, and indeed variation can improve the chance of recall. Variation in spacing can also help recall. So rather than repeating an advertisement regularly over a short period of time, it may be better to space the communication over a longer period. The evidence seems to show that various combinations of the space and content of advertisements may work together to provide different results with memory.

Position and duration

The position and duration of the advertisement may also help recall (however, see Research Insight 4.3). The time elapsed from the start of a commercial break until the beginning of a commercial may significantly negatively impact unaided brand recall, with the first and last commercial in a break having an advantage over those in the middle (Pieters and Bijmolt, 1997). In many countries a premium is charged for advertisements at the start of the commercial break, since advertisers may lose viewers who do something else during the break but catch the first advertisement. It is also important to remember that increasing numbers of consumers will have pre-recorded programmes and may notice the first ad but then zap to the end of the commercial break, making it more difficult for advertisers to capitalize on order effect.

RESEARCH INSIGHT 4.3

Mulhern, F. (2009), 'Integrated marketing communications: from media channels to digital connectivity', *Journal of Marketing Communications*, 15, 2/3, 85–101.

In a digital age position and duration may no longer be of so much importance to advertisers or consumers. In this review paper, Mulhern describes how the digitization of media represents a major step change with data-driven ad placement being principally about logistics. Advertising algorithms will place advertisements in contextually appropriate locations. They are placed in real time and the algorithm becomes smarter every time someone clicks on the ad. The advertisements are interacting with and learning the consumer's online behaviour and in so doing can generate higher levels of precision in targeting.

 Access the online resources to read the abstract and access the full paper.

Pictorial and verbal cues

When we look at a visual stimulus, such as an advertisement, we tend to take in the images before we consider the text (Kroeber-Riel, 1986). However, while we may notice a picture we may not comprehend it fully just through the pictorial cue and use the text to support our understanding. Research shows that pictures have an advantage over words for memory retrieval. However, some words will evoke images better than others and have higher levels of 'imagery value'. If you think of the word 'bed' or 'chair', an image is likely to be called to mind more easily than for words such as 'justice' or 'fairness'. Such high imagery words are better remembered than low imagery ones (Richardson, 1980) because they are able to form both verbal and visual codes in the memory. Unnava and Burnkrant (1991) give the example of advertising the features of a camera. If you used the line 'brand X camera captures fast movement', the reader might form a verbal code but the words are unlikely to produce an image. However, if a picture, such as people on a roller coaster, is used together with the claim, the addition of the picture would help the attribute 'captures fast movement' to be remembered as both a verbal code and an image. The dual codes should make the brand more likely to be retrieved. Microsoft launched its Surface Tablet with a strong visual commercial, but added a rhythmic background sound illustrating the magnetic click of the keyboard with the screen, underlining one of the key functionalities of the product that it could be used just as a tablet or with the keyboard. This can be extended to the actual brand name, which can use high imagery words and appropriate visual imagery together— for example, the Apple brand with its distinctive logo (see Figure 4.17).

Figure 4.17 Apple—a brand with high imagery value
Source: Image courtesy of Barry Doyon.

Social learning: observational or vicarious learning

Much of our learning occurs in a social setting where we observe the behaviour of others and learn from it. This is built upon the theory of social learning, and in particular the work of the psychologist Albert Bandura (1965, 1969). Social learning theory is concerned with the role played by vicarious, symbolic, and self-regulatory processes in people's behaviour. It sees human behaviour as influenced by observation, that humans use symbols to help analyse their experiences, and that people select and organize the stimuli around them in a self-regulatory manner. Observational learning is often used in marketing, as we regularly learn the specifics of how to do something by observing others. If you are in a new country and want to use the buses you may first observe what others are doing. Similarly, if you are using an automatic ticketing machine at an airport, you learn by observing others around you (see Figure 4.18). That we are prepared to learn like this is important, as it means that consumers will do some of the work for marketers and may even mean that businesses can reduce staff costs where consumers help themselves.

Observing the behaviour of others may also lead to us replicating such behaviour. As an example, we might watch the James Bond film *Spectre* and see James Bond sipping Bollinger champagne or wearing Tom Ford clothes and sunglasses. If we retain these images and are motivated to replicate them, millions of pounds worth of product placement investment will have been worthwhile. Utilizing observational learning is beneficial to marketers to explain how to use their products. Didactic or educational

Figure 4.18 Observational learning may occur by watching others
Source: © iStock.com/Mlenny.

Figure 4.19   National Dengue Prevention Campaign

Source: Copyright © 2017 National Environment Agency, Singapore. All rights reserved.

advertisements may engage the viewer with how to use a complex new product. When micro-waves were introduced, many such advertisements appeared giving instructions on how to use the machine, often supplemented by in-store demonstrations. Today advertisements for smartphones often do the same to show the various applications available. Sometimes such learning takes a more formal approach where it is important that people learn exactly how to do something. In many countries mosquitoes are a major problem, bringing illness and even death. Therefore teaching people how to limit the impact of mosquitoes in their home environment is essential. The Singapore government advertises the '5-Step Mozzie Wipeout' (see Figure 4.19), which uses words and pictures to simplify learning, on both above and below the line communications materials such as print and out-of-home advertisements, brochures, etc. throughout the country.

Sometimes we learn by accident, particularly if we are very interested in something. A child might be engaged in a specific activity because it is fun (such as a sport), but may be learning speech or coordination without knowing it. The use of tablet devices is said to be helping students learn because the range of apps available gives them access to more varied and enjoyable ways to learn. So again, children may feel that what they are doing is a game, but they may incidentally be learning vocabulary or maths or some other skills (see Research Insight 4.4).

RESEARCH INSIGHT 4.4

Kerrane, B. and Hogg, M.K. (2013), 'Shared or non-shared? Children's different consumer socialization experiences within the family environment', *European Journal of Marketing*, 47, 3/4, 506–24.

Children learn in many different ways, including formal learning at school, but one of the most important contexts for learning is the family. This study brings a consumer culture theory perspective to understanding the processes of children's consumer socialization practices within the family. The paper highlights the great variety, within families, in terms of parenting styles and interactions, sibling relations, and communication styles.

 Access the online resources to read the abstract and access the full paper.

Conclusions

Understanding how consumers learn and remember is central to understanding consumer behaviour. It is particularly important to companies in their efforts to market their brands. They want to know how to spend their budgets most cost effectively to ensure the best result. The **main approaches to learning** are behavioural and cognitive learning. We may note that at times our learning may be more behavioural in nature, a matter of stimulus and response or reacting to a conditioned or unconditioned stimulus. In considering **behavioural learning** we looked at the issues around both classical and operant conditioning, using a range of examples to show where each was relevant in marketing. Celebrity endorsement as an example of classical conditioning was considered in Consumer Insight 4.1, where we looked at the ways that celebrities from around the world are associated with brands in order to elicit positive feelings towards those brands. We also considered the application of operant conditioning in marketing through sales promotions and loyalty card schemes.

Alongside this approach, we know that consumers also learn about brands and are able to recall attributes and experiences of brands when they are in buying situations, and this is in line with the **cognitive learning approach**. From this perspective, the consumer is viewed as an information processor, and the focus is on internal mental behaviour, with studies often using experiments. The emphasis is on understanding what is happening in the consumer's mind, mediating between the stimulus/input and response/output. Practitioner Insight 4, focusing on the Nutracheck app, looked at how consumers learn to manage their diet and calorie intake through a process that aids comprehension and retention in memory.

The importance of understanding **memory**, and how consumers store information in their long- and short-term memories, is critical for marketers, and was examined in Consumer Insight 4.3. Marketers need to find ways to help get their message into the long-term memory and perhaps more importantly to help the consumer **retain and retrieve information** from memory at the point of purchase. By understanding better how memory works and how we may forget and remember things, marketers should be able to devise appropriate marketing communications strategies. Finally, we examined **social learning** and in Research Insight 4.4 we explored learning within the family context.

This knowledge of learning enables organizations to make positive links to their brand. Case Study 4 focuses on Havaianas flipflops to demonstrate how an understanding of learning can assist brand development.

Review questions

1. What are the key differences between operant conditioning and classical conditioning?

2. Explain the difference between observational learning and passive learning.

3. What are the stages that a consumer may go through when they are information processing?

4. Explain the key differences between sensory, short-term, and long-term memory.

5. Analyse the ways that memory is used in memory retrieval in consumer purchase situations.

6. Explain the importance of social learning for understanding consumer behaviour.

Discussion questions

1. Encoding can be helped by brands that incorporate a key benefit of the product and are easily remembered. Identify three brands that do this and explain how it is achieved.

2. Find and analyse two advertisements that use classical conditioning. Identify the unconditioned and conditioned stimulus. Why do you think they work?

3. Find specific examples of different reinforcement schedules. Identify whether they are fixed or variable and make an assessment of why each type is used in this circumstance and their likely success.

4. Develop an associative network of your own. Try starting with the following, 'breakfast', 'Friday night', or 'Starbucks', or choose your own. How many different types of nodes do you get, including products, brands, actions, thoughts, and people?

5. From your understanding of learning theory, analyse the use of product placement in a TV show or film of your choice. List the types of placement that occur, and explain how these might influence consumer behaviour.

Access the online resources to test your knowledge further and complete the Multiple Choice Questions for Chapter 4.

CASE STUDY 4

Learning Brazilian

Most young people have heard of the Havaianas brand of flipflops. In this case study we consider the history of the brand and how we have learned what the brand stands for. While all consumers learn, this case illustrates that the brand has to ensure how they learn and that they learn the right things to ensure success.

What are the first things you think of when someone says Brazil to you? Maybe you think of football, but then perhaps sunshine, beautiful bodies, having fun, bright colours and sunlight, beach life. And if you are on the beach you usually need a pair of flipflops. Flipflops are basically a piece of rubber with two straps. They are simple and practical, but one thing we can learn from Brazil is that even the simplest functional item can become a coveted brand. Over the last 20 years the Havaianas brand has been transformed from cheap footwear worn by maids, fishermen, and agricultural and construction workers to the chosen footwear of catwalk models and film actors, as well as consumers all over the world.

The brand was developed in the late 1950s based on the Zori sandals worn by Japanese immigrants in Brazil. These were made from fabric straps and rice straw soles, and Havaianas have maintained the textured rice pattern on the footbed of the sandals. At the beginning of their life cycle, their outstanding features were their cheapness and functionality. They were durable and sold largely in street markets—anyone could afford them. They were limited to five basic colours—black, blue, green, red, and yellow, all with a white sole. But as they were cheap and Brazilian they were often packed by tourists and taken home as souvenirs, and inevitably their fame spread. However, one of the problems with Havaianas was their functionality and cheapness. They became primarily perceived merely for their practicality, and so in the 1990s sales declined and the company began to reposition the brand.

In revamping the brand what did Havaianas hope to achieve? They wanted to maintain their identity as a democratic brand, one that could be worn by everyone, but they needed to instil more of the qualities associated with being Brazilian—fun and colourfulness, and even a bit of an irreverent attitude (see Figure 4.20). So new colours and improved styling were backed up by an extensive advertising campaign. The line of the campaign was 'Havaianas—everyone wears them' and featured famous Brazilians such as actress Malu Mader, the world champion football player Bebeto, basketball player Hortencia, and model and actress Luana Piovani. Today 30 million pairs are exported annually to 80 markets and they are worn everywhere, not just on the beach. They are still cheap, but not as cheap as they used to be—at least three to four times their original price. As the shoes were taken up by opinion leaders and stars such as Jennifer Aniston and surf champion Kelly Slater, it became socially acceptable to wear them in an ever wider variety of circumstances. In other words, they were no longer just beachwear. They even appeared on the runway during a John Paul Gaultier show and in the gift bags received by actors at the 2003 Oscars Ceremony.

Figure 4.20   Havaianas as a symbol of Brazilian lifestyle

Source: Image courtesy of Havaianas.

The brand hasn't stood still either; it has developed a range of flipflops, including exclusive ones studded with Swarovski crystals, and it caters for all age ranges including babies. Havaianas Slim were introduced with thinner straps to please the more feminine of their customers. Now Havaianas are extending their brand and their strategy. If you go on the Havaianas website you will see what other products you can buy, such as bags and boots. They opened a concept store designed by one of Brazil's best known architects, Isay Weinfeld, in São Paulo's Rua Osca to extend the Havaianas experience (see Figure 4.21). Here, Havaianas are displayed in market-like stalls, with the lighting carefully managed to give the feel of being outdoors, and you can

Figure 4.21   Havaianas concept store in Sao Paulo
Source: Image courtesy of Havaianas.

customize your sandals in all kinds of ways. The store, a profusion of colour and fun, has become a tourist attraction in its own right. Increasingly Havianas has built its collaborations with artists, designers, and architects, and integrated the resulting products into window displays, point of sale material and even the design of their ads.

Table 4.2 presents some of the associations identified for the brand from market research commissioned by Havaianas.

Cognitive response		Emotional response	
Before 1994	**Today**	**Before 1994**	**Today**
Original associations • Durable • Don't smell (hygiene) • Useful: 'comfort' • Worn by the poor • Good cost_benefit relation • Traditional: just one model • Only five colours	**New associations** • 'Sandal style' • Fashion sandals (more styles and colours) • 100% natural • 100% Brazilian **Maintained associations** • Excellent cost–benefit relation • Accessibility • Comfort • Durability • Hygiene	• Practical • Functional • Protects the feet of the poor at low cost, i.e. poor person's slipper	• Brazilian national identity • Tropical • Beach • Heat • Holidays • Joy and relaxation • Physical and emotional well-being • Comfort • Fashion • Customization • Sexy

Table 4.2   Havaianas brand associations—cognitive and emotional
Source: Adapted from Silva et al. (2010).

Questions

1. Use any learning theories discussed in the chapter to explain the development of the Havaianas brand.

2. Either from your own personal experience with the brand, or from what you have read here and on the Havaianas website, develop an associative network for the brand.

3. Take another popular brand of your choice and list the emotional and cognitive responses you think that the brand produces among consumers who buy it (and if you can, those who don't).

Sources: Anderson et al. (2010): Silva et al. (2010); WARC (2011); Khalpada et al. (nd); havaianas-store. com interbrand.com melissa.com.br/en

References

Anderson, J.R. (1993), *Rules of the mind*, Hillsdale, NJ: Lawrence Erlbaum.

Anderson, S., Nobbs, K., Wigley, S.M., and Larsen, E. (2010), 'Collaborative space: an exploration of the form and function of fashion designer and architect partnerships', *SCAN Journal of Media Arts Culture*, 7, 2 http://eprints.hud.ac.uk/11458/1/WigleyCollaborative.pdf (accessed 1 May 2017).

Bandura, A. (1965), 'Influence of models' reinforcement contingencies on the acquisition of imitative responses', *Journal of Personality and Social Psychology*, 1, 589–95.

Bandura, A. (1969), *Principles of behaviour modification*, New York: Holt, Rinehart and Winston.

Bettman, J.R. (1970), 'Information processing models of consumer behaviour', *Journal of Market Research*, 7, 3, 370–6.

Bitterman, M.E. (2006), 'Classical conditioning since Pavlov', *Review of General Psychology*, 10, 4, 365–6.

Blackwell, R.D., Miniard, P.W., and Engel, J.F. (2006), *Consumer behaviour* (10th edn), Mason, OH: Thomson Higher Education.

Burrell, I. (1997), 'Penguin wins its suit as Puffin gets the crumbs in battle of the biscuits', *The Independent*, 19 March, http://www.independent.co.uk/news/penguin-wins-its-suit-as-puffin-gets-the-crumbs-in-battle-of-the-biscuits-1273690.html (accessed 18 July 2017).

Economist (2003), 'The death of the jingle', http://www.economist.com/node/1570553 (accessed 18 July 2017).

econsultancy.com (2012), http://econsultancy.com/uk/blog/11204-dumb-ways-to-die-smart-ways-to-do-viral (18 July 2017).

Foxall, G.R., Goldsmith, R.E., and Brown, S. (1998), *Consumer psychology for marketing* (2nd edn), London: International Thomson Business Press.

Gewirtz, J.C. and Davis, M. (2000), 'Using Pavolvian higher-order conditioning paradigms to investigate the neural substrates of emotional learning and memory', *Learning and Memory*, 7, 257–66.

Heath, R. (2012), *Seducing the subconscious*, Chichester: Wiley–Blackwell.

Holden, S.J.S. and Vanhuele, M. (1999), 'Know the name, forget the exposure: brand familiarity versus memory of exposure context', *Psychology and Marketing*, 16, 479–96.

interbrand.com, 'What about Brazilian brands', http://www.rankingmarcas.com.br/downloads/2010/what_about_brazilian_brands_english.pdf (accessed 18 July 2017).

Jansson-Boyd, C.V. (2010), *Consumer psychology*, Maidenhead: Open University Press.

Kelly, G.A. (1955), *The psychology of personal constructs*, New York: Norton.

Kerrane, B. and Hogg, M.K. (2013), 'Shared or non-shared? Children's different consumer socialization experiences within the family environment', *European Journal of Marketing*, 47, 3/4, 506–24.

Khalpada, N., Lakhanpal, R., Moreira, L., Singh, J., and Sontakke, Y. (nd), 'Havaianas—international expansion', http://media2.intoday.in/businesstoday/images/Havaianas-International-Expansion-BT-version.pdf (accessed 15 July 2017).

Kroeber-Riel, W. (1986), Die inneren Bilder der Konsumenten: Messung, Verhaltenswirkung, Konsequenzen für das Marketing, *Marketing ZFP*, 8, 81–96.

Krugman, H.E. (1965), 'The impact of television advertising: learning without involvement', *Public Opinion Quarterly*, 29, 349–56.

Lee, A.Y. (2002), 'Effects of implicit memory on memory-based versus stimulus-based brand choice', *Journal of Marketing Research*, 39, 440–54.

MacGregor, J.N. (1987), 'Short-term memory capacity: limitation or optimization?', *Psychological Review*, 94, 107–8.

marketingweek.com (1997), 'Penguin forces Asda redesign', http://www.marketingmagazine.co.uk/article/60455/penguin-forces-asda-redesign (accessed 18 July 2017).

Miceli, G. and Pieters, R. (2010), 'Looking more or less alike: determinants of perceived visual similarity between copycat and leading brands', *Journal of Business Research*, 63, 1121–8.

Miller, G. (1956), 'The magical number seven, plus or minus two: some limits on our capacity for processing information', *Psychological Review*, 63, 81–7.

Mulhern, F. (2009), 'Integrated marketing communications: from media channels to digital connectivity', *Journal of Marketing Communications*, 15, 2/3, 85–101.

Narisetti, R. (1994), 'P&G files suit against its customer about sale of private-label products', *Wall Street Journal*, 8 September, p.A2.

Newell, A. and Simon, H.A. (1972), *Human problem solving*, Englewood Cliffs, NJ: Prentice Hall.

Nunes, J.C. and Drèze, X. (2006), 'The endowed progress effect: how artificial advancement increases effort', *Journal of Consumer Research*, 32, 4, 504–12.

Pieters, R.G.M. and Bijmolt, T.H.A. (1997), 'Consumer memory for television advertising: a field study of duration, serial position, and competition effects', *Journal of Consumer Research*, 23, 362–72.

Pornpitakpan, C. (2012), 'A critical review of classical conditioning effects on consumer behavior', *Australasian Marketing Journal*, 20, 282–96.

Richardson, J.T.E. (1980), *Mental imagery and human memory*, London: Macmillan.

Schacter, D.L. (1996), *Searching for memory*, New York: Perseus Books.

Shapiro, S., Lindsey, C., and Krishnan, H.S. (2006), 'Intentional forgetting as a facilitator for recalling new product attributes', *Journal of Experimental Psychology: Applied*, 12, 251–63.

Silva, S.C., Souza, M.J., and Freyre Filho, F. (2010), 'Understanding the internationalisation process of Havaianas: the important role of brand', *Encontros Científicos: Tourism and Management Studies*, 6, 9.

Skinner, B.F. (1953), *Science and human behavior*, New York: Free Press.

theinspirationroom.com (2012), http://theinspirationroom.com/daily/2012/metro-dumb-ways-to-die/ (accessed 18 July 2017).

Till, B.D. and Busler, M. (2000), 'The match-up hypothesis: physical attractiveness, expertise, and the role of fit on brand attitude, purchase intent and brand beliefs', *Journal of Advertising*, 29, 1–13.

Till, B.D. and Priluck, R.L (2000), 'Stimulus generalization in classical conditioning: an initial investigation and extension', *Psychology and Marketing*, 17, 1, 55–72.

Till, B.D., Stanley, S.M., and Priluck, R. (2008), 'Classical conditioning and celebrity endorsers: an examination of belongingness and resistance to extinction', *Psychology and Marketing*, 25, 2, 179–96.

Unnava, H.R. and Burnkrant, R.E. (1991), 'An imagery-processing view of the role of pictures in print advertisement', *Journal of Marketing Research*, 28, May, 226–231.

Vanhuele, M., Laurent, G., and Drèze, X. (2006), 'Consumers' immediate memory for prices', *Journal of Consumer Research*, 33, 2, 163–72.

Völckner, F and Sattler, H. (2007), 'Empirical generalizability of consumer evaluations of brand extensions', *International Journal of Research in Marketing*, 24, 2, 149–62.

WARC (2011), 'Sao Paulo Alpargatas: Havaianas—identity, Cannes Creative Lions', São Paulo: Creative Effectiveness Awards.

Warlop, L. and Alba, J.W. (2004), 'Sincere flattery: trade-dress imitation and consumer choice', *Journal of Consumer Psychology*, 14, 1/2, 21–7.

Wildschut, T., Sedikides, C., Arndt, J., and Rotledge, C. (2006), 'Nostalgia: content, triggers, functions', *Journal of Personality and Social Psychology*, 91, 975–93.

Zauberman, G., Ratner, R.K., and Kim, B.K. (2008), 'Memories as asset: strategic memory protection in choice over time', *Journal of Consumer Research*, 35, February, 715–28.

5

PERCEPTUAL PROCESSES

Introduction

Imagine that you are in a car, driving down a busy road into the city. On either side of the road are billboards and shops with signs above them and posters in their windows. There are bus shelters with more advertising displayed on their sides; you pass taxis and buses, all with stickers advertising local businesses. You may be listening to a commercial radio station while you drive. It is not possible for you to pay attention to this vast array of stimuli; you would not want to and indeed it would not be safe to do so. The way in which stimuli are perceived, attended to, and interpreted is vital for our understanding of consumer behaviour. How and whether we notice a stimulus is dependent on our perception. Perception is closely bound up with the nature of the stimulus itself, the environment in which it is placed, and our ability and willingness to perceive the stimuli. We have to make choices about which perceptual stimuli we will attend to. Not only can perception be limited, but it is also highly subjective; our own situation, past experiences, and preferences all affect how we perceive things. Marketers need to ensure that their messages are not only perceived, but attended to and interpreted by consumers in the way that they wish them to be. An understanding of the perceptual process is integral to success in this, and ultimately an effective marketing campaign. In this chapter, we begin by taking a close look at the perceptual process, focusing on the mechanisms of exposure, attention, and interpretation and how they are used in marketing. We then move on to some of the areas of marketing associated with perceptual theory, including perceptual mapping, perceived risk, semiotics, and price perceptions.

LEARNING OBJECTIVES

Having read this chapter, you will be able to:

1. Define the **perceptual process** and discuss the stages in detail.

2. Describe and analyse the mechanisms underlying **exposure** and how this is used in marketing.

3. Recognize the **nature and role that sensory receptors** play in the perceptual process.

4. Understand how consumers pay **attention** to sensory stimuli.

5. Demonstrate an understanding of how **interpretation** of stimuli occurs, and appreciate how **gestalt psychology** is used in marketing.

6. Describe some of the ways that marketing uses this understanding of perception, such as **perceptual mapping, perceived risk, repositioning, price perception, and semiotics**.

The perceptual process

Perception *is the process through which information in the form of stimuli in the environment is selected, organized, and interpreted through the sense organs.* The process by which we perceive is illustrated in Figure 5.1, and forms the basis for the structure of this chapter.

Exposure

This sequence of steps begins with exposure to stimuli—the visual effects, smells, or sounds we hear in marketplace encounters.

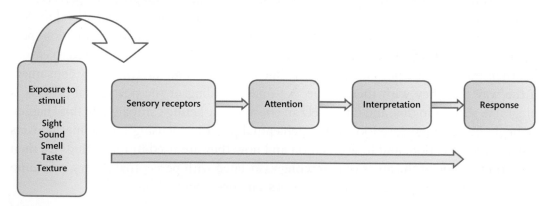

Figure 5.1   The perceptual process

Exposure is about *ensuring that the stimulus is in the appropriate place for consumers to have access to it*. At this stage stimuli are only analysed for their simple physical properties, with little information conveyed. Successful exposure can depend on many things. Siemon Scamell-Katz of TNS Magasin (an international shopper strategy consultancy) comments on the difficulties companies face when trying to ensure that their brand receives successful exposure when placed in visually noisy places such as supermarkets. He says that we can only process about five pieces of information at once, and this becomes particularly difficult when we are in an environment with over 20,000 products, each containing a number of different visual elements. One experiment, conducted by TNS Magasin to examine exposure, placed various products in unfamiliar shelves around the supermarket; for example, lager was located in the cereal aisle and chocolate bars were shelved among the cat foods. When asked, customers had not noticed the out-of-context products because they were effectively blind to what they did not expect to see.

Exposure is linked to physical positioning, and this can be managed by marketing and advertising. The Spanish organization ANAR (which deals with child abuse) developed an outdoor advertisement using lenticular print technology, a technique which gives the illusion of depth and can change or move as it is viewed from different angles. ANAR used this technology to embed a message that could only be read by people under a height of 1.35 metres (i.e. mainly children). They wanted to communicate a message to children who were potential victims of abuse, but without their adult aggressors viewing the message. Adults saw an image of an unharmed child with the message '*Sometimes child abuse is only visible to the child suffering it*'. However, those under the height of 1.35 metres saw the same child with cuts and bruises with the caption '*If somebody hurts you, phone us and we'll help*'.

Consumers can also limit their own exposure to stimuli, a form of **selective exposure** which is *the active seeking and avoidance of stimuli*. During a commercial break, viewers may switch to another channel, leave the room before their TV programme resumes, or, with time delay recording, fast forward through the advertisements. Similarly, consumers can subscribe to agencies which ensure that they do not receive unsolicited mail, advertising, or telemarketing. Children are particularly susceptible to exposure to products and messages that parents may not want them to see. Increasingly, governments are looking to limit the times when advertising for products high in sugar, salt, and fat may be advertised to children, and bodies such as Ofcom in the UK, the Australian Broadcasting Authority, and the Federal Communications Commission in the USA are looking to regulate internet content deemed inappropriate for children. In the UK, a ban on the advertising of food or drink high in fat, salt, or sugar (HFSS) across all non-broadcast media targeted at under-16s was introduced in July 2017 (Committee of Advertising Practice, https://www.cap.org.uk).

Selective exposure may also involve perceptual vigilance and perceptual defence. **Perceptual vigilance** *is when a consumer consciously or unconsciously filters stimuli for relevance*. Perceptual vigilance will depend on the person, their situation, and the nature of

Figure 5.2   Different approaches to cut through perceptual defence   *Source*: Image courtesy of NSPCC.

the stimulus. People who do not drive are unlikely to be interested in car advertisements; someone about to get married may be very interested in advertisements for dresses and venues, but once married the relevance of these products immediately diminishes.

   Perceptual defence *is when a consumer inhibits perception of potentially threatening or unpleasant stimuli.* For example, smokers may avoid the government health warnings on packs of cigarettes. One of the most common areas where people activate perceptual defence is charity advertising, largely because they feel fatigued at seeing unpleasant images or try to avoid them because they cannot or are unwilling to contribute to the charity. In response, charities have looked to break through this defence with ever more shocking images or use a juxtaposition of words and pictures to create impact, such as in the advertisement for the NSPCC (Figure 5.2) which uses more up-to-date and familiar imagery of young people using a mobile phone and social media. Research has shown that shocking ads do work, but often by eliciting responses of surprise, interest, and compassion (Cockrill and Parsonage, 2016).

Sensation and the perceptual process

We receive sensations through our sensory receptors—eyes, ears, nose, mouth, and skin—but it is the process by which we select, attend to, organize, and interpret these sensations that is most important to the marketer (see Research Insight 5.1). We may have preferences for certain colours or tastes, or we may associate particular smells with happy or sad moments in our past. Lindstrom (2008) suggests that the smell of Johnson & Johnson's baby powder has a similar impact on people the world over. As well as smell, there are numerous studies on the effects of colour. Van Doorn et al. (2014) demonstrated how the colour of a mug can influence how consumers rate the hot beverage it contains; coffee served in white mug is rated as less sweet than coffee served in a blue or transparent mug.

RESEARCH INSIGHT 5.1

Simons, D.J. and Chabris, C.F. (1999), 'Gorillas in our midst: sustained inattentional blindness for dynamic events', *Perception*, 28, 1059–74

Simons and Chabris (1999) conducted an experiment which appears to show that in many situations we do not even perceive objects that are directly in front of us—this is known as inattentional blindness. In their experiment a woman dressed as a gorilla passed in front of a group playing basketball. Observers had been asked to note the number of passes of the ball and many failed to see the gorilla. Previous research has shown that conscious perception requires attention, and that when attention is fixed on another object or, as in this case, a task intentional blindness may occur.

 Access the online resources to read the abstract and access the full paper.

In the retail context, retailers want to know if the colours they use in their stores influence consumer purchases. Babin et al. (2003) found that consumers reacted most favourably to shop interiors painted in cool colours; consumers rated and expressed relatively greater shopping intentions in a blue interior than in an orange one. However, it is clear that such preferences are very subtle, as Babin et al.'s research also showed that when colour is combined with different lighting intensities preferences can change; for example, the reaction to an orange store interior is improved when it is combined with soft lighting. Bellizzi et al. (1983) suggested that the colour red can speed up behaviour and so may be useful in a fast food restaurant environment. Even online shopping can be influenced by differences in sensory stimuli, such as colour, borders, type style, and sound, and it has been found that the atmospherics of an online environment can influence the pleasure experienced by shoppers (Eroglu et al., 2003).

Sight

Levine (2000) suggests that sight, or visual attention, accounts for about 80 per cent of human perception. Given this central role in our perception it is not surprising that colours have deep-rooted cultural meanings. In many Western countries, it is assumed that a baby dressed in blue is a boy, while girls are associated with pink clothing, an interpretation of these colours that emerged around the 1940s (Paoletti, 2012). Colours can also provoke or enhance various emotions, and psychologists have attempted to map out the effect of colours on our feelings. Red is generally understood to be the colour of passion, excitement, and energy, and is often used by companies wishing to express these qualities through their brand. The Virgin group logo conveys energy and confidence, while the trademarked red sole of Christian Louboutin shoes is a distinctive aspect of that brand, capturing its energy and glamour. In China, the colour red has traditionally symbolized health and wealth, and is associated with weddings and special occasions—bridal gowns are traditionally red, and newly married couples receive gifts of money in red packages. There is a strong cultural aspect to how colours are perceived, and it is important for companies operating in international contexts to be aware of this.

In addition, we often relate certain colours to certain roles in society, mainly because of the associations we make between colours and attributes. Black or dark blue is worn by the police, and white by health practitioners. Dark colours may establish authority, while the white coats worn by pharmacists, doctors, or nurses often represent hygiene and cleanliness. The association of white with purity has been used by the skincare brand Clinique. Clinique's branding of their 'medical' skincare range uses simple crisp white packaging with pale green text—the aim of which is to emulate the cleanliness and simplicity of the product inside (see Figure 5.3). Green and white is also the colour palate used by the Simple skincare brand whose unique selling point is the lack of perfume and colour for those with sensitive skin.

But white, like most other colours, has a cultural significance and mistakes are easily made. United Airlines had to remove the white carnations their assistants had been given to wear on Pacific routes as white is strongly associated with death and mourning in that region (Aslam, 2006). Colours become associated with brands and even movements. Since the early 1990s, pink has become associated with breast cancer awareness campaigns worldwide. Brands often distinguish themselves by differences in colour—Pepsi uses the colour blue which distinguishes it from Coca-Cola's red (Labrecque and Milne, 2012).

Figure 5.3　Clinique skincare product

Source: iStock.com/ AnthonyRosenberg.

Another aspect of sight relates to our expectations in relation to the shape of the products being consumed. Experimental research by Nestlé (Lenfant et al., 2013) has shown how the shape of dark chocolate pieces can impact on how the chocolate is regarded in terms of both texture and flavour perceptions. Round and rectangular chocolate shapes were rated highest in terms of texture, whereas wing-shaped chocolates were perceived as most flavourful. Some of the issues around how consumers are influenced by colour in their choices are explored in Research Insight 5.2.

RESEARCH INSIGHT 5.2

Soars, B. (2003), 'What every retailer should know about the way into the shopper's head', *International Journal of Retail Distribution and Management*, 31, 12, 628–37.

From a range of research studies Soars (2003) identifies the likely effects of different colours. These include yellow being the colour that the human eye normally notices, while red is often used to emphasize masculinity and play down femininity.

 Access the online resources to read the abstract and access the full paper.

Figure 5.4   Using size to get attention   *Source*: Image supplied by The Advertising Archives.

Visually, the size and shape of the object and the environment in which it is placed are also important. While we may be attracted by something that is large or out of the ordinary, small things can also focus our attention. The Volkswagen Beetle, known for being a small car, used this to its advantage in its advertising (Figure 5.4) by making smallness a virtue and using a tiny picture of the VW against a stark background, accompanied by lines such as 'Think small' and 'It makes your house look bigger'. Here, it is not only the smallness that attracts our attention but also the environment in which the object is placed.

Companies also have to ensure that their product or advertisement is seen in the 'right' environment (see Consumer Insight 5.1). Luxury brand owners will prefer their brands to be stocked in Harrods in London or Takashimaya in Singapore because the environment of the store rubs off on the brand. Similarly, advertisers take care where to place their advertisements in TV schedules, aiming to ensure a fit between the brand and the target audience's viewing interests. In-game advertising features in many popular video and PC games, and the perceptual fit between the brand being advertised and the target audience is important for the success of the campaign. An example is the case of Burger King featuring in the game Pro Evolution Soccer 2013 (Hang and Nairn, 2016).

CONSUMER INSIGHT 5.1

Spotting your favourite coffee shop

How we consume our coffee around the world varies hugely, but in major cities coffee shop chains, with their distinctive branding, are a familiar sight. How do they compete on the high street? One way is to make sure that we perceive, and pay attention to, the brand with which we are familiar (see Figure 5.5). When we spot the colour and logo of a familiar brand, be it in Melbourne or Stockholm, we know what to expect and may feel safe and comfortable. Therefore consistency and distinctiveness in the visual presentation, colour, and style are critical.

Figure 5.5   A famous coffee shop   *Source*: © iStock.com/ilbusca.

An interesting trend is towards ensuring that the store design retains the brand distinctiveness, but also speaks to the local market. Starbucks famously tries to have an individualized design aspect for each of its stores, while retaining the familiar Starbucks branding (Wilson, 2014). So, for example, Starbucks has embarked on updating and revamping its London stores to reflect the variations in its markets, with the St John's Wood store having low-key branding in dark colours, while the Westfield Stratford shop uses more prominent imagery of the Starbucks branding (Handley, 2013). Similarly, Costa Coffee has reported how it adjusted its in-store design in Shanghai to relate to the younger consumers using it compared with the UK market (Mortimer, 2011)

Questions

1.   Consider two famous coffee shop logos. What is distinctive about their visual presentation?

2.   Read the paper summarized in Research Insight 5.2. Choose another high street brand and, using the colour analysis developed in this paper, try to assess what feeling they are trying to communicate to their customers.

Sources: Mortimer (2011); Handley (2013); Wilson (2014).

 Access the online resources and follow the web links to learn more about this topic.

Sound

A feature of modern life is that we are bombarded with sound as we go about our daily lives, a key source being the music we hear in shops and restaurants. Just as with colour, the music played is designed to enhance or change people's mood to encourage purchase. One early study (Millman, 1982) found that shoppers spent 38 per cent more time in a grocery store when slow music was played compared with fast music. Lantos and Craton (2012) identify a range of factors that impact a consumer's response to music used in advertising, including their personality, social class, culture, and mood state when listening to the music. Music creates emotion, and some people may respond more to music that creates a sad response (Schellenberg et al., 2008; Eerola et al., 2016). Lantos and Cranton (2012) discuss how reactions to music are complex, such that a disliked genre of music may be appreciated if it is particularly upbeat and catchy. In 2012, South Korean musician PSY released 'Gangnam Style', an upbeat catchy song, with a distinctive dance featured in the accompanying video. The song and video enjoyed worldwide popularity, and by mid-2017 had over 2.94 billion views on YouTube. Both the music and the dance moves have been taken up in a range of commercial contexts. For example, PSY appears, dancing to 'Gangnam Style', in the advertisement for Wonderful Pistachios. In the advertisement for E-Lites, a company producing electronic cigarettes, a baby's first steps are the 'Gangnam Style' dance (see Figure 5.6).

Smell

Consumers generally expect certain products to have particular fragrances. Household cleaning products often have a lemony odour, while wood polish may smell of lavender. Milotic (2006) identifies the most commonly used terms to describe odours were floral,

Figure 5.6   Screenshot from the E-Lites commercial showing a baby dancing to 'Gangnam Style'
Source: Image courtesy of Zandera Ltd.

herbal, fruity, sweet, green, woody, spicy, animal, and citrus. Smells can elicit emotions in people, particularly in relation to memory, and so certain smells can evoke nostalgic thoughts and memories. Of all the senses, smell is considered to be most closely linked to emotion because the olfactory bulb in the brain detects smells and relates them to the limbic system which connects emotion and memory (Milotic, 2006). Fragrances can also be stimulating or relaxing. We spoke to Category Director of Dettol, Frederique Hull, to understand how the senses, and especially smell, play an important part in understanding how consumers perceive different products (see Practitioner Insight 5).

Consumers also categorize pleasant and unpleasant smells. Based on our cultural backgrounds, we come to regard some smells as acceptable and others as not. We may mask body odour by using deodorants, and the smell of our homes by using air fresheners. Supermarkets may ensure that the smell of freshly baked bread is pumped through the store, but are equally concerned to minimize and remove the smells from the fish counter. The advertisements for Febreze build directly on this point, showing how use of this product masks the other smells assumed to 'stick' to our clothes.

Some Asian bank brands are embracing the ideas around engaging customers' senses as a way of enhancing their service interaction. Standard Chartered in Hong Kong has created a special fragrance for its showcase Lan Kwai Fong branch. The fragrance is used to convey an upmarket, high quality, and warm feel for its customers, thus enhancing their experience in the branch and ultimately developing greater brand loyalty (Faure-Field, 2013). Similarly, Lloyds Bank in South London makes use of the fragrance of white tea and thyme to make customers feel welcome in the bank (Milligan, 2016).

PRACTITIONER INSIGHT 5

Frederique Hull, Category Director of Dettol, Reckitt Benkiser

Consumers relate to hygiene and germ awareness in different ways, and this is very noticeable when you look across countries. In the USA consumers are typically very concerned and use a lot of anti-bacterial products. In Russia there is generally a lower awareness of germs, whereas in Germany while people are aware, they have a lower concern and a feeling that the immune system needs to develop to cope with germs. In some developing countries there may even be confusion as to what germs are and where they are to be found. For example, in some countries people think that insects and dust contain germs or that they grow on your skin, so understanding how consumers perceive germs and hygiene is very important to how products are developed and marketed.

One also has to consider the role that disinfectant products play in people's lives. Most of the time people are not too worried about germs; they are busy looking after their family and home, and what they would prefer is a product that cleans and kills germs so they don't have to bother with an extra step in the whole cleaning process. But when there is a health scare such as A/H1N1 (swine flu), sales increase rapidly. There are also certain times when people want to use a disinfectant such as Dettol. Parents are extra vigilant when their children are sick, and people often do an extra clean and disinfect when they move into a new house.

Fragrance and texture are very important sensory stimuli in the choice of hygiene products. For Dettol antiseptic liquid, the initial perception needs to be one of a strong hospital-like smell. This gives consumers confidence and is the anchor of efficacy for the brand. The packaging also supports this; it is understated and the clear brown liquid says 'I am effective'. On the other hand, our soap products should not have a texture and fragrance that reminds someone of a hospital theatre but they still need to signal the efficacy of the brand, so we have different fragrances, but ones in keeping with the brand's attributes. Therefore it is important to get the right balance in terms of the texture and fragrance which is congruent with the product. A really unusual fragrance, such as pineapple, would create a completely different association. In the kitchen we know that lemon is a popular fragrance as people associate lemon with being able to cut through grease, but another fragrance such as vanilla might be perceived as interfering with the smell of the food and has connotations of stickiness as it is often associated with sweet things. Packaging is also very important when consumers choose products. We know from focus group research that an opaque pack or one with a sleeve is always considered to be a more effective cleaning product than one that is presented in a clear container. Therefore a product such as our Power and Pure multipurpose kitchen spray, which is designed to tackle tough kitchen cleaning tasks, is presented in an opaque package.

Touch and texture

Touch is an important, but underrated, sense. Underhill (2009) says that more than ever people want to touch the things that they are going to buy, and yet this raises questions about the role of touch in online environments (see Consumer Insight 5.2). Many products are marketed on the basis of texture. The strapline for Galaxy chocolate—'Why have cotton when you can have silk'—emphasizes the positioning of Galaxy as a distinctively smooth-textured chocolate. Fabric conditioner is a product that was developed purely to improve the texture and feel of clothes after they have been washed; a similar job is achieved with hair conditioner. Both are products that were not readily available 50 years ago but are innovations designed to match consumers' preferences for smooth or soft textures. Preferences for texture vary greatly, giving companies a good opportunity to market food items such as juice or yoghurt as either 'smooth' or 'with bits', thus matching differences in consumer tastes. Consumer Insight 5.2 further explores issues of consumer preferences in texture.

CONSUMER INSIGHT 5.2

Are you an NFT (need for touch) consumer?

The word 'haptic' derives from the Greek and refers to the sense of touch. In the marketing context we see it used to mean 'the active seeking and pickup of information by the hands' (Peck and Childers, 2003: 36). Peck and Childers performed a number of experiments to see how people responded to different touch situations. They found that product characteristics, individual differences in people, and the nature of the situation all affected the motivation to obtain haptic product information. They were also interested in the growth of non-touch media and how it might impact on people's shopping motivations. They suggested that eventually there might be a substitute for the sense of touch, although they stated that this was probably the most difficult sense to replicate. They suggested that the internet was going to be particularly successful for marketing products that consumers do not perceive to have material properties, such as books, music, and DVDs, and therefore are not dependent on their haptic properties for sales.

Retail anthropologist Paco Underhill (2009) recognized the importance of the tactile in shopping, which is one of the few opportunities that we have to touch things without inhibition. When goods are sealed or packed away in cabinets we are deprived of this important sensory experience. Others have recognized that senses are interrelated, especially touch and smell (Krishna et al., 2010). Although some would argue that internet and catalogue shopping is restricted by consumers' inability to touch the goods before buying (Peck and Childers, 2003), there are many successful online-only clothing stores such as ASOS (http://www.asos.com), The Outnet (https://www.theoutnet.com), and Figleaves (http://www.figleaves.com). Stores such as these exist throughout the world, for example Coco Fashion, selling Asian and Korean street fashion, and Kira Plastinina in Russia. In addition, there are internet versions of well-known stores such as Gap, TopShop, and Banana Republic. Presenters on TV shopping channels often talk about the feel and touch of the product to convey its texture and weight to prospective customers.

Questions

1. How have online clothing stores managed to overcome the problem of lack of touch on the internet?

2. Imagine you are opening a new clothes shop. How would your knowledge of sensory perception influence how you would design the store?

Sources: Peck and Childers (2003); Underhill (2009); Krishna et al. (2010).

 Access the online resources and follow the web links to learn more.

We learn to expect products to have a certain type of feel or even weight about them. Lindstrom (2008) reported an experiment conducted with Bang & Olufsen remote controls. A hundred participants were given two remote controls, one with aluminium inside and the other without. The participants felt that the lighter control was broken just because it felt lighter than they expected. Even after it was explained to them that the lightweight one was completely functional, they still preferred the heavier one. Evaluations of how some product or brand feels are based on objective evaluations (e.g. how heavy it feels), but in the context of previous experiences and associations with that evaluation (e.g. heavy feels good, light feels broken). This example emphasizes the importance of appreciating the social nature of our interpretation of sensory inputs. Research Insight 5.3 considers an example of the importance of touch sensations in online retail contexts.

RESEARCH INSIGHT 5.3

Overmars, S. and Poels, K. (2015), 'A touching experience: designing for touch sensations in online retail environments', *International Journal of Design*, 9, 3.

In this experimental study, the researchers investigated how different online product presentation formats (static versus interactive interfaces) would lead to different types of emotional, or hedonic, responses from consumers. They found that interactive online interfaces that encouraged stroking gestures led to more positive emotional responses from users. This finding has important implications for web design, since it demonstrates the importance of bringing the online tactile product experience closer to reality for online consumers.

 Access the online resources to read the abstract and access the full paper.

Taste

Taste preferences are highly specific to individuals and cultures. KitKat sells a green tea flavour variant in Japan, which would probably not be popular in European countries. Our taste preferences may also change as we grow older. Importantly, what tastes good to one person may not to others, which is why food product manufacturers ensure that their brands are thoroughly taste-tested before being brought to market. Marmite, the savoury spread brand, made a virtue out of the fact that people appear to be divided on whether they like the taste of the product or not, i.e. they either love it or hate it. In previous advertisements, Marmite actually showed scenes of salespeople chasing possible customers to get them to try the spread even though they clearly did not want to.

For those popular brands which are familiar to us and which we like, it may be difficult for our brains to distinguish the taste from our image of the brand (see section in Chapter 2 on neuromarketing). As Montague (2006) notes, experts in the field know that flavour is actually a composite perception only partly built from the taste (whether it is sweet, sour, or bitter, etc.). Other factors involved in our taste perception include texture, temperature, the way the product is presented, and expectations from our knowledge of the brand and our previous history with it.

There are also ethical issues about the taste of food that we should consider. In contemporary Western cultures, where obesity is a major health issue, food companies are accused by some of creating food products with tastes and textures that make them more appealing—tastes we become addicted to and ultimately crave. Kessler (2010) calls this 'hyperpalatability', which is defined as flavour that further stimulates the appetite, and it is thought that these foods may have an addictive potential because of increased potency due to certain nutrients or additives (Meule, 2015). Foods rich in fat, sugar, and salt are often also combined with textures that are easy to chew to create 'feel good' tastes. Many scientists and commentators are critical of these heavily processed foods, arguing that they are damaging to health and bear more similarity 'to drugs of abuse than to the natural energy resources people consumed historically' (Gearhardt et al., 2011: 140).

Sensory thresholds

We all have limits to how well our senses are able to respond to stimuli. The **absolute threshold** *is the minimum amount of stimulation that can be picked up by any of our senses.* Advertisers have to ensure that their communications can be seen or heard; therefore getting the right level of background music on TV advertisements and the right size of print on posters can be very important for the success of their communication. The **differential threshold** *is the point at which we notice a difference between two stimuli.* If you buy a product that claims that it contains a new and improved formula, can you tell or taste the difference between this and the old version of the brand? Whether or not product changes are communicated to consumers is a concern of marketers. A company may have had to change the ingredients of a product, but may prefer not to communicate the changes to customers as this might involve costs and possibly brand-switching. They may decide to conduct blind taste tests to see if consumers notice the difference in ingredients. Obviously in some cases marketers may want to inform their customers of the difference, especially if the product has been improved as part of a relaunch.

Often small differences in the size or price of a product are not noticed by customers. Referred to as the 'grocery shrink ray', this approach is sometimes used by marketers to reduce the size of products but charge the same amount (Northrup, 2017). It may be such a small difference that most people do not notice that they are getting less product for their money. However, it is becoming a major consumerist cause; the British consumer organization 'Which?' investigated the issue of consumer goods being produced in reduced size packs but with prices remaining the same (Allen, 2012) and concluded that this was an 'underhand way to raise prices'. They called for clearer labelling to indicate packaging changes. In the USA, The Consumerist (comsumerist.com) champions the cause of the consumer and highlights what it considers to be inappropriate market behaviour. It regularly highlights brands that have suffered from the grocery shrink ray, such as Aussie, a brand of hair care products made by Procter & Gamble, whose bottle redesign led to a reduction from 33.8 to 29.2 fluid ounces.

In perceptual terms, the **just noticeable difference (JND)** *is the minimum change in a stimulus to be noticed by the majority of people.* The nineteenth-century experimental psychologist Ernst Weber identified that the size of the just noticeable difference threshold appeared

Figure 5.7   How chocolate wrappers have changed

Source: Image Courtesy of Robert Opie and The Museum of Brands.

to be related in a law-like way to the magnitude of the initial stimulus. **Weber's law** tells us that *the stronger the initial stimulus, the more difference would be required for the change to be noticed*. In marketing, Weber's law has mostly been applied to the small changes in the design of packaging one sees over time, which are difficult for most consumers to notice individually. Take a look at the brands of sweets and chocolates shown in Figure 5.7 from the Museum of Brands and Packaging and see which wrappers look familiar. You will notice that some no longer exist, but there will be others that you recognize for their distinctiveness and similarity to the brands you see on the shelves today, such as Rolo, Bounty, Bournville, and Fry's Turkish Delight.

Crucially, Weber's law is also very important for pricing as it determines the levels of price differences that consumers will notice and respond to. When shopping for groceries we are typically happy if we find a promotion or item on sale that has 50p or 50 cents off. However, if we visited a major designer shop during sales time, a reduction of 50p would seem ludicrous and inappropriate in that context. This is because the initial stimulus of the much higher price has to be recognized by a similarly large change in the sale price. This is why promotions are often represented in terms of percentages.

Adaptation

Adaptation *is the extent to which people's awareness of a stimulus diminishes over a period of time.* Schwarz (2004) reported that in 1973 only 13 per cent of Americans thought that air-conditioning in cars was necessary, whereas in 2004 this figure was 41 per cent and today air-conditioning in cars is a norm in the USA. When we become accustomed to something, it becomes the norm. Sensory adaptation is when our sensory receptors diminish in sensitivity, enabling the body to function in unfamiliar situations by filtering out the initial strength of the stimulus. Four areas where sensory adaptation is important are sight, touch, smell, and sound. In consumer behaviour, marketers need to be aware that what was once unusual will gradually become unremarkable. This is important for developing the creative content of advertisements and for businesses to consider when they need to try something different to overcome adaptation.

Attention

Attention *is the mental activity given to a stimulus.* One of the most important aspects of attention is that it is selective. We are exposed to such a large amount and variety of marketing stimuli that we have to select what we pay attention to. Pieters and Wedel (2007) found that attention varied depending on the different processing goals that consumers had. For example, in situations where the consumer is trying to learn about the brand (brand evaluation), greater attention is paid to the textual information associated with the brand and less to the visuals. This is relevant to those contexts where a consumer is buying a product for the first time. They are likely to undertake a brand-evaluation process, whereby attention is paid to the detail of what is said about the brand on the packet, but with brand familiarity this becomes less important for future purchases.

We can also divide our attention between different activities, which means that we may be looking at content and advertisements on multiple screens (e.g. laptops, tablets, TV, smartphones) almost simultaneously. Increasing access to media in the twenty-first century has led to a rapid rise in the prevalence of polychromic or media multitasking (simultaneous use of multiple media streams) (Uncapher et al., 2016). It is important for marketers to try to understand how consumers allocate their attention over multiple screens. Given that there are more TV channels than ever before and more types of media, marketers increasingly have to deal with advertising clutter. Recent research (Angell et al., 2016) has shown that when the multitasking is congruent, i.e. the tasks being undertaken are somehow related (e.g. watching a soccer game on TV, and tweeting about the same soccer game), and when the secondary activity entails a higher level of social interaction (e.g. sending tweets or texts), then ad recall and recognition increases. There are various estimates of the thousands of promotional messages that target us each day, but what is evident is that companies are finding increasingly innovative ways of cutting through this clutter (see Consumer Insight 5.3).

CONSUMER INSIGHT 5.3

Gaining and retaining attention through social media

In 2003, Old Spice introduced body wash for men and amassed millions of fans with a campaign that targeted men and women, promoting what might happen if Old Spice body wash was used. The success was largely due to the presence, style, and charisma of American actor Isaiah Mustafa, also known in the campaign as 'The Man Your Man Could Smell Like'.

In 2011 the company wanted to increase the fan base on YouTube, Facebook, and Twitter. It created an interactive experience where 'The Man Your Man Could Smell Like' responded directly to his fans on the internet, answering questions or making suggestions related to questions that they had about Old Spice, i.e. highly personalized messages to fans.

How did Old Spice do this? The company began the campaign using YouTube, since it allowed user comments to be posted and had a wide existing fanbase for Old Spice. Using a program that identified mentions of Old Spice from a range of social networking sites, the company wrote and produced nearly 200 personalized videos. They began by hitting mainstream celebrities, influencers, and fans of Old Spice, but about 70 per cent were created in response to the man or woman in the street. On Twitter, Old Spice gave consumers a timeline to watch the campaign unfold and allowed additional questions to 'The Man Your Man Could Smell Like'. The company also posted responses on Old Spice's Facebook page for increased word of mouth. Thus the concept of a brand message swiftly became a brand conversation across platforms and media. On the first day of the campaign there were 5.9 million YouTube views and by the end of the week this had increased to 40 million. Twitter followers increased by 2700 per cent. Over three days 'The Man Your Man Could Smell Like' offered President Obama tips on how to court a lady, gave his support to libraries, and introduced a new catchphrase to the world.

Nobel (2013) reports on research from Harvard Business School which identifies successful viral advertising as having four steps:

- attracting viewers' attention

- retaining their attention

- getting viewers to share what they have seen with others

- persuading viewers.

In the case of Old Spice the key aspect is that the viewer's attention is grabbed and retained by the fact that the attention is actually focused on them—the Old Spice man is speaking directly to you!

Questions

1. Think of some examples of social media advertising that have gained and retained your attention. How have they done it?

2. Many believe that the success of social media advertising is sharing with others. What makes you want to share an advertisement with your friends? Think about how you would use this to market a product of your own.

Sources: Fernandez (2011); WARC (2011); Nobel (2013).

 Access the online resources and follow the web links to learn more.

Getting the consumer's attention

To gain consumers' attention in a cluttered environment companies have to think of novel, different, and relevant ways to get noticed. Movement can be used to grab people's attention, particularly when they are not expecting it. While we expect movement in a TV or cinema advertisement, we are not expecting it in a magazine, billboard poster, or sign. The neon cowboy sign in Las Vegas uses movement to capture attention (see Figure 5.8). Digital displays that change every so often use movement to grab our attention; other billboards may create a feeling of movement—for example, showing a bottle being poured. Such approaches disrupt our expectations of the world around us, expectations that arc based on schemas, beliefs, and feelings that we build up over time and through learning about

Figure 5.8   Neon cowboy sign in Fremont Street, Las Vegas   *Source*: © iStock.com/slearmonth2.

our environment. Movement breaks through to grab our attention even when we were not previously looking at the advertisement.

Schemas *are cognitive frameworks that are used to organize and interpret information.* Schemas help us to organize our world and interpret stimuli easily. We take shortcuts to interpret similar things because we have had experience of them before. So if we travel to Asia and are offered tea in a cup without handles we can still interpret it as an object for containing liquid, as it is similar enough to the schema of a teacup that we are used to.

Another technique to cut through clutter is to place something in an unusual or unlikely setting. Berns et al. (1997: 1272) express **novelty** as a *'deviation from the expected likelihood of an event on the basis of both previous information and internal estimates of conditional probabilities'.* Something can be novel because the stimulus has not been seen before or because it is in an unusual context. They found that certain parts of the brain respond to novel stimuli often without any conscious awareness. Contrast can also be used to gain people's attention, such as the use of black and white advertisements in a magazine or on television where we are expecting to see colour.

Sound can also be used as a contrast, and advertisers often use a combination of sound and visually arresting images to aid recall. The British financial services comparison website GoCompare used the strong visual image of a caricatured opera singer (with comic-like hair and corkscrew moustache in full evening dress) singing the benefits of the company, in opera style, to prospective customers. Sex can also attract attention, although there are issues around ensuring the viewers' attention is not focused on the sexual content over the brand. Sex can appear in many guises, and a recent TV campaign by Marks & Spencer was described as 'food porn' (Brownsell, 2010) because of the way the food was temptingly shown, and the use of a soft and sultry female voice-over and music, all designed to seduce the viewer. Emotion can also attract the consumer's attention. Particular images or sounds resonate with our emotions. The John Lewis Christmas advertisements are particularly successful in depicting scenarios that form deep emotional resonance with customers through the use of character, story, and music, and are an eagerly awaited cultural event each year. The 2017 campaign (Figure 5.9), which followed the story of a young boy and his friendship with an imaginary monster, attracted a great deal of media attention and analysis in the run-up to Christmas 2017.

The use of shock to gain attention

The use of shock to gain attention is perhaps the most interesting and controversial way in which advertisers gain awareness, but it can be fraught with danger since businesses have to ensure that they do not alienate existing and potential customers. Experiments have shown that shock advertising can increase attention and memory and influence behaviour in appropriate contexts (Dahl et al., 2003). One of the most famous businesses to use shocking images regularly in its advertising campaigns is Benetton. In the 1980s and

Figure 5.9 The John Lewis Christmas advert 2017: 'Moz the Monster'   *Source*: Image courtesy of John Lewis.

1990s, Benetton provoked controversy with advertisements showing a nun kissing a priest, a dying AIDS victim, and a child soldier holding a human bone. One of the most disliked images was of a newborn baby still covered in blood. The images provoked varying responses, particularly in different cultures. The nun kissing the priest was condemned in many Catholic countries, while the UK seemed to take a particular dislike to the newborn baby. Despite this, many of the advertisements received awards. Today Benetton advertisements still court controversy. They recently produced an advertisement in their so-called 'Unhate' campaign showing Pope Benedict XVI kissing Ahmed el-Tayeb, a senior Egyptian imam. The Vatican threatened to take legal action unless the advertisement was removed. Benetton's advertisements gain attention largely because they are challenging our expectations.

There are numerous images and messages that shock. These can be sexual, involve age or religion, or just be unusual behaviour. What people find shocking in advertisements is often culturally defined. In 2005, one of the TV advertisements that provoked the most complaints in the UK was for KFC, showing women in a call centre speaking with their mouths full. Of the 1,671 complainants to the Advertising Standards Authority (www.asa.org), many were particularly concerned about the example it might be setting children in terms of bad table manners.

Shocking advertisements can backfire on the company. A Brazilian advertisement for the World Wildlife Fund brought strong condemnation for the line 'the tsunami killed 100 times more people than 9/11' and showing a host of airplanes flying into New York. In a somewhat different example, the Italian firm Dolce & Gabbana had to remove an advertisement that showed a man towering over a woman, with other men in the background, because of its aggressive sexual implications.

Interpretation

Once people have attended to a stimulus, whether it is an advertisement or a new brand on the supermarket shelf, they may allocate meaning to it. Perception is highly subjective, and two people seeing the same advertisement or event may visualize and interpret it quite differently. Our interpretation may depend on our existing schemas, and in some cases interpretation may be primed by the use of certain images or colours already associated with the brand. This might be the case when we see the colour purple and think of Cadbury's Dairy Milk chocolate, or the green of the Starbuck's logo. Interpretation will also depend on the personal relevance of the stimulus and our particular preferences. In three experimental studies, Chernev (2001) found that participants regularly interpreted information that supported their existing established preferences more than information that countered their beliefs. Finally, companies have to bear in mind that even when an advertisement or the packaging on a brand is powerful in accosting the senses and grabbing attention, if it is for a product category that the customer is not interested in, the likelihood of personal relevance is limited and therefore there is no motivation to interpret the message.

Interpretation and organization: Gestalt psychology

The stimuli in our environment are not perceived separately. Perception in practice is largely about putting meanings to the things we see around us, and therefore we use our memory and experience to interpret the images we see. This often means that we add something to ensure completeness, as naturally we want to make sense of our environment. Gestalt psychology explains much of how the human brain looks for completeness. The meaning of **Gestalt** is roughly 'whole' but above all it refers to *how people look for meaning and patterns in the stimuli in the environment*. The implications of Gestalt for consumer behaviour were developed by a group of German psychologists in the late 1800s and early 1900s, who examined how people interpreted the whole above individual features. Above all they were interested in how people organized stimuli into shapes and patterns for completeness and order. A number of principles which reflect how people organize their environment have been derived from Gestalt psychology.

Principle of closure

Closure *is the tendency for people to fill in the 'missing' elements of an incomplete picture.* When we see an incomplete stimulus there is a tension, which is released when we complete it. Figure 5.10 shows two triangles which are incomplete, but we can readily make them out.

Advertisers involve the consumer and potentially promote retention using the principle of closure. Well-known lyrics may be used with some words missing or slogans will be incomplete, encouraging the consumer to complete them mentally. Visual closure may be successful with either words or images. A classic example using words was a Christmas campaign for J&B whiskey where the letters J and B were left out of the words Jingle Bells. A more recent example can be seen in the Audi campaign shown in Figure 5.11.

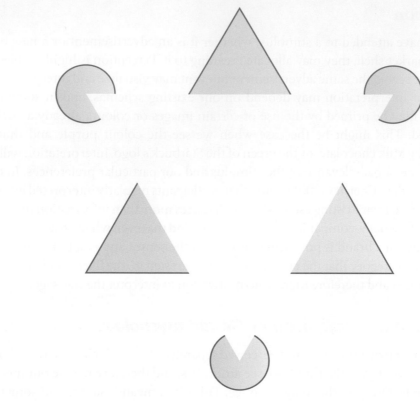

Figure 5.10   The principle of closure

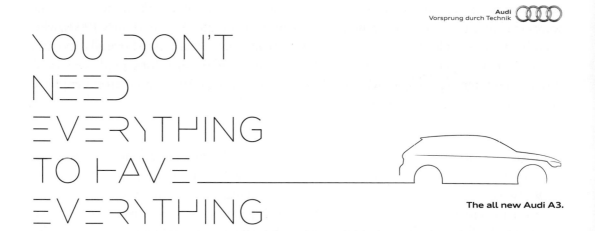

Figure 5.11   This Audi advertisement provides a good example of the principle of closure

Source: Image printed with permission of Audi and courtesy of Bartle Bogle Hegarty (www.bartleboglehegarty.com).

The principle of similarity

Humans naturally group objects of similar physical similarity together. **Similarity** *refers to how things that are similar to one another are perceived to be more related to each other than those that are dissimilar.* In Figure 5.12 it is easy to pick out the cross in the centre of the image because it is made up of similar square shapes, and is distinct from the other shapes in the picture. When manufacturers extend product lines they usually maintain the design of the packaging so that consumers can easily categorize the new product as part of the existing brand. By the same principle, own-label products often use similar colours and shapes to those of well-known brand names.

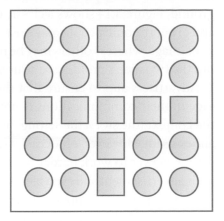

Figure 5.12   The principle of similarity

The principle of proximity

When we see visual stimuli close together we are more likely to assign them to a group. The **principle of proximity** states *that the things we see close together are perceived to be more related than things that are seen as farther apart.* In Figure 5.13, the viewer is more likely to see three groups of black and red circles, rather than a set of black dotted lines and a set of red dotted lines. The nearness (or proximity) of the lines is stronger than the similarity of the colours.

In marketing practice, retailers tend to group together products that complement one another, such as tights close to shoes and handbags in a department store, or hamburgers and buns alongside barbeque equipment.

The principle of figure and ground

In organizing stimuli, individuals tend to distinguish those that are prominent in the environment. The prominent element is the figure and the context in which it is seen is the ground. The more familiar the figure is the more likely it is to be noted, but sometimes

Figure 5.13   The principle of proximity

it is unclear which part is the figure and which is the ground. Figure 5.14 shows a classic example of figure and ground; some people may see a vase as the dominant image, whereas others may be more likely to pick out the two men's profiles as the dominant figure.

Advertisers aim to ensure that the dominant message in their communications is not drowned out by the context (the story, the setting, or even the personalities used). However, on occasion they may wish to get the viewer to work harder to view the message of their advertisement and even blend the 'figure' into the 'ground'. Figure 5.15 shows a German advertisement for the World Wildlife Fund with the line 'The rainforest does not die alone', showing parched earth but also the clear outline of a parrot against it. This appears to symbolize the connection between the rainforest and

Figure 5.14 The principle of figure and ground

Source: Image supplied by Shutterstock.

Figure 5.15 Tropical trees never die alone   *Source:* Image courtesy of Ogilvy & Mather.

the creatures within it, and is a powerful image created from the use of the Gestalt principle of figure and ground.

Marketing and perception

There are a number of areas in marketing where the nature of perception and how companies are able to manage their consumers' perceptions are particularly important. We shall examine perceptual mapping, perceived risk, repositioning, and semiotics.

Perceptual mapping

Perceptual maps are visual representations of the marketplace from the customers' perspective. They effectively provide managers with a map of how consumers view the products and brands in the market in comparison with other brands, and also in relation to how the company sees the brands. By giving a visual representation of the market, companies may be able to ascertain clearly where their brand lies relative to its competition (Kim et al., 2007; Nestrud and Lawless, 2008). Perceptual maps are developed from attribute ratings, where selections of product attributes are scored by consumers along semantic scales (e.g. very good through to very bad) or using bipolar scales (e.g. firm versus soft). Such judgements are then analysed to identify key variables influencing consumers' choices and preferences. Customer familiarity with products is important for companies, but the visual representations used to remind consumers of different brands are also important. The products are evaluated by participants, who may rate a product by attribute or consider similarities and differences between groups of alternatives. Brands are then represented on a visual map of perceived space as shown in Figure 5.16. Judgement from managers and researchers is required when labelling and interpreting these perceptual map diagrams, since the computer package generating the analysis is unable to label or interpret the axes.

Perceptual maps are useful for a number of reasons. First, they are a visual representation from the consumers' rather than the company's perspective of brands and their relations with other brands. Second, they can show where there may be potential gaps in the market for new product development. Finally, by showing the company where their brand lies compared with their competitors, the company can consider changes to their brand that might improve its position. These may take the form of product improvements, or could be changes in message to communicate to the consumers attributes of the brand that they currently do not perceive as being associated with it.

The perceptual map shown in Figure 5.16 is specific to brands of laptops and the axes show important discriminatory perceptions by consumers, namely performance and aesthetic appearance. Perceptual maps can also be used for identifying usage differences among products. If you think about eating cereal and toast, are these only perceived as breakfast foods or are they also used as an afternoon or evening snack by some people?

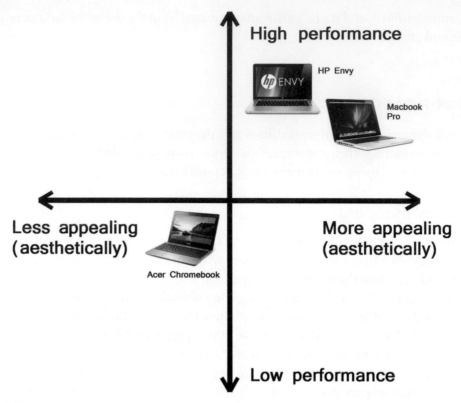

Figure 5.16   Perceptual map for laptops   *Source*: Image courtesy of Brandon Ford.

Perceived risk

While there may be a degree of objective risk in choosing to drive a fast car or going for a bungee jump, many of a consumer's decisions are also informed by perceived risk. The degree of perceived risk may depend on the nature of the consumer, and how they perceive the information provided to them. Bauer (1960) first introduced the idea of perceived risk, which he envisaged as having two dimensions, uncertainty and adverse consequences. In three experimental studies Fedorikhin and Cole (2004) found that mood was important, and specifically that people in a positive mood buying a new product were less risk averse than consumers who were in a negative mood. Like other aspects of perception, perceived risk is relative, and people's behaviour is mediated by their subjective perceptions of risk. There are a number of situations where perceived risk is likely to increase. These include the following.

- **A completely new offering to the market**, although probably less risk is involved in a new fast food product than in a new type of digital device which may also incur risk through its technological complexity.

- **Where there is little information about the product or service**, so travelling to a relatively unknown holiday destination may produce more perceived risk.

- **Where there are major differences among brands**, so there is a risk of inferior choice.

- **Where the consumer has limited experience of the product class**.

- **Where the purchaser may be likely to be judged by others for the purchase decision**.

In some cases marketers will want to reduce consumer's perception of risk, such as when marketing financial loans or more risky financial products such as stocks and shares. In other cases marketers may actually want to heighten consumer's perception of risk. Advertising for toothpaste regularly shows the consequences that plaque may bring about, amplifying consumer's fears and worries about the risks of tooth decay, and thus encouraging them to buy certain brands of toothpaste. An advertisement for Cancer Research UK cleverly juxtaposes a young girl eating a cake, an image that most would find inoffensive, with information regarding the potential consequences of overeating, thus trying to get across the idea that even apparently harmless food consumption has potential consequences as overweight and obese people have a greater propensity to certain cancers. Another example of perception of risk is shown in Research Insight 5.4.

RESEARCH INSIGHT 5.4

Baker, M.A., Shin, J.T., and Kim, Y.W. (2016), 'An exploration and investigation of edible insect consumption: the impacts of image and description on risk perceptions and purchase intent', *Psychology & Marketing*, 33, 2, 94–112.

This research examines a marketing problem of globally significant environmental importance: How do we encourage consumers to have favourable reactions to edible insect food products? Looking at a range of consumption situations, the study examined consumer risk perceptions in relation to the consumption of edible insects. The authors find that in a retail setting, actual insect images that appear on product packages dissuaded consumers by increasing perceptions of functional, social, physical, and psychological risks. They also showed that vague product descriptions were more preferable than explicit descriptions, especially when an edible insect image was not visually present. A final important finding was that social and physical risk perceptions received more salient impacts of settings than functional and psychological risk perceptions.

 Access the online resources to follow the link and read the full article.

Six types of perceived risk are most commonly recognized as affecting consumer behaviour. **Financial risk** *is the perception of a likely financial loss.* Financial risk is relative. Those with little money may perceive greater financial risk in buying situations where those with more money would not (Bertrand et al., 2006). Updating a mobile phone may seem like a small financial outgoing for some, while for others it will represent a major purchase and therefore being sure to buy the most appropriate phone for their needs is important.

Performance or functional risk is *the perception of how well the product will perform its expected task*. This may involve the technical aspects of a product, such as face creams that advertise that they will reduce the appearance of wrinkles or sanitizers that say they kill 99.9 per cent of germs. It may also be more intangible, as when someone buys a new suit for work with the hope that it may make them appear more professional and appropriate for the business environment. Companies may issue money-back guarantees to help reduce perceived performance risk before purchase.

Physical risk is *the perception of harm that a product or service might have*. Most prescription drugs now have lengthy descriptions of their potential side effects. Consumers often find it difficult to know when food is past its best and may cause a risk to their health. In 2011, the UK government decided that food should only carry 'use by' or 'best before' dates (indicating the point after which the food was unsafe), while 'sell by' and 'display until' labels (which emphasize the optimum time for eating) were removed to deter consumers from throwing out food that could still be consumed safely. This change was meant to give the labels greater clarity and reduce consumer confusion, although reports suggest that these terms are still not clear in consumers' minds (Leib et al., 2016). Other countries follow similar practices; for example the Foods Standards Code of Australia and New Zealand has guidelines for 'best before' and 'use by' dates.

Social risk is *the personal and social risk that may arise from a purchase*. Social risk is associated with having the 'wrong' product or brand. For example, teenagers may feel that it is very important to have the 'right' brand of mobile phone or to wear the coolest clothing brand (Piacentini and Mailer, 2004). In Copenhagen, many young people cycle, but wearing a helmet is regarded by some as unstylish and thereby carries a social risk. The company Nutcase developed its marketing and promotions strategy for cycling helmets ('I love my brain') to counteract this social risk and in so doing reduce the physical risk to cyclists. The company launched the 'Outdoor Fitting Room', a series of poles around Copenhagen, each indented with a helmet. People are invited to lean over and try out the helmet, and are encouraged to have their photo taken and placed on the Nutcase Denmark Facebook page through the incentive of the chance of winning a free helmet (see Figure 5.17).

Psychological risk is *the risk that reflects the individual's perception of themselves*. It reflects how well purchases fit with a consumer's self-perception (discussed in more depth in Chapter 7). For example, many consumers believe themselves to be highly ethical but still make purchases from companies that they do not consider to be so. The psychological risk is embodied in how they feel about such purchases (Szmigin et al., 2009) and how it reflects on their self-identity.

Time risk is *the risk embodied in the uncertainty regarding the time required to buy or learn to use the product*. Time is critical to marketing as many products and services are time-bound and require consumer time as an input, for example choosing convenience food or traditional

Figure 5.17   The Nutcase logo and model wearing a Nutcase helmet
Source: Image courtesy of Nutcase-Helmets.

cooking (Usunier and Valette-Florence, 2007). People may choose to put their savings into a building society or bank rather than in shares as the time involved in learning how to use the financial markets may seem like too great a commitment. Similarly, we might decide not to try to learn a new language because of the potential time commitment to become proficient in that language.

Repositioning

As perception is a subjective phenomenon it can be difficult for companies to manage how people perceive their brands. A key aspect of repositioning is to find ways of changing people's existing perceptions of a brand (see Consumer Insight 5.4). Of course, this may be difficult if a company has invested money over a period of time.

CONSUMER INSIGHT 5.4

Repositioning Lucozade

Lucozade was invented by a British chemist in the 1920s, and was found to be particularly effective for people who had been ill and lost their appetite since the glucose was in a form (a drink) that was easily assimilated by the body. Beecham bought the brand in 1938, and throughout the 1950s and 1960s Lucozade was very successful, positioned as a drink for times of illness. However, between 1974 and 1978 the brand's sales declined by 30 per cent, largely as a result of lower levels of sickness, fewer flu epidemics, and increased vaccination. In the 1980s Beecham completely repositioned the brand as a carbonated energy drink aimed at a broader market. To accomplish this, a new marketing campaign was developed involving a focus on sport and exercise, promoting the drink as a delicious refreshing energy drink. Daley Thompson, a British Olympic gold medal winning athlete, was chosen to advertise Lucozade as a refreshing drink that restores energy. From a perceptual perspective, Beecham successfully moved people's subjective perception of Lucozade as a drink for convalescents to a drink that supports sporting activity and revives energy (see Figure 5.18).

Since then the brand has developed its position in what is known as the energy drink sector, a growth sector of the soft drinks market, against competitors such as Red Bull and Powerade. It provides a number of different products aimed at satisfying hydration and energy needs. Over the years the brand has used many sporting superstars to advertise the brand, including footballer Michael Owen and rugby union player Jonny Wilkinson. With a target age range of 16–24, Lucozade has also used musicians such as British rapper Tinie Tempah and former Blink 182 drummer Travis Barker in its 'celebration of energy' campaign. The latest addition to Lucozade products is Revive, an enhanced and flavoured water marketed alongside its energy drinks.

Questions

1. Can you think of other brands that have repositioned themselves? Why did they? What was the nature of their repositioning and how successful do you think they have been?

2. If you were developing a new soft drink today for this age group, how might you position it against existing brands in the market?

Sources: Smith (1992); O'Reilly (2011); www.brandrepublic.com

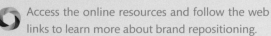 Access the online resources and follow the web links to learn more about brand repositioning.

Figure 5.18 Lucozade before and after repositioning

Source: Image of the classic Lucozade advert before repositioning is courtesy of Paul Carrington. Image of Lucozade after repositioning is supplied by The Advertising Archives.

Price perception

Price perception is another important issue for marketing. Consumers often make assumptions about the quality of products based on price. Similarly, they will make assessments of what the price of goods is likely to be based on the environment in which they are placed. Therefore it is very important for brand owners to ensure that their products are stocked in the stores that best reflect the price being charged. Customers become familiar with stores such as H&M and TopShop having clothes that are reasonably priced. Recently, these stores have introduced guest designers, such as Kenzo, Stella McCartney, and Jimmy Choo for H&M, and Top Shop has also teamed up with designers such as Marques Almeida to develop a set of limited edition design collections. While these designer ranges are associated with high-end prices, the collaboration with high street stores may suggest that the shops are trying to associate their brands with higher prices. Once connected with high-end brand names, customers may be more willing to pay the higher price charged for these products, or for products in those stores more generally. However, price perceptions work both ways, and in the past high-end brands have introduced diffusion ranges at lower prices. In 2017 the designer Victoria Beckham announced that she would be producing an exclusive diffusion line for the American retailer Target. While such moves may result in capture of a larger share of the market, it can also change their consumers' perception of the brand and reduce its perceived status.

Semiotics

It is clear that perception is subjective and open to interpretation, and therefore much of our reading of marketing communications is through the signs we pay attention to and interpret from advertising, packaging, and even the layout of shops. We use mental shortcuts based on our existing knowledge, experience, culture, and social preferences to simplify and manage the world. The signs in the environments we face trigger these shortcuts, and thus affect how we interpret them. From our experience, certain colours, shapes, clothing, and even jobs are associated with certain other things; many of these associations are deeply embedded and difficult to change. If we think about the winter festival of Christmas and the images associated with it, certain colours may spring to mind (red, green, gold), but importantly we often focus on the social aspects of the festival, perhaps the family meal and being with friends. Over time, Coca-Cola has associated itself successfully with Christmas, and indeed Coca-Cola's Christmas advertisements have become an event in themselves. One of the associations that Coca-Cola has with Christmas relates to 'the family Christmas' because of the advertising imagery that has been built by the brand. In 1931, Coca-Cola commissioned Swedish-American artist Haddon Sundblom to paint Santa Claus for the company's Christmas adverts. Sundblom created a portly warm character with a beard, purposefully crafted to look like a grandfather (see Figure 5.19). The colour red, synonymous with Coca-Cola, is also the traditional colour used for Santa Claus's outfit. The company benefited from the associations it was able to build between Coca-Cola and the family values associated with Christmas through a series of advertisements, to the extent that, for

Figure 5.19   Coca-Cola Christmas advertising   *Source*: Image supplied by The Advertising Archives.

many people, Coca-Cola represents American traditions and values (Oswald, 2012). This is a case of marketing semiotics, where the brand is linked through 'semiotic networks' with the consumer's view of the world.

Semiotics 'interprets reality in terms of cultural codes that structure phenomena into signs and meanings' (Oswald, 2012: 9). **Semiotics** *is concerned with exploring the links between signs and symbols and the meanings they signify and convey.* The use of signs to interpret our world goes back as far as Hippocrates, who looked at medical symptoms as signs on the body. But the origins of semiotics were developed by the Swiss linguist Ferdinand de Saussure and the American philosopher Charles Sanders Pierce. Pierce represented semiotics as comprising three elements: an object, a sign, and an interpretant in a triadic relationship (see Figure 5.20).

A sign is just that—a sign. On its own, this element may be just a word, a colour, a smell, or a flavour, and has no intrinsic meaning until linked with something else. A sign always stands for something else in the mind of others in a particular context or culture, and this is where the link to the interpretant is made. Red is just a colour, but it may stand for different things for different people, such as danger or stop or hot water or Santa Claus. 'Red' creates a sign in the mind of someone, and this effect of the

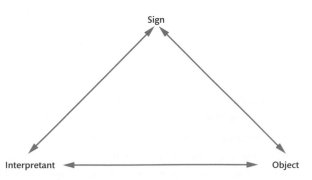

Figure 5.20   Triad of semiotics

Source: *Introduction to communication studies* (2nd edn), Fiske, J. (© 1990), Routledge, reproduced by permission of Taylor & Francis Books UK.

initial sign (red) on the person taking it in is known as the interpretant of the initial sign. The interpretant is the effect or the mental concept developed in someone's mind, and therefore represents a process of the sign's meaning forming into a further sign by interpretation. In the case of the Christmas advertisement for Coca-Cola, which on its own is just an image (the sign), the interpretant is what it represents in terms of being part of a family, celebrating, giving presents. For another person, the word Christmas might have a very different interpretant, perhaps a more religious effect or, if Christmas is not a feature of their cultural context, very little effect at all. As Mick (1986: 199) notes, 'Ultimately, the interpretant is transformed into a language or other symbolic code by which it is shared with and transmitted through the social environment'. The object is the thing that the sign is referring to, and thus the sign represents the object. In this example, the object is the drink Coca-Cola.

The symbolic function of a product or service depends on context and culture. As Oswald (2012) notes, when DeBeers entered the Chinese market in 1994, diamond rings were not symbolic of weddings in China. While in the West the diamond ring had been associated with long-lasting love and romance, the Chinese recognized the need for persistence in the marriage commitment, somewhat different to the romantic Western ideals. Therefore the diamond ring was positioned by DeBeers for the Chinese man to affirm his reliability rather than a sign of romantic love. DeBeers successfully entered this market by understanding that marriage in China is about persistence and commitment, and that associating the diamond ring with these values would be important for growing this market.

When a symbolic association becomes embedded in society or convention, the association acts as a code shaping how people behave, so in many countries a diamond engagement ring is part of the code for marriage. Similarly, a mother seeing an advertisement showing a family picnic on a sunny day, featuring a particular brand of suntan lotion, may think of family values and enjoying time safely with her children where they are not at risk of getting sunburn. But as Levy (1959) notes, teenagers may interpret the family picnic as 'kid stuff' from which they want to break away (see also Research Insight 5.5).

RESEARCH INSIGHT 5.5

Levy, S. (1981), 'Interpreting consumer mythology: a structural approach to consumer behaviour', *Journal of Marketing*, 45, 3, 49–61.

In this classic theoretical paper from the 1980s, Sidney Levy analyses the myths and interpretations associated with food preparation and consumption by American housewives. While he writes here about associations such as raw food and representing avant-garde dining, similar interpretations might be made with today's food choices.

 Access the online resources to read the abstract and access the full paper.

Conclusions

The **perceptual process** was explored, and we examined the stages and explained each through a number of advertising and communications examples. We looked at the mechanisms underlying **exposure** and how this is used in marketing. The example of the Spanish organization ANAR provided insights into how technology can be used to manage consumer's exposure to stimuli.

We considered the **nature and role of sensory receptors**, and the effect of sight, sound, smell, taste, and texture on how consumers behave. In Consumer Insight 5.1 we examined the role of the senses in helping consumers to pick out their preferred brand from an abundant set of choices—in this case, spotting their favourite coffee shop. Practitioner Insight 5 further examined how marketers use this understanding of the sensory aspects of consumption when devising product formulations, packaging, and promotions for disinfectants.

When exploring how consumers pay **attention** to stimuli, we looked at how social media was used in the case of Old Spice (Consumer Insight 5.3) to ensure that attention was on the brand and that the brand message was retained by consumers.

Interpretation was considered, and the principles of **Gestalt psychology** were described and illustrated through examples from marketing.

We described the techniques derived from an understanding of perception. **Perceptual mapping** was introduced, with the illustration of laptop brands, and we also looked at **perceived risk**, with Research Insight 5.4 focusing on risk perceptions relating to consumption of edible insect products. **Repositioning** was explored in Consumer Insight 5.4, where we examined how Lucozade had been repositioned over the years. Finally, we examined how **semiotics** is used in interpreting consumer behaviour, and also how **price perceptions** are formed.

Review questions

1. Outline the key stages in the perception process. Select one brand, and describe how the stages of the process can be mapped out for consumer perceptions of this brand.

2. In consumer perception terms, what is exposure? How is this relevant for marketers?

3. Highlight the key importance of each of the senses for marketing. Where do you consider each sense to be of most importance?

4. Explain what is required for successful attention to occur. How is this related to interpretation?

5. What is meant by Gestalt? Explain the importance of figure and ground for successful interpretation of an advertisement.

6. For each type of perceptual risk consider an example, which might help or hinder marketers.

Discussion questions

1. Look at the colours and lettering used by any two fast food restaurants that you are familiar with. How do you think the colours work for the brand? What alternative colours might they have used and why? Explain your arguments using perception theory as discussed in this chapter.

2. Consider tastes you do and don't like and analyse why. Are there cultural differences that may affect the foods you prefer? Can you explain this in perception theory terms?

3. Soars (2003) suggests the following scents and their effects:

   • sweet basil lifts mood, improves mental clarity and memory

   • bay relieves nervous exhaustion and melancholy

   • ginger relieves confusion, loneliness, and anxiety

   • lime cheers, uplifts, and purifies.

   Devise a set of suggestions for marketing situations where each scent might be successfully used.

4. Choose a Benetton advert from their 'Unhate' campaign. What do you think they were trying to achieve with this campaign? Why is this campaign in particular shocking? Use the research covered in this chapter to help you answer this question.

5. Draw a conceptualized perceptual map for brands of toothpaste and breakfast cereal, and assign appropriate axes. Are there key differences between brands and are they similar across product categories? How might you explain these differences and similarities?

6. Consider what elements there might be in a semiotic triad for the following signs: 'blue', 'Italian', and 'silk'. In each case try to link them with a brand or product category if possible.

Access the online resources to test your knowledge further and complete the Multiple Choice Questions for Chapter 5.

CASE STUDY 5

Real or fake: how consumers perceive brand symbolism in the luxury handbag market

In this case we look at the luxury handbag market, and focus on consumer perceptions towards brand symbols and their prominence for both authentic and counterfeit brands. We introduce a consumer taxonomy based on wealth and need for status, and consider how this translates into how brands are perceived and used for status signalling. We then consider some of the issues around counterfeit brands and how consumers perceive them.

Luxury handbags

Luxury goods and brands are a massive market, and seem to be impervious to the global recession. The overall global market grew at 4 per cent in 2016 to an estimated €1.08 trillion in retail sales value. (D'Arpizio et al., 2016). Luxury handbags are a particularly buoyant market, representing one of the fastest growing segments in the overall luxury market. The consumer base for luxury brands has grown in recent years because of the rising number of wealthy consumers worldwide, the growing global middle class, and the increasing consumer demand for branded products (Research and Markets, 2016). Much of the appeal of these highly priced bags lies in their ability to signal status and exclusivity to other consumers, using a code that is recognizable only in certain groups. This form of brand communication requires an understanding of the brand language and codes, which in turn relies on consumers being able to perceive and interpret the language of the luxury brand. But this is a complex language of symbols and styling, and brands mark their products differently in order to be more or less visible.

Consumers and brand prominence

Research by Han et al. (2010) has introduced the idea of brand prominence, which refers to the extent to which the branded product is visibly marked. They describe 'loud' and conspicuous branding, readily perceived and recognized by consumers, which contrasts with 'quiet' or discrete branding that is recognizable only to a select few. Both Louis Vuitton and Chanel bags might be described as loud brands, since they have visual cues that are instantly recognizable, in contrast with the more discrete cues represented by brands such as Hermès and Bottega Veneta, which are considered to be quieter.

Han et al. (2010) propose that luxury handbag consumers can be placed into a taxonomy which categorizes consumers into four main classes based on wealth and their need for status. This taxonomy enables a better understanding of how consumers perceive and relate to different brands to be achieved. The categories are as follows.

Patrician This group possesses significant wealth, and have a low need to consume for the sake of prestige. They will pay a premium for understated brands—those considered quiet or discreet. They are principally concerned with associating with other patricians (rather than dissociating from other groups) and use brand cues as a way of doing so. A typical brand that might appeal would be Hermès, with its very quiet and subtle brand markings.

Parvenus This group has considerable wealth but not the connoisseurship necessary to interpret subtle signals, and they use more obvious brand cues to signal their status. They are concerned with dissociating themselves from the 'have-nots', while clearly associating with the 'haves'. This group would be drawn to the distinctive LV of the Louis Vuitton bag.

Poseurs These consumers are highly motivated to consume for the sake of it, but tend to be less wealthy. They are motivated to associate with those they perceive as having wealth (the parvenus) and thus are more likely to turn to counterfeit products in place of authentic or original brands. This group seek out fake versions of loud or conspicuous brands, such as those favoured by parvenus.

Proletarians In this context, this term refers to people who are not driven to consume for the sake of status or interested in signalling prestige through consumption. They are not particularly interested in luxury brands.

How brands are perceived will vary for each consumer class, but it is important to recognize the role of fake brands, and how they are perceived, in relation to the luxury handbag market.

Counterfeit brands

Authentic luxury brands communicate exclusivity and status through high price, but for many consumers, these high prices mean that these brands are not available to them, which in turn feeds the market for counterfeit goods (Geiger-Oneto et al., 2013). Counterfeit goods are identical in appearance to authentic brands, displaying the brand name, but selling at a vastly reduced price (see Figure 5.21).

A fake Louis Vuitton wallet can sell for $40, while an authentic one costs $765 in the Louis Vuitton store (Ortiz, 2013). A consumer considering buying both may use a range of visual cues to assist the purchase. On visual cues alone, the two look very similar, although close scrutiny will reveal a number of differences, mainly in terms of quality of material used and attention to detail in production. However, at a superficial level, the fake could pass as an authentic wallet.

Figure 5.21   Market stall selling counterfeit handbags   *Source*: © iStock.com/contrastaddict.

Why do consumers buy fake brands? For those who are seeking to associate with prestige in some way (the poseurs) counterfeit luxury brands provide one way of signalling their status to other people at a fraction of the price (Wiedmann et al., 2012). This is the main reason for their purchase, but in a very disposable culture they allow consumers to keep up with handbag trends without a massive financial outlay (Gentry et al., 2006). However, in other respects counterfeits are limited in the value offered to consumers. Frequently, these products are not up to standard, may break down or fade, or even be damaging to consumers (Wiedmann et al., 2012). Also, these products may have limited social value, since those in the know (parvenus and patricians) are likely to perceive these goods to be of inferior quality and judge the counterfeit consumers accordingly (Sundie et al., 2006).

Questions

1. From your understanding of consumers' perceptions of luxury handbags, what advice would you offer Louis Vuitton to minimize brand damage caused by fake versions of its products?

2. This YouTube video (http://www.youtube.com/watch?v=9Vp8LXXMZwQ#at=67) shows a range of differences between authentic and fake versions of the Chanel 2.55 handbags. Watch it and list as many differences as you can between the two. What steps does Chanel take to minimize and protect its brand?

3. From your understanding of perceived risk (outlined in this chapter) provide a detailed analysis of the types of risk associated with (a) luxury handbags and (b) fake handbags.

4. Taking another luxury product category (e.g. watches or shoes), find examples of quiet and loud brands and analyse these in terms of types of consumers of the brands. Can you find any limitations of the four-class approach (Han et al., 2010)? Can you find luxury contexts where it does not apply neatly? Have you any suggestions for how this model might be improved upon?

Sources: Sundie et al. (2006); Gentry et al. (2006); Han et al. (2010); Wiedmann et al. (2012); Geiger-Oneto et al. (2013); Ortiz (2013); Research and Markets (2016).

References

Advertising Standards Association, www.asa.org.uk/About-ASA/Our-history.aspx (accessed 4 March 2017).

Allen, E. (2012), 'Supermarket "shrink ray": how shoppers are paying the same for ever smaller products', *Daily Mail*, 19 April, http://www.dailymail.co.uk/news/article-2131927/Our-shrinking-foods-How-manufacturers-making-everyday-products-smaller-keeping-prices-same.html (accessed 4 March 2017).

Angell, R., Gorton, M., Sauer, J., et al (2016), 'Don't distract me when I'm media multitasking: toward a theory for raising advertising recall and recognition', *Journal of Advertising*, 45, 2, 198–210.

Aslam, M.M. (2006), 'Are you selling the right colour? A cross-cultural review of colour as a marketing cue', *Journal of Marketing Communications*, 12, 1, 15–30.

Babin, B.J., Hardesty, D.M., and Suter, T.A. (2003), 'Color and shopping intentions: the intervening effect of price fairness and perceived effect', *Journal of Business Research*, 56, 7, 541–51.

Baker, M.A., Shin, J.T., and Kim, Y.W. (2016), 'An exploration and investigation of edible insect consumption: the impacts of image and description on risk perceptions and purchase intent', *Psychology & Marketing*, 33, 2, 94–112.

Bauer, R.A. (1960), 'Consumer behaviour as risk taking', in R.S. Hancock (ed.), *Dynamic marketing for a changing world*, Chicago, IL: American Marketing Association, pp.389–98.

Bellizzi, J.A., Crowley, A.E., and Hasty, R.E. (1983). 'The effects of color in store design', *Journal of Retailing*, 59, 1, 21–44.

Berns, G.S., Cohen, J.D., and Mintun, M.A. (1997), 'Brain regions responsive to novelty in the absence of awareness', *Science*, 276, 1272–5.

Bertrand, M., Mullainathan, S., and Shafir, E. (2006), 'Behavioral economics and marketing in aid of decision making among the poor', *Journal of Public Policy & Marketing*, 25, 1, 8–23.

Brownsell, A. (2010), 'M&S axes long-running "food porn" ad strategy', *Marketing Magazine*, 22 March, http://www.marketingmagazine.co.uk/article/991680/m-s-axes-long-running-food-porn-ad-strategy (accessed 4 March 2017).

Chernev, A. (2001), 'The impact of common features on consumer preferences: a case of confirmatory reasoning', *Journal of Consumer Research*, 27, 475–88.

Cockrill, A. and Parsonage, I. (2016). 'Shocking people into action: does it still work?', *Journal of Advertising Research*, 56, 4, 401–13.

Dahl, D.W., Frankenberger, K.D., and Manchanda, R.V. (2003), 'Does it pay to shock? Reactions to shocking and nonshocking advertising content among university students', *Journal of Advertising Research*, 43, 3, 268–80.

D'Arpizio, C., Levato, F., Zito, D. et al. (2016), 'Luxury goods worldwide market study, Fall–Winter 2016', *Bain Report*, 28 December 2016, http://www.bain.com/publications/articles/luxury-goods-worldwide-market-study-fall-winter-2016.aspx (accessed 3 March 2017).

Eerola, T., Vuoskoski, J. K., and Kautiainen, H. (2016), 'Being moved by unfamiliar sad music is associated with high empathy', *Frontiers in Psychology*, 7, 1176.

Eroglu, S.A., Machleit, K.A., and Davis, L.M. (2003), 'Empirical testing of a model of online store atmospherics and shopper responses', *Psychology & Marketing*, 20, 2, 139–50.

Faure-Field, S. (2013), 'Why customer "sensation" is important in Asian retail and premium banking (Part 2)', *Asian Banking and Finance*, 11 September, http://asianbankingandfinance.net/retail-banking/commentary/why-customer-sensation-important-in-asian-retail-and-premium-banking-part-0 (accessed 4 March 2017).

Fedorikhin, A. and Cole, C.A. (2004), 'Mood effects on attitudes, perceived risk and choice: moderators and mediators', *Journal of Consumer Psychology*, 14, 1/2, 2–12.

Fernandez, J. (2011), 'How the Old Spice hunk took over the world', *Marketing Week*, http://www.marketingweek.co.uk/how-the-old-spice-hunk-took-over-the-world/3030137.article (accessed 4 March 2017).

Gearhardt, A.N., Davis, C., Kuschner, R., and Brownell, K.D. (2011), 'The addiction potential of hyperpalatable foods', *Current Drug Abuse Reviews*, 4, 140–5.

Geiger-Oneto, S., Gelb, B.D., Walker, D., and Hess, J.D. (2013), ' "Buying status" by choosing or rejecting luxury brands and their counterfeits', *Journal of the Academy of Marketing Science*, 41, 3, 357–72.

Gentry, J.W., Putrevu, S., and Shultz, C.J. (2006), 'The effects of counterfeiting on consumer search', *Journal of Consumer Behaviour*, 5, 3, 1–12.

Han, Y.J., Nunes, J.C., and Drèze, X. (2010), 'Signaling status with luxury goods: the role of brand prominence', *Journal of Marketing*, 74, 4, 15–30.

Handley, L. (2013), 'Starbucks wants bespoke design for every store', *Marketing Week*, 26 June, http://www.marketingweek.co.uk/news/starbucks-wants-bespoke-design-for-every-store/4007167.article (accessed 4 March 2017).

Hang, H. and Nairn, A. (2016), 'Defend the indefensible: helping children cope with the implicit influence of online game advertising', *Advertising in new formats and media: current research and implications for marketers*, Bingley: Emerald, pp.379–95.

Kessler, D. (2010), *The end of overeating: taking control of our insatiable appetite*, London: Penguin.

Kim, D.J., Kim, W.G., and Han, J.S. (2007), 'A perceptual mapping of online travel agencies and preference attributes', *Tourism Management*, 28, 591–603.

Krishna, A., Elder, R.S., and Caldara, C. (2010), 'Feminine to smell but masculine to touch? Multisensory congruence and its effect on the aesthetic experience', *Journal of Consumer Psychology*, 20, 410–18.

Labrecque, L.I. and Milne, G.R. (2012), 'Exciting red and competent blue: the importance of color in marketing', *Journal of the Academy of Marketing Science*, 40, 5, 711–27.

Lantos, G.P. and Craton, L.G. (2012), 'A model of consumer response to advertising music', *Journal of Consumer Marketing*, 29, 1, 22–42.

Leib, E.B., Rice, C., Neff, R. et al. (2016), 'Consumer perceptions of date labels: national survey', *Safety*, 23, 54, 19.

Lenfant, F., Hartmann, C., Watzke, B. et al. (2013), 'Impact of the shape on sensory properties of individual dark chocolate pieces', *LWT-Food Science and Technology*, 51, 2, 545–52.

Levine, M.W. (2000), *Levine and Shefner's Fundamentals of sensation and perception* (3rd edn), Oxford: Oxford University Press.

Levy, S. (1959), 'Symbols for sale', *Harvard Business Review*, July/August, 117–124, reprinted in Rook D. (ed.) (1999), *Brands, consumers, symbols, and research*, Thousand Oaks, CA: Sage, pp.203–12.

Levy, S. (1981), 'Interpreting consumer mythology: a structural approach to consumer behaviour', *Journal of Marketing*, 45, 3, 49–61, reprinted in Rook, D. (ed.), *Brands, consumers, symbols, and research*, Thousand Oaks, CA: Sage, 1999, pp 514–29.

Lindstrom, M. (2008), *Buyology: how everything we believe about why we buy is wrong*, London: Random House.

Meule, A. (2015), 'Addiction: back by popular demand: a narrative review on the history of food addiction research', *The Yale Journal of Biology and Medicine*, 88, 3, 295.

Mick, D.G. (1986), 'Consumer research and semiotics: exploring the morphology of signs, symbols, and significance', *Journal of Consumer Research*, 13, 196–213.

Milligan, B. (2016), 'Branch banking takes on a new fragrance for 2017', BBC News, http://www.bbc.co.uk/news/business-38380465 (accessed 4 March 2017).

Millman, R.E. (1982), 'Using background music to affect the behavior of supermarket shoppers', *Journal of Marketing*, 46, 86–91.

Milotic, D. (2006), 'The impact of fragrance on consumer choice', *Journal of Consumer Behaviour*, 3, 2, 179–191.

Montague, R. (2006), *Why choose this book? How we make decisions*, New York: Dutton.

Mortimer, R. (2011), 'Costa's £10m tongue', *Marketing Week*, 6 October, http://www.marketingweek.co.uk/analysis/essential-reads/costas-10m-tongue/3030691.article (accessed 4 March 2017).

Nestrud, M.A. and Lawless, H.T. (2008), 'Perceptual mapping of citrus juices using projective mapping and profiling data from culinary professionals and consumers', *Food and Quality Preference*, 19, 431–8.

Nobel, C. (2013), 'Advertising symbiosis: the key to viral videos', *Harvard Business School Working Knowledge*, http://hbswk.hbs.edu/item/advertising-symbiosis-the-key-to-viral-videos (accessed 4 March 2017).

Northrup, L. (2017), 'Grocery shrink ray makes yogurt smaller, salt slightly bigger', *Consumerist*, 4 January, https://consumerist.com/2017/01/04/grocery-shrink-ray-makes-yogurt-smaller-salt-slightly-bigger/ (accessed 3 March 2017).

O'Reilly, L (2011), 'Lucozade features musicians for first time in brand repositioning', *Marketing Week*, http://www.marketingweek.co.uk/lucozade-features-musicians-for-first-time-in-brand-repositioning/3024936.article (accessed 4 March 2017).

Ortiz, P. (2013), 'Fake designer handbags: hard to find and easy on the eye but feeling is believing', *Daily News*, 14 June, http://www.nydailynews.com/new-york/feeling-believing-fake-handbags-article-1.1373364#ixzz2a3NDezVO (accessed 4 March 2017).

Oswald, L.R. (2012), *Marketing semiotics: signs, strategies, and brand value*, Oxford: Oxford University Press.

Overmars, S. and Poels, K. (2015), 'A touching experience: designing for touch sensations in online retail environments', *International Journal of Design*, 9, 3.

Paoletti, J.B. (2012), *Pink and blue: telling the boys from the girls in America*, Bloomington, IN: Indiana University Press.

Peck, J. and Childers, T. (2003), 'To have and to hold: the influence of haptic information on product judgements', *Journal of Marketing*, 67, 35–48.

Piacentini, M. and Mailer, G. (2004), 'Symbolic consumption in teenagers' clothing choices', *Journal of Consumer Behaviour*, 3, 3, 251–62.

Pieters, R. and Wedel, M. (2007), 'Goal control of attention to advertising: the Yarbus implication', *Journal of Consumer Research*, 34, 2, 224–33.

Research and Markets (2016), 'Global handbags market: industry analysis and outlook (2016–2020)', http://www.researchandmarkets.com/reports/3797962/global-handbags-market-industry-analysis-and-outlook (accessed 3 March 2017).

Schellenberg, E.G., Peretz, I., and Vieillard, S. (2008), 'Liking for happy- and sad-sounding music: effects of exposure', *Cognition and Emotion*, 22, 218–37.

Schwarz, B. (2004), *The paradox of choice: why more is less*, New York: HarperCollins.

Simons, D.J. and Chabris, C.F. (1999), 'Gorillas in our midst: sustained inattentional blindness for dynamic events', *Perception*, 28, 1059–74.

Smith, G. (1992), 'Lucozade: a case history', IPA Effectiveness Awards, www.warc.com

Soars, B. (2003), 'What every retailer should know about the way into the shopper's head', *International Journal of Retail Distribution and Management*, 31, 12, 628–37.

Sundie, J., Ward, J., and Geiger-Oneto, S. (2006), 'Schadenfreude as a consumption-related emotion: feeling happiness about the downfall of another's product', *Advances in Consumer Research*, 33, 96–7.

Szmigin, I., Carrigan, M., and McEachern, M. (2009), 'The conscious consumer: taking a flexible approach to ethical behaviour', *International Journal of Consumer Studies*, 33, 224–31.

Uncapher, M.R., Thieu, M.K., and Wagner, A.D. (2016). Media multitasking and memory: differences in working memory and long-term memory. *Psychonomic Bulletin & Review*, 23, 2, 483–90.

Underhill, P. (2009), *Why we buy*, New York: Simon & Schuster.

Usunier, J.-C. and Valette-Florence, P. (2007), 'The time styles scale: a review of developments and replications over 15 years', *Time and Society*, 16, 2/3, 333–66.

Van Doorn, G.H., Wuillemin, D., and Spence, C. (2014), 'Does the colour of the mug influence the taste of the coffee?', *Flavour*, 3, 1, 10.

WARC (2011), 'Old Spice: the man your man could smell like', https://www.warc.com/content/article/effies/old_spice_the_man_your_man_could_smell_like/94320 (accessed 18 December 2017).

Wiedmann, K. P., Hennigs, N., and Klarmann, C. (2012), 'Luxury consumption in the trade-off between genuine and counterfeit goods: what are the consumers' underlying motives and value-based drivers?', *Journal of Brand Management*, 19, 544–66.

Wilson, M (2014), 'Can Starbucks make 23000 coffee shops feel unique?', *Fast Design*, 18 August https://www.fastcodesign.com/3034441/starbucks-secrets-to-make-every-store-feel-unique (accessed 27 February 2017).

6

ATTITUDE THEORY AND BEHAVIOUR CHANGE

Introduction

Encouraging consumers to feel positively towards products and brands is an important aim for marketing. Companies recognize that consumers are more likely to buy products that they feel good about. Take, for example, Triodos Bank (Figure 6.1), which started operations in the Netherlands in the late 1960s and has since opened further branches in European countries. It has a mission to make its customers' money work for positive social, environmental, and cultural change and to promote sustainable development. Triodos Bank's objectives are promoted in communications with consumers, enhancing their feelings about the bank and encouraging development of positive attitudes towards banking with them. Consumer attitudes are important in marketing terms, since they represent the beliefs and evaluations that consumers hold towards marketing offerings. A key aspect of attitudes is their role in influencing behaviour. Some consumers may form favourable attitudes towards a brand and then purchase it, while others may have negative attitudes and thus avoid it. Aside from influencing how we consume products and brands, consumer attitudes can also influence other aspects of consumption, such as how we talk about our experiences with brands to other consumers, thus spreading word-of-mouth communications (see Chapter 8).

Figure 6.1 Banking with Triodos *Source*: Image printed with permission from Triodos Bank.

LEARNING OBJECTIVES

Having read this chapter, you will be able to:

1. Define the *concept of attitudes* as used in consumer marketing.

2. Understand the *main components of attitudes*—the tri-component model, the unidimensionalist model, and the hierarchy of effects model.

3. Discuss and evaluate the *main approaches* to attitude theory.

4. Identify the differences between *compensatory and non-compensatory* models and understand how they can be used in consumer decision-making.

5. Explain the various approaches *to attitude change*, including persuasion models such as the elaboration likelihood model.

6. Demonstrate and assess the *value of attitude theory* for marketing practice.

Defining attitudes

At the simplest level, an attitude is made up of what you think, what you feel, and what you do. The definition proposed by Fishbein and Ajzen (1975: 6) suggests that **attitude** is *'a learned predisposition to respond in a consistently favourable or unfavourable manner in relation to some object'*. From this definition it is clear that attitudes are *learned* (through experiences in the world), have an *evaluative dimension* (favourable/unfavourable), have *intensity* (strong attitudes versus weak attitudes), and have *consistency* and *stability* (tend not to change much and align with our other attitudes) (Oskamp and Schultz, 2005). Importantly, this definition suggests that attitudes have a link to behaviour, giving a predisposition to act in a certain way. It is this link with behaviour that makes the study of attitudes so interesting to marketers. When discussing attitudes it is important to specify the target object about which attitudes are being gathered and explored. This is known as the **attitude object/act** which can be defined as the *thing about which the attitude is held, and can include brands, services, ideas, people, and behaviours* (Herr and Fazio, 1993). This may be behaviour (e.g. smoking), an object (e.g. Marlboro cigarettes), or a person (e.g. Brad Pitt).

If we think about consumer attitudes towards debt, the various aspects of this definition will become clearer. Consumers learn about and form views on debt through interactions with family, friends, other consumers, and various media, as well as the marketplace offerings they are exposed to. From these interactions and experiences, consumers are likely to hold a relatively stable position (positive or negative) towards debt, which in turn informs and influences their behaviour towards debt. If you come from a family setting where saving is valued and borrowing discouraged, you are likely to avoid building up large debts. However, there are situations where it is difficult to avoid accumulating debt (if you are getting a mortgage, or taking out a student loan to pay for fees), and in those contexts you are likely to adjust your attitude and behaviour. Therefore contexts of consumption are important as a key influence on consumer attitudes and subsequent behaviour, as is evident in Consumer Insight 6.1 where the changing environment around credit and debt is discussed.

CONSUMER INSIGHT 6.1

Attitudes to credit and debt

Credit has become a common feature of consumer lives in the late twentieth and early twenty-first centuries. This has been an almost worldwide phenomenon, with credit card usage in some Asian countries increased by up to 500 per cent (Kang and Ma, 2007). Peñaloza and Barnhart (2011) studied the cultural meanings that white middle-class Americans associated with credit and debt, and considered how attitudes compared with the previous generation's views. A dominant theme emerged that debt was necessary in order to fund the 'must haves' associated with a middle-class American lifestyle—buying a house, a car, a college (university) education. Taking on debt was a *normal* way of funding this lifestyle. O'Loughlin and Szmigin (2006) found that students in the UK and Ireland also accepted debt as part of normal life. This increased debt resulted in students being more confident in their consumer roles; they were also less thrifty in an environment where credit was the norm. In a recent study of student attitudes towards debt, Zerquera et al. (2016) identified three main approaches to debt: debt avoiders or averters, debt minimizers, and debt acceptors, who fully accepted carrying multiple forms of debt as an integral part of the college-going experience.

Data from the UK suggests that attitudes towards debt have changed. While UK consumers became more debt-tolerant from the 1990s up to around 2005, there has since been a shift to a more cautious approach, prompted by the economic climate. Consumers realize that they cannot refinance their mortgages in the ways they might have done previously. Recent Mintel data from the USA (Mintel, 2016a) shows that as the economic climate picks up, consumers are spending their savings on pursuing more experiential type activities, such as vacations and dining out. In the UK consumer confidence in relation to borrowing has been affected by the decision to leave the EU, which is likely to lead to consumers being cautious about their personal finances. And across Europe, consumers are concerned about the impact of Brexit on their own country's economic stability, which also leads to more cautious attitudes towards money, debts, and saving (Mintel, 2016b).

Questions

1. Ask three people you know, ideally of different ages, about their thoughts and attitudes towards debt. Ask them if they have tried to reduce their debt in the last few years and why?

2. From these discussions outline how you think their current attitudes to debt might be described.

Sources: Kang and Ma (2007); Szmigin and O'Loughlin (2010); Mintel (2011, 2016a, 2016b); Peñaloza and Barnhart (2011); Lane (2012); Zerquera et al. (2016).

 Access the online resources and follow the web links to learn more about consumer debt.

Main components of attitudes

The tricomponent model

Generally, attitudes are thought to comprise three main components: *affect* or feelings, *behaviour* or conations, and *cognitions* or beliefs (Henderson and Hoque, 2010).

The **affective component** relates to the *emotional connection the consumer has with the target object about which the attitude is formed*. If we think about the emotional aspect of our attitude towards buying books on Amazon, we may feel enthusiastic about the prospect of a bargain, but we may also feel angry as we recall stories of Amazon avoiding paying tax in the European countries within which it is trading. The affect refers to the fundamental feelings related to the attitude, which are often represented as liking or disliking.

The **behavioural component** refers to *the action or behaviours associated with the attitude object*. This may be an intention to stop smoking, or an intention to start composting household waste. This component covers the 'doing' aspect of the attitude, the action about which the attitude is formed. Note, however, that intended actions are not necessarily carried out.

The **cognitive component** refers to the beliefs and thoughts the individual has in relation to the target attitude object, its character, and its relations to other things. We may hold a belief that running every day is good for our fitness. We may also believe that being fit is preferable to being unfit and perhaps overweight. These are cognitions that can be related to the behaviour of buying new running shoes.

Together, these elements combine to give the tri-component model, also called the ABC model: affect (feeling), behaviour (doing), and cognition (knowing). The ABC model is useful in terms of thinking about the components of attitudes, but does not provide marketers with a sense of how these elements are related, or how they combine to produce attitudes (Grimm, 2005).

The following example makes this clear. The Livescribe Smartpen is a ballpoint pen with an embedded computer and digital audio-recorder, and its main function is to save written words (through transferring them onto a computer) and to synchronize these notes with any audio-recording that is made (see Figure 6.2). The Livescribe Smartpen is

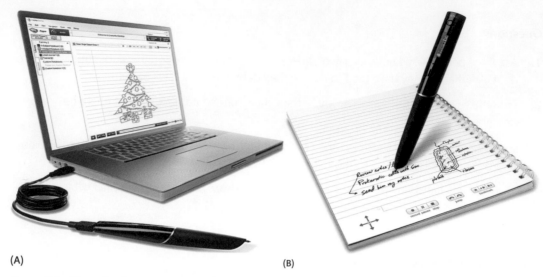

(A)   (B)

Figure 6.2   Livescribe Smartpen   *Source*: Image courtesy of Honcho PR.

aimed at situations where notes are taken (e.g. in meetings or classrooms) and its main benefit is captured in the strapline 'Never miss a word' (see the company website http:// www.livescribe.com/uk/).

If we analyse this product in terms of the tri-component model, we can see how each of the ABC elements are related.

A. Affect—in terms of affect (feelings), the consumer may be positive, excited, and enthusiastic about trying the Livescribe Smartpen.

B. Behavioural (conations)—the consumer decides to buy and use the Livescribe Smartpen, based on their feelings and beliefs about it.

C. Cognitions (beliefs)—the consumer may form cognitions (beliefs) about the Livescribe Smartpen along the lines that it has great functionality and will improve their note-taking skills. While consumers may be able to generate many beliefs associated with the target attitude object (in this case the Livescribe Smartpen), only those that are *important* to consumers, known as salient beliefs, will inform the attitude they form in relation to it. **Salient beliefs** *are the most relevant beliefs for any given person at the time the attitude is considered.*

Together these three components may translate into the attitude, but this model does not tell us how these elements come together. We have no idea how important one is in relation to the others, and it is often difficult for marketers to influence attitudes using this approach. However, the three main components of attitudes found in this model (affect/feelings, behaviour, and cognitions/beliefs) do form the basis of many of the more structured models of attitudes, as we shall see in our discussion of the multi-attribute models of attitudes. In Research Insight 6.1, we consider a study of attitudes in the context of online group buying.

RESEARCH INSIGHT 6.1

Suki, N.M. and Suki, N.M. (2017), 'Modeling the determinants of consumers' attitudes toward online group buying: do risks and trusts matter?', *Journal of Retailing and Consumer Services*, 36, 180–8.

Adopting a quantitative approach, this research investigated the basis of consumers' attitudes towards online group buying (OGB) sites, such as Groupon and LivingSocial in the United States. This study found that website trustworthiness was the most important predictor of consumers' attitudes towards OGB sites. The authors concluded that managers must reassure consumers in terms of transaction security, so that consumers feel these transactions are less risky, and hence develop more positive attitudes towards this type of consumption behaviour.

 Access the online resources to read the abstract and access the full paper.

Hierarchy of effects

Although the ABC model does not indicate the level of contribution and interrelationship of the three attitude components, it represents a sequence of steps that arise when consumers form attitudes (Alexandris et al., 2012). Using this approach, the starting point for attitude formation can be any of the components (affect, behaviour, or cognition), and different implications for marketers emerge depending on the starting point (Beatty and Kahle, 1988). This is known as the hierarchy of effects, and there are four main types of hierarchy that are useful for marketers, summarized in Table 6.1.

The *high involvement or standard learning hierarchy*, represented by the sequence 'cognitions → affect → behaviour', assumes that the consumer is actively engaged in a rational decision-making process. Here the consumer starts with a set of beliefs, and probably searches for more information to bolster or develop these beliefs from which an affective response (or preference) is developed before the behaviour is completed. This hierarchy

Hierarchy and sequence	Main emphasis
High involvement (standard learning) hierarchy: cognitions → affect → behaviour	High involvement, consumer engaged in extensive research to develop beliefs, emphasis on *cognitive information processing*
Low involvement hierarchy: cognitions → behaviour → affect	Consumer drawing on limited knowledge, *behavioural learning* important here
Emotional hierarchy: affect → behaviour → cognitions	Experiential aspects of the consumption setting, importance of *experiential or hedonic consumption*
Behavioural hierarchy: behaviour → cognitions → affect	Emphasis on consumers responding to consumer context, impulse type buys, behavioural approach important.

Table 6.1   Hierarchy of effects

is relevant for attitude formation in high involvement consumption contexts, such as when a consumer is considering purchasing a laptop. The consumer undertakes an extensive search, but also develops an affective or emotional connection with the brands available. The HP Spectre is marketed as their thinnest laptop ever, while retaining a very high processing specification. However, the experiential aspects of the laptop are also emphasized in its advertising message, which suggests a potential emotional attachment to the brand: 'Artisan materials and striking craftsmanship create an experience unlike anything else. With a breathtaking composition that's 10.4 mm thin and full Intel® Core™ i5 or i7 power, this luxurious Laptop is completely irresistible.' (http://store.hp.com/UKStore/Merch/Offer.aspx?p=c-hp-spectre). Finally, the consumer acts (makes a purchase) based on the evaluation of their beliefs and feelings, with beliefs dominating this attitude formation process.

The *low involvement hierarchy* has the sequence 'cognitions → behaviour → affect'. Here, the consumer starts with a set of beliefs about the consumption object, but the knowledge they are drawing on may be limited, and it is not as essential for them to undertake extensive research. Often, the thinking and action stages are quite close, with the consumer forming an emotional response (how they feel about the brand or service) after the purchase. Consider going to buy a new pair of running shoes. You will have some knowledge to draw on—for example, about the type of shoe required, the shops where they can be bought, and an acceptable price range. However, going to a store such as Decathalon, and seeing what products are available in your size and price range, will greatly impact on the purchase made. Following purchase, the consumer may establish an emotional connection to the product/brand purchased. This hierarchy is distinctive in that it is relevant for relatively familiar consumption situations. In such contexts, the consumer relies greatly on their own knowledge and beliefs to inform their attitudes towards the consumption object.

The *behavioural hierarchy*, represented by 'behaviour → cognitions → affect', emphasizes behaviour first, and from this the consumer forms beliefs and then feelings in relation to the consumption object. A consumer may impulsively purchase a new Essie nail polish shade, but it is only through the act of wearing the nail polish that she feels that this colour suits her (or not) and thus forms an attitude towards the nail polish, and perhaps towards the Essie brand in particular.

The *emotional hierarchy*, represented by 'affect → behaviour → cognitions', is more experiential in nature, assuming that a consumer acts based on emotional triggers. The feeling comes first, followed by consumption. After consumption the consumer will think through and form an attitude towards the target attitude object. A consumer may be looking for a new dress for a special occasion, such as her twenty-first birthday party. In this context, she may make her decision based on how a dress makes her feel—glamorous—then she makes the purchase, and, following that, evaluates and forms beliefs about the item. Was the price right? Can she wear it for other occasions? Did the dress feel 'just right'? In this hierarchy, emotions and feelings dominate the attitude formation process.

Understanding the various hierarchies of effects, and how they relate to attitude formation for different types of consumer contexts, is useful for marketers as it has implications for the ways that marketing efforts can be emphasized. An example of the emotional hierarchy can be seen with the American lifestyle clothing brand Hollister Co. Hollister places great emphasis on the experiential aspects of the in-store retail environment, trying to emulate a multisensory experience (using smells, textures, music, visuals, and lighting) to encourage an emotional connection with, and affective response to, the brand. This emotional connection is the main underpinning component of attitudes towards the brand, from which beliefs and action towards the brand emerge, and is a vital part of Hollister's retailing strategy.

Contrast this with the marketing of personal computers, where beliefs are likely to dominate attitude formation and hence it is important for marketers to ensure that their brands are promoted in such a way as to emphasize the brand attributes most important to consumers. Chillblast is a UK-based computer manufacturer, launched in 2001 (http://www.chillblast.com/). It very quickly developed a reputation for offering high specification, superior quality PCs at a reasonable price, supported by outstanding customer service. Chillblast has won a series of major awards in the UK computer press, and the company highlights these successes on their webpage ('UK's Most Awarded PC Manufacturer') and in all their communications as an assurance to consumers of the quality of the product and service offering (see Figure 6.3). This kind of communication influences the development of consumer beliefs in a highly complex and involved consumer context.

The uni-dimensionalist model

An alternative way of considering attitudes is the uni-dimensionalist model (Lutz, 1991). This can be viewed as an evolution of the tripartite approach because, while the same three

Figure 6.3   Image from the Chillblast website

Source: Printed with permission from Chillblast at www.chillblast.com.

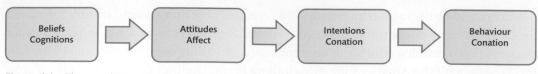

Figure 6.4   The uni-dimensionalist model   *Source*: Lutz (1991).

components are present, how they are linked conceptually is different. The cognitive and behavioural components are separated from attitude such that attitude is considered to be uni-dimensional, i.e. consisting of only the component affect which can be described as the degree of liking/disliking, favourability/unfavourability towards the attitude object. There-fore the belief and behavioural elements present in the tripartite model are now considered to be antecedents (beliefs) or consequences (intention to behave) of attitude. Thus the uni-dimensionalist view proposes that we can see a causal flow through the components from beliefs to behaviour, which reflects the consistency of the tripartite model (see Figure 6.4).

Main theoretical perspectives on attitudes

There are three main categories of attitude theories: balance theories, motivational theo-ries, and multi-attribute expectancy-value theories.

Balance theory of attitudes

Heider's balance theory of attitudes considers the relationship between a person (a consumer), their perception of an attitude object (often a brand), and their perception of some other person or object that has a connection with this brand (e.g. a celebrity) (Lee et al., 2011). The person seeks a balance or alignment between these three elements. If the three elements feel at all unbalanced, the consumer adjusts their perception of one (or more) of the elements to bring all three into balance (Dalakas and Levin, 2005). A consumer may have a positive impression of swimmer Ryan Lochte who was associated with a number of brands including Speedo, and so feel similarly positively towards Speedo because of its connection with Lochte. However, in 2016 it emerged that he had embellished a story that he had been robbed at the Rio Olympics. Speedo dropped their sponsorship of Lochte in order to minimize the damage and to reduce any imbalance consumers may feel in relation to the Speedo—Lochte association.

Balance theory can also be considered when looking at the tri-component model of atti-tudes (affect, behaviour, and cognitions). There is a psychological drive to ensure that all three elements are balanced; if they are not, feelings of discomfort may arise and the con-sumer may adjust one of the components to bring them into line (Woodside and Chebat, 2001). Many people eat fast food (behaviour) and enjoy its taste and convenience (affect), but recognize that too much fast food is bad for their health and may lead to obesity (cognition). From a balance theory perspective, these are not in line with each other, and therefore the consumer changes one element to bring them to a more consistent direction. They could stop eating fast food (i.e. bring their behaviour in line with their thoughts about fast food and health), but they may also adjust their thoughts to support their fast food consumption. A common view expressed by people is that 'I do not eat enough of it to impact my weight or health'. This shift in cognition (belief) allows the three elements to be balanced and the consumer to develop an attitude that is in line with their behaviour—consuming fast food.

Linked to balance theory is the **theory of cognitive dissonance** (Festinger, 1957). **Cognitive dissonance** *is the state of having inconsistent beliefs and attitudes.* Cognitive dissonance is important in consumer behaviour as it is based on the belief that people need consistency or consonance between their behaviour and their attitudes. People will change their behaviour or their attitudes to maintain consistency and reduce feelings of unease (dissonance) that are present where an attitude or behaviour is inconsistent with some other information. Cognitive dissonance often emerges in relation to consumers eating fast food—after consumption consumers may try to downplay the health problems associated with fast food, and perhaps even emphasize the convenience benefits. Research Insight 6.2 looks at cognitive dissonance relating to deceptive packaging, and how this affects attitudes and subsequent buying behaviour.

RESEARCH INSIGHT 6.2

Wilkins, S., Beckenuyte, C., and Butt, M.M. (2016), 'Consumers' behavioural intentions after experiencing deception or cognitive dissonance caused by deceptive packaging, package downsizing or slack filling', *European Journal of Marketing*, 50, 1–2, 213–35.

This study examined the issue of deceptive packaging, focusing on consumer expectations in terms of pack fill (how much product they could expected to receive, given package size), cognitive dissonance (was there a discrepancy between expected and actual pack fill, and how this made them feel), and subsequent behavioural intentions around the product (would they purchase it again?). They confirmed a link between consumer expectations and cognitive dissonance, and discussed the importance for firms of not risking damage to their brand's reputation and consumer loyalty to the brand through these kinds of packaging practices.

 Access the online resources to read the abstract and access the full paper.

Motivational theories: the functional theory of attitudes

The functional theory of attitudes was proposed by Katz (1960). This approach is called a motivational theory of attitudes, and the theoretical idea is that in order to change attitudes it is important to first understand the motives (or functions) underpinning the attitudes (Kardes, 1993). According to this theory, advertising and marketing campaigns are most persuasive when they address the motives underlying the attitude targeted for change. This is an important theory for understanding consumer behaviour.

There are four main functions that attitudes can serve for people: *utilitarian, value-expressive, ego-defensive,* and *knowledge-based* (Russell-Bennett et al., 2013). The first is the **utilitarian function**, which stems from the idea that *consumers seek maximum utility and value from their consumption* (Grewal et al., 2004). The utilitarian function of attitudes is characterized by consumers seeking (and maximizing) rewards in their consumption and avoiding punishment. If you think about bottled water, you might think that the product fulfils your need for thirst, but it is also portable and handy when you are out and about. You place value on these useful aspects of the bottled water, and therefore you are seeking to fulfil a utilitarian motivation through your consumption, which informs your positive attitudes towards it.

Marketers of products and brands serving utilitarian functions benefit from recognizing that there is a greater likelihood that consumers will form positive attitudes if there is a good match between the consumer need and the brand which satisfies that need. Looking to other product categories, a consumer suffering from a headache may take ibuprofen for pain relief, which removes the pain they are suffering; this is a form of reward in theoretical terms. The packaging for Nurofen (Figure 6.5) illustrates the utilitarian function of attitudes, emphasizing the benefits following use of this brand—easy to swallow, fast and effective pain relief.

The second motivational function is the **ego-defensive** function. Here attitudes *have the function of defending our self-image,* making us feel better about ourselves (Kardes, 2001). Think about the grooming routines and rituals we undertake in the morning. We gargle with mouthwash to ensure that our breath does not smell unpleasant, and we put on deodorant to mask our natural body odours. We are hiding aspects of ourselves that we do not want others to experience. Fundamentally, this is what the ego-defensive function of attitudes is concerned with— protection of our sense of self, and ensuring that we control aspects of our selves that are deemed unacceptable in some way. Personal hygiene products such as Nivea's deodorant Invisible for Black and White (see Figure 6.6) are often discussed in terms of ego-defensive attitudes. This product incorporates a formula which does not stain black (or dark clothes) and

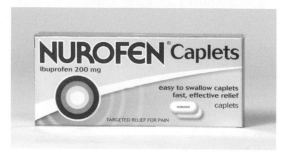

Figure 6.5 Nurofen as an example of utilitarian function

Source: Image courtesy of Reckitt Benckiser.

Figure 6.6 Nivea Invisible for Black & White deodorant

Source: © iStock.com/mrtom-uk.

also prevents white clothes from yellowing, thus protecting the consumer from having unsightly stains on their clothes which may make them feel self-conscious. In addition, the deodorant offers 48-hour dryness, giving the consumer confidence and security.

The third motivational function is the **value-expressive function**, or the social identity function (Shavitt, 1990; Schossler, 1998). This is concerned with *the drive to express important aspects of the self* (Grewal et al., 2004) and, linked to this, of the self that one aspires to be. This function is characterized by consumers using products and brands to project, rather than hide, some aspect of themselves or of how they would like to be perceived. An example of value-expressive function of brands is found in the luxury brand Louis Vuitton, which expresses the values of luxury, quality, and authenticity to the consumer, and thus communicates the status of the wearer. Louis Vuitton has collaborated with artists, including the Japanese artists Takashi

Figure 6.7   The Louis Vuitton/Kusama Collaboration
Source: iStock by Getty Images.

Murakama and Yayoi Kusama (see Figure 6.7) and more recently the Chapman brothers, to emphasize symbolic meanings for the brand around cultural authenticity. Wearing a bag designed by a great artist brings the consumer closer to the artist, expressing the consumer's cultural capital.

Finally, the **knowledge function** *relates to the human need to have a meaningful, stable, and organized view of the world,* 'involving forming accurate judgements about an object or issue' (Kardes, 1993: 169). The example of consumers choosing a mobile phone is useful for explaining this function. Often consumers find that they are looking to change their mobile phone because they have finished their contract and are eligible for a new one. If your current handset is a Nokia and you have been happy with this brand, you are likely to draw on your positive experience and knowledge about Nokia as you look to get a new handset. In this context, knowledge-based attitudes, built around brand and product information, act as a frame of reference to help the consumer understand and make sense of the consumption context of upgrading their phone.

These knowledge-based attitudes provide structure for consumers to evaluate new information. Another example may be a mother who has a positive attitude towards

Johnson & Johnson baby skincare products (see Figure 6.8), based on her experience with the brand. If Johnson & Johnson were to launch a new range of baby toy products, parents with a positive attitude towards Johnson & Johnson, based on their knowledge function, may be willing to try it. The knowledge-based function is important for marketing in helping to understand and predict consumer attitudes towards brand extensions and diversifications, since it helps consumers to organize and simplify new experiences.

Products, services, and brands can activate the motivational concerns of consumers. The examples outlined in this section provide instances where a product can be categorized as satisfying one predominant function, but products and brands can often serve multiple functions (Shavitt, 1989, 1990). A car is a good illustration of a multi-functioned product, since it can relate to both utilitarian concerns (e.g. around safety and performance) and value-expressive concerns (such as implied social status). Another example of a multi-functioned product is described in Consumer Insight 6.2.

Figure 6.8 Johnson & Johnson baby skincare products

Source: © iStock.com/evemilla.

CONSUMER INSIGHT 6.2

Attitudes towards tents from a functional theory perspective

Oase Outdoors is a Danish company that specializes in camping equipment, and is the parent company of the popular tent brands Outwell and EasyCamp (see Figure 6.9). These brands serve different markets. Outwell is an innovative camping brand, aimed at the family market, where quality and reliability are

(A)   (B)

Figure 6.9 Outwell tent and EasyCamp Carnival tent   *Source*: Images courtesy of Oase Outdoors.

important. In contrast, EasyCamp (http://www.
easycamp.com) is a budget range, producing
easy-to-pitch tents at a reasonable price. They
have a range called Carnival, aimed at the festival
market, which is 'light and bright, easy to use and
exudes an element of fun'.

From a functional theory of attitudes perspective, these tents are satisfying different
motivational functions. For the young person
buying a tent for a festival, the EasyCamp
brand meets their utilitarian needs of being
cheap and easy to pitch. Longevity of use (and
re-use) is not a primary concern. In fact, many
festival-goers seek cheap 'disposable' tents

Figure 6.10   Outwell brand extensions
Source: Image courtesy of Oase Outdoors.

that they can leave behind, which is an environmental concern and issue for festival organiz-
ers (Watson, 2016), For festival-goers, the tent may serve a secondary value—expressive function
around having a bright, colourful, and trendy tent that matches the mood of the festival event,
allowing them to express their social identity through use.

There may be similar motivational functions in place for the middle-class family buying a tent, but
they operate differently. The utilitarian function may be very important, not just in terms of how easy
the tent is to pitch, but also in terms of its innovative materials and design features, such as ventilation,
window design, and living space. Additionally, there is a strong value-expressive aspect to the Outwell
brand, viewed as a lifestyle tent brand. Ego-defensive motivations may also be at play, in terms of the
middle-class family being assured that they have the 'right' brand of tent that enables them to project
their aspirational self-image relating to their family role. Knowledge functions operate in terms of
helping buyers make sense of product information and lines available, as well as buying affiliated
products (brand extensions), such as an Outwell carpet for inside the tent (see Figure 6.10).

Questions

1.   How might a camping equipment company use the ideas of differing motivational functions to
     market its products to different consumer segments?

2.   Think of another brand that markets products to different target groups and identify the moti-
     vational functions served by their different products.

Sources: Kardes (1993); Shooter (2010); Watson (2016).

 Access the online resources and follow the web links to learn more.

Multi-attribute models of attitudes

The final category we are considering is the multi-attribute models of attitudes. Multi-
attribute models are used to understand and measure attitudes, and they work by

unpacking the many aspects or attributes of the attitude object (remember, this is what we are forming our attitude about) and attempting to work out how important each of these is to consumers.

The expectancy-value model

The basic multi-attribute model has three elements:

- *attributes* are the characteristics or features of the attitude object
- *beliefs* about the extent to which the object has the attributes
- *evaluations* are the levels of importance attached to the attributes.

If we take the example of attitudes towards Nespresso coffee (the attitude object), attributes might include characteristics such as flavour strength, caffeine level, aroma, colour, and coffee density. Beliefs would be the extent to which the consumer believes that Nespresso has these attributes. For example, a consumer may believe that the flavour is not strong enough, and so rate the coffee low on that belief. Finally, the evaluation measure is trying to gain a sense of how important that attribute is to the consumer. The same consumer may feel that the flavour strength is extremely important, and if he believes that Nespresso is lacking in that attribute then this is likely to reduce how he rates Nespresso overall. This model offers a way for marketers to unpack the range of factors that influence our overall attitude and evaluation of a brand, and to gain a sense of how important these factors are to consumers. Such an understanding can inform many aspects of product and brand development from the actual product design itself through to devising advertising campaigns to emphasize attributes viewed as important by consumers.

The most influential multi-attribute model—the Fishbein model (Fishbein and Azjen 1975)—also uses three components of attitude and, in a similar fashion, aims to establish the relative importance of each and how they inform consumer attitudes. This model aims to represent the mental calculations that consumers perform when developing attitudes and represents this by a numerical score. This model is also known as the **expectancy-value model**, which suggests *that people form attitudes towards objects (e.g. brands) based on their expectations and evaluations of the attributes that make up the brand.* Such models describe how these components relate to each other in order to produce attitudes. They have had a wide range of applications, including attitudes towards condom use in social marketing (Gabler et al., 2004), attitudes and intentions towards music piracy (Chiou et al., 2005), and attitudes towards counterfeit luxury goods (Phau and Teah, 2009). In order to explain this model more fully, it is useful to unpack and revisit some key terms.

The first is **attitude object**, which is *anything towards which we hold an attitude* (as discussed already in this chapter). As stated earlier, this can be a product, brand, service, or even idea, but the attitude object must be clearly defined. Sony may be interested in consumer attitudes towards Sony generally, but perhaps more useful for the company is to establish attitudes towards the latest Sony PlayStation specifically as the attitude object (or indeed any of its specific brands). In fact, Fishbein was concerned that the attitude measurement was as specific as possible, and suggested that we measure the attitude towards a behaviour, rather than an object (e.g. the attitude to buying the Sony PlayStation).

Next it is important to revisit beliefs. **Beliefs** are the *thoughts the consumer holds, which describe the object of the attitude, its charac-teristics, and its relations to other objects.* While a consumer may hold many beliefs in relation to the attitude object, the most salient beliefs (already described in this chapter) will have

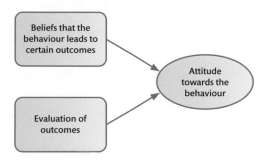

Figure 6.11 Relationship between beliefs, evaluations, and attitudes

greater importance for the consumer in that context. This is important for attitude stud-ies, since the attitude is formed based on the beliefs that are important to the consumer. Remember, beliefs in themselves do not indicate a particular attitude, i.e. beliefs do not have an affective (good or bad) component. For example, you may hold beliefs about different brands of mobile phone, but that in itself does not indicate whether you feel positively or negatively towards them. **Evaluation** refers *to the process of determining how valuable, or important, something is to us.* In the context of attitudes, evaluation refers to the process of judging the consequences of the beliefs associated with the attitude object. The evaluation of beliefs provides a way of unpacking the importance attached to each salient belief influencing attitude formation, since it provides a sense of how important each belief is to the consumer's attitude towards the object. Figure 6.11 shows graphically how these elements are related.

These elements form the building blocks of multi-attribute attitude models. The purpose of this approach is to express the relationships between these three elements as a way of representing how consumers form attitudes. In the consumer's mind, each belief is assigned a value, which is then multiplied by their evaluation scores. These values are combined across all the beliefs, and finally added to provide an overall atti-tude score.

Taking this approach to understanding attitudes requires that the person commis-sioning the research accepts that consumers can and do mentally assign values to each of the belief and evaluation components, and the multiplication of these can produce a score which represents their attitude towards an object. The beliefs must be salient, and these tend to be the first few that a respondent gives to an open-ended question such as 'Tell me what you think about …'. They may be different in different situations; for example, your beliefs regarding buying ice-cream will vary with the time of year. In Practitioner Insight 6, we spoke to Edward Langley, Head of Environment Research at Ipsos MORI (the leading provider of social research to the public services in the UK), to discover just how important research into consumer attitudes and beliefs is when plan-ning environmental initiatives. He also provides some insights into how attitudes are measured and tracked.

PRACTITIONER INSIGHT 6

Edward Langley, Head of Environment Research, Ipsos MORI

For some areas of consumer behaviour, it is very important to get a picture of the differences in people's beliefs and attitudes. Where there are issues that can divide communities, such as forms of energy, housing, or new transport links, it is very important for those involved to really understand how people differ in their positions.

In 2009, the Welsh Government launched the new Sustainable Development Scheme *One Wales: One Planet*. This scheme defined sustainable development as enhancing the economic, social, and environmental well-being of people and communities, achieving a better quality of life for our own and future generations in ways which promote social justice and equality of opportunity, and enhancing the natural and cultural environment and respecting its limits. In order to further the Sustainable Development Scheme the Welsh Government wanted to understand differences in people's beliefs and attitudes around sustainability. In 2012 we produced a survey for them which identified the Welsh population segmented on the basis of their values, beliefs, attitudes, and behaviours, with a view to help target and support interventions designed to deliver sustainable behaviours. To do this we had to identify the nature of relevant values (e.g. self-enhancement, openness to change, beliefs related to environmental and economic sustainability, and attitudes to such things as living in Wales, climate change, and sustainable lifestyles). Appropriate questions were developed and administered to a sample of over 1,500 people from across Wales, the responses from which enabled the project partnership to build a segmentation model. Six segments were identified: enthusiasts (17 per cent), pragmatists (21 per cent), aspirers (15 per cent), community-focused (20 per cent), commentators (12 per cent), and self-reliant (16 per cent). We also looked at the nature of each group in terms of demographic dimensions. From this we were able to build up a picture of the type of sustainable behaviours and attitudes prevalent in Wales; we could also see where consistencies and inconsistencies between attitudes and behaviour may lie. The community-focused segment favoured the economy over the environment, which they viewed as the concern of an 'alternative lifestyle'. Despite this they are concerned about waste, are committed recyclers, and are the second most likely group to say that they don't throw away much food. The youngest segment, with nearly half under 35, are aspirers. While they are concerned about the environment and climate change, they also consider success and wealth to be important values and are below average for 'recycling everything'. Such detailed analyses of attitudes will give policy-makers a much more nuanced understanding of how consumers might respond to initiatives and how they see such measures fitting in with their own beliefs and lifestyles. It can help to develop appropriate and targeted actions and communications.

This study was delivered in partnership with AD Research & Analysis Ltd and Cardiff University.

Theory of planned behaviour

Attitude theory has evolved to represent more fully the range of influences on attitude formation and intentions to behave in a certain way, and a revised and expanded version is the theory of planned behaviour (Figure 6.12).

The revised model includes **behavioural intention**, which is the *intention to act in some way*. Behaviour is determined by intentions, which are influenced by our attitudes. To illustrate, instead of investigating consumers' attitudes towards Saucony training shoes, the theory of planned behaviour would investigate consumers' attitudes towards *running in Saucony training shoes*. The subtle shift in emphasis focuses attention on the consumer's attitude towards the behaviour (running) attached to using the product, brand, or service, and provides a more accurate predictor of whether or not the behaviour will take place.

Here, behavioural intention is also influenced by the way in which the consumer pays attention to, and takes on board, the beliefs of key social influencers. Social influences are represented by the **subjective norm** concept, which *represents perceptions of specific significant others' preferences as to whether one should or should not engage in the behaviour* (Han et al., 2010). The subjective norm refers to the people who may influence the consumer in their consumption lives (e.g. parents, siblings, partner/spouse, friends, boss) and will vary from context to context. Your boss may be an important social influencer in terms of the clothes you wear to work, but your friends are likely to be more influential regarding the clothes you wear on a Friday night.

Just as the expectancy-value model focuses on calculating the scores for attitudes based on beliefs and evaluations, a similar approach is adopted in the theory of planned behaviour. However, additionally scores are calculated for the subjective norm and perceived behaviour control concepts. There are two aspects to the subjective norm. First, we have **normative**

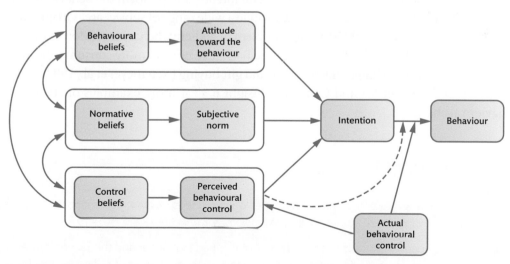

Figure 6.12 Theory of planned behaviour

beliefs which are the *individual's perception about relevant or significant others' beliefs that the individual should engage in the behaviour or not* (Ajzen, 2012). In the running example, a normative belief might be 'My friends think that it is a good thing for me to wear Saucony running shoes when I go out running'. It is worth pointing out that the response to a statement such as this represents the subjective perception of the participant, rather than an objective account of whether the friends really would think it a good thing to wear Saucony shoes. The second aspect of the subjective norm is the **motivation to comply,** which is *the extent to which the consumer wishes to comply with or conform to the perceived preferences of these important people* (Ajzen, 2012). A motivation to comply item might be 'It is important to me that my friends think I am wearing good running shoes'. The subjective norm score is calculated by multiplying the various normative belief and motivation to comply scores, and then adding them together.

The theory of planned behaviour includes the concept of **perceived behavioural control**, which is *the person's perception of how easy or difficult it is for them to perform the behaviour*. Perceived behavioural control gives an indication of an individual's own confidence in successfully performing the behaviour. For example, a consumer may have the intention of travelling to an IKEA store to buy a flatpack shelf unit. Perceived behavioural control may relate to how confident the consumer feels that the store stocks the item she wants; it may also include her confidence in her DIY skills and ability to follow the instructions. Other factors can also interfere with the consumer's control over their intended behaviour, including skills, abilities, and knowledge (internal), and time, opportunity, and dependence on others (external). The point is that perceived behavioural control accesses the range of factors that may intervene between deciding to do something and actually managing to do so.

Finally, the attitude, subjective norm, and perceived behavioural control scores are weighted (with respect to the relative importance of each of these components) and are then added together to provide a measure of the behavioural intention to perform the behaviour. Applications of the theory of planned behaviour include a wide range of subject areas from physical exercise (Ajzen and Driver, 1992) through problem or addictive behaviours (Morojele and Stephenson, 1992; Schlegl et al., 1992; Devries and Backbier, 1994) to more consumption-related behaviours such as recycling (Boldero, 1995) and gift buying (Netemeyer et al., 1993).

See Research Insight 6.3 and Consumer Insight 6.3 for more examples of attitude and behavioural change.

RESEARCH INSIGHT 6.3

Yang, H.C. and Wang, Y. (2015), 'Social sharing of online videos: examining American consumers' video sharing attitudes, intent, and behavior', *Psychology & Marketing*, 32, 9, 907–19.

In this research paper, the authors used the Theory of Planned Behaviour and the Technology Acceptance Model to examine attitudes, intent, and behaviour towards sharing of online videos. Taking a mixed-method approach, the findings suggests that US consumers are more willing to share online videos if they hold positive attitudes towards this practice, and that their stronger intention to share online videos did translate into a higher number of online videos shared. The authors also found that subjective norms influence consumers' online video sharing intent and behaviour—that is, if other people important to you think it's acceptable, then this is likely to impact on your attitudes and intentions to share online videos!

 Access the online resources to read the abstract and access the full paper.

CONSUMER INSIGHT 6.3

Attitude change in social marketing

Within social marketing, attitude theories are fairly widely used to inform interventions aimed at attitude and behavioural change. Such strategies often aim to influence and change behaviour by modifying the beliefs that individuals hold. This is especially important, given that these beliefs underline their attitudes, their perceptions of social norms and their motivations to comply, and support their sense of personal control over the situations in which the behaviour takes place. Examples of some recent social marketing campaigns based around attitude change include the following:

Road safety

Arrive alive DRIVE SOBER® is a Canadian campaign, which has been running for 25 years and aims to change attitudes towards drink driving and encourage sober driving. This campaign uses a wide range of marketing communications techniques, including social media (Twitter, YouTube, Facebook) and a mobile phone app (the 'Arrive Alive Mobile App') to raise awareness of the risks associated with drink driving (Leonard, 2013).

Clothes recycling

Schwopping M&S/Oxfam: to encourage consumers to donate their unwanted clothes to Oxfam, the charity runs a scheme, in partnership with Marks & Spencer, where donors receive a £5 M&S shopping voucher for donating clothes to Oxfam. This campaign operates at the behavioural aspect of attitudes, trying to encourage people to change their behaviour through a reward. The campaign has been running successfully since 2008, and more recently M&S have launched an online platform (Shwop Shop), where consumers can buy items of clothing that used to belong to celebrities (including models, actors, and popstars). This operates more at the beliefs and motivation level, encouraging consumers to view buying recycled clothes as a high status activity.

Sources: Leonard (2013); http://www.arrivealive.org http://www.oxfam.org.uk/shop/shwop-shop http://corporate.marksandspencer.com/plan-a/our-stories/partnerships/oxfam

Questions

1. From your understanding of attitude theory, devise a set of questions you might use to inform a study tracking attitudes towards recycled clothes. Look back over the various theories covered in this chapter, and try and map your questions onto the theoretical concepts (such as listing beliefs, evaluations of beliefs).

2. What do you think are the benefits and disadvantages associated with measuring and tracking attitude change?

3. Consider the kind of communications campaign you might put together using attitude theory to lessen the impact of binge drinking in cities at night. Consider who your targets would be and what the different elements of your campaign would include.

Access the online resources and follow the web links to learn more about social marketing and attitude change.

Critique of multi-attribute models of attitudes

While these theories have been widely used in academic research in social marketing and health sciences, their use in commercial marketing has not been widespread. There are a number of reasons for this. As the expectancy-value model takes account of the impact of social influences through the subjective norm construct, it works best for behaviours for which individuals are solely responsible (known as volitional control). The emotional aspects of consumption are not clearly dealt with in this model, although some studies have overcome this limitation by including emotions (such as regret or guilt) in the model (Ajzen, 2011). Overall, these multi-attribute models can be difficult to administer in practice, since there are a number of elements to be measured, leading to fairly lengthy questionnaires. Generally these models have proved most useful where people have quite strong opinions and are aware of the opinions of others, including social and personal issues such as contraception, smoking, and health-related topics. However, it is important to recognize the contribution that such models have made to help understand consumer behaviour. First, they have reduced to clear and simple terms the key elements that contribute to behavioural intentions. Second, their diagnostic properties have been found useful for identifying how people perceive and evaluate the attributes of a brand. In terms of understanding an attitude to a particular brand, if it is possible to determine a person's beliefs and evaluations of those beliefs, the company can identify what it might do in terms of changing any of those elements or introducing new beliefs that might be relevant to their brand.

Compensatory and non-compensatory models

An important feature of the multi-attribute models discussed so far is that they are compensatory in nature. **Compensatory models** *are made up of a number of beliefs and use a scoring system to derive a final score—a low score in one belief/evaluation can be compensated by a higher score in another.* In attitude research, the beliefs are often weighted equally, implying that they have the same importance. However, we know that for some purchase decisions just one belief or evaluation of belief may be the overriding factor in behavioural intent. Consumers may use different types of **decision rules** to identify what is the best choice for them. For example, if you are choosing a new TV but you live in a small flat, while you might have many positive beliefs regarding the quality and style of alternative brands, your decision might be totally dependent on the size of the TV. This is what we call a **non-compensatory model**, i.e. *one overriding factor or attitude is dominant in the choice process*. A number of different decision rules may be used in non-compensatory models. If a customer uses the **conjunctive decision rule** it implies that *they will choose a brand based on minimum levels for each of any key evaluative attributes*. Any brand that meets all the cut-off points will be considered for purchase. Using the **lexicographic decision rule** the customer would *rank the evaluative attributes by their importance*. They would then begin by considering the attribute most important to them and pick the brand that performs best. If brands tie, the consumer looks to the next most important attribute and so on. The **elimination-by-aspects decision rule** *ranks evaluative aspects by importance again and establishes a minimum cut-off point for each attribute*. Ranking begins with the most important attribute; a brand that does not meet the satisfactory cut-off point is eliminated and the remaining brands are evaluated on the next most important and so on until one brand remains. Full examples of all these rules are provided in Case Study 6.

In summary, we have considered in some detail three main categories of attitude model:

(1) balance theory, and the associated theory of cognitive dissonance

(2) motivational function theories of attitudes

(3) multi-attribute models, including discussion of the expectancy-value model, the theory of planned behaviour, and compensatory and non-compensatory models of attitudes.

We will now go on to consider how these can be used to influence behaviour change among consumers.

Attitudes and behaviour change

As we discussed earlier in this chapter, attitudes are learned, and are amenable to change and influence using the processes associated with consumer learning (Chapter 4). The influences on attitude formation are wide-ranging, but can relate to personal experiences, social influences, and marketing. The main opportunities for marketing to influence attitudes relate to the theoretical explanations offered for attitude formation and, building on the main approaches covered in this chapter, we will now consider how attitudes can be changed.

Changing the basic motivational function

This strategy builds on Katz's motivational theory of attitudes, which comprises four functions: utilitarian, value-expressive, ego-defensive, and knowledge. This approach to attitude change involves understanding the motivational needs driving attitude formation,

Figure 6.13 Comparing 'Simply M&S' with 'Your M&S' labels
Source: Images courtesy of Marks & Spencer.

and ensuring that there is a match between consumer need and the ability of the product or brand to meet this need. The launch of 'Simply M&S' food by the British retailer Marks & Spencer might be considered as satisfying utilitarian needs—offering good value for money, a simple product, at a particular quality level. The 'Simply M&S' label contrasts with the 'Your M&S' slogan, which ran across all product lines, including food, and served a more value-expressive social identity function, where cost and value were emphasized less and the link to identity was provided through the use of the word 'your'. Both campaigns are shown in Figure 6.13.

Altering components of the multi-attribute model

Marketers need to understand attitudes not only towards their products and brands, but also towards those of their competitors. Companies engage in brand-tracking exercises examining consumer attitudes towards their brands, and from this try to establish key aspects of the brand attributes that appeal to consumers. If companies understand how consumers feel about their offerings and those of their competitors, they are in a better position to understand what it is about the product category that is important to consumers, and thus to adjust or add new attributes based on this research. Linked to this approach, organizations or companies may attempt to change consumer beliefs about their offering. The Fairtrade organization launched a campaign in 2017 (Vizard, 2017), to change consumers' attitudes to fair trade products. By focusing on the emotional aspects

Figure 6.14   An advertisement from the Fairtrade campaign 'Don't Feed Exploitation'
Source: Image courtesy of the Fairtrade Organisation, and Christopher Terry.

of fair trade products instead of rational factors, the campaign 'Don't Feed Exploitation' centred on what unfair trade looks like, and how we as consumers have a role to play (Figure 6.14).

It is clear from the expectancy-value model and the theory of planned behaviour models, that evaluations of beliefs are also important, and this may be a useful route for influencing or adjusting consumer attitudes. Governments aiming to discourage young people from excessive alcohol consumption may seek to use social marketing efforts to influence them to change their evaluation of the consequences of drinking heavily. This approach was used in the Alcohol Advisory Council of New Zealand's campaign which sent out powerful messages about the consequences of excessive drinking, with the strapline 'Was last night really worth it?'. By showing a range of consequences across different contexts (such as a girl on a hospital bed looking bruised and dishevelled, and a family scene where a father figure is sitting alone looking ashamed of himself), the campaign encouraged consumers to pause and think about the potential consequences of heavy drinking, and ultimately, through changing beliefs, to influence attitudes and behaviour with respect to heavy drinking. In the past companies have also tried to directly influence the beliefs that people hold about their competitor's brands in a bid to make their brand appear superior. However, this can be dangerous as competitors can respond in kind and ultimately this can result in legal action (Beard, 2015)

Consumer Insight 6.4 provides another example of influencing consumer attitudes.

CONSUMER INSIGHT 6.4

Consumer attitudes to data and privacy

There is a growing acceptance of the use of big data in business, i.e. that companies can access a wealth of data about their customers in order to develop more tailored and innovative products or services. What consumers think and feel about their personal data, and the level of trust they have that the company will protect their information, is a key issue for marketing. Research shows how consumers' attitudes towards privacy and sharing data vary by situation, as well as by the company or organization involved. A study by Quint and Rogers (2015) examined consumer views on 'What is the future of data sharing?' collecting information from over 8,000 consumers from the USA, the UK, Canada, France, and Mexico. Aside from identifying the types of data consumers feel are the most sensitive pieces of information, (address, mobile telephone number, name and date of birth), Quint and Rogers (2015) identified four main types of mindsets around data sharing.

- Defenders (43 per cent) have a negative attitude towards sharing data, and will take defensive actions to protect it from companies (such as making up personal details to avoid giving away real information, or taking steps to limit companies from tracking them online).

- Savvy and in control (24 per cent) are happy to share data with companies for added value, but will take defensive actions at times to protect it from companies.

- Resigned (23 per cent) have a negative attitude towards sharing data, but do not do anything to actively avoid providing it to companies.

- Happy go lucky (10 per cent) are happy to share data with companies for added value, and do not take any actions to avoid sharing it with companies.

Younger generations are more likely to be in the savvy and in control group, and this is expected to grow in the next few years. There has also been an increase in consumer complaints relating to how companies are sharing their personal information. The Direct Marketing Commission (DMC) produced a report showing that consumers are worried and confused over consent and third-party data (Roderick, 2017). These cases often involved complex supply chains, where the original consent (or lack of consent) had been disregarded, thus breaking DMA Code. This kind of breach can cause serious reputational damage, making consumers distrustful of companies and forming negative attitudes towards consenting to data sharing.

Questions

1. Discuss your attitudes towards data sharing in online shopping contexts with two or three other people. Do you think you can classify yourselves into one of the four categories from the Quint and Rogers (2015) study? How useful are these categories for thinking about attitudes towards data sharing? Can you think of situations where they would be more or less applicable?

2. Using your knowledge of consumer attitude theory, analyse consumer attitudes towards sharing their personal data in a range of online shopping contexts (e.g. financial services, airline, clothes shopping). Analyse consumer attitudes from two different perspectives. Which theory of attitudes is most useful and in which context?

Sources: Quint and Rogers (2015); Roderick (2017).

 Access the online resources and follow the web link to learn more.

Elaboration likelihood model

One model that is useful for considering the mechanisms of attitude change is the elaboration likelihood model (ELM) (Petty and Cacioppo, 1986). The ELM focuses on the ways that consumers respond to communication messages, and is shown in Figure 6.15.

The ELM details the psychological processes by which attitudes are created and changed, providing insights into how attitudes can be formed or modified. Central to this model is the **elaboration continuum**, *which describes the amount of thought (elaboration) given to an advertising message or persuasive communication* (Petty and Briñol, 2012). Elaboration likelihood ranges from high (deep critical engagement) to low (less engagement), and the ways in which information is processed will depend on the level of engagement. As shown in Figure 6.15, high elaboration (greater thinking and engagement) leads to central route processing, and low elaboration (less thinking) leads to peripheral route processing.

High elaboration tends to accompany highly involved consumer situations, and typically involves the consumer systematically and critically engaging with the information in the advertising message (O'Keefe, 2008). The highly involved consumer is likely to pay attention to the information, and then carefully evaluate new information in relation to their existing knowledge and develop an attitude based on logical reasoning. When consumers are motivated to pay attention to an advertising message, they consciously think about the ad and tend to take a logical central route to decision-making. This is known as *central route processing*—they make greater use of information that relates to the product features in evaluating the product (Rucker and Petty, 2006). The

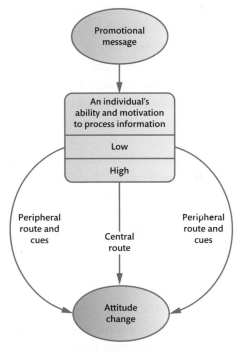

Figure 6.15   The elaboration likelihood model

Source: Petty, R.E. and Cacioppo, J.T., *Communication and persuasion: central and peripheral routes to attitude change*, published 1986, New York: Springer-Verlag, reproduced with permission of SCSC.

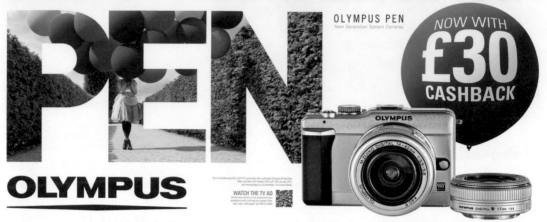

Figure 6.16 Olympus PEN camera advertising campaign   *Source*: Image courtesy of Wallop Design.

advertisement for the Olympus PEN camera (Figure 6.16) provides a good illustration of a persuasive communication that mainly aims to encourage central route processing to elicit deep thinking and engagement about the brand. This advertisement is engaging, is information oriented (with good use of text and engaging images), and also has a QR code, which takes consumers to the online TV advertisement ('Watch the TV ad'), encouraging deeper engagement with the brand.

When elaboration likelihood is low (i.e. when people are less likely to pay attention to persuasive messages), they make less effort to evaluate new information and bring less of their own information to bear in forming their attitude to the product or service (Petty and Briñol, 2012). Here, *peripheral route processing* occurs, where consumers pay less attention to the persuasive arguments in advertising messages but instead are influenced by the surface characteristics of the advertisement or product. The emphasis is on the images used, the speakers (often celebrities), and the use of emotional connections between the product/brand and the consumer. The 2016 campaign by Chinese mobile brand Huawei, featuring the Hollywood stars Scarlett Johansson and Henry Cavill, provides a good illustration of peripheral processing. The ad for its new P9 smartphone follows the actors through the day, as they send each other snaps from film sets and exotic locations, getting increasingly competitive with each image shared. It is fun and engaging, and connects with audiences on an emotional level.

Communications messages can draw on both central and peripheral routes to encourage deeper elaboration and engagement, as demonstrated in the award-winning print advert for the Prostate Cancer Foundation (Figure 6.17). This image is definitely eye-catching and captures the viewer's attention (peripheral processing route), but then draws you in to read the small print which informs you about detection methods for prostate cancer, which are connected to the image in the advertisement ('The early detection examination for prostate cancer no longer takes place where it would be expected. A simple blood test in the crook

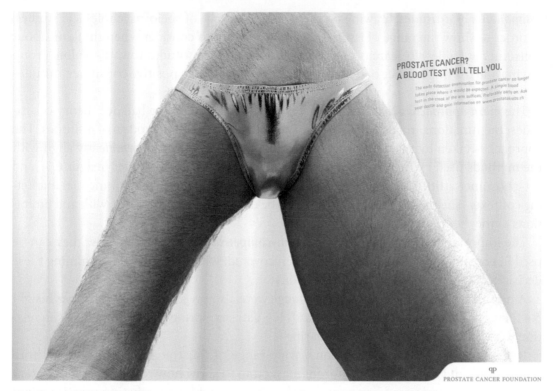

Figure 6.17   Prostate Cancer Foundation   *Source*: Image courtesy of Jung von Matt (www.jvm.com).

of the arm suffices. Preferably early on. Ask your doctor and gain information on www.
prostatekrebs.ch'). The textual part of the advertisement encourages deeper engagement,
and hence a central processing route.

Understanding the routes to persuasion is important for marketers, since it encourages a deeper appreciation of the circumstances under which the different routes to attitude formation and change are likely to occur. Knowing the impact that levels of involvement and motivation have on the ways that consumers engage with marketing cues is a useful starting point when devising content and messages for marketing strategies.

Conclusions

Attitudes are important for marketers and can act as both an obstacle to their strategies and as a way of helping to ensure that they fully understand their consumers. In this chapter, we *defined the concept of attitudes* as used in consumer marketing, emphasizing the importance of the link between attitudes and behaviour, as explored in Consumer Insight 6.1 which examined attitudes towards credit and debt. We then discussed the *main components of attitudes*, drawing on theory from a range of socio-psychological studies, in order to show the range of issues that are important to consider when thinking about consumer attitudes. Research Insight 6.1 focused on the attitudes towards online group buying and the importance of trustworthiness for developing positive consumer attitudes in this situation.

The *main approaches to attitudes* were presented, including the balance theory of attitudes, the functional theory of attitudes, and the multi-attribute models of attitudes. The approaches taken by academics when studying attitudes do not always neatly align with the methods used by marketing practice (as demonstrated in Consumer Insight 6.3), and yet 'consumer attitudes' are frequently examined and called upon in commercial marketing contexts. The mismatch in approach may be due to some of the issues with and limitations of the theories discussed in this chapter.

The importance of *compensatory and non-compensatory models* and how they can be used in consumer decision-making was then covered, with Case Study 6 examining these decision rules in the context of buying a house.

A number of approaches to *attitude change* were also presented, and Consumer Insight 6.4 focused on consumer attitudes towards big data, exploring some of the issues in relation to attitudes to data privacy and sharing.

In this chapter, we have drawn on a wide range of illustrative examples from both commercial and social or not-for-profit marketing to show how relevant and important attitudes are to understanding consumer behaviour, and *how marketing practice might work with and build on this theory*. Above all, understanding the components of attitudes can help marketing professionals better position and reposition their brands in the market.

Review questions

1. Define attitudes, and comment on the various components of attitudes.

2. What do you understand by the term 'hierarchy of effects'? Provide illustrations of your own from four different contexts, mapping these onto each of the hierarchy of effects outlined in the chapter.

3. Describe balance theory, and comment on how it is useful for marketing. Provide two different illustrations of balance theory.

4. What do you understand by the term 'cognitive dissonance'? How can marketers use this theory to inform their activities?

5. Explain the functional theory of attitudes and illustrate with examples.

6. Describe the evolution of, and the components within, the theory of planned behaviour.

7. In terms of attitude theory, what is meant by compensatory and non-compensatory models?

8. What are the main approaches to attitudinal change? Give illustrations drawing on each of the main theoretical approaches to attitudes.

Discussion questions

1. Choose any consumer context, and analyse a range of brand offerings within that category in terms of the functional theory of attitudes (you may wish to revisit the analysis of tents provided in Consumer Insight 6.2).

2. Attitudes are commonly referred to and used in marketing practice, but marketing managers rarely draw on the theory of planned behaviour to inform their studies of consumer attitudes. Why do you think this might be the case? What evidence can you find to back this up?

3. You have been asked by your local community to develop a strategy to encourage greater use of public transport. Based on your understanding of attitude theory, what would you advise them?

4. Access the Online Resource Centre and follow the web link to learn about the global homeless charity Depaul (https://int.depaulcharity.org/our-work/where-we-work-0). Use your knowledge of attitude theory and measurement to work out how you would examine attitudes towards donating to Depaul. Approach this issue using two completely different theories. Which one is most useful/appropriate? What recommendations would you make for trying to assess attitudes towards donating to this charity?

Access the online resources to test your knowledge further and complete the Multiple Choice Questions for Chapter 6.

CASE STUDY 6

Decision rules when buying a house

In this exercise, we consider the case of a consumer buying a house, and specifically how they might come to a purchase decision based on the type of decision rule they use. You must be familiar with the material in this chapter on both the compensatory and non-compensatory decision rules (conjunctive, lexicographic, elimination by aspect) in order to analyse this material.

Attributes (B_i)	House 1	House 2	House 3	House 4
Price	4	5	3	6
Proximity to school	2	4	6	4
Size of garden	2	3	4	4
Location	6	5	2	3
Renovation required	4	3	4	1
Size of kitchen	6	5	5	4

Table 6.2   Key attributes rated for each house

Imagine you are buying a new family house. While there are likely to be a number of key features or attributes of the house that would be important to you, you are probably aware that your perfect house may not exist, or will be too expensive, or at the very least will have some drawbacks. Often in decisions like this we have to consider what is most important to us, and even make compromises in areas that are less important. We are going to look at a range of attributes and their evaluations, and consider how the different models (and rules) might lead to the development of different attitude scores and ultimately decisions.

Attributes and evaluation scores

Table 6.2 contains information comparing four potential houses in terms of attributes that you might consider to be important when making a house purchase. Taking each attribute in turn, we have come up with a hypothetical rating for each house according to the importance of that attribute. Looking at 'price', house 4 ranks best on this feature, since it is the highest score of 6. For 'location', houses 1 and 2 rate the highest (scored 6 and 5, respectively).

In Table 6.3, we provide an evaluation of these attributes, which is the weighting for the importance of each of these attributes to the consumer. For this house buyer, 'location' and 'size of kitchen' are the most important attributes, and hence are given the highest evaluation scores (4 each), while the size of the garden is the least important feature (with a score of 1).

Attributes (B_i)	Evaluation score (E_i)
Price	3
Proximity to school	2
Size of garden	1
Location	4
Renovation required	1.5
Size of kitchen	4

Table 6.3   Evaluation scores for each attribute

Attributes (B_i)	Evaluation score (E_i)	House 1	House 2	House 3	House 4
Price	3	4 × 3 = 12			
Proximity to school	2	2 × 2 = 4			
Size of garden	1	2 × 1 = 2			
Location	4	6 × 4 = 24			
Renovation required	1.5	4 × 1.5 = 6			
Size of kitchen	4	6 × 4 = 24			
Total attitude score $\Sigma B_i \times E_i$		72			

Table 6.4   Attitude calculations based on compensatory model

Application of the compensatory model

You will recall that the compensatory model is one where all the key attributes and evaluations are included. Compensation occurs because a low evaluation on one particular attribute can be compensated for by a high evaluation on another attribute.

Using this approach to determine the attitude towards each house, you need to use the following calculation:

where Σ is the sum total, B_i is the attribute ranking for each house, E_i is the numerical evaluation rating for each attribute, and n is the total number of attributes. All the numerical scores required to find the attitude values are provided in Tables 6.2 and 6.3. From this information and the equation, you can calculate the attitude score for each house. Table 6.4 provides the calculations for house 1, to show this process.

Calculate the attitude scores for the other houses, and from this information work out which house would be chosen.

Application of non-compensatory models

Conjunctive decision rule

Now consider that, rather than using a compensatory rule, you use the *conjunctive decision rule*, where you choose a product or brand based on the minimum attribute score for each of any key attributes. Any brand that meets *all* the cut-off points will be considered for purchase. In our example, the cut-off point for attributes is 3 for every attribute *except* 'price', where the cut off is 4, and 'location', with a cut-off of 5 (see Table 6.6). Table 6.5 gives the calculations for house 1, to show this process.

Now, calculate the cut-offs for the other houses, and from this information work out which house would be chosen. Remember, use the key attributes provided in Table 6.2 (you do not need to use the evaluation scores this time). Is the same house chosen as when applying the compensatory model?

Lexicographic decision rule

Looking at the other non-compensatory rules, now try and apply the *lexicographic decision rule* to calculate attitudes towards the houses. Using the lexicographic rule the customer would rank the

Attributes (B_i)	Cut-off	House 1	House 2	House 3	House 4
Price	4	4 (Yes)			
Proximity to school	3	2 (No)			
Size of garden	3	2 (No)			
Location	5	6 (Yes)			
Renovation required	3	4 (Yes)			
Size of kitchen	3	6 (Yes)			
Meets all attribute cut-offs		No			

Table 6.5 Calculations based on non-compensatory model: conjunctive rule

evaluative attributes by their importance, and would then choose the house (or brand or product) which performs best on the attribute most important to them. In the event of a tie between two options, the consumer looks to the next most important attribute and so on. Using Table 6.6, where attributes are ranked in importance with price most and size of kitchen least important, you can work out which house would be chosen based on the lexicographic rule.

Elimination-by-aspects decision rule

Finally, you can work out which house would be chosen based on the *elimination-by-aspects decision rule*, where evaluative aspects are ranked by importance and a minimum cut-off point is established for each attribute. Ranking begins with the most important and a brand that does not meet the satisfactory cut-off is eliminated; the remaining brands are evaluated on the next most important and so on until one brand remains. Using the information provided in Table 6.6 about ranking and cut-off points, calculate which house would be chosen using this approach.

General questions

Once you have completed the exercise discuss with your classmates what differences you note. What did you notice about how different the results were and why they were different? Were there any surprising results? What recommendations for marketing do you have following this exercise?

Attributes (B_i)	Ranking	Cut-off points
Price	1	4
Proximity to school	2	3
Size of garden	3	3
Location	4	5
Renovation required	5	3
Size of kitchen	6	3

Table 6.6 Ranking and cut-off points

References

Ajzen, I. (2005), *Attitudes, personality and behaviour*, Maidenhead: Open University Press.

Ajzen, I. (2011), 'The theory of planned behaviour: reactions and reflections', *Psychology & Health*, 26, 9, 1113–27.

Ajzen, I. (2012), *'Theory of planned behavior'*, in P.A.M. Van Lange, A.W. Kruglanski, and E.T. Higgins (eds), *Handbook of theories of social psychology*, Vol. 1, London: Sage, pp.438–59.

Ajzen, I. and Driver, B.L. (1992), 'Application of the theory of planned behaviour to leisure choice', *Journal of Leisure Research*, 24, 3, 207–24.

Alexandris, K., Tsiotsou, R., and James, J. (2012), 'Testing a hierarchy of effects model of sponsorship effectiveness', *Journal of Sport Management*, 26, 5, 363–78.

Beard, F. (2015), 'The effectiveness of comparative versus non-comparative advertising: do "strictly" comparative ads hurt credibility of non-professional service brands?', *Journal of Advertising Research*, 55, 3, 296–306.

Beatty, S.E. and Kahle, L. R. (1988), 'Alternative hierarchies of the attitude-behavior relationship: the impact of brand commitment and habit', *Journal of the Academy of Marketing Science*, 16, 2, 1–10.

Boldero, J. (1995), 'The prediction of household recycling of newspapers—the role of attitudes, intentions and situational factors', *Journal of Applied Psychology*, 25, 5, 440–62.

Chiou, J.S., Huang, C.Y., and Lee, H.H. (2005), 'The antecedents of music piracy attitudes and intentions', *Journal of Business Ethics*, 57, 2, 161–74.

Dalakas, V. and Levin, A.M. (2005), 'The balance theory domino: how sponsorships may elicit negative consumer attitudes', *Advances in Consumer Research*, 32, 91–7.

Devries, H. and Backbier, E. (1994), 'Self-efficacy as an important determinant of quitting among pregnant women who smoke: the phi pattern', *Preventive Medicine*, 23, 2, 27–37.

Festinger, L. (1957), *A theory of cognitive dissonance*, Stanford, CA: Stanford University Press.

Fishbein, M. and Ajzen, I (1975), *Belief, attitude, intention and behavior*, Reading, MA: Addison-Wesley.

Gabler, J., Kropp, F., Silvera, D.H., and Lavack, A.M. (2004), 'The role of attitudes and self-efficacy in predicting condom use and purchase intentions', *Health Marketing Quarterly*, 21, 3, 63–78.

Grewal, R., Mehta, R., and Kardes, F.R. (2004), 'The timing of repeat purchases of consumer durable goods: the role of functional bases of consumer attitudes', *Journal of Marketing Research*, 41, 1, 101–15.

Grimm, P.E. (2005), 'Ab components' impact on brand preference', *Journal of Business Research*, 58, 4, 508–17.

Han, H., Hsu, L.T.J., and Sheu, C. (2010), 'Application of the theory of planned behavior to green hotel choice: testing the effect of environmental friendly activities', *Tourism Management*, 31, 3, 325–34.

Henderson, S. and Hoque, S.F. (2010), 'The ethnicity impact on attitudes toward country of origin for products with different involvement levels', *Journal of International Consumer Marketing*, 22, 3, 271–91.

Herr, P.M. and Fazio, R.H. (1993), 'The attitude-to-behavior process: implications', in A. Mitchell (ed.), *Advertising exposure, memory and choice*, Hillsdale, NJ: Lawrence Erlbaum, pp.119–40.

Kang, T.S. and Ma, G. (2007) 'Recent episodes of credit card distress in Asia', *BIS Quarterly*, June, 55–68.

Kardes, F.R. (1993) 'Consumer inference: determinants, consequences and implications for advertising', in A. Mitchell (ed.), *Advertising exposure, memory and choice*, Hillsdale, NJ: Lawrence Erlbaum, pp.163–93.

Kardes, F.R. (2001), *Consumer behaviour and managerial decision making* (2nd edn), Upper Saddle River, NJ: Prentice Hall.

Katz, D. (1960), 'The functional approach to the study of attitudes', *Public Opinion Quarterly*, 24, 163–204.

Lane, P. (2012), 'Austerity's children', *Harvard International Review, From the Blogs*, Summer, 4–5, http://hir.harvard.edu/blogpat-laneausteritys-children/ (accessed 4 March 2017).

Lee, H.M., Lee, C.C., and Wu, C.C. (2011), 'Brand image strategy affects brand equity after M&A', *European Journal of Marketing*, 45, 7/8, 1091–111.

Leonard, A. (2013), 'Arrive Alive app—a road map', presented at World Social Marketing Conference, Toronto, 21–23 April.

Lutz, R.J. (1991), 'The role of attitude theory in marketing', in H.H. Kassarijian and T.S. Robertson (eds), *Perspectives in consumer behavior* (4th edn), Glenview, IL: Scott, Foresman, pp.317–39.

Mintel (2011), 'Consumer attitudes towards debt—UK', http://oxygen.mintel.com/display/638223/# (accessed 20 February 2017).

Mintel (2016a), 'American lifestyles—US', http://www.mintel.com/press-centre/social-and-lifestyle/americans-cash-in-on-recession-savings-in-pursuit-of-experiential-activities-entertainment-markets-thrive-while-clothing-and-household-markets-take-a-hit (accessed 23 February 2017)

Mintel (2016b), 'European consumers more concerned over Brexit economic impact than the UK', http://www.mintel.com/press-centre/social-and-lifestyle/european-consumers-more-concerned-over-brexit-economic-impact-than-the-uk (accessed 20 February 2017)

Morojele, N.K. and Stephenson, G.M. (1992), 'The Minnesota model in the treatment of addictions: a social psychological assessment of changes in beliefs and attributions', *Journal of Community and Applied Social Psychology*, 2, 1, 25–41.

Netemeyer, R.G., Andrews, J.C., and Durvasula, S. (1993), 'A comparison of three behavioural intentions models: the case of Valentine's Day gift giving', *Advances in Consumer Research*, 20, 1, 135–41.

O'Keefe, D.J. (2008) 'The elaboration likelihood model', in W. Donsbach (ed.), *International encyclopaedia of communication*, Vol. 4, Boston, MA: Blackwell, pp 1475–80.

O'Loughlin, D. and Szmigin, I. (2006), '"I'll always be in debt": Irish and UK student behaviour in a credit led environment', *Journal of Consumer Marketing*, 23, 6, 335–43.

Oskamp, S. and Schultz, W. (2005), *Attitudes and opinions*, Hillsdale, NJ: Lawrence Erlbaum.

Peñaloza, L. and Barnhart, M. (2011), 'Living U.S. capitalism: the normalization of credit/debt', *Journal of Consumer Research*, 38, 4, 743–62.

Petty, R.E. and Briñol, P. (2012), 'The elaboration likelihood model', in P.A.M. Van Lange, A.W. Kruglanski, and E.T. Higgins (eds), *Handbook of theories of social psychology*, Vol. 1, London: Sage, pp.224–45.

Petty, R.E. and Cacioppo, J.T. (1986), *Communication and persuasion: central and peripheral routes to attitude change*, New York: Springer-Verlag.

Phau, I. and Teah, M. (2009), 'Devil wears (counterfeit) Prada: a study of antecedents and outcomes of attitudes towards counterfeits of luxury brands', *Journal of Consumer Marketing*, 26, 1, 15–27.

Quint, M. and D. Rogers (2015), *What is the future of data sharing? Consumer mindsets and the power of brands*, Report, Center on Global Brand Leadership, Columbia Business School.

Roderick, L. (2017), 'Confusion around consent and data sharing still reigns', *Marketing Week*, 6 January.

Rucker, D.D. and Petty, R.E. (2006), 'Increasing the effectiveness of communications to consumers: recommendations based on elaboration likelihood and attitude certainty perspectives', *Journal of Public Policy and Marketing*, 25, 1, 39–52.

Russell-Bennett, R., Härtel, C.E., and Worthington, S. (2013), 'Exploring a functional approach to attitudinal brand loyalty', *Australasian Marketing Journal*, 21, 1, 43–51.

Schlegl, R.P., Davernas, J.R., and Zanna, M.P. (1992), 'Problem drinking: a problem for the theory of reasoned action', *Journal of Applied Social Psychology*, 22, 5, 358–85.

Schossler, A. (1998), 'Applying the functional theory of attitudes to understanding the influence of store atmosphere on store inferences', *Journal of Consumer Psychology*, 7, 4, 345–69.

Shavitt, S. (1989), 'Operationalizing functional theories of attitude', in A.R. Pratkanis, S.J. Breckler, and A.G. Greenwald (eds), *Attitude structure and function*, Hillsdale, NJ: Lawrence Erlbaum.

Shavitt, S. (1990), 'The role of attitude objects in attitude functions', *Journal of Experimental Social Psychology*, 26, 124–48.

Shooter, A. (2010), 'Carry on glamping! That's GLAMOROUS camping … and here's how you do it with your family this summer', *Daily Mail*, 8 July, www.dailymail.co.uk/femail/article-1292925/Carry-glamping-Thats-GLAMOROUS-camping-heres-family-summer.html (accessed 4 March 2017).

Suki, N.M., and Suki, N.M. (2017). 'Modeling the determinants of consumers' attitudes toward online group buying: do risks and trusts matters?', *Journal of Retailing and Consumer Services*, 36, 180–188.

Szmigin, I. and O'Loughlin, D. (2010), 'Students and the consumer credit market: towards a social policy agenda', *Social Policy and Administration*, 44, 5, 598–619.

Vizard, S. (2017), 'Fairtrade hunts for emotional connection in strategy shift', *Marketing Week*, 23 February.

Watson, T. (2016), 'How do we get festival goers to think a bit more "green" and tidy up after themselves?' Economy, 20 September, http://www.ecnmy.org/engage/festival-goers-think-green-tidy/ (accessed 23 February 2017)

Wilkins, S., Beckenuyte, C., and Butt, M.M. (2016), 'Consumers' behavioural intentions after experiencing deception or cognitive dissonance caused by deceptive packaging, package downsizing or slack filling', *European Journal of Marketing*, 50, 1–2, 213–35.

Woodside, A.G. and Chebat, J.C. (2001), 'Updating Heider's balance theory in consumer behavior: a Jewish couple buys a German car and additional buying–consuming transformation stories', *Psychology & Marketing*, 18, 5, 475–95.

Yang, H. C., and Wang, Y. (2015), 'Social sharing of online videos: examining American consumers' video sharing attitudes, intent, and behavior', *Psychology & Marketing*, 32, 9, 907–19.

Zerquera, D.D., McGowan, B.L., and Ferguson, T.L. (2016), 'Yes, no, maybe so: college students' attitudes regarding debt', *Journal of College Student Development*, 5, 5, 609–13.

spare
me the
guilt chip.

7

PERSONALITY, SELF, AND MOTIVATION

Introduction

Consumption is central to how we define and think about ourselves. The brands we use, and how we use them, can act as signifiers to others about who we are and how we see ourselves. While just a few generations ago people were mainly defined in terms of their occupation, now consumption is central to many people's sense of identity. How we see ourselves influences how we perceive products, brands, and marketing stimuli. When thinking about personality and self, it is important to recognize how personality impacts on our motivations in life. The first part of this chapter examines a range of perspectives on personality, self, and identity, and then considers different ways to conceptualize notions of self to aid understanding of consumer behaviour. We consider how these concepts apply in marketing, and finally examine the key concepts of motivation theory and the methods used for researching motivation.

LEARNING OBJECTIVES

Having read this chapter, you will be able to:

1. Understand the *main psychological and socially oriented perspectives on personality and self*.

2. Explain the meaning of the **multiplicity of self**, and understand the relevance of different aspects of self to consumer behaviour.

3. Identify the links between **personality and self in marketing practice**, including the mechanisms of symbolic consumption and the association between personality, values, and lifestyles.

4. Explain the relevance of **psychographics** to marketing practice.

5. Define the key concepts of **motivation**, and differentiate the meanings of needs, wants, and desires.

6. Critically analyse the usefulness of **Maslow's hierarchy of needs and Herzberg's dual factor theory**.

7. Critically assess the main approaches to **researching motivation**.

Different perspectives on personality and self

In pre-modern society, an individual's identity was determined by just a few factors, such as power and status in society, as well as occupation. For those born into nobility there was a code for behaving, speaking, and dressing; the same could be said for someone born a servant (Kellner, 1992). Roles and expectations were established and static. Things are very different in today's world. There is more freedom, and identity is no longer entirely dependent on a person's place of birth or social status. A number of variables now come into play, with brands and consumption playing a key role as distinguishers of identity.

Many marketing practitioners recognize that how people make decisions around consumption are influenced by their perceptions of themselves and how they would like to be seen. Underpinning the Apple Mac campaign of 2007 (I'm a Mac, I'm a PC) was the strong identification consumers had with the Apple brand, and the distance they felt between themselves and Microsoft products. If you haven't seen the advertisement, you can watch it on YouTube. This campaign is an example of self-image and brand image alignment (or congruence). The idea was for the viewer to associate with the qualities of the more desirable person (the Mac). The campaign also emphasized the *avoidance* of brands (the PC), those for which there was an incongruence between self-image and brand image. Both brands were effectively anthropomorphized—they became people.

Marketers aim to ensure that brand image is consistent with the consumer's self-image. However, this is a complex arena, where identifications with brands are often based on how consumers see themselves now and in their past, and how they imagine and aspire to be in the future. When thinking about personality and identity, there are a number of key perspectives that are relevant to consumer research, falling into more individualist psychological perspectives in comparison with socially oriented perspectives. Both approaches are relevant to understanding the role of personality and identity in relation to consumer behaviour, and each can provide useful insights into identity and consumption. How personality and identity are defined will vary depending on the theoretical approach taken, and in the course of this chapter that will become clearer.

Psychological perspectives on personality

The psychological perspective defines **personality** *as the combination of the characteristic patterns of thoughts, feelings, and behaviours that make up an individual's distinctive character* (Kassarjian, 1971). Personality stems from within the individual and remains fairly stable throughout life. This perspective includes psychoanalytic theories and trait theories.

Psychoanalytic theories

Psychoanalytic theory holds that there are inner forces outside our awareness or consciousness that are directing our behaviour. The founder of psychoanalytic theory was the Austrian neurologist Sigmund Freud. While his theories have been the source of much debate, his work has had a major effect on motivation and personality research in marketing and consumer behaviour.

According to Freud (1923), the mind is divided into the conscious and the unconscious. The conscious includes everything we are aware of (including memory since it can be retrieved easily and brought into our awareness), while the unconscious refers to the feelings, thoughts, urges, and memories that lie outside our conscious awareness. It is the unconscious that drives all human motivation and, according to Freud, personality is made up of the interplay between three elements—the id, the superego, and the ego.

- The **id** *corresponds to primary needs, focused on immediate gratification, directing a person's psychic energy towards pleasurable acts without regard to the consequences.* This represents the biological forces driving humans.

- The **superego** *reflects the rules, values, and norms imposed by society, and serves as the person's conscience working to prevent the id from seeking selfish gratification.* This represents a form of societal force.

- The **ego** *represents the interests of the individual, ensuring the necessary arbitration between the demands of id and constraints of superego.* This is a form of human consciousness.

While Freudian analysis may provide some interesting insights into the underlying forces at play, such analyses are rarely applied in marketing and consumer behaviour research. However, Freudian psychology informed the methods and tools of in-depth interviewing to delve into consumer motives, often located below the level of conscious awareness, which have had a lasting impact. A psychoanalytical approach to understanding why someone engages in a high risk sport (e.g. paragliding) would ask questions that aim to dig deep into the underlying motives of behaviour, and how the individual balances the pleasures of participating in consumption activities against societal norms and expectations around risky behaviours.

Some theorists, such as Swiss psychiatrist Carl Jung in his work on archetypes, developed their own version of psychoanalytic theory. Jung's concept of the **archetype** relates to *the stable characters that capture basic ideas, feelings, fantasies, and visions that seem constant and frequently re-emerge across different times and places.* These characters, such as the hero, the outlaw, and the sage, are recognizable across cultures, and appear over and over again in films, songs, novels, and popular culture (Woodside, 2010). According to Jung, these archetypes prompt humans to react to the world in a selective fashion, and help explain why people can hold certain myths and images across cultures. The success of the Oprah Winfrey brand draws on the 'sage' archetype, with Oprah viewed as an individual with wisdom and experience of life who is looked to for guidance. The Oprah brand is hugely successful not only in the USA, but also in other countries, such as Saudi Arabia where she is viewed as an inspiration for many women who feel trapped (Zoepf, 2008). In marketing and advertising, archetypes are used as a way of making connections with consumers, to develop more compelling brand stories for communicating with them. An example of the use of archetypes in practice is found in the work of the market research company Kantar Millward Brown (see Practitioner Insight 7). We spoke to the group account director Graham Staplehurst to get an understanding of how they put Jung's theory of archetypes into practice.

PRACTITIONER INSIGHT 7

Graham Staplehurst, Group Account Director, Brand & Communications, Kantar Millward Brown

Since brands communicate with consumers, and consumers listen, they develop a relationship with those brands based both on *what* the brand says and *how* it says it. The tone of voice adopted by a brand is part of the set of mental associations—the knowledge, memories, and feelings that create the brand's representation in the consumer's mind. Market researchers have found that consumers can describe the impact of this tone of voice—an otherwise intangible quality—through measures of brand personality.

Brand personality is particularly suited to investigation using sensitive and careful techniques. Its earliest use was in qualitative research, when moderators started using projective techniques to help consumers articulate their feelings about brands and provide depth to their descriptions of brands. A typical projective technique would be to ask the respondent to imagine that the brand 'comes to life' and you meet them at a party. Answers to probing questions about how the brand looks, how it is dressed, who it is with, what it drinks, what car it drives, and so on can help identify the nature of the brand as it exists in the consumer's mind, and help marketers understand what and how they should communicate in future. Most brands play only very superficial roles in consumers' lives, and it is only through constant repetition that advertising imprints upon the brain.

Therefore a measure used to determine the existence and nature of any brand personality must act upon simple and slender perceptions, particularly when qualitative research is not available. The CharacterZ approach developed by Kantar Millward Brown is based on archetypes. Archetypes are easily recognized personality types or characters commonly found in story-telling across all cultures. The archetypes are based on universal metaphors rooted in psychological and sociological analysis of stories and dreams, for example by Jung and Campbell. An archetype can be quickly sketched and recognized. It is this instant recognition that makes it such an appropriate model to apply to the measurement and description of brands. CharacterZ uses a system of ten archetypes: Joker, Seductress, Rebel, Hero, Wise, King, Mother, Friend, Maiden, and Dreamer (see Figure 7.1).

Figure 7.1   Kantar Millward Brown brand personality archetypes   *Source:* Image courtesy of Kantar Millward Brown.

For example, the King archetype expresses a personality with power, leadership, strength, importance, and charisma.

Respondents are asked to choose at least four words to describe a brand from a list of 24, which were selected through extensive qualitative and quantitative piloting. The relative levels of association of each word with a brand determine its strongest traits and these in turn determine its archetype. Many of the strongest brands historically are Wise—they are trustworthy expert partners for the consumer, skilled at the product or service they provide. IKEA is a Dreamer, providing creative ideas and preaching its unique ideals. Red Bull is a true Hero, brave and adventurous, while Irn Bru is a Rebel, defiantly different. Brands can change. IBM, which had been seen as a Wise brand, has recently evolved into a King, with its growing business success reflected in more confident assertive messages.

CharacterZ was used to help Burger King understand its brand better in the UK. Analysis showed that Burger King and its key competitors McDonald's and KFC were all seen at the simplest level as Joker archetypes. None are 'serious' food, their communications often feature toys, children, and families, and their consumer experience is one of fun. CharacterZ was able to probe below this level and identify some revealing differences about the brands. McDonald's was more of a 'straight' Joker—playful, fun, and friendly. Its personality related to humorous communications, including the clown Ronald McDonald. In contrast, KFC had aspects of the Mother about it—generous sharing qualities typified by the 'bucket' sharing offers for families. Burger King had two distinct aspects not present in either of these competitors—the Rebel and the Seductress. Burger King communications had used a stronger American tone and its King advertising character was designed to have a more edgy appeal to younger adults. The Seductress was the more desirable nature of the food itself—perceived to be more authentically sourced and cooked. These insights helped the advertising agency create a new campaign with a tone of voice absolutely suited to the brand, ensuring that the message resonated with the target group and built on existing brand memories.

While psychoanalytic theories laid the groundwork for much research in the area of personality, trait-based theories have been used extensively in studies into the effect of personality on consumption.

The trait-based view of personality

According to the **trait-based approach**, *personality is regarded as the sum of a set of traits or qualities about a person, and these can be used to predict or explain consumption behaviour.* This view works on the basis that traits can be assessed and evaluated. The trait-based approach assumes a *quantitative approach* to personality, which is viewed as comprised of a set of traits. According to the trait-based view of the self, an individual's personality is composed of definite predispositional attributes (traits) and it can be described in terms of a particular combination of these traits. It is assumed that traits are common to

Trait	Definition and key study
Materialism	The degree to which a consumer is overly concerned with physical objects and material goods (Richins and Dawson, 1992)
Consumer innovativeness	Generalized tendency toward innovations applicable across product classes (Goldsmith and Hofacker, 1991)
Consumer ethnocentrism	The idea that ethnocentric individuals view their group (or culture) as superior to others, and therefore that in consumer terms there is a strong preference towards buying domestic rather than foreign-produced goods (Shimp and Sharma, 1987)
Frugality	'The degree to which consumers are both restrained in acquiring and in resourcefully using economic goods and services to achieve longer-term goals' (Lastovicka et al., 1999: 88)
Consumers' spending self-control	'The ability to monitor and regulate one's spending-related thoughts and decisions in accordance with self-imposed standards' (Haws et al., 2012: 697).

Table 7.1   Examples of single-trait theories

many individuals, but the exact combination reflects the personality of the individual. Traits are relatively stable and exert fairly universal effects on behaviour regardless of environment.

Some consumer researchers distinguish between single-trait and multi-trait approaches to personality. In the **single-trait approach** the *focus is on one trait that is particularly relevant to a situation*. This approach does not suggest that other traits are irrelevant, but rather focuses on how one trait alone can impact on consumption. For example, a social marketing researcher may be trying to establish the links between smoking and personality. Here they may look at the effect of the personality trait 'anxiety' on smoking. Table 7.1 provides details of some key traits that have been used in consumer behaviour and marketing.

The **multi-trait approach** is *concerned with a number of personality traits taken together and how they combine to effect consumption*. So, returning to the smoking example, the researcher would be interested in the effect of anxiety in combination with other personality variables (such as shyness, conscientiousness, openness) on smoking. For both these approaches, prediction of behaviour is important to researchers, and multi-trait approaches have generally been used to enable prediction of behaviour since they offer a more detailed and complex picture of the relationships between personality and behaviour.

Many psychologists agree that there are five main personality types, which constitute a stable and robust structure of personality. The 'Big-Five' factor structure, developed by McCrae and Costa (1990), proposes the main traits of extroversion, agreeableness, conscientiousness, neuroticism (or emotional stability), and openness (sometimes referred to as intellect). This model has been widely applied in social psychology and consumer research, such as studies of customer service performance and personality (Harris and Fleming, 2005) and of smoking and personality (Adams and Nettle, 2009). A Swedish study (Axelsson et al., 2011) showed how personality impacted on how likely people are to take medicine. People who score highly on the neuroticism scale (likely to be fairly anxious) were found to be less likely to stick to their doctor's prescribed medication. On the other hand, people who are influenced by conscientiousness tend to be very careful and methodical in following the doctor's prescription. A study such as this can inform social marketing campaigns, recognizing that different consumer communication and education may be needed depending on personality type.

According to recent research from the psychographic agency Mindset Media, there is a link between common personality traits and consumers' TV viewing choices (Bulik, 2010). For instance, viewers of *Dancing with the Stars*, the American reality dance show, tend to be traditional in their personalities, unlike viewers of the cartoon comedy *Family Guy*, who are more likely to be 'rule-breakers' or rebels. Knowing this link between personality traits and viewing preferences might help marketers to match brands to audiences in the commercial breaks for these shows. Brands associated with risk-taking (e.g. Harley-Davidson) are more likely to connect with viewers of *Family Guy* than safe brands (e.g. Volvo), which may appeal to the traditionalists watching *Dancing with the Stars*. This approach has some appeal for marketing on the basis that consumers may choose products that fit their personality or boost their personality in areas where they feel weak.

Brand personality and traits

Once we understand the nature of people's personality, we can apply such theories to brands. Some brands even use characters to represent the brand. The Energizer Bunny appears to signify an upbeat, happy, and indefatigable personality, in line with the idea of the long-lasting batteries. The French Michelin Man has existed since 1898, and not only does he visually capture the tyre brand but he represents friendliness, gentleness, and above all safety. Aaker (1997) devised a **brand personality scale**, which *describes the underlying brand dimensions of sincerity, excitement, competence, sophistication, and ruggedness*. These dimensions can apply to both retail and product brands (Möller and Herm, 2013). There is some overlap with human personality traits (e.g. sincerity–agreeableness, excitement–extroversion, competence–conscientiousness), although the brand personality dimensions of sophistication and ruggedness do not obviously map onto the human personality dimensions. Aaker explains that these dimensions tap into those things that consumers desire but do not necessarily have. High-end brands (such as Cartier and Chanel) encourage consumer aspirations around class and glamour, while more rugged brands (such as G-SHOCK or Marlboro) emphasize ideals of strength and masculinity (Figure 7.2). Despite the extensive use of brand personality in consumer behaviour, some are sceptical of the anthropomorphic approach (i.e. giving human qualities to

Figure 7.2 Advertisements for Cartier and G-SHOCK watches, illustrating the sophistication of the former contrasted with the ruggedness of the latter. The idea is that consumers choose brands with distinctive personalities that represent aspects of the self that they wish to express or enhance
Source: Images courtesy of Cartier and Casio.

brands) and question whether it is a lens that adds clarity to understanding brands (Avis and Aitken, 2015). Nevertheless the development of a brand personality continues to be adopted by consumer companies.

For example, in 2015 Magnum developed two new flavours, Magnum Pink (raspberry flavour) and Magnum Black (coffee flavour), initially based on a gendered approach—pink for girls and black for boys. However, they soon recognized that such stereotyping was prescriptive and archaic (see Chapter 10), and instead they developed a campaign that highlights 'the different sides of consumers' personalities.

Marketing Week reported the brand manager of Magnum at Unilever UK as saying, 'None of us are the same person all the time and we have different sides to our personalities and moods' (Millington 2015). The two ice creams represent two sides of a personality. The raspberry is supposed to be fun, playful, and light-hearted, but still sophisticated and upmarket. The black is elegant, cool, and confident, the more refined side of our personality (Figure 7.3). Research Insight 7.1 looks at perceptions of website personality and how this impacts on consumer attitudes.

RESEARCH INSIGHT 7.1

Shobeiri, S., Mazaheri, E., and Laroche, M. (2015), 'How would the e-retailer's website personality impact customers' attitudes toward the site?', *Journal of Marketing Theory and Practice*, 23, 4, 388–401.

This study is a survey of consumer attitudes towards an e-retailer's website, looking specifically at the website personality (defined as the brand personality of an online product or service, usually represented by a website) and how this related to site involvement and site attitudes. The authors found that the five dimensions of website personality (enthusiasm, sophistication, genuineness, solidity, and unpleasantness) are not equally effective in shaping consumer reactions to a site. While enthusiasm has a positive effect and unpleasantness has a negative effect on both site involvement and site attitudes, some other dimensions only influence site attitudes (genuineness), or site involvement (solidity), or neither attitude nor involvement (sophistication). The authors discuss how online marketers should pay extra attention to enthusiasm and unpleasantness because these two personality dimensions played a major role in influencing user site involvement and attitudes.

 Access the online resources to read the abstract and access the full paper.

Figure 7.3   Magnum Pink and Black   *Source*: Image courtesy of Unilever.

A social perspective on identity and self

Sociology has made distinctive contributions to the study of personality, mainly in terms of broadening understanding of personality and identity to encompass the influence of social forms and social arrangements and their impact on how people view themselves (Heine, 1971). One major theoretical perspective on this is symbolic interactionism.

Symbolic interactionism

A more socially oriented view of identity follows the **symbolic interactionist perspective** which *sees the self as emerging out of the mind, which develops out of social interaction, and patterned social interaction as forming the basis of social structure* (Mead, 1913). The mind is the thinking part of the self (Stets and Burke, 2003: 130), but this perspective stresses the *importance of other people* in forming how we think about ourselves, particularly in relation to the ways that meanings are defined by social consensus (Ligas and Cotte, 1999). We tend to behave in ways that match how we imagine other people will react towards us. Consumers want to fit in with other people's expectations, but how does our understanding of ourselves fit with others' understanding of who we are? The **self-concept** refers to *the sum total of our thoughts, feelings, and imaginations as to who we are* (Rosenberg, 1979). This approach is based on the idea that people define themselves by how others judge them and how they believe that others judge them. While the self-concept represents the content and structure of the beliefs that a person holds about him/herself, and how these are evaluated, these self-assessments can be distorted. People are particularly conscious of their physical appearance. The leisure, beauty, dieting, fashion, and clothing markets thrive on people wanting to send out the 'correct' messages to others as to the way they look in order to stimulate preferable judgements about themselves.

The Adidas 2011/2012 'All Originals' advertisement builds on this idea by showing how you can show your individuality by wearing Adidas, but still connect with other people more widely. The 2012 TV advertising showed people from around the world, representing their home, their passions, and their joy of life, connected by the tagline 'Adidas is All In'—with the word 'All' connecting them to a bigger whole. The print campaign featured shots from gigs of four of the UK's top music artists (Plan B, Example, DJ Caspa, and The Enemy), all wearing Adidas clothing, with the tagline 'All Originals', emphasizing the message that everyone can be individual when wearing this brand.

Multiplicity of self

Consumer research has moved away from the idea that identity is unitary, fixed, and stable, and instead views it as dynamic (Shankar et al., 2009), comprising different aspects of the self associated with the different roles and situations we occupy in our lives. Some roles are more active than others, depending on the situations we are in and how central to our sense of self

Aspect of self	Definition	Summary statement
Actual self	The core sense of self which is enduring and stable across situations	'The person that I believe I actually am'
Ideal self	The self we aspire to be like, often as important to what we do in the consumption arena as our sense of our actual self	'The person that I would ideally like to be'
Social self	Sometimes referred to as the 'looking glass self', this is how consumers believe that they are seen by significant others	'The person that I believe others see me as being'
Ideal social self	How consumers would like to be seen by significant others	'The person that I would ideally like others to see me as being'
Situational self	Recognizes the self-concept as a dynamic entity, where different aspects of self are activated depending on different situations the consumer is in, and who they are interacting with in that situation	'The person I believe I am in particular situations'
Extended self	The idea that our possessions and belongings form such a close connection to us and our past that they come to represent us in some way; the extended self can explain a variety of consumer and human behaviour, and helps us to understand the connections that we feel towards items and brands that are special to us in some way (Belk, 1988)	'The way that my personal possessions are linked to me'
Possible selves	'Personalized representations of one's self in future states' (Cross and Markus, 1991: 230): these can be both positive selves (how they might aspire to be) and negative selves (the imagined futures they wish to avoid), and this motivates behaviour both towards and away from certain consumption practices	'The person I would like to become, could become, may be afraid of becoming'
Negative selves	Refers to the person you are not, and do not want to become: Banister and Hogg (2001) have examined the negative self in depth, arguing that the 'push' of the negative self (away from what you do not want to be) is more powerful than the 'pull' of the ideal self (towards what you want to be); they also distinguish between the undesired self ('so not me') and the avoidance self ('just not me')	'The person I am not, or do not want to be'

Table 7.2   Aspects of self

they are, and social identity (Tajfel, 1979)—the sense of who we are based on different group memberships—can be a powerful driver in shaping how we act in different situations. Your role as a student or employee may be more active and central than your role as a cyclist, which may only emerge at weekends or on vacation. Table 7.2 gives a set of the key definitions used in the literature to refer to the multiplicity of self. Research Insight 7.2 provides an example of how the negative self has been used in the domain of brand avoidance and anti-consumption, and links to environmentally oriented avoidance behaviour.

The importance of situation and context is captured in the idea of the **malleable self** (Aaker, 1999), which acknowledges *that people will act differently according to the situation, influenced by social roles, cues, and the need for self-presentation.* Take, for example, the act of 'going out for lunch' (Figure 7.4). This can be analysed in terms of the selves that are

Figure 7.4 'Going out for lunch'—different selves in different consumption contexts

Source: Zizzi images courtesy of Zizzi; Pizza Hut image © Radu Bercan/Shutterstock.com.

activated in different consumption contexts—each of these selves may reflect a form of social self, but they differ in relation to situational contexts. For a young mother, a visit to Pizza Hut for a child's birthday party reflects her actual self, enacting her 'mother identity', whereas a trip to Zizzi, a more upmarket chain of restaurants, may be reflective of a social self, the type of place she would perhaps go with a group of girlfriends where good food is the priority but is still within a fairly reasonable price range. Finally River Café, an upmarket restaurant in Hammersmith, London, where Jamie Oliver worked before becoming a TV chef, may be reflective of a more ideal social self, a possible self, and one perhaps not easily available to her, but nonetheless desirable in terms of status attached to the venue.

RESEARCH INSIGHT 7.2

García-de-Frutos, N., Ortega-Egea, J.M. and Martínez-del-Río, J. (2016). Anti-consumption for environmental sustainability: conceptualization, review, and multilevel research directions. *Journal of Business Ethics*, https://doi.org/10.1007/s10551-016-3023-z.

A recent stream of consumer behaviour research has focused on the area of anti-consumption (Lee et al., 2009) and how consumers avoid certain brands and products for a host of reasons, including what is communicated about them. In this conceptual paper by García-de-Frutos et al., the authors review the most recent literature on anti-consumption in environmentally oriented situations, and examine the role of individuals and organizations in achieving environmental sustainability. They comment that environmentally oriented anti-consumption gives some power to individuals who are willing to express their environmental concerns in a way that corporations will listen.

 Access the online resources to read the abstract and access the full paper.

The idea of multiple selves is important for marketers, especially in terms of understanding consumers' aspirations and ideals of who they *want* to be, as much as their ideas of who they *do not want* to be. The ideal self is relevant to consumption in terms of people buying brands they believe will help them achieve their ideal self. The perfume industry benefits from consumers' aspirations to access designer lifestyles. While designer clothes are beyond the financial means of many consumers, perfumes represent a more affordable way of experiencing the designer brand. Similarly, negative possible selves can act as incentives for future behaviour, representing the idea of ourselves that we reject or wish to avoid. Consumer Insight 7.1 provides an example of the negative self in action, and how the company Abercrombie & Fitch responded to the wearing of their brand by celebrities they did not want associated with the brand.

CONSUMER INSIGHT 7.1

Abercrombie & Fitch and Mike 'The Situation' Sorrentino

While many companies enjoy celebrity endorsement of their brands, in some instances this backfires, as was the case when Abercrombie & Fitch's clothes were worn by the cast members of the US MTV show *Jersey Shore*. The company put out a press release announcing that it had offered compensation to Mike 'The Situation' Sorrentino, one of the show's stars, to get him to stop wearing the company's products on the show. The retailer was concerned that associating the brand with the raucous behaviour of Sorrentino would damage its image. In this context, Mike Sorrentino did not fit the company's customer aspirations, and was indeed a version of a negative or avoidance self for those consumers. However, the *Jersey Shore* star alleged that the offer never happened, and that the company concocted the press release as a publicity stunt to create brand awareness.

Questions

1. Can you find any examples of consumers using brands in ways deemed unacceptable to the brand owner?

2. Given your understanding of how consumers use brands to construct their identity, what would you recommend the company to do in this situation?

Sources: Hughes (2011); http://www.abercrombie.co.uk/anf/investors/investorrelations.html

 Access the online resources to learn more.

The symbolic interactionist perspective implies that each of us has many selves, and different products are required to support these selves. Valued objects such as cars, homes, and even attachments to sports teams or national monuments are used to define the self when these are incorporated into the extended self. Consumer identity can be developed through the products and brands consumed to help us construct the 'story of ourself' (Shankar et al., 2009). If you imagine getting ready for a night out, you might use special shower gel (e.g. Gucci Envy rather than Nivea), you might mix high street fashion with some designer items (e.g. wearing TopShop skinny jeans with a D&G top), you might wear your 'going out' Diesel shoes, and straighten your hair with GHD straighteners. Together, these items help you to get ready, but also enable you to become the 'you' you want to display to the world. These examples show how brands can become a central part of how we see ourselves, and are so wrapped up in our identity that they are almost part of us.

This fits with Belk's extended self (see Table 7.2), where people consume goods and brands as part of an overall 'identity project'. They are engaged in constructing an identity and using consumption as a means to do so (Ahuvia, 2005). This is what is meant when we talk about the narrative approach to identity, and this fits with the consumer culture theory (CCT) perspective of the consumer (Arnould and Thompson, 2005: 871). According to this perspective, identity is a major and continuous preoccupation of individuals, residing in a personal narrative—the story that consumers construct and play out as they make life choices and decisions (see also Consumer Insight 7.2).

CONSUMER INSIGHT 7.2

Virtual displays of self

With the rise of social media, and in particular apps such as Pinterest and Instagram, a key trend has been towards consumers showing off their consumption activities through the pictures they post (Chahal, 2013). Whether it be pinning products you own or aspire to own on Pinterest, or postings on Instagram and Facebook of cakes baked and craft items produced, consumers are increasingly using photography to communicate quickly with others. In doing this, they are also producing and reproducing something of themselves in these formats, and thus these postings are a form of identity display and expression. The idea of consumers using brands to communicate various aspects of themselves has emerged in recent research (Hollenbeck and Kaikati, 2012). However, a form of impression management is taking place (Goffman, 1959), with consumers navigating clashes between their actual and ideal selves through their posts (including hiding consumption of certain brands). Recent research into how people manage their online persona or virtual identity has shown that the ways in which people engage with image-sharing social networking sites (such as Instagram and Pinterest) is linked to their level of self-monitoring (the extent to which they are concerned to tailor information to present a particular self-image). Low self-monitors, who are less likely to be included by social cues, interact more intensely with Pinterest than Instagram (Kim et al., 2017).

Another interesting aspect of this is how viewers use social media during commercial breaks. For years, marketers have known that consumers do many things during the commercial break (making a cup of tea, flicking through channels, etc.), but recently viewers have turned to 'second screen conversations' on Twitter and other social media during ad breaks, checking out what other viewers are saying about the show. Brands are trying to find ways to connect to viewers during commercial breaks, and inserting messages through Twitter appears to be one way of doing this. A viewer watching the US TV show *Glee* may turn to her smartphone during the break to see what other Gleeks (Glee fans) are tweeting about the show. While she may not be watching the TV when a Pepsi ad appears on the screen, she might see when Pepsi's Twitter account sends a related message with the hashtag #Glee. In this way the brand is connecting with the viewer at the heart of the conversation taking place on Twitter. The success or failure of this approach will relate to how convincing the presence of the brand is and the fit between the brand and viewer personality.

Questions

1. Spend some time on the various social media you use (e.g. Instagram, Facebook, Snapchat, Pinterest) and consider the extent to which you and your friends construct your identities through your consumption activities. Do you do this? Do you see any patterns in who does/does not use consumption in this way? From your experiences, do you see a link between type of social media used and self-monitoring?

2. How might this awareness of consumers' use of social media as a way of expressing their brand use and identity be useful for marketers?

Sources: Goffman (1959); Lawler (2011); Hollenbeck and Kaikati (2012); Chahal (2013); Kim et al. (2017).

 Access the online resources and follow the web links to learn more about the importance of social media to marketers.

People are able to find identities to associate with through many websites and blogs, often linked to fashion. The blog of Italian fashionista Nicoletta Reggio shows her daily life with links to specific brands she buys (Figure 7.5), all set within an enviable Italian identity (www.scentofobsession.com). Now married, Nicoletta also posts thoughts on the new home she is creating. Other sites, such as Donnamoderna.com, show a wider range of identity roles including health and food, but also look for real-life models to be represented on their pages, thus making a link to people's real lives.

Sport England used a narrative approach in its ground-breaking This Girl Can campaign. Sport England had found that millions of women are afraid of being judged when exercising and so they avoid it. Sport England rejected using celebrities as role models, and featured real women and their stories of how they got into sport and what it did for them. The ads showed ordinary women of all sizes exercising and that, as the website notes, it is 'normal' for women to 'sweat and jiggle'. In other words the campaign showed women what it really looked

Figure 7.5 An image of Nicoletta Reggio from the 'My Closet' section on her blog

Source: Image printed with kind permission from Nicoletta Reggio from www.scentofobsession.com.

like to exercise and that it wasn't always pretty. It seeks to tell the real story of women who play sport by using images that are the complete opposite of the idealized and stylized images we are used to seeing. 'Sweating like a pig, feeling like a fox' (Figure 7.6) and 'I kick balls, deal with it' are among the hard-hitting lines used in the campaign to prompt a change in attitudes and help boost women's confidence. The campaign links to people's

Figure 7.6   Advertisement from Sport England's 'This Girl Can' campaign

Source: Image supplied by The Advertising Archives.

individual stories by allowing visitors to the site to make their own posters using the This Girl Can app.

Personality and self in marketing practice

Symbolic consumption

Symbolic consumption is the *tendency of consumers to rely and focus on the meanings attached to goods, beyond their physical properties,* and provides an important means by which consumers define themselves. Consumer goods are capable of serving consumers in this way because of the symbolic meaning that is embedded in the offering. Contained within the symbolism are the messages that an individual may wish to transmit to socially significant referents. However, these messages will only be successfully communicated if the symbolism in the offering is socially recognized. Therefore a shared understanding of symbolic meaning facilitates the capabilities of products as communicators of self-identity, and depends upon the individual's knowledge of the codes involved.

Thus consumption symbols provide an important way of communicating with others in the world. Yet not all product categories serve as identical means of communication. Products such as cars, clothes, homes, and leisure activities are very visible and are used by many to make a statement. A consumer wearing a Rolex watch may be communicating success, wealth, and status to others. We attach meanings to symbols in our constructed realities (Elliott and Wattanasuwan, 1998), and the ability to recognize such meanings is at the heart of marketing culture. These symbols are associated with

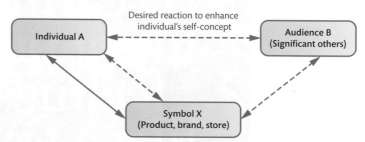

Figure 7.7   Symbolic meaning of goods, consumer self-concepts, and related audience

Source: Grubb and Grathwohl (1967: 25). Printed with permission from The American Marketing Association.

self-definition, which leads to symbolic consumption. Grubb and Grathwohl (1967) proposed a framework mapping out the relationships between the symbolic meaning of products/brands, consumers' self-concepts, and related audiences (see Figure 7.7).

A person (individual A) uses a product or brand (Symbol X) to achieve self-enhancement. This process relies on the socially agreed meanings attached to the product/brand (Symbol X) being transferred to and associated with the consumer. Critical to this process is the role of other significant people or audiences, and their attributions of meanings and associations with the brand. The person uses the brand in the hope that significant others notice, that the positive associations the person has with the brand are also held by significant others (friends, peers, family), and that, by extension, significant others transfer that meaning to the person. To illustrate, consider a nine-year-old boy who is a keen footballer and rates Cristiano Ronaldo as a player (Figure 7.8). Ronaldo wears Nike football boots, and so the child wears the boots in order to enhance his sense of footballing self ('I can play football like Ronaldo'), but also to enhance his status and standing in the eyes of other children who interpret the wearing of these boots as a signal of high football performance. By wearing the football boots he transfers and communicates the socially agreed meaning of the boots to himself and in the process achieves self-enhancement in both a private and public sense—the child is transferring the socially attributed meanings of the product or brand to himself.

It is obviously important that the brand and its associations are congruent with the image consumers have or want to have of themselves. According to Ericksen and Sirgy (1992:

Figure 7.8 Application of the process of the symbolic meaning of goods attached to brands
Source: Image of Ronaldo's football boots is taken from the Summer 2013 CR7 collection, courtesy of Nike Inc.

409), **self-congruity** *refers to the extent to which a product image matches a consumer's self-image,* and **ideal congruity** *refers to the extent to which the product image matches the ideal self-image.* The theory of 'image congruency' recognizes that consumers select products, brands, and retailers that correspond to their self-concept (Sirgy, 1982).

Linking identity and values

Increasingly, companies are recognizing the importance of understanding consumer values and making clear links to the identity of the organization. Asda in the UK has talked about its efforts to ensure that the brand personality ('cheeky and honest', emphasizing everyday low prices) resonates with consumer values across all its marketing communications (Baker, 2013).**Values** are *our desired end-states in life and preferred paths to achieving them, constituting the purposes and goals for which we believe human life should be lived.* Rokeach's list of values (Table 7.3) proposes that there are two main sets of values guiding our behaviour: terminal values, linked to the goals we seek in life, and instrumental values, representing the means, paths, and behavioural standards by which we pursue these goals (Rokeach, 1974). Another popular model of values influencing behaviour is offered by Schwartz (1994), who proposed a theory of 10 types of values, distinguished by their motivational goals of power, achievement, hedonism, stimulation, self-direction, universalism, benevolence, tradition, conformity and security.

An example of the use of values in consumer marketing can be found on Martin Lewis's money saving website moneysavingexpert.com. This site is a forum for consumer tips across many consumer domains and sectors, encouraging consumer-to-consumer interactions and communications. A key theme underpinning the resource is one of consumer empowerment, celebrating frugal and shrewd consumer behaviour. In terms of values, this taps into primary terminal values around security and a sense of accomplishment, but also speaks to secondary instrumental values, especially demonstrating self-control and imagination to make savings

Terminal values	Instrumental values
A comfortable life	Imaginative
A sense of accomplishment	Ambition
A world at peace	Broad-mindedness
A world of beauty	Capable
An exciting life	Cheerful
Equality	Clean
Family security	Courageous
Freedom	Forgiving
Happiness	Independent
Inner harmony	Intellect
Mature love	Obedience
National security	Helpful
Pleasure	Polite
Salvation	Logic
Self-respect	Love
Social recognition	Honest
True friendship	Responsibility
Wisdom	Self-control

Table 7.3   Rokeach's list of values

based on information gleaned from the website. Examples of companies that adapt and respond to consumer trends and values are John Lewis and Innocent, which both build their core brand values in line with consumer needs and values (Cuddeford-Jones, 2013).

Psychographics

It is intuitively plausible that personality differences are related to the types of product/brand purchased, and the assumption of links between character and consumption is evident in many perfume and car advertisements. Researchers have even tried to find links between perfume preferences and personality, measured through the 'Big-Five' (Janssens and De Pelsmacker, 2009). However, reviews of research (Kassarjian and Sheffet, 1981; Foxall and Goldsmith, 1988) show that findings linking personality to brands and products are equivocal, with empirical results generally not repeated. At best, personality measures explained about 10 per cent of variation in consumer behaviour. Lifestyle segmentation, referred to as **psychographics**, is based on *building a picture (sometimes literally) based on demographics, alongside activities, interests, and opinion variables.* Lifestyle and personality are different, but closely related; personality refers to internal characteristics, and lifestyle refers to external manifestations of how a person lives. The advantage of lifestyle segmentation such as psychographics is that it can be done at a very general level (i.e. a population), at a product level (i.e. by typifying people by their attitude to healthy food or fashion), or by brand (i.e. the different types of purchasers of a particular car brand).

VALS™ framework: a lifestyle segmentation tool

VALS™ (acronym for Values and Lifestyle) is *a trade-marked segmentation system, based on US adult consumers, where subjects are grouped into eight segments using the VALS™ questionnaire, which consists of questions around primary motivations and resources* (Strategic Business Insights, 2016). Originally created in the 1970s, this revised framework has been developed to improve its ability to explain and predict consumer behaviour. The VALS™ framework classifies people in groups based on the two main dimensions of primary motivation (ideals, achievement, and self-expression) and resources (income, education, self-confidence, intelligence, leadership skills, and energy).

The central idea is that these traits, in combination with consumer demographics, can explain and predict behaviour. The VALS™ system has eight main segments, based on the subject's resource base (generally categorized as high or low) and the extent to which they are motivated in life by their ideals, by achievement, or towards self-expression. Figure 7.9

Demographic and Behavior Snapshots Highlight the Vibrancy of Using VALS™

Primary Motivation		Ideals		Achievement		Self-Expression		
	Innovators	Thinkers	Believers	Achievers	Strivers	Experiencers	Makers	Survivors
Psychological Descriptors	Sophisticated In Charge Curious	Informed Reflective Content	Literal Loyal Moralistic	Goal Oriented Brand Conscious Conventional	Contemporary Imitative Style Conscious	Trend Seeking Impulsive Variety Seeking	Responsible Practical Self-Sufficient	Nostalgic Constrained Cautious
	Percent of Innovators	Percent of Thinkers	Percent of Believers	Percent of Achievers	Percent of Strivers	Percent of Experiencers	Percent of Makers	Percent of Survivors
Total US	10	11.3	16.5	14	11.5	12.7	11.8	12
Median age	47	58	53	41	30	24	48	69
Married	62	73	62	70	32	20	64	45
Work full time	67	52	40	65	45	42	56	13
Own a tablet or e-reader	36	25	9	19	6	14	7	4
Contributed to environmental organization in past year	20	11	2	4	2	3	4	1
Own a dog	39	40	43	52	44	41	57	38
Bought new or different auto-insurance policy in past year	17	16	16	18	15	16	22	14
Buy food labeled natural or organic	24	15	8	10	4	9	8	4
Used hair color at home to cover gray	7	11	15	9	2	1	9	11
Media trusted the most:								
TV	11	25	43	26	38	24	33	54
Radio	15	11	7	7	7	6	12	11
Internet	42	30	21	35	32	48	26	4
Magazines	10	9	7	7	4	3	7	5
Newspapers	23	25	23	24	18	19	22	24

Source: VALS™/GfK MRI Spring 2012.

Figure 7.9   Overview of VALS™ segments

Source: Strategic Business Insights (SBI); www.strategicbusinessinsights.com/VALS

provides an overview of the segments, linking each to some key forms of consumer behaviour such as internet usage, purchase of organic foods, and exercise habits.

The value of a system such as this lies in its ability to explore in depth consumers who are similar demographically, but display different consumption habits and behaviour. Innovators and Achievers may be similar in terms of age and work patterns, but Achievers are much less likely to buy organic foods than Innovators, which may be explained in terms of their goals and drives.

Not all companies use the VALS™ system, but many take a similar approach to segmenting consumers based on lifestyle characteristics. Research sponsored by Coca-Cola Retailing Research Council (2016) considers the different ways that consumers in Eurasia and Africa use e-commerce and how these might impact on different types of shopping behaviours—Potentials, North Stars, Uninvolved, and Autopilots (see Figure 7.10). By categorizing consumers into a typology based on their personality and other variables, marketers can anticipate the brand categories that these consumers are most engaged with. For example, members of the category North Stars are both highly connected with mobile devices and are high spenders; they are forward thinking, early adopters, and want to be constantly connected to their mobile devices.

Psychographics provides very useful information about consumers, drawing on multiple data sources which results in a detailed categorization of the drivers of consumers' behaviour (Beckland, 2011). This focused categorization allows for more targeted marketing.

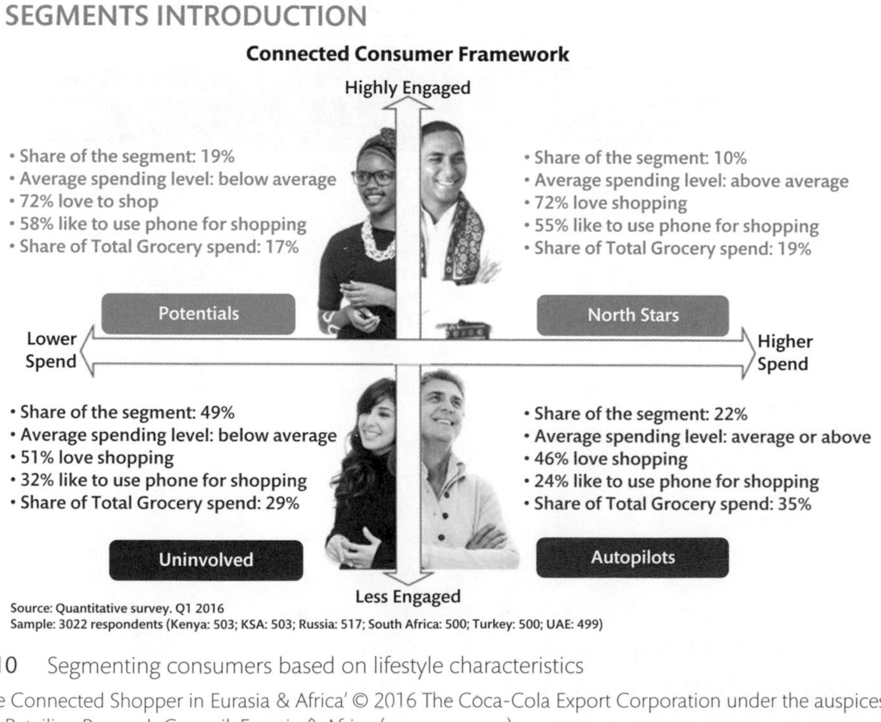

SEGMENTS INTRODUCTION

Connected Consumer Framework

Highly Engaged

• Share of the segment: 19%
• Average spending level: below average
• 72% love to shop
• 58% like to use phone for shopping
• Share of Total Grocery spend: 17%

• Share of the segment: 10%
• Average spending level: above average
• 72% love shopping
• 55% like to use phone for shopping
• Share of Total Grocery spend: 19%

Potentials   **North Stars**

Lower Spend ← → Higher Spend

• Share of the segment: 49%
• Average spending level: below average
• 51% love shopping
• 32% like to use phone for shopping
• Share of Total Grocery spend: 29%

• Share of the segment: 22%
• Average spending level: average or above
• 46% love shopping
• 24% like to use phone for shopping
• Share of Total Grocery spend: 35%

Uninvolved   **Autopilots**

Less Engaged

Source: Quantitative survey. Q1 2016
Sample: 3022 respondents (Kenya: 503; KSA: 503; Russia: 517; South Africa: 500; Turkey: 500; UAE: 499)

Figure 7.10   Segmenting consumers based on lifestyle characteristics

Source: 'The Connected Shopper in Eurasia & Africa' © 2016 The Coca-Cola Export Corporation under the auspices of the Coca-Cola Retailing Research Council, Eurasia & Africa (www.ccrrc.org).

Motivation

Motivation *describes the processes that cause people to behave in a particular way.* Why does one person choose chocolate for a snack while another chooses an apple? Why do some people spend time following the latest celebrities while others investigate their family genealogy? What needs and wants are being fulfilled for people by different products and activities? Marketers want to know the answers to such questions in order to communicate appropriately in terms of what needs and wants their products will fulfil. In addition, marketers need to understand their consumers' motivations in order to develop new products and services that people do not even know that they need or want yet. Imagine a life without your mobile phone, laptop, or tablet. These are all relatively new inventions, the benefits of which were unknown to people 50 years ago, yet are now considered to be necessities by many. Motivations for purchase may be purely functional in some cases, such as buying a sandwich when we are hungry; the motivations for purchase of many other products can be more complex. Many people consider more than just their need for telling the time when buying a watch. Wearing an Omega watch says something about the wearer, their social status, and the distinction that the watch conveys.

Needs, wants, and desires

We may use the terms needs, wants, and desires interchangeably in everyday speech, but in consumer behaviour they have quite specific and distinct meanings. A person is motivated when a need is aroused that they wish to satisfy. This motivation relates to a state of tension that exists when there is a difference between our actual and our desired state. The motivation is the drive to remove this tension. You may be thirsty, which leads to a tension in how you actually feel (thirsty) compared with how you would like to feel (satiated). You will be motivated to drink a glass of water, or a cup of tea, or a bottle of beer to satisfy your thirst. **Needs** are *the result of the difference between the actual and desired states,* such as not having any music to play at the gym, while **wants** are *specific manifestations of the motives and are linked to a specific goal object* such as having an iPod so you can listen to music at the gym. Finally **desires** have been described as *'temporal wants which may or may not have a biological basis'* (Oliver, 1996: 144). To illustrate, I may desire a fresh orange juice, whether or not I am actually thirsty.

How consumers choose to reduce the tension arising from the difference between their actual and ideal states is an important question for marketers, since companies want consumers to use their products and brands to close this gap. Companies engage with consumers to show them how the company's brand offers benefits that can satisfy some consumer need, whether functional or symbolic. Consumer choices are driven by a range of factors. If we consider the example of buying a car, it is clear that cars can serve different needs. For a recent graduate starting their first job some distance away from her home, with no public transport connections, a car serves primarily a utilitarian need as she needs to travel to and from work. In contrast, cars can also satisfy more hedonic needs, as demonstrated by the tag line 'the ultimate driving machine' used by BMW to indicate the pleasure to be gained from driving a high performance car.

When consumers are compelled to act in a way that removes or reduces the tension between their actual and desired state, there has to be a goal that the person is trying to achieve or accomplish. Such goals may be generic, product-specific, or brand-specific (Jansson-Boyd, 2010).

At work in the morning you may feel like a cup of coffee and do not mind making yourself a cup of instant coffee. This would be a generic goal. Alternatively, you might want to have a latte or cappuccino and decide to go to a café; this would be product-specific. However, you might also have a preference for a specific brand, such as Starbucks or Caffe Nero, and with such a brand-specific goal you might be motivated to walk for five minutes to your favourite supplier. This process may be influenced by a range of factors, including personality, perception, learning, and attitudes. In Consumer Insight 7.3, we describe the motivations around the development and adoption of innovative products.

Cultural differences determine how needs are translated into consumption. While we all need food and shelter, the houses we live in and the food we eat differ hugely across continents. Sometimes this is determined by the geography and climate, but it is also influenced by our cultural preferences. So, while a British student might choose a sandwich for lunch, a Singaporean might have dumplings or satay. Needs can also be classified as biogenic or psychogenic. **Biogenic needs** *or innate needs enable us to survive* and include the need for food, water, and shelter, while **psychogenic needs** *are socially acquired needs and include the need for status, affiliation, self-esteem, and prestige.* While we all need food to survive, it may also answer psychogenic needs. What you choose to eat may be affected by cultural differences, making you averse to eating certain foods (e.g. crickets are commonly eaten in Thailand, but this is unpalatable to US and UK consumers), while eating in particular restaurants may be answering your need for status or prestige. Restaurants in major cities are often booked up months in advance, but this seems to make such places even more desirable to consumers who want to eat and be seen in such places. Research Insight 7.3 expands some of the issues around functional and hedonic needs.

CONSUMER INSIGHT 7.3

The IKEA effect

In his book *Payoff: the hidden logic that shapes our motivations*, Dan Ariely refers to our fondness for our own creations as 'the IKEA effect'. The pride we have over an artefact that we have created ourselves is nothing new. In the 1940s the idea of cake mixes was first introduced and they were potentially incredibly convenient because housewives only had to add water, mix, and bake. To the surprise of the makers the mixes did not sell well, and it was not due to the taste. The problem was that it was just too simple; by only adding water the result was little more in terms of the effort involved than buying the cake from a shop. When the company changed the formula so that eggs and milk had to be added rather than just water the cake mixes became much more popular.

Ariely describes the cake mix story as illustrating how effort and ownership relate to motivation. In particular we are motivated to make a little more effort because the ownership we then feel makes us enjoy the product more. Ariely also notes that we are strongly motivated by our sense of identity. Companies have recognized this by allowing us to individualize products. For example we can choose different interior layouts for our cars, design our sports shoes, create our own sweets, or customize garments.

Questions

1. What other products or services might usefully use the 'the IKEA effect'?

2. Today lots of foods are ready prepared but there are also TV programmes and books that encourage us to cook from scratch. List and discuss the different motivations that may be present in our behaviour when we use ready prepared food and when we cook from scratch.

3. Are there products and services where the IKEA effect could not take place? What are they and why do you think motivation would not be a factor?

Sources: Norton et al. (2012); Park (2013); Ariely (2016).

 Access the online resources to learn more.

RESEARCH INSIGHT 7.3

Lowe, M.R. and Butryn, M.L. (2007), 'Hedonic hunger: a new dimension of appetite?', *Psychology & Behavior*, 91, 432–9.

In this literature review paper the authors argue that, for many people, food consumption is increasingly driven by pleasure rather than the functional need for calories. The environment is such that for most people there is a constant availability of highly palatable food: 'some individuals experience frequent thoughts, feelings and urges about food in the absence of any short- or long-term energy deficit'. The authors refer to this as 'hedonic hunger', reflecting the psychogenic qualities that food has today.

 Access the online resources to read the abstract and access the full paper.

Motivational conflict

People are driven to avoid negative results as well as to achieve positive goals. In some cases this may result in conflict—for example, you want to lose weight but you are tempted to indulge in choosing a dessert. Research also shows that people differ in their motivational profiles (Kramer and Yoon, 2007). Some people have a greater inclination to approach specific goals and therefore will have a greater sensitivity to positive outcomes, while others may be more sensitive to avoiding negative outcomes. There are three main motivational conflicts that marketers need to be aware of and which they can use to their advantage.

Approach–avoidance conflict *is when a desired goal also has negative consequences.* If you buy (approach) designer label clothes you may not want (avoid) people knowing how much you paid for them. Perhaps the most obvious approach–avoidance conflict concerns food, and particularly food high in calories such as chocolate or cakes. Often marketers will position their products in a way that recognizes their indulgence but also suggests that the consumer deserves it. A classic line which was used to advertise dairy cream cakes was 'Naughty … but Nice', thus recognizing a consumer's potential approach–avoidance conflict with a highly calorific but enjoyable food. Today, however, manufacturers are looking to make traditionally indulgent products such as potato crisps with fewer calories, often aiming them directly at those concerned about their weight and ostentatiously promoting their guilt-free status as in the example of Pop Chips (Figure 7.11) which have less than 100 calories per serving.

As almost all consumer behaviour is about choosing among alternatives, most of us experience what is termed approach–approach conflict on a regular basis. **Approach–approach conflict** *is when you have to choose between two or more equally attractive alternatives.*

Figure 7.11   Pop chips advertisement with US star Katy Perry
Source: Image courtesy of Pop Chips (www.popchips.com).

If you imagine being in a restaurant choosing a main course, there may be two or three dishes that you would like. In making the final choice you probably experience some approach–approach conflict as you would really like to taste them all, but you try to ensure that you make a choice you will be happy with, and not feel any dissatisfaction about—a form of cognitive dissonance (see Chapter 6). Some restaurants deal with this approach–approach conflict by providing tasting menus where you can have a selection of small dishes.

The final motivational conflict is known as avoidance–avoidance conflict. In **avoidance–avoidance conflict** *the choices available all have some apparent negative consequence.* Finance is an area of potential avoidance–avoidance conflict as consumers often do not see the benefit of an insurance plan or savings scheme, may be concerned about the risk associated with stocks and shares, and so have to be persuaded of the benefits of financial products. An advertisement for the US Bank of Mauston Christmas Saving Club has the tagline 'The Bank of Mauston makes saving for Christmas worth the wait with its Christmas Club account'. The campaign attempts to resolve two potential avoidance goals—saving (for Christmas) throughout the year set against the other possibilities which are dealing with all Christmas costs in one go or, worse, getting into debt for Christmas. Consumer Insight 7.4 examines aspects of motivational conflict in relation to health-related behaviours.

CONSUMER INSIGHT 7.4

'Will you take the stairs?' Turning approach-avoidance into approach-approach

Helen Nuki works for the behavioural economics research agency Monkey See. One morning when her daughter Litzi asked for another biscuit, Helen showed her the information on the packet that indicated the ingredients, and why it was probably a good idea not to eat too many. Litzi complained that one is always told about how bad things are for you and not how good they are. This is a typical approach–avoidance problem; we like biscuits (approach) but they generally contain a lot of calories, so we shouldn't eat too many (avoidance).

Helen took this problem and turned it around so that something people tend to avoid (climbing the stairs) was labelled in a positive way by telling them how many calories they would burn. You may think that this is still approach–avoidance, as while people may feel positive about burning calories they probably still don't like climbing stairs, but there is more to it than that. Most people recognize that they are not active enough and the challenge is to find relatively easy ways to help them that do not require a massive change. Most of us can climb a few more stairs without too much pain (approach) and we feel good about knowing how many calories we have burned (another approach), much easier than running a marathon (avoidance!).

But you still have to think about how you can encourage people to take the stairs. Suri et al. (2014) tested different signs either using a command, 'Take the stairs,' or a question, 'Will you take the stairs?' (Figure 7.12). The researchers found that different signs worked better in different situations. Overall they concluded that while telling people to take the stairs sometimes has a bigger immediate impact, asking people has a longer-lasting effect (See also Chapter 2, Consumer Insight 2.1 about nudging behaviour).

Questions

1. How else might you get people to use the stairs? Consider what theories of motivation you might use.

2. This is an example of encouraging people to do more, but what about when you want people to do less? We know that many people eat more food and drink more alcohol than is good for them. Discuss how you could use motivational theories to get people to reduce their consumption?

3. What happens when you have to market a product (such as a funeral plan or insurance) which would be categorized as avoidance–avoidance because there is no upside to the purchase? Can you think of ways you might motivate people to purchase such services?

Sources: Bates (2009); Suri et al. (2014); Reddy (2015).

Figure 7.12 'Take the Stairs' sign used by Suri et al. (2014)

Source: Suri, G., Sheppes, G., Leslie, S., Gross, J. J., Stairs or escalator? using theories of persuasion and motivation to facilitate healthy decision making, *Journal of Experimental Psychology: Applied*, 2014, Vol. 20, No. 4, 295–302, American Psychological Association, reprinted with permission.

 Access the online resources to learn more.

Maslow's hierarchy of needs

Maslow's hierarchy of needs (Figure 7.13) is one of the most frequently quoted theories of motivation (Maslow, 1954). It is important for many reasons, not least because it differentiated between intrinsic and extrinsic needs and emphasized the importance of intrinsic needs for human development. An **intrinsic need** *is an internal motivation* that comes from within the person, such as the need for food, water, and sex, but it can also be emotional, such as the need for love and friendship. On the other hand, an **extrinsic need** will *require some return or goal from the external environment*, such as a reward in the form of money or prestige. Consider how people are motivated to play computer games; some may enjoy just playing on their own or with friends (intrinsic motivation), while others may prefer to go on gaming sites that offer financial rewards (extrinsic motivation). Prior to Maslow, researchers had emphasized biological needs in relation to human motivation, but Maslow introduced the idea of people having deficiency needs and growth needs. In Maslow's theory one has to achieve each level of deficiency need (physiological, safety, social, and esteem needs) before moving to the next level.

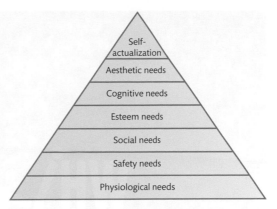

Figure 7.13 Diagrammatic representation of Maslow's hierarchy of needs

According to Maslow's hierarchy, if you did not feel safe it would be difficult to move to the level of looking for social relations and affiliation with others, and similarly if these social needs had not been met, looking for recognition and esteem would be difficult. Once these deficiency needs were met the individual could move to growth needs. Originally Maslow only included self-actualization as a growth need, but later this was reclassified to include cognitive need (the need to understand and explore) and aesthetic need (the need for beauty and order) below self-actualization (the realization of one's potential), which in turn is below self-transcendence where the fulfilment goes beyond the self to help others realize their potential (Maslow, 1971).

There are many criticisms of Maslow's theory. First, it is a theory that is not based on any empirical, experimental, or clinical data. Second, Maslow believed that a person has to satisfy each level before moving to the next; it would not be possible to move to the social needs before the physiological needs were satisfied, which suggests that poor people could not have meaningful relationships. Culturally, there are many differences in what motivates people—people can starve or give up their lives for a cause, which suggests that they can reach a level of self-actualization or transcendence by negating some of the lower levels of the hierarchy. What has been referred to as the gratification/activation aspect of the theory is also a problem. The theory states that once a lower-order need is gratified, its importance is reduced and a higher-order need is activated, increasing the importance of that higher-order need to the individual. But such a gratification/activation process has not been supported (Oliver, 1996). Others have questioned the key element of Maslow's theory—that basic needs exist for all. Perhaps, for example, we do not all have a need for self-actualization or esteem. Finally, times change, and different needs may take on differential importance. In many countries people are aware of the dangers of terrorism and that bombs may be planted in public spaces, such as on public transport. We have to take these factors into account as we function in our lives, but it does not mean that we feel completely safe while we carry out our daily activities. Indeed, safety is a need that seems

Figure 7.14   Volvo car advertisement emphasizing safety

Source: Image courtesy of Volvo Cars (www.volvocars.com).

to pervade much of what we do. We want to be safe on the roads; we want to be sure that the food we eat and the medicines we take are safe. Volvo have used the need for safety to market their cars for years, recognizing that people will feel more secure in a brand of car which advertises its safety record. Their recent campaign, shown in Figure 7.14, emphasizes their Whiplash Protection System (WHPS) which reduces the likelihood of whiplash damage in an accident.

It is clear to see how marketing recognizes deficiency needs; even if most people in the Western world have food and shelter, they may still be enticed by advertisements that offer additional qualities (e.g. nutritional value) or amounts (two for the price of one), or security such as in gated communities. In Research Insight 7.4, we describe work looking at the how the hierarchy of needs applies in consumer lives.

RESEARCH INSIGHT 7.4

Tikkanen, I. (2007), Maslow's hierarchy and food tourism in Finland: five cases, *British Food Journal*, 109, 9, 721–34.

Using case study methodology, the author identified five sectors of food tourism where the needs and motivations could be linked with Maslow's hierarchy of needs. For example, the kinds of food tourism that are based on social needs include festivals that attract tourists and local residents and food trails where tourists can create their own experiences. The social motives identified include having social interaction with others and the creation of a community spirit around food.

 Access the online resources to read the abstract and access the full paper.

Alternatives to Maslow

Although Maslow's hierarchy of needs is probably the best-known motivation theory, alternative models have been proposed. Alderfer's ERG theory (Alderfer, 1969) comprises three stages—existence, relatedness, and growth. Existence covers the basic necessities, including food, water, and shelter, and activities (such as being employed) through which we achieve these. Relatedness covers needs that involve relations with significant people, and activities that provide sharing including companionship, marriage, and friendship at work. Finally, growth involves a person realizing their potential. At first sight there does not appear to be a huge difference between Maslow and Alderfer, although some suggest that Alderfer overcomes some of the overlapping of categories (e.g. affiliation and prestige) that are found in Maslow's model.

Another view on motivations is provided by Herzberg's dual factor theory (Herzberg, 1968). Although this theory was developed in the organizational context, it has been tested in empirical consumption situations, which Maslow and Alderfer's have not. The key to Herzberg's theory is the presence of satisfiers and dissatisfiers. In the context of his research, dissatisfiers were aspects of the context of a job (working conditions, organizational policies, the boss's approach), while satisfiers were about the job content (the achievement and satisfaction derived from the work). Critical here is that these two factors operate separately; context factors cause dissatisfaction when absent because they are essentially what you expect at a most basic level. So, when buying a book you expect it to have page numbers, or if you buy a new table lamp you expect it to have a plug attached. These are also referred to as hygiene factors. Satisfiers create satisfaction and motivation, but their absence does not produce dissatisfaction but rather a neutral state. It is important not to think of the dual factor theory as bipolar between dissatisfaction and satisfaction; rather we should concentrate on the two independent entities of satisfaction and dissatisfaction:

No satisfaction _____ Satisfaction

Dissatisfaction _____ No dissatisfaction

If we apply this to a consumption situation, we can imagine a number of scenarios including some that might include both satisfaction and dissatisfaction. One could, for example, experience dissatisfaction with the layout of a store but satisfaction that the store makes fresh sushi every day. Importantly, it allows companies to differentiate products and services along lines of satisfaction and no dissatisfaction. Imagine, for example, that you are an internet company selling clothes. A way to reduce dissatisfaction might be to ensure that returns are pre-paid—this aspect of customer services will not impact the level of satisfaction that a person feels with the product that they purchase, but may reduce the possible dissatisfaction they feel when returning something that does not fit and help to remind them to return to your site.

Motivation research

Motivation research became popular in the 1950s. It developed from Ernest Dichter's work with companies, which stressed the psychological and emotional content of consumption choices (see Chapter 1), and from Freudian theories that emphasized unconscious motives. An important aspect of the Freudian approach is to identify hidden and often suppressed motives that people are unable to express in a straightforward survey or interview. Marketers were interested in identifying the symbolic roles that products played in people's lives, but were difficult to express. As discussed already, motivation research tried to understand the true motives for consumers' choice or rejection of a brand or product, i.e. what that product symbolized for them. Motivation research comes in many forms, such as projective techniques, role play, word associations, and even clay modelling. Consumer Insight 7.5 provides information about one such technique, the thematic apperception test (TAT).

CONSUMER INSIGHT 7.5

The thematic apperception test

The thematic apperception test was developed by the clinical psychologists Christiana Morgan and Henry Murray in the 1930s (Morgan and Murray, 1935). It consisted of a series of often ambiguous pictures which participants were asked to talk about. It has been used primarily for clinical research, in particular personality disorders, but it has also been widely used in personality research and marketing contexts (Rook and Levy, 1983). In Rook and Levy's study, which showed men and women in various grooming rituals including applying make-up and blow-drying hair, participants were asked to write stories about and around these pictures. The stories revealed issues that participants had with social norms around grooming rituals, and some complex motives and fantasies. The authors concluded:

> So far these various grooming tales show that the consumption of bathroom furnishings, hair dryers, soaps, makeup, shampoos, colognes, shavers, underwear, and so on, affords complex ways of expressing one's sexual and social striving. The products are not merely aids to cleanliness and sensory pleasure; they are means to coping systematically with the demands for growing up in particular ways in American society.

(Rook and Levy, 1983: 333)

Figure 7.15 An example of a thematic apperception test

Source: Ueda, T. (2012), 'Creating value with sales promotion strategies that avoid price discounting', in G.E. Smith (ed.), *Visionary pricing: reflections and advances in honor of Dan Nimer* (*Advances in Business Marketing and Purchasing*, Vol.19), Emerald Group Publishing, Bingley, pp.213–56. Reproduced with permission from Emerald Group Publishing Ltd.

Studies such as these help marketers, and especially creatives in advertising agencies, to understand and identify appropriate ways of communicating their brands in line with how they are perceived by their customers.

Questions

1. Look at the picture in Figure 7.15. Discuss with a colleague what you think might have just happened and what might happen next.

2. What products and brands might these people be using? What products and brands might they not use?

Sources: Morgan and Murray (1935); Rook and Levy (1983).

 Access the online resources and follow the web links to learn more about the use of thematic apperception tests and see more examples of them.

Commentators such as Vance Packard (1957) criticized motivation research because they thought it had the potential to manipulate consumers (see Chapter 1). Some psychoanalysts criticized motivation research for misapplying their techniques in a business situation. Another problem with motivation research is that the results depend on the researcher's interpretation, and different researchers may produce different results (Avis and Aitken, 2015). It also requires an understanding of often very complex data in which the researcher needs to be carefully trained (Donoghue, 2000). Participants themselves may also feel uncomfortable about being asked to engage in role-playing exercises (Steinman, 2008).

However, it is important to recognize that, despite these arguments, motivation research still has value since it has the potential to be a rich source of data regarding consumers' beliefs and motivations which might not be reached using traditional survey methods. In particular, participants are unlikely to be aware of the purpose of the exercise, and so are unaware of what their responses might mean and therefore are less likely to give the answer that they think the interviewer is looking for. Motivation research also offers a further dimension to other research methods. It provides additional information about consumers' behaviour and decision-making, and often hypotheses developed from such research are further verified using other techniques (Steinman, 2008). These insights into motivations are useful for marketers as they reveal the deep-rooted reasons driving behaviour and thus enable companies to form deeper connections with consumers through their brand communications.

The means–end approach

Businesses would like to know why people are motivated to purchase a particular brand or behave in a certain way. The means–end chain model assumes that what we choose to buy or do is linked to an end-state that we want to achieve, such as belonging, security, or good health. In other words, the product offers the means to an end other than just its purchase. The technique that is used to identify these end-states is called laddering; researchers ask questions that lead the consumer up a ladder of abstraction from the attributes of the product they have bought through to the desired end-states achieved. From such laddering, researchers produce 'hierarchical value maps'. Figure 7.16 shows the hierarchical value map for clothing store attributes. Functional attributes such as a pleasant store atmosphere and clear shop layout lead to more abstract ideas such as feeling well, fun to shop, and an end-state of contentment. So a storeowner could deduce from this that a convenient layout within a pleasant store makes consumers feel good, and when feeling content these consumers may be more amenable to purchasing from that store.

Conclusions

This chapter focused on the central role that personality, identity, and motivation play in consumer behaviour. While there are many different **perspectives on personality and self**, in this chapter we discussed the main approaches in terms of definitions of self, the extent to which the internal or external aspects of self are emphasized, and the primary functions of the self-concept in each approach. As Practitioner Insight 7 shows, such theories are

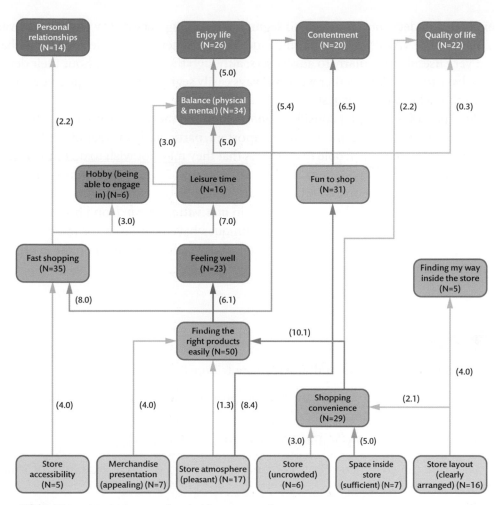

Figure 7.16 Hierarchical value map for clothing store attributes

Source: Wagner (2007). Reproduced with permission from Emerald Group Publishing Ltd.

currently used by companies such as Kantar Millward Brown in the development of CharacterZ, a system of ten archetypes which they have used in their commercial work for global brands including Burger King.

Theories such as ***multiplicity of self*** can be very useful to marketing as they recognize that we may be made up of different selves at different times in our lives and in different situations. Recognition of even negative aspects of self have proved useful to campaigns such as that of Sport England in getting women to engage in activities without feeling uncomfortable about themselves and how they look. Relating ***personality to marketing practice***, it is important to appreciate that an individual's personality represents a set of characteristics that can be used to describe consumer segments. This has been the backdrop to the sections about the way that the concepts of personality and identity apply in marketing contexts.

We explained in detail one approach to segmentation using personality and identity variables, namely the VALS™ psychographics and lifestyle scheme. Lifestyle approaches have proved very useful, particularly to advertisers, although they are not without their detractors. We have to consider whether we can always easily segment groups of people as neatly as such approaches would suggest.

The final part of this chapter considered ***motivation*** and the role it plays in our choices of products and brands. What is increasingly important, particularly in areas of public health, is finding ways to motivate people to do things that they may not wish to do but which are probably going to improve their health. Consumer Insight 7.4 explored some of the issues around how we can get people to take the stairs, a relatively easy way to increase activity. We explored some of the techniques involved in ***motivation research*** and how they might be used in marketing. Again, while these techniques have been used for many years we should remember that they have their detractors and are very dependent on the interpretation by the researcher.

Review questions

1. Explain how the id, ego, and superego contribute to personality.

2. Define the different aspects of self, and provide an example of each from your own experience.

3. What is symbolic consumption? Why is this useful for marketers?

4. Describe the congruency concept, and provide two different examples of it in practice.

5. Discuss the advantages and disadvantages of psychographics in consumer behaviour.

6. Why is it important to understand consumer motivation when thinking about personality?

Discussion questions

1. Access the Online Resource Centre and follow the link to the website http://www.teefury.com/ How can this brand/product best be understood in terms of personality and identity theory?

2. Take a look at the 'This Girl Can' website (http://www.thisgirlcan.co.uk). What theories of self are being used here? Do you think that these are successful? How else might you use personality to encourage people to be more active?

3. Can you really link products and brands to personality? Search the internet to find your own examples of companies using personality and lifestyle approaches to segment consumers. Compare these approaches with the VALS™ system, and comment on the similarities and differences. Where do you think lifestyle approaches are likely to be most useful to marketers?

4. Consider Maslow's and Herzberg's theories built around motivation. How realistic do you think they are in the twenty-first century? Read the paper by Tikkanen (2007) on food tourism in Finland and consider which other products or services might benefit from this treatment.

Access the online resources to test your knowledge further and complete the Multiple Choice Questions for Chapter 7.

CASE STUDY 7

Using profiles to understand the Indian consumer

Examining lifestyles alongside demographics has been one method business has used to get closer to understanding the lives and in some cases the personality and motivation of consumers around the world. This case examines some of the lifestyle issues relevant to Indian consumers.

In 10–15 years, the Indian economy could be as big as China's is today. India's population of well over one billion people is getting richer but, unlike China, India's population will remain relatively young for many years to come. Goldman Sachs (2016) reported that there were currently 440 million millennials and 390 million Generation Z teens and children in India; 65 per cent of the population was born after 1980. India is culturally diverse with 1,500 dialects and many different faiths, ethnicities, customs, foods, and dress styles. It is also varied geographically, with some richer, more literate, areas around Mumbai and Bangalore contrasted with poorer, less well educated states in the east of the country. This may be a problem for Indian development; in the state of Bihar, 67 per cent of women are illiterate, and while overall growth in India is impressive, about 400 million Indians are still living on less than $1.25 a day. Maslow's hierarchy is only too evident in an Indian phrase highlighting what are life's essentials—'*roti kapda aur makaan*'—or 'food, clothing, and shelter'.

But things are definitely changing. The economic growth of eight of the highest performing Indian states has led to remarkable upward mobility for their residents. In 2012, these states accounted for 14 million consuming-class households, which was over half of India's total, and along with the two million consuming-class households in the four very high performing city states, these 12 states accounted for 58 per cent of Indian consuming households in 2012.

The Western idea of self is about the individual and their personality, but the Indian self has a stronger social identity with the individual often subsumed by the social in a need to conform. This need to conform may in turn drive behaviour, although there is some evidence that the individual self is becoming more important under Western influence. Prasad Narsimhan, Virgin Mobile's chief marketing officer, notes that the most important aspect of young Indians is that they like to network. They see networking as creating possibilities, and brands need to identify how to help them. This thinking has led to presenting the young in advertisements as very different from their parents' generation. The internet provider Bharti Airtel has used the idea of impatience in their advertising for Airtel Broadband. Their advertisements show a group of young people impatient to get on with their lives, download data, find new trends, and communicate with friends. This campaign, with the tagline 'Impatience is the New Life: Live it with Airtel Broadband', is aimed at attracting consumers aged under 25.

When thinking about the Indian consumer's lifestyle one must consider a range of factors (family status, extended family, community and caste, peer group, and personal ability, as well as personality). Many young Indians will undertake peer group benchmarking based on 'people like me' with a similar geographical location and education. In India children do not leave home early, and so family status has a strong influence on how they see themselves. But the younger generation may be doing better financially than their elders, which may create particular tensions. India now boasts seven million college graduates a year. A student from a top business school may be earning a salary way beyond what his father earns. When young Indians reach a goal in their career they are likely to celebrate with aspirational products such as premium car brands or expensive watches. Although similar to the aspirations of young successful people in other contexts, the symbolism attached has a resonance deeply connected to their family history. Being Indian is said to be an amalgamation of personality traits, ethnicities, and the melting pot aspect of living in India.

The McKinsey Global Institute (2007) identified five economic classes based primarily on disposable income (Table 7.4). These classes help companies understand their consumers, and they offer a sketch of a typical consumer for each. These descriptions provide a glimpse of the range of lifestyles of Indians today.

Beyond these lifestyles based on economic differences, others have developed additional profiles of Indian consumers. These include the following.

1. **Young** and **restless**—young people in all income segments who are influencing their parents' spending or spending their own money. Some have part- or full-time jobs which gives them scope for spending money without the responsibility of a family. The young and affluent among them will be eating out, going to movies, and clubbing. Dress is modern and they are looking for new fashions at affordable prices. Some work in IT or call centre type jobs; they are college-educated city dwellers, often working odd hours, and they want to be able to shop when they are off duty. Some will be married (both working) with children and will be looking to improve their lifestyles through appropriate services.

2. **The bold and the beautiful**—they have money or are getting it and want to show it. This group includes yeppies (young entrepreneurial professionals) and yippies (young international professionals). Truly self-made, they enjoy premium weekend getaways and travel outside India regularly, and their focus is on their career. The raffles (rural affluent farm folk) treat farming as a business.

3. **The golden folks in high spirits**—although India is a young nation, there are also plenty of old people. These are the wealthy retired. Typically, older Indians have remained close to their children, but that may change in the future as the lifestyles of the young themselves change.

Economic class and description	Consumer sketch
Deprived—This is the poorest group, typically unskilled or low-skilled workers. They may well struggle to find employment throughout the year, settling for seasonal or part time employment.	Mangu (43) and his wife Basanti (35) live and work in a poor rural district in central India. They have five children and Mangu's mother lives with them. They do not have a regular income and life is a struggle. They rely on government-subsidized food and health care. Mangu is wondering whether to move to the city like many he knows have done. While he might find construction work and Basanti might work as a maid, they would have to live in a crowded slum with few amenities. They want their children to get a basic education as a means of getting out of poverty.
Aspirers—These are usually small-scale shopkeepers or farmers, or low-skilled industrial or service workers. Although they are not deprived, they still struggle and spend almost half their income on basic necessities.	Ramnath (43) graduated from high school and is an electrician. His wife Lakshmi is at home bringing up their three children and looking after her in-laws. They have some additional income from a small grocery shop run by Ramnath's father. They own an LPG stove, a small TV, and an iron, and use an electric rod for heating water. Most of their household articles are second-hand.
Seekers—These are varied in terms of employment, age, and attitudes. They range from young college graduates to traditional white-collar employees, mid-level government officials, and medium-scale traders and business people.	Suresh (35) is a commerce graduate who works as an accountant in a private company and his wife is a nursery teacher. They spend almost half their income on food and rent for their two-bedroom apartment. Educating their two children is a priority, and they spend a large amount of their budget on sending them to private school. They live comfortably with a second-hard car, a colour TV, a music system, a mobile phone, a refrigerator, and some jewellery. Suresh is ambitious and aspires to luxuries and to own his own flat.
Strivers—People in this band and upwards are considered successful in Indian society. They work as business people in cities, professionals, senior government officials, and richer farmers in villages. They have stable sources of income and a reasonable wealth base.	Yash (32) and Radha (30) are college graduates from prosperous families. Yash works in a multinational bank and Radha is juggling a job as a marketing manager and a weekend course in interior design. They have bought a two-bedroom flat. They are brand conscious, with a Honda car and a Sony TV, air conditioners, and a washing machine. They holiday annually in India or neighbouring countries.
Global Indians—These are senior executives, large business owners, and top tier professionals. Recently, there are also increasingly upwardly mobile graduates who are commanding premium salaries from international companies and therefore may be young. They are global in their tastes and enjoy a high standard of living.	Rahul (40) is vice-president of a large IT company. He gained his MBA from the Indian Institute of Management. His wife is a senior executive in a leading ad agency. They have bought a four-bedroom apartment. They have a flat-screen TV and a Bose audio system alongside many other impressive lifestyle products. They have a full-time cook, maid, and chauffeur. They have two cars and regularly travel abroad to Europe and the USA.

Table 7.4   McKinsey's five Indian economic classes

Interesting features of the Indian consumer market include the fact that 40 per cent of the population is vegetarian, that it is the largest market in the world for milk, and that it is also one of the largest spirits market in the world. There is demand for cars and scooters, and personal transportation is currently the second-largest category of personal consumption because of the lack of public transport.

It is difficult to make generalizations about how Indians respond to Western brands. It appears that they do not have the same preference for foreign brands that Chinese consumers have. Coca-Cola bought the leading Indian Cola, Thums Up, with a view to ditching it and enabling Coke to take over the market, but local managers recognized that Indians preferred Thums Up, so it remained on the shelves next to Coke. Coke also has to compete with global brands, notably Pepsi. In 2015, 30 per cent of Indian teens had never tried Coke. Pepsi had more successfully engaged with the youth market through the appeal of cricket and Bollywood, with Virat Kohli, the vice-captain of the Indian cricket team, and Ranbir, a Bollywood celebrity, as its brand ambassadors.

Both Pepsi and Coke were targeting youth, but Pepsi represented them as impatient, confident, and rebellious, while Coke decided that for every extrovert there were likely to be five introverts and that many teenagers were not super-confident. Coke realized that many Indian teens do not get to meet one another over cups of coffee, as most do not live in large cities, and so they marketed Coke as the perfect ice-breaker—the universal need of young people to meet one another. Teens were urged to bond over a Coke with the tagline *Taste jo har dil chahe!* (Taste that every heart desires). Coke also took on board the different cultural traditions of India, using a similar approach in ads showing a bride and groom in an arranged marriage getting to know one another. Young, Bollywood stars Alia Bhatt and Siddarth Malhotra depicted a young married couple awkward in each others' company to begin with but who bond over a bottle of Coca-Cola (You can watch the ad on Youtube). Coke experienced over 5 per cent increase in consumption following the ad.

Some believe that the social nature of identity in the country has led to greater assimilative and accommodative tendencies in terms of acceptable brands. This may have led to the adoption of multinational brands as Indian. Such brands include Lifebuoy, Dettol, Philips, Colgate, Cadbury's, Bata, and more recently Hyundai, Nokia, McDonald's, and Samsung. For example, Colgate is a brand which has long been part of the Indian household, despite the presence of many domestic brands, such as Promise, Vicco, and Dabur, and other multinationals such as Pepsodent. Above all, Colgate is not seen as a foreign brand and it cannot be outperformed on functionality. Brands such as this appear to receive a high degree of loyalty across the country, while a brand like Kellogg's had a tough time because Indians were loath to give up their calorie-rich breakfasts. Other premium brands have to compete in a more difficult market. While Nike, Adidas, and Reebok all have some loyal buyers, if a discount is offered they appear to become interchangeable. Why? Because from the Indian consumer's point of view they all have enough image value, and they prefer a premium brand at a bargain price rather than just sticking to one premium brand. Goldman Sachs (2016) has identified seven key consumption desires of Indian consumers (see Figure 7.17). International designer brands such as Diesel, Armani, and Gucci have opened stores in the major cities to meet the increasing desire for luxury brands.

But Indian brands are increasingly popular, with brands such as Tata, Godrej, and Bajaj amongst the most popular. Successful brands often modify their products to suit the Indian market. Nokia, for example, modified one of its mobile phones with a built-in flashlight that truck drivers used on poorly lit roads. 'Indianizing' also has to do with keeping prices at levels that are manageable for the average Indian consumer.

Questions

1. Taking into consideration the lifestyles presented and the seven key desires in Figure 7.17, what Western products/brands which you are familiar with might appeal to the different profiles and why? Consider some consumer issues that might affect their introduction into India.

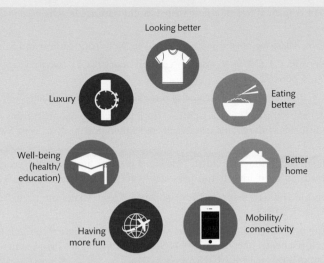

Figure 7.17   Consumption patterns across seven key desires
Source: Image courtesy of Goldman Sachs Global Investment Research.

2. If the social self is important in Indian culture, what impact might this have on an individual's consumer behaviour? How might a marketing organization capitalize on the idea of the social self?

3. If you were marketing sports goods, how might you differentiate your brand to different segments of Indian consumers?

4. Pepsi and Coca-Cola used different approaches to their marketing in India. Consider the strengths and weaknesses of each approach. If you were Coca-Cola how would you differentiate the indigenous brand Thums Up from the global brand?

Sources: McKinsey Global Institute (2007); Prasad (2010); Subramanyeswar (2010); McKinsey and Co. (2014); Chakrapani (2015); Goldman Sachs (2016); WARC (2016); Dutta (nd).

References

Aaker, J.L. (1997), 'Dimensions of brand personality', *Journal of Market Research*, 34, 3, 347–56.

Aaker, J.L. (1999), 'The malleable self: the role of self-expression in persuasion', *Journal of Marketing Research*, 36, 1, 45–57.

Adams, J. and Nettle, D. (2009), 'Time perspective, personality and smoking, body mass, and physical activity: an empirical study', *British Journal of Health Psychology*, 14, 1, 83–105.

Ahuvia, A.C. (2005), 'Beyond the extended self: loved objects and consumers' identity narratives', *Journal of Consumer Research*, 32, 1, 171–84.

Alderfer, C.P. (1969), 'An empirical test of a new theory of human needs', *Organizational Behavior and Human Performance*, 4, 2, 142–75.

Ariely, D. (2016), *Payoff: the hidden logic that shapes our motivations*, New York: Simon and Schuster.

Arnould, E.J. and Thompson, C.J. (2005), 'Consumer culture theory (CCT): twenty years of research', *Journal of Consumer Research*, 31, 4, 868–82.

Avis, M. and Aitken, R. (2015), 'Intertwined', *Journal of Historical Research in Marketing*, 7, 2, 208–31.

Axelsson, M., Brink, E, Lundgren, J., and Lötvall, J. (2011), 'The influence of personality traits on reported adherence to medication in individuals with chronic disease: an epidemiological study in West Sweden', *PLOS One*, 6, 3, e18241.

Baker, R. (2013), 'Cutting through the price clutter', *Marketing Week*, 27 June, http://www.marketingweek.co.uk/analysis/essential-reads/asda-creating-brand-personality/4007059.article (accessed 8 April 2014).

Banister, E.N. and Hogg, M.K. (2001), 'Mapping the negative self: from "so not me" … to "just not me"', *Advances in Consumer Research*, 28, 1, 242–8.

Bates, C. (2009), 'Scaling new heights: piano stairway encourages commuters to ditch the escalators', http://www.dailymail.co.uk/sciencetech/article-1218944/Scaling-new-heights-Piano-stairway-encourages-commuters-ditch-escalators.html (accessed 10 November 2016)

Beckland, J. (2011), 'The end of demographics: how marketers are going deeper with personal data', *Mashable*, 30 June, http://mashable.com/2011/06/30/psychographics-marketing/ (accessed 25 May 2017).

Belk, R.W. (1988), 'Possessions and the extended self', *Journal of Consumer Research*, 15, 2, 139–68.

Bulik, B.S (2010), 'You are what you watch, market data suggest', *Advertising Age*, 1 November, http://adage.com/article/news/research-links-personality-traits-tv-viewing-habits/146779/ (accessed 25 May 2017).

Chahal, M. (2013), 'Social media: this is what my stuff says about me', *Marketing Week*, 11 April http://www.marketingweek.co.uk/trends/social-media-this-is-what-my-stuff-says-about-me/4006169.article (accessed 8 April 2017).

Chakrapani, A. (2015), 'Consumer behaviour and preferences of Indian consumers towards apparel purchase in retail markets of India', *Innovative Journal of Business and Management*, 4, 4, 94–100.

Coca-Cola Retailing Research Council (2016), 'The connected shopper in Eurasia and Africa', https://prod-wp.pub.coke.com/wp-content/uploads/sites/24/2016/07/Winning_with_the_Connected_Shopper_in_Eurasiaan-dAfricaCoca_Cola_Retailing_Council_FINALJune2016.pdf (accessed 18 October 2017).

Cross, S. and Markus, H. (1991), 'Possible selves across the life span', *Human Development*, 34, 4, 230–55.

Cuddeford-Jones, M. (2013), 'Designed for lives of customers', *Marketing Week*, 11 July, http://www.marketingweek.co.uk/analysis/marketing-tactics/design/designed-for-lives-of-customers/4007234.article (accessed 8 April 2017).

Donoghue, S. (2000), 'Projective techniques in consumer research', *Journal of Family Ecology and Consumer Sciences*, 28, 47–53.

Dutta, D. (nd), 'Indian consumers', http://thirdeyesight.in/articles/Indian_consumer_A_do-it-yourself_kit.pdf (accessed 1 May 2017).

Elliott, R. and Wattanasuwan, K. (1998), 'Brands as symbolic resources for the construction of identity', *International Journal of Advertising*, 17, 2, 131–45.

Ericksen, M.K. and Sirgy, M.J. (1992), 'Employed females' clothing preference, self-image congruence, and career anchorage', *Journal of Applied Social Psychology*, 22, 5, 408–22.

Foxall, G.R. and Goldsmith, R. (1988), 'Personality and consumer research: another look', *Journal of the Market Research Society*, 30, 2, 111–25.

Freud, S. (1923), *The ego and the id*, London: Hogarth Press

García-de-Frutos, N., Ortega-Egea, J.M., and Martínez-del-Río, J. (2016), 'Anti-consumption for environmental sustainability: conceptualization, review, and multilevel research directions', *Journal of Business Ethics*, https://doi.org/10.1007/s10551-016-3023-z.

Goffman, E. (1959), *The presentation of self in everyday life*, New York: Anchor.

Goldman Sachs (2016), 'India consumer close-up', http://www.goldmansachs.com/our-thinking/pages/macroeconomic-insights-folder/rise-of-the-india-consumer/report.pdf (accessed 6 November 2016).

Goldsmith, R.E. and Hofacker, C.F. (1991), 'Measuring consumer innovativeness', *Journal of the Academy of Marketing Science*, 19, 3, 209–21.

Grubb, E. and Grathwohl, H. (1967), 'Consumer self-concept, symbolism and market behavior: a theoretical approach', *Journal of Marketing*, 1, 4, 22–7.

Harris, E.G. and Fleming, D.E. (2005), 'Assessing the human element in service personality formation: personality congruency and the five factor model', *Journal of Services Marketing*, 19, 4, 187–98.

Haws, K.L., Bearden, W.O., and Nenkov, G.Y. (2012), 'Consumer spending self-control effectiveness and outcome elaboration prompts', *Journal of the Academy of Marketing Science*, 40, 5, 695–710.

Heine, P.J. (1971), *Personality in social theory*, Chicago, IL: Alpine.

Herzberg, F. (1968), 'One more time: how do you motivate employees?', *Harvard Business Review*, 46, 1, 53–62.

Hollenbeck, C.R. and Kaikati, A.M. (2012), 'Consumers use of brands to reflect their actual and ideal selves on Facebook', *International Journal of Research in Marketing*, 29, 4, 395–405.

Hughes, S.A. (2011), 'Mike "The Situation" Sorrentino sues Abercrombie & Fitch', *Washington Post*, 16 November, http://www.washingtonpost.com/blogs/celebritology/post/mike-the-situation-sorrentino-sues-abercrombie-and-fitch/2011/11/16/gIQAglmNRN_blog.html (accessed 8 October 2016).

Janssens, W. and De Pelsmacker, P. (2009), 'Smells like me—personality and perfume choice', *International Journal of Market Research*, 51, 4, 465–80.

Jansson-Boyd, C.V. (2010), *Consumer psychology*, Maidenhead: Open University Press.

Kassarjian, H.H. (1971), 'Personality and consumer behavior: a review', *Journal of Marketing Research*, 8, 4, 409–18.

Kassarjian, H.H. and Sheffet, M.J. (1981), 'Personality and consumer behavior: an update,' in H.H. Kassarjian (ed.), *Perspectives in consumer behavior*, Glenview, IL: Scott Foresman, pp 160–80.

Kellner, D. (1992), 'Popular culture and the construction of postmodern identities', in S. Lash and J. Friedman (eds), *Modernity and identity*, Oxford: Blackwell, pp.140–56.

Kim, D.H., Seely, N.K., and Jung, J.H. (2017), 'Do you prefer Pinterest or Instagram? The role of image-sharing SNSs and self-monitoring in enhancing ad effectiveness', *Computers in Human Behavior*, 70, 535–43.

Kramer, T. and Yoon, S.-O. (2007), 'Approach–avoidance motivation and the use of affect as information', *Journal of Consumer Psychology*, 17, 2, 128–38.

Lastovicka, J.L., Bettencourt, L.A., Hughner, R.S., and Kuntze, R.J. (1999), 'Lifestyle of the tight and frugal: theory and measurement', *Journal of Consumer Research*, 26, 1, 85–98.

Lawler, R. (2011), 'SyncTweet will sync TV ads with your Twitter stream', http://gigaom.com/2011/08/26/synctweet/ (accessed 11 January 2012).

Lee, M., Motion, J., and Conroy, D. (2009), 'Anti-consumption and brand avoidance', *Journal of Business Research*, 62, 2, 169–80.

Ligas, M. and Cotte, J. (1999), 'The process of negotiating brand meaning: a symbolic interactionist perspective', *Advances in Consumer Research*, 26, 609–14.

Lowe, M.R. and Butryn, M.L. (2007), 'Hedonic hunger: a new dimension of appetite?', *Psychology & Behaviour*, 91, 432–9.

McCrae, R.R. and Costa, P.T. (1990), *Personality in adulthood*, New York: Guilford Press.

McKinsey Global Institute (2007), 'The "bird of gold": the rise of India's consumer market', *McKinsey Report* http://www.mckinsey.com/insights/asia-pacific/the_bird_of_gold (accessed 11 May 2017).

McKinsey and Company (2014), 'India's economic geography in 2025: states, clusters and cities. Identifying the high potential markets of tomorrow', *Insights India*, October, https://www.mckinsey.com/global-themes/asia-pacific/understanding-indias-economic-geography (accessed 5 November 2016).

Maslow, A. (1954), *Motivation and personality*, New York: Harper.

Maslow, A. (1971), *The farther reaches of human nature*, New York: Viking Press.

Mead, G.H. (1913), 'The social self', *Journal of Philosophy, Psychology and Scientific Methods*, 10, 14, 374–80

Millington, A. (2015), 'Magnum launches two new flavours as it looks to become top indulgent treat', *Marketing Week*, https://www.marketingweek.com/2015/04/08/magnum-launches-two-news-flavours-as-it-looks-to-become-top-indulgent-treat/ (accessed 6 November 2016).

Möller, J. and Herm, S. (2013), 'Shaping retail brand personality perceptions by bodily experiences', *Journal of Retailing*, 89, 4, 438–46.

Morgan, C.D. and Murray, H.A. (1935), 'A method for investigating fantasies: the thematic apperception test', *Archives of Neurology and Psychiatry*, 34, 2, 289–306.

Norton, M., Mochon, D., and Ariely, D. (2012), 'The IKEA effect: when labor leads to love', *Journal of Consumer Psychology*, 22, 3, 453–60.

Oliver, R.L. (1996), *Satisfaction: a behavioural perspective on the consumer*, New York: McGraw-Hill.

Packard, V.O. (1957), *The hidden persuaders*, New York: McKay.

Park, M. (2013), 'A history of the cake mix, the invention that redefined "baking"', http://www.bonappetit.com/entertaining-style/pop-culture/article/cake-mix-history (accessed 18 October 2017).

Prasad, S. (2010), 'Why some slumdogs feel like millionaires: the theory of multiple poverty lines', https://2016.esomar.org/web/research_papers/Happiness_2212_Why-some-slumdogs-feel-like-millionaires-and-some-millionaires-like-slumdogs.php (accessed 18 October 2017).

Reddy, S. (2015), 'How to get people to take the stairs', http://www.wsj.com/articles/how-to-get-people-to-take-the-stairs-1424145648 (accessed 9 October, 2016)

Richins, M.L. and Dawson, S. (1992), 'A consumer values orientation for materialism and its measurement: scale development and validation', *Journal of Consumer Research*, 19, 303–16.

Rokeach, M. (1974), 'Change and stability in American value systems, 1968–1971', *Public Opinion Quarterly*, 38, 2, 222–38.

Rook, D.W. and Levy, S.J. (1983), 'Psychosocial themes in consumer grooming rituals', *Advances in Consumer Research*, 10, 329–33.

Rosenberg, M. (1979), *Conceiving the self*, New York: Basic Books.

Schwartz, S. H. (1994), 'Are there universal aspects in the structure and contents of human values?', *Journal of Social Issues*, 50, 4, 19–45.

Shankar, A., Elliott, R., and Fitchett, J.A. (2009), 'Identity, consumption and narratives of socialization', *Marketing Theory*, 9, 1, 75–94.

Shimp, T.A. and Sharma, S. (1987), 'Consumer ethnocentrism: construction and validation of the CETSCALE', *Journal of Marketing Research*, 24, 8, 280–9.

Shobeiri, S., Mazaheri, E., and Laroche, M. (2015), 'How would the e-retailer's website personality impact customers' attitudes toward the site?', *Journal of Marketing Theory and Practice*, 23, 4, 388–401.

Sirgy, M.J. (1982), 'Self-image/product-image congruity and advertising strategy', in V. Kothari (ed.), *Developments in marketing science*, Vol. 5, Marquette, MI: Academy of Marketing Science, pp.129–33.

Steinman, R.B. (2008), 'Projective techniques in consumer research', in J.B. Belloit and T.R. Johns (eds), *Northeast Association of Business, Economics, and Technology, Proceedings of the 30th Annual Meeting*, pp.253–61.

Stets, J.E. and Burke, P.J. (2003), 'A sociological approach to self and identity', in M. Leary and J. Tangney (eds), *Handbook of self and identity*, New York: Guilford Press, pp.128–52.

Strategic Business Insights (2016), 'The VALS™ survey', http://www.strategicbusinessinsights.com/vals/ustypes.shtml (accessed 20 December 2016).

Subramanyeswar, S. (2010), 'Brand loyalty: Indian consumers value substance over style', *Admap*, September, 32–34, http://www.warc.com/ (accessed 23 May 2014).

Suri, G., Sheppes, G., Leslie, S., and Gross, J.J. (2014), 'Stairs or escalator? Using theories of persuasion and motivation to facilitate healthy decision making', *Journal of Experimental Psychology: Applied*, 20, 4, 295–302.

Tajfel, H. (1979), 'Individuals and groups in social psychology', *British Journal of Clinical Psychology*, 18, 2, 183–90.

Tikkanen, I. (2007), 'Maslow's hierarchy and food tourism in Finland: five cases', *British Food Journal*, 109, 9, 721–34.

Wagner, T. (2007), 'Shopping motivation revised: a means–end chain analytical perspective', *International Journal of Retail & Distribution Management*, 35, 7, 569–82.

WARC (2016), 'Coca-Cola: winning the preference battle with Indian teens', http://www.warc.com.ezproxye. bham.ac.uk/Content/ContentViewer.aspx?MasterContentRef=67e266ad-dbe2-40ab-bd82-9e476f32d8ef& q=indian+consumers&CID=A108230&PUB=WARC-PRIZE-ASIA (accesssed 8 November 2016).

Woodside, A.G. (2010), 'Brand-consumer storytelling theory and research', *Psychology & Marketing*, 27, 6, 531–40.

Zoepf, K. (2008), 'Saudi women find an unlikely role model: Oprah', *New York Times*, 18 September, http://www. nytimes.com/2008/09/19/world/middleeast/19oprah.html?_r=0 (accessed 22 May 2017).

PART 3

MACRO-VIEW OF CONSUMPTION

Where are we going?

Future trends in consumer behaviour

Macro-view

Consumers in society and the market: groups, social processes, culture, and repeat purchasing behaviour

Micro-view

The individual consumer: individual decision-making, learning, perception, attitudes, personality and motivation

How we arrived here

Historical context and contemporary perspectives on consumption

8

GROUPS, SOCIAL PROCESSES, AND COMMUNICATIONS

Introduction

People do not consume in isolation. Who you are with, who you know, which groups you identify with, those you feel antipathy towards—all these and many more social states and processes affect how you consume. Companies make use of this knowledge to shape the ways they market to consumers. This chapter will focus on groups, and on the processes within and across groups that impact upon how people consume. We consider how marketing uses this knowledge for the purposes of developing products and brands and communicating with different groups, or people within those groups. A particularly important group is the family, and a later part of this chapter focuses on consumption within the family context.

3. Understand the *importance of social power and social connectedness*, and how we communicate within and across groups, both face-to-face and in electronic environments (word of mouth (WOM) and e-word of mouth (eWOM)).

4. Identify the role of the *family* on consumption.

5. Analyse the *nature of social class structures* and their impact on consumption behaviour.

Reference groups

Understanding the types of people we associate with or with whom we would prefer not to associate with is fundamental to marketing. Many products are purchased and consumed in a public setting, so we see what other people buy and often associate beliefs, attitudes, and behaviours with them. The Belgian-based company Ecover produces ecologically sound cleaning products, and its brand imagery is important for communicating those values to consumers. If we see a consumer buying Ecover cleaning products (Figure 8.1), we may assume that they are committed to environmental beliefs and attitudes.

Reference groups are those groups that are used by a person as a basis for comparison and guidance when forming their beliefs, attitudes, and behaviours. Reference groups were first defined by Hyman (1942) as reference points that individuals use to evaluate their situation. Park and Lessig (1977: 102) developed the concept to include 'an actual or imaginary institution, individual or group conceived as having significant relevance upon an individual's evaluations, aspirations or behaviour'. This broadens the idea of reference groups from an individual person to an institution (real or imaginary).

Types of reference group

Reference groups can be described across two dimensions—membership and attractiveness of the group. Membership groups are those to which we belong (termed contactual, identificational, or associative) and those which we no longer wish to be associated with (disclaimant). There are also groups to which we aspire to belong (aspirational) and others which we wish to avoid entirely (avoidance or dissociative). Table 8.1 shows the main types of reference group

Figure 8.1   Ecover cleaning products   *Source*: Image courtesy of Ecover.

Attractiveness	Membership	
	Member	Non-member
Positive	Contactual or associative	Aspirational
Negative	Disclaimant	Avoidance or dissociative

Table 8.1   Group membership
Source: Adapted from Assael, H. (1998), *Consumer behavior and marketing action* (6th edn), Mason, OH: South-Western College Publishing. Printed with kind permission from the author.

Contactual or associative groups are generally *close groups with which we interact regularly and where there is a degree of proximity*. This closeness may be through family or friendship ties. or through mutual interests such as work, a hobby, or a sporting interest. Carling's 'Belong' campaign, illustrated in Figure 8.2, emphasized the power of belonging represented by groups. Carling showed groups of friends standing up for one another in adverse situations, such as in outer space or Arctic conditions, suggesting that Carling could support belonging to a group of like-minded young men.

A **disclaimant** group *is one that we currently belong to, or perhaps belonged to in the past, but no longer want to associate ourselves with*. At college a person may be part of a social group that drinks alcohol, but if the group then experiments with soft drugs they may no longer join

Figure 8.2   Carling advertisement demonstrating the power of belonging
Source: Image courtesy of Beattie McGuinness Bungay.

in with them (Figure 8.3). Disclaimant groups may be transitional groups from our past that we are trying to move on from (e.g. school friends going in different paths). People may also belong to groups that they would prefer others not to know about as they feel that knowing this could lead to stigmatization by others. For example, we may not want others to know we belong to a dieting group or a particular political group as we might feel it would affect how others perceive us

Figure 8.3 Disclaimant groups, reflecting shifting interests among friends

Source: © iStock.com/sturti.

Aspirational groups are composed *of people that the consumer can identify with or admire (often from afar), and aspires to be like in some way.* Often the aspirational group is actually an individual representing some state or position we aspire to be like. We may respect them for their skills (such as sports personalities) or for their style and glamour or their lifestyle (such as famous actors). We may try to emulate them through the consumption of certain products or brands. Many people now follow fitness and lifestyle celebrities on Instagram and Snapchat, such as Clean Eating Alice and The Body Coach. Often such vloggers are marketing products and brands as well as a lifestyle that many would aspire to. The vlogger Zoella (Zoe Sugg) is a fashion, beauty, and lifestyle vlogger, who also posts about issues around mental health and well-being. Her blog is exceptionally popular with young girls and young women who look up to and aspire to aspects of her life (see Figure 8.4).

Figure 8.4 Screenshot from www.zoella.co.uk

Source: Zoella (2017) homepage (online). Available at: zoella.co.uk (accessed 22 September 2017).

Dissociative or avoidance groups *are groups we have negative feelings towards and whom we avoid being associated with.* They differ from disclaimant groups in that we have never been members of such groups, and we associate negative feelings with them for their intrinsic qualities rather than because we or they have changed. We do not wish to emulate the way they look or behave and may associate certain products or brands with them that in turn we feel negative towards. Japan is well known for its different fashion groups among young people, many of which appear very extreme such that other young people avoid associating with them. One such group were Ganguro girls (see Figure 8.5) whose distinguishing features were their tanned skin, platform shoes, short dresses, and white lipstick. Ganguro girls suffered harassment and avoidance by others. Interestingly, as the trend died down, many tanning salons were closed. Often we may just wish to avoid certain products or brands that we associate with others in a wish to ascertain our individuality, such as choosing to buy a different brand of car or holiday destination to our parents.

If a brand becomes associated with a group that many others wish to dissociate themselves from, it can be damaged. Brand-conscious football hooligans adopted Burberry, which had for years been associated with making raincoats for royalty and the rich and famous, and as a result the distinctive 'Burberry check' became something that many people in Britain no longer wanted to be seen in. In particular, the Burberry check became associated with so-called 'chavs', a derogatory term defined by the *Oxford English Dictionary* as 'a young lower-class person typified by brash and loutish behaviour and the wearing of (real or imitation) designer clothes'. Burberry was a brand that had moved from being associated with aspirational groups to being associated with dissociative groups. However, Burberry skilfully repositioned itself away from the traditional check and back to a

Figure 8.5   Ganguro girls   *Source*: Image courtesy of Gozogomo (http://dozodomo.com/).

nostalgia-inspired, but still cutting-edge, fashion image. The company introduced a range of product lines that were quirky and difficult to emulate, with classically beautiful English models with an 'aristocratic' air, such as Stella Tennant and Emma Watson. Building such associations over a period of years has enabled Burberry to remove the 'chav' label and made it once again an aspirational brand. In Research Insight 8.1 we look at how disassociative groups can be an important influence on consumers and their self-image.

RESEARCH INSIGHT 8.1

White, K. and Dahl, D.W. (2006) 'To be or not to be? The influence of dissociative reference groups on consumer preferences', *Journal of Consumer Psychology*, 16, 4, 404–14.

Through an experimental research design this paper concluded that the tendency to avoid products associated with dissociative reference groups is often driven by concerns for self-presentation or self-image.If a product was to be consumed in public then consumers were more likely to avoid choosing a product associated with a dissociative group and be more susceptible to reference group influence. The authors concluded that consumption choices in their study revealed a desire to present a positive self-image to important others.

 Access the online resources to read the abstract and access the full paper.

Reference groups are also classified as formal or informal. A **formal group** is one that is usually formed by some kind of outside structure, and it is likely to have a formalized constitution and set of rules of conduct for members. Examples of formal groups include being a member of a golf club and adhering to the strict dress codes associated with such a club. Formal groups can impact consumption when they exert power, often in terms of institutional expectations where individuals are required to conform. Many companies have 'dress-down days', where employees are expected to dress casually, but often the group exerts power such that there is a standardized approach to 'smart casual' in such contexts.

An **informal group** is formed by *a group of individuals who have some sort of commonality but no formal connection to each other.* They may get together because they have a mutual interest (such as gardening or singing), through common values (e.g. a boycotting group), or through friendship. Some formal and informal groups may be of more interest to marketers than others. A gardening group can be a target for particular products, but a boycotting group is unlikely to be so. Similarly, you may find informal groups within a formal group. Thus you may work within a large organization (formal group), but within that be part of an informal book group or five-a-side football team. While it is very useful for marketing to engage with such informal groups, it can be difficult to identify and reach them. However, it can be easier if they have some kind of mutual interest, such as reading or sport, as they are more likely to engage with relevant product information and then communicate within the informal group. Popular books now regularly include information about activities for book groups, with suggestions for further reading. Similarly, Facebook groups (whether initiated by a company or by enthusiasts) and the use of hashtags to identify and manage Twitter conversations and promotions all make conversations on particular topics easier to identify and manage by companies.

In summary, there are many different ways of viewing the types of reference groups to which consumers belong or are influenced by, and these are summarized in Table 8.2.

Reference group influence

Mechanisms of reference group influence

Leigh (1989) recognized that reference group influence can be direct from the reference group to individual members, or indirect through an individual observing the behaviour of group members and altering his/her own behaviour because of it. The importance of reference groups for marketing is the influence that they can bring to bear on others, particularly in terms of which products or brands are bought and how different groups consume them. There are three main mechanisms of reference group influence: informational, utilitarian, and value-expressive (Park and Lessig, 1977).

- **Informational group influence** *is when a consumer uses the reference group to actively get information from opinion leaders or expert groups.* The person will attribute benefits to the product through its association with the group or individual, but does not necessarily have any personal interaction with them. We might purchase the same equipment as a celebrity cook or gardener, or we might follow the guidance of groups giving consumer advice, such as 'Which?' for consumer goods or 'The Motley Fool' for financial products.

- **Utilitarian reference group influence** *is when a person is influenced in their choice of brand by the preferences of those with whom they socialize, including family members and work colleagues.* The decision to purchase a brand will be influenced by the

Reference group type	Definition
Associative or contractual	Close groups with which we interact regularly and where there is a degree of proximity
Disclaimant	A group that we currently belong to, or perhaps belonged to in the past, but no longer want to associate ourselves with
Aspirational	Composed of people that the consumer can identify or admire (often from afar), and aspires to be like them in some way
Dissociative or avoidance group	A group with which the individual wishes to avoid being associated and feels a sense of dis-identification
Formal	A formal group is usually formed by some kind of outside structure, and is likely to have a formalized constitution and set of rules of conduct for members
Informal	An informal group is formed by a group of individuals who have some sort of commonality; they may get together because they have a mutual interest or through friendship

Table 8.2   Types of reference group

wish to satisfy the expectations others have, and in some cultures this utilitarian influence can be very strong. Research with second-generation Punjabis in Britain (Sekhon and Szmigin, 2011) found that family influence was very strong in terms of purchasing particular brands.

- **Value-expressive influence** *is when someone buys a particular brand to enhance their image and because they admire characteristics of people who use the brand.* Central to value-expressive influence is the idea that we want to be like others whom we admire or respect in society. Companies often develop ads, which link their brand visually with attractive models or characters with a view to enhancing the image of their brand through this connection (see Figure 8.6).

Figure 8.6   Tom Ford models   *Source*: Image supplied by The Advertising Archives.

In Consumer Insight 8.1 we look at how reference group influences on social media can impact on consumer aspirations to appear like various celebrities and vloggers.

CONSUMER INSIGHT 8.1

Transformation through social media—how aspiration impacts the way we look

Young people are increasingly influenced by social media, following celebrities and friends on Instagram, Facebook, and Snapchat. Vloggers and bloggers such as The Body Coach, Kayla Itsines, and The Food Medic act as aspirational role models, which many young people want to emulate. Increasingly, such social media inspiration may impact on what people do, eat, and look like. This may be very positive; for example, research has shown that environmental cues can aid people who are pursuing a weight-control goal (Stämpfli et al., 2016), and it is possible that social media images may work in a similar way. Such sites have also started showing transformation pictures of people who have followed the blogger's diet and exercises, and lost weight and become fitter as a result. Taking exercise selfies, posting status reports, and following lifestyle and exercise regimes can be inspirational and motivational, especially when people see posts where individuals have lost a lot of weight (Vaterlaus et al., 2015). It is likely that the more popular or well known the blogger is, the more likely people will be to follow their advice. An experimental research study (Tal and Wansink, 2016) presented three randomly divided groups of people pictures of groups of people who were described as being linked to veganism. The first group were celebrities, the second were 'uncool' hippies, and the final group was used as a control. Following this the first two groups were asked to sample a vegan cupcake. The research found a higher tasting rating for the 'cool' celebrity group than the 'uncool' hippy group, suggesting the influence of linking food to aspirational social images.

Questions

1. Take a look at some of the vloggers and bloggers who post transformational pictures. What pictures and messages do they use to inspire people? How and why do you think they work?

2. What might be the drawbacks of such aspirational reference groups for young people?

3. Some apps can make you beautiful without you having to do anything. See, for example, the Chinese app Meitu. Check out what people are saying about the app (e.g. http://www.theverge.com/2017/1/19/14316486/meitu-anime-filter-beautiful-memes) and consider what the implications of such an app might be for marketing other self-enhancement products.

Sources: Vaterlaus et al. (2015); Stämpfli et al. (2016); Tal and Wansink (2016).

 Access the online resources and follow the web links to learn more.

Reference groups influencing public versus private consumption

Bearden and Etzel (1982) examined how reference group influence varied in relation to where consumption occurs (private versus public) and the extent to which it is considered

	Public	
Product / **Brand**	*Weak reference group influence on product choice*	*Strong reference group influence on product choice*
Strong reference group influence on brand choice	**Public necessities** — Because it is a necessity, e.g. car, suit, or wristwatch, the influence for the product will be **weak**. But it will be seen by others, so the influence for the brand is **strong**.	**Public luxuries** — Because it is a luxury, e.g. golf clubs, yacht, or skis, the influence for the product should be **strong**. Because it will be seen by others, the influence of the brand is also **strong**.
Weak reference group influence on brand choice	**Private necessities** — This would be a product consumed out of public view but which almost everyone owns, such as a mattress or refrigerator. As a necessity, the product influence is **weak** and as it is not seen by others the influence for the brand also tends to be **weak**.	**Private luxuries** — This would be a product that is not commonly owned and unlikely to be conspicuous, but would still convey meaning about the status of the owner, e.g. an ice-cream maker. As a luxury the influence of the product is **strong**, but as it is not seen by others the influence for the brand is **weak**.

Necessity — Luxury

Private

Figure 8.7   Model of reference group influence on consumption
Source: Adapted from Bearden and Etzel (1982).

a necessity or a luxury, and this work has been very influential in helping understand reference group influence on consumer behaviour. Figure 8.7 gives an overview of the model, indicating the flows of influence we would expect to see for luxury and necessity products and brands consumed in public and privately.

How we decide which goods and services are a luxury or a necessity changes over time and across different cultures. What we can see in this work is that the influence of reference groups is high for products and brands that are typically consumed in public spaces, and this is even more so when the item is a luxury (in contrast with necessities). So, according to this model, the purchase of ski equipment (publicly consumed, luxury or non-essential purchase) is subject to very high reference group influence. In contrast, watch brands (publicly consumed, most often considered an essential purchase) would also be subject to reference group influence, but this would be slightly less than the ski equipment example. Bearden and Etzel (1982) then considered products consumed in private and concluded that the reference group influence is strong for luxury privately consumed goods (they give the example of an ice-cream maker) , whereas it is weak for privately consumed necessity goods (something that virtually everyone owns, such as a mattress). In their original work, Bearden and Etzel classified mattresses, floor lamps, and refrigerators as public necessities with weak reference group influence. However, the kitchen has become a focal point for socializing for many in Western countries, and the brands we own are more conspicuous and susceptible to reference group influence. Brands such as Smeg, Aga, or Lavazza coffee are associated with aspirational reference groups, and coffee makers are often shown in a social setting (Figure 8.8) or recommended by celebrities.

Figure 8.8   Advertisement for Lavazza coffee   *Source*: Image supplied by The Advertising Archives.

Development of conformity

For the concept of reference groups to be useful to marketers, there has to be some degree of conformity that results from group membership (see Research Insight 8.2). **Conformity** can be defined as *adoption of behaviour resulting from real or perceived pressure to comply with a person or group*. If you are with a group of friends and they all want to watch a football match, but you would prefer to go shopping, you may conform to their decision because their friendship is more important to you than going shopping.

Mann (1969) identified four types of conformity: normative, informational, compliance, and internalization.

- **Normative conformity** applies *when a person wants to fit in with the group or is afraid of being rejected by them and will publicly accept the group's view even if privately they do not agree.*

- **Informational conformity** *occurs when someone actively looks for guidance from the group where they lack knowledge or are in an ambiguous situation.*

- **Compliance** *refers to publicly changing behaviour to fit in with the group but privately disagreeing, i.e. a behavioural shift without an attitudinal one.*

- However, **internalization** *involves both an attitudinal and behavioural change in favour of the group.*

RESEARCH INSIGHT 8.2

Asch, S.E. (1955), 'Opinions and social pressure', *Scientific American*, 193, 5, 31–5.

The classic experimental study of the power of conformity in groups is found in Asch's work from the 1950s. Asch asked student participants, in a group setting, to estimate the length of a line (a form of a vision test). He manipulated the experimental setting such that all but one of the group were assistants of the experimenter and had been asked to provide the (same) wrong answer to the question. One member of the group was not in on the experiment, but he often also gave the wrong answer. In later experiments, when subjects wrote down their responses and thus kept them private, conformity dropped, suggesting the importance of public compliance.

 Access the online resources to read the abstract and access the full paper.

If someone is using a neighbourhood recycling scheme, normative conformity may dominate in the early stages of recycling, when they sort and recycle packaging in order to fit into neighbourhood norms and expectations. They may then enter a period of informational conformity, where they chat to other neighbours and consult specialist websites to learn more about recycling. Compliance may occur if people recycle but perhaps disagree with and resent the time taken, but most likely a process of internalization will occur when they are recycling because they believe in the value and importance of this behaviour.

Of course, many people will not conform; this may be because of a difference of opinion and independence of decision-making or because they are rejecting the group's norms. As we shall see later, individuals may also resist if they feel that the group is pressurizing them into conformity.

How group norms influence conformity

Venkatesan (1966) developed some of the early ideas on conformity in the context of consumer decision-making and concluded that in a group situation, and where it is difficult to assess the quality of the product, individuals will accept the information provided by others in the group. However, where group pressure appears to limit independent choice, people react to reassert their freedom to decide—a process known as reactance.

Reactance is *a motivational state, which acts as a counterforce to threats to a person's freedom.* It can be a powerful force if groups of people feel that their freedom is compromised. In the realms of popular and consumer culture, Earls (2009) describes the social pressure to grieve for the death of Princess Diana (through the placing of floral tributes at her home in Kensington Palace), and how the literary magazine *Granta* expressed reactance by calling the pressure to conform 'floral fascism'.

Much conformity comes about through excepted norms that people wish to conform to in order to be part of a group. However, marketers can use the idea of not conforming to successfully show how individualism can be very attractive. Unilever's Axe body spray for men brought out an ad entitled 'Find your magic' showing a diverse array of men who did not fit the stereotypical image of a masculinity with lines such as 'Who needs the six pack when you've got the nose?', implying that conforming to stereotypes was unnecessary if you had other qualities (Figure 8.9).

Figure 8.9　Axe body spray 'Don't Change Your Profile' campaign　　*Source*: Image courtesy of Unilever.

Social power and reference groups

Another important area to consider is social power. Understanding the role of power in group influence is largely derived from the work of French (1956), French and Raven (1959), and Raven (1993). Defining social power as potential influence, they examined types of influence in various organizational and family settings, and developed six bases of social power: coercive, reward, legitimacy, expert, reference, and informational. Raven (1993) further developed the social power framework to provide a more elaborate understanding of how power influences people.

- **Reward power** *may be present when a person responds to the influence of the group and is rewarded in some way.*

- **Coercive power** *means that conformity to the group is brought about through the threat of punishment.*

- **Legitimate power** *is where the referent is seen to have authority by virtue of their position in the particular context,* often achieved in service businesses through the use of uniforms to show authority.

- **Expert power** *is when we are influenced to behave or purchase something by someone who we recognize has particular expertise, for example a doctor or scientist.*

- **Referent power** is similar, *although the influence stems from our admiration of the qualities of a person, and how we try to imitate those qualities by copying their behaviour,* often evident in the way we consider celebrities.

- **Informational power** is based on *logical argument and knowledge that someone may have acquired from experience or through the nature of their job.* A person or group has informational power because they know something that others would like to know.

Raven highlighted the importance of recognizing how these forms of power can be personal or impersonal in character. Personal influences of reward and coercive power relate to the approval (or sanction) of those close to us. Personal approval from others in a friendship group of young people, say for having the 'right' mobile phone, can be as powerful as being ridiculed (and therefore punished) for wearing outdated sports gear. In advertising, legitimate power is sometimes attempted through the use of actors wearing white coats in ads for products such as dental hygiene or cosmetics.

Originally, expert and referent power were examined only in positive forms, but on some occasions we resist this power. Consider the celebrity chef Jamie Oliver who is an expert in the world of cooking and food. Yet when he was involved in a campaign to introduce healthy meals into UK schools, many parents rejected his message, arguing that the school meals were expensive and were not particularly popular with their children, which led to many of them providing less healthy packed lunches (Adams, 2012).

For informational power, Raven suggested that it may be effective if the information comes in an indirect form as a hint or suggestion. Personal hygiene products used to be sold in highly explicit ways with advertisements suggesting what brand to use if you suffered from 'BO' (body odour), but advertisers found more subtle ways of describing what their brands could achieve, for example Dove deodorants emphasize the skincare aspect of their deodorant products. Research Insight 8.3 considers the different ways that group influence and power occur in the running community.

RESEARCH INSIGHT 8.3

Thomas, T.C., Price, L.L., and Schau, H.J. (2013), 'When differences unite: resource dependence in heterogeneous consumption communities', *Journal of Consumer Research*, 39, 5, 1010–33.

While much of the theory around consumption groups and communities emphasizes the importance of similarity within groups, the authors of this paper adopt a different perspective—they consider how consumption communities or groups cope with heterogeneity (difference), and how this can be handled to ensure that the community sustains itself. Adopting a CCT perspective, the authors study the distance-running community, which has grown from a niche male-dominated group to a more mainstream community attracting all types of runners for all sorts of motives. They discuss how the community draws on and activates social and economic resources to overcome tensions and difficulties to develop a thriving community.

 Access the online resources to read the abstract and access the full paper.

Opinion leaders and opinion seekers

Rogers and Cartano (1962: 435) described **opinion leaders** as '*individuals who exert an unequal amount of influence on the decisions of others*'. Lazarsfeld et al. (1944), in their study of the 1940 US presidential election, found that the media had little direct influence on the public, but rather influence flowed from the media to opinion leaders who then passed on information to a broader public. This became known as the two-step flow of communication (Figure 8.10) and was further tested in consumer purchases (Katz and Lazarsfeld, 1955).

The idea that a small group of influential people can accelerate or stop the adoption of a product has become central to our idea of what an opinion leader is, which Gladwell (2001) calls 'The Law of the Few'. He identifies those who are well connected, knowledgeable, or persuasive as connectors, mavens, and salesmen. See also Consumer Insight 8.2 for more on types of opinion leaders.

- **Connectors** *are people who tend to know lots of other people, often from different subcultures to their own*, not necessarily very well but well enough to pass on information to others.

- **Mavens** *are collectors and brokers of information, but they use this information and want to start discussions with others or*

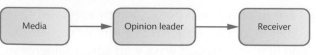

Figure 8.10 Two-step flow of communication

respond to requests. They are the kind of people who have inside knowledge of what is going on in the marketplace. Market mavens (Feick and Price, 1987) are very engaged with consumption and often pass on information about products they have not necessarily bought themselves (see Chapter 3).

- **Salesmen** *are the arch persuaders, people who will not accept 'no' for an answer and are always looking for an opportunity to get their message across to someone else.*

While opinion leaders are an important group to understand, so too are those on the receiving end of the communication. **Opinion seekers** *are people who seek opinions and information to help their purchase decision.* Engel et al. (1990: 42) recognized the reciprocal nature of opinion seeking and leading, stating that 'When we actively seek advice from another, that person becomes an opinion leader'. Opinion seeking acts as a form of product information search; consumers seek opinions and information to make better purchase decisions, effectively a form of external information search (see Chapter 3).

CONSUMER INSIGHT 8.2

Hierarchies of opinion leadership

Examining how opinion leaders influence other consumers is a concern for many in business. Companies and organizations are keen to understand the hierarchy of influence, as demonstrated in a report by the Future Foundation (Econsultancy, 2010), which classified opinion leaders into three distinct types. Focusing on how they share information about brands, news, and personal experiences, this report revealed three distinct, but interrelated, types of opinion leader.

1. Hub urbanites share information through social media and instant messaging services. They are highly motivated to start discussing stories in order to get a reaction and gain recognition.

2. Email evangelists share ideas through email and other social media, aiming to reach more diverse networks than the hub urbanites, and are motivated to share, educate, and inspire.

3. Offline influencers are more likely to pass on information face to face or on the phone. They have small networks, but often pass on online content to an offline audience. They want to help others, offer advice and guidance, and be helpful.

This study also found that the amount of international contacts in an opinion leader's network is higher in nations such as India, Hong Kong, and the UAE. These markets tend to have a high proportion of hub urbanites and email evangelists.

Increasingly, it is social media where opinion leaders have the most impact. Key opinion leaders (KOLs) are influential public figures—celebrities, actors, models, or sporting personalities—who are perceived to be experts in certain fields, especially personal appearance. They have become hugely popular in China and are used extensively to market brands as they have the potential to reach millions of potential customers. Chinese website topklout.com even created a list of the most influential KOLs based on data from social media sites such as Sina Weibo and WeChat that have millions of daily users.

Maybelline is a recent example of just how powerful such KOLs can be in marketing. Through the power of the KOL celebrity Angelababy they sold 10,000 lipsticks in just two hours. They promoted a live internet stream of Angelababy and other KOLs trying and choosing different lipsticks from Maybelline. As the celebrities tried different products, customers could leave messages and comments on the message board and were able to purchase products through a direct link in the video stream.

Recent research into sustainable car choices, specifically electric and flexible fuel vehicle adoption, has shown that opinion leaders are important in influencing adoption of eco-innovative products (Jansson et al., 2017).

Questions

1. Think about your friends. If you had to categorize them in terms of opinion leadership, what would be their distinguishing features?

2. How is information passed within your reference groups and who are the critical information providers?

3. Think about the media you might use to promote a new band. What would you choose and why?

Sources: Econsultancy (2010); Jansson et al. (2017); http://marketingtochina.com/top-5-chinese-key-opinion-leaders/ http://socialbrandwatch.com/chinas-social-media-top-100-kols-chart/ http://socialbrandwatch.com/maybelline-sells-10000-lipsticks-china-within-two-hours/

 Access the online resources and follow the web links to learn more.

Opinion leaders or easily influenced individuals?

Increasingly we are seeing the importance of certain people with influence on others (see also Practitioner Insight 8, where Andrew Tenzer discusses reaching affluent millennials). Nevertheless, while the idea of opinion leaders has been widely accepted, some have suggested that the picture may be more complex. Watts and Dodds (2007) rejected the idea that some people are more influential than others and exert a disproportionate amount of influence on the community. Rather, they concluded that information flow does 'not succeed because of a few highly influential individuals influencing everyone else, but rather on account of a critical mass of easily influenced individuals influencing other easy-to-influence people' (Watts and Dodds, 2007: 454). Their model shows how influence can flow in both directions between leaders and followers, and that it can develop over a number of steps in a schematic network (Figure 8.11). The television in the centre represents the

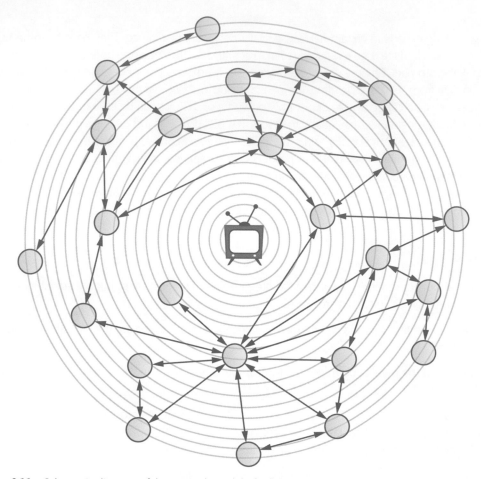

Figure 8.11 Schematic diagram of the network model of influence

Source: Watts, D.J. and Dodds, P.S. (2007), 'Influentials, networks, and public opinion formation', *Journal of Consumer Research*, 34 (4), 441–457. By permission of Oxford University Press.

mass media where much of our information is gathered, and around this we see individuals receiving and passing on information, with some clearly more active than others.

Watts (2007) uses the example of the revival of Hush Puppies in the USA to say that just because a few fashionistas in New York began to wear them, this may not have solely caused the brand's subsequent revival. According to Watts, it is more likely that the success of this trend related to there being a critical mass of easily influenced people influencing other easy-to-influence people. He uses the terms 'accidental influentials' to capture the idea that getting a large number of ordinary people to reach out and influence other people is the best way to spread the message about a brand. Increasingly, social messaging is doing just that as messaging apps such as WhatsApp, Facebook Messenger, Viber, and WeChat have a huge number of users. Sixty-two per cent of millennials are said to be loyal to brands that engage through these channels, and importantly they act as a constant networking medium among friends (Rohampton, 2017). Read more about the importance of certain millennials in Practitioner Insight 8.

PRACTITIONER INSIGHT 8

Andrew Tenzer, Head of Group Insight at Trinity Mirror plc, previously Head of Insight Global & EMEA, BBC Global News Ltd

Throughout history we have placed people into groups. This comes from a basic, and often subconscious, human need to categorize the world known as 'social categorization theory'—we simply stop seeing people as individuals. These types of label are useful to reduce complexity, but the problem is that we assign characteristics to them, which can often lead to stereotyping and are simply not true. This can be a concern for the marketing industry, particularly as marketers have always sought to define and target groups of consumers based on such labels.

Millennials is the latest group that advertisers are looking to reach, even though there is still no consensus on when the generation starts and ends. This is very worrying from a marketing perspective, as how can we target them if we don't know exactly who they are? Despite this lack of clarity, this group has generated huge amounts of coverage not only within the industry, but also in the mainstream media. It appears that growing up in an era of rapid technological change, the likes of which were not experienced by older generations, has elevated the status of millennials amongst marketers. This cohort are so sought after because they're considered young, influential, and therefore extremely attractive to brands.

This led us at the BBC to ask a few simple questions. Are millennials really all they're cracked up to be? Are they a unique generation, the likes of which we've never seen before?

Millennials are one vast homogenized group of 16–34-year-olds and it's obvious that they aren't all the same. We at the BBC set out to identify the millennials who do embody the attributes often seen as synonymous with this vast target group. We quickly discovered that when we apply a filter of affluence, things start to get very interesting. Non-affluent millennials account for 84 per cent (788 million) of all millennials worldwide and, contrary to popular belief, in terms of attitudes they aren't all that different from older generations:

- 68 per cent of non-affluent millennials agree with the statement 'I look after my appearance/image' versus 65 per cent of people aged over 35.

- 48 per cent of non-affluent millennials agree with the statement 'I am a brand conscious person' versus 44 per cent of people aged over 35.

Naturally, there are some small generational differences, but these are not as vast or extreme as we're often led to believe.

What about affluent millennials who represent just 16 per cent (155 million) of the global millennial universe? The same data tells a very different story:

- 79 per cent of affluent millennials agree with the statement 'I look after my appearance/image' versus 68 per cent of non-affluent millennials

- 67 per cent of affluent millennials agree with the statement 'I am a brand conscious person' versus 44 per cent of non-affluent millennials

Affluent millennials are unique not only within their own demographic group but also in comparison with older generations, including affluent ones. This tells us that the industry's perception of millennials just doesn't match up to the reality—it's the affluent subset that should be considered the 'real millennials'.

Even though we applied a filter of affluence, closer analysis of the data revealed that not even all affluent millennials are the same. As a result, we took this one step further and segmented this group to identify the most valuable segment for targeting. Within the affluent millennials cohort, there are three distinct segments.

1. 'The Crowd' are attitudinally no different from non-affluent millennials, because they have a local outlook and don't have much of a relationship with brands.

2. 'The Understated' have a fleeting relationship with brands but aren't brand loyal.

3. 'The Supercharged' are the extreme affluent millennials—the opinion leaders of today and tomorrow. They are very global in their outlook and have a deep emotional relationship with their favourite brands.

So why should brands concentrate their efforts on 'The Supercharged'? First, they are much more influential in business, early adopters of the latest technology, opinion leaders, and commercially receptive brand ambassadors. As shown below, it is The Supercharged who are more likely than the average 16–34-year-old to be the senior business decision-maker, i.e having overall responsibility for purchase decisions within a business and more likely than the other groups to have the latest technology and be communicating with others about their new products and services.

- Senior business decision-maker: The Supercharged ($i = 444$), The Understated ($i = 275$), The Crowd ($i = 191$).

- 'Having the latest technology products is very important to me': The Supercharged ($i = 316$), The Understated ($i = 150$), The Crowd ($i = 81$).

- 'I regularly inform friends and family on new products/services': The Supercharged ($i = 286$), The Understated ($i = 133$), The Crowd ($i = 87$).

- 'My favourite brand plays an integral role in my life': The Supercharged ($i = 386$), The Understated ($i = 103$), The Crowd ($i = 90$).

(The index scores i used above are versus an average for 16–34-year-olds, which we take as $i = 100$. Therefore The Supercharged with an index of 316 are 216 per cent more likely than the average 16–34-year-old to agree that 'having the latest technology products is very important to me'.)

The BBC reaches 87 per cent of The Supercharged on a monthly basis. We are offering agencies and advertisers the chance to plan campaigns aimed at this group on BBC.com and BBC World News. Taking this one step further, using first party data, advertisers will be able to buy campaigns against The Supercharged on BBC.com.

Expert influentials

Expert influentials are people who have real power to influence the marketplace. This can be due to their expertise and/or the nature of the message. In 2012, the BBC showed a documentary 'Eat, Fast and Live Longer', which was written and presented by the doctor Michael Mosley. This led to the popularity of the '5:2 diet' where people effectively fast for two days, and then eat what they like for the remaining days of the week. Numerous books are available to people who want to follow the diet, although there is a lack of research evidence regarding its safety and effectiveness (Trueland, 2013).

We also need to consider whether the influence comes about because of the kinds of people that are communicating or because of how they communicate with others. Watts (2007) argues that the power of celebrities, such as Oprah Winfrey in the USA and Richard and Judy in the UK, to advocate a previously unknown book—which then becomes a bestseller—is more to do with their celebrity power through the mass media than word of mouth. But ordinary people can use the power of mass communication to influence public opinion dramatically. A notable example of this is Dave Carroll's YouTube video 'United Airlines breaks guitars'. Musician Dave Carroll composed a country and western style song (posted with a comic video on YouTube) which expressed his frustration with United Airlines, who he alleged had damaged his guitar and subsequently offered poor customer service.

At the time of writing, his video had over 17 million hits and his song became a bestseller on iTunes in Canada. Carroll himself has become a celebrity, and has founded a website Gripevine (https://gripevine.com/) which aims to help consumers and companies handle and resolve customer complaints. Does this mean that anyone can influence the market if they have the right message? Doubtless Carroll benefited from the viral nature of his video, but it also struck a chord with many who have been frustrated by airlines' lack of care and above all his video was a highly professional communications tool.

The search for cool

For companies trying to discover influential people who can affect whether a brand or product will be successful, identifying trendsetters—those who set the agenda for what is worn, played with, eaten, watched, and listened to—is crucial. Marketers believe that where these 'cool' (usually young) people lead, the rest will follow. Nancarrow and Nancarrow (2007: 135) describe cool as 'an advanced form of knowledge about commodities and consumption practices'. These people have been termed urban pioneers, trendsetters, and alpha consumers, and those who follow them, seeking to identify what will become cool, have been termed 'coolhunters'. In the last 20 or so years an industry has been built on developing research methods, following young people, and trying to engage with them in ways which will help to develop products and brands to appeal to a wider market. Techniques of coolhunting include ethnography, shop-alongs, and accompanied shopping trips. Coolhunters follow blogs and conversations on Facebook and Twitter. Commercially there are many problems with coolhunting. First, not all trends will have mass market appeal. Second, the techniques rely on interpretation by the coolhunters and companies as to how to turn a trend into a popular consumer product. Getting to know where the latest trends are happening is so important that London's Central St. Martins School of Art has introduced a course on coolhunting in London which describes the phenomenon as 'an increasingly crucial area for many large companies, fashion designers, stylists, makers and the fashion industry in general' (arts.ac.uk, 2017), and indeed places in East London, such as Shoreditch and Clerkenwell (madeinshoreditch.co.uk), have become renowned for their fashion forward influence (Johnson, 2013) (Figure 8.12). According to Warren and Campbell (2014), people and brands become cool by understanding what is considered normal, obeying the rules considered necessary, and then diverging from the rules considered expendable or unnecessary. Brands interested in showing how cool their products are should highlight features of independence and uniqueness. But ultimately, it is important to recognize that what is considered cool by one group may be too different for another, and therefore not be considered cool by them. Finally, and perhaps most importantly, once something that was cool becomes mass market, it loses its coolness. As the strategic planning director of one US advertising agency put it, 'By the time a celebrity had worn it, it had appeared in *InStyle* and then everybody wanted it right now … and then it was over in a few weeks' (Grossman, 2003: 4).

Figure 8.12   Fashion in Shoreditch, East London

Social connectedness: the importance of word of mouth

Early studies of diffusion and mass communication revealed that it is rare for people to respond only to mass media information without transmission through personal ties as well (Katz and Lazarsfeld, 1955; Rogers, 1962). **Word of mouth (WOM)** is *an informal communication, either positive or negative, about goods, services, and sellers.* WOM occurs in both face-to-face contexts and electronic contexts (mostly online), when it is often referred to as eWOM. This social contact between people is an important part of our social lives, as too are the social communications we share around consumption (e.g. telling one another about products, whether they work or not, where to buy them, how to get the best deal, and what to avoid). Understanding how such social connectedness works is important to marketers and is the focus of this section.

Firms want to effect WOM communication; they try to get consumers both to pass on information about their brand and to recommend it. **Endogenous WOM** is *when conversations happen among consumers as part of their natural communication and when they are just passing on information about their experiences with a product or brand.* **Exogenous WOM** occurs as a *direct result of the firm's marketing.* You can see how this works in practice in Consumer Insight 8.3. Firms may have a problem creating successful exogenous WOM, as consumers may identify ulterior motives and this could affect their WOM activity and their willingness to pass on information (Verlegh et al., 2004).

CONSUMER INSIGHT 8.3

Endogenous and exogenous WOM in action

When creating a buzz around a brand, product, or service, organizations recognize the power of WOM and make considerable effort to create positive WOM around their offering.

Endogenous WOM is considered the most authentic form of brand communication, since it tends to be bottom-up, emerging through consumer-to-consumer interactions around the brand. There are a number of high profile examples of singers and bands becoming famous through the power of WOM. The Arctic Monkeys had two British number ones and a fastest-selling debut album, and won many major wards without any commercial backing. They built a strong local following in Sheffield and gave away demos at their gigs. They encouraged their fans to upload their music on social networking sites and even banned record company scouts from their performances.

In China, the Reckitt Benckiser liquid antiseptic brand Dettol had found little growth outside the big cities. Reckitt Benckiser distributed 48,000 samples to 4,000 influencer mums in its WOM campaign, encouraging them to try one sample and share ten. The campaign also included gamification elements to encourage WOM discussion. Overall brand awareness increased by a factor of 5 and sales increased by 86 per cent. Allowing consumers to try out a product is known as product seeding, and is particularly useful when you are trying to target new customers who may not have heard of the brand.

A good example of a company successfully using both endogenous and exogenous WOM was provided by the Japanese fashion company Uniqlo when it launched in Singapore in 2009. Uniqlo

Figure 8.13 Uniqlo store in Shinjuku Takashimaya, Japan *Source*: Image courtesy of Uniqlo Stores.

had a relatively low awareness in Singapore, and the advertising agency Tribal DDB was briefed to launch the first stores there (see Figure 8.13). The agency was surprised to find that only 16 per cent of the highly fashionable Singaporeans had heard of Uniqlo, and that most could not even pronounce the brand name. The agency found that Uniqlo actually had an established fan site on Facebook (endogenous WOM). The agency worked with the fan, asking him to put up some information, although most of it was his own. After just one week Uniqlo had 5,000 Facebook fans in Singapore.

Questions

1. Can you find other examples of these forms of WOM?

2. Do you think that consumers can detect or are sceptical of companies' attempts to create WOM?

3. What other suggestions would you have for companies to use these ideas to create positive WOM for their brands?

Sources: Lynskey (2005); Samson (2010); Thorniley (2011); Dougherty (2015).

Access the online resources and follow the web links to learn more about WOM and see further examples.

The power of eWOM

Although a number of the examples in this chapter include eWOM, it is worth saying a little more about its power for consumer behaviour today. **eWOM** has been defined by Hennig-Thurau et al. (2004: 39) as *'any positive or negative statement made by potential, actual or former customers about a product or company, which is made available to a multitude of people and institutions via the internet'*. Many websites are developed by consumers and are primarily for the purpose of reviewing products and services; marketers generate others. Consumers appear to visit both if they are looking for advice and information. A national survey in the Netherlands examined information seeking by consumers planning holidays, and found that 49 per cent visited a marketer-generated site and 36 per cent a consumer-generated site (Bronner and de Hoog, 2010).

There has been a growth in sites such as TripAdvisor where consumers share their own product experiences with others. eWOM is powerful because it is able to influence people on a global scale. Researchers have emphasized that people tend to trust others who are similar to themselves (Eccleston and Griser, 2008). Perhaps that is why many sites tend to specialize in a particular area, such as Mumsnet which supplies specialist knowledge and discussion for new and existing mothers, or Grannynet designed for grandparents who are helping to look after their grandchildren.

Many commercial sites, such as Hotels.com, encourage feedback that can help other consumers make decisions. Amazon asks customers for reviews of goods, which enable other customers to make decisions when choosing to buy online. There are many online consumer communities, dedicated forums, or websites where online communities share and discuss their interests. Examples include the Lego Ideas, an online creative community (https://ideas.lego.com/dashboard), and BeautyTalk, an online community for beauty fans created by the beauty company Sephora. The key to these online consumer communities is that they are dedicated to specific areas of interests, where consumers can share ideas, tips, advice, and reviews, and just talk about whatever topic they like. For companies, the benefits are that consumers can act as advocates for their brands, and potentially also offer insights into consumer behaviour (Claveria, 2016). There are also discussion forums and sites within sites, such as Appreciation Society on Facebook, with thousands of members 'for those who love or are addicted to ASOS.com'. All of these are examples of companies attempting to manage eWOM and online communities, and recognizing their importance and value.

Market research companies recognize the importance of eWOM, with Nielsen Research reporting in 2015 that 66 per cent of respondents across 50 worldwide markets trusted online consumer posts (Nielsen, 2015). While WOM has always been important in influencing consumer behaviour, social media has transformed the ways that social influence work, taking this to another level by encouraging consumers or users to incorporate their 'friends' opinions into the purchasing process. Further, recent research (De Langhe et al., 2015) has shown that consumers are very reliant on other users' rating scores, but that these scores are not actually good indicators of product quality. A few bad reviews could be detrimental to the success of any company or organization; this is an issue covered in more detail in Consumer Insight 8.4.

CONSUMER INSIGHT 8.4

The problem with online reviews

Simonson and Rosen (2014) suggest that three things usually inform customers' purchase decisions: their prior beliefs, a firm's marketing, and input from other people and information services. They refer to this as the influence mix and we are currently seeing the increase in influence of other people and information services, often in the form of online reviews.

Nevertheless there has been growing concern that online reviews have been manipulated, and a complaint to that end was upheld against TripAdvisor by the UK's Advertising Standards Authority in 2012 (Advertising Standards Authority, 2012). In 2013, Samsung was fined $340,300 by Taiwan's Fair Trade Commission for paying people to post negative messages about their competitor HTC (Chang, 2013). One study suggests that 16 per cent of restaurant reviews on Yelp are fake (Luca and Zervas, 2015). While organisations such as TripAdvisor are becoming better at identifying false reviews and consumers are getting better at choosing the sites and reviewers to trust, others are concerned that legal action will need to be taken against fake or manipulated reviews in the future (Mathews Hunt, 2015).

It is likely that consumers will continue to rely on the influence of online reviews. Evidence from research commissioned by Google in 2011 shows that typically consumers consult 10.4 information sources when making a purchase, which seems to imply that in the future this will be considered a better information provider than traditional marketing.

Questions

1. Why do you think online reviews are so popular?

2. What suggestions would you make to consumers using online reviews, knowing that these reviews may be fake?

3. How can companies reassure their customers that their reviews are genuine?

Sources: asa.org.uk; Chang (2013); Simonson and Rosen (2014); Luca and Zervas (2015); Mathews Hunt (2015).

 Access the online resources and follow the web links to learn more.

From e-word of mouth to crowdsourcing and user-generated content

The internet provides somewhere for people to meet to share and explore ideas and creativity. Surowiecki (2005) identifies several examples where a solution to a problem results from a number of people working on that problem. Earls (2009) described this as comparable to the whiteboard in the movie *Good Will Hunting*, where mathematicians were invited to contribute solutions to posted problems. A number of people can help to provide a solution partly by building on one another's ideas; this is known as crowd-sourcing. The term **crowdsourcing** was coined by Howe (2006) and described as 'the act of a company or institution taking a function once performed by employees and outsourcing it to an undefined (and generally large) network of people in the form of an open call'. Wikipedia is a form of crowdsourcing, as are many of the consumer online forums, but increasingly companies are looking to consumers and independent producers to crowdsource new ideas or business propositions. An issue with crowdsourcing is that the solution becomes the property of the company, rather than individuals being paid for their creative input, and as such represents a form of internet exploitation (Postigo, 2003). Others have argued that the crowd gets to see the result of their creativity and this would not happen without an organization to put that creativity into action (Brabham, 2008). For example, the internet T-shirt company threadless.com invites people to send in their designs; members then vote on their favourite styles and the highest scoring designs are printed and sold on the website.

Creators can make a living from taking part in crowdsourcing. iStockphoto sells royalty-free stock photography. Clients purchase credits to buy stock images and photographers receive 20 per cent of the purchase price every time their image is downloaded. Here we see how harnessing the power of the crowd can generate business in often different and better ways for producers and consumers. Earls (2009) suggests that crowdsourcing can lead to cheaper solutions for consumers; this is evident in iStockphoto where consumers no longer have to pay high royalty charges for images. Researchers have recently identified that the best crowd for identifying solutions is probably not the largest possible, and smaller crowds may have too few willing collaborators, so there is likely to be a differing ideal size depending on the type of problem (Guazzini et al., 2015).

The role of social media

Much user-generated content has arisen through the growth of social media, blogs, Instagram, Facebook, Flickr, and microblogs such as Twitter. All depend on people creating content and then sharing it with their friends. The number of people now using social media is phenomenal; in 2017, Facebook had over 1.86 billion active users monthly and Twitter had 317 million active users monthly. Such social media allows everyone to easily follow what others are doing and have instant conversations with a wide range of people. According to Statista.com the celebrities with most followers on Twitter in 2017 were Katy Perry, Justin Bieber, Barack Obama, and Taylor Swift—in that order! Twitter has also been highly influential in the rapid dissemination of information relating to disasters, political events, and requests for help from individuals in threatening or dangerous situations. In 2014 the UK's Food Standards Agency identified Twitter as a key social media platform for sharing feelings of being unwell. The agency followed and correlated words such as puke, vomit, and 'vomcano', used to describe the highly contagious norovirus. From the Twitter data they developed an algorithm, which predicts outbreaks of norovirus with a very high accuracy rate of 70 per cent (Pulsar Platform, 2016) (Figure 8.14).

Figure 8.14 Key words relating to norovirus, crowdsourced by FSA staff
Source: Contains public sector information licensed under Open Government Licence v3.0.

The family

The family is an example of a specific reference group that exerts some of the most important social or group influences on individual consumption decisions. The family shapes consumption behaviour through acting as a source of informational, utilitarian, and value-expressive influence. Research shows that families play a particularly important role in providing information to their members, especially young adult consumers (Bravo et al., 2006; Epp and Price, 2008; Kim et al. 2009). Families are especially important in terms of consumer socialization, representing one of the key influences on our consumption because of the frequency of interactions and close relations between family members, at least during the early years. Increasingly, we hear about the influence children have on parents' consumption behaviour (Shoham and Dalakas, 2005).

Family structure and roles

For years the traditional view of families was based on the family unit comprising two adults (mother and father), each undertaking clearly defined roles based on gender stereotypes and parent–child familial interactions. However, as family structures have changed some firms have represented this in their advertising (see Figure 8.15). It has long been recognized that family decision-making is a joint (rather than individual) process, and that family members can occupy different buying roles depending on the nature of the product/service being consumed (see Research Insight 8.4). Typically, parents are the decision-makers and ultimate purchasers or buyers, but other family members also fulfil important roles, such as initiating purchases, influencing the purchasing process and as ultimate users of many purchases. This approach provides a useful description of the influences on family decisions, but it does not provide many insights into the complexity and variation of family decisions.

Figure 8.15 Still from McCain's 'We Are Family' advertisement

Source: Image courtesy of McCain and adam&eveDBB.

RESEARCH INSIGHT 8.4

Henkel, A.P., Boegershausen, J., Ciuchita, R., and Odekerken-Schröder, G. (2017), 'Storm after the quiet: how marketplace interactions shape consumer resources in collective goal pursuits', *Journal of the Association for Consumer Research*, 2, 1, 26–47.

This qualitative research focuses on the experiences of nine families after they learn that a child is disabled, and considers the consumption challenges the family faces given their new circumstances. The authors look at how family goals and purposes change, and how consumption is aligned towards achieving these goals, offering insights into marketplace interactions at times of transition.

 Access the online resources to read the abstract and access the full paper.

Research into family choices around holiday destinations has typically focused on roles and power relations, exploring the relative influence of each family member on the decision process. Wu et al. (2010) found that children were active participants in the decision process around holiday choices, but parents act as gatekeepers filtering out those attractions they judge inappropriate. So, although children are actively involved in making decisions, the range of options available may be limited by the parents.

In relation to fashion and clothing purchases, Boden (2006) suggests that children are influencing parents' clothing consumption, and that parents welcome this development. Parents are relying on children to help them decide what is fashionable or trendy to wear, a form of reverse socialization whereby children are teaching parents.

Sociocultural trends and impact on family consumption

Although we see changing family structures, in 2015 the majority of children around the globe still lived in two-parent families. However, children are more likely to live with one parent, in blended or foster family arrangements, or with no parents in North America, Europe, and Oceania than in Asia and the Middle East. The proportion of young adults who are married is in decline, and unmarried cohabitation is increasingly popular in many areas including Europe, and Central, South, and North America (www.worldfamilymap.org).

Chalmers (2016) identified five trends that were changing the nature of families.

- A decline in marriage alongside increasing diversity in family make-up.

- The number of children born outside marriage is increasing, with nearly 15 per cent of children in OECD countries living in single-parent households.

- Parenting is delayed as people prefer to establish themselves in careers before becoming parents.

- Smaller families; in almost all countries globally, family size is reducing.

- Children are staying at home longer, particularly where living costs have increased and the impact of the global recession is still felt.

Over the last two decades in the UK lone-parent families have increased by nearly 19 per cent (General Lifestyle survey, 2016).

Research shows that the involvement of children in consumption decisions is related to family type. Where children live with a single parent, they tend to be more involved in talking about and shopping for goods than children from two-parent or blended families (Tinson et al., 2008). The research attributes this to the complexity of the family arrangement (more complex family arrangements lead to less child involvement), but one-parent households may also expect greater participation of children in important decision-making.

Italy has the highest rate of older births in Europe. The trend towards later parenting is partly fuelled by societal trends around women in the workplace, with many women now in professional occupations. Changing sex roles have led to a shift in how decision-making responsibility is allocated. More equal distribution of family decision-making is evident, with children having more involvement where there is a less traditional approach to sex roles. However, despite advances in equality in division of labour within households, women still take most of the responsibility for household chores (Asher, 2011), which can impact on approaches to shopping and consumption.

Linked to the trend for late parenting is that such parents tend to have higher disposable incomes and are more likely to spend more money on their children, sometimes regarding children as extensions of themselves in terms of clothing and entertainment purchases. The launch of children's ranges by designers such as D&G, Gucci, and Stella McCartney, with the endorsement and patronage of celebrities (e.g. Jennifer Lopez for Gucci) in their marketing campaigns, captures this trend. A marked trend in recent years is the closure of the parent–child distance (see Consumer Insight 8.5). The proximity in tastes between parents and children is manifest in consumption of leisure activities (music, festivals, restaurants, games consoles), clothes (e.g. H&M, D&G, Stella McCartney, etc.), and even books (with the *Harry Potter* series being popular with both adults and children). The games console market demonstrates some interesting patterns of consumption as families spend leisure time together. Recent data from the USA indicates that 62 per cent of parents whose children are gamers play video games with them at least once a week (Entertainment Software Association, 2016), and consoles such as the Nintendo Wii, Sony Playstation, and Microsoft Xbox 360 are moving into the family living space.

Ekström et al. (1987) emphasized the importance of taking a reciprocal view of family decision-making and consumer socialization for a more realistic research perspective. In their paper they looked at the influence of parents on children and of children on parents in learning about consumption. They found evidence of **parental yielding**, *which is when a parental decision-maker is influenced by a child's request and 'surrenders'*, a range of tactics used by children (such as informing, persuasion, and reasoning strategies), and also the idea of **reverse socialization**, *which is where parents acquire consumer skills from their children*. This is evident in the area of technology (e.g. using the internet). Children also influence parents in relation to celebrity/popular culture, environmental issues, and ethical issues.

CONSUMER INSIGHT 8.5

You never actually own a Patek Philippe

The luxury watch market is a lucrative business as watches have become increasingly associated with a person's image and identity. Watches can demonstrate your taste and aesthetic sense. The website bestwatchbrandsguide.com suggests that a high-end luxury watch 'is indispensable when trying to advance yourself at your job, or even romantically'. High-end watches are also valuable because they retain their value and can be sold for more than their original purchase price (Adams, 2013). The ongoing value of high-end watches has been translated into an interesting marketing campaign by Swiss luxury watch manufacturer Patek Phillipe.

The Patek Phillippe brand is strongly identified with family subgroups, with advertisements based around mother–daughter and father–son relations. The campaign is called 'Generations' and its tagline is 'You never actually own a Patek Philippe. You merely look after it for the next generation'. The campaign focuses on the connections between parent and child over the life course, emphasizing how the brand is an important part of the development of the relationship. The brand is central to the developing mother–daughter relationship and identification, supporting the particular social dramas, rituals, and stories of that relationship. One advertisement focuses on mother and daughter enjoying a range of grooming rituals associated with 'dressing up' (e.g. putting on jewellery, hair fixing), and another shows an older mother–daughter pairing, this time sharing a special moment which, although not explicitly stated, is most likely an important and defining occasion such as an engagement. Another advertisement shows a father and son on a tennis court (Figure 8.16). The ads link the rituals and dramas within these important relationships with the presence of the Patek Phillippe brand.

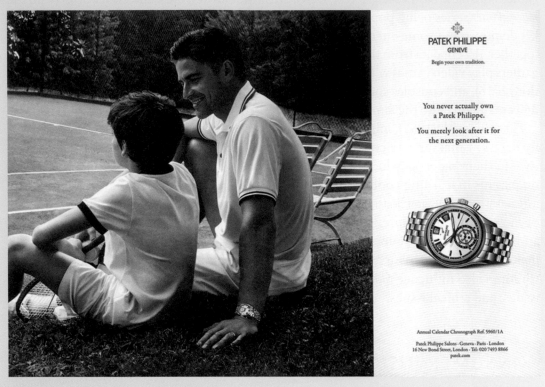

Figure 8.16   Patek Philippe 'Generations'   *Source*: Images supplied by The Advertising Archives.

Questions

1. Identify two or three other brands that use a family relationship. What is the nature of the relationship and why do you think that the family context is suitable?

2. Look at some recent advertising for some other high-end watch brands. How do they convey the value aspect of such watches addressed in this consumer insight. Can you link their communication approaches to any other theories in this chapter (e.g. word of mouth, opinion leaders)?

Sources: Adams (2013); www.bestwatchbrandsguide.com

 Access the online resources and follow the web links to learn more.

Social class structures and impact on consumption

As already suggested in this chapter, consumption behaviour and practices can play an important role in marking distinction and reflecting social position. Max Weber (1978) defined **status groups** *as communities of people linked together on the basis of wealth, status, and power.* Marketing is interested in how these communities share similar tastes and consumption practices. One area where marketers have used this extensively is in the cat-egorization and classification of consumers based on social class position. These systems reflect divisions, or groups, of people based on a composite measure of income, occupa-tion, and education. Two commonly used approaches in the UK are the Joint Industry Committee for National Readership Surveys (JICNARS) and that used by the Office of National Statistics (ONS) where occupation alone is taken as an indicator of social class, but which reflects newer employment patterns.

The focus of these classification systems tends to be the resources available to people, with the emphasis on economic resources. Such classification systems are still commonly used in the UK for both policy/government and commercial purposes, in particular to identify appropriate products and services for particular groups and to target these differ-ent groups. According to Bourdieu (1984), people draw on three different types of resource (economic, social, and cultural capital) to compete for status, referred to as symbolic capital (Holt, 1998). Economic capital relates to the financial resources available to the individual, while social capital covers the relationships and social networks that influence behaviour. Cultural capital, i.e. knowledge that is accumulated through upbringing and education (Bourdieu, 1984), consists of a set of 'socially rare and distinctive tastes, skills, knowledge and practices' (Holt, 1998: 3). According to Bourdieu, people's tastes are predominantly a marker of class. Although an individual may have economic capital and consume brands and products that may confer social standing, without the necessary skills associated with high cultural capital, they will not occupy a higher social position.

In 2013 a new classification was developed in the UK, derived from the BBC's 2011 Great British Class Survey, the largest survey of social class conducted in Britain. The sample was nationally representative and the survey included detailed questions relating to social, cultural, and economic capital (Savage et al., 2013) (Table 8.3).

The role of class and status has been explored in a number of consumer behaviour stud-ies, including research into the status consumption habits of upper-middle-class Turkish women (Üstüner and Holt, 2010), men's participation in DIY projects and how this links to identity (Moisio et al., 2013), and teenagers' use of brands as a form of social communica-tion (Piacentini and Mailer, 2004).

There is a growing body of research looking at disadvantaged consumers, which examines how people living with severe resource constraints cope (e.g. Hamilton and Catterall, 2005; Baker et al., 2005; Piacentini et al., 2013). Where consumers are lacking in economic, physical, cultural, and social resources, they are less likely to fully access the consumer market and thus lose out in the marketplace. Many studies have established that those living on low incomes tend to rely more on cash than on bank accounts and often miss out as they do not qualify for discounts (e.g. through direct debit payment options). A report into broadband/internet usage (Consumer Focus, 2010) showed that the benefits associated with use of the internet, especially for price comparison purposes, were not viewed as particularly relevant for low income consumers, since many in this category do not have the bank accounts or credit facilities to enable access to these deals. Socially

Social class	Percentage in sampled population	Description
Elite	6	Very high economic capital (especially savings), high social capital, very high highbrow cultural capital
Established middle class	25	High economic capital, high status of mean contacts, high highbrow and emerging cultural capital
Technical middle class	6	High economic capital, very high mean social contacts, but relatively few contacts reported, moderate cultural capital
New affluent workers	15	Moderately good economic capital, moderately poor mean score of social contacts, though high range, moderate highbrow but good emerging cultural capital
Traditional working class	14	Moderately poor economic capital, though with reasonable house price, few social contacts, low highbrow and emerging cultural capital
Emergent service workers	19	Moderately poor economic capital, though with reasonable household income, moderate social contacts, high emerging (but low highbrow) cultural capital

Table 8.3 Summary of social classes

Source: © Savage et al (2013). Adapted and reproduced under the Creative Commons Attribution 3.0 Unported licence.

responsible marketers need to ensure that they have channels which do not exclude lower income consumers in this way.

Conclusions

Our purpose in this chapter was to develop current thinking around the role of groups and social processes on consumption behaviour, and in so doing introduce the reader to some of the implications for marketing and brand communications.

We have *defined the reference group concept* and described the types of reference group which impact on consumption behaviour. We have highlighted how contactual, disclaimant, avoidance, and aspirational groups are used in consumer behaviour. We explained the increasing importance of aspirational groups, with people following a range of celebrities on social media, and Research Insight 8.1 showed how disassociative groups can be an important influence on presentation of self-image.

The *processes of reference group influence* were described, including the importance of informational, utilitarian, and value-expressive mechanisms of influence. Distinctions between goods consumed in public or in private were drawn, and related to luxury and necessity goods. In Research Insight 8.2 we described Asch's classic study of the development of conformity, an important mechanism for compliance within reference groups. Case Study 8 looks at gym membership, and the mechanisms of group and social influences on how young people use gyms.

We have looked at *social power and social connectedness* within and across groups. Marketers need to be aware of the importance that reference groups play in the lives of their customers and how people discuss issues and products among themselves. Increasingly, the use of the internet and social media has meant that these discussions are faster, geographically spread, and can impact a company very quickly. Consumer Insight 8.2 showed the increasing importance of KOLs in the social media land-scape and the importance of identifying influential people, while Consumer insight 8.3 explored how word-of-mouth communications work, focusing on the launch of Uniqlo in Singapore as an example of companies attempting to use social media to cre-ate buzz around their brand. The importance of reaching the 'supercharged' influential millenials was presented by Andrew Tenzer in Practitioner Insight 8. While customers will spread good news about new products they have liked or advertisements they have found interesting or funny, they will also be quick to pass on negative information, as has been the case for companies such as Amazon, Google, and Starbucks when they were identified as possibly evading taxes (Barford and Holt, 2013). Online reviews are an essential part of word-of-mouth, both positive and negative, and Consumer Insight 8.4 showed just how much consumers rely on them today even though some may not be that reliable.

Finally, we paid attention to both *the family* and *social class* as important influences on consumers. One of the most important reference groups is the family, and understanding the changing role of families and family roles within the broader context of communi-ties and social class structures is vitally important for marketing in terms of developing appropriate products and services and identifying different segments within the broader family grouping.

Review questions

1. List the main types of reference group relevant to consumer behaviour and explain their relevance. Provide an example of each.

2. What are the main mechanisms of reference group influence? Can you provide examples of each in relation to grocery shopping?

3. Why is conformity relevant for consumer behaviour?

4. Define opinion leadership. Give examples of where opinion leadership might be successfully used by marketing companies.

5. What is WOM? Consider some ways that eWOM could be used by companies.

6. How is family decision-making relevant for marketing in the twenty-first cen-tury?

7. What do you think we should consider using social class for? How might it be useful for studying consumer behaviour?

Discussion questions

1. If you were producing a matrix of 'reference group influence on product and brand decisions' (Bearden and Etzel, 1982), what products, which are important to you, would you place in the four squares?. How do you think they might vary if your parents or friends were doing this?

2. Identify and analyse situations where conformity with the group might affect an individual's behaviour. How might the situation impact on the product, service, and/or brands purchased? What recommendations would you have for marketers seeking to influence consumer behaviour in these situations?

3. Visit a consumer-generated review website and a marketer-generated website. What differences do you notice between them? Examine some consumer comments on both and assess how a consumer might make a decision based on these comments. How would a consumer identify whether the reviewer was an expert or had a similar lifestyle to them.

4. Identify a crowdsourcing site. Make an assessment of what the site owner is getting out of crowdsourcing and what the producer/consumer does. From your understanding of reference group influences, analyse how this site operates in consumer behaviour terms.

5. Read Simonson and Rosen's (2014) paper. Under the section 'How much does opinion matter' they classify product classes where online opinion may be important. Do you agree with their classification? What else might be important?

6. Identify one or two current trends in fashion, food, games, or music that you think a cool hunter might be interested in. Consider how they might be adapted for a larger market.

7. Given the changes in family composition identified in this chapter, suggest how marketing companies might capitalize on these changes. Think about how this might be relevant in a low involvement purchase context and then a high involvement context.

8. Look at the new social classes identified by Savage et al. (2013). Consider some of the major consumption issues that might impact the different groups identified.

Access the online resources to test your knowledge further and complete the Multiple Choice Questions for Chapter 8.

CASE STUDY 8

Group and social influences on gym culture

This case focuses on the male gym market in the UK, looking at some of the key trends influencing this market and its growth in consumer terms. We consider gym users as an example of a consumption community, and present some insights into going to the gym from their point of view. The questions focus on (1) how the gym community can be analysed in terms of the key concepts from this chapter, and (2) how the community deals with tensions and difficulties within the community.

Trends in gym usage in the UK

Latest figures from the market research company Mintel indicate that in 2016 one in eight (12 per cent) of the British population use health and fitness clubs, and over half (52 per cent) of current users of health and fitness clubs visit three or more days a week (Mintel, 2017). Working out in gyms is a popular activity for young people. In the UK, the most recent Mintel data shows that 19 per cent of young adults (aged 16–25) are members of a sporting club or gym, as are 18 per cent of the 25–34 age group (Mintel, 2015).

Gyms have become important spaces for people to work on their bodies and discipline their physical selves in the pursuit of improved physical condition and general well-being. Reasons for using a gym include building muscles, losing weight, toning up and looking better, keeping fit and healthy, and increasing performance in a particular sport (*Muscle and Strength*, 2006). The social aspect of the gym is also important, and friendship groups can be a powerful motivator in terms of both joining the gym and working out together. The gym is a public space, and working out in the gym provides a place for consumers to scrutinize or 'check out' other users, to compare themselves with, and possibly learn technique from, others. In addition, media and popular culture can influence trends in gym usage in terms of body ideals being affected by the media and also in terms of practices. Since the 2012 Olympics, there has been a shift in perception among women regarding desired body shapes, with more young women aspiring to achieve an athletic body like Jessica Ennis. This shift is likely to lead to some women doing more resistance and weight training in their efforts to achieve that physique.

Another cultural shift is in how working out at gyms, and the practices associated with them, has shifted in the popular imagination as a result of featuring in the MTV shows *Jersey Shore* and *Geordie Shore*. Magazines such as *Men's Health* and *Men's Fitness* often feature articles based around the work-out habits of the stars of these shows (see Figure 8.17).

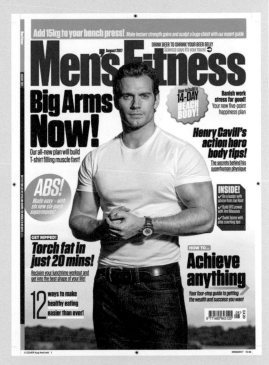

Figure 8.17   Example front cover of the magazine *Men's Fitness*

Source: Image courtesy of *Men's Fitness*, Dennis Publishing Ltd.

Linked to this is a shift in perceptions of protein drinks, which are becoming mainstream and normalized among the gym-using public.

Group aspects of gym use

In interviews collected for this case study, we investigated how gym users view themselves and other users, and what they think of shifts in the way that gyms are being used. There were a number of frustrations for those who viewed themselves as regular serious gym users compared with lighter users, who had different motives for going to the gym. This comes through in this interview with Michael, who considers himself to be 'a serious bodybuilder':

> I get frustrated when people are in the gym, dressed in inappropriate clothing, on their mobiles and just sitting on machines talking. I have an intense regime and I feel these people just slow down and ruin my experience in the gym.

When discussing appropriate usage of the gym, for Michael there is a code of practice which includes what to wear and how to behave. This contrasts with some of the lighter users, who are more socially oriented in their motives. This is shown in the quote from Jon, a part-time social gym goer:

> I would describe myself as a part time-gym goer. For me it is more of a social reason; I like to go to the gym with my friends and then go out and party at night. I guess it's more of a 'yeah I go to the gym' thing.

Clearly, the social dimension is important for Jon, and he views the gym as something he does with friends and as a part of his evening going-out ritual. Going to the gym is a badge that signifies the kind of person he is ('I go to the gym'). Jon goes on to talk about the way that images and trends in popular culture impact his gym life, and it becomes clear that TV shows, such as *Jersey Shore*, do have an influence:

> Personally I don't really watch these programmes [Jersey Shore and Geordie Shore], *but the people I socialize with certainly do. They constantly mention names such as Mike 'The Situation' and use the terms GTL—gym, tan, laundry. I go more for the social aspect, but my mates like to emulate what they have watched on TV.*

Jon mentions one of the main characters from MTV's *Jersey Shore*, Mike 'The Situation' Sorrentino, who is looked up to and emulated by his friends. All the male characters from *Jersey Shore* are well known for their physiques, and are often shown displaying their 'ripped' bodies. These characters also have their own language and terminology based around going to the gym, which has filtered into the public discourse in gyms (as demonstrated in Jon's quote). GTL ('gym, tan, laundry') is a phrase coined by Sorrentino, and refers to the routine done on a daily basis to ensure that he (and people who want to be like him) look and feel good. According to Sorrentino, 'You gotta GTL every day to make sure you're looking your best bro. If your shirt looks bad it makes the whole product look bad' (Urban Dictionary, 2010).

Similarly, there are gym users who are driven by more body-conscious motives, as shown by Rory, who works out to achieve a set goal and for a healthy lifestyle:

> I really enjoy going to the gym and working out with some of the experienced bodybuilders. Myself, I want to get ripped, and talking to people who really understand nutrition and working out is a great help for me, especially as you can see that they know what they are on about.

A current trend in popular culture is towards men having a 'ripped' appearance, as mentioned by Rory, which means that there is a lot of muscle mass and low body fat—this is the look that features heavily in health magazines and manuals, such as *Men's Health*.

Rory also reveals that one of his motives for going to the gym relates to the guidance he seeks from other gym users, viewing the gym as a place to access expertise on both exercise and nutrition. It is not necessarily the gym staff who provide this support, but rather other gym users, experienced bodybuilders, emphasizing the strong social angle to his gym consumption.

Another aspect of their discussions around the gym relates to how the market has evolved to meet their changing needs and demands. This is seen in the access to protein-based products that are viewed as an important part of the serious bodybuilder's regime. As Michael says:

> *Looking at the community as a whole, I guess becoming more common we have seen benefits. I remember protein used to be really expensive, hard to come by but now companies seem to be offering various types of supplements helping me get my protein intake for the day—it's now a lot easier and more convenient than eating six chicken breasts and ten eggs!*

Similarly, the growth in the market for supplements has changed gym user's perceptions of these products, probably due to increased familiarity with and awareness of them, and also de-stigmatization of their use. According to Rory:

> *I have changed my opinion on supplements; I used to think it was unnatural but companies communicating with the market has really helped me understand that it's a great and effective way of getting into shape, keeping healthy quickly and conveniently which is a real added benefit in such busy day-to-day lifestyles. Having a shake stops me from choosing unhealthy take-away and fast food!*

Gym users are seeing some benefits of the community becoming more popular and commercial. A few years ago, the protein community was avoided as something that is fake, unnatural, and illegal, and was surrounded by banned substances such as steroids for people who just wanted to get bigger. As mentioned already, the use of protein supplements and drinks has become mainstream, supported by popular culture reference points. In an interview in the magazine *Men's Fitness*, Sorrentino offered his fitness tips, which included: '*eat every few hours. Aim for small meals per day—three meals and three protein shakes* (*Men's Fitness*, 2010).

The gym and fitness market is evolving, and people are starting to see the benefits of working out, which leads them to have quite different goals from gym consumption. The sector is now more appealing and profitable for business investment, and consequently businesses are expanding markets and investing in research and development of new products and nutrition to help people achieve their goals. Drug screening is being used on products to make them safer, natural, and normal. This is where the hard core community are now starting to see the benefits of a more mixed (or heterogeneous gym user)—because of the expanding market the core community has access to a wider variety of nutritional supplements that are cheaper, taste better, and are more readily available. With increased participation, what were once seen as 'freaks of nature' are now seen as 'wow that's really impressive' and 'role models', since there is a greater awareness and understanding of the effort and commitment needed for improved physical condition and well-being.

Questions

1. This case covers a range of issues around gym users. Analyse the gym community in terms of key concepts of reference group influences and motives for group membership.

2. From your analysis of the gym community, and your understanding of the material in Thomas et al. (2013), describe how the gym community draws on and activates social and economic resources to overcome tensions and difficulties within the community.

Sources: Muscle and Strength (2006); *Men's Fitness* (2010), *Urban Dictionary* (2010); Thomas et al. (2013); Stewart and Smith (2014); Mintel (2015, 2017).

Thank you to Lee Swinnerton (Lancaster University) for collecting the data for this case. All interviews were conducted in December 2012. All participants' names have been changed for this case work.

References

Adams, S. (2012), '"Jamie Oliver drove children away from school meals", says Prue Leith', *The Telegraph*, 10 June, http://www.telegraph.co.uk/health/healthnews/9322595/Jamie-Oliver-drove-children-away-from-school-meals-says-Prue-Leith.html (accessed 7 May 2017).

Adams, A. (2013), 'Wrist watch brands and models of high value', http://www.forbes.com/sites/arieladams/2013/01/10/wrist-watch-brands-models-of-high-value/ (accessed 26 July 2017).

Advertising Standards Authority (2012), https://www.asa.org.uk/rulings/tripadvisor-llc-a11-166867.html (accessed 27 July 2017).

arts.ac.uk (2017), http://www.arts.ac.uk/csm/courses/short-courses/business--management-and-science/cool-hunting-fashion-online/ (accessed 15 December 2017).

Asch, S.E. (1955), 'Opinions and social pressure', *Scientific American*, 193, 5, 31–5.

Asher, R. (2011), *Shattered: modern motherhood and the illusion of equality*, London: Harvill Secker.

Assael, H. (1998), *Consumer behavior and marketing action* (6th edn), Mason, OH: South-Western College Publishing.

Baker, S.M., Gentry J.W., and Rittenburg, T.L. (2005), 'Building understanding of the domain of consumer vulnerability', *Journal of Macromarketing*, 25, 2, 128–39.

Barford, V. and Holt, G. (2013), 'Google, Amazon, Starbucks: the rise of tax shaming', *BBC News Magazine*, 21 May, http://www.bbc.co.uk/news/magazine-20560359 (accessed 27 July 2017).

Bearden, W.O. and Etzel, M.J. (1982), 'Reference group influence on product and brand purchase decisions', *Journal of Consumer Research*, 9, 332–341.

Boden, S. (2006), '"Another day, another demand": how parents and children negotiate consumption matters', *Sociological Research Online*, 11, 2, http://www.socresonline.org.uk/11/2/boden.html (accessed 27 July 2017).

Bourdieu, P. (1984), *Distinction: a social critique of the judgement of taste* (transl. R. Nice), London: Routledge.

Brabham, D.C. (2008), 'Crowdsourcing as a model for problem solving', *International Journal of Research into New Media Technologies*, 14, 1, 75–90.

Bravo, R., Fraj, E., and Martínez, E. (2006), 'Differences and similarities in measuring family influences on young adult consumers: an integrative analysis', *European Advances in Consumer Research*, 7, 104–11.

Bronner, F. and de Hoog, R. (2010), 'Consumer-generated versus marketer-generated websites in consumer decision making', *International Journal of Market Research*, 52, 2, 231–48.

Chalmers, H. (2016) 'How to market effectively to parents and families', WARC.com (accessed 20 February 2017).

Chang, J.M. (2013), http://abcnews.go.com/Technology/samsung-fined-paying-people-criticize-htcs-products/story?id=20671547 (accessed 21 April 2017).

Claveria, K. (2016), 'Beyond Facebook: four types of online communities and best practices on how to use them', *VisionCritical*, 26 August, https://www.visioncritical.com/types-of-online-communities-best-practices/ (accessed 21 July 2017).

Comm, J. (2010), *Twitter power 2.0: how to dominate your market one tweet at a time*, Hoboken, NJ: John Wiley.

Consumer Focus (2010), 'Broadband minded? Overcoming consumers' barriers to internet access', Report, Consumer Focus, http://www.onecommunity.org/reports/broadband-minded-overcoming-consumers-barriers-to-internet-access/ (accessed 21 July 2017).

De Langhe, B., Fernbach, P.M., and Lichtenstein, D.R. 'Navigating by the stars: investigating the actual and perceived validity of online user ratings', *Journal of Consumer Research*, 42, 6, 817–33.

Dougherty, J. (2015), 'Word of mouth campaigns that rocked', http://www.cision.com/us/2015/03/9-word-of-mouth-campaigns-that-rocked/ (accessed 21 April 2017).

Earls, M. (2009), *Herd: how to change mass behaviour by harnessing our true nature*, Chichester: John Wiley.

Eccleston, D. and Griser, L. (2008), 'How does Web 2.0 stretch traditional influencing patterns?', *International Journal of Market Research*, 50, 5, 575–90.

Econsultancy (2010), 'Global study shows majority of digital word of mouth is positive', https://econsultancy.com/nma-archive/35354-global-study-shows-majority-of-digital-word-of-mouth-is-positive (accessed 15 December 2017).

Ekström, K.M., Tansuhaj, P.S., and Foxman, E.R. (1987), 'Children's influence in family decisions and consumer socialization: a reciprocal view', *Advances in Consumer Research*, 14, 1, 283–7.

Engel, J.F., Blackwell, R.D., and Miniard, P.W. (1990), *Consumer behavior* (6th edn), Chicago, IL: Dryden.

Entertainment Software Association (2016), 'Sales, demographic and usage data: essential facts about the computer and video game industry', http://essentialfacts.theesa.com (accessed 21 July 2017).

Epp, A.M. and Price, L.L. (2008), 'Family identity: a framework of identity interplay in consumption practices', *Journal of Consumer Research*, 35, 1, 50–70.

Feick, L.F. and Price L. L. (1987), 'The market maven: a diffuser of marketplace information', *Journal of Marketing*, 51, 83–97.

French, J.R.P. (1956), 'A formal theory of social power', *Psychological Review*, 63, 181–94.

French, J.R.P. and Raven, B. (1959), 'The basis of social power', in D. Cartwright (ed.), *Studies in social power*, Ann Arbor, MI: Institute for Social Research.

General Lifestyle Survey (2016), https://www.ons.gov.uk/peoplepopulationandcommunity/birthsdeathsandmarriages/families/bulletins/familiesandhouseholds/2016 (accessed 13 September 2017).

Gladwell, M. (2001), *The tipping point*, London: Abacus.

Grossman, L. (2003), 'The quest for cool', *Time*, 30 August, pp.2–6.

Guazzini, A., Vilone, D., Donati, C. et al. (2015), 'Modeling crowdsourcing as collective problem solving', https://arxiv.org/pdf/1506.09155v2.pdf (accessed 21 April 2017).

Hamilton, K.L. and Catterall, M. (2005), 'Towards a better understanding of the low income consumer', *Advances in Consumer Research*, 32, 1, 627–32.

Henkel, A.P., Boegershausen, J., Ciuchita, R., and Odekerken-Schröder, G. (2017), 'Storm after the quiet: how marketplace interactions shape consumer resources in collective goal pursuits, *Journal of the Association for Consumer Research*, 2, 1, 26–47.

Hennig-Thurau, T., Gwinner, K., Walsh, G., and Gremler, D. (2004), 'Electronic word-of-mouth via consumer-opinion platforms: what motivates consumers to articulate themselves on the internet?', *Journal of Interactive Marketing*, 18, 1, 38–52.

Holt, D.B. (1998), 'Does cultural capital structure American consumption?', *Journal of Consumer Research*, 25, 1–25.

Howe, J. (2006), 'Crowdsourcing: a definition', http://www.crowdsourcing.typepad.com/ (accessed 26 July 2017).

Hyman, H. (1942), 'The psychology of status', *Archives of Psychology*, 269, 1–95.

Jansson, J., Nordlund, A., and Westin, K. (2017), 'Examining drivers of sustainable consumption: the influence of norms and opinion leadership on electric vehicle adoption in Sweden', *Journal of Cleaner Production*, 154, 176–87.

Johnson, G. (2013), Clerkenwell cool is London at its best, *Huffington Post* http://www.huffingtonpost.co.uk/gareth-johnson/clerkenwell-cool-london_b_2804896.html (accessed 20 April 2017).

Katz, E. and Lazarsfeld, P. (1955), *Personal influence*, New York: Free Press.

Kim, C., Lee, H., and Tomiuk, M.A. (2009), 'Adolescents' perceptions of family communication patterns and some aspects of their consumer socialization', *Psychology and Marketing*, 26, 10, 888–907.

Lazarsfeld, P., Berelson, B.R., and Gaudet, H. (1944), *The people's choice*, New York: Duell, Sloan and Pearce.

Leigh, J.H. (1989), 'An extension of the Bourne typology of reference group influence on product-related decisions', *Journal of Business and Psychology*, 4, 1, 65–85.

Luca, M. and Zervas, G. (2015), 'Fake it till you make it: reputation, competition and Yelp review fraud http://people.hbs.edu/mluca/FakeItTillYouMakeIt.pdf (accessed 21 April 2017).

Lynskey, D. (2005), 'Fast and furious', *The Guardian*, 30 September, http://www.guardian.co.uk/music/2005/sep/30/popandrock.arcticmonkeys (accessed 29 July 2017).

Mann, L. (1969), *Social psychology*, New York: John Wiley.

Mathews Hunt, K. (2015), 'Gaming the system: fake online reviews v. consumer law', *Computer Law and Security Review*, 31, 1, 3–25.

Men's Fitness (2010), 'The situation: how to get my abs!', http://www.toofab.com/2010/11/03/the-situations-revealing-interview/ (accessed 28 July 2017).

Mintel (2015), 'Health and fitness club usage', *Health and Fitness Clubs–UK–July 2015*, http://store.mintel.com/health-and-fitness-clubs-uk-july-2015 (accessed 20 October 2017).

Mintel (2017), 'Health and fitness club usage', *Health and Fitness Clubs–UK–July 2017*, http://store.mintel.com/health-and-fitness-clubs-uk-july-2017 (accessed 20 October 2017).

Moisio, R., Arnould, E.J., and Gentry, J. (2013), 'Productive consumption in the class-mediated construction of domestic masculinity: do-it-yourself (DIY) home improvement in men's identity—work', *Journal of Consumer Research*, 40, 2, 298–316.

Muscle and Strength (2006), 'Why do you go to the gym poll', http://www.muscleandstrength.com/forum/threads/106-Why-do-you-go-to-the-gym (accessed 26 July 2017).

Nancarrow, C. and Nancarrow, P. (2007), 'Hunting for cool tribes', *Consumer Tribes*, B. Cova, R.V. Kozinets, and A. Shankar (eds), Oxford: Butterworth-Heinemann, pp.129–43.

Nielsen (2015), 'Global trust in advertising: winning strategies for an evolving media landscape', http://www.nielsen.com/eu/en/insights/reports/2015/global-trust-in-advertising-2015.html (accessed 21 April 2017).

Park, C.W. and Lessig, V.P. (1977), 'Students and housewives: differences in susceptibility to reference group influence', *Journal of Consumer Research*, 4, 2, 102–10.

Piacentini, M.G. and Mailer, G. (2004), 'Symbolic consumption in teenagers' clothing choices', *Journal of Consumer Behaviour Theory and Practice*, 3, 3, 251–62.

Piacentini, M.G., Hibbert, S.A., and Hogg, M.K. (2013), 'Consumer resource integration amongst vulnerable consumers: care leavers in transition to independent living', *Journal of Marketing Management*, 30, 1/2, 201–19.

Postigo, H. (2003), 'From Pong to Planet Quake: post-industrial transition from leisure to work', *Communication and Society*, 6, 4, 593–607.

Pulsar Platform (2016), http://www.pulsarplatform.com/blog/2016/pulsar-case-study-how-twitter-can-help-predict-a-norovirus-vomcano/ (accessed 22 April 2017).

Raven, B.H. (1993), 'The bases of power: origins and recent developments', *Journal of Social Issues*, 49, 4, 227–51.

Rogers, E. (1962), *Diffusion of innovations*, New York: Free Press.

Rogers, E.M. and Cartano, D.G. (1962), 'Methods of measuring opinion leadership', *Public Opinion Quarterly*, 26, 3, 435–41.

Rohampton, J. (2017), 'Five social media trends that will dominate 2017', *Forbes*, 3 January, https://www.forbes.com/sites/jimmyrohampton/2017/01/03/5-social-media-trends-that-will-dominate-2017/#1543a8306ffe (accessed 20 April 2017).

Samson, A. (2010), 'Product usage and firm-generated word of mouth: some results from FMCG product trials', *International Journal of Market Research*, 52, 4, 459–82.

Savage, M., Devine, F., Cunningham, N. et al. (2013), 'A new model of social class? Findings from the BBC's Great British Class Survey experiment', *Sociology*, 47, 2, 219–50.

Sekhon, Y. and Szmigin, I. (2011), 'Acculturation and identity: second generation Indian Punjabis', *Consumption Markets Culture*, 14, 1, 79–98.

Shoham, A. and Dalakas, V. (2005), 'He said, she said … they said: parents' and children's assessment of children's influence on family consumption decisions', *Journal of Consumer Marketing*, 22, 3, 152–60.

Simonson, I. and Rosen, E. (2014), 'What marketers misunderstand about online reviews', *Harvard Business Review*, January–February, 23–5.

Stämpfli, A.E., Stöckli, S., and Brunner, T.A. (2016), 'A nudge in a healthier direction: how environmental cues help restrained eaters pursue their weight-control goal', *Appetite*, 110, 94–102.

Stewart, B. and Smith, A.C.T. (2014), 'The significance of critical incidents in explaining gym use amongst adult populations', *Qualitative Research in Sport, Exercise and Health*, 6, 1, 45–61.

Surowiecki, J. (2005), *The wisdom of crowds: why the many are smarter than the few*, New York: Anchor.

Tal, A. and Wansink, B. (2016), 'What would Brad Pitt eat? How popularity can make food tasty', *Journal of Nutrition Education and Behavior*, 48, 7, S89.

Thomas, T.C., Price, L.L., and Schau, H.J. (2013), 'When differences unite: resource dependence in heterogeneous consumption communities', *Journal of Consumer Research*, 39, 5, 1010–33.

Thorniley, T. (2011), 'Uniqlo thrives on digital marketing', *Market Leader*, www.marketingsociety.com/the-library/uniqlo-thrives-digital-marketing (accessed 27 May 2014).

Tinson, J., Nancarrow, C., and Brace, I. (2008), 'Purchase decision making and the increasing significance of family types', *Journal of Consumer Marketing*, 25, 1, 45–56.

Trueland, J. (2013), 'Fast and effective?', *Nursing Standard*, 28, 16, 25–7

Urban Dictionary (2010), http://www.urbandictionary.com/define.php?term=GTL (accessed 18 July 2017).

Üstüner, T. and Holt, D.B. (2010), 'Toward a theory of status consumption in less industrialized countries', *Journal of Consumer Research*, 37, 1, 37–56.

Vaterlaus, J.M., Patten, E.V., Roche, C., and Young, J.A. (2015), '#Gettinghealthy: the perceived influence of social media on young adult health behaviours', *Computers in Human Behavior*, 14, 151–7.

Venkatesan, M. (1966), 'Experimental study of consumer behavior conformity and independence', *Journal of Marketing Research*, 3, 4, 384–7.

Verlegh, P.W.J., Verderk, C., Tuk, M.A., and Smidts, A. (2004), 'Customers or sellers? The role of persuasion knowledge in customer referral', *Advances in Consumer Research*, 31, 304–5.

Warren, C. and Campbell, M.C. (2014), 'What makes things cool? How autonomy influences perceived coolness', *Journal of Consumer Research*, 41, 2, 543–63.

Watts, D.J. (2007), 'Challenging the influentials hypothesis', *Word of Mouth Marketing Association*, 3, 201–11.

Watts, D.J. and Dodds, P.S. (2007), 'Influentials, networks, and public opinion formation', *Journal of Consumer Research*, 36, 441–57.

Weber, M. (1978), *Economy and society*, Berkeley, CA: University of California Press.

White, K and Dahl, D.W. (2006), 'To be or not to be? The influence of dissociative reference groups on consumer preferences', *Journal of Consumer Psychology*, 16, 4, 404–14.

Wu, K., Holmes, K., and Tribe, J. (2010), ' "Where do you want to go today?" An analysis of family group decisions to visit museums', *Journal of Marketing Management*, 26, 7/8, 706–26.

9

CULTURE

Introduction

Culture is often considered to be an important influence on how people behave. When we talk about culture, we are really talking about all the aspects of a society that distinguish members of that society, or group, from those of another. Culture is the shared understandings, meanings, and customs which together act as a 'blueprint' to guide behaviour and to help people live and function in ways that are appropriate and acceptable to others within that same culture. Culture shapes and guides everyday consumption behaviours, and celebrates special life events from birthdays to weddings and funerals. Certain aspects of culture are stable and resistant to change, while others are malleable. In this chapter we focus on understanding culture and its relevance and impact on marketing practice.

LEARNING OBJECTIVES

Having read the chapter you will be able to:

1. Identify and appreciate the elements of culture.

2. Understand the three **elements of the cultural system**.

3. Explain how **cultures are classified** and assess the value of these classifications.

4. Appreciate the nature of **cultural myths and rituals**.

5. Consider the ways that culture is important for **marketing communications**.

6. Recognize the relevance of **subcultures** (demographic and consumption-based), how these relate to culture, and the implications for consumer behaviour.

Defining culture

Culture *is the sum total of learned ideas, beliefs, values, knowledge, and customs that regulate the behaviour of members of a particular society.* There are a number of aspects of this definition and each will be treated in turn.

Culture is learned or inherited

Culture is learned through socialization, which involves learning through social interactions, making observations, and actively processing information to form impressions and understandings about everyday practices. Such learning includes enculturation and acculturation.

Enculturation *refers to how an individual learns the traditional content of his/her native culture.* Cultural practices and values are assimilated through this process, which mostly takes place within the family. The development of food tastes provides a good illustration of enculturation in operation. Through observational learning children mimic the choices of adults, and their dietary choices are reinforced through overt social rewards such as praise. Bitter gourd is a popular vegetable in South Asia that is used in curries and prized for its nutritional and medicinal qualities; it is also very bitter, and is definitely an acquired taste. However, various processes of learning come into play (e.g. habituation, learning to like the taste in your mouth, and repeated exposure leading to instrumental learning (Chapter 4), reinforced via praise from parents), which result in the child growing to enjoy (or at least endure!) the taste of the gourd.

Many people find themselves moved from their original culture. In such cases a different kind of learning occurs. **Acculturation** relates *to the idea of movement between places or cultural contexts.* In Penaloza's study of the experiences of Mexican immigrants living in the USA, she defined **consumer acculturation** as '*the general process of movement and adaptation to the consumer cultural environment in one country by persons from another country*' (Penaloza, 1994: 33). The study was concerned with processes and conditions that shaped acculturation experiences and outcomes. The main outcomes were:

- *assimilation*, where the consumers entering the new culture abandon Mexican culture in favour of US culture;

- *maintenance*, where aspects of both cultures are maintained;

- *resistance*, privileging Mexican culture over US culture and in so doing rejecting aspects of the new culture;

- *segregation*, where there is a separation of cultural needs, with evidence of Latino consumer culture being kept distinctly separate from mainstream US culture.

Penaloza described how institutions of society (family, school, church) alongside marketing agents are important in the process of acculturation. An example of such marketing efforts is found in Unilever's Vive Mejor programme (Adweek, 2009). Vive Mejor takes the form of a website and social media presence, all in Spanish, providing helpful lifestyle, cooking, and beauty tips for 'Latina moms' in the USA. From an acculturation perspective, this programme enables Hispanics living in the USA to maintain their 'Spanishness' while living in another country. Research Insight 9.1 considers some other issues around consumer acculturation.

RESEARCH INSIGHT 9.1

Luedicke, M.K. (2015), 'Indigenes' responses to immigrants' consumer acculturation: a relational configuration analysis', *Journal of Consumer Research*, 42, 1, 109–29.

In this paper, the author charts the literature on acculturation research, and then goes on to explain findings from a multiyear interpretive study which explored how indigenous consumers interpreted and responded to immigrant consumer acculturation practices in a rural Austrian town. The article contributes a broader conceptualization of consumer acculturation, highlighting four sources of ethnic group conflict in a consumer acculturation context: (1) a gradual sell-out of the indigenous community, (2) a crumbling of their authority, (3) a violation of equality rules, and (4) indigenes being torn between contradictory micro- and macro-social morals].

 Access the online resources to read the abstract and access the full paper.

Beliefs, values, knowledge, and customs

We refer to beliefs, values, knowledge, and customs in terms of their contribution to culture. As discussed in Chapter 6, **beliefs** are *the thoughts an individual holds about some object, idea or person*. **Values** *are the deep-rooted and enduring beliefs or ideals about what is good and desirable and what is not*. Values tend not to be situation specific; rather, they are more generally held, and act to guide and shape behaviour. Many people care about the ethical treatment of animals and have turned to vegetarian or vegan diets. Those who do eat meat also need to be reassured that their beliefs and values as to how animals should be treated are engaged with (see Figure 9.1). As Jeremy Rix outlines in Practitioner Insight 9, this is not necessarily always how we might expect them to engage.

Figure 9.1   Lidl RSPCA/free range meat advertisement   *Source*: Image supplied by The Advertising Archives.

PRACTITIONER INSIGHT 9

Jeremy Rix, Managing Director, OKO

Do you care about how the meat you eat is produced? To what extent do you think about animal welfare when you're in the meat aisle at your local supermarket? Choosing to buy and eat meat is associated with many different beliefs and customs which manufacturers need to understand in order to identify the appropriate messages that resonate with their consumers' values.

Buying meat seems, on the surface, to be relatively simple. Shoppers throw packs of it into their trolleys apparently without thought. But contained within consumer decisions to buy meat are complexities which we needed to understand fully in our work with Winterbotham Darby—the largest supplier of continental meats into UK retail. They have been working with farming and manufacturing partners across Europe and Compassion in World Farming for a number of years to improve animal welfare standards in their supply chain. Their aim now is to make higher animal welfare a key part of their brand and strategy. The question was how to communicate this to retailers and consumers.

OKO's initial extensive desk research found little good quality research in the public domain about consumer views and understanding of animal welfare. Research—often using focus groups and simple quantitative surveys—just didn't take into account the complexity underlying buying decisions for meat.

We developed a more nuanced approach. We recruited and ran semi-ethnographic research with 22 UK families who purchased continental meat. Over a period of several months we tracked their purchasing and consumption behaviour, and interviewed them regularly, carefully avoiding priming them on animal welfare issues. At the end of the research, we conducted longer reflective discussions that tackled animal welfare as part of the buying decision. Finally, we quantified our findings used a layered questionnaire designed to measure key themes identified in our ethnographic research.

We found that consumers deal with the complexity of buying meat by dissociating themselves from responsibility. They don't want to think about how meat is produced, and the farming and production of meat is complicated. This presents significant risks for manufacturers and retail brands in *not* tackling animal welfare issues.

- Consumers see manufacturing and retail brands as responsible for animal welfare.

- Consumers assume animal welfare standards in the supply chain are higher than they are.

- Consumers' underlying animal welfare concerns could be activated to become conscious drivers of retailer and product choice.

The key driver of meat purchase at shelf edge is quality (with price a close second). However, quality as a high level, simplified attribute is comprised of a range of more specific components, for example:

- ingredients used in the product

- level of animal welfare

- what the animals are fed

- method/process of making the product

- where the product is made

- where the animals are farmed

- breed of animal used.

There are too many issues to consider and trade-off during the seconds in which they make the decision to buy, so consumers simplify this complexity to a level which enables a relatively straightforward purchase. Although they don't appear to consider animal welfare explicitly at shelf edge, it is one of the *key factors* that feeds implicitly into their assessments of quality.

For Winterbotham Darby the implications were clear. Rather than talking about animal welfare explicitly and creating complexity by forcing consumers to trade off numerous factors in their decision to buy, they needed to think about how to talk about quality in a way that resonates.

Ultimately this comes down to a single word: 'care'. As one of our participants put it:

You want to know that the people who make these products care. They care about their farms. They care about the animals. They care about doing things properly. Because if they don't care about all those things, how could you trust them to care about the quality of the product itself?

In Asian countries there is a clear respect for elders that is often not present in some Western cultures. When Singapore celebrated its 50-year anniversary of independence they used illustrations of elders and their experiences as representing the cultural values of the nation. But culture is dynamic, and as more countries encounter the issues of an ageing population there is some evidence that younger generations may be losing their respect for older people. For example, the Singapore newspaper *The Straits Times* reported (Seow Bei Yi, 2017) how a NIMBY (not in my back yard) attitude had developed in some areas of Singapore, with residents not wishing to have elder care homes built in their area.

Knowledge *refers to the familiarity with people or things, which can include understandings, facts, information, and descriptions gained through experience and education.* Since culture comprises the prevailing norms, practices, beliefs, and values held by a particular group in society, understanding of these can be described as cultural knowledge. Words can immediately conjure up images and meanings within the culture to which they belong. The Korean word 'nunchi' reflects Korean values of hospitality and the ability to read a guest's needs. A Korean host is expected to read their guest's requirements, and asking for food and drink is considered impolite. The word is shorthand for a set of complex but shared values specific to that culture.

Customs *are the norms of behaviour that have been passed from generation to generation.* These serve to control basic behaviour within a culture around the core facets of life, such as the division of labour within the home or how to celebrate rites of passage. It is customary in many cultures to leave a tip in service encounters—a gratuity for a service performed. The approach to tipping varies with culture and is influenced by local customs (Lynn and Starbuck, 2015). In the USA, there is a strong tipping culture; in restaurant settings it is usual to leave 15–20 per cent as a tip (anything less suggests that you are unhappy with the restaurant service). In other countries, such as Japan, tipping is not the custom, and indeed to tip someone is viewed as rather insulting.

Culture regulates the behaviour of members of a particular society

Culture is communicated to members of society through a common language and commonly shared symbols. In the consumer world, advertising provides models for

Figure 9.2   Enculturation of family fun

Source: Image printed with kind permission from Cognation Mountain Biking Trails South Wales, Neath Port Talbot County Borough Council.

behaviour and also reinforces desired modes of behaviour and expectations. The promotional material for Cognation, an organization encouraging mountain bike and trail use in South Wales, UK, provides a good example of how cultural learning can shape consumer behaviour (Figure 9.2). This image shows a family out on their bikes, with the bold message 'Family Fun Day' labelled across the picture. A number of cultural messages are communicated here: the tagline 'Family Fun Day' emphasizes the point that this is a family activity; the way the family is dressed shows us the appropriate clothing and equipment needed for this type of activity; finally, the order of cycling (parents at the back, children at the front) conveys a message around the protective role of parents towards their children. All these together provide a clear example of how consumers are enculturated to practices that are developed and reinforced around cultural understanding of what constitutes 'family fun'.

Increasingly, most cultures are concerned about their impact on the environment. People of island cultures may be particularly concerned about exhausting their local resources, but the way people deal with their environment and issues of waste and sustainability differ. In Japan, for example, waste has become an issue of regret through the term *mottainai*, which expresses a sense of regret at wasting the value of a resource. Alongside the mantra of reduce, reuse, recycle, *mottainai* introduces the concept of respect for objects. The postwar generation of Japanese had to live in a resource-poor time, and some say that *mottainai* developed from this time. *Mottainai* expresses a reverence for objects even when they are old and unloved, and communicates the inherent value in anything, encouraging people to use objects fully for as long as possible, to take good care of objects, and to cherish everything. Increasingly, *mottainai* is reflected on a daily basis in Japan. For example in Tokyo, buildings are often fitted with toilets flushed by wastewater. There has also been a resurgent fashion for *furoshiki*, a type of wrapping cloth used in the eighth century to protect valuable items. Today, it is often used to replace plastic bags (Taylor, 2015) (Figure 9.3).

The movement of cultural meaning

Another aspect of understanding learning within culture relates to how cultural meaning moves between the different aspects of society that make up culture (see Chapter 7). Figure 9.4 shows how meaning moves from the existing 'out there' in the wider cultural world to meaning for individual consumers, which then shapes their consumer behaviour. According to McCracken (1986), cultural meaning is influenced by cultural categories (how the culture organizes time, space, nature,

Figure 9.3   A *furoshiki* shopping bag

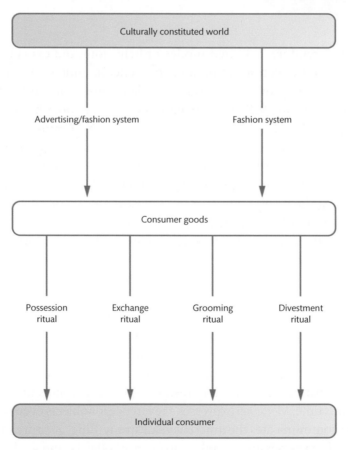

Figure 9.4   Movement of cultural meaning

Source: McCracken, G. (1986), 'Culture and consumption: a theoretical account of the structure and movement of the cultural meaning of consumer goods', *Journal of Consumer Research*, 13, 1, 71–84. By permission of Oxford University Press.

the sacred, and society) and cultural principles (the values, ideals, norms, and beliefs that allow things to be grouped into cultural categories, ranked, and interrelated). McCracken's diagram can be used to demonstrate how the meaning associated with consumer goods transfers to consumers through cultural understanding of the world (e.g. catwalk parades of high fashion, worn by celebrities) and via consumption-related acts (e.g. fashion, grooming, and possession rituals). An analysis of current hipster culture provides an illustration of this model in action. The term 'hipster' actually dates back to the USA of the 1940s describing a subculture built around the popularity of jazz music (http://www.micar.com/origins-of-the-hipster/). The term was derived from 'hip' meaning 'in the know'. This is the initial part of the *culturally constructed world* of what a hipster originally meant, as shown at the top of McCracken's diagram. Over time the hipster became associated with different ideas including its current incarnation which includes a concern with ethical sourcing of goods, creative fashion practices, and alternative culture that is associated with less well-known bands (not jazz) and the arts. This has occurred through the advertising and fashion system. The hipster of the twenty-first century is culturally constructed by groups of people who have engaged with the cultural construction over time. The rituals of McCracken's transfer of meaning framework are well illustrated by hipsters who are associated with certain types of products, including grooming rituals and even divestment rituals. A stereotypical British hipster male might wear thick-rimmed glasses, have hair cut short on the sides but slicked back on top, and sport a carefully groomed beard (Figure 9.5).

Figure 9.5   A stereotypical British male hipster

The cultural system

A cultural system is comprised of three main elements, which together help to understand the culture: ecology, social structure, and ideology. Ecology refers to the physical geography of a place, and how culture evolves and adapts to suit that environment. In warm climates, people wear light clothes, much of their social life is outdoors, and air conditioning in buildings is common. Contrast this with colder climates, where warm clothes and jackets are worn, leisure activities are more indoor-based, and heating in buildings is important. Motorbikes in the USA have to be made tougher and more durable than those for sale in Japan, as the typical motorbike rider in the USA will want to cross rough terrain while in Japan they are more likely to be used for urban travel. Natural resources shape

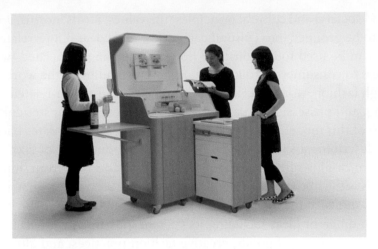

Figure 9.6   Japanese mobile compact kitchen
Source: Image courtesy of Toshihiko Suzuki and Atelier Opa (http://www.atelier-opa.com/).

cultural practices, but so too does technological advancement. Japan is a population-dense country, where domestic space is scarce. Space-saving devices, such as the shopping bag that unfolds to produce an ironing board and the mobile compact kitchen (Figure 9.6), are useful and popular among Japanese consumers.

Social structure tells us about the way that orderly social life is maintained in a culture. This is often seen in the representation of stereotypical gender roles in advertising, which reinforce the dominant social structure of domestic life. Historically women have been shown engaged efficiently in the household tasks, while men are removed from this environment or only marginally engaged with it. But as more women work outside the home and more men work part time (Poole, 2014) and engage in social media and blogs (e.g. http://dadbloguk.com or http://dadwhoblogs.co.uk), it has been found that men resent being marginalized in the domestic sphere (Coskuner-Balli and Thomson, 2013). Increasingly, advertisers are looking to present men and fathers as positive domestic role models (see Figure 9.7).

The final aspect of the cultural system relates to **ideology**, which reflects *the mental characteristics of a people*, building on the assumption that members of a society possess the same world view, ethos, ideas, and principles. Hip-hop music is popular in Brazil, and is used by young marginalized people living in the favelas (slums) to comment on and try to change their lives and Brazilian society as a whole (Pardue, 2005). More than acting as a form of musical expression, hip-hop music is an important way for young Brazilian men and women to express their ideology of social consciousness, truth-telling, and transformation. In some cases ideology can be played out through brands that have meaning to that culture. In countries around the world Coca-Cola has become ubiquitous, so when a country develops its own cola brand, such as Turka Cola in Turkey, this represents a sense of achievement through their ability to compete with a global superpower. It says 'We have arrived' (Gobé, 2007). Turka Cola is now sold in many countries, including Cuba and France,

Figure 9.7   A Sainsbury's campaign showing a father baking with his child
Source: Image supplied by The Advertising Archives.

and its advertising gently pokes fun at its global ambitions and US competitor by using US star Chevy Chase who, on drinking Turka Cola, starts displaying Turkish characteristics.

Classification of cultures

Core societal values

We know that cultures emerge and form in relation to core societal values, which in turn shape behaviour and practices. While many authors have described the various dimensions of culture, one of the main ways that different cultures are discussed is in terms of their emphasis on collectivism versus individualism (Triandis, 1995). Although this is quite a blunt instrument for categorizing cultures, it does provide some insights into the key concerns and values that influence people's behaviour in different cultures. Collectivist cultures, such as those of Portugal, Indonesia, Venezuela, and Japan (de Mooij and Hofstede, 2002; Bu et al., 2013), are characterized by a focus on collective well-being, and in these cultures people tend to prioritize the group's goals over personal goals. The 2009 Converse Japan advertising campaign recognizes the collectivistic influences in its society. The advertisement shows Japanese schoolgirls and schoolboys, all in identical school uniform, wearing various different Converse styles and coloured shoes. The advertisements are striking, as they contrast the traditional Japanese school uniforms with the colourful Converse shoes and thus show the schoolchildren expressing their individuality while retaining a strong sense of social connection to others.

In more individualistic cultures, such as the USA, UK, and Australia, people's behaviour is mainly determined by personal goals, which may overlap with collective goals. In South Australia container deposit legislation allows people to collect a deposit for each drinks container they return to a recycling depot. This incentive encourages people to recycle at the individual level, but also leads to a wider societal and community benefit associated with greater levels of recycling behaviour and reduced littering.

Although it is helpful to see broad cultural differences, it would be wrong to assume that everyone in a certain culture is a collectivist or an individualist—rather, these provide a general way of understanding how society is shaped within a culture. This, in turn, is helpful to marketers in understanding the best way to communicate their brand message to each different culture. For example in Chinese Tier One cities, rather than sticking to accepted roles regarding suitable types of car for up-and-coming executives (usually a Western sedan style) there is a trend to show individualism, for example by buying SUVs which would have traditionally been seen as inappropriate (Morgan, 2015).

Dimensions of cultural values

Core societal values are important in understanding cultures and underpin the various dimensions of culture that help us understand how different people act and behave around the world. One of the most famous categorizations is the Dutch consumer behaviour researcher Geert Hofstede's dimensions of culture, which were developed from a work-based study of IBM employees (Hofstede, 1984, 2001). Hofstede identified the main dimensions of culture as individualism, masculinity, power distance, uncertainty avoidance, and long-term orientation. Although they have been criticized over the years (these criticisms will be discussed in the next section), these dimensions have been widely used. This approach does provide some useful insights for understanding consumption in different cultures. We will now look at each of Hofstede's dimensions.

Individualism *refers to the ways in which individual goals are balanced against collective or group goals, with individualistic cultures prioritizing the individual's goals over those of the collective (and vice versa).* This dimension refers to the strength of the ties people have with others within the community, with high individualism characterized by a lack of interpersonal connection and little sharing of responsibility, whereas low individualism is applicable in cultures where there is strong group cohesion. The German advertisement for Coca Cola Light emphasizes individuality in its strapline 'Nur du, bist du', which translates as 'Only you are you'. According to Hofstede's framework, Germany is a highly individualistic culture, and this advertisement emphasizes the way that the drink resonates with and supports the maintenance of this particular dimension of German culture.

Masculinity *refers to motives that are classified as either achievement-oriented, with an emphasis on heroism, assertiveness, and material reward (labelled masculine in Hofstede's terms), or more consensus-oriented, where the emphasis is on cooperation, modesty, caring, and quality of life (labelled feminine in Hofstede's terms).* Sweden is often considered to be a feminine culture (de Mooij and Hofstede, 2002) where quality of life, caring, and cooperation are valued. A more masculine culture is one such as Slovakia (Sidle, 2009), and the digital campaign for Miele S8 vacuum cleaner provides an illustration of this (Figure 9.8). The agency behind the campaign used a billboard to turn a well-known tunnel in Slovakia into a vacuum cleaner pipe which sucked

Figure 9.8   The Miele tunnel billboard

Source: Image printed and supplied with kind permission of Mayer/McCann Erickson, Slovakia, and Miele.

up everything—including cars and trucks going through the tunnel. The strong and powerful imagery of the advertisement suited this cultural context.

Power distance (PD) *refers to how people in a culture view power relationships and the degree to which they accept superior and subordinate relationships.* Cultures with high PD tend towards a hierarchical structure, with an unequal distribution of power. In low PD cultures a flatter structure of relations exists, with power shared and well dispersed. Malaysia is considered to score highly on the PD dimension (de Mooij and Hofstede, 2002), implying a hierarchical structure, whereas Austria, Israel, and Denmark have low PD scores (Aguinis et al., 2012), suggesting a flatter structure.

Uncertainty avoidance (UA) *relates to how a cultural group feels about ambiguity, and the extent to which the members of the culture avoid uncertainity (and accordingly avoid risk), or embrace risk (and uncertainty).* It refers to the degree of anxiety members of a society feel when in uncertain or unknown situations. High UA cultures avoid ambiguous situations whenever possible, whereas low UA cultures enjoy novel events and value differences. Austria is a culture that scores reasonably highly on the UA scale, suggesting that Austrians tend to avoid ambiguity and reduce risks by relying on rules, laws, and regulations. China, on the other hand, is a country that scores relatively low on the UA dimension, implying that it is a culture that enjoys novelty and difference, as well as ambiguity (Aguinis et al., 2012).

Long-term orientation (LTO) *reflects the degree of focus on the future the society has which relates to the time orientation of the culture and its perspectives on time and tradition.* Cultures with a long-term orientation tend to display characteristics associated with perseverance. These cultures are likely to save and invest, and exhibit thriftiness and persistence in achieving results in the long term. In contrast, shorter-term cultures tend not to save so much for the future, but instead focus on achieving quick results. China is a country with a long-term orientation, and the China Construction Bank (Asia) ran a successful campaign in 2008 aimed at reinforcing the shared values that parents have for their children about the importance of education and building a successful career and future. The company adopted a multi-platform approach, including sponsorship of *Are You Smarter Than a 5th Grader?*, a family TV programme in the USA, in which children pitch their intelligence and wit against adults. Association with the programme made sense for the company. The show emphasized the importance of education and being smart for long-term gains, and this echoes the China Construction Bank's underpinning brand values. Of course, while some marketers want to capitalize on the particular cultural identities of countries, others can see an opportunity for undermining cultural characteristics, as was the case with the Norwegian soft drink Solo described in Consumer Insight 9.1.

CONSUMER INSIGHT 9.1

How to be un-Norwegian

In their book *Cultural Strategy*, Holt and Cameron (2012) question cultural orthodoxy by stating that cultural innovations can undermine the status quo, just as changes in society create demand for new and different cultural innovations. This is what Solo, a soft drink from Norway, did through a combination of traditional and social media. Above all, the communications strategy built upon a cultural conundrum—Norwegians are both proud and frustrated by their modesty as a nation.

Solo is a soft drink, but for too long it was modest in its ambitions. Although it was drunk by Norwegians on special occasions, it had been losing market share to global brands such as Fanta. The strategy to rebuild the brand was constructed around the idea of making Norwegians proud of Solo by imbuing it with the same confidence as a global brand. Solo was aware that young people's perception was very important in the choice of soft drinks, both for themselves and in the family context, and they wanted to build an identity sympathetic to the young and also use them as a channel to talk to one another about Solo. Solo decided that its route to getting young people's attention was to challenge modesty and do something 'un-Norwegian' by sticking its neck out and advertising in the USA. The campaign began with a billboard on Sunset Boulevard in Los Angeles using lines such as 'Shocking but true—the world's best soft drink is yellow and Norwegian'. To enlist engagement, Norwegians were then able to upload their own billboards onto video screens on Sunset Boulevard with endorsements on Twitter from US celebrities such as Paris Hilton and Lindsay Lohan. This was followed by a competition where winners were able to get their pictures on a digital billboard with the line 'A Norwegian soft drink with an American Dream'. The line below the Solo brand name was always 'Soon to be world famous—all modesty forgotten!'. The brand was not really trying to become world famous; what it wanted was to be noticed by Norwegians. Above all, the idea of a Norwegian brand acting in an un-Norwegian way appears to have resonated with young people, who in turn shared their responses on Facebook and other social media—a true cultural innovation. By advertising in the USA Solo was not concerned about marketing to the USA, as the brand could not actually be bought there. It wanted its consumers at home to realize that it had big ambitions. Following this, Solo undertook an initiative with DHL allowing Norwegians to send a bottle of Solo to anyone in the world. Recipients sent photos of themselves with Solo from 130 countries using Facebook and other online initiatives.

The campaign was noticed by 80 per cent of the target group and sales increased by over 7 per cent.

Questions

1. If Norwegians are modest, what other national cultural stereotypes are you familiar with? Are they useful for marketing?

2. Solo used a national stereotype as the basis for their cultural innovation. What other characteristics might be used (e.g. gender, age, occupation) and how?

Sources: Ehrlich (2012); Holt and Cameron (2012); Larsen (2012).

 Access the online resources and follow the web links to learn more about Solo.

Critiques of Hofstede

It is important to note that much criticism has been levelled at Hofstede's work (Baskerville, 2003; Fang, 2010; McSweeney, 2016) (see Research Insight 9.2). This criticism includes issues around measurement and sampling. The original study was based on one organization only, it was undertaken at a time of political instability which may have influenced the dimensions, and there was a lack of inclusion of people from socialist and less affluent countries in the sample. Hofstede's assumptions about culture have also been criticized. For example, the categorization assumes that national identity translates to cultural identity, and therefore ignores the variations within a culture/cultural group.

RESEARCH INSIGHT 9.2

McSweeney, B. (2016), 'Collective cultural mind programming: escaping from the cage' *Journal of Organizational Change Management*, 29, 1, 68–80.

The methodological approach of this study is to draw on research from multiple disciplines to critique the way that management disciplines use the ideas of national culture (as advanced by Hofstede and others). The paper argues that this approach to national culture is very limited, confining analysis of culture to misleading explanations of how organizations and individuals act, and argues that other approaches are needed.

 Access the online resources to read the abstract and access the full paper.

Culture norms and rules for behaviour

Within any culture there are norms of behaviour which refer to the accepted main ways of behaving. These norms are shaped by the underpinning values or principles of a culture. Cultural norms are rule-bound, and in any culture there tends to be a fairly complex set of rules for behaviour. These norms can be either enacted (explicitly decided on) or crescive (meaning embedded in the culture). Crescive norms are often not formally noted—rather, learning about the culture takes place through experiences and interactions within that culture. Crescive norms can be further broken down into customs, mores, and conventions.

Customs *are the norms of behaviour that have been passed from generation to generation.* These serve to control basic behaviour within a culture, around the core facets of life. For example, in Japan it is the custom to always take your shoes off before entering someone's home. **Mores** *are particular forms of custom and have a strong moral overtone.* Mores often involve a taboo or forbidden behaviour, and violation of mores is met with strong censure from other members of a society. For example, some cultures strongly condemn people sleeping together before they are married. **Conventions** *are also a specific form of custom, and relate to the norms for the conduct of everyday life.* These are often subtle and not always easy for people outside a culture to learn. For example, they may include conventions around how to behave and dress at a dinner party, or what time to arrive. While in some parts of the world arriving late might be frowned upon, in many Latin cultures it is not. If you are invited to dinner in Chile for 20:00, you would not be expected to arrive before 20:15 or even 20:30. This knowledge of cultural norms is important for marketers, especially in terms of showing consumers how products might fit into their consumption patterns.

Making sense of culture: the role of myths and rituals

In addition to the norms of a culture, it is important for cultures to have stories and practices which help provide a collective sense of its values and what is important to the culture. Two key aspects of this are myths and rituals.

A **myth** *is a story that contains symbolic elements that express shared emotions and ideals of a culture.* Myths serve the function of emphasizing how things in a culture are interconnected; they maintain social order by authorizing a social code. According to Woodside et al. (2008: 98), 'a myth is a traditional story about heroes or supernatural beings', and it often features a conflict between two opposing forces.

Myths provide psychological models for individual behaviour and identity. Effectively, these stories present cultural ideals and direction, and can provide consumers with guidelines about their world (see Consumer Insight 9.2).

CONSUMER INSIGHT 9.2

Consumer archetypes and myths

Stories are very powerful in people's lives as a way of communicating, and marketing companies strive to create brand myths, or stories, in order to produce powerful emotional connections with consumers. Sometimes marketers use the idea of myth creation to build or invent a myth around their brand. An interesting example is found in the clothing brand Jack Wills. According to the company's founders:

> Our registered trademark 'Fabulously British' defines our inspiration: British heritage, style and culture. We interpret these traditional starting points in our contemporary way, playing off the tensions that are created between old and new, formal and casual. This eccentric, dandyish British style is the essence of our Fabulously British concept, and is reflected across our brand: from our product and store design to our graphical output and events.

> (www.jackwills.com).

The company attempts to create an emotional connection with consumers, portraying itself as a heritage brand with a long history (named after the grandfather of one of the founders), with a key role to play in a particular form of British culture.

Questions

1. Think of some archetypes that you are familiar with and consider how they are reflected commercially. You might start by considering how they are used in advertising and retailing, as well as in digital marketing contexts.

2. Access the Online Resource Centre and follow the web link to Entreproducer to find out more about creating audience archetypes. For a product category of your choice, think about how you might develop a social media campaign based around one central archetype (e.g. the hero, the seductress, the friend/buddy).

Sources: Vernon (2010); Clark (2012); www.jackwills.com

 Access the online resources and follow the web links to learn more about Jack Wills, Entreproducer, and other organizations that make use of archetypes and myths.

Myths are often used in a nostalgic way in advertising, encouraging consumers to look back in time and remember the 'good old days' (often involving an element of re-imagining the past). Classic examples of this include the Ridley Scott advertisement for Hovis bread with the imagery of a boy cycling over cobbled streets to deliver bread, the voice-over of an old man yearning for the past, a brass band playing, and the overall implication of a more wholesome, better life. This is a very British advertisement, picking up on specific cultural cues, which would not translate to other cultures. Myths as traditions can readily be translated into a lifestyle concept when they become connected with specific commodities as the Consumer Insight 9.3 on Danish idea of *hygge* shows.

CONSUMER INSIGHT 9.3

Hygge: myth or reality?

Sometimes an aspect of a country's culture can become so influential that it almost develops into a commodity. This has been the case with the concept of Danish *hygge*. But how much of *hygge* is myth and how much reality? *Hygge* has been described as a feeling of cosy contentment, but its influence and the desire for *hygge* has become a fashion and lifestyle phenomenon. So in marketing terms at least it is definitely reality.

In 2016 Denmark was ranked first in the *World Happiness Report* (Helliwell et al., 2016) which suggests that the Danish lifestyle is one that others might want to emulate. While some might think of living in Denmark as a combination of cold and dark for a large part of the year, the Danish Tourist Board has made sure that the world gets to know about the positive side of Danish life through the concept of *hygge*, which includes cosy social gatherings in front of a roaring fire or a snowy day spent at a Christmas market (Figure 9.9). Scandinavian design has always been popular with fashion-forward cosmopolitans, and now the Danes are adding to this but not so much with clean lines and muted colours but with something altogether warmer. Candles and bedsocks and all things cosy feature in the *hygge* way of life.

Figure 9.9   Bedsocks and a roaring fire: part of the concept of Danish *hygge*

Possibly people want to recreate the sense of cosiness that the term suggests; there have been numerous books published recently about *hygge* and how to create it in the non-Danish world. Indeed, trying to recreate a sense of *hygge* seems to have become more to do with consumption than anything else. As one commentator says:

> I have seen *hygge* used to sell cashmere cardigans, wine, wallpaper, vegan shepherd's pie, sewing patterns, a skincare range, teeny-tiny festive harnesses for dachshunds, yoga retreats and a holiday in a 'shepherd's hut' in Kent.

(Higgins, 2016)

But while some sing the praises of *hygge*, others are more sceptical, suggesting that this sense of cosiness is not always extended to outsiders in Denmark, possibly because you need to know the rules of *hygge* which seem to include not talking about politics or religion. So while some may long for a bit more cosiness in their lives, for others the positive picture of a warm Danish lifestyle is more myth than reality.

Questions

1. Why do you think cosiness is so attractive?

2. What aspects of your culture do you think have been commodified?

3. In your view how do the commodified versions match your experience?

4. Consider an aspect of your culture. What are the good things about it and what are not so good? In your experience how do outsiders deal with it?

5. Do you think that some aspects of a culture are developed to keep outsiders at a distance? Why might that be?

Sources: Booth (2016); Buerger (2016); Higgins (2016); Helliwell et al. (2016); Thomson (2016); visit-denmark.co.uk

 Access the online resources and follow the web links to learn more.

Rituals are very important in the transfer of meaning within cultures. The term **ritual** *refers to a symbolic and expressive activity, often comprising multiple behaviours which occur in a fixed sequence and are repeated over time* (Rook, 1985). There are many rituals in our lives; some can be viewed as sacred and relating to broad cultural or religious values (e.g. the ritual of removing shoes before entering a mosque), but others are considered more mundane, such as putting out one's clothes ready for work the following day. Within marketing, rituals have been applied to understand consumption, and six main types of ritual have been identified.

The main types of consumer ritual

Grooming rituals *are those private behaviours that consumers undertake to aid the transition from private to public self (and back again).* Rituals associated with getting ready for a night out (showering, putting on make-up, choosing outfit) prepare the consumer as they move from their private space to a more public and social space.

Possession rituals *are the rituals associated with transforming mass-produced products from the marketplace into more personal products for the home or workplace.* For example, home purification, which involves burning a sage smudge stick to 'cleanse and remove the residual or negative energy left behind by the previous occupants', is a ritual favoured by New Age practitioners (Allegheny, 2010). This product enables the new homeowners to make the house spiritually theirs.

Gift-giving rituals *are the rituals surrounding giving presents to others.* These rituals may be extensive, including obtaining/finding the gift, giving the gift, receiving the gift, and gift reciprocation. While gifts have an economic value, they also have a symbolic value which emphasizes the social connections between people. Sanrio, owner of the Hello Kitty brand, lists its principal business as the 'sale of social communication gifts'. Japanese people have a deep gift-giving tradition, and Hello Kitty is a brand that plays on this cultural practice.

According to the Sanrio Company website 'Giving someone a cute Hello Kitty letter set doesn't just say "let's stay in touch"—it gives them a means to do so'. Figure 9.10 shows a range of Hello Kitty products.

Self-gifts *are a specific example of gift giving, where consumers purchase self-gifts as a way of regulating their behaviour.* We may buy a gift as a treat or a reward for some success, but also as a way to cheer ourselves up if we are having a bad day. Companies often encourage self-gifting; for example, an advertisement for the fashion company J. Crew, suggested 'Before you lavish your loved ones with gift upon gift this holiday season, take the time to treat yourself …'.

Holiday rituals *are the rituals associated with both tourism holidays and culturally bound holiday seasons* (such as Christmas, Easter, and Eid). Holidays are important rituals, and represent consumers suspending their everyday lives and performing particular ritualistic behaviours. Many of the main film companies schedule their major film releases to coincide with the holiday season (Easter, Summer, Christmas), tapping into family rituals around holidays and cinema-going.

Rites of passage rituals *are those rituals that mark a change in a person's social status.* Examples of such changes include a child's first day at school, getting married, becoming a parent, and even getting divorced. In the USA, the baby shower party is a way of marking the beginning of a new chapter in people's lives, i.e. becoming a parent, and baby showers are also becoming popular in other cultures.

Elements of the ritual

According to Rook (1985) there are a number of elements that are common to rituals. As with other aspects of culture, these are not formally noted down, but are learned through immersion in the culture. First there are **ritual artefacts**, *which are the objects and products that accompany or are consumed in a ritual setting.* These artefacts often communicate specific symbolic messages understood by ritual participants. There is also a **ritual script** which *guides the use of the ritual artefact—which artefacts to use, by whom, the sequence of use, and the types of comment that accompany the ritual.* **Ritual performance roles** *are the roles occupied by people involved in the ritual as they perform according to the script.* Finally, there is a **ritual audience**, *who are the people who witness or are involved in the ritual in some way* beyond those involved in the particular performance roles.

Tea drinking is a ritual which can be analysed to reveal these elements. The ritual artefacts include the tea, the teapot, the milk, the crockery, and the cakes, but also the location or venue (e.g. Fortnum and Mason, London, or the Victoria Room, Sydney) (see Figure 9.11). The script could include aspects such as the sequence of service within the tearoom, what additions are appropriate (milk, lemon, honey, sugar), and when it is appropriate to pour milk. In terms of performance roles, there will be roles around service within the tearoom, who pours the tea, and the appreciative recipient of the tea. Finally, the audience (other than those directly involved) may refer to other customers in the tearoom, as well as those whom you talk to about the tea (word of mouth). When you compare tea drinking around the world it can be seen that the elements may differ. Each culture has its own rituals, and these can be a very important aspect of that particular culture.

SANRIO / CHARACTERS LOGO

Figure 9.10 Hello Kitty products and logo showing the range of characters

Source: Images courtesy of Sanrio.

Figure 9.11 Afternoon tea in The Victoria Room, Sydney
Source: Image courtesy of The Victoria Room, Sydney.

Rites of passage

Rites of passage *are a specific type of ritual that marks a change in a person's social status.* These rites can relate to changes that are a natural aspect of the consumer's life course, for example moving from the world of the child to the world of the adult (such as becoming a teenager, moving out of the family home), but also to changes in people's lives which are more individual and specific in nature (e.g. being made redundant or facing a serious illness). However, in contemporary consumer society the markers of this transition (from child to adult) are not always obvious or clear-cut, as explored in Research Insight 9.3.

RESEARCH INSIGHT 9.3

Jaimangal-Jones, D., Pritchard, A., and Morgan, N. (2010), 'Going the distance: locating journey, liminality and rites of passage in dance music experiences', *Leisure Studies*, 29, 3, 253–68.

Jaimangal-Jones, himself a DJ, and his co-authors studied four major dance music festivals over four years using participant observation and focus groups to understand how people experienced these events. They found that, for many, the journey to the festivals and the experience of these unfamiliar places for the first time acted as a rite of passage that was socially constructed as a pilgrimage or source of spiritual fulfilment. Engagement with the rite of passage includes certain behaviours such as dressing up in extravagant, day-glo, and often revealing clothes.

 Access the online resources to read the abstract and access the full paper.

Since rites of passage relate to times of change, it is clear that people go through many changes over their life course, and marketing has a role to play in providing consumers with the goods and services they need as they move through these stages from engagement rings to retirement homes.

Culture and communication

It is important to understand culture in terms of giving meaning to objects, activities, and practices. Culture plays an important role in terms of the content and tone of advertising and marketing messages, and an understanding of the various aspects of culture informs communications (see Consumer Insight 9.4).

Apart from understanding cultural values and beliefs, it is important to appreciate the various customs and norms influencing the ways that people behave, which may impact on how they incorporate consumption into their daily lives. The Philips Augmented Reality Mugs Campaign worked in that context as a response to the cultural norms around male grooming.

In addition, an important aspect of understanding culture's impact on consumption lies with the idea of sacred and profane consumption, and how this exists in various cultural settings.

CONSUMER INSIGHT 9.4

Philips in Taiwan

The advertising campaign for Philips grooming products in Taiwan is a good illustration of a culturally informed campaign. Taiwanese men prefer a clean-shaven look, and the challenge for Philips was to interest them in facial hair and grooming in order to increase sales of shaving products. Philips created a campaign around Augmented Reality Mugs, clear glass mugs with facial hair stickers. The mugs were presented at selected salons in Taiwan, and drinking from one gave the consumer an indication of how he might look with facial hair (as shown in Figure 9.12). Interested customers were offered a coupon for 50 per cent off Philips' grooming kits.

Questions

Can you think of any other contexts where a culturally informed campaign has been used, or would be useful in your culture?

1. Think of some specific cultural consumption contexts where this type of approach might be suitable?

Sources: Young (2012); Riley-Adams (2012).

 Access the online resources and follow the web links to learn more about this Philips, Taiwan campaign.

Figure 9.12 Stills from the Augmented Reality Mugs Campaign
Source: Image courtesy of Philips, Taiwan.

Sacred and profane consumption

In the consumer context, **sacred consumption** *is used to refer to objects and events that are 'set apart' from normal activities, and are treated with some degree of respect or awe*. In contrast, **profane consumption** *is the term used to capture those consumer objects and events that do not share the 'specialness' of sacred objects*. In the key article on sacred and profane consumption by Belk et al. (1989), the authors describe the properties of the sacred aspects inherent in consumer behaviour and the processes by which consumers sacralize and de-sacralize dimensions of the experience described.

Sacred items are not necessarily associated with religion, but most religious items tend to be regarded as sacred. Sacred consumption can be applied to places, people, and events. The Vatican in Rome holds special religious significance for many Catholics around the world. The site of the Holy Thorn Tree on Wearyall Hill in Glastonbury, Somerset, is regarded as one of Britain's most important symbols of Christendom, and attracts visitors and pilgrims as a result. The tourism industry builds on the idea of creating sacred places in order to connect with tourists and to elevate holiday destinations to sacred and special places in consumers' minds. For example, the idyllic remote holiday island, a 'taste of paradise', is sold in this way as a special place that is set apart from the pressures of everyday life, representing a form of escape for consumers.

People can also have sacred status, mainly when they are idolized and set apart from others. This idea is easily applicable to religious figures (such as Mother Theresa or Ghandi), but it can also be applied to individuals who have achieved sacred status for other reasons, such as musical or sporting prowess. Elvis Presley is sacred in the eyes of his fans, many of whom go on a pilgrimage to his home Graceland (which is now a museum) to honour his memory. In their study of distance runners and hip-hop culture Chalmers and Arthur (2008) found that shoes held a sacred status. In running brands the status changed as technical functionality developed, but in hip-hop culture Nike Airforce 1 and Adidas superstars were defined by their symbolic qualities, giving them a more permanent sacredness.

Events such as football matches can also take on sacred status. Fans travel long distances to support their teams, and they often sing songs and chants particular to their team (or it can be their national anthem if it is an international game). The singing of 'You'll Never Walk Alone' by Liverpool FC fans at the beginning and end of every match is highly ritualistic. Team colours are obviously symbolic. Particular players can have iconic significance for fans, receiving extra applause if they come on as a substitute, and some, such as David Beckham, maintain global cult status long after their football playing days are over. The pitch itself can also be a sacred space, with fans going to stadiums when they close and digging up a piece of the pitch.

Appreciating the difference and symbolism associated with profane and sacred consumption is especially important from a marketing perspective in terms of ensuring that a company gets things right when they enter a market (see Research Insight 9.4). If an organization breaks the conventional norms and values in some way, it is important that they have a keen awareness and understanding of this and therefore what impact it might have on consumers' reactions to their communications. To begin with, though, consumers have to engage with the commercial world, and language can have a major impact on how different cultures are able to engage.

RESEARCH INSIGHT 9.4

Jafari, A. and Suerdem, A. (2012), 'The sacred and the profane in Islamic consumption', *Advances in Consumer Research*, 39, 1, 427–9.

The authors challenge the portrayal of Islam as a rigid ideological system and demonstrate that in their everyday life consumption activities (the profane), Muslims constantly (re)interpret religious guidelines of Islam (the sacred) as cultural codes rather than rigid rules. They show how Muslims interpret the sacred Islamic guidelines in multiple ways to shape their everyday consumption practices.

 Access the online resources to read the abstract and access the full paper.

Sacralization and objectification

Attaching sacred meaning to profane consumption is often a challenge for marketers, but this is an important objective in terms of trying to imbue products and brands with distinctiveness and 'specialness' in the consumer's eyes. As sacralization is about giving special status to objects, marketing companies attempt to do this through the use of memorabilia associated with special places (e.g. a key ring from Graceland; a festival or concert T-shirt). This process is known as **objectification** *whereby sacred qualities are attributed to mundane items.* **Contamination** *is when objects associated with sacred events or people become sacred in their own right (e.g. items belonging to famous people).*

An associated process is that of **desacralization**, *which is when a sacred item or symbol is removed from its special place.* This can be seen in instances where an iconic object is mass produced—for example, souvenir reproductions of the Eiffel Tower or the use of religious symbols in mainstream jewellery. D&G attempted to make rosary beads a mainstream fashion item by putting models on catwalks wearing rosary beads as necklaces. This caused uproar and upset among Catholics and the Catholic media who considered it sacrilegious (*Courier Mail*, 2010). Similarly, the Christian cross has been used in mainstream fashion with a variety of designs available on the market, often bejewelled (Figure 9.13).

Figure 9.13   A man wearing rosary beads as a fashion item
Source: © iStock.com/korionov.

In this situation, the special aspect of the iconic object (the Christian cross) is eliminated, turning the objects into inauthentic commodities (no longer a prayer object, but now a fashion necklace). The central premise of desacralization is that objects and activities can move from one sphere to another, that some things that were formerly regarded as sacred have moved into the realm of the profane, and that some everyday phenomena are now regarded as sacred. Events can also undergo such a transformation from sacred to more profane (e.g. the commercialization of Christmas, the touristic exploitation of the sinking of the Titanic), although this is not without danger of criticism since this transformation is against the central values and beliefs of many people within a culture, and can never be accepted.

Subcultures

Within any culture, there exist subcultures (sometimes referred to as microcultures) which are important to marketing since these often capture meaningful links and connections between groups in society. Subcultures share similar values and tastes, and in many ways exhibit the same qualities and characteristics of a culture. The main distinction is that they are smaller in size. **Subcultures** can be defined in *terms of shared demographic characteristics (e.g. age, regionality, ethnicity) or in terms of shared consumption interests.*

In marketing, the term subculture is widely used to refer to any subgroup of consumption, although early usage implied some kind of subversive activity against mainstream society. Punks in the UK in the 1970s were concerned with individual freedom and being anti-establishment, and used their clothes, music, and behaviour to demonstrate their alternative views.

Subcultures may share demographic characteristics (e.g. in terms of age, race, gender, class), but there is usually a consumption dimension to membership in terms of the adoption of various symbols in the consumer world to signify membership of the group, identifiable ways of dressing (at least to the subcultural group), and shared interests and music styles. Both demographic characteristics and shared consumption interests can be useful for marketers when examining subcultures (see Research Insight 9.5).

RESEARCH INSIGHT 9.5

Hebdige, D. (1979), *Subculture: the meaning of style*, London: Methuen.

Dick Hebdige's 1979 book *Subculture: the meaning of style* provides a deep understanding of subcultures from a sociological and cultural studies perspective. In this book, Hebdige describes and discusses Britain's post-war youth subculture styles (such as Teddy boys, mods, and punks) as symbolic forms of resistance, with these groups setting themselves apart from the mainstream in terms of values, politics, and behaviour.

 Access the online resources to find out more about this book.

Subcultures based on demographic characteristics

A number of criteria can be used to look at subcultures of society defined by demographic characteristics. Here we look at subcultures based on age, sex roles, region, ethnicity, and religion.

Age-based subcultures

Age is often used by marketers to define market segments, on the premise that people of a similar age share similar sets of experiences and can be engaged in a meaningful way through shared cultural reference points. There are many examples of age-based subcultures that are used in marketing (see Table 9.1 for some illustrations). Age-based subcultures can refer to groups of consumers at key stages in their life course (e.g. tweens, teenagers, pensioners). The other use of age-based subcultures is with reference to generationally based subcultures, groups of people who were born at certain key points in history (e.g. Baby Boomers, Generation X, and Millennials), and the marketing interest is in this group of people as they move through the life course.

Tweens		
Definition		
Usually 8–12 years, although there is a slight variation in definitions (e.g. Mintel (2011) defines this group as aged between 10 and 12).		
Main points of relevance		
• Consumers in training, first steps into independence in marketplace interactions.		
• A key characteristic of this group, making them attractive to marketers, is that they are beginning to make independent purchases. Tweenage girls tend to develop a keen interest in pop music, and are more likely than tweenage boys to listen to music and have music systems in their bedroom. Tweens are like mini-teenagers, starting to exhibit similar emotional and symbolic aspects of purchasing and consumption. For an interesting application of marketing to this group, see Consumer Insight 9.5.		

Teens		
Definition		
Teens is the term used to refer to all youths in the 13–18 age group, although this is a wide-ranging age group, with the needs of young teens being different from those of older teens.		
Main points of relevance		
• In commercial terms, teenagers represent a large and important market, with estimates suggesting that the US market is worth around $200 billion (Brafton, 2010). Teens are difficult for marketers to reach, since often just as marketers have worked out how to engage with young people using the latest communications tools, teenagers have moved on to something new (Roberts and Scott, 2009).		
• Teens are tech-savvy (often called digital natives), are heavy users of social media, and like interactive content. Many companies targeting this market include strong interactive elements to their campaigns.		
• Research into smartphone usage by teens shows that the rise in the number of low-priced Android-based phones on the market and the availability of free apps is popular among teens (Shields, 2011).		

Generation X		
Definition		
Varies as being born somewhere between 1962 and 1985.		
Main points of relevance		
• Grew up under largely Conservative governments at a time of economic recession. Douglas Coupland's novel *Generation X,* about the lifestyles of young adults during the late 1980s, popularized the use of this term.		
• Although their needs are likely to be diverse and typical of anyone at this stage of life, it seems that this cohort are more pessimistic about their financial future, are used to cheap imports, are suspicious of marketing, and want straightforward talk and evidence to support claims.		

Generation Y or Millennials		
Definition		
Born between 1980 and 2000		
Main points of relevance		
• Both in the West, often as children of Baby Boomers (also known as the Me generation), and in China (as a result of the one-child policy). Tend to have been brought up to be high in confidence and self-involved.		
• High rates of materialism and technology addiction. They are the generation that record everything through social media.		
• They have less civil engagement and involvement in politics than previous generations.		

Table 9.1   Key age-based subcultures relevant for marketing

Baby Boomers
Definition   Those born between 1945 and 1964, sometimes regarded as Baby Boomer Cohort 1 (1946–1955) and Cohort 2 (1956–1964).
Main points of relevance   • Baby boomers are those people born after the Second World War at a time marked by optimism and economic security. This group of people were the original 'teenagers', coming of age during the 1960s.   • They have been the source and power behind many recent economic changes, but also played a key part in major social and cultural changes in the second half of the twentieth century.   • Because of its sheer size, this is a substantial and important market, with high levels of savings and disposable income available.

Table 9.1   *(Continued)*

CONSUMER INSIGHT 9.5

Age compression and the tweenager

Increasingly, age compression is being seen in the toys and activities of children. This means that younger children are becoming interested in toys and products that in the past would have been targeted at an older age. One result of this is the development of a new subcultural age category, the tweenager, which refers to children in the pre-teen age group. While various definitions exist, the general view is that this term applies to children aged 8–12 (Clarke, 2003), clearly emphasizing their pre-teen status. Products for the tweenager now abound. In the UK, the toy store Hamleys opened a hair and nail bar in 2009, which according to the company is the first dedicated hair salon for children. Hamleys says it is particularly popular with 7–8-year-old girls, suggesting even more age compression.

In 2010, the singer Mariah Carey launched a new fragrance called Lollipop Bling. Produced in collaboration with Elizabeth Arden and Bazooka Candy Brands, the brand is inspired by Carey's song *Candy Bling* and the story of her engagement ring being presented inside a lollipop package. The fragrance and its packaging are inspired by all things confectionery: sweet smelling, brightly packaged, and with a free gift of Ring Pop, an edible confectionery ring. The supporting website (http://www.lollipopbling.com/) plays the song on a continuous loop, and encourages extended consumer interactions through a game, a messaging service (Candy Gram), and news about future products (Gotta Have It! and Latest Goodies). This is a case of three major companies combining forces to target this age group very effectively.

Questions

1. Can you think of any ethical issues raised by this case?

2. What other product categories do you think are likely to be targeted to tweenagers?

3. Are there any lessons in this approach that can be used in social marketing campaigns aimed at this age group, say to encourage exercise or healthy eating?

Sources: Clarke (2003); Hawks (2010); *Marketing Week* (2010); Tansel (2010).

 Access the online resources and follow the web links to learn more about Lollipop Bling and other tweenage products.

However, marketers need to be careful about assuming that generations are comparable across national and cultural boundaries. In China, Japan, and South Korea there have been six, six, and four generational groups, respectively, during the time span 1940–2000, all defined differently and with different names and birth periods. It would be a vast oversimplification to assume that Millennials in China are equivalent to Millennials in the USA, Germany, or South Korea, despite sharing some traits such as being highly connected via social networking sites.

Subcultures based on sex roles

Sex roles relate to society's expectations about the appropriate attitude, values, and behaviour of men and women. Examples of sex-role-based subcultures include Mumsnet, the web-based organization that connects mothers and parents in the UK, and Fathers4Justice, the fathers' rights campaigning group. While sex roles are the point of connection, it is also useful to recognize that these groups can unite in their resistance to stereotypical sex role norms that the subculture does not relate to or connect with, as mentioned already in this chapter. Typically, advertisements in many countries maintain the stereotypical sex roles of the nurturing mother and father who provides for the family by going out to work.

Regional, ethnic, and religious subcultures

We can feel a connection and affiliation with other people linked to our regional and ethnic identifications. Within the UK, there are regional subcultures based on county variations. The Yorkshire Tea brand, owned by Taylors of Harrogate, has a strong regional identity and is presented as the favoured tea brand of Yorkshire people, signifying their shared connection with the place. Ethnic subcultures, representing around 15 per cent of the UK population, are also important. Some companies serve specific ethnic groups. Boots sell the Mumtaz range of halal baby foods for Muslims. For companies marketing to ethnic groups there is the danger of appearing tokenist, and ending up with marketing communications that are based around stereotypical imagery of an ethnic group. In 2001 an advertisement for Chicken Tonight was taken off air after the Hindu community complained that the campaign ridiculed their religion by using a Hindu prayer to advertise the meat sauce when some sections of their faith forbid the eating of meat (Singh, 2004).

Marketing needs to engage appropriately with ethnic audiences. Research (Ivanič et al., 2014) has shown that consumers have a well-developed ability to discern whether or not the spokesperson is similar to them. They find it easier to recall and understand the message and in turn develop a more favourable attitude towards the brand if they are. This may be why Rent-A-Wheel used African American comedian Kevin Hart in its ads targeted at the generation of hip-culture African Americans, using a fast-paced urban dialect. Nevertheless, many feel that they are not represented in products and advertising. In Brazil, people of African descent have protested about their lack of commercial representation by hold-

Figure 9.14   'Não me vejo, não compro!'—'I don't see myself, I don't buy'

Source: Image courtesy of revistadonna.com.

ing up placards in front of ads and products showing only white models with the words, 'Não me vejo, não compro!' meaning 'I don't see myself, I don't buy' (see Figure 9.14). Some businesses are concerned to reflect the cultural reality of the society in which they operate. For example, Lloyds Banking Group released research in December 2016 which identified the diversity of British society and whether or not that is reflected in advertising (http://www.lloydsbankinggroup.com/reflectingmodernbritain). As a result they have aimed to show a more inclusive view of British society in their advertising (Figure 9.15).

Figure 9.15   Lloyds Bank's 'he said yes' campaign

Source: Image courtesy of Lloyds Banking Group.

Religion represents one of the central institutions shaping consumer culture. It provides a point of affiliation for subcultures within a national culture, and these subcultures are based around the consumption of certain products which are symbolically and ritualistically associated with the celebration of religious ceremonies and holidays. Within the Catholic faith, the First Holy Communion is a ceremony that represents a person's first reception of the sacrament of communion. In Mediterranean Catholic countries, this is a major event in a child's life, particularly for girls. There are many shops that cater specifically for this market, and some even put on a First Holy Communion clothing fashion parade to show off the dresses and accessories. Other examples of religion-based subcultures impacting on consumer behaviour can be found in Jewish consumers following a kosher diet and celebrating a son's bar mitzvah, and Islamic consumers following a halal diet.

Subcultures based on consumption communities

Many companies have been keen to influence and nurture brand communities around their brands through creating branded social space. Starbucks set up the 'My Starbucks Idea' site (http://mystarbucksidea.force.com/), which aimed to develop a sense of community among its customers by encouraging them to share ideas and suggestions for new types of drink.

Community as a concept has a long history in sociology and anthropology, but its emergence in consumer behaviour research stems from the 1990s, with the publication of the paper by Schouten and McAlexander (1995) on subcultures of consumption, which focused on Harley-Davidson owners, or HOGs (Harley Owners Group). Over the years, the focus has subtly changed from an interest in subcultures of consumption (Schouten and McAlexander, 1995) to consideration of brand communities (Muniz and O'Guinn, 2001) through to the current emphasis on consumer tribes (Cova and Cova, 2002). While there are some differences in meaning, they all represent forms of subcultural consumption, and as such share common features with cultures. Just like a cultural group, these subcultures share values, beliefs, and knowledge, as well as customs and norms around ways of acting. We now consider subcultures of consumption, brand communities, and consumer tribes in more detail.

Subcultures of consumption

A **subculture of consumption** is defined as a group of consumers connected through a 'shared commitment to a particular product class, brand or consumption activity' (Schouten and McAlexander, 1995: 43). The Harley-Davidson community is the classic example of a subculture of consumption (see Research Insight 9.6). The defining characteristics of subcultures of consumption are an identifiable ethos underpinning the subculture, core values that are accepted to varying degrees by all adherents, and expression of these values in certain products and their usage. An interesting recent example of a brand that inspires a subculture of consumption is Fred Perry. This brand has a website (http://www.fredperrysubculture.com/) where it brings together and promotes the way that music, film, fashion, and other aspects of popular culture connect with the Fred Perry brand.

RESEARCH INSIGHT 9.6

Schouten, J. and McAlexander, J.H. (1995), 'Subcultures of consumption: an ethnography of the New Bikers', *Journal of Consumer Research*, 22, 3, 43–61.

In their analysis of Harley-Davidson Owners, subcultures of consumption were characterized by having an identifiable ethos, by sharing core values that are accepted to varying degrees by all adherents, the expression of these values in certain products and their usage, and that members relate to other members through product and brand usage.

 Access the online resources to find out more about this book.

Brand communities

Brand community is a similar concept to subculture, but the focus is very much on the shared admiration of a brand. According to Muniz and O'Guinn (2001), a **brand community** is a non-geographically bound community of people, who are connected through brand admiration, with a structured set of social relations. Muniz and O'Guinn defined brand community as sharing a consciousness of kind, rituals, and traditions, and also a moral responsibility to the brand. This was important, as it related to the idea of the brand community sustaining itself, and its members feeling a duty to ensure that the brand community thrives. BMW is an example of a brand that evokes strong brand community, with its own website (http://www.bimmerfest.com/) and events that promote the sense of brand community. There are three key aspects of brand community.

- *Consciousness of kind* is the recognizable connection to the brand and each other, the 'we-ness' of the brand community. Here the connection among people has great importance for understanding brand communities. For MacUsers, often cited as the seminal consumption community, the identification with the Apple Macintosh brand, and the strong recognition of other users, implies a strong connection to the values and ethos of the company and brand.

- *Rituals and traditions* associated with the consumption community are those vital social processes by which meaning of the community is reproduced and transmitted within and beyond the community (e.g. shared consumption experiences with the brand). These rituals may involve storytelling and sharing of brand stories to create and maintain community around the brand, but also celebrate the history of the brand. Apple had a history of ritualistic unveiling of new products by the late Steve Jobs at company conferences, amid great media attention and consumer interest.

- *Moral responsibility* to the brand is a shared sense of duty to the community as a whole, and individuals within, which involves looking out for and helping other members in their consumption of the brand. This is often about coalescing around the brand in favour of this brand over others.

One final aspect of brand communities is the anti-brand community. As a backlash against capitalism, there is a growing resistance to corporate globalization, and there have been some recent high profile examples of consumers who are actively opposing brands or companies, and in the process forming anti-brand communities around certain brands. Anti-brand communities, similar to brand communities, are non-geographically bound communities based on a structured set of social relationships (Hollenbeck and Zinkhan, 2010). In anti-brand communities, consumers form networks or communities in opposition to specific brands (e.g. Marlboro cigarettes) and/or in opposition to corporate brands (e.g. the anti-Starbuck's community http://www.ihatestarbucks.com/). Essentially, consumers take on social activist roles; anti-branding demonstrations are emerging as a new form of consumer activism. The damage that this can cause companies is considerable, and while the internet offers great opportunities, in cases of brand transgression there can be major negative implications for companies.

Consumer tribes

Consumer tribes are an extension of the brand community idea. **Consumer tribes** are *a group of people emotionally connected by similar consumption values and usage, who use the social 'linking value' (Cova, 1997: 297) of products and services to create a community and express identity*. The consumer tribes concept builds on ideas emerging from Maffesoli's work on neo-tribes (Maffesoli, 1988), taking them into the consumption context. Consumer tribes are similar to subcultures of consumption and brand communities in the sense that the collective is connected through their shared passion for a brand or consumption practice. The difference, however, is that consumption tribes recognize the multiple nature of consumption collectives and that consumers may belong to several collectives, or tribes, at the same time. Just as an individual has different aspects of their self, through membership of multiple tribes, consumers can express different aspects of their identity.

Cova and Cova (2002) emphasized the playful aspect of tribal consumption, and argued that one does not need to feel commitment or responsibility to the brand. Tribes are transient, in the sense that they emerge and grow, but they can also disappear as members of the tribe keep changing. Finally, tribes are entrepreneurial, as tribe members try and customize or produce market offerings to meet their needs. Unlike subcultures and brand community, tribal membership does not dominate consumers' lives, nor do members feel a strong moral obligation to the tribal collective. Tribes are prominent in consumer culture, as evidenced in the range of tribes discussed by Cova et al. (2007). They can emerge around consumption practices (e.g. surfers, clubbers), consumer brands (e.g. the Alfisti tribe who are committed to the Alfa Romeo brand), or in response to popular cultural trends (e.g. the Twilight Moms, a tribe sharing a passion for the Twilight series, its author. and its stars). Tribes are distinct from other ways of thinking about consumption collectives in that, from this perspective, they place less emphasis on the product or service, but instead focus on the linking value that connects consumers and hence is key to understanding (and supporting) consumer-to-consumer relations, and ultimately engendering affective based loyalty.

The form and nature of subcultures reflect major cultural and demographic trends within wider society, and clearly these tribes closely reflect popular cultural trends. Increasing cultural diversity and consumer affluence will impact on subcultures of consumption, as consumers are exposed to a wider range of influences (at a global level) and have resources available to participate in tribes. The relevance of understanding tribes is seen in the popularity of tribal marketing, with many companies embracing these ideas in their effort to understand their consumers better and to form greater connection to their brands. This is exemplified in the case of Oreo (see Case Study 9) in their use of tribal marketing to celebrate 100 years of Oreo.

Conclusions

We began this chapter by stressing how culture is learned through enculturation and acculturation. Culture is about where we come from, and what we have grown up with, but as acculturation attests sometimes we have to move between cultures too. It is vitally important for marketers to fully understand the extent, range, and depth of different cultures where they are defined by geography, age, religion, ethnicity, or even consumption. Our **definition of culture** has centred on the contents of culture, but has also given consideration to the role that culture serves as a blueprint for our lives. The important **elements of the cultural system** include ecology and the very often simple differences between climate and terrain that can impact on what products serve the consumer best and the design of those products to suit how they will be used. Social structure shapes culture and the roles people play in that culture and, as we have increasingly seen, genders are unwilling to be stereotyped into traditional roles. Finally, people can express their personal and social ideology through their consumption activities as in the hip culture of Brazil and even the brand of cola they buy.

Our section on the **classification of cultures** looked at core societal values which can shape behaviour and practices. We took a closer look at the dimensions of cultural values, drawing on Hofstede's classification. Consumer Insight 9.1 focuses on how the Norwegian brand Solo challenged the cultural characteristics associated with Norway as a way of drawing attention to itself.

We described the nature of **cultural myths and rituals** and how these can be translated into lifestyle and consumption as in the case of the Danish *hygge* concept explored in Consumer Insight 9.3. Through the framework of McCracken's Movement of Meaning (Figure 9.4) we examined the consumption rituals of hipsters, including possession, grooming, and divestment rituals. How rites of passage are played out can be a very important part of the establishment of cultural understanding, and Research Insight 9.3 focused on this in relation to dance music festival attendees.

We examined a range of ways in which culture is important for **marketing communications**, including advertising tone and message, and in understanding sacred and profane consumption. Consumer Insight 9.4 provided an example of a culturally informed campaign—Philips grooming products in Taiwan.

We have also discussed in detail the various **subcultural groups** that are important for marketing, linking them to our understanding of culture more generally. We focused on demographic-based and consumption-based subcultural groupings. Consumer Insight 9.5 highlighted how marketers target products and brands at tweenagers, while Practitioner Insight 9 discussed some of the issues around understanding how values and beliefs about animal welfare impact on consumer choices. Research Insight 9.6 described the classic study of Harley-Davidson Owners (HOGs) as a subculture of consumption. When thinking of culture in these terms, it is important to remember that the cultural landscape has both a permanent and a dynamic quality. While people will continue to have similar religious and ethnic affinities, culture associated with age, gender, and sexuality has changed dramatically and will undoubtedly continue to do so. Marketing has to be aware of and sensitive to trends that are affecting the way that culture influences consumption practices.

Review questions

1. Explain the difference between enculturation and acculturation.

2. How does acculturation work? What are the main processes and why is this useful for marketers to know about?

3. What are the main perspectives on culture, and in what key ways do they differ?

4. Think of a culture that has a particular ideology that may be played out in behaviour, attitudes, or even brands. How is that ideology communicated and why is it important to people?

5. Define the following terms in the context of culture: learning, knowledge, customs, and norms.

6. What are the key dimensions of culture as identified by Hofstede? What do you think might be the problems with Hofstede's dimensions? Analyse your culture of birth using the dimensions?

7. What are myths and why are they relevant for understanding culture? Think of a myth that you are aware of that has been important to marketing. How has the meaning been transferred to consumer goods?

8. What are the main rituals associated with consumer culture? Can you provide your own examples of each?

9. What are the key issues around communication and culture?

10. What is the difference between demographic and consumption-based subcultures? Can you provide examples of such subcultures?

Discussion questions

1. Consider the material on the dimensions of culture. Read the paper by McSweeney (2016) (Research Insight 9.2) and, together with your understanding of culture, discuss what you think the main problems are with this approach.

2. Find an advertisement that you feel has a strong cultural dimension to it. Analyse this from the dimensions of both the culture perspective and the CCT perspective. Which offers greater insights and value for marketers?

3. Use McCracken's framework of cultural meaning to consider how possession, exchange, grooming, and/or divestment rituals might work for a recent fashion innovation of your choice.

4. Can you think of key rituals in your life where consumption plays a significant role? Other than advertising, in what ways might marketing and social marketing use these ideas to influence consumer behaviour in some way?

5. Choose a consumer collective and analyse it in terms of the three main perspectives on consumption-based subcultures: subcultures of consumption, brand community, and consumer tribes. Which do you think is most useful for understanding these consumption-based subcultures?

◐ Access the online resources to test your knowledge further and complete the Multiple Choice Questions for Chapter 9.

CASE STUDY 9

Oreo's 100th birthday celebrations

This case focuses on the company Oreo and its 100th Anniversary Campaign (June 2012) as an illustration of the development of bonded loyalty created through the extensive use of social media, and on how to use social media to 'build brand love'. Oreo provides an interesting example of a company appropriating and applying the ideas of tribes of consumption, making extensive use of social media to facilitate and reinforce the sense of tribal connections around the brand.

Background to case

The Oreo biscuit was developed and first produced by the National Biscuit Company (now known as Nabisco, and owned by Kraft) in 1912. A chocolate sandwich cookie (or biscuit) with a creamy white filling, it has become an iconic symbol of US culture, and its 'twist, lick, dunk' ritual resonates with people all over the world. Oreo is the world's best-selling cookie, sold in more than 100 countries.

To celebrate the 100th anniversary of the Oreo cookie, a global social media campaign was devised, based around the iconic 'twist, lick, dunk' ritual.

According to John Ghingo, senior director for Oreo Global,

> In today's hectic world, people have more responsibilities and pressures than ever before. Despite this, the simple act of enjoying an Oreo cookie and glass of milk continues to speak to a universal human truth: inside all of us ... there's a kid that deserves to be set free every once in a while.

This was the basis of the campaign, which aimed to inspire people to relive the magic of youth.

Social media as part of the Oreo campaign

Activities across social media platforms were critical to the success of this campaign, and there were a range of key activities driving the campaign. The central campaign was around the 100 consecutive 'Daily Twists', portraits created from straws, empty glasses, milk, and Oreo cookies. These were shared over Facebook, Tumblr, and Pinterest, and through the Daily Twist website. These reflected trending events, holidays, and major news events, and were not without controversy. To coincide with Gay Pride, Oreo posted an image of a multicoloured cookie with the message 'Proudly Support Love', which attracted a quarter of a million 'likes' on Facebook. However, this posting divided fans, drawing criticism from Christian groups.

Another key event was the Guinness World Record event which aimed to set the record for the most 'likes' on a Facebook post in 24 hours. This was promoted globally through their social media platforms and the Oreo website, and was also picked up by various online media outlets and local press. The Guinness event received 25,000 'likes' in the first 60 seconds of launching publicly and achieved a total of 114,619 'likes'.

A number of activities were organized over the anniversary year. According to the company, the 100th Anniversary Campaign connected 40 million people worldwide and attracted 8.5 million Facebook 'likes', and on Twitter the #OreoMoment hashtag became a trending topic, with birthday treats reaching nearly 15 million people.

Tribal marketing

For Sarah Hofstetter, President of 360i Foods (the digital agency that led the Oreo campaign), Kraft had to find out how to bring the campaign to centre stage as people were eating Oreos across the world but in different social settings: 'Brands today need to act as media companies and invite people to share content ... Social media is a conversation, not a one-night stand'. Taking a consumer tribes approach is a useful way for companies to think about how they create connections, and thus bonded loyalty, with consumers.

According to Cova et al. (2007: 21), 'where once tribes were seen as transformative to their members, we are beginning to see how they are transformative to business and communicative practices and through them, to society itself'. The challenge for companies is to understand the dynamics of tribes and to support consumers' involvement with the tribe, and in so doing align marketing efforts with the tribe's values. Central to tribal marketing activities is the use of social media, since this presents a way for companies to connect with consumers. Figure 9.16 shows a framework for how firms can build bonding loyalty through supporting the tribe (Mitchell and Imrie, 2011).

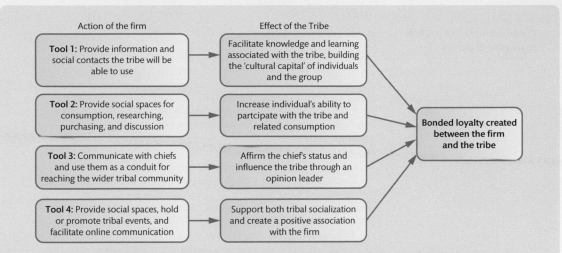

Figure 9.16   Building bonded loyalty through a firm's support of the tribe (Mitchell and Imrie, 2011)

Source: Mitchell and Imrie (2011). Reproduced with permission from Emerald Group Publishing Ltd. Oreo as a consumption tribe

The tribal marketing approach to building loyalty can be used as a way of analysing Oreo's successful campaign (see Table 9.2).

Proposed action of the firm to support the tribe	Examples of Oreo activities
1. Company should provide information and social contacts that the tribe will be able to use, which can facilitate knowledge and learning associated with the tribe, building the cultural capital of individuals and the group.	• Daily Twists campaign, present across multiple platforms. Encouraged interest and engagement with the campaign across platforms. Built cultural capital through engagement with wider sociocultural events at the time. • Oreo set up a 100th Birthday Facebook page to provide a focal point for activities, and for information dissemination (http://www.facebook.com/oreo/app_192670807490788). According to company information, Oreo's Facebook community grew from 2 million to 60 million fans.
2. Provide social spaces for consumption, researching, purchasing, and discussion, increasing the individual's ability to participate with the tribe and related consumption.	• Active management of Facebook page, offering opportunities for consumers to connect; for example, a posting 'OREO cookies make every day a little more _____' attracted 7,749 comments. • Daily Twists postings reflect topical events, and their tongue-in-cheek graphics make them ideal for sharing on other platforms (Pinterest, Twitter, Facebook). Reflecting topics in the news and popular culture resonate with the interests and concerns of tribe members in a playful way. • Show participation and care of their tribe, for example through celebrating fans' birthdays (Fan Lisa T. was born in 1912—the same year Oreo cookies were introduced. Wish her a special happy birthday below!), and the creation (and posting on YouTube) of a short film showing 'Thousands of Oreo cookie fans are celebrating the kid inside. Watch below to learn how you can join the movement!'

Table 9.2   Analysis of the Oreo campaign

Proposed action of the firm to support the tribe	Examples of Oreo activities
3. The company communicates with chiefs and uses them as a conduit for reaching the wider tribal community. It affirms the chief's status and influences the tribe through an opinion leader.	• The main tribe 'chief' is the child at the centre of the campaign message 'Celebrate the kid inside'. The global reach of the campaign is demonstrated through a series of commercials, run in 15 countries, building on the Oreo 'twist, lick, dunk' ritual. The commercials bring the Oreo moments to life by transforming routine adult activities into something fun and playful—as the adults discover their inner children, the children hold up signs that say 'Next Stop: Childhood' and 'Recess for Everyone!'. • Award-winning advertising campaign to support engagement with the brand; the advertisement is titled 'Oreo Explanation' and in it a little girl introduces her father to the 'twist, lick, dunk' ritual during a play tea party. The winning advertisement is part of a Europe-wide campaign, with similar ads starring French and German children. • Live Daily Twist Finale—on the last day of the campaign (2 October) Oreo set up a virtual office in Times Square, New York City, to produce the final Daily Twist advertisement. In order to connect and include global fans, fans were able to submit ideas between 8 a.m. and 10 a.m. via Oreo's Twitter and Facebook pages.
4. Provide social spaces, hold or promote tribal events, and facilitate online communication, which can support both tribal socialization and create a positive association with the firm.	• Oreo devised the AmbassadOREO campaign, whereby Oreo (in consultation with fans) chooses an ambassador (an AmbassadOREO) to communicate with the tribe and promote their brand propositions and rituals. • Global AmbassadOREO Program—These brand evangelists gathered in New York City to share their childlike moment. They take an oath to help Oreo extend its movement to recapture and spread the wonder of youth and become part of the mission to 'celebrate the kid inside' when they return home. • According to Oreo, AmbassadOREO honorees were chosen in unique ways by each country. In the Philippines, a Facebook contest called on fans to submit family photos that creatively formed the number 100 with Oreo cookies. In Ecuador, lucky consumers who found a 'golden ticket' in their package of Oreo cookies were entered in a raffle for the chance to represent their country in New York as an AmbassadOREO. In China, AmbassadOREO honorees had to earn points by completing Oreo missions throughout the year. In the USA, millions of Oreo Facebook fans had the chance to vote for five national winners from video submissions of fans demonstrating their passion for the Oreo brand.

Questions

1. Oreo has been presented here as an example of a consumer tribe. Can you analyse this case material from (a) a brand communities perspectives and (b) a subculture of consumption perspective? What similarities and contrasts can you make between the three perspectives (tribes, brand communities, subcultures of consumption) based on this analysis?

2. Can you analyse the Oreo case in terms of myths and rituals around consumption?

3. What next for Oreo? What do you suggest the company does next in order to sustain this successful social media campaign?

Sources: Cova et al. (2007); Shayon (2012); MacPherson (2012); Elliot (2012); *PR Newswire* (2012); Jacques (2012).

References

Adweek (2009), 'Unilever expands Vive Mejor initiative', *Adweek*, 16 July, http://www.adweek.com/news/advertising-branding/unilever-expands-vivemejor-initiative-106120#1 (accessed 21 April 2013).

Aguinis, H., Joo, H., and Gottfredson, R.K. (2012), 'Performance management universals: think globally and act locally', *Business Horizons*, 55, 4, 385–92.

Allegheny (2010), 'Home purification—how to do sage smudge ceremony', http://alleghenycandles.wordpress.com/2010/05/01/home-purification/ (accessed 30 November 2012).

Baskerville, R.F. (2003), 'Hofstede never studied culture', *Accounting, Organizations and Society*, 28, 1, 1–14.

Belk, R.W., Wallendorf, M., and Sherry, J.F., Jr (1989), 'The sacred and the profane in consumer behavior: theodicy on the Odyssey', *Journal of Consumer Research*, 16, 1, 1–38.

Booth, M. (2016), ' Hygge: Why the craze for Danish cosiness is based on a myth', https://www.theguardian.com/world/shortcuts/2016/sep/04/hygge-denmark-danes-cosiness-wealth-antidepressants-scandinavians (accessed 22 October 2017).

Brafton (2010), 'Marketers can tap into $200 billion marketing by targeting teens', http://www.brafton.com/news/marketers-can-tap-into-200-billion-market-by-targeting-teens-800014942 (accessed 9 November 2012).

Bu, K., Kim, D., and Son, J. (2013), 'Is the culture–emotion fit always important? Self-regulatory emotions in ethnic food consumption', *Journal of Business Research*, 66, 8, 983–8.

Buerger, M. (2016), 'Scandinavian design is more than just IKEA', https://www.washingtonpost.com/lifestyle/home/look-beyond-ikea-to-understand-scandinavian-design/2016/01/25/0f001ce4-becc-11e5-bcda-62a36b394160_story.html (accessed 1 February 2017).

Chalmers, T.D. and Arthur, D. (2008), 'Hard-core members of consumption-oriented subcultures enactment of identity: the sacred consumption of two subcultures', http://www.acrwebsite.org/volumes/v35/naacr_vol35_472.pdf (accessed 1 February 1 2017).

Clark, B. (2012), 'Three steps to creating audience archetypes for smarter content marketing', http://entreproducer.com/audience-archetypes/ (accessed 20 July 2013).

Clarke, B. (2003), 'The angst, anguish and ambitions of the teenage years', *Young Consumers: Insights and Ideas for Responsible Marketers*, 4, 3, 27–33.

Coskuner-Balli, G. and Thomson, C.J (2013), 'The status costs of subordinate cultural capital: at-home fathers' collective pursuit of cultural legitimacy through capitalizing consumption practices', *Journal of Consumer Research*, 40, 2, 19–41.

Courier Mail (2010), 'Catholics angry as celebrities hijack rosary beads as a fashion statement', 11 July, http://www.couriermail.com.au/lifestyle/catholics-angry-as-celebrities-hijack-rosary-beads-as-a-fashion-statement/story-e6frer4f-1225890174772 (accessed 8 November 2012).

Cova, B. (1997), 'Community and consumption: towards a definition of the "linking value" of product or services', *European Journal of Marketing*, 31, 3/4, 297–316.

Cova, B. and Cova, V. (2002), 'Tribal marketing: the tribalisation of society and its impact on the conduct of marketing', *European Journal of Marketing*, 36, 1–27.

Cova, B., Kozinets, R.V., and Shankar, F.A.C. (eds) (2007), *Consumer tribes*, London: Routledge.

de Mooij, M. and Hofstede, G. (2002), 'Convergence and divergence in consumer behavior: implications for international retailing', *Journal of Retailing*, 78, 1, 61–9.

Ehrlich, S. (2012), 'Solo make thousands of their fans famous', http://blog.contagiousagency.com.au/solo-makes-fans-famous/ (accessed 17 December, 2017).

Elliot, S. (2012), 'The Oreo turns 100, with a nod to the past', *New York Times*, 27 February, http://www.nytimes.com/2012/02/28/business/media/the-oreo-turns-100-with-a-nod-to-the-past-advertising.html?_r=0 (accessed 13 July 2013).

Fang, T. (2010), 'Asian management research needs more self-confidence: reflection on Hofstede (2007) and beyond', *Asia Pacific Journal of Management*, 27, 1, 155–70.

Gobé, M. (2007), *Brandjam: humanizing brands through emotional design*, New York: Allworth Press.

Hawks, A. (2010), 'Mariah Carey launches "Lollipop Bling" perfume and ring pop candy', http://starcasm.net/archives/52913 (accessed 28 June 2012).

Hebdige, D. (1979), *Subculture: the meaning of style*, London: Routledge.

Helliwell, J., Layard, R., and Sachs, J. (eds) (2016), *World Happiness Report 2016*, http://worldhappiness.report/wp-content/uploads/sites/2/2016/03/HR-V1_web.pdf (accessed 22 October 2016).

Higgins, C. (2016), 'The Hygge consipiracy', https://www.theguardian.com/lifeandstyle/2016/nov/22/hygge-conspiracy-denmark-cosiness-trend (accessed 1 February 2017).

Hofstede, G. (1984), *Culture's consequences: international differences in work-related values* (abridged edn), London: Sage.

Hofstede, G.H. (2001), *Culture's consequences: comparing values, behaviors, institutions and organizations across nations* (2nd edn), London: Sage.

Hollenbeck, C.R. and Zinkhan, G.M. (2010), 'Anti-brand communities, negotiation of brand meaning, and the learning process: the case of Wal-Mart', *Consumption, Markets & Culture*, 13, 3, 325–45.

Holt, D. and Cameron, D. (2012), *Cultural strategy*, Oxford: Oxford University Press.

Ivanič, A.S., Bates, K., and Somasundaram, T. (2014) 'The role of the accent in radio advertisement to ethic audiences', *Journal of Advertising Research*, 54, 4, 407–19.

Jacques, A. (2012), '100 years of Oreo: how the iconic cookie brand is using social media', http://www.prsa.org/Intelligence/Tactics/Articles/view/9713/1046/100_years_of_Oreo_How_the_iconic_cookie_brand_is_u#.WezsOltSzIU (accessed 3 March 2013).

Jafari, A. and Suerdem, A. (2012), 'The sacred and the profane in Islamic consumption', *Advances in Consumer Research*, 39, 1, 427–9.

Jaimangal-Jones, D., Pritchard, A., and Morgan, N. (2010), Going the distance: locating journey, liminality and rites of passage in dance music experiences, *Leisure Studies*, 29, 3, 253–68

Larsen, S. (2012), 'Solo: soon to be world-famous', *WARC*, http://www.warc.com.ezproxye.bham.ac.uk/Content/ContentViewer.aspx?MasterContentRef=ef2da8ef-b06c-46a1-ad08-e613009a9181 (accessed 9 June 2013).

Luedicke, M.K. (2015). 'Indigenes' responses to immigrants' consumer acculturation: a relational configuration analysis', *Journal of Consumer Research*, 42, 1, 109–29.

Lynn, M. and Starbuck, M.M. (2015), Tipping customs: the effects of national differences in attitudes toward tipping and sensitivities to duty and social pressure, *Journal of Behavioral and Experimental Economics*, 57, 158–66.

McCracken, G. (1986), 'Culture and consumption: a theoretical account of the structure and movement of the cultural meaning of consumer goods', *Journal of Consumer Research*, 13, 1, 71–84.

MacPherson, R. (2012), 'Oreos mark 100 years of "twist, lick, dunk" ', *ABS-CBN News*, https://ph.news.yahoo.com/oreos-mark-100-years-twist-lick-dunk-213454102.html (accessed 21 July 2014).

McSweeney, B. (2016), 'Collective cultural mind programming: escaping from the cage', *Journal of Organizational Change Management*, 29, 1, 68–80.

Maffesoli, M. (1988), *Le temps des tribus: le déclin de l'individualisme dans les sociétés de masse*, Paris: Librairie des Méridiens.

Marketing Week (2010), 'Mariah Carey targets young with sweet-inspired fragrances', *Marketing Week*, 24 June, http://www.marketingweek.co.uk/mariah-carey-targets-young-with-sweet-inspired-fragrances/3015087.article (accessed 1 December 2012).

Mintel (2011), ' "Teens" and "tweens" technology usage', *Mintel*, http://store.mintel.com/teens-and-tweens-technology-usage-uk-november-2011 (accessed 20 December 2012).

Mitchell, C. and Imrie, B.C. (2011), 'Consumer tribes: membership, consumption and building loyalty', *Asia Pacific Journal of Marketing and Logistics*, 23, 1, 39–56.

Morgan, B. (2015), *Impact*, 8 January, 14–15.

Muniz, A.M., Jr and O'Guinn, T.C. (2001), 'Brand community', *Journal of Consumer Research*, 27, 4, 412–32.

Pardue, D. (2005), 'Brazilian hip-hop material and ideology: a case of cultural design', *Image and Narrative*, 10, 23–31.

Penaloza, L. (1994), 'Atravesando fronteras/border crossings: a critical ethnographic exploration of the consumer acculturation of Mexican immigrants', *Journal of Consumer Research*, 21, 1, 32–54.

Poole, G. (2014), 'Society still doesn't like the idea of stay-at-home dads', http://www.telegraph.co.uk/men/relationships/fatherhood/11122773/Society-still-doesnt-like-the-idea-of-stay-at-home-dads.html (accessed 3 February 2017).

PR Newswire (2012), 'A cookie with a mission: Oreo welcomes first "AmbassadOREO" honorees from around the globe to New York City,' *PR Newswire*, http://www.prnewswire.co.uk/news-releases/a-cookie-with-a-mission-oreo-welcomes-first-ambassadoreo-honorees-from-around-the-globe-to-new-york-city-170476916.html (accessed 13 July 2013).

Riley-Adams, E. (2012), 'Ogilvy Action Taiwan makes augmented reality mustaches', *Agency Spy*, http://www.mediabistro.com/agencyspy/ogilvyaction-taiwan-makes-augmented-reality-moustaches_b35190 (accessed 20 May 2013).

Roberts, J. and Scott, S. (2009), 'The teen commandments', *Marketing Week*, 20 May, http://www.marketingweek.co.uk/the-teen-commandments/2065514.article (accessed 8 April 2014).

Rook, D.W. (1985), 'The ritual dimension of consumer behavior', *Journal of Consumer Research*, 12, 3, 251–64.

Schouten, J. and McAlexander, J.H. (1995), 'Subcultures of consumption: an ethnography of the New Bikers', *Journal of Consumer Research*, 22, 3, 43–61.

Seow Bei Yi (2017), 'A little less Nimby', *Straits Times*, 19 February, http://www.straitstimes.com/singapore/housing/a-little-less-nimby (accessed 19 February 2017).

Shayon, S. (2012), 'Oreo's Daily Twist finale goes live and crowdsourced from Times Square', *Brand Channel*, http://www.brandchannel.com/home/post/2012/09/28/Oreo-Daily-Twist-Finale-092812.aspx (accessed 13 July 2013).

Shields, R. (2011), 'HTC rivals BlackBerry's dominance of teen market', *Marketing Week*, 6 July, http://www.marketingweek.co.uk/sectors/telecoms-and-it/htc-rivals-blackberrys-dominance-of-teen-market/3028141.article (accessed 20 December 2012).

Sidle, S.D. (2009), 'Building a committed global workforce: does what employees want depend on culture?', *Academy of Management Perspectives*, 23, 1, 79–80.

Singh, S. (2004), 'Why ads don't reflect UK ethnic population', *Marketing Week*, 22 April, http://www.marketingweek.co.uk/why-ads-dont-reflect-uk-ethnic-population/2019104.article (accessed 31 July 2014).

Tansel, U. (2010), 'Effects of age compression on traditional toys and games', http://blog.euromonitor.com/2010/10/effects-of-age-compression-on-traditional-toys-and-games.html (accessed 10 February 2017).

Taylor, K. (2015), 'Avoiding waste with the Japanese concept of "mottainai" ', http://www.abc.net.au/radio-national/programs/philosopherszone/avoiding-waste-with-the-japanese-concept-of-mottainai/6722720 (accessed 5 June, 2017).

Thomson, C. (2016), 'The Danish concept of "hygge"—and why it's their latest successful export', https://theconversation.com/the-danish-concept-of-hygge-and-why-its-their-latest-successful-export-67268 (accessed 1 February 2017).

Triandis, H.C. (1995), *Individualism and collectivism*, Boulder, CO: Westview Press.

Vernon, P. (2010), 'Jack Wills: the Sloane Ranger rides again', *Observer*, 9 May, http://www.guardian.co.uk/theobserver/2010/may/09/polly-vernon-jack-wills-preppy-fashion-teenagers-success (accessed 30 November 2012).

Woodside, A.G., Sood, S., and Miller, K.E. (2008), 'When consumers and brands talk: storytelling theory and research in psychology and marketing', *Psychology & Marketing*, 25, 2, 97–145.

Young, K. (2012), 'Philips "augmented reality mugs" give hairless men faux facial hair', *Trendhunter*, 31 May, http://www.trendhunter.com/trends/augmented-reality-mugs (accessed 20 March 2013).

10

PATTERNS OF BUYER BEHAVIOUR

Introduction

So far in this book we have considered consumer behaviour from the perspective of the individual as part of a larger social group, or set within a specific subculture such as teenagers, or a broader cultural setting such as their country or ethnicity. In this chapter we consider consumers in the light of research that has studied their actual purchasing behaviour. Consumer panel data, measuring the behaviour of thousands of consumers in different parts of the world, has been analysed by researchers to explain differences in purchasing behaviour. Such research is used in this chapter to draw implications to aid our understanding of consumer behaviour. Although the data does not tell us *why* people buy in the way they do, by showing *how* they buy the information can be used by marketing managers when considering their competitive strategy and to make decisions regarding whether to target new, existing, or both types of customer.

LEARNING OBJECTIVES

After you read this chapter, you will be able to:

1. Analyse the concept of **repeat buying** and understand the implications for **brand loyalty** and market share.

2. Identify what **patterns of purchasing from consumer panel data** can tell us about the state of a brand.

3. Explain the different ways of considering **brand loyalty**.

4. Recognize the importance of **light and heavy buyers** of a brand.

5. Understand the importance of **mental** and **physical availability** for the success of a brand.

6. Understand the significance of what **patterns of buyer behaviour** tell us about segmentation, differentiation, and distinctiveness.

What are repeat buying and brand loyalty?

As consumers we are all subject to repeat buying. There may be some examples where we do not ever buy the same product or brand again—perhaps we dislike the taste or the texture, or perhaps we feel that it has not performed in the way advertised. For most goods and services, however, we are likely to be back in the market to purchase regularly, whether that is every few days, say in the case of bread or milk, or every week for foodstuffs such as meat and vegetables. Obviously some items may be stored for longer, such as frozen or tinned food, and some are used over a period of time, such as jars of instant coffee or bars of soap. Even these products may vary considerably in how long it is before we buy them again. Imagine, for example, a person who does not drink much coffee but keeps a jar in the house in case of visitors. The same person buys cereals once a week because they have children who eat them every day for breakfast. Although both products will be used over time, the different consumer needs and preferences of the household dictate when the product will be repeat-purchased. There may even be products that we buy more than once a day—chocolate bars for example, although perhaps we should not! The point is that we all have a regularity to our purchase patterns, which is linked to consumer needs.

If we want to examine how people repeat buy we can use consumer panel data that records people's purchasing over extended periods (often, over a year or longer) so that we can see what brands are bought repeatedly and how often the consumer chooses alternative brands. Typically, panels are large representative samples of people. In Japan, for example, the consumer research company Sci-Personal has a panel of around 50,000 men and women across the country who use a portable terminal like that shown in Figure 10.1 to

Figure 10.1   Scanning a barcode for a consumer panel
Source: Image supplied and printed with kind permission from INTAGE Inc.

scan barcodes on products purchased. Often this data is then combined with attitudinal and demographic information.

Purchasing patterns from consumer panel data

Repeat buying over time

Table 10.1 is a fictionalized and simplified table giving data about four people's purchasing habits over a nine-week period. Let us consider the different brands to be various types of coffee. A, B, and C are different brands of coffee purchased, and 0 means that no purchase takes place. In this case, we see both the variety in the coffee purchased and the frequency with which it is purchased, and how this varies across four different people.

Person 1 seems to have a preference for brand A but then in week 5, after a gap of two weeks, switches to B. In week 8 they return to brand A again, but in week 9 buy brand B. It might be that they have discovered brand B and it has entered their repertoire of brands (perhaps because of taste), or that when brand A is not available they choose brand B as an alternative. Person 2 also has two weeks of buying brand A and then a gap followed by more brand A, then C, then B, and then C again. We cannot tell from this data the reason for their move from brand A or indeed whether in week 10 they might not return to brand A again. Person 3 switches from C to B, but purchases coffee at regular intervals—this may be because brand B was cheaper than brand C in week 7. The final person bought coffee only once in the nine-week period. This might be a person who buys instant coffee for guests but does not drink it herself.

Most brands are actually not bought that often, and when they are bought it is at irregular intervals. East et al. (2008) suggest that there are a number of reasons for this. First, most brands are just bought infrequently; East et al. suggest that a typical US household buys a particular coffee brand only about three times a year and the product category about nine times a year. Second, the intervals may vary as customers stockpile (e.g. buy more when there is a price promotion) and at other times they may run out. Of course, there are

		Brands of coffee purchased each week								
Weeks		1	2	3	4	5	6	7	8	9
Person	1	A	A	0	0	B	0	0	A	B
Person	2	A	A	0	0	A	C	B	C	0
Person	3	C	0	0	C	0	0	B	0	0
Person	4	0	0	0	0	0	0	0	A	0

Table 10.1   Hypothetical repeat purchasing over nine weeks

exceptions to this. You may well have brands that you buy far more frequently; indeed if you are a 'coffee addict' you might buy coffee every week.

Purchase frequency

The analysis of repeat buying data is managed by considering the 'purchase occasion', i.e. the frequency of purchase. This is a useful approach as it recognizes that some purchase occasions may mean that more than one unit of the brand is bought on a particular occasion. When buying instant coffee it is most usual to buy a jar at a time, but when buying yoghurt it would be more usual for a family to buy this in bulk for consumption throughout the week. Fixed time periods (e.g. a month or a quarter) are followed to analyse repeat purchasing behaviour, as this allows repeat buying for any brand to be presented using two variables:

(1) **penetration**, i.e. the number of people who buy an item in a given time period;

(2) **purchase frequency**, i.e. the average number of times they buy in the time period.

This means that we can calculate sales for a brand by multiplying penetration (the number of buyers) by purchase frequency (how often they buy the brand). A brand may be big because a few buyers buy it very often or because it has lots of buyers who do not buy it so often. From this data, companies can see how their customer base is made up, i.e. lots of buyers, buying infrequently, fewer buyers who buy the brand a lot, or a combination of both.

What has been found from the analysis of many product categories in many markets is that:

> *the penetration of brands may differ a lot but the average purchase frequency of any brand tends to be similar.*

This is an important finding in terms of understanding how consumers' behaviour actually affects the market, and questions some assumptions about what brand loyalty really means.

To illustrate the importance of the difference between the penetration of brands and their average purchase frequency we show an example from an analysis of the instant coffee market in the USA (Table 10.2).

It is worth explaining that two important measures of market size discussed throughout this chapter are defined as follows:

$$\text{market share } (\%) = \frac{\text{total purchase of the brand}}{\text{total purchases of the category}}$$

$$\text{penetration } (\%) = \frac{\text{number buying the brand at least once}}{\text{total number of potential customers}}$$

Brand	Market share (%)	Penetration or percentage buying	Average purchase per buyer
Any instant coffee	100	67	6.7
Maxwell House	19	24	3.6
Sanka	15	21	3.3
Tasters Choice	14	22	2.8
High Point	13	22	2.6
Folgers	11	18	2.7
Nescafé	8	13	2.9
Brim	4	9	2.0
Maxim	4	9	2.0
Other brands	13	20	3.0
Average	11	17	2.8

Table 10.2   Penetration and purchase frequency for the US coffee market
Source: Ehrenberg and Scriven (1996).

Although the brands may be unfamiliar (this is an example from some time ago, but one which clearly illustrates the importance of penetration), what we can see is that the coffee market at the time was made up of eight players accounting for 87 per cent of the market share and a number of small brands which together held 13 per cent of the market. The penetration or percentage buying is the percentage of households that bought any coffee (67 per cent) and below this in the table is what percentage of this total figure was bought by each brand (e.g. 24 per cent for Maxwell House). If you add up the percentages for each brand you will see that it comes to over 100; this is because many people buy more than one brand of coffee. The average purchase rate is simply the number of times on average the brand was bought. This ranges from a low of 2.0 times to a high of 3.6 for the market leader.

Near-stationary markets

It is important at this point to note that the markets we are considering here are well established rather than new. An important feature of them is that they do not change much. This is known as a **near-stationary market** which is *an established mature market which appears stable over a period of several months or a year*. Of course some markets do change over longer periods, and this can be for all kinds of reasons including changing tastes and priorities, or the introduction of innovative technology. For example, the music industry has seen records replaced by tape recordings, then CDs, and more recently downloading and streaming music on digital music services such as Spotify. An example of change in taste is the move away from beer drinking in Britain and an increase in lager and wine consumption, which can be explained by a behavioural change to lighter drinks and the environments in which people prefer to consume alcohol.

Looking at the numbers in Table 10.2 and in many different markets, the trends in the data are broadly similar, and Ehrenberg and Scriven (1996) noted the following important points about purchase behaviour.

- The market shares for the coffee brands differ up to six times and for penetration around four times, but the average purchase frequencies do not show such great differences. They are all broadly around the average of 2.8. This tells marketers that whether they are a big brand or a small brand they need to reach the market average purchase rate to succeed in that market.

- As market share declines, average purchase frequencies tend to go down. This is referred to as **double jeopardy**, which *is the phenomenon whereby brands with smaller market share have fewer buyers and those fewer buyers buy the brand less often*. Again, this can act as a warning signal to brand owners; there are real advantages in being a bigger brand, as you tend to have more buyers buying more often. Further information about double jeopardy is provided in Consumer Insight 10.1

- Where there are discrepancies, they can usually be easily diagnosed and explained. Analysing the market in this way can give the brand owner the opportunity to find out if there is a problem and what it might be due to. In the coffee example, Brim had a slightly low average purchase frequency of 2.0. Checking the previous year's data showed that this was due to the one-off negative effect of a fire in a warehouse (Ehrenberg et al., 2004).

CONSUMER INSIGHT 10.1

Defection in the car market

Double jeopardy can affect the rate of brand switch. Defection from a brand will depend to some extent on its market share. Brands with a larger market share both win and lose more customers in a year than brands with a smaller market share, but their *relative* loss will be less. In other words, their size allows them to sustain customer defections and capitalize on repeat purchasing. The smaller you are, the greater such losses are relative to your share of the market. Table 10.3 is an example of repeat purchasing of brands of cars in the Thai market. The patterns that are seen here are also found in North America and Europe (Colombo et al., 2000; Bennett, 2005). However, defection rates from service industries are somewhat lower, at around 3–5 per cent (Sharp, 2010).

Brand	Market share (%)	Market penetration (%)	Repeat purchase (%)
Toyota	46	61	56
Other	24	32	47
Honda	10	18	31
Nissan	8	15	33
BMW	7	9	30
Mitsubishi	5	10	29
Average	17	24	38

Table 10.3   Repeat purchasing in the Thai car market
Source: Bennett and Graham (2010).

Questions

1.   What do you notice about the biggest brand's repeat purchase rates?

2.   What does this tell you about brand loyalty?

3.   Why do you think defection rates from services might be lower?

Sources: Colombo et al. (2000); Bennett (2005); Bennett and Graham (2010); Sharp (2010).

 Access the online resources and follow the web links to learn more about the concept of double jeopardy and repeat purchase rates.

Brand loyalty: explaining how we buy

In Chapter 3 we considered the effect of having a lot of choice. Barry Schwartz (2004) described how his supermarket held 61 types of suntan lotion and 80 brands of pain relievers. Most of us are familiar with going into the supermarket and seeing shelves full of different types of shampoo or toothpaste. Currently, Colgate lists 49 types of toothpaste on its website (colegate.co.uk) including Total Advanced, Total Sensitive, Sensitive Whitening, Cavity Protection, and Deep Clean Whitening.

In the fast-moving consumer goods (FMCG) sector, having a wide range of product types under the same brand name is a worldwide phenomenon. Figure 10.2 shows a selection of toothpastes in a retail outlet in the UK. We know that the relative importance of FMCG purchases is low—buying toothpaste or suntan lotion is not like buying a house or a car. Choosing a brand that the consumer subsequently finds that they do not like is not going to have a significant economic impact on most buyers. These are relatively low risk purchases. We may exhibit inertia, randomly choose brands, or engage in variety-seeking behaviour (see Chapter 3). For the most part, our shopping is frequently bought, and in

Figure 10.2   Toothpaste choice   *Source*: Image courtesy of Frankie Roberto.

purchasing low priced goods where we encounter little risk we 'develop *habits* to simplify the repetitive choice-situation' (Ehrenberg, 1988: 5). However, while all brands are bought at roughly the same rate, a brand that has higher market penetration will have more customers buying it, and that is ultimately what makes the difference to market share. The importance of penetration cannot be underestimated, and most changes in market share are due to large movements in penetration and small increases in loyalty (Romaniuk and Sharp, 2016).

What does repeat purchasing tell us about brand loyalty?

Understanding how consumers actually purchase over repeated occasions allows us to consider what brand loyalty really means. In particular, we can consider whether brand loyalty implies that you do not buy other brands, how often you have to buy the same brand to be considered brand loyal, and whether the brand loyalty that we see in consumer panel data might reveal nothing more than habit or inertia which could be broken by a sales promotion or discount on a competing brand (see Research Insight 10.1).

Ehrenberg defined **brand loyalty** as '*any tendency for people to buy the same brand again, whilst usually also buying other brands*' (Ehrenberg and Scriven, 1996: 3). Rather than consumers relentlessly switching from one brand to another, they shop from a repertoire of brands (see Chapter 3), all of which are acceptable to them, and from these they choose different brands at different times. They are not switching from brand to brand without any apparent reason, but choosing from a selected group of brands, all of which are acceptable to them.

These alternative ways of considering what brand loyalty is have major implications for how companies manage their brands. Should a company try to improve brand loyalty or increase the penetration of the brand? It could be argued that if companies tried to make customers more satisfied, they would retain more and increase their market share. So an important question for companies is whether they should aim to retain customers or acquire more?

RESEARCH INSIGHT 10.1

Brown, G.H. (1953), 'Brand loyalty—fact or fiction?', *Advertising Age*, 43, 251–8.

In 1953, Brown published a paper entitled 'Brand loyalty—fact or fiction?' which summarized analysis of consumer panel data for items such as margarine, toothpaste, and coffee over a year-long period. This seminal work was the starting point for research using consumer panel data to identify brand loyalty. Brown examined the purchasing habits of 100 members of the 610 families in the USA involved in the panel to identify whether there were differences in their purchase profiles. He identified four types of loyalty, which he called undivided, divided, unstable, and no loyalty.

 Access the online resources to read the abstract and access the full paper.

Sharp (2010) argues that trying to increase brand loyalty is a waste of time. This is largely because of the nature of double jeopardy discussed in Consumer Insight 10.1. A large company will have more repeat buyers just because it has so many more buyers than a small company—the more customers you can get, the more likely you are that some of them will repeat buy, so size really does make a difference. This happens in all types of consumer goods and in all countries tested (Romaniuk and Sharp, 2016). Of course, you will also lose customers but, as noted in Consumer Insight 10.1, this tends to be relatively fewer for a large company. Double jeopardy implies that it is not possible to change your defection rates without first drastically increasing your market share. Much defection occurs outside the company's control and is particularly troublesome for smaller companies. For example, if you are a small local delicatessen or dog-walking service operating in one locality, and your customer moves to another area, they will no longer be able to use your services and will have to find alternatives. There is little you can do about this unless you can open more branches throughout the country, perhaps by developing a franchise.

Light and heavy buyers—which matter most?

Of course, consumers have different tastes and make different choices. Examining consumer panel data for many different brands shows that most have a lot of light buyers who buy the brand only occasionally. Such people are often also light users of the product category but may buy from a wide repertoire of brands. These are people who do not buy much of the product category, and when they do they like to vary the brands they buy. There are also heavy users of a product category, but interestingly they are often seen to buy relatively few brands. Here we might suggest that as heavy users of the product category they have identified the brands they like best and stick to them. For example, consumer panel data from the UK shows that just 4 per cent of people who buy Coca-Cola once a week were responsible for a quarter of its sales volume (Sharp, 2010). If we were the marketing manager for Coca-Cola, we might think about targeting our marketing at these heavy buyers, since they have developed a relationship with Coca-Cola and will probably notice our marketing communications. But it is difficult to make heavy buyers even heavier buyers as they may have already reached saturation point.

An alternative strategy would be to focus marketing effort on the infrequent buyers who, while they do not buy often in absolute terms, actually account for most of the brand's total customers. While it might be argued that they are more of a challenge, marketing to them could be an important defensive strategy as they may be prone to 'forget' the brand or readily switch to Pepsi or own-label brands as they do not appear to have any particular affiliation with Coca-Cola beyond occasionally buying the brand. As they account for a large number of Coca-Cola's buyers, they cannot be ignored and need reminding to buy the brand. This argument is in line with what we have learned about low involvement. We argued in Chapter 3 that marketers often want to increase involvement with their brand; to do so you may at the very least remind such occasional or low involved consumers that your brand is still there and prompt them to buy it (if only now and again). In the matter of influence, successful marketing is most likely to create more light than heavy buyers, and marketers do need light buyers to buy their brand and a few of them to buy the brand again in the time period. To become a big brand you have to reach out and attract as many of these light category buyers as you can (Romaniuk and Sharp, 2016). These differences between a company's heavy and light buyers are examined further when we consider the Pareto law.

The Pareto law

The Pareto law suggests that 80 per cent of your sales come from only 20 per cent of your customers. In practice, a company's heaviest customers may actually account for around 50 per cent of your sales in a year. This would mean that light and medium buyers are also accounting for 50 per cent, and so their importance cannot be overlooked. Table 10.4 provides information on the body spray and deodorant category from the USA and shows the Pareto law in action. Whether the brand has a 16 per cent or a 1 per cent market share, the percentage of heavy buyers in a 12-month period is around 50 per cent. See also Research Insight 10.2 for a method of evaluating a new brand.

Brand	Market share (%)	Percentage volume accounted for by heaviest 20% of buyers in 12 months
Sure	16	53
Lynx	14	53
Impulse	8	55
Soft and Gentle	7	52
Rightguard	7	51
Dove	6	48
Mum	1	46

Table 10.4   The Pareto law and the deodorant market
Source: Sharp (2010).

The law of buyer moderation

When we look at the range of buyers for a brand, we are always looking over a particular time period—how many consumers buy in a month, six months, or a year. However, companies obviously need to plan over longer time periods to ensure that they have the appropriate marketing strategy. Do heavy and light buyers stay the same year after year? Anschuetz (2002) looked at the leading brand of ketchup in the USA using IRI panel data over two years. The brand had both high brand name recognition and large market share. Anschuetz first analysed only those customers who bought any ketchup in both years. Then he divided Year 1 consumers into groups that differed in terms of their volume contribution and value to the brand. He found, perhaps not surprisingly, that non-buyers of the brand were the largest group buying nothing in Year 1, while light buyers who bought only once contributed about 14 per cent of the brand's volume (see Table 10.5). Those who

Buyer group	Percentage of sample (%)	Frequency in Year 1	Brand volume (%)	
			Year 1	Year 2
Non-buyers	45	0	0	14
Light	22	1	14	15
Medium	25	2–4	43	36
Heavy	9	5+	43	34
Total	100		100	100

Table 10.5   All buyers of ketchup across two years

Source: IRI Panel Data from Aschuetz, N. (2002), 'Why a brand's most valuable customer is the next one it adds', *Journal of Advertising Research*, January/February, 15–21.

bought two to four times were classified as medium buyers and contributed 43 per cent to volume, while the 9 per cent of customers who were heavy buyers (buying more than five times) also accounted for 43 per cent of volume. Anschuetz then compared Year 1 and Year 2 purchasing, looking at those who had purchased in both Year 1 and Year 2 and how often they had purchased. Interestingly, those who bought nothing in Year 1 contributed to 14 per cent of Year 2's volume and when combined with light buyers from Year 1 this rose to 29 per cent of Year 2's volume. Although still very important for the brand's volume, the medium and heavy buyers in Year 2 contributed less than in the previous year. This illustrates that just because non-buyers do not buy in one time period it does not mean that they will not buy in the next, even if the period is as long as a year. Light, moderate, and even non-buyers in a particular year should not be ignored; while as individual units they deliver less profit for the brand, they deliver overall a large number of units sold which contributes to the revenue and profit of a brand selling to a mass market. This is termed the **law of buyer moderation** and is *the tendency for light buyers to become heavier and heavier buyers to become lighter* (Sharp, 2010).

RESEARCH INSIGHT 10.2

Ehrenberg, A.S.C., Uncles, M.D., and Goodhardt, G.J. (2004), 'Understanding brand performance measures: using Dirichlet benchmarks', *Journal of Business Research*, 57, 12, 1307–25.

The Dirichlet model is a theoretical model that can be used to evaluate a new brand to see how it is fairing in the marketplace. This study takes an example from Campbell's who had launched a premium priced Tastes of the World soup in Britain. The brand had low loyalty-related measures compared with the bigger competitors in the market. It seemed that Tastes of the World would not succeed in this market until Campbell's was introduced to the double jeopardy effect by its marketing advisors. Using the Dirichlet model it was possible to see that in this case the impact of double jeopardy was that repeat buying levels would be predictably lower for such a small brand. The brand's problem was not the level of repeat buying, but that it just needed more customers.

 Access the online resources to read the abstract and access the full paper.

Blips in a household's buying can arise for all sorts of reasons. One household may appear as a heavy buyer of breakfast cereal one year but not the next year, perhaps because a child who liked cereal has now left home or the family are going through a phase of different breakfast menus. Or maybe a household buys a lot of burgers in Year 1 but none the next year because they only cook burgers on the barbecue and the weather in Year 2 was not as good as in Year 1. While there can be many reasons, for marketers the message is not to assume that the patterns that occurred in one year will be replicated in the following year; the evidence reveals that markets are dynamic and are often outside the control of the business.

Patterns of buyer behaviour and market segmentation

As noted in Chapter 3 we often buy a number of brands in a product category because the risk of trying different brands is low, we may seek variety, or it just does not matter enough to us which brand we buy. We may have some favourites that form our repertoire of brands, which inevitably means that each brand's customers are also another brand's customers. For example, in a given period in the UK 65 per cent or more of buyers of Diet Coke, Fanta, Lilt, and Pepsi also bought regular Coca-Cola (Sharp, 2010). Obviously Coca-Cola is a particularly large brand, and so all soft drink brands have to compete with it. The **duplication of purchase analysis** explains this phenomenon and is described as '*the degree to which brands within a category share their buyers with each of the other brands*' (Sharp, 2010). Sharp considered a number of product categories and generally found that in most cases a brand will share its customers with others in that category. However, there is some deviation from this norm. For example, in the ice cream market Walls Carte D'Or is a strong market leader with whom all brands share customers, while the two brands Ben & Jerry's and Häagen Dazs share double the customers they share with other brands. In other words, if you are a buyer of Ben & Jerry's, you are very likely to regularly buy Häagen Dazs. This has implications for segmenting consumers. In particular, it suggests that companies should be careful when assuming that their brand appeals to a very different segment of consumer than their competitors. It also suggests that competition is more about mental and physical availability (see the section 'Implications for marketing' later in this chapter) rather than brand positioning or the brand's history or even its quality (Romaniuk and Sharp, 2016). Some functional product forms do seem to have an impact. For example, diet soft drinks tend to share customers. Duplication of purchase analysis can be useful in helping a marketing manager see which other brands are also bought by their customers and whether, as in the ice-cream example, they have a particularly close competitor. It also shows that brands gain most new customers from the biggest brands, to whom they also lose most customers. Duplication of purchase analysis can provide a guide to the product category based on what consumers actually buy, and perhaps also on how they use brands. It may also give an insight into how companies go about segmenting their markets and how consumers respond to this.

For example, the UK cereal market used to be considered to be made up of two categories—hot (such as porridge) and cold (such as cornflakes)—but panel data showed that so-called cold breakfast cereals also sold well in the winter, and investigations revealed that consumers were simply turning their cold cereals into hot by pouring warm milk on them (Sharp, 2010) (see Figure 10.3). Such data helps managers to

Figure 10.3   Consumers can defy situational segmentation

Source: © iStock.com/dulezidar.

understand consumers better and to recognize that their segmentation categories may not always match up with how consumers actually use products.

How insights from research with consumer panel data can be used in practice is further explained by Tom Lloyd, from Metametrics UK, in Practitioner Insight 10.

PRACTITIONER INSIGHT 10

Tom Lloyd, Director, Metametrics UK

Metametrics is a company specializing in marketing analytics. Here, Tom Lloyd talks about the impact of the work done by Ehrenberg and his colleagues on practical marketing.

The work done by Ehrenberg and his colleagues has very significant practical implications for businesses today. In my experience there is no common, robust shared view amongst marketing practitioners as to 'how marketing works'.

But Ehrenberg's buyer behaviour principles provide a robust framework that we can use to make predictions and sensible decisions. Unlike many other marketing models, which are mainly theoretical, the buyer behaviour principles are empirical, and can be very easily demonstrated and validated. The advantage of this is that the marketing manager does not have to 'believe' the model; he/she simply has to plot the data. For the brands in your market, does share correlate highly with penetration and less with loyalty/frequency? It is interesting to see how brands almost always follow the established pattern, and it is also interesting to look into any odd outliers that do not.

We can then give simple practical guidance to managers.

- All brands essentially work in the same way. There are almost no 'niche' brands or 'special'/ unusual brands in terms of buyer metrics (e.g. brands with a few customers who buy them very loyally). Brands are just large or small.

- Which key performance indicators (KPIs) are valuable? For example, traditional brand funnels that categorize consumers into those aware, trialists, occasional users, regular users, and loyal users are widely used but in reality provide little helpful insight—the buyer behaviour principles explain why all brand funnels within a category tend to be the same shape; they are just bigger or smaller depending on brand size.

- Setting sensible growth targets—if you want your 5 per cent share brand to be a 10 per cent share brand, it will need to look like a typical 10 per cent brand in terms of its buyer metrics. This provides very helpful insights into the marketing challenges in achieving that scale. What level of penetration will we need and how much will it cost us in advertising and trial activity to do that?

- Generating growth—to grow you almost always need to increase penetration. Frequency and loyalty strategies almost never work. This is a counter-intuitive leap for many marketers. They ask, 'Surely it's easier to get existing buyers to buy more than to get new buyers?' The reality is that growing penetration does not mean attracting totally new buyers who have never bought you. It is mostly a case of reminding lapsed buyers to buy you again. The evidence for this can be easily seen by looking at the dynamics of the fastest growing successful brands. Even though they probably pursued different strategies, if they grow at all, they almost always do so by increasing the number of buyers they have.

- Learn from other brands. It is interesting how little analysis marketers undertake of the buyer metrics of successful growing brands even in their own categories. This is most likely because marketers believe that brands behave so differently that you cannot learn very much about one brand by looking at any others. By challenging this misconception there is actually a huge amount of insight to be gained from this type of analysis, and this is a practice that should be encouraged.

Finally, we should not ignore the internal organizational and cultural issues involved in communicating buyer behaviour principles. It is a radical shift for a marketer to accept that growing their brand means attracting a lot of disloyal buyers who will buy their brand occasionally. Or that there are rules that dictate that most brands behave in the same way and that their brand is not 'special' or different in terms of its buyer metrics (although it will, of course, be unique in its creative positioning). Even though these principles are not 'models' but simple empirical observations that anyone can make, attempts to disseminate the learning within organizations have often failed simply because of the radical shift in understanding that is required and the perceived threat to marketing's role.

How duplication of purchase impacts segmentation

Consumer panel data also shows where there are real perceived differences in brands leading to different market segments. The market for flavoured milk in Australia includes brands with distinct attributes. One brand, Dairy Vale, is perceived as sweet and luxurious, and is also considered as suitable for children. Max is marketed to males, and two other brands, Feel Good and Take Care, are 'healthy' brands targeted at women. Table 10.6 shows that most brands, following the law of duplication of purchase, shared about half their customers during the period examined with the largest brand, Farmers Union. However, note that the distinctly 'male' brand Max had no overlap of customers with the two 'healthy' female brands Feel Good and Take Care, revealing clear consumer preferences resulting from the brands' segmentation strategies. Indeed, segmentation by gender is an approach that has been used by other product categories as illustrated in Consumer Insight 10.2.

CONSUMER INSIGHT 10.2

Men are hungry, women deserve a treat

In a number of product categories you will see that companies have chosen to segment by gender. Carlsberg introduced a low alcohol spritzer drink named Eve, while Wrigley's 5 Gum (chewing gum) has flavours such as Cobalt, Pulse, and Flood, names that are reminiscent of aftershave fragrances, and the gum is presented in what has been described as a package designed to look like a box of condoms (Carter, 2010). But it is probably in chocolate that we can see the biggest gender divide. The Yorkie Bar began with a decidedly masculine trucker advertising the chocolate bar from Nestlé, which some years later was followed by the line 'It's not for girls' (see Figure 10.4). Television advertisements showed women trying to buy Yorkie by wearing false beards or dressing up as builders. Snickers also has a masculine

Figure 10.4   Yorkie it's *not* for girls!
Source: Image printed with permission from Nestlé.

feel, most recently using the line 'You are not you when you are hungry'. In one advertisement the veteran actress Joan Collins is transformed back into a football player once she has eaten her Snickers bar. In the past, brands like Flake and Galaxy have clearly been targeted at women with messages of indulgence and taking time away from the hurly burly of everyday life. The latest addition to the female chocolate line is diet chocolate Crispello. Cadbury launched the lower calorie Crispello after apparently identifying that women are becoming more health conscious and therefore buying fewer chocolate bars, with annual sales falling by over 6 per cent (Bartlett, 2012). The strap line for Crispello is 'A little treat for you'. Gender stereotyping has always been an issue in marketing and particularly advertising. While some products may continue to be presented in a gender-specific context one commentator, Stephen Bayley, has suggested that increasingly desirable products, especially those with a technological element, will be presented in a gender-free manner. He said: 'We are all scrabbling to [get] the same status symbols—the most desired objects of recent years are gender-free objects; that is an extraordinary change to be happening now'.

Questions

1. Given what you now know about duplication of purchase, how successful do you think such gender-based advertising would be?

2. Suggest some likely overlapping purchases in the chocolate bar sector?

3. In what other sectors might one find such overlapping purchase behaviour and why?

4. What other products are you aware of that use gender stereotypes? Why do you think they use them? Do you think they are useful?

Sources: Carter (2010); Bartlett (2012); Chahal (2016).

 Access the online resources and follow the web links to see other examples of organizations that have chosen to segment by gender.

Buyers of brand	Percentage of buyers who also bought brand				
	Farmers Union	Dairy Vale	Take Care	Max	Feel Good
Farmers Union	–	21	8	6	5
Dairy Vale	43	–	5	5	5
Take Care	52	16	–	0	20
Max	45	20	0	–	0
Feel Good	53	27	33	0	–
Average	48	21	12	3	8

Table 10.6 Duplication of purchase between flavoured milk brands
Source: Sharp (2010).

Do you need to differentiate your brand?

When buying a brand, to what extent does a consumer have to feel that there is something particularly different about it which motivates their purchase? If you were choosing between different brands of ice cream, for example, would you have to be struck by something very different to the other brands that would make you choose this brand? The reality is that there is not a great deal of difference between brands in any category. Imagine that each day you tried a different brand of shampoo but did not know which brand was which—would there really be that much variation in your experience or the performance of the brands? Of course, there would be slight differences in colour, perfume, and texture, but how much would that matter to you? There are situational differences that can affect customers. You may choose Lynx shower gel because it is stocked in your supermarket (where you happen to be buying other goods); you may actually really prefer Adidas shower gel, but it's not stocked in that store. When you go on holiday you may wish to take smaller packs of shampoo and conditioner and so choose from the brands that produce these holiday-sized packs. There is also differentiation by price, but within a competitive set customers of one brand will be similar to those of another. One might expect H&M customers to be broadly similar to Primark customers, and Gucci customers to be similar to Prada customers. Of course this does not preclude Primark or H&M customers from also visiting Gucci and Prada, and vice versa, but this will not be of great importance to the managers of Primark. Studies across products and services in different countries and using different methods reveal consistent patterns (Sharp, 2010: 123).

1. Buyers of a brand perceive very weak differentiation—yet this does not stop them loyally buying a particular brand.

2. A brand's level of perceived differentiation is very similar to that of their rivals.

Table 10.7 illustrates that relatively few of a brand's regular buyers see it as either different or unique.

Brand	Different (%)	Unique (%)	Either (%)
Coca-Cola	8	13	19
Diet Coke	9	8	15
Pepsi	7	10	15
Fanta	8	5	12
Pepsi Max	9	10	19
Schweppes	6	9	13
Canada Dry	10	9	17
Average	9	9	16

Table 10.7   Brand user perceptions of differentiation in the soft drink category (UK)
Source: Sharp (2010).

Similar patterns are found across different product categories unless there are exceptional functional differences. Therefore Aldi, a food retailer that does not stock national brands, was considered by 67 per cent as 'different' from other supermarkets, and Subway, a sandwich-based fast food brand, scored 50 per cent in comparison with McDonald's, Domino's, and KFC (Romaniuk et al., 2007) (see Figure 10.5). The message generally seems to be that consumers do not require differentiation in their brand to purchase it. Research Insight 10.3 looks at brand differentiation in more depth.

What matters to consumers?

As brands are continually looking to catch the consumer's attention, branding helps consumers to remain loyal while creative advertising reminds them about new and different brands. There is plenty of evidence to show that brand image impacts consumers' choice of brand, but even the leading brand in a market with strong brand images will, for most people, be just one brand in their repertoire. Therefore media strategies need to maximize reach and keep reminding customers of their presence (Sharp et al., 2012). However, does this mean that consumers have a different kind of relationship with the brands that they are more loyal to? The evidence from the research we have been discussing in this chapter would tend to suggest that this kind of loyalty is just a fact of life. It is a feature of habit, dependent on what is readily available, familiarity, and even a lack of really caring in some cases (Sharp, 2010), and does not reflect a deeper kind of connection. It may be that some of us do have different types of relationships with brands; we may feel strongly (positive or negative) about some brands, but that in itself does not mean that we do not buy other brands. Brand communities (see Chapter 9) do exist and people in such communities often exhibit strong positive feelings about their chosen brand (Schau and Muniz, 2002; Casaló et al., 2008), but the question that Sharp and his colleagues address is whether this really matters in terms of the brand's market share and penetration. These 100 per cent loyal buyers tend to be light category, low value customers. Of course, many consumers are passionate about brands

(A)   **(B)**

Figure 10.5 Subway and Aldi, perceived as different by consumers
Source: Subway © iStock.com/ivanastar; Aldi © iStock.com/SeanPavonePhoto.

that are dear to them. The most often cited are Apple (Muniz and Schau, 2005) and Harley-Davidson (Schouten and Alexander, 1995), but if you explore other brand communities such as The Purse Blog you will find consumers passionate about many other brands—in this case premium handbag brands such as Louis Vuitton, Chanel, and Jimmy Choo. Even if you love Chanel bags, it does not mean that that is the only brand you buy. Both Apple and Harley-Davidson have repeat purchasing levels that are broadly what would be expected in their categories; in the case of Apple it is higher, but there is also the fact that switching from Apple would require changing operating systems (Sharp, 2010).

RESEARCH INSIGHT 10.3

van Marrewijk, A. and Broos, M. (2012), 'Retail stores as brands: performances, theatre and space', *Consumption Markets and Culture*, 15, 4, 374–91.

In this paper Van Marrewijk and Broos provide an interesting perspective on how retail stores develop brand distinctiveness from a consumer culture theory perspective. The authors explore how management and shop assistants in Oger, a Dutch fashion store, communicate and construct the brand to consumers. This in-depth ethnographic analysis of the Oger retail setting provides many insights into how organizations manage the spatial settings within the retail store to communicate differentiation in an effort to maximize consumer loyalty and relationships.

 Access the online resources to read the abstract and access the full paper.

While there may be some consumers who exhibit these kinds of highly loyal preferences, generally having a brand repertoire gives you more choice. By having a range of goods in mind the consumer has this choice but without the mental effort of constantly re-evaluating all the potential brands available, and this can be both convenient and reassuring. Therefore it is important that marketing managers recognize that they need to be in the consumer's repertoire but not to expect total loyalty from them. Romaniuk and Sharp (2016) conclude by saying that it is unusual for people either to buy only one brand across purchase occasions, or to buy a different brand on every purchase occasion. For the effect of seasonality on sales figures see Consumer Insight 10.3.

CONSUMER INSIGHT 10.3

Seasonality—do you sell more soup in the winter?

While stationary markets, if looked at over a period of time, seem fairly stable, there are some fluctuations throughout the year. The time of year and sales promotions are sure to have an effect on monthly sales figures. In the UK people buy mince pies at Christmas and chocolate eggs at Easter, and in Singapore and Malaysia Chinese New Year is celebrated with the consumption of pineapple pastries. In the northern hemisphere more soup is sold in the winter and more ice cream in the summer, while in countries such as Singapore, where the temperature varies very little, ice cream is sold all year round. Soup may be considered a seasonal product. Evidence shows that soup is bought at a higher rate in the winter than in the summer (Wellan and Ehrenberg, 1990). Research using the Dirichlet model (see Research Insight 10.2) revealed that, largely, people who only bought in the peak season made up the difference in sales. In other words, the seasonal effect in this case was due to those people who did not buy in the off-season but bought during the winter months, while the rest retained a fairly steady rate of purchase throughout the year. This was an important finding, as the traditional view had been that those who bought all year round increased their purchases during the peak season. This knowledge helped decisions such as when to advertise and how to deal with the off-season dip with regard to production and cash flow issues (Ehrenberg et al., 2004). By doing this type of analysis, companies can identify whether they have different types of segmented markets and can introduce appropriate marketing and internal organizational responses to help manage these differences.

Questions

1. With the knowledge from this consumer insight, if you were the marketing manager for a European soup company how would this impact your marketing communications?

2. Consider some other products that might be impacted by seasonality (e.g. sun cream, turkeys). How might you manage the seasonality of these products?

Sources: Wellan and Ehrenberg (1990); Ehrenberg et al. (2004).

 Access the online resources and follow the web links to see other examples of seasonal products.

Implications for marketing and advertising

If light, moderate, and even non-buyers are important for a brand, in terms of reach a company should consider media that are going to allow it to target more customers than it currently has—simply put, every non-buyer is a potential buyer. This may mean attention to distribution and sales force activity alongside marketing communications. Brands have to make the invest-ment to reach more potential consumers. To enable this, brands need to develop:

- mental availability—the propensity for the brand to be thought of in buying situations;

- physical availability—how easy is the brand to buy and find (Romaniuk and Sharp, 2016: 10).

This is particularly difficult for a small brand as with a limited budget the temptation may be to focus only on the smaller segment of apparently more profitable consumers, but for the brand to grow it needs to be bought by as many consumers as possible. To do that it has to be thought of by customers (mental availability) and easily available to buy (physical availability) by as many people as possible. Small brands in emerging markets may be regionally based and therefore suffer because they do not have significant distribu-tion networks. As identified in Consumer Insight 10.4, shopping across channels (includ-ing the internet) is now common in many countries and therefore having a multi-channel presence is important to build physical availability. But it is also important to know what your customers 'do' in the channels they visit. For example Bain & Co. (2013) found that across 27 countries, while customers transact regularly online, physical branches are still the most important for opening new bank accounts. Only Germany and the Netherlands have online account openings that are comparable with those at physical branches.

Another important implication of this research is for marketing managers to understand the nature of loyalty among their customers. The goal of the 100 per cent loyal customer is not only unlikely but not necessarily worthwhile in terms of how much they actually buy. A large brand may have a relatively high number of 100 per cent loyal customers, although for a small brand this will be much less (the double jeopardy effect), but 100 per cent loyal users are generally light users of the category, purchasing fewer items than others, and so effectively they do not have much chance of being disloyal (Ehrenberg et al., 2004). As such, they may not be that useful to the brand.

There are also implications for the creative message. In particular, according to Anschuetz (2002), it is important that the brand's message connects inclusively across all types of user. A message, or indeed choice of media, that is too exclusive will not allow the brand to grow as it will not reach or appeal to a wide enough cross section of potential users.

CONSUMER INSIGHT 10.4

How global brands get penetration in emerging markets using physical and mental availability

Products and brands face a variety of barriers to mental and physical availability in different markets, but there are also many ways of overcoming such barriers. The First National Bank of South Africa achieved physical availability by developing and growing its customer base through becoming the market leader in mobile banking. In some product categories in some countries it may be an issue of how the product is currently used or perceived, such that it is not thought appropriate for certain uses or only considered for certain occasions (mental availability). For example, in India those who consume alcohol often see wine as a drink only for particular celebratory situations, which limits its purchase possibilities, but unlike in most Western countries there is also a fear of buying fake wine.

Similar cultural and economic issues impact the uptake of other products, but some companies have found ingenious ways of defeating these barriers. For example, Thailand is a strong market for haircare products and Western brands are sought after, but the large bottles that Westerners might buy are often too expensive for most shoppers in Thailand. L'Oreal, Unilever, and Proctor & Gamble have overcome this by offering smaller bottles which, although more expensive per gram, mean that people are able to give themselves a treat and has allowed penetration of the market by ensuring appropriate physical availability and, by getting people to use the brands, has also increased mental availability.

This need for mental and physical availability has an impact on how you present your brand to the market. In particular, it reveals the importance of not limiting the target of your marketing. In the USA the fast growing Goya Foods is Hispanic in origin and specializes in Hispanic food products but ensures that it markets these to all Americans. Similarly, the Quorn brand which markets meat-free protein dishes does not position itself as a vegetarian substitute but rather a healthy eating brand.

Questions

1. What tactics might you use to alter the mental availability problem of wine in India?

2. A problem for many brands is that they are thought only suitable for certain occasions such as gifts or for other celebrations. Think of any brands that you are aware of that fall into this category. What might you do to change this? You should consider all marketing mix possibilities.

3. If you were introducing a new herbal tea into your home market, how would you manage its physical and mental availability?

Sources: Wragg and Regan (2012); Wentz (2013); Bayne et al. (2014); Romaniuk and Sharp (2016).

 Access the online resources and follow the web links to learn more.

Growing a brand's distribution into a previously unrepresented area is an important strategy because it reaches potential buyers who have not readily been able to gain access to the brand. Not only are light or non-buyers given access to the brand, but heavy buyers also have improved availability. This is a strategy that multiple retailers, such as Tesco, often pursue. In addition to Tesco Extra and superstores, often located on the outskirts of towns, Tesco has populated urban and inner-city areas with its Tesco Express stores, thus making the opportunity for consumers to buy from them that much greater (see Figure 10.6).

Ehrenberg and his colleagues have shown that a careful analysis of data often provides an explanation for why consumers are actually behaving in a way that is different to what is expected by marketers. For example, when Unilever ran a promotion that offered extra

(A)   (B)

Figure 10.6   Tesco Express and Tesco Extra   *Source*: Images printed with permission of Tesco Stores Ltd.

product with their leading UK laundry powder, they assumed that this would be particularly attractive to the brand's heavy buyers. However, analysis of the data showed the exact opposite; the extra product promotion appealed to recent non-buyers and light buyers (Ehrenberg, 1988). This illustrates that one does not have to have a complete change in attitude to brands to buy a different one; this is further explored in Consumer Insight 10.5.

CONSUMER INSIGHT 10.5

Do consumers always change their attitudes when they switch brands?

An area of contention in marketing is whether attitudes produce behaviour or behaviour influences attitudes—of course, both may occur in different situations (see Chapter 6). If we look at patterns of behaviour over time we can see that often even highly loyal buyers of a brand will buy other brands at some point. If we can switch easily between different brands, it seems to suggest that our attitudes to brands are not absolute in the sense that we prefer one above the other in every circumstance. Ehrenberg et al. (2004) argue that the nature of the polygamous consumer is the outcome of many years of past experience, and consumers do not change their beliefs and evaluations of brands in a way that constantly affects their brand choice. Therefore a consumer's behaviour, i.e. which brands they have bought in the past, is probably the best predictor of what they will do in the future. Indeed, rather than assuming that consumers have very different attitudes to different brands, it is far more likely that, within a product category, how someone feels about Brand A is not that different to how they feel about Brand B (Barwise and Ehrenberg, 1985). This suggests that a 'me-too' brand is quite viable if it can gain market penetration and share. At issue here is also how people feel about brands—their emotional attachment. Romaniuk and Sharp (2016) say that this can happen but typically is a relatively weak emotion and marketers should be wary of placing too much importance on relationships with brands. They identified from research across 500 brands in 24 product categories and 23 countries that explicit rejection of brands is generally low. What is more important is mental availability.

However, many marketers and business strategists see differentiation as an important strategic option. For example, Michael Porter (1985) identified differentiation as one of three generic business strategies. A problem for differentiation is that it can usually be quite easily copied, especially in service businesses, and so any competitive advantage may be short-lived. The perceived need to differentiate has led to product innovation, which ultimately is a good thing for consumers, but it is rare for a brand in a product category to remain an innovator for long; most brands catch up fairly quickly.

Questions

1. Identify two or three 'me-too' brands in different product categories. Do you consider them to be successful and why?

2. Choose two or three differentiated brands in different product categories. How have they differentiated themselves? Have they been copied?

3. In your opinion, what are the pitfalls and opportunities of these two approaches?

Sources: Barwise and Ehrenberg (1985); Porter (1985); Ehrenberg et al. (2004).

 Access the online resources and follow the web links to learn more about consumers' attitudes when switching brands.

Price-related promotions may be developed in the hope that they will appeal to potential customers of the brand, but this may not be the case. Ehrenberg et al. (1994) looked at 150 promotions in Britain, Germany, Japan, and the USA, and found that there were no before-to-after sales increases following the promotion and very few new buyers. In addition, repeat buying following the promotion was not affected. Their conclusion was that price promotions generally just bring the purchase occasion forward for existing customers. Research Insight 10.4 is about an additional important category of buyers, lapsed buyers, who are those people who have purchased in the past but since defected to another brand.

RESEARCH INSIGHT 10.4

Romaniuk, J. and Nenycz-Thiel, M. (2016), 'Lapsed buyers' durable brand consideration in emerging markets', *Journal of Business Research*, 69, 9, 3645–51.

This research examines consumers with a mixed brand buying history, attempting to understand the lapsed buyer, i.e. consumers who have purchased a brand in the past but have since defected to another brand. Looking at data across 26 brands, in a range of markets, the authors found that lapsed buyers hold more positive attitudes towards the brand than never-buyers of the brand, and that lapsed buyers are *not less likely* to consider the brand in the future than other non-customers. This shows the importance of considering the buyer's full past history with the brand, not just current status, in theoretical models and when modelling brand choice or customer lifetime value for durables in emerging markets.

 Access the online resources to read the abstract and access the full paper.

Does your brand need to be distinctive?

We have discussed how differentiation does not appear to be that important to consumers; rather, their past purchasing history (their behaviour) seems to be a better indicator of which brands they will choose in the future. However, a brand needs to be distinctive; above all, customers need to be able to spot it and recognize it. As discussed already, distinctive elements might be colours, logos, or taglines, or they might be celebrities associated with the brand. Critical for the marketer is that the customer identifies the brand and that this builds awareness, or reminds or reinforces their memory of the brand and makes it easier to choose. There are many examples of successful distinctiveness, but those discussed here are particularly well known. The Nike 'swoosh' logo alongside the powerful tagline 'Just do it' is distinctive and is used in all its advertising and point of sale material, and is even placed on many of its clothes as part of the design. Similarly, people across the world recognize the four circles of the Audi logo (Figure 10.7). To succeed in distinctiveness, the brand has to have something that is both unique and ubiquitous, i.e. when you choose your distinctiveness you need to stick with it and ensure that consumers can see it everywhere so that it acts as a trigger in their memories to identify the brand. This inevitably means a lot of investment in communicating to the consumer over time. It does not matter whether this distinctiveness is preferred by consumers; rather, what matters is that over time consumers connect such distinctiveness with that brand, such that a particular feature, such as the oil company Shell's distinctive red and yellow shell or the purple of Cadbury's Dairy Milk, can almost replace the brand name or other identifying feature.

An important message for companies advertising their brand to experienced consumers of the product class is that you can rarely imbue attributes that will differentiate it greatly from its competitors. Similarly, it will be difficult to increase customers' loyalty to the brand because, as previously discussed, these factors generally vary little from one brand to another. However, if a brand is publicized effectively, more people will be aware of it, interested in it, feel it may be worth trying, and so bring it into their consideration set. This does not preclude advertising that is aimed at informing the public, such as a price cut, a special promotion, or a new flavour, size, or package type.

Most of the time, however, marketers need to remind people that their brand is there. While copy and visuals need to be noticed and get into consumers' memories, this does not mean that a particular message is required or indeed that the advertising itself needs to be particularly outstanding (see Figure 10.8). What is necessary is that the brand is remembered. Perhaps counter-intuitively, the

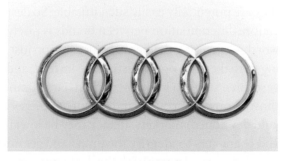

Figure 10.7   The distinctive Audi logo
Source: Roberto Lusso/Shutterstock.com.

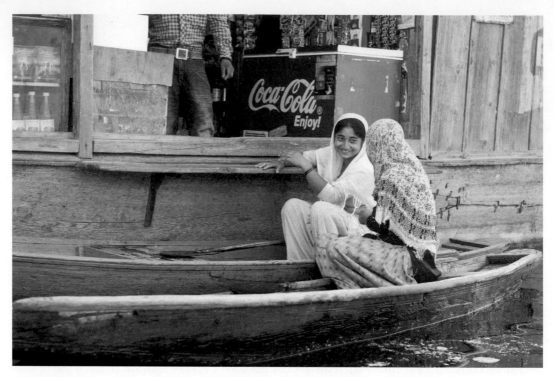

Figure 10.8 Coca-Cola ensures that its presence is everywhere   *Source*: © iStock.com/Pavliha.

job may be easier for brands that are closer to and more substitutable by other brands. Why? Because the advertising does not have to try to change people's attitudes or behaviours around a particular product type, i.e. the functional differentiating factors. For example, if your preference for breakfast is Shredded Wheat, it may be much easier to convince you to try a new brand that is similarly constituted to Shredded Wheat than to get you to try a brand of muesli or even croissants as alternatives. Therefore Ehrenberg et al. (1997: 11) believe that the less difference between brands, the easier it may be for advertising to 'nudge choice behaviour', but at the same time such brands must retain defensive reinforcement as they are potentially easily substitutable. So despite the rhetoric for differentiation and innovation, differentiation between brands is rarely sustainable for long and might not even be worthwhile as it is deliberately focusing on just part of a market. Companies should be looking to make their brand distinctive instead, and to do this Romaniuk and Sharp (2016) suggest three steps to implementation. First, brands need to reach all category buyers as only those exposed to your brand's distinctive asset can build a memory of it. In some emerging (and developed) markets literacy may be low; this may mean simply using shapes, colours, and characters to identify the brand and get noticed (see Chapter 5). Second, it is necessary to link the brand name with the distinctive asset and these connections must be a noticeable part of all communications. Finally, to do this one must be consistent in the message and ensure that every exposure to the brand counts. Such consistency also relates to packaging as often companies are tempted to update packaging, but this will also mean that for some time at least the customer has to search harder to find your brand. Therefore the reasons for changing packaging should be carefully considered.

Loyalty programmes and price promotions

The data presented in this chapter has major implications not only regarding *who* companies target but also *how* they do it. As we have seen, it is likely that inclusive advertising appeals will be more successful than those that are obscure or clearly exclude a large proportion of a potential market. Sharp (2010: 54) is particularly critical of loyalty programmes, saying that they 'generate small or no shifts in market share'. Above all, he says, they are skewed, more than other marketing actions, towards heavier, more loyal brand buyers. This is because these buyers have a greater economic incentive to sign up, whereas many light buyers may not see the point of signing up. Sharp's argument is that this severely restricts the reach of such programmes. On the other hand, we know that some loyalty programmes have been very successful for companies despite being very expensive to run.

One of the most notable of these is Tesco who teamed up with the analysis agency dunnhumby to make sure that the loyalty programme they used, the Clubcard, yielded results beyond just being an incentive for customers. They use the information they receive to target their customers more effectively. The amount and extent of the data they glean from their customers is so comprehensive that it acts as their own consumer panel. They carefully analyse the data to encourage heavy users of certain products to use more and non-users of other products to try them. For example, they might find that while a customer buys many of their toiletries from Tesco, they never buy shampoo, so vouchers for shampoo can be targeted to such customers. They might also find that someone else never buys meat from them, but in this case they would avoid offending what could be a vegetarian and instead offer more vegetable-based promotions. In this case the loyalty programme is built primarily on the information it provides Tesco rather than the incentive effect (East et al., 2008).

Conclusions

In this chapter, **repeat buying** habits and the implications for **brand loyalty** were explored with the conclusion that, on the whole, the repeat purchase rate of brands does not vary a great deal; the major differentiating factor is the size of the brand and how many customers it has. We also identified the importance for companies to have a range of loyalty profiles among their customers.

We have analysed **patterns of buying behaviour** through consumer panel data in order to shed light on explaining *how* consumers buy products and the ways in which this information can be used by marketing managers. Critical for marketing and the successful development of market share are mental and physical availability, which should help increase penetration.

We have considered the phenomenon of double jeopardy and its impact on **brand loyalty and repeat purchasing** using defection in the car industry (Consumer Insight 10.1) as a good example of this. Of great importance to marketers is the argument that increasing brand loyalty can be a difficult task which may have very little effect on increasing a company's market share. In the FMCG sector, inertia or random choice sometimes dictates the purchasing decisions of consumers. In sum, a brand that has higher market penetration will have more customers who buy it, and that is ultimately what makes the difference to market share.

Data illustrating the Pareto law in action in the deodorant market (Table 10.4) highlighted the differences between **light and heavy buyers** of a brand and the **law of moderation**. Research Insight 10.2 introduced the Dirichlet model as a method of evaluating the sales performance of a new brand. Overall, it is important for marketers to understand that light and heavy buyers may change their habits from one year to the next.

Market segmentation and differentiation were covered and their implication for marketers made clear through the phenomenon of **duplication of purchase**. Companies need to consider how to make their offering distinctive, but not so distinctive that they do not naturally fit into a repertoire of brands. Consumer Insight 10.5 presented an interesting debate around differentiation and buyer attitudes, noting that whilst differentiation is an important strategic option, being a 'me-too' brand is also a viable option if it can gain penetration and market share.

Practitioner Insight 10 supplemented these theories by showing how marketers use empirical buyer behaviour principles in everyday business decisions. We also learnt from the case of the Tesco Clubcard that there are other methods of collecting huge swathes of consumer behaviour information in a way tailored to your company's specific needs.

Review Questions

1. What does double jeopardy tell us about the difference between small and large brands in a market?

2. Explain what the Pareto law can tell us about heavy and light buyers of a brand.

3. Explain how understanding the law of buyer moderation might be useful to a company introducing a new brand into the market.

4. What is the difference between distinctiveness and differentiation?

5. Why is a company's penetration and coverage so vital to its success in the market?

Discussion Questions

1. Consider ways that brands of cosmetics and confectionery could increase their market penetration.

2. Ehrenberg distinguishes between promiscuous and polygamous consumers. Can you think of any situations or product purchases where you are more likely to be one than the other? Why should this be?

3. Choose two product categories and list as many brands as you can within them. Consider which brands you think will be subject to duplication of purchase and which will not. What are the reasons for your choices?

4. Consider how brands might increase their mental and physical availability.

5. In this chapter we identified that diet soft drink brands tend to have considerable customer overlap. In what other functional products might you expect to find such overlap?

Access the online resources to test your knowledge further and complete the Multiple Choice Questions for Chapter 10.

CASE STUDY 10

Repertoire shopping in China

This case highlights a number of issues that have been discussed in this chapter, but in a particular cultural context. It shows that shopping habits are not that different wherever you look. But it also raises important questions for a brand entering a new market in terms of winning customers and managing its growth.

Do Chinese people shop any differently from the rest of the world? It is commonly believed that brands matter to Chinese shoppers. In studies by Bain & Co. it is clear that the brand is an important factor in choice for both food and non-food categories, with more than 60 per cent of Chinese shoppers listing the brand as being among their top considerations in their decision-making process. What is interesting is that while the choice of brand is important, this does not mean that consumers stick to only one or two of their favourites. A series of studies by Bain & Co. and Kantar Worldpanel (2012) show that, just like everywhere else, the Chinese consumer shops from a repertoire of brands.

Repertoire shopping

Bain and Kantar studied 26 of the top consumer goods categories across four areas: beverages, packaged food, personal care, and home care. This accounted for more than 80 per cent of the FMCG market. The research involved 40,000 households in urban China and barcode scanners were used to record purchases; 373 cities in 20 provinces and four major municipalities were represented. China's cities are ranked in five tiers. The large cities of Beijing, Shanghai, and Guangzhou Shenzen are in the first tier, followed by a second tier of 20–30 cities, mostly developed provincial capitals. The third tier of about 20–30 cities includes less developed provincial capitals and comparably developed non-capital cities. There are over 200 cities in the fourth tier, while the fifth tier are county level cities. China's urban population exceeded its rural population for the first time in 2011, and increasingly Chinese workers are leaving rural regions to move to the city. There are now 160 cities with a population of a million or more.

Thus the survey represents a huge range of very different shopping options available in China from those in the modern urban Tier 1 cities, which include hypermarkets, supermarkets, and convenience stores, to the more traditional corner grocery stores, speciality stores, and department stores in the smaller cities (see Figure 10.9).

Figure 10.9 Supermarket shopping in China

Source: © iStock.com/pengpeng.

It was found that, in most cases, when consumers buy more times within a product category, they also buy more brands in that category. Bain and Kantar call this 'repertoire behaviour'. Their research showed that this repertoire purchasing is similar for heavy and average shoppers in a category. As consumers increase their purchasing within a particular product category, they are likely to try more different brands. For example, the Chinese are heavy purchasers of biscuits, with an average household buying 6.2 brands in 2012. Those that bought most frequently (the top 20 per cent) bought about 10.4 brands. Similarly, while average shoppers, who bought facial tissues 6.7 times in 2012, chose between three or four brands, the heavy shoppers, who bought facial tissues 14 times in the year, chose between five or six brands. Therefore the research concludes that a brand's heavy buyers are also likely to be heavy buyers of competing brands.

This repertoire behaviour appears to be consistent. It appears to exist whether the category is in the development stage or a more mature stage. For example, colour cosmetics (mascara, eye shadow, foundation, and lipstick) is an emerging product category in China compared with many other countries, as less than 40 per cent of households had bought in this category at the time of the research. Chinese women have not been using colour cosmetics on a daily basis, as is the case in other Asian countries, and they spend much less money on them, but as they begin to buy this product category more frequently, they purchase a wider range of brands. For example, women who purchase these products more than three times a year buy on average 2.86 brands, and when they purchase them more than five times over two years the average number of brands increases to 4.1.

The same laws as in other markets apply in China, for example the law of double jeopardy (Table 10.8). In Table 10.8 we see that in China, Colgate has double the market share of the local brand LSL. This can be explained by its penetration being 46 per cent versus LSL's 23 per cent. It also has a slightly higher purchase frequency. This undermines what Romaniuk and Sharp (2016) refer to as the myth that Chinese consumers shop primarily on price. Other evidence supports this, as a 2016 report from McKinsey (Zipser et al., 2016) shows that Chinese consumers are increasingly trading up to premium products in many areas including skincare, cars, sports, and fashion.

Brand	Market share (%)	Household penetration (%)	Average purchase frequency (number of times purchased)	Average share of category purchased (%)
Crest	19	57	2.8	29
Colgate	14	46	2.5	26
Zhonghua	12	43	2.4	25
Darlie	11	35	2.7	26
LSL	6	23	2.2	23
Hei Mei	3	14	1.9	18
YNBY	3	14	2.2	20
Bamboo	2	9	2.0	19
LMZ	2	9	1.7	17
Sensodyne	0.3	2	1.5	13
Average	**7**	**25**	**2.2**	**22**

Table 10.8   Illustration of the double jeopardy law—toothpaste in China (annual figures for 2011)
Source: Kantar Worldpanel China.

Similarly, the duplication of purchase law can be seen in Chinese haircare purchases. Data shows that customer overlap across brands varies from around two-thirds of each brand sharing with Pantene to under a fifth sharing with a much smaller brand Clear (Faulkner et al., 2014). In their research Faulkner et al. suggest that although the data for some product categories (e.g. toothpaste and biscuits) shows the possibility of a subset of consumers more loyal to local brands or resisting global ones, this could also be due to distribution issues with some outlets only stocking local brands.

'Loyalist' shoppers

There do appear to be some product categories where currently Chinese consumers are more loyal, buying the same brand repeatedly. Labelled as loyalist behaviour, the categories this covers include baby formula, nappies, beer, milk, carbonated soft drinks, and chewing gum. For these products, an increase in buying frequency has not translated into buying more brands. Bain and Kantar (Bain & Co. and Kantar Worldpanel, 2012) suggest two reasons for such loyalist behaviour. First, in these product categories there may be more limited brand choices, and, second, in some cases buying the particular brand has become a habit. However, it should still be noted that these loyalists are a small group, accounting for only 10 per cent of total brand sales in these categories.

The research identified that leading brands in all the repertoire categories had one thing in common—they all had relatively high rates of penetration. For example, in toothpaste Crest had 57 per cent penetration compared with an average of 15 per cent for the other top 20 brands, even though its repeat purchase is not very different from these brands. It is also the category leader, with a

15 per cent market share. Similarly, Oreo has a penetration of 46 per cent which is about three times the national average for the top 30 brands. Oreo also has the highest rate of repurchasing frequency at 3.3 times per household in 2011. Even for the leading brands in a category, more than 40 per cent of shoppers are only buying the brand once a year.

The findings from the research show a number of other important factors.

1. There appears to be no difference in repertoire and loyalist behaviour in terms of whether the brand is foreign or locally owned. The Chinese consumer is looking for brands they consider to be safe and trustworthy, whether they are home grown or from abroad. They will not necessarily take note at the point of sale as to whether they are buying a foreign or a local brand.

2. Where shoppers live appears to impact on repertoire behaviour. Shoppers living in Tier 1 or Tier 2 cities buy more brands in a category than those living in Tier 3–5 cities. For example, in 2011 the average family in Beijing, Shanghai, and Guangzho made 22 purchases of biscuits and bought nine different brands, while those in a Tier 5 city bought four brands, on average 11 times. However, in loyalist categories such as milk and beer there does not seem to be a great difference among cities.

3. Repertoire behaviour does not vary by a person's stage in their life cycle. Some may think that young shoppers are less brand loyal, while older shoppers like to stick to tried and tested brands. This does not appear to be the case; the only difference found was that young families bought more biscuits, sweets, and yogurt brands, but that may well be because they are at a stage where they are just consuming more of that product category.

Questions

1. Explain the reasons for brand loyalty in different tiers of city.

2. Would you expect to see repertoire behaviour increase in Tier 3–5 cities and if so why?

3. What does the case tell us about penetration versus brand loyalty?

4. What recommendations would you make to a foreign FMCG brand entering China for the first time?

5. Would you expect the loyalist brands to change? How and why?

Sources: Bain & Co. and Kantar Worldpanel (2012); Bolger (2012); Yu and Lannes (2013); Faulkner et al. (2014); Romaniuk and Shar (2016); Zipser et al. (2016); www.chinanormal.com

References

Anschuetz, N. (2002), 'Why a brand's most valuable customer is the next one it adds', *Journal of Advertising Research*, January/February, 15–21.

Bain & Co. (2013), 'Customer loyalty in retail banking' (global edn), http://www.bain.com/publications/articles/customer-loyalty-in-retail-banking-2013.aspx (accessed 1 March 2017).

Bain & Company and Kantar Worldpanel (2012), 'What Chinese shoppers really do but will never tell you', http://www.bain.com/Images/BAIN_REPORT_What_Chinese_shoppers_really_do_but_will_never_tell_you_.pdf (accessed 17 December 2017).

Bartlett, E. (2012), 'Why Cadbury's Crispello bar "for women" leaves a nasty taste', *The Telegraph*, 3 October, http://www.telegraph.co.uk/women/womens-life/9581866/Why-Cadburys-chocolate-for-women-leaves-a-nasty-taste.html (accessed 17 December 2017).

Barwise, P.T. and Ehrenberg, A.S.C. (1985), 'Consumer beliefs and brand usage', *Journal of the Market Research Society*, 27, 81–93.

Bayne, T., Samuels, B., and Sharp, B. (2014), 'Marketing banks: target new, not loyal customers', *Admap*, April, 40–1.

Bennett, D. (2005), *What car will they buy next?*, Report 19, Ehrenberg–Bass Institute for Marketing Science, Adelaide.

Bennett, D. and Graham, C. (2010), 'Is loyalty driving growth for the brand in front? A two-purchase analysis of car category dynamics in Thailand', *Journal of Strategic Marketing*, 18, 7, 573–85.

Bolger, M. (2012), 'China's cities', http://www.ccmm.ca/documents/presentations/2011_2012/12_03_22_1_ChinaCities.pdf (accessed 27 October 2017).

Brown, G.H. (1953), 'Brand loyalty—fact or fiction?', *Advertising Age*, 43, 251–8.

Carter, M. (2010), 'Men buy Mars, women prefer Galaxy: gender targeting is advertising industry's secret weapon', *The Independent*, 18 March, http://www.independent.co.uk/life-style/food-and-drink/features/men-buy-mars-women-prefer-galaxy-gender-targeting-is-advertising-industrys-secret-weapon-1922941.html (accessed 17 December 2017).

Casaló, L.V., Flavián, C., and Guinalíua, M. (2008), 'Promoting consumer's participation in virtual brand communities: a new paradigm in branding strategy', *Journal of Marketing Communication*, 14, 1, 19–36.

Chahal, M. (2016), 'Gender stereotyping is about people not just women', https://www.marketingweek.com/2016/10/05/unilever-gender-stereotyping-is-about-people-not-just-about-women/ (accessed 15 June, 2017).

Colombo, R., Ehrenberg, A.S.C., and Sabavala, D. (2000), 'Diversity in analyzing brand-switching tables: the car challenge', *Canadian Journal of Marketing Research*, 19, 22–36.

East, R., Wright, M., and Vanhuele, M. (2008), *Consumer behaviour: applications in marketing*, London: Sage.

Ehrenberg, A.S.C. (1988), *Repeat buying* (2nd edn), Oxford: Oxford University Press.

Ehrenberg, A. and Scriven, J. (1996), 'Brand loyalty under the microscope', unpublished paper.

Ehrenberg, A.S.C., Hammond, K., and Goodhardt, G.J. (1994), 'The after-effects of price related consumer promotions', *Journal of Advertising Research*, 34, 4, 11–21.

Ehrenberg, A., Barnard, N., and Scriven, J. (1997), 'Differentiation or salience', *Journal of Advertising Research*, 37, 6, 7–14.

Ehrenberg, A.S.C., Uncles, M.D., and Goodhardt, G.J. (2004), 'Understanding brand performance measures: using Dirichlet benchmarks', *Journal of Business Research*, 57, 1307–25.

Faulkner, M., Truong, O., and Romaniuk, J. (2014), Uncovering generalized patterns of brand competition in China, *Journal of Product and Brand Management*, 23, 7, 554–71.

Muniz, A.M., Jr, and Schau, H.J. (2005), 'Religiosity in the abandoned Apple Newton brand community', *Journal of Consumer Research*, 31, 737–47.

Porter, M. E. (1985), *Competitive advantage: creating and sustaining superior performance*, New York: Free Press.

Romaniuk, J. and Nenycz-Thiel, M. (2016). 'Lapsed buyers' durable brand consideration in emerging markets', *Journal of Business Research*, 69, 9, 3645–51.

Romaniuk, J. and Sharp, B. (2016), *How brands grow: Part 2*, Melbourne: Oxford University Press.

Romaniuk, J., Sharp, B., and Ehrenberg, A.S.C. (2007), 'Evidence concerning the importance of perceived brand diffferentiation', *Australasian Marketing Journal*, 15, 42–54.

Schau, H.J. and Muniz, A.M., Jr (2002), 'Brand communities and personal identities: negotiations in cyberspace', *Advances in Consumer Research*, 29, 344–349.

Schouten, J. and McAlexander, J.H. (1995), 'Subcultures of consumption: an ethnography of the new bikers', *Journal of Consumer Research*, 22, 3, 43–61.

Schwartz, B. (2004), *The paradox of choice: why more is less*, New York: HarperCollins.

Sharp, B. (2010), *How brands grow*, Oxford: Oxford University Press.

Sharp, B., Wright, M., Dawes, J.L. et al. (2012), 'It's a Dirichlet world: modeling individuals' loyalties reveals how brands compete, grow and decline', *Journal of Advertising Research*, 52, 2, 1–10.

van Marrewijk, A. and Broos, M. (2012), 'Retail stores as brands: performances, theatre and space', *Consumption, Markets and Culture*, 15, 4, 374–91.

Wellan, D.M. and Ehrenberg, A.S.C. (1990), 'A case of seasonal segmentation', *Market Research Society*, 30, 1, 35–44.

Wentz, L., (2013), 'A leader in Latin-influenced food market, Goya enters baby aisle', *Advertising Age*, http://adage.com/article/hispanic-marketing/a-leader-changing-market-goya-enters-baby-food-aisle/243089/ (accessed 29 October 2017).

Wragg, C., and Regan, T. (2012), 'Marketing food: Quorn's appeal', *Admap*, November, 32–3.

Yu, J. and Lannes, B. (2013), 'Chinese shopping behaviour: China's repertoire shopping', *Admap*, 48, 1, 36–8.

Zipser, D., Chen, Y., and Gong, F. (2016), 'The modernization of the Chinese consumer', http://www.mckinseychina.com/wp-content/uploads/2016/03/The-Modernization-of-the-Chinese-Consumer_EN.pdf (accessed 27 October 2017).

PART 4

WHERE ARE WE GOING?

Where are we going?

Future trends in consumer behaviour

Macro-view

Consumers in society and the market: groups, social processes, culture, and repeat purchasing behaviour

Micro-view

The individual consumer: individual decision-making, learning, perception, attitudes, personality and motivation

How we arrived here

Historical context and contemporary perspectives on consumption

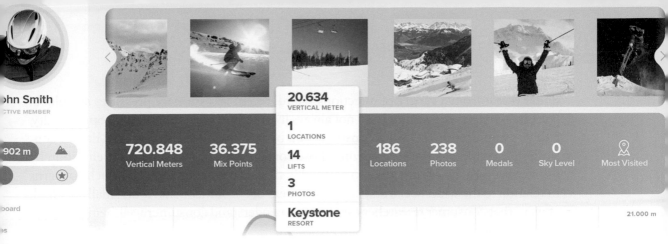

11

FUTURE TRENDS IN CONSUMER BEHAVIOUR

Introduction

So far in this book we have shown how consumer behaviour has developed into a coherent and systematic academic perspective. While there are diverse ways of considering how the consumer behaves, a key element has been the development of a set of tools and analytical approaches drawn from psychology, economics, sociology, cultural studies, and anthropology that help improve our understanding of the complexity of consumption in the modern world. We have also shown something of this complexity, considering the different perspectives on consumption and examples from a range of contexts.

However, consumers change, and so do the contexts in which they consume. Where does consumer behaviour go next? What developments in consumer behaviour are we likely to see? And what are the theories, frameworks, tools, and methods that will help us understand these changes? We suggest three main areas where consumer behaviour may be susceptible to change. The first is the domain of technology induced change. This is a thread that runs through this chapter, but we examine it specifically in terms of technology, sociocultural contexts, and its manifestations in virtuality, and the move away from ownership of goods towards access-based models of ownership. One of the most important areas that combines technology and social interaction is the field of big data that is already bringing major changes to how consumers are researched and understood. The second thread is around sustainability, not only environmental sustainability but also economic sustainability and a wider perception that the Western economic model of growth may be under threat from a variety of directions. Third, recent recessionary pressures at a global level remind us that consumers do not always live in times of abundance and opportunity, and it is important to consider constraints on behaviour and the impact this has on consumers and the organizations serving those consumers. Issues around misbehaviour, by both consumers and firms, are also covered in this chapter, and we discuss such concerns in relation to the wider social and cultural context of consumer behaviour. Finally, we look at ways that consumer researchers are trying to understand consumer well-being through the theme of transformative consumer research.

LEARNING OBJECTIVES

After reading this chapter you will be able to:

1. Identify a range of **technological trends and developments** and consider their relevance for consumer behaviour.

2. Understand what **big data** is and how it is being used.

3. Appreciate the range of issues around **sustainability and sustainable consumption** that are important, and consider how these will impact consumers in the future.

4. Understand a range of current social and financial **pressures** and how they may impact consumer behaviour.

5. Discuss what constitutes **misbehaviour** on the part of the consumer and the firm and recognize marketing's role in this and its impact on society.

6. Consider the relevance of **transformative consumer research** for dealing with issues around consumer well-being.

Technology trends impacting consumer behaviour

Monitoring consumer trends around the world is important, especially given that technology and environments change at an incredible pace. Organizations such as trendwatching.com and futurefoundation.net specialize in identifying global consumer trends and business ideas. The importance of digital and social media in consumers' daily lives in terms of providing useful information and advice is clear, but in the coming years there is likely to be an increase in popularity for products, apps, and services that work for consumers by reminding them to behave 'better'. This trend has been labelled the **quantified self** (Wolf, 2010), and refers *to the idea that tracking metrics can lead to self-improvement in some way*. Examples include the Nike+ Fuelband, which uses an accelerometer to track all daily activity and calorie intake, and can monitor its wearer's efforts against preset goals. The trend towards wearable technology is best seen to date with the appearance of 'smart watches', devices that can communicate with a modem, wireless headset, or the wearer's smartphone. The smart watch may include features such as a camera, a compass, a mobile phone, and GPS navigation. Early pioneers included the Sony SmartWatch and the Pebble SmartWatch, more recently joined by the Apple Watch (Figure 11.1). However, research has shown that this move towards increased measurement/quantification of self has some negative effects. Etkin (2016) demonstrates that consumers who track and quantify their daily activities—through such technologies as the MyFitnessPal app or the FitBit—may experience decreased enjoyment and engagement in these activities, and a decline in subjective well-being.

Figure 11.1 The Apple Watch
Source: Lukas Gojda/Shutterstock.com.

The new technological trends are not only manifested in hardware. Software developments are also significant. One area where software is key is the adoption of apps by doctors and physicians to monitor and improve health outcomes. Epocrates (https://online.epocrates.com) is a medical app, supporting doctors as they look up drug information and interactions, find other providers for consultations and referrals, and calculate patient measurements such as body mass index. There are many health-related apps for consumers as well. The Red Cross First Aid app (http://www.redcross.org.uk/What-we-do/First-aid/Mobile-app) provides consumers with simple step-by-step instructions to guide them through everyday first aid scenarios, such as responding to someone having a heart attack or dealing with burns. Another example, launched in Australia, is the Antibiotics Reminder app, which reminds patients to take their prescribed medicines.

Self-monitoring technology has already had an impact on companies in the health and fitness sector (see Figure 11.2). Gym companies can offer their clients portable monitors to provide data on performance, including heart rate, distances run, and weights lifted. Companies can work together to offer tailored benefits to consumers based on performance data. The health insurer Vitality Life & Health, for example, offers a range of benefits to policy holders, which involve consumption of other companies' products and services: Vitality policy holders can access a reduced membership fee for Virgin Active gym (40 per cent reduction), can get a price reduction on running shoes bought from Sweatshop, and can collect points (based on gym usage) which can be redeemed through various commercial partners (including cinema and holiday companies).

Responsibility for health may soon devolve more towards the individual and less towards the state as these new systems, techniques, and technologies enable people to monitor their own health performance. With such information, consumers may be considered accountable for their own health choices, raising ethical and political questions around responsibilities in

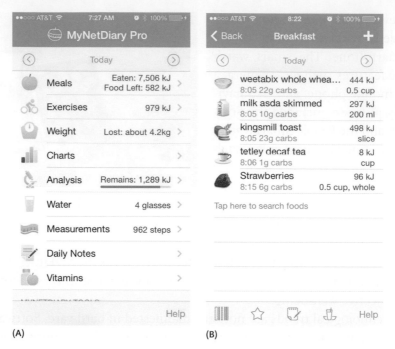

Figure 11.2 Example of self-monitoring technology: an app from MyNetDiary called Calorie Counter Pro
Source: Image courtesy of MyNetDiary Inc.

relation to health and well-being. Issues also emerge in relation to ownership of data; this information is valuable to the business customers of the companies providing the tracking tools for targeting their marketing to individuals and identifying market trends. This is not merely an issue for health technologies but applies to a range of new technologies that provide, deliberately or otherwise, extensive data about the users of those technologies.

Another technological trend is evident in how consumers share their interests, likes, and experiences from the real world through social media platforms. Posting images and messages on Facebook, Twitter, Instagram, and other social media applications has become a key part of many people's lives and of their consumer experiences. For example, the tourism sector has embraced the use of radio frequency identification (RFID) to allow consumers to share their touristic experience via their social media apps, and many resorts are using RFID to integrate digital experiences with offline sports activities to improve customer experience (Wheelwright, 2017). Figure 11.3 shows an example of RFID data output relating to a ski trip.

Other key technologies centre on location-based information. The familiar barcode is an early example of this group of technologies: encoded information, typically about a product, that can be read by an optical scanner. More recently, **QR (quick response) codes**, which are *optical machine-readable barcodes that record and store information related to items* (Dean, 2013), have been used for a range of marketing and information dissemination purposes. QR codes offer a method of adding web-based content to real-world messages, objects, or locations. A QR code looks similar to a bar code, but is scanned from a QR reader on a smartphone or tablet to connect to web content. QR codes can be placed

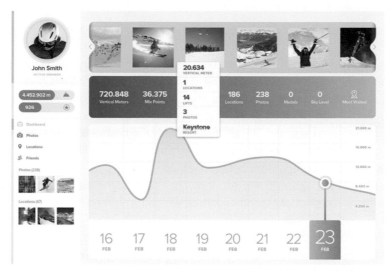

Figure 11.3   Example of RFID output from a ski trip   *Source*: Image courtesy of Datapine.

on packaging, advertisements, websites, carrier bags, key rings, newspapers, banner ads, T-shirts, invoices—any place where the target consumer is able to access these codes and where they have the means to scan them.

It is worth noting that QR codes are particularly effective in situations that can provide consumers with real-time updates, especially where there is a constant flow of information such as schedules at train stations and bus stops, restaurant specials, or airline bookings. Deutsche Bahn's NFC system is a QR-based system which allows users to simply scan a QR code to check in and out of the train station.

QR codes showed great promise but have failed to dominate as they were expected to a few years ago. They have been shown to have a number of disadvantages; poor physical placement in particular has given them a bad reputation amongst business professionals and a lack of enthusiasm on the part of consumers. Redundant or wrong information is another key problem. As Lucie Milosavljevich outlines in Practitioner Insight 11, companies have to respond to digital developments rapidly.

PRACTITIONER INSIGHT 11

Lucie Milosavljevich, Senior Analyst, Consumer Sector—Grant Thornton UK LLP

Consumers have more power than ever before. Over the past decade, the balance of power between consumers and brands has changed irrevocably. This is largely a consequence of two things: the recession that wreaked havoc on the global economy in 2007–8

and the launch of the first iPhone, coincidentally also in 2007, which led to mainstream adoption of smartphones.

The recession, and its impact on household budgets and discretionary spending, forced consumers to assess their spending priorities. With the need to save money prioritized over the need to save time, Britain became a nation of bargain hunters who shopped around for the best deals, for example splitting a weekly food shop between several supermarkets as well as doing weekly top-up shops in the fast-emerging convenience stores. The ability to identify the best value deal was further enhanced by the increasing use of smartphones and the growing popularity of online shopping, allowing quick and easy price and product comparisons between retailers.

In the intervening years, although the economy has seen some stabilization, consumers have retained many of their recessionary spending habits, which has forced companies to adapt to consumer demands and use of technology.

Online retail has grown from around 3 per cent of all retail sales in 2007 to around 14 per cent in 2016 (Mintel Online Retailing, 2016). However, these days there is more to online retailing than just purchasing. It remains the most accessible way for consumers to compare pricing on products but, through the growth of more visual apps like Instagram and the rise of bloggers and vloggers, it is increasingly a source of lifestyle inspiration. This emphasis on lifestyle is a relatively recent development in consumer behaviour as it allows consumers to demonstrate their individuality, either through products they own or, increasingly, experiences they have. Consumer Insight 11.1 looks at some of these issues in relation to the shopping mall of the future.

The adoption of social media has presented a unique set of challenges that companies have had to address in order to remain relevant to modern consumers. First it has levelled the playing field for smaller companies, allowing them to access consumers around the world with greater agility than some of their larger counterparts. It has also made companies of all sizes much more accountable to their consumer base, as a bad review of a product or customer service can be incredibly detrimental. Finally, it has reinforced the need for companies to have an omnichannel presence that allows consumers to browse their products or services in person, in store, or online, whether on a computer or a mobile. All of these touch-points with the consumer must be consistent in terms of style, service, and brand.

Back in 2007 few would have predicted the pace of change the past decade has seen. Though social media has been an obvious success story, other innovations, such as the iPod, have become almost obsolete in a very short space of time. For companies looking to attract consumer spend, backing the right technology can be problematic. For example, many hotels invested in iPod docking stations for their guests but are now faced with guests who no longer have iPods but do require seamless, consistent, and reliable WiFi connections for their numerous smartphones and tablets.

Looking 10 years into the future it is likely that the ways in which we shop today will start to feel outdated. In the short term, the pressure on companies to meet consumer demands is incredibly high and, given the context of economic pressures around weakened sterling, increased employment costs, and business rates, puts them in a difficult position of managing financial margins alongside innovation. In the longer term, the use of technology, such as virtual and augmented technologies, offers huge potential in allowing consumers to more accurately visualize products they are purchasing before having to part with their money. The success in summer 2016 of

Pokemon Go showed a willingness of consumers to engage with these newer technologies, and if companies are able to tap into this to help, for example, a consumer visualize how a new piece of jewellery will look with their outfit or how a new oven will look in their new kitchen, the potential for the technology is huge. The one thing that is certain, though, is that it will be consumer adoption of the technology that will decide whether or not it is a success. In the meantime, companies will have to pay even more attention to consumer behaviour and hope that this allows them to back the most relevant technology.

CONSUMER INSIGHT 11.1

The shopping mall of the future

With the rise of online retail, we might think that the shopping mall is an outdated concept and under threat from online competition. However, this is not the case, and shopping malls are starting to evolve and adapt beyond being practical locations where shoppers go purely to make multiple retail transactions. The five largest malls in the world are all in Asia, with China's New South China Mall in Dongguan occupying 2.9 million square metres of space. The role of the mall in consumers' lives is changing. With more people living in smaller spaces there is a greater need for public spaces where people can get together and socialize. People are looking for more engaging shopping experiences, where socializing is facilitated. Sustainability concerns are causing some consumers to prefer mixed-use spaces, where they can live, shop, and work all within walking distance, rather than having to drive out to suburban malls. Finally, the e-commerce revolution and the rise of digital technologies are fundamentally reshaping consumer expectations and shifting the function of stores toward useful and entertaining customer experiences (O'Shea, 2017). These global trends are leading mall operators to rethink how malls are devised and operated, and to constantly consider how they can stay relevant for consumers, and thus drive growth.

Key ideas driving the way malls are going are as follows.

1. *Differentiating the consumer offering, with a focus on experience and convenience.*

   While online shopping gives consumers the ultimate in convenience, malls can differentiate themselves in terms of value-added elements such as offering concert space and arts centres, spas and fitness clubs, and other community-based initiatives.

   Examples:

   - Xanadu, a mall 30 km from Madrid, has positioned itself as a place for parents to spend quality time with their children. The mall has a ski slope, go karts, a cinema, and bowling alleys.

   - The Mall of America in Minnesota has an underwater aquarium, a Nickelodeon theme park, and a gaming and entertainment centre called SMAAASH.

- In the Dubai Mall, 'Fashion Avenue' is an area dedicated to luxury brands and services tailored to upmarket consumers, with its own separate outside entrance and parking area.

2. *Transforming the mall experience by leveraging technology and multichannel strategies.*

The digital transformation of retail can present new opportunities for malls to engage consumers throughout their decision journeys. They can do this through relationship building with consumers, before, during, and after the visit, finding ways of engaging customers through compelling content through social media and proprietary sites and apps, as well as loyalty programmes. Loyalty programmes can provide the means for malls to establish a direct relationship with customers that goes beyond each visit to the mall, and they can also reach out to their consumers with customized offers, gift ideas, and other targeted advertisements based on real-time intelligence and location-based marketing. For example, 313@Somerset shopping mall in Singapore used beacon technology to offer shoppers various options for receiving hyper-targeted messages, deals, and other content based on their proximity inside the property.

3. *Exploration of new formats and commercial real estate opportunities.*

Finally, malls are looking at new formats and styles, making them quite unrecognizable compared with malls in the past. Open-air malls to give the feel and impression of a town centre, sometimes incorporating other real estate (e.g. work and residential spaces), such as the Sino Ocean Taikoo Li in Chengdu, China, which is an outdoor mall with streets. Incorporating more natural ambiance into the design of enclosed malls is a major trend, with plants, trees, wooden walls and floors, waterfalls, and lots of glass to let in natural lighting becoming more common as a way of letting malls blend in with their surroundings. The key to such mixed-use developments is to offer consumers the opportunity to have access to an integrated community in which to live, work, and shop. For example, Langham Place, a 59-storey complex in Hong Kong, includes retail space, a five-star hotel, and class A office space, and the mall is connected to the subway with its own tunnel. Its 'expresscalator' takes consumers up four levels in a matter of seconds, and there is a retail-lined downward spiral path, shaped like a corkscrew, to get shoppers back down.

Questions

1. What are the key benefits to consumers of visiting shopping malls in comparison with online shopping or shopping in local high street locations?

2. How do you think shopping malls will evolve in the next 20 years? What do you imagine will happen to local shopping?

3. Do you think that there are any negative aspects of these developments in mall shopping?

Sources: Fantoni et al. (2014); Tea (2016); AI (2017).

Access the online resources and follow the web links to learn more.

Augmented reality techniques combined with geotargeting are used to allow information to be presented to customers at various points during their journeys. Geotargeting uses GPS locational data generated by a user's smartphone to provide text alerts or in-app information as they move around an area. This may simply alert them to the existence of a store or service, or give details of offers or voucher codes. Geotargeting is used where the business has data about the individual user, and therefore can identify that user, which means that the information presented can be tailored. The multimedia campaign from Tequila Herradura's Ultra brand uses location technology to connect with consumers via Foursquare's online-to-offline discovery platform and on Facebook (Kaplan, 2016).

Big data

The new tools described in the previous section have the potential to change our sense of self in the world, acting not only as mirrors for self-improvement, discovery, and knowledge, but also in how we engage with other people (Giesler, 2012). For marketers, they offer opportunities to develop greater connectivity and conversations with consumers. New technologies inevitably raise issues in terms of how businesses apply the knowledge they acquire from and about consumers. To understand some of these issues we need to consider a key aspect: the role of what has become known as 'big data'. This is a somewhat vague term that can embrace everything from datasets gathered by large scientific experiments and surveys to the extremely large datasets that are generated by business digital processes, media searches, and social media interactions. Of most interest in the context of consumer behaviour are forms of what might be called 'found data' (Harford, 2014). Examples of found data include credit card transactions, Google search data, and mobile phone transactions.

For consumer researchers there is an important methodological aspect of big data, namely that rather than using data to support theories, researchers can identify patterns in big data without forming a hypothesis (Lycett, 2013) and hence develop new theories of how consumers behave and respond to marketing actions. Researchers often refer to the three Vs of big data (Lycett, 2013; Gandomi and Haider, 2015).

1. **Volume**, which is the magnitude of the data typically stored in terabytes, petabytes, and zettabytes. A terabyte equates to 1500 CDs or 220 DVDs or about 16 million Facebook photos (Gandomi and Haider, 2015). It has been estimated that by 2020 the digital universe will be around 44 zettabytes, where a zettabyte is equivalent to 250 billion DVDs (Erevelles et al., 2016).

2. **Velocity** is the speed at which data is being created, analysed, and acted upon, allowing companies to make decisions based on evidence of what is happening in real time. They can see what products, brands, colours, flavours, etc., are popular at any time and what consumers are saying about their products on social media.

3. **Variety** refers to the unstructured behavioural quality of big data. While structured data from scanners, records, and databases have been collected for some time, unstructured data includes blogs and text messages, videos, images, and audio recordings (Erevelles et al., 2016).

Commentators have suggested that there are other Vs to consider with big data; importantly these include veracity and value. Erevelles et al. (2016) point out that not all big data about consumers will be accurate (veracity), and the ever increasing amounts of data raise the issue of what is important and what is not (value). This is something that is increasingly going to tax those who analyse the data and the marketers who need to put the analysis into action. Where the data is used successfully it can be a very powerful tool. One now well-documented example is when Target used consumer insights to predict a woman's pregnancy (Hill, 2012). Once information like this is known, it can be powerfully used to influence purchases and develop long-term customer relationships (Erevelles et al., 2016)

These kinds of data have obvious applications in business and marketing, where they can be applied to extending the understanding and prediction of consumer attitudes, needs, and purchasing decisions. But they have other impacts too. Big data can be used to extend transparency around the provenance and authenticity of goods, playing a part in consumer decisions around ethical and environmental issues. This is especially the case if combined with blockchain technology to improve the tracking of goods (Popper and Lohr, 2017). Big data will change how markets are researched and what can be done with the data. For example, geospatial data can be used to identify where and when consumers will shop, making prediction of consumer behaviour possible as well as helping in product development. For example Netflix analysed the streaming behaviour of its 33 million subscribers to help identify the likely success of remaking the original series 'House of Cards' (Carr, 2013).

However, there are caveats attached to the use of big data (Hofacker et al., 2016). For one thing, big data suffers from the usual problem of statistical data—it is good at showing correlation but poor at establishing causation. This is exacerbated by the tendency of big data practitioners to avoid making hypotheses that can be effectively tested by the data. In this regard it goes against trends seen elsewhere that emphasize qualitative data-gathering methods which have the benefit of delving further into the causes of behaviour. Then there is the question of data quality. Big data involves a variety of data sources with a range of data types and structures collected from diverse sources including internet and mobile data, data from the 'internet of things', industrial data, and scientific data. The range of types and structures makes for great difficulty in combining data sources. Added to this is the huge volume of data involved, which makes it very difficult to make sound assessments of quality in a timely fashion (Cai and Zhu, 2015). Research Insight 11.1 considers how contemporary technology is impacting on the passion for consumption.

RESEARCH INSIGHT 11.1

Kozinets, R., Patterson, A., and Ashman, R. (2017), 'Networks of desire: how technology increases our passion to consume', *Journal of Consumer Research*, 43, 5, 659–82.

This paper takes a consumer culture theory approach to looking at how contemporary technology is impacting on the passion for consumption. Drawing on participant observation and depth interview data, this study focused on online food image sharing (e.g. on food networks and food blogs), and showed the ways in which technology increases the desire for sharing and consumption of these kinds of images.

 Access the online resources to read the abstract and access the full paper.

Sustainable worlds, sustainable consumption

Contemporary consumer culture is dominated by ideas around abundance and excess. Much of marketing is aimed at selling goods and services that enhance people's sense of self; the underlying premise is that the 'self' is a never-ending project, to be worked on and developed, and that products and brands are available to satisfy potentially endless needs. However, this raises a number of ethical issues. First, the focus on materialism raises questions about the role of goods in people's lives. Why are material goods so desired? What happens if we try and step out of that system, consume less, and have a lifestyle less focused on buying things? Further, resource shortages, the increased economic power of countries outside the Western bloc, and climate change together are likely to lead to a reappraisal of both individual and social attitudes to consumption. What are the implications of this for our understanding of consumption and consumer behaviour?

The emergence of the voluntary simplicity (VS) movement in various guises in the 1970s, as a simpler way of living, provided one route for consumers to opt out of some of the demands of consumer and marketplace cultures. There is also, since the recession of 2008, the distinct possibility that constraints on consumption will be necessary rather than voluntary. At the moment austerity is a political concept that largely focuses on cuts in government spending, but in future we may be facing a kind of austerity that has more in common with the rationing that Second World War populations in Britain and Europe experienced. It is too soon, and possibly too gloomy, to say that this is necessarily the case, but one consequence of this may be what has been called mindful or conscious consumption (Sheth et al., 2011; Meier et al., 2017), where consumers are motivated to be more careful and aware of their consumption. The trend towards less ownership may be partly analysed in terms of sustainable consumption. These ideas are developed in the following sections.

Voluntary simplicity

Voluntary simplicity refers to a lifestyle choice where people opt to limit material consumption and free up resources, such as time and money, which they believe will raise the quality of their life (Huneke, 2005). Voluntary simplicity can involve a wide spectrum and variety of practices and values. Shaw and Newholm (2002) describe this spectrum as ranging from consumers who fully embrace the ideas around reducing consumption, driven by ethical concerns to own and use fewer goods (Research Insight 11.2), through to those consumers who simply 'refine' their consumption towards ethical standards (e.g. buying Fairtrade coffee in their supermarket), enabling them to continue to have similar levels of consumption, but to consume differently and in line with their ethical concerns. Similarly, Huneke (2005: 546) distinguishes between 'highly committed simplifiers' and 'less committed simplifiers' who change their behaviour, but not in highly disruptive way.

RESEARCH INSIGHT 11.2

Peyer, M., Balderjahn, I., Seegebarth, B., and Klemm, A. (2017), 'The role of sustainability in profiling voluntary simplifiers', *Journal of Business Research*, 70, 37–43.

Using objective measures of income level and expenditure on durable goods, this research, undertaken in Germany, identifies a sizeable market segment of moderate voluntary simplifiers (14.4 per cent of total population). This group represents a target market for both green products and potentially for products that can meet consumer trends towards lower consumption (e.g. access-based consumption; more durable goods; second-hand purchasing; repairing). These moderate voluntary simplifiers represent a move towards more sustainable models of consumption, which don't necessitate a wholesale removal from the market.

 Access the online resources to read the abstract and access the full paper.

Conscious consumption

The global outlook, particularly in Western cultures, towards environmental and ethical concerns (Huneke, 2005) has changed, and so has the attitude to voluntary simplification. While this concept was regarded as radical 30 years ago, it is now regarded as more relevant to society (Elgin, 2009). Many commentators argue that contemporary consumer culture cannot be maintained for long, with the threats of climate change and peak oil (the point when oil supplies decline after reaching the highest rates of extraction) resulting in a situation where consumers must be conscious of their consumption activities. Kantar Millward Brown reported that following the world financial crisis, Japanese consumers, traditionally willing to pay a premium for convenience, were increasingly likely to be spending more time to save money. The *danshari* movement, derived from the Japanese for throwing away and letting go, has resulted in many books and television programmes focused on reducing conspicuous consumption and identifying low cost alternatives. This increased awareness of the issues around sustainable living, such as composting and recycling, has been increasingly encouraged by governments and therefore normalized by some countries such as Germany and the UK (Defra, 2017). Awareness of what one does is encapsulated in the concept of mindfulness, which is further discussed in Research Insight 11.3.

RESEARCH INSIGHT 11.3

Bahl, S., Milne, G.R., Ross, S.M. et al. (2016), 'Mindfulness: its transformative potential for consumer, societal, and environmental well-being', *Journal of Public Policy & Marketing*, 35, 2, 198–210.

In this paper the authors propose the concept of mindfulness in consumption as a way of having a positive impact on consumer well-being. One area they look at in detail is the idea of mindful consumption as an approach to promoting more pro-social behaviours, including being less materialistic, being more environmentally oriented, and supporting consumers to be less wasteful. The authors make suggestions that consumers, institutions, and policy-makers could adopt to promote mindful consumption.

 Access the online resources to read the abstract and access the full paper.

Consumers are more conscious of the conditions in which the products they use are made and increasingly use resources such as GoodGuide.com to identify the best choices in terms of healthiness. Firms in turn try to become more transparent about their practices; Johnson & Johnson's Earthwards presents information about the origins of products, but as Adams (2014) states this is still about brands deciding what information they are prepared to impart. As consumers find it easier to access information and use it, brands will have to respond and disseminate all that is required. Initiatives such as Wikichains, which is looking to build a crowdsource platform of information on companies' supply chains, will help consumers to become even more conscious in their consumption and ensure that firms are fully transparent.

Following the global recession of 2008–9, there has been an increase in self-reliance among consumers, with more people moving from consumption to production (Burch, 2012). For example, the increasing popularity of allotments in the UK is a shift towards more self-sufficient consumers and contributes to a rise in the barter economy, where people trade goods and skills (Hallsworth and Wong, 2015). Car boot sales and online auction sites, such as eBay, have meant that consumers can trade or sell their unwanted possessions to others instead of throwing them out. There are also numerous websites (such as freecycle.org) dedicated solely to giving away unwanted items free, thus reducing waste that could otherwise end up in landfill sites. Consumer Insight 11.2 describes some of the ways in which consumers are demonstrating and celebrating acts of conscious consumption.

CONSUMER INSIGHT 11.2

Celebrating conscious consumption and production

Increasingly people and organizations are engaging with a more mindful approach to consumption. For example, take a look at DIY lifestyle Singapore http://diy-lifestyle.org/about.html which encourages people to support local producers, find greener ways to travel, and be aware of what and why they are buying new things. While some organizations such as the Adbusters Media Foundation are openly anti-consumersist, the idea of buying nothing as celebrated in this organizations 'Buy Nothing Day' (Corner, 2011) is probably not acceptable to most people. However, increasingly consumers are taking care over what they buy, perhaps buying less or being more mindful in their consumption. As a result companies are taking note and trying to engage with conscious consumption. One of the best known for engaging with a mindful approach to production is Patagonia which pioneered the use of recycled bottles to make fleece jackets and recently ran an ad campaign which ostensibly discouraged shoppers from buying their products with the line 'Don't buy this jacket'. The idea behind it was supposedly to get consumers to examine their own consumption behaviour (Gelles, 2015). Another brand that has engaged with conscious production is H&M, whose Conscious Collection consists of clothes crafted from sustainable, organic, and recycled materials (Figure 11.4).

Figure 11.4 Advertisement for H&M's 'Conscious Collection'g

Source: Image supplied by The Advertising Archives.

Questions

1. What do you think of companies such as Patagonia suggesting that consumers don't buy products as part of their marketing?

2. Can you think of other factors related to conscious production and consumption that companies might use to their advantage?

Sources: Gelles (2015); https://www.adbusters.org/bnd/

 Access the online resources and follow the web links to learn more about conscious consumption.

Shift towards an ownerless economy?

Consumer practices are also shifting in relation to ownership, with people considering what they can live without and alternative ways of accessing goods and services. For many of these consumers, owning goods and services is not critical; rather, it is the experiences and solutions that are valued and required. Many commentators have discussed how important it is for consumers to share their experiences via social media, such as Twitter and Facebook. Importantly, this sharing and the associated social media updates are acting as status symbols for consumers in the way that possessions have in previous times (Malnight and Keys, 2013). Posting your holiday photos on Facebook is driven by a need to share the experience, but the number of 'likes' is also important for many. In this context, ownership is becoming less valued. The example of Vélib in Paris and Santander bikes in London (Figure 11.5), services that provide access to a fleet of bicycles parked across these city centres, illustrates the appeal of this mode of consumption access. Once registered with the service, you receive a smart key that unlocks the bike from its docking station; you then make your journey and return the bike to any of the docking stations dotted around the capital. The pricing scheme is devised to encourage short trips. Apart from removing the burden and responsibility of ownership, this mode also removes the fear of theft and the lack of safe parking. Contemporary issues around ownership and consumption are considered in Research Insight 11.4.

Figure 11.5   Santander Cycle Hire in London
Source: Graphical_Bank/Shutterstock.com.

RESEARCH INSIGHT 11.4

Schaefers, T., Lawson, S.J., and Kukar-Kinney, M. (2016), 'How the burdens of ownership promote consumer usage of access-based services', *Marketing Letters*, 27, 569–77.

This paper builds on the recent consumer research work on access-based consumption by Bardhi and Eckhardt (2012) to consider the relationship between how consumers view the burden of owner-ship (risks and responsibilities that accompany owning goods), access-based usage levels, and sub-sequent decisions to own goods (or not). Looking at data from a US car-sharing provider, they found that there is a link between access-based service usage and risk perceptions. The lower financial commitment inherent in an access-based service makes it a viable alternative to ownership. Where consumers are more concerned with performance risks associated with ownership, they are more likely to have made use of access-based services. In situations where consumers are uncertain about the social consequences of ownership, they tend to have higher access-based service usage. The research also found that higher usage of an access-based service increases the likelihood that con-sumers subsequently reduce ownership.

 Access the online resources to read the abstract and access the full paper.

Other companies benefiting from this trend towards access rather than ownership modes of consumption include Fashion Hire (luxury handbags, where you can rent a Cha-nel handbag for £130 per month), Zipcar (car sharing), and Netflix (film and media rental). The term 'asset-light generation' has been used to describe the behaviour of young people who are part of a growing trend towards storing and streaming music and documents digi-tally in a move away from physically owning books, CDs, magazines, and TV (Fitzgerald, 2012). Companies such as Netflix and Spotify are leaders in the field of streaming enter-tainment. Of course, borrowing is nothing new; in the past most people obtained their books from libraries, and paying a subscription was a common model in the early days of libraries. This subscription model has been extended to products such as mobile phones and software, and is likely to become more common. For example, Hyundai is introducing a subscription-based model for its new range of electric cars (Stocksdale, 2017). And as we see in the Consumer Insight 11.3, the idea is extending further into a range of consumer goods that would once have been purchased outright.

Recession consumption and sustainability

At times of recession, people often change their consumer behaviour in response to the constraints on their economic budget; such material constraints can also be detrimen-tal to people's identity. One study of European men identified very different coping strategies and feelings of loss when previous consumption habits could no longer be maintained (O'Loughlin et al., 2017). We have already mentioned possible impacts on attitudes and behaviour of the experience of recession and austerity. Russia has recently suffered a number of negative events that have impacted the social mood of the country; the collapse of the rouble and subsequent reduction in real incomes, the decrease in oil prices, and wars in Ukraine and Syria have increased anxiety levels. A three-year study by a cultural insight company has identified how marketing has responded to such anxiety through advertsing that emphasizes protection, nature, technology, trusted traditions, and supportive community (Murphy, 2017). Protection comes in the form of products that act 'against' something, such as cleaning products. Protection also comes in the form of the Hero (see Chapter 7)—a physically strong superhero or animal such as a tiger or bear that provides brands with metaphors of power and energy. The use of nature in marketing is particularly prevalent in personal care and food advertisements as an antidote to danger, and the copy emphasizes the product's natural ingredients. Another code is 'tender care', which conveys a caring form of protection, and in Russian culture is associated with women who represent care and experience as consumers. Finally, in Russian collectivist culture (see Chapter 9), the support of family and friends is increasingly vital at a time of anxiety, and brands are taking on the role of supporter

Some consumers tighten their belts and avoid taking on debt, which can have a major impact on business. During recessions, higher-end more expensive categories (e.g. cars, kitchens) tend to do badly, as consumers are fearful of taking on new debts when jobs and future incomes are not guaranteed. Companies in these product categories have to allay these fears when promoting their products. In 2009, Hyundai developed a finance package whereby they offered an assurance to all customers that if in the year following the purchase of a Hyundai car they lost their income, they could return the car. This assurance was an attempt to offer some safety to consumers in uncertain times; of the million vehicles sold since the agreement began only 350 cars were returned based on the agreement. Many hailed this as a very effective marketing campaign, and the approach was copied by General Motors and Ford (Anon., 2011a). In 2011, Hyundai stopped this assurance programme, declaring that it was no longer needed since America was coming out of the recession.

The recession has had an impact on leisure activities outside the home, with recent evidence from Keynote (2015) showing how eating out and going to the cinema decreased in the immediate aftermath of the recession, but have started to stabilize as consumers emerge from the recession. At times of recession, anything to do with home entertainment usually does well, as people spend more time indoors and cheer themselves up through greater expenditure on broadband and satellite TV packages (Easier Finance, 2008).

In terms of more essential purchases, such as food and energy, consumer spending patterns show less variation, mainly because there is less scope to cut down on these items.

Consumer volatility is a characteristic of recessions—people reassess their expenditure. At times of recession, consumer 'savviness' tends to go up, as does usage of websites offering money saving advice, such as moneysavingexpert.com. Recent reports suggest that almost all shoppers, across all socio-economic groups and all age groups, now use coupons (PitneyBowes, 2013).

A major trend in the retail sector is the increasing popularity of smartphone digitally based discount vouchers or codes, fuelled by changes in mobile technology but also a response to recessionary pressures on consumers. This implies that marketers should be investing particularly where consumers are considering changes in expenditure, and are also willing to invest time looking for and collecting coupons and discount vouchers. However, this is the reverse of what many companies do during a recession, and it is often marketing budgets that are the first to be hit. In Consumer Insight 11.3 we discuss how the trend towards renting, rather than owning, occurs in the luxury market.

CONSUMER INSIGHT 11.3

Living a life of borrowed luxury

A recent consumer trend taking hold in a number of countries is the growth in rental culture, where consumers are renting, rather than owning, cars and properties in their bid to save money during the recession. As people's confidence in this new consumption mode increases, we are witnessing consumers with slightly more discretionary income going further in their rentals, and renting designer gowns, shoes, and handbags for short periods of time (anything from a few days to a month or so). This is what is coming to be known as 'borrowed luxury'.

Rental companies are found in many categories, including designer dresses (Rent the Runway https://www.renttherunway.com, Girl Meets Dress http://www.girlmeetsdress.com), handbags (Bag Borrow or Steal http://www.bagborroworsteal.com/borrow), watches (Borrowed Time Watches http://borrowedtimewatches.com), and luxury cars (Dream Car Hire http://www.dreamcarhire.com/ and Elite Rent https://www.eliterent.com/en/).

The attraction of this approach is that it assuages any guilt consumers may feel about such expenditure—they can have a small amount of luxury without the negative feelings that may accompany extravagant spending. It also removes the hassle and cost associated with the maintenance and insurance of expensive items. The Borrowed Time Watches club offers luxury watch rentals for men, with different levels of membership reflecting the needs and passions of its members, from 'executive' for enthusiasts who want an all-year membership through to 'basic' which suits the occasional wearer. In Milan, the Circle Club emerged as a way of enabling people who are already fairly wealthy to access designer jewels, luxury cars, and customized watches in order to convey greater wealth than they perhaps have. Its members pay about $26,000 to join, and this entitles them to a number of points. These points are then used to 'pay' for use of a range of luxury items (including boats, helicopters, and small planes!). When members' points run out, they pay the fee again. Another attraction of renting is that consumers can keep 'refreshing' their wardrobe, while keeping costs down. This fits with the recent analysis by trendwatching.com (Trendwatching, 2016) on the Future of Luxury, where it is identified that increasingly connected consumers want luxury that fits with their quintessential self, is available on demand, and plays to their concerns for sustainable futures. These consumers have the power to transform the who, where, and when of luxury.

Questions

1. What factors do you think will influence the wider uptake of this trend?

2. Try and think about different types of consumers (different age groups; income bands; different country contexts) and consider the issues for them in terms of considering renting rather than owning.

Sources: Castonguay (2006); Wilkinson (2007); Hevrdejs (2011); Scharf (2012); Trendwatching (2016); http://borrowedtimewatches.com/ http://www.bagborroworsteal.com/ http://www.dreamcarhire.com/ http://www.eliterent.com/ http://www.girlmeetsdress.com/ http://www.renttherunway.com/

 Access the online resources and follow the web links to learn more about the growth in rental culture.

Despite the recession, sustainability appears to have maintained some significance amongst consumers. For instance, a recent Unilever survey showed that a third of consumers surveyed expressed a preference for sustainable goods and brands (Unilever, 2017). While it has been suggested that millennials may be more narcissistic than previous generations, one survey in 2014 showed that they were in favour of caring for others and their environment (Nielsen, 2014). They expressed concern for family, with 63 per cent of the sample saying that they had a responsibility to care for elderly parents. When they care about something, millennials share it on their social media accounts, and this includes their favourite social and political causes. They are often willing to spend more on goods and services from companies that are sustainable and give to society or are ethical in their approach to business. Advertisers that can engage with this in a way that millennials see as authentic and useful, as in the G-Star raw ad that is turning an environmental problem into a positive alternative (Figure 11.6), may be perceived positively. A further global report by Deloitte (2017) shows a similar concern among millennials that businesses should not focus only on financial success but contribute to employment, society, education, and the environment. For businesses, this means that a greater understanding of communicating with customers on social media and responding to their concerns will be required. They also need to recognize that millennials value product attributes beyond price and quality; provenance, fairness, and environemental sustainability will be aspects they will look for in the brands they favour.

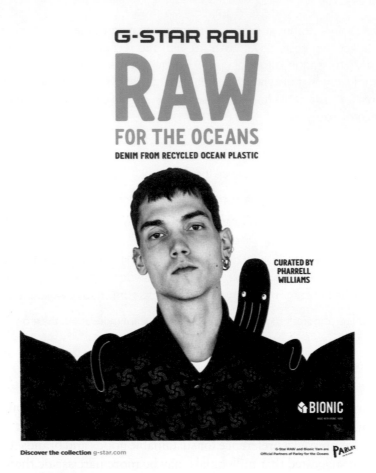

Figure 11.6 G-Star Raw 'for the oceans' advertisement

Misbehaviour

Much of this book has focused on attempting to explain and explore the ways that consumers behave, assuming that the consumer is acting according to the socially agreed norms of the marketplace. If you stop and think about a recent shopping experience, you may consider that you knew the way to behave in the store, how to interact with sales staff and other customers, and generally how to navigate the various aspects of the retail encounter. Many organizations are focused on customer satisfaction ratings, and have the philosophy that the customer is always right.

However, some types of consumer behaviour are definitely not what we would expect—some consumers can be deviant and dysfunctional in the way they act (Daunt and Harris, 2012). While some dysfunctional behaviours may occur in marketplace contexts and are linked to the acquisition of goods and services (e.g. compulsive buying, in-store abuse of staff, theft), others can be linked to product misuse (such as addictive or compulsive buying/consuming of food, drugs, or alcohol). **Consumer misbehaviour** is the term used to capture these types of behaviours, and is defined as *'behavioral acts by consumers, which violate the generally accepted norms of conduct in consumption situations, and thus disrupt the consumption order. It represents the dark, negative side of the consumer'* (Fullerton and Punj, 2004: 1239).

When we discuss the dark side of consumption, we are talking mainly about consumer misbehaviour, although a range of terms are used including deviant customer behaviour (Moschis and Cox, 1989), jay customers (Lovelock, 1994), and dysfunctional customer behaviour (Harris and Reynolds, 2003). All the definitions share a common focus on consumer behaviour that violates social norms of the exchange encounter. As we discussed in Chapter 9, social norms tend to be formed through customs, rules, laws, and values of a cultural context. Underlying the deviant nature of the consumer misbehaviour definition is the assumption that consumers know the 'accepted' norms of the encounter. Not all forms of consumer misbehaviour are clear cut; for example, the knowing purchase of counterfeit goods is common today, and the relationship of this activity to prevailing social norms is ambiguous and contested (Maman, 2010). Further, discussions of the dark side of consumer behaviour encompass issues in terms of disruption for other consumers and for the environment and society at large. It is also important when considering the darker aspects of consumption to question the broader ramifications of marketing practices, and the negative consequences associated with excess in contemporary consumer culture.

It is important when talking about misbehaviour to remember that companies misbehave too. Many companies have been fined for pollution and for mis-selling financial products, and drugs companies for improper marketing of certain drugs.

Piracy and counterfeit goods

In 2016 the OECD reported that imports of counterfeit and pirated products amounted to around 2.5 per cent of global imports. While most of us may think of counterfeiting as only affecting high-end luxury brands such as handbags and perfume, the fact is that almost anything from machine parts to chemicals can be counterfeited, although the most counterfeited product is footwear (OECD, 2016). Importantly this behaviour can harm lives. Many developing countries suffer from counterfeit pharmaceuticals, toys, electrical products, and even baby foods (OECD, 2016). In such cases the consumers may be unaware that the brand is not genuine; however, in many countries consumers will know that the luxury brand bags, belts, and watches being sold in the streets are counterfeit, and some would say that if they purchase such items they are being complicit in cheating the owners of the real brand. Another argument is that these usually poor refugees need to find a way to live. The sellers of such fake goods in Spain have actually developed their own brand. It is called 'top manta' named after the blanket (*manta*) on which they display their goods. The manteros buy their goods from Chinese importers and, rather than selling the trainers as copies of Nike or Adidas trainers, they now attach the manta logo (Burgen, 2017). Time will tell whether they will be as popular as the fakes.

The other increasingly problematic form of piracy is digital piracy, including e-books, music, films, and computer games. Technology has been important in tackling such piracy through digital rights management (DRM) systems which make it difficult to reproduce and distribute such products (Sinha et al., 2010). There has been much opposition to DRM, notably in terms of its inconvenience to legitimate customers because it is claimed that it stops both innovation and competition and works can be difficult to access if the DRM scheme changes (https://www.eff.org/issues/drm). From a consumer perspective we have to consider who would buy pirated goods and why they would do it. Research suggests that although negative incentives can be a strong deterrent for some consumers, they can actually increase the likelihood of piracy for others. Positive incentives such as better functionality seem to reduce the likelihood of piracy (Sinha and Mandel, 2008).

Piracy is not bad for all producers. For example, books have become bestsellers through pirated PDFs before publication (Bullas, nd), which suggests that however distribution comes about it is usually good for business. Others have tried to bring piracy audiences back into legal downloading. For example MUSO Retune is an analytics product which helps owners market their content to illegal uses to enable them to reconnect to licensed content such as Spotify or iTunes.

Deviant acquisition behaviour

The term deviant acquisition behaviour refers to consumer misbehaviour in acquiring goods. Black Friday, the day after Thanksgiving in the USA, is regarded as the start of the holiday shopping season when shops offer sales and special offers. In recent years, most major retailers have opened extremely early and offered promotional sales to kick off this important shopping period. There have been stories from the USA of consumers behaving badly during the Black Friday sales (Figure 11.7), with one report stating that customers rushing towards early morning (5 a.m.) deals in Wal-Mart pushed employees against stacks of merchandise (Barbaro, 2006). There have been reports of injuries and deaths associated with Black Friday sales (http://blackfridaydeathcount.com/). Although this is an extreme example, behaviour such as this is expected at sales time, and has almost become part of the retail mythology around major sales events.

Other problematic behaviours include skipping payments, late payments, breaking rental agreements, and aggressive behaviour towards staff or other customers. These are a pervasive part of everyday customer behaviour (Fullerton and Punj, 2004) and are sometimes deliberate or a result of thoughtlessness, but can also occur when a customer does not have control over the situation or lacks knowledge or experience of roles and responsibilities. Marketers can ease such situations by providing clear guidance and information on how to behave in certain situations, such as queuing guidelines in banks or posters alerting customers how to behave in their interactions with staff. Two particularly problematic forms of consumer misbehaviour are found in compulsive shopping and theft—the negative consequences of each can be far-reaching.

Figure 11.7   Typical scenes from a Black Friday sale in the USA
Source: Image courtesy of Martin Thuresson.

Compulsive buying

Compulsive buying is *an unusual obsession with shopping such that it significantly affects the person afflicted*. It is considered to be a form of deviant acquisition behaviour. Those people who buy in a compulsive way have a strong preoccupation with shopping, often characterized as uncontrolled, which has significant negative consequences. Most often these consequences are financial (since many buy excessive amounts that cannot be afforded), but there can also be serious personal and emotional consequences, such as stress and broken relationships. For compulsive buyers, it is the experience of shopping and the accompanying emotions that drive their behaviour. Various estimates of this phenomenon in the USA suggest that it affects 3–6 per cent of the population (Koran et al., 2006; Rose and Segrist, 2012). A number of causes have been suggested, ranging from a psychological basis (such as low self-esteem, low mood, as a way of coping with stress and anxiety, and as a form of fantasy) through to a more socially oriented basis, including a form of materialistic value endorsement, dissatisfaction with identity, or as a way of exercising power and control in relationships (O'Guinn and Faber, 1989; Elliott et al., 1996; Dittmar, 2005). Contemporary consumer culture, which emphasizes materialism, can heighten the problem for compulsive buyers, and those with low self-esteem or self-worth are particularly vulnerable. It is important for companies to be aware of the potential (unintended) consequences of their marketing messages. However, we should also consider the prevalence of store cards which are frequently offered with an immediate discount at the point of sale; these may impact compulsive shoppers in terms of how much they are able to spend if they amass a number of such cards.

Theft

In marketplace contexts, consumers have a sense of what they think is honest and acceptable behaviour, which is informed by cultural and societal values and beliefs. As discussed already, people generally know how to behave in shops and how to interact with sales staff. A real problem for companies, and society, is consumer theft. When talking about theft it is important to appreciate the spectrum of dishonest behaviours that may fall under that heading. Many people shopping in supermarkets think it is acceptable to try grapes, as if they are a free sample, yet there is no sign saying 'Help yourself to grapes'. However, many consumers rationalize this as acceptable and not even dishonest, since the act is considered to be so insignificant compared with the profits that the supermarkets make. At the other end of the spectrum are organized gangs of shoplifters stealing to order. In this section we are referring to the more significant acts where the thief (acting on their own or in a gang) leaves the store with goods that have not been paid for. Although shoplifting is criminal behaviour, and hence primarily the domain of criminologists, it is also consumer behaviour (albeit deviant behaviour), since it is 'part of people's conduct in their role as consumers' (Fullerton and Punj, 1997: 336). Clearly, this is a problem that represents a cost for many companies, and so it is important for businesses to have strategies for handling consumer theft.

Consumer theft *refers to the desire to steal as a way of acquisition of consumer objects,* and is a significant phenomenon affecting the experience of all consumers. It is costly for businesses and ultimately for consumers. One study from the USA suggests that one in every eleven people who walk into a shop will leave with at least one item that has not been paid for (National Association for Shoplifting Prevention, 2011), and in recent years there have been well-publicized cases of celebrities being caught shoplifting (e.g. Anthony Worrall Thompson in the UK, and Winona Ryder and Lindsay Lohan in the USA).

The recent rise in more middle-class shoplifters has been explained in terms of their stealing goods to maintain a standard of living, rather than to sell them on to make money. The Centre for Retail Research in Nottingham, UK, tracks projected losses from retail crime in the Christmas season. Their research covers 19 countries and the data provides an interesting snapshot of how retail crime is viewed in different countries. Retail crime comprises shoplifting, staff theft, and supply chain fraud. In nearly all countries (except the USA) shoplifting is the single most significant form of retail theft. The countries worst hit by shoplifting are the USA (£23.7bn), followed by the UK (£5.2bn), Germany (£4.6bn), France (£4.3bn), and Italy (£3.4bn) (Bamfield, 2012).

The most popular items for consumer theft are those that are CRAVED—**C**oncealable, **R**emovable, **A**vailable, **V**alued, **E**njoyed, and Disposable (Barkham, 2012). Items that are in high demand, easily disposed of (i.e. sold or passed on), and in small mobile formats are popular items. Reports of the 'most popular items stolen' emerge annually in the UK and the USA, and these often includes expensive cuts of meat, cheese, alcohol, small electrical items such as toothbrushes and DIY tools, electronic gadgets such as video games, smartphones, and laptops, razor blades, and designer clothing and shoes (Barkham, 2012 ; Oxley,

2015). Although specific data is not available for all countries, Barkham (2012) reports that cheese is the most popular item stolen across the world!

Product factors influencing whether or not people steal are linked to the CRAVED aspect of the product, but also the product may be one that is embarrassing (e.g. condoms) or illegal (e.g. cigarettes or alcohol to youths). Environmental factors are also relevant, and may emanate from the marketing context, particularly the way that products are presented to make them look attractive and enticing. Merchandising of goods may also make it seem easy for thieves to steal goods or switch tags. Some consumers seek the thrill and excitement of thieving (which may be a contributory factor in adolescent and youth thefts). Another important consumer factor may relate to attitudes towards the store and big business in general. Consumers may justify their theft by suggesting that the environment encourages it, and the company somehow deserves it and can absorb the cost, and so it is a victimless crime. Finally, the moral development of consumers may be a factor influencing their views on stealing, and they may not see stealing as wrong. Linked to this are their beliefs around the extent to which thieves think they can get away with stealing.

Finally, it is worth noting the increase in other forms of retail crime, as reported in the British Retail Crime Survey (BRCS, 2017), linked to advances in technology and practices around shopping and accessing goods. With the increase in e-business and card transactions online there has been a rise in e-crime and fraud in retail contexts. Retailers estimated that 53 per cent of the total cost of fraud conducted against them online in 2015–16 was cyber-enabled fraud. This was about 15 per cent of the total cost of crime, or around £100 million.

The main challenge for marketers is to discourage shoplifting. Measures in place include making access to expensive goods difficult, often by locking them away (e.g. perfumes and jewellery) or by having them available behind a counter (e.g. sales of razor blades and spirits in convenience stores). While these strategies may not be ideal in terms of consumer experience, they are adopted to reduce shoplifting opportunities. Other theft-reducing devices include the use of security tags on merchandise which are deactivated or removed for reuse at the cash register. The costs of these thefts need to be covered somehow, and often consumers pay the price for lost merchandise and the costs of security systems through higher prices.

The problem of overconsumption

Some of the problems associated with excessive consumption have been mentioned in our discussion of the issues around sustainability and consumption. When we talk of over consumption, we are referring not only to the problems associated with levels of consumption that are unsustainable for the planet's resources, but also those that pose health problems for consumers. In a global context, two significant problematic areas of excessive consumption relate to food and alcohol.

The obesity crisis

A global obesity epidemic was first identified in the 1990s by the World Health Organization (WHO, 2016). Although initially considered a problem associated with developed countries, records show that rates are rising worldwide, and most dramatically in urban settings.

Obesity levels have more than doubled around the world since 1980 (WHO, 2016). In the UK the latest figures state that 26 per cent of adults and 16 per cent of children are obese. The picture in the USA is similar, with 35.7 per cent of adults and 16.9 per cent of children and adolescents reported as obese in 2012 (Food Research & Action Center, 2012). Reports from other countries also suggest that rising obesity levels are a problem. In Brazil, 48.5 per cent of the population are overweight and 15.8 per cent are obese (BBC, 2012). The number of overweight people in China is also on the rise, with one adult in four reported to be overweight or obese, and this figure is higher in urban areas (Howard, 2012). This increase is partly related to the vast change in lifestyles oriented towards greater use of processed food and supermarkets, and a drop in physical activity as a result of huge economic expansion (Bristow, 2010).

Paradoxically, many developing countries (such as India) are facing the dual challenge of suffering from both under- and overnutrition. In Mexico, where the tap water is unreliable, soft drinks are a popular alternative; in the Middle East, the increasing wealth of Bedouins and their tradition of feasting has led to overeating in a climate where exercise is not favoured.

The data on the relationship between income level and obesity is mixed. In the UK, there is a pattern of greater obesity among the most deprived in society (Booth et al., 2017). In the USA, the disparities between high and low income consumers and obesity levels are weakening—morbid obesity appears to affect all socio-economic groups (Booth et al., 2017). However, the Food Research & Action Centre (FRAC) reports that those living on low incomes are more vulnerable to becoming obese for reasons including limited access to quality healthy fresh produce, greater reliance on cheaply produced processed foods, and greater exposure to the marketing of obesity-promoting foods (e.g. fast food restaurants, TV advertisements).

When discussing the problem of global obesity, many commentators point to the role of the global food industry in producing more cheap processed foods, high in fat and sugar, which leads to 'passive overconsumption' of energy and ultimately results in higher levels of obesity (Swinburn et al., 2011). In 2016 the UK government published a plan to tackle childhood obesity, saying that it would make long-term sustainable changes which could 'only be achieved through the active engagement of schools, communities, families and individuals' (HM Government, 2016). However, others believe that more responsibility for obesity should be taken by manufacturers for the way high calorific food is marketed in what has been termed the 'obesogenic environment' (Jones et al., 2007; Szmigin and Gee, 2017).

Excessive and irresponsible alcohol consumption

Excessive alcohol consumption is another major global problem. The WHO conducts an annual survey, the Global Information System on Alcohol and Health, and the most recent data shows the developed world as having the highest alcohol consumption levels. Many Eastern European countries have high consumption, risky patterns of drinking, and, accordingly, high levels of alcohol-related deaths and disabilities. The global pattern among young people is towards higher levels of alcohol use and binge drinking (WHO, 2014). In the UK, the levels of alcohol consumption among the 16–24 age group remain high (Office of National Statistics, 2017), although young people are less likely to consume alcohol than other age groups (46.0 per cent of those aged 16–24 years reported drinking alcohol in the previous week, compared with 64.2 per cent of those aged 45–64 years). When they do drink, the younger age group is more likely to 'binge' on their heaviest drinking day. This is the most problematic form of drinking, representing a risky consumption behaviour for young people.

Researchers from a range of disciplines, including public health, criminology, psychology, and social marketing, have focused on the issues around alcohol consumption, seeking to understand the drivers of excessive consumption. A number of studies have highlighted the central role that drinking and drunkenness play in many young people's social lives (Griffin et al., 2009; Smith and Foxcroft, 2009). Reasons for drinking alcohol are diverse, and include the social function that it plays in young people's lives (Szmigin et al., 2008), its importance in how young people act out the gender roles associated with being young (Abel and Plumridge 2004; Likis-Werle and Borders, 2017), and the hedonistic appeal of the deliberate and determined drunkenness that characterizes contemporary youth culture. The marketing and retailing practices around alcohol and the UK drinking culture are important considerations. Over the last 10 years, the alcohol industry has changed the way that alcohol is marketed in a number of ways, such as developing new alcohol products that encourage new ways of drinking (e.g. new higher strength alcohol products to be consumed as 'shots'). The industry has also engaged in greater use of price promotions and point-of-sale materials in bars and retail environments, which encourages higher consumption. Consumer Insight 11.4 explores alcohol marketing and how it impacts alcohol consumption.

CONSUMER INSIGHT 11.4

Does the marketing of alcohol influence consumption?

The role of the alcohol industry in promoting alcohol consumption has been the focus of much government and media attention in the UK in recent years. In 2009, The Showbar Club in Warrington, UK, was in trouble for encouraging irresponsible drinking through its 'Two Bob Tuesdays' promotional event (see Figure 11.8). Entry to the event was £5, and following that all drinks were sold for 10 pence (colloquially, 'two bob'). The company defended this promotion as follows: 'They will only be allowed to have one drink at a time. It's not irresponsible. Other places have had promotions of drink at 1p a time—now that is irresponsible' (Jenny Keep, Manager of Showbar, quoted in *Verge Magazine* (2011)). Other nightclubs, such as the Tokyo Club in Oldham, Greater Manchester, have been criticized for offering all-inclusive drinks promotions (BBC, 2009).

Figure 11.8 Alcohol promotion for 'Happy Hour'   *Source*: © iStock.com/ManuelVelasco.

Novel approaches to alcohol packaging, often reflecting consumer trends, have emerged in recent years, and some have argued that these have contributed to excessive alcohol consumption. 'Suck & Blow' jelly shooters are a case in point—these plastic shot cups are sold to individual and corporate clients as 'The most fun way to do a party shot ever!' The idea is that consumption is accomplished through the combined effort of two people, one blowing and the other sucking, leading to very quick consumption of the alcoholic jelly.

Cell Drinks, who make pre-packaged spirit (PPS) drinks sold in flexible packaging via unique vending machines, ran into problems with their advertising. One of the main appeals of this drink is that consumers can hold the drink while dancing, and it will not spill. The no-spill aspect of its packaging was emphasized in its advertising campaign of 2011, where it showed young people in various scenarios (a free-runner running and jumping over buildings while holding the drink, a girl raver dancing frantically while holding the drink) who were not spilling the drink. The Advertising Standards Authority (ASA) found that the advertisements appealed to under-18s and ruled that they should be withdrawn.

Questions

1. To what extent do you think marketing and the alcohol industry contribute to excessive alcohol consumption among young people?

2. Can you think of ways in which marketing could be used to dissuade young people from drinking so much?

Sources: Measham (2008); Anon. (2011b); ASA (2011); *Verge Magazine*, 2011; www.suckandblow.com

 Access the online resources and follow the web links to learn more about the marketing of alcohol.

Transformative consumer research

Transformative consumer research (TCR) *refers to a stream of research that focuses on benefiting consumer welfare and quality of life across the world.* While high quality and rigorous research has been a central plank of much consumer welfare research over the years, what distinguishes TCR work is that it emphasizes the dissemination and sharing of valuable findings (Mick et al., 2011), in ways that are geared towards having effective and impactful outcomes. A key aspect of TCR work is the recognition that in order to develop effective consumer welfare solutions to real consumer problems it is important to include all stakeholders in the research from early on, and for these stakeholders to be involved throughout the whole project. The TCR perspective lends itself to problems and contexts where there is a consumer welfare implication. The global problems around food well-being are important and have been the focus of TCR work (Block et al., 2016), as has addiction (Martin et al., 2012), poverty (Corus et al., 2016), and risky consumption behaviour among youths (Mason et al., 2013).

A typical TCR approach to a consumer well-being issue would aim to inform interventions to address the problematic behaviour by including relevant stakeholders in all aspects of the intervention, from research through to design of campaign materials and evaluation of impact of the campaign. For example, research for Alcohol Research UK reports that there has been a steady increase in the amount of alcohol consumed by older age groups in recent years, and that a growing number of older people are at risk of alcohol-related harm (Wadd et al., 2011). However, alcohol problems are often difficult to detect in older people because of complex physical and social problems, including a lack of awareness amongst health professionals in recognizing alcohol misuse, or barriers for older people seeking to access help. From a TCR perspective, health and social care workers would be included to inform the health and social care perspective, community-based public service workers (such as community police and the fire service) might be included, since they often interact with and see the consequences of the effects of alcohol consumption and may have something to contribute, and substance misuse practitioners might also be included. The approach might be closer to action research, with the focus on the impact of the research to bring about social change. This is an important theme in current consumer research as it goes beyond understanding how and why consumers purchase and use products to identifying problems in consumption and helping to improve consumers' lives in a holistic way. It is possible that TCR will become an important stream in consumer research which can also inform welfare policy.

Conclusions

When the certainties of the growth economy are removed and the economic and financial parameters are shifting it becomes imperative to understand how consumer behaviour responds to these new conditions. In this chapter we have addressed a range of issues that are likely to have a major impact on consumer behaviour. The **technological trends and developments** in marketing are likely to increase; on the one hand they give marketers incredible access to consumers through **big data**, but on the other hand businesses need to know what to do with that data and what it is telling them about consumers. Alongside this, as Practitioner Insight 11 from Grant Thornton tells us, business will constantly have to change to keep up with technological advances, and this can be costly.

Issues around **sustainability and sustainable consumption** were discussed in this chapter, and in Consumer Insight 11.2 we focused on Buy Nothing Day as an example of an international voluntary simplicity initiative. Increasingly people are showing themselves to be more conscious in their consumption activities, and particular segments such as Millennials may be particularly vocal in how they expect companies to behave in line with their expectations.

Another important theme in this chapter related to how **consumers are responding to global recessionary pressures**. Consumer Insight 11.3 looked at how consumers are changing the ways that they access luxury goods, with a greater move towards rental and hiring. We also identified different ways that cultures such as Russia may respond to local and world problems in the messages that they use in their advertising.

We also looked in detail at **misbehaviour** and recognized marketing's role in this and its impact on society, with Consumer Insight 11.4 focusing on the issues around the marketing and consumption of alcohol. There are many forms of misbehaviour including piracy and theft. The solutions which help both consumers and businesses may not be easy to find. Finally we considered the relevance of **transformative consumer research** to dealing with issues around consumer well-being.

In terms of marketing's future, there are important points to consider, not least the role that marketing and business has played in creating the conditions that have led to some of the problems discussed here (e.g. advertising foods high in fat/sugar to children, and developing alcoholic products that encourage swift consumption of high alcohol content short drinks). Questions are raised as to whether marketers should be involved in advising people on 'life choices'. Further, marketers need to think about consumer trust and cynicism. Chylinski and Chu (2010) comment that consumer cynicism is commonly related to suspicion, mistrust, scepticism, and distrust of an agent's or organization's motives, and can lead to reactions such as dissatisfaction, alienation, resistance, and hostility towards the organization. However, they point out that this is a fairly under-researched area, and it is difficult to say what the consequences of consumer cynicism are. Some consumers may engage in consumer activism (similar to the Buy Nothing Day discussed in Consumer Insight 11.2) while others may boycott particular stores and brands, and voluntary simplicity and more conscious consumption may also result.

It is difficult to predict what methods and approaches will be most used in the coming years. The very fact of big data will determine how some research is conducted, as discussed in this chapter. but alongside that it is likely that semiotics, anthropology, and visual research will be equally important as businesses try to understand *why* people behave in the way they do, not just *what* they buy. The text and visuals that are now freely available as data on social media will mean that such data can be mined for insight and sentiment. However, one of the biggest challenges is likely to be what companies do with all this data in terms of translating it into new products and appropriate marketing.

In this book we have examined consumer behaviour from many angles—from a historical perspective, from the view of different disciplines such as psychology, sociology, and economics, and from new approaches including consumer culture theory and transformative consumer research. It is difficult for any of us to predict the future, but perhaps one of the most significant changes and opportunities for businesses is how consumers have become enabled and empowered in recent years. Consumers have more control and are more involved than ever before. They provide and use content, and have access to information and can use it instantly. Whether it is choosing and purchasing products and services, taking charge of their finances or healthcare, deciding what to share on social media, or when and where to have an item delivered, they are able to take control, and companies need to understand and meet these consumer demands both in the products, services, and experiences they develop and the in way they market to consumers. Companies need more than ever to have their finger on the pulse of what consumers want and carefully examine how they are actually behaving in order to identify their current and future needs and wants.

Review Questions

1. Describe and discuss two main technological developments that are impacting on consumer behaviour.

3. What is your understanding of the difference between voluntary simplicity and conscious consumption?

4. What are the key reasons behind the trend away from ownership towards borrowing and renting?

5. How does compulsive consumption differ from excessive consumption? Can you identify the factors leading to each type of compulsive consumption?

6. What are the key characteristics of consumer crime?

7. What does CRAVED stand for?

8. What is transformative consumer research, and why is it relevant to the study of consumption?

Discussion Questions

1. What apps do you have? How do you use them? Discuss with your classmates which apps are most popular, and try to categorize the main reasons why you buy and use apps. Do you think that they lead to more consumption?

2. Consider what you think are the main ethical issues around piracy. Can it ever be right to purchase counterfeit products?

3. If you had to reduce your consumption, how would you do it? What changes to your lifestyle would you make and how do you think it would affect you?

4. Can you identify codes such as the Russian 'tender care' in your culture that seem to be particularly relevant to current economic and/or social trends. What are they and why do you think they are used?

5. Consider different products or services you might borrow rather than buy. What are the advantages and disadvantages?

6. Discuss what you consider to be consumer theft. Are some types of theft worse than others and if so why?

7. What do you consider are the main drivers for young people to drink excessively?

⊙ Access the online resources to test your knowledge further and complete the Multiple Choice Questions for Chapter 11.

CASE STUDY 11

Are you a virgin consumer?

In this case we examine the idea of the virgin consumer. The fast pace of innovation and changes in contemporary society mean that in many consumer contexts everyone is at times a virgin consumer, unfamiliar with the brands, services, apps, and experiences they come across on a daily basis. In this Case Study, we discuss this in more depth, and offer some suggestions for connecting with virgin consumers.

The website trendwatching.com identifies a recent trend in consumer behaviour which they describe as the 'virgin consumer'. The reason for this term is more to do with the constant innovation and development of new and unfamiliar products, services, brands, and experiences that become available every day than the nature of the consumers themselves; indeed, such virgin consumers are usually highly experienced. Trendwatching.com say that virgin consumers want new things, they look for them and lust after them, and they want to experiment and have fun. In the twenty-first century, not only are there lots of new things for consumers to experience, but the choice is overwhelming and there is much more on the way, with China alone granting millions of new patents.

In the past new brands might take a long time to become popular as consumers were wary and preferred to stick with tried and trusted brands. Today new brands may become trusted quickly for a number of reasons. Why? People are less concerned about the value of the old 'trusted' brand; indeed choosing new unknown brands can offer novelty, authenticity, and a feeling of discovery, and the risk associated with trying new brands is much lower because consumers are easily able to share information. Consumers discover new products and services through their social networks. They receive recommendations and reviews, and ask friends and followers to improve and validate their buying decision. The actual sharing of information can become a business in itself; the coupon site Groupon has used referrals from friends and colleagues to drive sales of 40 million since its launch in 2008. Trendwatching.com has recently published some facts regarding social connections and the impact they have on brands:

- three-quarters of Facebook users have 'liked' a brand

- over 50 million users 'like' brands every day

- Juicy Couture found that their product purchase conversion rate increased by 160 per cent after installing social sharing features

- Incipio Technologies, a gadget accessory retailer, found that referrals from Facebook had a conversion rate double the average.

It is important to remember that different cultures may be looking for different experiences. Although social media is a worldwide phenomenon, it is going to be used in many different ways. China's largest food and drinks company built the success of its new product, an organic juice called Loahs, on the Farmville mania gripping China in 2009 by encouraging social media game players to plant organic products in their virtual gardens, produce organic juice, and then share it with their friends. Therefore the campaign raised awareness, which led to 130 million virtual bottles being shared with friends. Sales jumped by 30 per cent. Trendwatching.com suggest three important approaches for engaging with consumer virgins.

1. Cast off industry convention—this means thinking about how your consumers live now and what they want, rather than developing existing products (see Chapter 2 on discontinuous innovations). The product also needs to be intuitive to use—no messing about with instruction manuals. Thermostats may seem like an unlikely product to be developed in a new way to meet consumer needs. Nest has achieved this and produced a product that looks good and is not overly technical (see Figure 11.9). The company posts that three out of four people can install it within 30 minutes. Nest learns people's schedules and is programmed to save energy. They also provide an app so that if you are coming home early you can turn up your heating so your home is warm when you arrive (see www.nest.com).

2. Explain your brand—a virgin brand is going to be new to consumers so it has to be explained, and one way that new brands are doing this is telling stories about their brand and then finding ways to keep the story in the consumers' minds. When you go on the Welsh jeans manufacturer Hiut it has a section entitled 'Story'. Here they tell you that the jeans are made in Cardigan in Wales which used to have Britain's biggest jeans factory

(A)   (B)

Figure 11.9 Left the Nest Thermostat UK app for an iPhone; right, a Nest thermostat
Source: Image courtesy of Nest Labs.

producing 35,000 pairs a week for decades. When the factory closed down, people lost their jobs but not their skills. Hiut, although a small company, wants to offer the opportunity for some of those people to use their skills again. To stimulate consumer demand, and also to engage more effectively with its consumer base, Hiut created the History Tag. The History Tag harnesses the potential for storytelling through objects by creating a mechanism (the History Tag) allowing consumers to develop and track their personal history with the company's jeans. Each pair of jeans is issued with a unique number, which the consumer registers (and activates) on the company website. They are then encouraged to upload photographs of themselves wearing the jeans as a way of preserving memories associated with wearing the jeans (see Figure 11.10). The message on the

Figure 11.10 Hiut advertising campaign   *Source*: Image courtesy of Hiut Denim Co. (http://hiutdenim.co.uk).

website also encourages consumers to think about how they preserve these memories, and reinforces the point that their jeans are made to a high standard and are built to last: 'And that's the genius of making a product to last. It will give our objects more meaning. It will mean we throw things away less. Because it attaches the stories to the objects that we love' (hiutdenim.co.uk).

3. Finally, trendwatching.com warns companies not to expect commitment from their consumers. Rather than expecting a long-term relationship, companies need to embrace the fact that consumers may want variety, so alternatives such as streaming or renting products rather than selling them may be the best solution. What is clear is that renting can work for any kind of product, not just films and music—now you can even rent your clothes (see thesixosix.com). As this site notes, many people want clothes not a closet.

Questions

1. What new products, brands, or experiences do you think will appeal to virgin consumers? Try to think about ways that a brand is delivered, not just what it is?

2. What new ideas or brands have you recently adopted? What do you like about them and why?

3. Write a history for a new brand/experience/service of your choice. Think about what you would emphasize, e.g. history, sustainability, novelty, exclusivity.

Sources: Yu and Lannes (2013); trendwatching.com www.hiutdenim.co.uk www.nest.com

References

Abel, G.M. and Plumridge, E.W. (2004), 'Network "norms" or "styles" of "drunken deportment"?', *Health Education Research Theory and Practice*, 19, 5, 492–500.

Adams, T. (2014), 'Brands must embrace the future of fully conscious consumption', *The Guardian*, https://www.theguardian.com/sustainable-business/brands-data-conscious-consumption (accessed 17 July 2017).

Al, S. (2017), 'All under one roof: how malls and cities are becoming indistinguishable', *The Guardian*, 16 March, https://www.theguardian.com/cities/2017/mar/16/malls-cities-become-one-and-same#img-3 (accessed 7 May 2017).

Anon. (2011a), 'Research review: technology adoption depends on customer relationships', *Teller Vision*, 1407, 3–4.

Anon. (2011b), 'Cell Drinks escapes censure from the Portman Group', *The Drum*, 25 August, http://www.thedrum.com/news/2011/08/25/cell-drinks-escapes-censure-portman-group (accessed 7 May 2017).

ASA (Advertising Standards Association) (2011), 'Adjudication on Cell Drinks', http://www.asa.org.uk/Rulings/Adjudications/2011/8/Cell-Drinks/SHP_ADJ_164359.aspx (accessed 7 May 2017).

Bahl, S., Milne, G.R., Ross, S.M. et al. (2016), 'Mindfulness: its transformative potential for consumer, societal, and environmental well-being', *Journal of Public Policy & Marketing*, 35, 2, 198–210.

Bamfield, J.A.N. (2012), 'Shoplifting for Christmas 2012: how criminals profit from the festive season', Centre for Retail Research, http://securityadvancement.com/wp-content/uploads/2012/12/Shoplifting+for+Christmas+2012+Study+US+3.pdf (accessed 7 May 2017).

Barbaro, M. (2006), 'Attention, holiday shoppers: we have fisticuffs in aisle 2', *New York Times*, 25 November, http://www.nytimes.com/2006/11/25/business/25shop.html?_r%C2%BC1&pagewanted%C2%BC2&ei%C2%BC5087%%200A&em&en%C2%BCe8b3e335cf3fa05c&ex%C2%BC1164603600&oref%C2%BCslogin&_r=0 (accessed 7 May 2017).

Bardhi, F. and Eckhardt, G.M. (2012), 'Access-based consumption: the case of car sharing', *Journal of Consumer Research*, 39, 4, 881–98.

Barkham, P. (2012), 'Why is cheese the most shoplifted food item in the world?', *The Guardian*, 10 January, https://www.theguardian.com/lifeandstyle/shortcuts/2012/jan/10/cheese-most-shoplifted-food-item (accessed 7 May 2017).

BBC (2009), 'MP blasts club's drink promotion', 27 January, http://news.bbc.co.uk/1/hi/england/manchester/7853882.stm (accessed 7 May 2017).

BBC (2012), 'Brazil health study shows growing weight problem', 11 April, http://www.bbc.co.uk/news/world-latin-america-17671253 (accessed 7 May 2017).

Block, L.G., Keller, P.A., Vallen, B. et al. (2016), 'The squander sequence: understanding food waste at each stage of the consumer decision-making process', *Journal of Public Policy & Marketing*, 35, 2, 292–304.

Booth, H.P., Charlton, J., and Gulliford, M.C. (2017), 'Socioeconomic inequality in morbid obesity with body mass index more than 40kg/m² in the United States and England', *SSM-Population Health*, 3, 172–8.

BRCS (2017), Retail Crime Survey 2016, https://brc.org.uk/media/116322/10081-brc-retail-crime-survey-2016_v6.pdf (accessed 30 October 2017).

Bristow, M. (2010), 'China faces obesity explosion', http://www.bbc.co.uk/news/world-asia-pacific-11368027 (accessed 7 May 2017).

Bullas, J. (nd), 'Is Piracy just free marketing?', http://www.jeffbullas.com/does-piracy-expand-your-market-for-free/ (accessed 22 July 2017).

Burch, M.A. (2012), 'Educating for simple living', Simplicity Institute, http://simplicitycollective.com/wp-content/uploads/2012/08/EducatingforSimpleLivingSimplicityInstitute1.pdf (accessed 7 May 2017).

Burgen, S. (2017), 'Original pirate material: Barcelona's street sellers form own fashion label', *The Guardian*, 7 July, https://www.theguardian.com/world/2017/jul/07/original-pirate-material-barcelonas-street-sellers-form-own-fashion-label (accessed 22 July, 2017).

Cai, L. and Zhu, Y. (2015), 'The Challenges of data quality and data quality assessment in the big data era', *Data Science Journal*, 14, 2, http://doi.org/10.5334/dsj-2015-002.

Carr, D. (2013), 'Giving viewers what they want', *New York Times*, 25 February, http://www.nytimes.com/2013/02/25/business/media/for-house-of-cards-using-big-data-to-guarantee-its-popularity.html (accessed 20 July, 2017).

Castonguay, G. (2006), 'The rich are choosing to live on borrowed luxury', *International Herald Tribune*, 7 November, http://www.nytimes.com/2006/12/07/business/worldbusiness/07iht-auto.3822935.html (accessed 7 May 2017).

Chylinski, M. and Chu, A. (2010), 'Consumer cynicism: antecedents and consequences', *European Journal of Marketing*, 44, 6, 796–837.

Corner, L. (2011), 'Buy Nothing Day: Adbusters' role in the global Occupy movement', *The Independent*, 20 November, http://www.independent.co.uk/news/world/politics/buy-nothing-day-adbusters-role-in-the-global-occupy-movement-6263205.html (accessed 7 May 2017).

Corus, C., Saatcioglu, B., Kaufman-Scarborough, C. et al. (2016), 'Transforming poverty-related policy with intersectionality', *Journal of Public Policy & Marketing*, 35, 2, 211–22.

Daunt, K.L and Harris, L.C. (2012), 'Exploring the forms of dysfunctional customer behaviour: a study of differences in servicescape and customer disaffection with service', *Journal of Marketing Management*, 28, 1/2, 129–53.

Dean, D.H. (2013), 'Anticipating consumer reaction to RFID-enabled grocery checkout', *Services Marketing Quarterly*, 34, 1, 86–101.

Defra (2017), 'Greening Government Commitments 2016 to 2020', London: Department for Environment, Food and Rural Affairs, https://www.gov.uk/government/publications/greening-government-commitments-2016-to-2020/greening-government-commitments-2016-to-2020 (accessed 2 May 2017).

Deloitte (2017), 'The Deloitte millenial survey 2017', https://www2.deloitte.com/global/en/pages/about-deloitte/articles/millennialsurvey.html (accessed 21 July 2017).

Dittmar, H. (2005), 'Compulsive buying—a growing concern? An examination of gender, age, and endorsement of materialistic values as predictors', *British Journal of Psychology*, 96, 4, 467–91.

Easier Finance (2008), 'Economic recession impacts broadband ISP migration', http://www.easier.com/17403-economic-recession-impacts-broadband-isp-migration.html (accessed 7 May 2017).

Elgin, D. (2009), *The living universe: where are we? Who are we? Where are we going?*, San Francisco, CA: Berrett-Koehler.

Elliott, R., Eccles, S., and Gournay, K. (1996), 'Revenge, existential choice, and addictive consumption', *Psychology & Marketing*, 13, 8, 753–68.

Erevelles, S., Fukawa, N., and Swayne, L. (2016), 'Big data consumer analytics and the transformation of marketing', *Journal of Business Research*, 69, 2, 897–904.

Etkin, J. (2016), 'The hidden cost of personal quantification', *Journal of Consumer Research*, 42, 6, 967–84.

Fantoni, R., Hoefel, F., and Mazzarolo, M. (2014), 'The future of the shopping mall', McKinsey Report, November 2014, http://www.mckinsey.com/business-functions/marketing-and-sales/our-insights/the-future-of-the-shopping-mall (accessed 7 May 2017).

Fitzgerald, E. (2012), 'An ever-connected generation is going asset-light', Eamonn Fitzgerald's Rainy Day Blog, http://www.eamonn.com/2012/12/05/an-ever-connected-generation-is-going-asset-light/ (accessed 7 May 2017).

Food Research &Action Center (2012), 'Overweight and obesity in the US', http://frac.org/initiatives/hunger-and-obesity/obesity-in-the-us/ (accessed 7 May 2017).

Fullerton, R.A. and Punj, G. (1997), 'What is consumer misbehavior?', *Advances in Consumer Research*, 24, 336–9.

Fullerton, R.A. and Punj, G. (2004), 'Repercussions of promoting an ideology of consumption: consumer misbehavior', *Journal of Business Research*, 57, 11, 1239–49.

Gandomi, A. and Haider, M. (2015), 'Beyond the hype: big data concepts, methods, and anlytics', *International Journal of Information Management*, 35, 137–44.

Gelles, D. (2015), *Mindful work: how meditation is changing business from the inside out*, London: Profile Books.

Giesler, M. (2012), 'How doppelgänger brand images influence the market creation process: longitudinal insights from the rise of Botox cosmetic', *Journal of Marketing*, 76, 6, 55–68.

Griffin, C., Bengry-Howell, A., Hackley, C. et al. (2009), ' "Every time I do it I absolutely annihilate myself": loss of (self-)consciousness and loss of memory in young people's drinking narratives', *Sociology*, 43, 3, 457–76.

Hallsworth, A. and Wong, A. (2015), 'Urban gardening realities: the example case study of Portsmouth, England', *International Journal on Food System Dynamics*, 6, 1, 1–11.

Harford, Tim (2014), 'Big data: are we making a big mistake?', *Financial Times*, 28 March, https://www.ft.com/content/21a6e7d8-b479-11e3-a09a-00144feabdc0 (accessed 2 May 2017).

Harris, L.C. and Reynolds, K.L. (2003), 'The consequences of dysfunctional customer behavior', *Journal of Service Research*, 6, 2, 144–61.

Hevrdejs, J. (2011), 'A frock on the clock?', *Chicago Tribune*, 28 January, http://articles.chicagotribune.com/2011-01-28/news/sc-cons-0127-save-savvy-renter-20110128_1_rental-cars-frock-late-fees (accessed 7 May 2017).

Hill, K. (2012), 'How Target figured out a teen girl was pregnant before her father did', https://www.forbes.com/sites/kashmirhill/2012/02/16/how-target-figured-out-a-teen-girl-was-pregnant-before-her-father-did/#433ddbac6668 (accessed 20 July 2017).

HM Government (2016), *Childhood obesity: a plan for action*, https://www.gov.uk/government/uploads/system/uploads/attachment_data/file/546588/Childhood_obesity_2016__2__acc.pdf (accessed 8 May 2017).

Hofacker, C.F., Malthouse, E.C., and Sultan, F. (2016), 'Big data and consumer behavior: imminent opportunities', *Journal of Consumer Marketing*, 33, 2, 89–97.

Howard, C. (2012), 'The big picture', *Economist*, 15 December, http://www.economist.com/news/special-report/21568065-world-getting-wider-says-charlotte-howard-what-can-be-done-about-it-big (accessed 7 May 2017).

Huneke, M.E. (2005), 'The face of the un-consumer: an empirical examination of the practice of voluntary simplicity in the United States', *Psychology & Marketing*, 22, 7, 527–50.

Jones, A., Bentham, G., Foster, C. et al. (2007), 'Tackling obesities: future choices: obesogenic environments—evidence review', Foresight Government Office for Science.

Kaplan, D. (2016), 'Tequila Herradura amplifies "sound of smoothness" with geotargeting on Facebook, Foursquare', *GeoMarketing*, 11 August, http://www.geomarketing.com/tequila-herradura-amplifies-sound-of-smoothness-with-geotargeting-on-facebook-foursquare (accessed 2 May 2017).

Keynote (2015), 'Leisure activity preferences of UK adults continue to evolve', Keynote Market Review Report, https://www.keynote.co.uk/press-release/12232015/leisure-activity-preferences-uk-adults-continue-evolve (accessed 7 May 2017).

Koran, L.M., Faber, R.J., Aboujaoude, E. et al. (2006), 'Estimated prevalence of compulsive buying behavior in the United States', *American Journal of Psychiatry*, 163, 1806–12.

Kozinets, R., Patterson, A., and Ashman, R. (2017), 'Networks of desire: how technology increases our passion to consume', *Journal of Consumer Research*, 43, 5, 659–82.

Leonardi, L. (2016) 'When to choose geofencing, geotargeting or beaconing for you location marketing', *Relate*, 4 August, https://www.appboy.com/blog/geofencing-geo-targeting-beaconing-when-to-use/ (accessed 2 May 2017).

Likis-Werle, E. and Borders, L.D. (2017), 'College women's gender identity and their drinking choices', *Journal of Addictions & Offender Counseling*, 38, 1, 16–32.

Lovelock, C. (1994), *Product plus*, New York: McGraw-Hill.

Lycett, M. (2013), 'Datafication: making sense of (big) data in a complex world', *European Journal of Information Systems*, 22, 4, 381–6.

Malnight, T.W. and Keys, T.S. (2013), 'A top ten for business leaders', *Economist*, http://www.economist.com/blogs/theworldin2013/2012/11/global-trends-2013 (accessed 7 May 2017).

Maman, A.-F. (2010), 'Buying non-deceptive luxury counterfeits: can we call it a misbehaviour?', http://www.marketing-trends-congress.com/archives/2010/Materiali/Paper/Fr/Maman.pdf (accessed 28 April 2017).

Martin, I.M., Kamins, M.A., Pirouz, D.M. et al. (2012), 'On the road to addiction: the facilitative and preventive roles of marketing cues', *Journal of Business Research*, 66, 8, 1219–26.

Mason, M.J., Tanner, J.F., Piacentini, M. et al. (2013), 'Advancing a youth-centred approach for risk behavior: foundations, distinctions, and research directions', *Journal of Business Research*, 66, 1235–41.

Measham, F. (2008), 'The turning tides of intoxication: young people's drinking in Britain in the 2000s', *Health Education*, 108, 3, 207–22.

Meier, B.P., Noll, S.W., and Molokwu, O.J. (2017), 'The sweet life: the effect of mindful chocolate consumption on mood', *Appetite*, 108, 21–7.

Mick, D.G., Pettigrew, S., Pechmann, C.C., and Ozanne, J.L. (eds) (2011), *Transformative consumer research for personal and collective well-being*, New York: Routledge Academic.

Moschis, G.P. and Cox, D. (1989), 'Deviant consumer behavior', *Advances in Consumer Research*, 16, 1, 732–7.

Murphy, J. (2017), 'Supportive strategy', *Impact*, 17, April, 16–17.

National Association for Shoplifting Prevention (2011), 'The shoplifting problem in the nation', http://www.shopliftingprevention.org/TheIssue.htm (accessed 7 May 2017).

Nielsen (2014), 'Millenials breaking the myth', http://www.nielsen.com/content/dam/corporate/us/en/reports-downloads/2014%20Reports/nielsen-millennial-report-feb-2014.pdf (accessed 21 July 2017).

OECD (2016), 'Global trade in fake goods worth nearly half a trillion dollars a year', http://www.oecd.org/newsroom/global-trade-in-fake-goods-worth-nearly-half-a-trillion-dollars-a-year.htm (accessed 22 July 2017).

Office of National Statistics (2017), 'Adult drinking habits in Great Britain: 2005 to 2016', https://www.ons.gov.uk/peoplepopulationandcommunity/healthandsocialcare/drugusealcoholandsmoking/bulletins/opinionsandlifestylesurveyadultdrinkinghabitsingreatbritain/2005to2016 (accessed 7 May 2017)

O'Guinn, T.C. and Faber, R.J. (1989), 'Compulsive buying: a phenomenological exploration', *Journal of Consumer Research*, 16, 2, 147–57.

O'Loughlin, D., Szmigin, I., McEachern, M. et al. (2017), 'Man thou art dust: rites of passage in austere times', *Sociology*, 51, 5, 1050-66.

O'Shea, D. (2017), '5 technologies reshaping retail in 2017', *Retail Dive*, 19 January, https://www.retaildive.com/news/5-technologies-reshaping-retail-in-2017/433954/ (accessed 28 October 2017).

Oxley, D. (2015), 'Why do people steal grocery meat and what do they do with it?', *MyNorthWest*, 5 June, http://mynorthwest.com/13592/why-do-people-steal-grocery-meat-and-what-do-they-do-with-it/, (accessed 27 October 2017).

Peyer, M., Balderjahn, I., Seegebarth, B., and Klemm, A. (2017), 'The role of sustainability in profiling voluntary simplifiers', *Journal of Business Research*, 70, 37–43.

Pitney Bowes (2013), 'The coupon renaissance', http://pressroom.pitneybowes.co.uk/the-coupon-renaissance/ (accessed 7 May 2017).

Popper, N. and Lohr, S. (2017), 'Blockchain: a better way to track pork chops, bonds, bad peanut butter?', *New York Times*, 4 March, https://www.nytimes.com/2017/03/04/business/dealbook/blockchain-ibm-bitcoin.html?_r=0 (accessed 2 May 2017)

Robinson, S. and Harris, H. (2011), 'Smoking and drinking among adults, 2009: a report on the 2009 General Life-style Survey', Office of National Statistics, http://doc.ukdataservice.ac.uk/doc/6737/mrdoc/pdf/6737report.pdf (accessed 7 May 2017).

Rose, P. and Segrist, D.J. (2012), 'Difficulty identifying feelings, distress tolerance and compulsive buying: analyzing the associations to inform therapeutic strategies', *International Journal of Mental Health and Addiction*, 10, 927–35.

Schaefers, T., Lawson, S.J., and Kukar-Kinney, M. (2016), 'How the burdens of ownership promote consumer usage of access-based services', *Marketing Letters*, 27, 3, 569–77.

Scharf, C. (2012), 'Accessible excess: how luxury marketing is changing', *TrendReports.Com*, 14 November, http://www.trendreports.com/article/luxury-marketing (accessed 7 May 2017).

Shaw, D. and Newholm, T. (2002), 'Voluntary simplicity and the ethics of consumption', *Psychology & Marketing*, 19, 2, 167–85.

Sheth, J.N., Sethia, N.K., and Srinivas, S. (2011), 'Mindful consumption: a customer-centric approach to sustainability', *Journal of the Academy of Marketing Science*, 39, 21–39.

Sinha, R.K. and Mandel, N. (2008), 'Preventing digital music piracy: the carrot or the stick?', *Journal of Marketing*, 72, 1–15.

Sinha, R.K., Machado, F.S., and Sellman, C. (2010), 'Don't think twice, it's all right: music piracy and pricing in a DRM-free environment', *Journal of Marketing*, 74, 40–54.

Smith, L. and Foxcroft, D. (2009), 'Drinking in the UK: an exploration of trends', Joseph Rowntree Foundation Report, http://www.jrf.org.uk/publications/drinking-in-the-uk (accessed 7 May 2017).

Stocksdale, J. (2017), 'Hyundai announces pricing for Ioniq Electric subscription service', Autoblog, 20 April, http://www.autoblog.com/2017/04/20/hyundai-ioniq-electric-unlimited-subscription-price/ (accessed 2 May 2017).

Swinburn, B.A., Sacks, G., Hall, K.D. et al. (2011), 'The global obesity pandemic: shaped by global drivers and local environments', *Lancet*, 378, 9793, 804–14.

Szmigin, I. and Gee, V. (2017) 'Mystification and obfuscation in portion sizes in UK food products', *Journal of Business Research*, 75, 176–84.

Szmigin, I., Griffin, C., Hackley, C. et al. (2008), 'Reframing "binge drinking" as calculated hedonism: empirical evidence from the UK', *International Journal of Drug Policy*, 19, 5, 359–66.

Tea, B. (2016), 'Case study: how shopping malls are adapting to the digital world', https://socialwall.me/en/author/brigitte-tea/ (accessed 2 May 2017).

Trendwatching (2016), 'The future of luxury', http://trendwatching.com/trends/the-future-of-luxury/ (accessed 5 May 2017).

Unilever (2017), 'Report shows a third of consumers prefer sustainable brands', Press Release, https://www.unilever.com/news/press-releases/2017/report-shows-a-third-of-consumers-prefer-sustainable-brands.html (accessed 2 May 2017).

Verge Magazine (2011), 'Warrington club comes under fire for 10p drinks student night', 27 September http://www.vergemagazine.co.uk/girls/2011/09/warrington-club-fire-10p-drinks-student-night/ (accessed 7 May 2017).

Wadd, S., Lapworth, K., Sullivan, M. et al. (2011), 'Working with older drinkers', Report for Alcohol Research, http://alcoholresearchuk.org/downloads/finalReports/FinalReport_0085 (accessed 7 May 2017).

Wheelwright, G. (2017), 'Tech on the slopes: how RFID is changing the experience of skiing and snowboarding', 12 April, https://www.geekwire.com/2017/whistler-blackcomb-uses-rfid-tech-to-marry-mobile-apps-to-skiing-and-boarding/ (accessed 5 May 2017).

WHO (2014), *Global status report on alcohol and health 2014*, Geneva: World Health Organization.

WHO (2016), 'Obesity and overweight fact sheet', June, http://www.who.int/mediacentre/factsheets/fs311/en/ (accessed 7 May 2017).

Wilkinson, T (2007), 'Italy's rich pay to look richer', *Los Angeles Times*, 18 February, http://articles.latimes.com/2007/feb/18/world/fg-bella18 (accessed 7 May 2017).

Wolf, G. (2010), 'The quantified self', http://www.ted.com/talks/gary_wolf_the_quantified_self.html (accessed 7 May 2017).

Yu, J. and Lannes, B. (2013), 'Chinese shopping behaviour: China's repertoire shopping', *Admap*, 48, 1, 36–8.

GLOSSARY

Absolute threshold is the minimum amount of stimulation that can be picked up by any of our senses.

Acceptance/rejection is when the consumer considers existing choice criteria and elaborates the message received to reach a point of acceptance or rejection of the information.

Acculturation relates to the idea of movement between places or cultural contexts.

Active learning involves the acquisition of knowledge before purchase, and therefore extensive information search.

Actual self refers to the core sense of self, that sense of self which is enduring and stable across situations.

Adaptation is the extent to which people's awareness of a stimulus diminishes over a period of time.

Affective component (of attitudes) relates to the emotional connection the consumer has with the target object about which an attitude is formed.

Aggregation is where the person becomes used to a new role and transforms within that role.

Anchoring is over-reliance on one piece of often irrelevant information to make a decision.

Approach–approach conflict is when you have to choose between two or more equally attractive alternatives.

Approach–avoidance conflict is when a desired goal also has negative consequences.

Archetype relates to the stable characters that capture basic ideas, feelings, fantasies, and visions that seem constant and frequently re-emerge across different times and places.

Aspirational groups are composed of people that the consumer can identify with or admire (often from afar), and aspires to be like in some way.

Attention is the mental activity given to a stimulus., and requires the focusing of attention, leading to perception and categorization of stimuli.

Attitude is a learned predisposition to respond in a consistently favourable or unfavourable manner in relation to some object.

Attitude object/act is the thing towards which the attitude is held, and can include brands, services, ideas, people, and behaviours.

Attributes are the characteristics or features of the attitude object/act.

Attributions arise when 'one evaluates the extent to which the initial product performance corresponds to one's level of aspiration vis-à-vis that product, and one then questions the cause of the outcome' (Weiner, 2000: 383).

Automatic mode is used to describe a human being that is operating routinely with little effort and no feeling of voluntarily being in control.

Availability heuristic refers to a situation where people judge the likelihood or frequency of something happening in the future by how easy it is to remember similar events.

Avoidance–avoidance conflict is when the choices available all have some apparent negative consequences.

Behavioural component (of attitudes) refers to the action or behaviours associated with the attitude object.

Behavioural intention is an intention to act in some way.

Behavioural learning is concerned with learning as a response to changes in our environment.

Beliefs are the thoughts an individual holds which describe the object of the attitude, its characteristics, and its relations to other objects.

Biogenic needs or innate needs enable us to survive, and include the need for food, water, and shelter.

Brand community refers to a non-geographically bound community who are connected through brand admiration, with a structured set of social relations.

Brand loyalty is 'any tendency for people to buy the same brand again, whilst usually also buying other brands' (Ehrenberg and Scriven, 1996:3).

Brand personality scale describes the underlying brand dimensions of sincerity, excitement, competence, sophistication, and ruggedness.

Choice architecture describes how the way a choice is presented influences the choice made.

Choice heuristics are processes which allow people to reduce the number of attributes to be considered for possible alternative choices.

Chunking is the grouping together of similar or meaningful pieces of information.

Closure is the tendency for people to fill in the 'missing' elements of an incomplete picture.

Coercive power is when conformity to the group is brought about through the threat of punishment.

Cognitive component (of attitudes) refers to the beliefs and thoughts the individual has in relation to the target attitude object, its character, and its relations to other things.

Cognitive dissonance is the state of having inconsistent beliefs and attitudes.

Cognitive learning theories focus on learning through internal mental processes and conscious thought.

Collective unconscious stores hidden memory traces inherited from the human ancestral past.

Compensatory models are made up of a number of beliefs and use a scoring system to derive a final score. Attributes are averaged such that a low score on one attribute can be compensated by a higher score on another attribute.

Compliance refers to publicly changing behaviour to fit in with the group but privately disagreeing, i.e. a behavioural shift without an attitudinal one.

Compliance heuristics are those heuristics built around the likelihood of choosing something based on complying with a request.

Comprehension is where the consumer searches (and identifies) meaning.

Compulsive buying is an unusual obsession with shopping such that it significantly affects the life of the person afflicted.

Conformity is the adoption of behaviour resulting from real or perceived pressure to comply with a person or group.

Conjunctive decision rule is when a consumer chooses a brand based on minimum levels for each of any key evaluative attributes.

Connectors are people who tend to know lots of other people, often from different subcultures to their own.

Consideration set includes brands from the evoked set that you might actually consider buying.

Consumer acculturation is 'the general process of movement and adaptation to the consumer cultural environment in one country by persons from another country' (Penaloza, 1994: 33).

Consumer ethnocentrism is based on the idea that ethnocentric individuals view their group (or culture) as superior to others, and therefore that in consumer terms there is a strong preference towards buying domestic, rather than foreign-produced, goods.

Consumer innovativeness is defined as a generalized tendency toward innovative behaviour applicable across product classes.

Consumer misbehaviour is a behavioural act by a consumer which violates accepted norms of consumption conduct.

Consumer theft refers to the desire to steal as a way of acquisition of consumer objects.

Consumer tribes are groups of people who are emotionally connected by similar consumption values and usage and who use the social linking value of products and services to create a community and express identity.

Consumption function maps the relationship between disposable income and level of wages.

Contamination is when objects associated with sacred events or people become sacred in their own right, for example items belonging to famous people.

Contactual or associative groups are generally close groups with which we interact regularly and where there is a degree of proximity.

Contexts of decisions are the environments within which consumption choices take place.

Continuous innovations are innovations that tend to create little change in consumption patterns and generally involve the introduction of a modified product rather than a totally new one.

Conventions are a specific form of custom, and relate to the norms for the conduct of everyday life.

Crowdsourcing occurs when a company or institution takes a function once performed by employees and outsources it to an undefined (and generally large) network of people in the form of an open call.

Culture is the sum total of learned ideas, beliefs, values, knowledge, and customs that together regulate the behaviour of members of a particular society.

Customs are the norms of behaviour that have been passed from generation to generation.

Decision rules are criteria used by consumers in the process of making a decision.

Declarative memory is specifically about knowing things. It is made up of two different types of memory systems, episodic memory and semantic memory, which remember different types of event.

Default is a preselected option without active choice.

Desacralization is when a sacred item or symbol is removed from its special place.

Desires are temporal wants which may or may not have a biological basis.

Differential threshold is the point at which we notice a difference between two stimuli.

Direct influence by a reference group refers to direct, often face-to-face, contact between members of a group.

Disclaimant group is one that we currently belong to, or perhaps belonged to in the past, but no longer want to associate ourselves with.

Disconfirmation paradigm is the difference between a consumer's pre-purchase expectations of the product's performance and their post-purchase experience.

Discontinuous innovation has a disruptive effect, and will require the establishment of new behavioural patterns by consumers.

Dissociative or avoidance groups are groups we have negative feelings towards and whom we avoid being associated with.

Double jeopardy is the phenomenon whereby brands with smaller market share have fewer buyers and those fewer buyers buy the brand less often.

Duplication of purchase analysis explains the degree to which brands within a category share their buyers with each of the other brands.

Dynamically continuous innovations create some change in behavioural patterns, but the magnitude of change is not very great.

Ego represents the interests of the individual, ensuring the necessary arbitration between the demands of the id and constraints of the superego.

Ego-defensive function (of attitudes) refers to the idea that attitudes can have the function of defending our self-image.

Ego involvement is when consumers perceive products or brands as relevant to their personal interests.

Elaboration continuum describes the amount of thought (elaboration) given to an advertising message/communication.

Elimination-by-aspects decision rule ranks evaluative aspects by importance and establishes a minimum cut-off point for each attribute.

Encoding refers to how information enters the memory.

Enculturation refers to how an individual learns the traditional content of his/her native culture.

Endogenous WOM is when conversations happen among consumers as part of their natural communication and when they are just passing on information about their experiences with a product or brand.

Endowment effect describes how highly we value what we already have, and it shows that people assign specific values to a thing relative to their situation.

Enduring involvement is 'the pre-existing relationship between an individual and the object of concern' (Houston and Rothschild, 1978: 3).

Engrams are neural networks connecting new memories with old ones.

Episodic memory refers to our memories of specific events and experiences, which have formed our autobiographical time line.

Evaluation refers to the process of determining how valuable, or important, something is to us.

Evaluative conditioning is defined as the changes in the liking of a stimulus (e.g. brand) linked to the pairing of that stimulus with other positive or negative stimuli (e.g. celebrity).

Evaluative criteria are those factors that we use to compare offerings to help make a choice.

Evoked set includes all brands the consumer is aware of which might meet their needs,.

eWOM is any positive or negative statement made by potential, actual, or former customers about a product or company, which is made available to a multitude of people and institutions via the internet.

Exchange value can be said to represent what the value of a good is to the consumer and therefore what it could be exchanged for, usually its price.

Exogenous WOM is word of mouth that occurs as a direct result of the firm's marketing efforts.

Expectancy-value model suggests that people form attitudes towards objects (e.g. brands) based on their expectations and evaluations of the attributes that make up the brand.

Expert power is when we are influenced to behave or purchase something by someone whom we recognize has particular expertise, for example a doctor or scientist.

Explicit memory is the conscious recollection of an experience.

Exposure ensures that the stimulus is in the appropriate place for consumers to have access to it. It involves sensory detection and registration through receptor organs.

Extended self refers to the idea that our possessions and belongings form such a close connection with us and our past that they come to represent us in some way.

Extinction is the decrease in the conditioned response which occurs when the unconditioned stimulus is removed from the conditioned stimulus.

Extrinsic need requires some return or goal from the external environment.

Fetishism of commodities is 'the disguising or masking of commodities whereby the appearance of goods hides the story of those who made them and how they made them' (Lury, 1999: 42).

Financial risk is the perception of a likely financial loss.

First-order conditioning occurs when a conditioned stimulus acquires motivational importance by being paired with an unconditioned stimulus, which is intrinsically aversive or rewarding.

Fixed interval schedule is when reinforcement is provided after a specific known period of time.

Fixed ratio schedule applies reinforcement after a specific number of responses.

Formal groups are formed by some kind of outside structure and are likely to have a formalized constitution and set of rules of conduct for members.

Framing refers to how we make a decision through the context in which a choice is presented to us.

Gestalt means 'whole' and refers to how people look for meaning and patterns in the stimuli in the environment as a whole rather than in terms of the individual parts.

Gift-giving rituals are the rituals surrounding giving presents to others.

Grooming rituals are those private behaviours that consumers undertake to aid the transition from private to public self (and back again).

Heuristics are methods to aid decision-making to arrive at satisfactory solutions by simplifying the complexity of assessing the probability and prediction of value in a choice situation.

Higher-order conditioning is the pairing of two conditioned stimuli.

Holiday rituals refer to the rituals associated with both tourism holidays and culturally bound holiday seasons.

Hyperbolic discounting refers to many people's inability to prefer future gains over current losses and where they place more emphasis on immediate pleasures and pains.

Id corresponds to primary needs, focused on immediate gratification, directing a person's psychic energy towards pleasurable acts without regard to the consequences.

Ideal or idealized self relates to the self we aspire to be like.

Ideal congruity refers to the extent to which the product image matches the ideal self-image.

Ideal social self-image is how consumers would like to be seen by significant others.

Identity schema represents one's understanding of oneself with respect to a particular role and is thus both personalized and often realistic.

Identity-ideal schema corresponds to how the person would like to become as one who enacts that role.

Ideology reflects the mental characteristics of a people, building on the assumption that members of a society possess the same worldview, ethos, ideas, and principles.

Implicit memory is remembering without conscious awareness.

Impulse purchasing is a sudden powerful urge to buy a product with little regard to the consequences of what we are buying.

Indirect influence occurs through an individual observing group members' behaviour and altering his/her own because of it.

Individualism refers to the ways in which individual goals are balanced against collective or group goals, with individualistic cultures prioritizing the individual's goals over those of the collective (and vice versa).

Inept set includes those brands that the consumer may have come across during their search or from previous experience but would not consider for this particular decision.

Inert set includes those brands not under consideration at all.

Informal groups are formed by a group of individuals who have some sort of commonality but no formal connection to each other.

Information search is the process by which we identify appropriate information to help aid our choice in a decision-making situation.

Informational conformity occurs when someone actively looks for guidance from the group where they lack knowledge or are in an ambiguous situation.

Informational group influence is when a consumer uses the reference group to actively obtain information from opinion leaders or experts in the group.

Informational power is based on logical argument and knowledge that someone may have acquired from experience or through the nature of their job.

Internalization involves both an attitudinal and behavioural change in favour of the group.

Interpretivist perspective stresses the subjective meaning of the consumer's individual experience and the idea that any behaviour is subject to multiple interpretations rather than one single explanation.

Intrinsic need is an internal motivation.

Involvement is the perceived relevance of a purchase to the consumer.

Just noticeable difference (JND) is the minimum change in a stimulus to be noticed by the majority of people.

Knowledge refers to the familiarity with people or things, which can include understanding, facts, information, and descriptions gained through experience and education.

Knowledge function (of attitudes) relates to the human need to have a meaningful, stable, and organized view of the world.

Law of buyer moderation is the tendency for light buyers to become heavier, and heavier buyers to become lighter.

Learning is the activity or process of acquiring knowledge or skill by studying, practising, or experiencing something.

Legitimate power is where the referent is seen to have authority by virtue of their position in the particular context.

Lexicographic decision rule is when the customer ranks the evaluative attributes by their importance.

Liminality is the period when a person is moving between roles in his/her life, and consequently is often unsure of him/herself.

Long-term orientation (LTO) reflects the degree of focus on the future the society has which relates to the time orientation of the culture and its perspectives on time and tradition.

Loss aversion describes the fact that most people dislike losses more than they like gains of an equivalent amount.

Malleable self refers to the idea that people will act differently according to the situation, influenced by social roles, cues, and the need for self-presentation.

Masculinity refers to motives that are classified as either achievement-oriented, with an emphasis in heroism, assertiveness, and material reward (labelled masculine in Hofstede's terms), or more consensus-oriented, where the emphasis is on cooperation, modesty, caring, and quality of life (labelled feminine in Hofstede's terms).

Materialism is a trait that captures the degree to which a consumer is overly concerned with physical objects and material goods.

Mavens are collectors and brokers of information, but they use this information and want to start discussions with others or respond to requests.

Memory is both a system and a process whereby information is received, sorted, organized, stored, and retrieved over time.

Mental accounting is when individuals allocate assets into separate non-transferable groupings to which they may assign different levels of utility.

Message-response involvement reflects the consumer's interest in marketing communications.

Microcultures are subgroupings within a culture, where people are classified based on shared demographic characteristics (e.g. age, regionality, ethnicity) or in terms of shared consumption interests.

Monomorphic opinion leaders are experts in a limited field.

Mores are particular forms of custom and have a strong moral overtone.

Motivation describes the processes that cause people to behave in a particular way.

Motivation to comply (MC) is the extent to which the consumer wishes to comply with or conform to the preferences of significant others.

Multi-trait approach (to personality) is where researchers are concerned with a number of personality traits taken together and how they combine to effect consumption.

Myth is a story that contains symbolic elements that express shared emotions and ideals of a culture.

Narrative approach (to identity) is where consumers are viewed as identity seekers and makers using marketplace resources to construct and express both individual and collective identities.

Needs are the result of the difference between the actual and desired states.

Near-stationary market is an established mature market, which appears stable over a period of several months or a year.

Negative self refers to the person you are not, and do not want to become.

Neuromarketing is 'the application of neuroscientific methods to analyse and understand human behaviour in relation to market and marketing exchanges' (Lee et al., 2007: 200).

Neutral operants are responses from the environment that neither increase nor decrease the probability of a behaviour being repeated.

Non-compensatory models are where some overriding factors or attributes are dominant in the choice process.

Normative beliefs (NBs) are the individual's perception about relevant or important others' beliefs that the individual should engage in a behaviour or not.

Normative conformity applies when a person wants to fit in with the group or is afraid of being rejected by them and will publicly accept the group's view even if privately they do not agree.

Norms are informal rules that govern behaviour.

Novelty refers to the deviation from the expected likelihood of an event on the basis of both previous information and internal estimates of conditional probabilities. Novelty can refer to the quality of being new, original, or unusual, and in marketing it can include new or unfamiliar products, services, brands, ideas, people, or experiences.

Objectification is the process whereby sacred qualities are attributed to mundane items.

Operant conditioning is the changing of behaviour through reinforcement following a desired response.

Opinion leaders are 'individuals who exert an unequal amount of influence on the decisions of others' (Rogers and Cartano, 1962: 435).

Opinion seekers are people who seek opinions and information to help their purchase decision.

Parental yielding is when a parental decision-maker is influenced by a child's request and 'surrenders'.

Passing off is the marketing of a good in a way that enables it to be mistaken for another brand. It relies on the phenomenon of stimulus generalization.

Passive learning is the acquisition of knowledge without active learning.

Penetration is the proportion of people who buy an item in a given time period.

Perceived behavioural control is the person's perception of how easy or difficult it is likely to be for them to perform a particular behaviour.

Perception is the process through which information in the form of stimuli in the environment is selected, organized, and interpreted through the sense organs.

Perceptual defence is when a consumer inhibits perception of potentially threatening or unpleasant stimuli.

Perceptual vigilance is when a consumer consciously or unconsciously filters stimuli for relevance.

Performance or functional risk is the perception of how well the product will perform its expected task.

Personal unconscious is a Jungian term that refers to anything which is not presently conscious but can be, holding previously conscious experiences and memories that have been repressed, forgotten, suppressed, or ignored.

Personality is the combination of the characteristic patterns of thoughts, feelings, and behaviours that make up an individual's distinctive character.

Persuasion heuristics refer to how consumers take short cuts when processing advertisers' messages.

Physical risk is the perception of harm that a product or service might have.

Polymorphic opinion leaders are experts in a number of areas, although generally within a particular category such as sport, fashion, food, or technology.

Positivist approach emphasizes the objectivity of science and the consumer as a rational decision-maker.

Possession rituals are the rituals associated with moving products from the marketplace to the home or workplace.

Possible selves are personalized representations of one's self in future states.

Power distance (PD) refers to how people in a culture view power relationships and the degree to which they accept superior and subordinate relationships.

Prediction heuristics are where the consumer is trying to predict an outcome such as 'If I buy a new mobile phone now, when will I need to update it?'

Priming is the alteration of people's behaviour outside their conscious awareness as a result of their first exposure to certain sights, words, sensations, or activities.

Principle of proximity states that things we see close together are perceived to be more related than things that are seen as farther apart.

Problem recognition is a realization that a problem needs to be solved through purchase.

Procedural memory is memory involved with knowing how to do things. and allows us to remember how to perform tasks and actions.

Product involvement is the perceived personal relevance of the product, based on needs, values, or interest.

Profane consumption is the term used to capture those consumer objects and events that do not share the 'specialness' of sacred objects.

Psychogenic needs are socially acquired needs and include the needs for status, affiliation, self-esteem, and prestige.

Psychographics is based on building a picture (sometimes literally) based on demographics, alongside activities, interests, and opinion variables.

Psychological risk is the risk that reflects the individual's perception of themselves.

Purchase frequency is the average number of times consumers purchase a brand in a given time period.

Quantified self refers to the idea that tracking metrics can lead to self-improvement in some way.

QR (quick response) codes are optical machine-readable barcodes that record and store information related to items.

Reactance is a motivational state which acts as a counterforce to threats to a person's freedom.

Recognition requires the memory to retrieve information by experiencing it again.

Recollection is when we reconstruct memory through a range of different narratives and bits of memory.

Reference groups are those groups that are used by a person as a basis for comparison and guidance when forming their beliefs, attitudes, and behaviours.

Referent power is influence that stems from our admiration of the qualities of a person, and how we try to imitate those qualities by copying their behaviour.

Reflective mode is used to describe when a person gives effortful attention to a mental activity, and this is often associated with considered choice and concentration.

Relearning is when you relearn something that you had previously learned, and the process of relearning helps you to remember and retrieve.

Representativeness heuristic is when we judge something on the basis of how similar it is to something else.

Retention is when learning has to be retained in the memory for future use.

Retrieval is the process whereby we remember and access our stored memories.

Reverse socialization is where parents acquire consumer skills from their children.

Reward power may be present when a person responds to the influence of the group and is rewarded in some way.

Rites of passage rituals are a specific type of ritual that marks a change in a person's social status.

Ritual refers to a symbolic and expressive activity, often comprising multiple behaviours which occur in a fixed sequence and are repeated over time.

Ritual artefacts are the objects and products that accompany or are consumed in a ritual setting.

Ritual audience is the people who witness or are involved in a ritual in some way.

Ritual performance roles are the roles occupied by people involved in the ritual as they perform according to the script.

Ritual script guides the use of the ritual artefacts—which artefacts to use, by whom, the sequence of use, and the types of comment that accompany the ritual.

Role schema contains shared representations, such as norms and cultural stereotypes about 'doing' a particular social role.

Sacred consumption is used to refer to objects and events that are set apart from normal activities, and are treated with some degree of respect or awe.

Salesmen (relating to opinion leaders) are the arch persuaders, who will not accept 'no' for an answer and are always looking for an opportunity to get their message across to someone else.

Salient beliefs are the most relevant beliefs for any given person at the time the attitude is considered.

Schemas are cognitive frameworks which are used to organize and interpret information.

Scientific approach in consumer behaviour emphasizes the objectivity of science and the consumer as a rational decision-maker.

Selective exposure is the active seeking and avoidance of stimuli.

Self-concept refers to the sum total of our thoughts, feelings, and imaginations as to who we are.

Self-congruity refers to the extent to which a product image matches a consumer's self-image.

Self-gifts are a specific example of gift giving, where consumers purchase self-gifts as a way of regulating their behaviour.

Self-schema are thoughts and feelings you have about yourself, based on past experiences, especially those resulting from your own experience and the feedback you receive.

Semantic memory involves the structuring of specific records, facts, concepts, and knowledge about the world we live in.

Semiotics is concerned with exploring the links between signs and symbols and the meanings they signify and convey.

Separation is the point of detachment or separation from the original group or status held by the individual.

Sign or symbolic value is the symbolic meaning consumers attach to goods to construct and participate in the social world.

Similarity refers to how things that are similar to one another are perceived to be more related to each other than to those that are dissimilar.

Single-trait approach (to personality) is where the focus is on isolating the key trait of interest and how this impacts on consumption.

Situational involvement is involvement with a product class or brand dependent on some other event.

Situational self recognizes the self-concept as a dynamic entity, where different aspects of self are activated depending on the different situations the consumer is in.

Social power is the degree of influence an individual or organization has among their peers and within society as a whole.

Social risk is the personal and social risk that may arise from a purchase.

Social self, sometimes referred to as the 'looking glass self', is how consumers believe they are seen by significant others.

Status groups are communities of people linked together on the basis of wealth, status, and power.

Stimulus generalization occurs when a stimulus similar to a conditioned stimulus (CS) elicits a similar conditioned response.

Storage is how the encoded information is retained in the memory.

Subcultures can be defined in terms of shared demographic characteristics (e.g. age, regionality, ethnicity) or in terms of shared consumption interests.

Subculture of consumption is defined as a group of consumers connected through a 'shared commitment to a particular product class, brand or consumption activity' (Schouten and McAlexander, 1995: 43).

Subjective norm construct represents a person's perceptions of specific significant others' preferences as to whether the person should or should not engage in the behaviour.

Sumptuary laws are laws that attempt to control and regulate permitted consumption activities.

Superego reflects the rules, values, and norms imposed by society, and serves as the person's conscience working to prevent the id from seeking selfish gratification.

Symbolic consumption is the tendency of consumers to rely and focus on the meanings attached to goods, beyond their physical properties.

Symbolic interactionism states that relationships with other people play a large part in forming the self.

Symbolic interactionist perspective views the self as emerging out of the mind, which develops out of social interaction, and patterned social interaction as forming the basis of social structure.

Terminal values are our desired end-states in life and preferred paths to achieving them, constituting the purposes and goals for which we believe human life should be lived.

Theory of cognitive dissonance is based on the belief that people need consistency or consonance between their behaviour and their attitudes.

Time risk is the risk embodied in the uncertainty regarding the time required to buy or learn to use the product.

Trait-based approach (to personality) regards personality as being the sum of a set of traits or qualities about a person, which can be used to predict or explain consumption behaviour.

Transformative consumer research (TCR) refers to a stream of research that focuses on benefiting consumer welfare and quality of life across the world.

Uncertainty avoidance (UA) relates to the way that a cultural group feels about ambiguity, and the extent to which members of a culture avoid uncertainty (and accordingly avoid risk), or embrace risk (and uncertainty).

Use value can be described as the value of a good to the consumer in terms of the usefulness it provides.

Utilitarian function (of attitudes) stems from the idea that consumers seek maximum utility and value from their consumption.

Utilitarian reference group influence is when a person complies with perceived expectations of those with whom they socialize, including family members and work colleagues.

VALS™ (acronym for Values and Lifestyle) is a trade-marked segmentation system, based on US adult consumers, where subjects are grouped into eight segments using the VALS™ questionnaire, which consists of questions around primary motivations and resources.

Value-expressive function (of attitudes) is concerned with the drive to express important aspects of the self and, linked to this, of the self that one aspires to be.

Value-expressive influence (of groups) is when someone buys a particular brand to enhance their image and because they admire characteristics of people who use the brand.

Values are the desired end-states in life and preferred paths to achieving them, constituting the purposes and goals for which we believe human life should be lived.

Variable interval is when the reinforcement occurs at some unknown but consistent rate.

Variable schedules are where reinforcement is provided on an irregular basis.

Volitional control is a state where there are no internal or external factors preventing performance of the behaviour.

Wants are specific manifestations of motives and are linked to a specific goal object.

Weak ties act as a bridge between other different but strong social networks.

Weber's law suggests that the stronger the initial stimulus, the more difference would be required for a change to be noticed.

Weights are the levels of importance attached to object attributes.

Word of mouth (WOM) is an informal communication, either positive or negative, about goods, services, and sellers.

INDEX

Note: Tables and figures are indicated by an italic *t* and *f* following the page number.